1775

ALSO BY KEVIN PHILLIPS

Bad Money

American Theocracy

American Dynasty

William McKinley

Wealth and Democracy

The Cousins' Wars

Arrogant Capital

Boiling Point

The Politics of Rich and Poor

Staying on Top

Post-Conservative America

Electoral Reform and Voter Participation

Mediacracy

The Emerging Republican Majority

1775

A Good Year for Revolution

KEVIN PHILLIPS

VIKING

VIKING
Published by the Penguin Group
Penguin Group (USA) Inc., 375 Hudson Street, New York, New York 10014, U.S.A.
Penguin Group (Canada), 90 Eglinton Avenue East, Suite 700, Toronto, Ontario, Canada M4P 2Y3
(a division of Pearson Penguin Canada Inc.)
Penguin Books Ltd, 80 Strand, London WC2R 0RL, England
Penguin Ireland, 25 St. Stephen's Green, Dublin 2, Ireland (a division of Penguin Books Ltd)
Penguin Group (Australia), 707 Collins Street, Melbourne, Victoria 3008 Australia
(a division of Pearson Australia Group Pty Ltd)
Penguin Books India Pvt Ltd, 11 Community Centre, Panchsheel Park, New Delhi – 110 017, India
Penguin Group (NZ), 67 Apollo Drive, Rosedale, Auckland 0632, New Zealand
(a division of Pearson New Zealand Ltd)
Penguin Books, Rosebank Office Park, 181 Jan Smuts Avenue, Parktown North 2193, South Africa
Penguin China, B7 Jaiming Center, 27 East Third Ring Road North, Chaoyang District,
Beijing 100020, China

Penguin Books Ltd, Registered Offices: 80 Strand, London WC2R 0RL, England

First published in 2012 by Viking Penguin, a member of Penguin Group (USA) Inc.

Copyright © Kevin Phillips, 2012
All rights reserved
Maps by Jeffrey L. Ward

ISBN 978-0-670-02512-1

Printed in the United States of America

BOOK CLUB EDITION

To the newest generation—William, Lindy, and Evan Phillips

Preface: Why *1775*

John Jay, president of the Continental Congress and later the first U.S. Chief Justice, opined years later that "the true history of the American Revolution can never be written . . . A great many of the people in those days were not at all what they seemed, nor what they were generally believed to have been."[1] If they were not—and some evidence and similar statements by others uphold Jay's point—perhaps it is best to let events, circumstances, suspicions, and necessities tell more of the tale. Less need be taken from the memoirs of the gentlemen, however worthy, whose portraits grace our currency, coinage, and postage stamps. Which is one of this book's underlying premises.

Seventeen Seventy-five, easy title that it is, stands for the somewhat forgotten and widely misunderstood first year of the American Revolution. If 1775 hadn't been a year of successful nation building, 1776 might have been a year of lost opportunity, quiet disappointment, and continued colonial status.

Although I will of necessity cover events both before and after 1775, the title means what it says: 1775 is the crucial, early-momentum year of the Revolutionary era. Still, the period profiled in these pages is not a standard January 1 to December 31 chronology. It is the larger sweep of a powerful start that put independence farther along earlier in time than most Americans realize.

Bluntly put, much of "the history" of the American Revolution suffers from distortion and omission tied to the twentieth century's excessive immersion in 1776 as a moral and ideological starting point. If July 4 of that year is truly the nation's birthday, then 1775 was little more than a number of months *in utero*. And this it categorically was not.

The infant named the United Colonies, born in 1775, was conceived during the Continental Congress of September and October 1774. The famous date, July 4, 1776, was actually a belated christening, with only a few godparents on hand. Indeed, the actual ceremony—the gathering, the signatures that bore witness—did not occur until August. Few thought the date or delay mattered. Nor was Thomas Jefferson the true father. Back in autumn 1774, Lady Liberty had never seriously dated him. He was still just Peyton Randolph's string bean of a nephew in remote Albemarle County, Virginia.

The initial purpose of this book, as contemplated in 2008, was to argue that *1775 was as important as 1776.* The finished book goes farther. It argues—and I hope substantiates—that in many respects, *1775 was more important than 1776.* The earlier year's cocky optimism, its advance guard of hundreds of new grassroots Patriot committees, its political gambles, and its unsung military successes enabled and entrenched de facto American independence. Moreover, it was begun powerfully enough to survive the crushing Patriot defeats and disillusionments that came in summer and autumn 1776 as the British Army and Royal Navy won major battles in and around New York. Much of the necessary underpinning of American self-governance—provincial congresses, local committees of safety, new seaport regulators, the flight of royal governors to small British warships obliged to provide cramped and humble quarters, and Patriot militia ordered to double as political police—had been put in place, as part of the spirit of 1775. Jefferson himself thought that the United Colonies already had de facto independence before the Declaration came along. As 1775 ended, the only place the British still controlled was occupied Boston.

A second spur to write on this topic came from my fascination over more than a half century with the periodic realignments of U.S. politics. My first book, *The Emerging Republican Majority,* written in 1966–1968 and published in 1969, predicted the beginning of a new Republican era in presidential politics. In 1993, when Bill Clinton was inaugurated, the departing GOP had held the White House for 20 of the last 24 years.

Two decades later, I am not sanguine. Both major parties seem chained to pernicious interest groups and tired ideologies. In 2008, given this context, it had seemed more rewarding to stop analyzing the present and instead to delve back into history and examine English-speaking North America's first political realignment, the 1774–1776 resort to war by which thirteen colonies quit the British Empire with such great consequence. That was an era of political hope and ambition to take seriously. The political realignment achieved amid revolution was unique—no other has come with simultaneous ballots and bullets, although the Confederacy tried in 1860–1861.

As for 1775 and 1776, no stretch is needed to talk about an emerging republican (small-*r*) majority or plurality. And despite exhaustion and disillusionment, much of this civic commitment hung on through 1782 and 1783. The U.S. Constitution, to be sure, was hammered out and ratified five years later by a somewhat different combination—one in which many persons who had been Tory-minded or neutrally inclined during the war came together with the wealthier Patriots to write more conservative national guidelines. Many of the farmers, artisans, laborers, and seamen—vocal rebels whose egalitarian postures circa 1775 had disquieted the northern commercial and southern plantation elites—opposed the new coalition a decade later. But although this further transformation is a fascinating one, this book does not pursue it. *Seventeen Seventy-five* focuses entirely on the early biases, ballots, and bullets that—literally—made the United States, albeit with the critical assistance of French and Dutch gunpowder.

My decision in 2008 to forgo current affairs for history had its own small backdrop. I had immersed myself between 2002 and 2008 in early twenty-first-century U.S. politics and the American political economy. In four sequential national election years, I had published books that sought to explain national predicaments and their implications—*Wealth and Democracy* in 2002; *American Dynasty: Aristocracy, Fortune, and the Politics of Deceit in the House of Bush* in 2004; *American Theocracy: The Politics and Perils of Radical Religion, Oil, and Borrowed Money* in 2006; and *Bad Money: Reckless Finance, Failed Politics, and the Global Crisis of American Capitalism* in 2008. All were best sellers, but the quandaries persisted.

The "financialization" of America—an ill omen I had been writing about since 1993—helped bring about a crash in 2008, but postcrash politics did not yield the needed far-reaching reform. Finance continued to sit in the catbird seat. Between 2008 and 2012, the relative economic decline of the United States and the shift of influence to Asia moved from theory to reality. The prospect is not cheering, but I have discussed it at sufficient length in earlier books. *Seventeen Seventy-five* represents a decision to write about a United States taking shape rather than one losing headway.

The present book completes another disillusionment-spurred cycle in my writing. Back in 1994 and 1995, after souring on a lobbyist-larded Washington preoccupied with Bill Clinton and Newt Gingrich, I opted to spend the next four years on a history project published in 1999 under the title *The Cousins' Wars: Religion, Politics, and the Triumph of Anglo-America.* This volume examined and sought to interrelate the three principal English-speaking civil wars—the English Civil War of the 1640s, the American Revolution, and the American Civil War—and their sequential role in the hegemonic rise first of Britain and then of the United States. The book was well received, and the change of subject matter and residence was restorative. Soon thereafter the Bush family's return to the White House in 2001 lured me back to my word processor, initiating the four 2002–2008 books mentioned above.

The Cousins' Wars, in turn, worked to seed this new book—first, by leaving a desire to revisit the American Revolution in greater depth, yet also by encouraging a second psychological holiday from national politics and the ups and downs of the Republicans and Democrats.

In its own way, to be sure, *1775* is a political book. My aim has been to view and describe the onset of the American Revolution in the thirteen colonies through much the same multiple lenses that I had first employed between 1966 and 1968 in *The Emerging Republican Majority.* That book ventured its prediction on the basis of my examining prior decades of national politics and presidential, state, and local election returns against a teeming backdrop of history, economics, major wars won or lost, geography, migration, culture, race, ethnicity, and religion. This was an in-depth fascination I had started developing as a teenager in 1956. National election patterns went from hobby to vocation. Most of that volume was written before I worked as assistant to the campaign manager in that year's Republican presidential effort. In fact, the early manuscript got me the job. The deeper I got into national politics, the more convinced I became that these various criteria served to explain most of the population's presidential-level psychologies, trends, and electoral decision making. Voting for president in the United States has not been a haphazard thought process.

If, over nearly a half century, my books have been characterized by one vein of ongoing original research, it has been this fascination—deepening, enlarging, and extending my knowledge of the grassroots United States. Back in 1968 or even 1980, I might have known which presidential candidate carried a fair number of the nation's individual counties, and I might have known the Republican or Democratic leanings of most congressional districts. No longer, of course. I have not kept up systematically on the detail of national elections since 1992, save for religion-related research in

2005–2006. That project was for a section of a larger volume, chapters that detailed the rise since the 1960s of conservative and born-again religious voters within the Republican Party's national coalition. In the United States, religion is rarely unimportant in national politics. The 1770s provide their own strong affirmation.

Since the 1990s, the balance of my research and writing has shifted from contemporary politics back into earlier history. The focus in *The Cousins' Wars* was on grassroots behavior and decision making during the periods leading up to and including the Revolution and the American Civil War. In researching *William McKinley,* my 2003 biography of the twenty-fifth president for Arthur Schlesinger's *American Presidents* series, my search included grassroots detail, especially in the Midwest, for the realigning character of the 1896 presidential election. Over the last few years, *1775* has required its own round of museums, libraries, and back roads, ranging from coastal New England, Canada, and Vermont to the Chesapeake and the upcountries of both Carolinas. Once again, I found that ethnicity and religion most often guided a man's choice of uniform—if he chose one—although many decisions were swayed by vocation, crops, hard times, or indebtedness.

I have tried to avoid too much detail on these matters. However, 50 years of some familiarity have bred not contempt for detail but appreciation. Proof matters. Elaboration is sometimes essential to understanding. Hopefully, a reasonable line has been drawn between documentation and minutiae.

In the process of reading and writing this book, my familiar methodology has buttressed my conclusion and vice versa. Taking all thirteen colonies together, no sweeping one-dimensional explanation of why 1774–1776 became a political and revolutionary watershed—be it ideology, economics, or religion—works everywhere, all of the time, or even most of the time. If anything, the upheavals of 1775 were laboratories for the *complexity* of local behavior and Revolutionary motivation.

History and Fashion

Unlike trends in men's and women's clothing, whose overnight shifts are documented avidly, fashions in American history change only slowly. The rapid inching-up of women's hemlines above the knees toward midthigh, first seen in the 1920s and again in the 1960s, was closely observed and widely taken as a national barometer of more permissive morality and speculative finance. Reinterpretations of American history, more glacial and less sensuous, occur over decades or generations, although old ones sometimes remain influential beyond their time.

The public, as opposed to the profession, has little interest. Historiography—the study of history and its processes—is dull stuff. A proposal entitled "The Role of the Consensus and Neo-Whig Schools in Shifting Public Perceptions of the American Revolution, 1946–1976" might win plaudits as Ph.D. ambitions go. However, as a published book it would be lucky to reach number 325,000 on Amazon.com. So this volume, including this preface, will tread carefully, but sometimes contextualizing comments are in order.

Briefly put, the ongoing, exaggerated American focus on 1776, which grew in the nineteenth century, became even more insistent after World War II. This was when historians of the so-called Consensus and later Neo-Whig schools—less than electric names, obviously—displaced the Progressive or Economic Determinist schools. The latter's own downfall had come from overstating economic factors and motivations in the Revolution. Deification of 1776 was further encouraged by the bicentennial commemorations in 1976, which, as Chapter 7 will amplify, promoted that single year as if it—or the Declaration of Independence—were a toothpaste or automobile. In recent decades, several scholars have gone so far as to describe the Declaration's portraiture as quasireligious.

Such legacies are not trivial, because they continue to weigh on national opinion. It has often been remarked, for example, that Washington officeholders pontificating on markets, taxes, and monetary policy are usually repeating the ideas of some dead economist, often one of whom the orator had no inkling. Similarly, Fourth of July speakers holding forth about the Declaration or the Spirit of 'Seventy-Six are often repeating the ideas of some deceased Consensus historian or trite bicentennial commemoration. Such are the ways that historical fashion can linger well beyond its expiration date.

For example, the theses offered by Consensus historians in the confident decades following World War II typically emphasized American distinctiveness and exceptionalism. Many played down internal divisions in the colonies, instead suggesting a considerable homogeneity of pro-Revolutionary opinion. In the words of Daniel Boorstin, the Revolution "was hardly a revolution at all" and bore little resemblance to upheavals in Europe.[2] If

Americans were not entirely united in 1775 and 1776, the argument went, they were not seriously divided either. Neo-Whigs were less consensus driven. Although they rejected social and economic causations, most singled out "more political, legalistic and constitutional" explanations of the Revolution's emergence. Patriot victory, pronounced one, represented "the triumph of a principle."[3]

The late 1940s, 1950s, and early 1960s were also a time when prominent thinkers imagined an "end of ideology" and a triumph of moderation. Others enthused over a "melting pot" bound to lessen ethnic and racial differences. Some homogenization was presumed, if not endorsed. The concept of Americanism became strong enough that the House of Representatives could establish a Committee on Un-American Activities. Beyond politics, for those of us old enough to remember the cooking of the 1950s, that too was bland. Jell-O was a staple; frozen pizza was a breakthrough.

More depth and attention to historical complexity developed in the 1970s and 1980s, abetted by the rise of specialties such as military history, as well as by cliometrics and neoprogressive emphasis on "bottom-up" economic history that analyzed the circumstances of ordinary folk. The first camp directed attention to internal conflict and civil war in Revolutionary America. The second latched on to social and economic discontent, not least in prewar cities and seaports. From a relatively conservative perspective, military historians were persuasive in maintaining that "close study of the areas committed to one side or the other supports the view that ethnic and religious differences were important determinants of Revolutionary behavior."[4]

Sophisticated information technology has been a particular boon, opening up new resources, making available specialized detail, and providing easy access to hard-to-find collections and publications. This, too, diminished misconceptions of relative colonial homogeneity and the oneness of political opinion. The Internet Revolution, especially in the 2000s, worked its own magic. Colonial America regained complexity and tension; Consensus and to a lesser extent Neo-Whig interpretations lost ground. Social, economic, and internal conflict-based explanations regained influence.

This book does not contend that a particular set of social and economic forces touched off the Revolution. On the contrary, no one set of causations played that role, because too many separate ingredients were involved. Of thirteen colonies, roughly half were economic and cultural amalgamates.

New York, New Jersey, Pennsylvania, and the Carolinas were conspicuously so. Social, economic, political, ideological, and religious forces all influenced local versions of the Revolution.

The last third of the twentieth century saw the new or further documentation of many innovations, local animosities, and competing interests. Consider the First Continental Congress in late 1774. It called for localities to set up committees of observation and inspection. By mid-1775, some 500 to 600 counties and towns had done so, many of them quickly developing loyalty-enforcement and regulatory mechanisms. The Revolution's committees, conventions, congresses, and associations, although recalling English Civil War terminology and precedents, were deployed more quickly and in much greater numbers. In Philadelphia, as research published during the 1980s showed, the local committee structure mushroomed between 1774 and 1776. What's more, as Chapter 5 will illustrate, committee membership became more radical in each stage. True, their politics and practices fell short of what emerged in France during the 1790s. But although the French analogy is limited, the number of Loyalist émigrés who fled the United States ultimately exceeded the count of Frenchmen who fled their revolution.[5]

Military historians have documented the civil war characteristics that the Revolution displayed in many areas. In New York, New Jersey, and the Carolinas, tabulations show that in roughly half of the battles in which militia participated, Americans were fighting Americans.[6] This bitterness continued to the war's end.

Population-minded scholars have shown how the rapid growth of the thirteen colonies worried British officials by the 1760s, pushing them toward restrictive measures like the Royal Proclamation of 1763, which sought to prohibit settlement west of the Appalachians. Unless western expansion could be stopped, it was feared that the colonies would soon be too populous to be restrained militarily. Migration to North America was for some years seen as threatening depopulation and loss of wealth in northern Ireland and parts of Scotland.

As for colonial economic growth and opportunity, it is now clear that especially after 1764, British policies unduly restricting paper money shrank the local money supply in some American colonies to an extent that throttled commerce and forced more people into debt. The expanding ranks of artisans, most notable in Boston, New York, and Philadelphia, grew restive in the pre-Revolutionary decade as their share of municipal wealth and income declined. Remedies they put forward included reducing or cutting off imports from Britain, as well as promoting the growth of American manufacturing enterprises that Parliament discouraged or flatly prohibited.

Powerful ethnic and religious divisions mocked notions of cultural and political homogeneity. Wartime loyalties were splintered and divided among emergent groups like Germans, Irish Catholics, Methodists, and Baptists, and despite nineteenth- and twentieth-century boosterism determined to praise their Patriotic fervor, probing scholars have documented something less. In New Jersey, for example, bitter divisions set Patriot Dutch Reformed adherents of the Coetus faction against Conferentie-faction congregations who took the Loyalist side. In South Carolina, Regular Baptist clergymen on the Patriot side failed to sway backcountry Separate Baptists, many of whom instead followed an unctuous pro-Tory preacher.

Sometimes the new detail has been double-barreled in its revisionist effect. Arthur Schlesinger, Sr., in 1917 a young Ohio historian, made a splash that year with his influential volume *The Colonial Merchants and the American Revolution, 1763-1776*.[7] Much of the revolutionary impetus of the 1760s, he argued, came from merchants, and the eventual Revolution represented a clashing of economic interests. Late twentieth-century research has amplified how different specializations within the urban merchant communities, not broad overall merchant status, best explained their Patriot-versus-Loyalist commitments. This upheld the salience of economic issues. However, the same research into Boston, New York, Philadelphia, Baltimore, Norfolk, and Charleston loyalties has shown how ethnicity and religion split the merchants, rebutting the notion of a largely economic clash of issues.

Ideally, this information should rebut the insistences of historians who claim a singular and paramount role for politics, economics, or religion. Part of that singularity is also a matter of definitions, which need not detain us here.

Historians and others who write for a popular audience tend to minimize or eliminate the quotations from scholarly tracts and from others in the field. This book does, too, but not always happily. As with *The Cousins' Wars* a decade and a half ago, and for that matter *The Emerging Republican Majority* forty-five years ago, the frameworks, general theses, and interrelations in this book are mine. However, when it comes to specifics of the new complexity, be they colonial money supplies, local merchant ethnicity and religion, the European munitions trade of 1774–1775, the evolution of Philadelphia Revolutionary committees, or the intramural tensions between

Coetus and Conferentie in what is now suburban New Jersey, the original spadework is someone else's. I have drawn on individual historians whose names and writings should add to the credibility of the points made.

If those names appear mostly in endnotes, I should acknowledge a particular debt to several groups of specialists in American history. One such combines the scholars and writers who have seen a great turning point in 1774's fierce response to the several Coercive Acts and its culmination in the First Continental Congress. A second related school hypothesizes an accelerating mid-1770s rejection of George III by American colonials—a psychological version of regicide, which helped the public to embrace republicanism over monarchy. This aided a steady 1775–1776 transfer of legitimacy to a new nation, a Congress, and a new framework of thirteen republican states. Yet another small group of scholars identifies 1775 as the bold, daring year from a military as well as popular opinion standpoint. Their conclusions evoke a vivid "spirit of 1775," not an ebbing "spirit of 1776." This early confidence was essential.

A fourth body of opinion explains the American Revolution as a civil war—a clear display of the sort of bitter fratricide in which existing and emerging religious, ethnic, and sectional divisions deepen in both politics and warfare. In 1774, Thomas Jefferson penned his own fears of "civil" war. Then in 1776 he insisted that a united "people" were separating themselves from another "people" in Britain. This book takes the "civil war" position.

A fifth category includes authors who have examined an opening year, 1774 or 1775, from the standpoint of one province, Massachusetts, Virginia, South Carolina, or Connecticut, where confrontation began early. Titles include *The First American Revolution: Before Lexington and Concord* (profiling Massachusetts in 1774), *1775: Another Part of the Field* (explaining Virginia during that year), and *The South Carolina Civil War of 1775.*[8] Doubtless there are others.

The Book's Plan

This volume's attempt to set out a new view of the United Colonies and how they managed to become the United States is divided into four parts. The structure can be summarized as follows:

Part I, the *Introduction,* is a single chapter designed to explain what the future United States was like in 1775, what the key events were between the summer of 1774 and the spring of 1776, and how they have been minimized or even pushed aside by a fixation on 1776. This discussion also previews several of the book's subjects, from the international gunpowder trade to Samuel Adams's backstage role in Massachusetts.

Part II, headed *The Revolution—Provocations, Motivations, and Alignments,* examines the multiple origins of the American Revolution. The Continental Congress and most of the provincial congresses met in secrecy—wisely, because what they were planning and plotting amounted to treason. But the principal circumstances and subject matter can be set out in six chapters, which address the political, religious, economic, and cultural frustrations and motivations that underlay their Revolution.

To establish the leading actors, Chapter 2 argues that four colonies— Massachusetts, Virginia, Connecticut, and South Carolina—made up the vanguard of the Revolution, contributing two thirds or even three quarters of its momentum and leadership. These four boasted roughly half of the population, more than half of the wealth, and much more than half of the thirteen colonies' political history. They were the old colonies, directly chartered by seventeenth-century kings (who granted territory west to the Pacific), proud of century-and-a-half- or century-old histories of defending against France, Spain, and a dozen Indian tribes, and equally proud of long-established assembly houses that considered themselves New World parliaments. Much of the colonial self-confidence and aggressiveness of 1774 and 1775 came from these four. Pennsylvania and New York, by contrast, although populous and important, lacked a parallel tradition and were foot draggers in revolutionary commitment.

Chapter 3 weighs the great importance of religion in the Revolution and puts it on a par with two other incitements to action: political and constitutional clashes with Britain, and North America's growing demand for economic self-determination.

Chapter 4 catalogues and assesses colonial economic circumstances and complaints, emphasizing twelve. These include shortages of currency and money, lack of land banks or other banks, growing colonial debt burdens, so-called enumerated commodities (tobacco, rice, et al.) that could only be shipped to Britain, objectionable taxes, oppressive maritime regulation and customs red tape, imperial trade constraints, attempts to limit American population growth, increasingly restrictive British land policies, the transfer to Canadian jurisdiction in 1774 of western territory claimed by leading colonies, constraint of colonial industries like iron making, hats, and woolens, and growing American desire to manufacture what had to be imported from

Britain. Simply put, the mushrooming colonies were already more populous than Holland or Switzerland, and British curbs and limitations that had been acceptable in 1750 were becoming unacceptable, even insulting.

The focus of Chapter 5 is on how the leading colonial cities—Boston, New York, Philadelphia, and Charleston—were particular seedbeds of revolution. Emphasis is put on seamen, artisans, and mechanics, and radical militias, the latter a real force in Philadelphia circa 1775.

The expansion of the colonial backcountry—from Maine to Georgia, but particularly in the south—was so pronounced that it unnerved the British. They feared not only the expense of Indian wars but that North America would soon populate beyond London's control. However, as Chapter 6 shows, the new southern backcountry settlements and large influx of poor whites also disturbed the coastal planter elites, who feared losing control of politics in the Carolinas and Georgia. In both Carolinas, white settlers who had arrived since 1750 outnumbered the preexisting coastal or low-country white populations by two or three to one. These latter-day settlers provided the framework of civil war in both Carolinas.

Chapter 7, "The Ideologies of Revolution," casts doubt on the role of abstract ideology or radical pamphleteers in bringing about the American Revolution, which some have asserted. Instead, it emphasizes five broadly ideological factors: *community* (the growth of American nationhood), *commerce* as resentment (colonial frustration over economic subordination*),* *constitutions* (competing British and American legal concepts), *Calvinism* (with its theology of republican religion and just war), and *conspiracy* (a long-standing English sensitivity further developed in America).

All of these angers and pressures contributed to the Revolution, albeit in different proportions from one colony to the next.

Having surveyed the principal causes and motivations, I've aimed in Part III to shift attention to the Revolution's major political and military arenas as they emerged and developed in 1775. For historians to describe battlegrounds and confrontations as taking real shape only in 1776 is misleading; it passes over much of the essential context of what happened and why.

In this new vein, Chapter 8 discusses "Fortress New England," which is meant literally. Although the Patriot elites in Virginia and the Carolinas were not far behind in their politics and mobilization calendar, the four New England colonies, all dating back to the seventeenth century, and all largely English by ancestry, were the most united and cohesive bloc. They were wedded to the belief that Englishmen in colonial Boston, Hartford, or Portsmouth had the same rights as Englishmen living in towns with those same names on the other side of the Atlantic. Because they had forced the issue, the major battles of 1775 were joined in New England or alongside it in upper New York or Canada. New England furnished most of the early soldiers.

The title of Chapter 9, "Declaring Economic War," means just what it says. In October 1774, the First Continental Congress called for a phased-in popular refusal to import British products, followed by a prohibition against the export to Britain of key commodities like tobacco, rice, and naval stores. This did nothing less than challenge the central economic premise of the imperial system. By April 1775, even before Lexington and Concord, Parliament was identifying nine of the thirteen colonies as rebellious because of their participation.

Chapter 10 underscores how the war tilted north during the summer of 1775 as the British, with many regiments immobilized in Boston, nervously turned to defending Canada against an invasion—and almost lost.

Chapter 11 lays out one of the least-known but highest-priority enterprises of 1774–1775—the global munitions contest to determine whether the would-be rebels would have the gunpowder and arms needed to revolt. For example, although obtaining munitions was only a sidebar to invading Canada, the British commander there in November 1775, General Guy Carleton, was so worried about Quebec falling to the Americans that he returned to Britain a transport stuffed with needed munitions because it was likely to be captured.

Difficult and mismanaged logistics dogged the British from the start, as Chapter 12 details. In late 1775, as war spread, there were too few escort vessels to guard military transports crossing the Atlantic and too few transports to move the British soldiers stuck in Boston to New York where they needed to be.

Chapter 13 details one of the most inept British strategies of 1775—the "southern expedition" conceptualized during the summer and put into motion by the king and Lord North during October and November. It was planned around an early 1776 naval and troop-transport rendezvous off Cape Fear, North Carolina, and it was botched so badly that the British and mercenary regiments expected to reach New York by spring did not get there until the summer, jeopardizing the 1776 invasion calendar.

British Admiral Samuel Graves's late-summer orders for the Royal Navy

xxii Preface: Why *1775*

to burn seaports along the New England coast became, as Chapter 14 details, a powerful Patriot point of condemnation. Although the Americans themselves were not beyond torching cities—Norfolk, Virginia, and possibly part of Manhattan in 1776—widely regarded as nests of Loyalists, Washington, Adams, and company handily won the propaganda war.

Chapter 15, "Red, White, and Black," looks at the British-laid plans of 1775 to have hostile Indians raid the American frontier, incite white indentured servants to run away to the British Army, and promise freedom to black slaves who would enlist in His Majesty's forces. Lord Dunmore, the royal governor of Virginia, pursued all three, but his tactics backfired and drove white Virginians toward independence.

Chapter 16 explains how the Britain of 1775 could not fight a major war without hiring large numbers of mercenaries. The Russians were approached first, but refused in November. That meant hiring Hessians, Brunswickers, and other Germans, but their employment offended public opinion in much of Europe, North America, and even Britain.

The Chesapeake region, centered on the thirteen colonies' largest estuary, had a large Loyalist population and might have been an effective British invasion route. Chapter 17 looks at who made that case and how British planners, literally and figuratively, missed the boat in Chesapeake Bay.

Chapter 18 looks at how the American Revolution was also an English-speaking civil war, principally in North America but also to an extent in the British Isles.

Between the summer of 1775 and June 1776, the Continental Congress produced a wide range of proclamations, declarations, and enactments that moved the United Colonies further and further toward independence, with little left undone. Chapter 19 looks at these various "almost-declarations" and makes the argument that the Declaration approved in July was anticlimactic and principally aimed at finalizing American withdrawal from the empire for legal, diplomatic, and treaty-making reasons. But it also had to be agreed to before the arriving British in New York harbor could disembark enough troops to scare New York and New Jersey back into the arms of King George.

Part IV, Chapters 20 through 26, goes beyond individual battles to interpret the overall meaning and significance of the principal campaigns and confrontations of 1775—the "long" 1775 that began in the late summer of 1774 and ended in the spring of 1776, when de facto American independence finally became de jure. From "The Battle of Boston," fought between the Coercive Acts of 1774 and British withdrawal in March 1776, to Britain's woeful "southern expedition," bungled from its conception in 1775 to its conclusion in Charleston Harbor, these were auspicious underpinnings for the United Colonies that often go unrecognized.

Several other points need to be made. To begin with, *1775* concentrates on the thirteen British North American colonies that mounted the Revolution. Five that did not—Quebec, Nova Scotia, Prince Edward Island (St. Jean), East Florida, and West Florida—are mentioned only in passing. There is an interesting larger context, which I discussed in *The Cousins' Wars*. However, to put it simply, these were new colonies created from captured territory in 1763 and either were run by the army or navy or, like Nova Scotia, Quebec, and the Floridas, were home to major British bases. Although each held Patriot sympathizers—as for that matter did Bermuda and the Bahamas—none of these colonies wanted to participate in the Continental Congresses. They were a different breed.

Secondly, in identifying the four vanguard colonies in Chapter 2, it may be well to offer a few sidebars. One powerful reason for picking Connecticut will be fleshed out in the several chapters that discuss military preparedness in 1775. All but independent under its royal charter, Connecticut did not have to change governments in 1775, and its chief executive, ardent Patriot Jonathan Trumbull, already in office for six years, served eight more through 1783. The colony was uniquely positioned between the three major hot spots of 1775—Boston, New York City, and Lake Champlain—and was uniquely able to raise and send regiments where needed. Trumbull, who worked closely with George Washington, deserves much more recognition than he has ever received.

As to why Virginia and South Carolina are identified as vanguard colonies and North Carolina is not, the latter was neither an old colony nor a national leader. But its rarely recognized importance in discouraging the 70-ship and seven-regiment southern expedition set in motion by King George and Lord North in October 1775 deserves a special mention.

The years 1774 and 1775 have more than their share of unsung heroes. Some of these have provided a further, welcome refreshment in this era of political disappointment.

Kevin Phillips
Litchfield County, Connecticut
April 2012

Contents

List of Maps

PART I

INTRODUCTION

CHAPTER I

The Spirit of 1775

In one sense it is doubtless true that nobody, in 1775, wanted war; in another sense it is almost equally clear that both the Americans and the British were aching for a showdown.

Henry Steele Commager and Richard B. Morris, *The Spirit of 'Seventy-six,* 1958

How do we account for the hostilities on Lexington Green? . . . Simple, in that control of munitions was crucial to both sides—to the Americans for making war, to the British for avoiding it.

Don Higginbotham, *The War of American Independence,* 1971

S uch was the arousal and spirit of 1775 that *rage militaire*—a patriotic furor, a passion for arms—swept the thirteen colonies that spring and summer, giving the American Revolution its martial assurance and its vital, if somewhat delusionary, early momentum. Great hopes took hold, and sedentary lawyers, publishers, and preachers pored over their libraries of English political and revolutionary precedents.

Lexington and Concord and Bunker Hill sowed confidence, and by summer, scarlet-coated military might had shrunk back to encircled Boston and a few fast-deserting companies in New York. Following these initial successes, Patriots soon developed "a national conceit of born courage in combat with a sudden acclaim for a superior form of military discipline, easily acquired"—that of a valorous and virtuous citizen soldiery.[1] It was all very heady.

Virtue, the old Roman credo, clad itself in a uniquely American garb. Hunting shirts, belts, and leggings became fashionable, what a later era might term militia chic. Even gentry-minded Virginians cast aside their imported velours and joined in. Before the opening of a June 1775 legislative session in Williamsburg, burgesses were recommended to attend in shirtmen's garb—frontier-type apparel—"which best suits the times, as the cheapest and the most martial." And "numbers of the Burgesses" did indeed come wearing "coarse linnen or canvas over their Cloaths and a Tomahawk by their Sides."[2] New Englanders, informed by Harvard and Yale scholars, boasted that no plausible European army could be large enough to overcome the combination of American space and just cause. In Pennsylvania, even erstwhile pacifist Quakers marched in a volunteer light infantry company nicknamed the "Quaker Blues," for which some were quickly read out of their monthly meetings.

Three thousand miles away, many British policy makers suffered from an opposite "empire militant" style of conceit. No colonial riffraff could hope to stand up to the professional armies of the world's preeminent imperium. The revolutionaries would scatter in panic after two or three of their well-known leaders were hung as traitors. General James Grant told amused listeners that he could march from one end of the American colonies to the other with 5,000 British regulars. The king's aide-de-camp, General Thomas Clark, thought he could do it with 1,000 men, gelding colonial males as he went.[3] Boston radicals, "Oliverian" at heart, were the trouble spreaders, subverting loyal and unwary subjects elsewhere. Through much of 1774 and 1775, even as British ministers transferred troops to hostile Boston, they naïvely emptied barracks elsewhere.

Clearly both sides misread some military and political realities. However, the rebels of 1775 had the better reason for confidence. Provincial boundaries of that era being imprecise, disputed, or vague, no researcher can hope to calculate the ratio of the thirteen-colony domain—from Maine (then a district of Massachusetts) south through Georgia—still effectively occupied by British soldiers or administered by functioning officials of His Majesty's government at year's end. Whatever the maps in Whitehall or St. James purported to show, the reality on the ground was stark: practically nothing.

Consider: in Virginia and both Carolinas, the summer of 1775 saw Crown-appointed governors ignominiously flee their unfriendly capitals for cramped but seizure-proof accommodations on nearby British warships. In February 1776, the governor of Georgia, all but powerless, finally decamped to a convenient frigate. In most places, the king's writ no longer ran. In all four southern colonies, Patriot-led provincial congresses and committees of safety had taken extralegal but effective control of government. Forts had been captured, munitions seized, sea actions fought, towns burned, and regiment after regiment mustered into the new Continental Army.

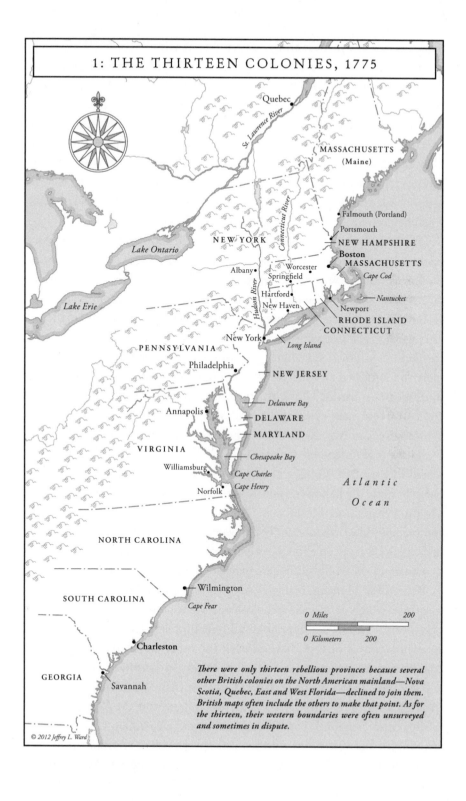

1: THE THIRTEEN COLONIES, 1775

Quebec

St. Lawrence River

MASSACHUSETTS
(Maine)

• Falmouth (Portland)

Portsmouth

NEW HAMPSHIRE

NEW YORK

Connecticut River

Lake Ontario

Boston
MASSACHUSETTS

Albany •   Worcester
           Springfield   *Cape Cod*

Lake Erie

Hudson River

Hartford •
New Haven

Newport

Nantucket

RHODE ISLAND
CONNECTICUT

New York

PENNSYLVANIA

Long Island

Philadelphia

NEW JERSEY

Delaware Bay

Annapolis •

DELAWARE

MARYLAND

VIRGINIA

Chesapeake Bay

Williamsburg •
           Cape Charles

Norfolk •   *Cape Henry*

Atlantic

Ocean

NORTH CAROLINA

Wilmington

SOUTH CAROLINA   *Cape Fear*

| 0 Miles | | 200 |
| 0 Kilometers | 200 | |

Charleston

GEORGIA

Savannah

There were only thirteen rebellious provinces because several other British colonies on the North American mainland—Nova Scotia, Quebec, East and West Florida—declined to join them. British maps often include the others to make that point. As for the thirteen, their western boundaries were often unsurveyed and sometimes in dispute.

© 2012 Jeffrey L. Ward

An ocean away, the punitive intentions of King George III also kept growing—from his late-1774 comment about looking forward to putting down rebellion in Massachusetts to his mid-1775 hope of hiring Russian mercenaries, only to settle by year end for Hessians and Brunswickers. Henry Howard, twelfth Earl of Suffolk and a principal secretary of state, had agreed that the Russians would make "charming visitors at New-Yorke, and civilize that part of America wonderfully."[4] A year before July 4, 1776, the die was all but cast. In fact, participants from King George to John Adams used precisely that phrase, first employed by Julius Caesar when he crossed the Rubicon in 49 B.C.

The reader can learn about these events and escalations in the history books, just not conveniently or in very much detail. Over two centuries, as the Revolutionary War became all but sanctified as "the single most important source for our national sense of tradition," public attention was diverted from the struggle's more complicated, less-inspiring realities.[5] Disregarding the necessities of munitions smuggling and using militiamen to suppress political dissidence, the origins of the republic became ever more romanticized around the assertion of 1776 as a moral and ideological watershed not just for North America but for the world. Events were also confected into neat celebratory symbols like Paul Revere's ride, George Washington's greatness, Benjamin Franklin's genius, Thomas Jefferson's Declaration of Independence, Betsy Ross's flag, and the seriously misrepresented Liberty Bell. Boston, Lexington-Concord, Philadelphia, and Valley Forge became the hallowed venues, with legend-building side excursions to Mount Vernon and Monticello. This adulation has served to minimize comprehension of what actually happened—not least how a *rage militaire* helped put down deep enough early foundations for American nationhood to withstand the disillusionments that mounted in the second half of 1776.

Behind the bunting, reality is not merely a corrective but a more gripping tale. Much of it is scarcely known. Massachusetts and Virginia did play central roles, just as schoolchildren properly learn. However, the sprawling canvas of 1775, beyond even the other eleven insurgent North American colonies, stretches to include events in Bermuda, the Bahamas and the West Indies, Canada, Ireland and the Irish Sea, London, Glasgow, England's Isle of Wight, the sea lanes off Holland and the Austrian Netherlands (now Belgium), Paris, Nantes, the smuggler-ridden Channel ports of Dunkirk and Ostend, the Prince-Bishopric of Liège (Europe's principal independent weapons contractor), and Hesse-Cassel and a half dozen other minor principalities in northern Germany, as well as Madrid, Gibraltar, Mediterranean Minorca, and West Africa's Slave Coast. Intrigue even reached the St. Petersburg palace of Catherine the Great, Russia's czarina, who scoffed at King George's Russian troop-hire request. All were venues where British or Americans, publicly or privately, sought critical assistance— mercenaries, munitions, or both. Competition and then confrontation were global.

Another essential subject is rebellion's political geography—the different degrees of involvement and intensity within the insurgent thirteen. New England's other three provinces, for example, were scarcely less motivated than Massachusetts. Self-governing Connecticut and Rhode Island, only nominal "colonies," were in Patriot political hands from the start. In New Hampshire, the royal governor, John Wentworth, soon took refuge in harborside Fort William and Mary. Then in August 1775, he sailed away to Boston on HMS *Scarborough,* which six months later also became home to Georgia's fugitive executive. In the South, despite the speed shown in driving out royal governors, important divisions lingered. As for the middle colonies—the future states of New York, New Jersey, Pennsylvania, Maryland, and Delaware—overall they included the highest ratio of doubters and temporizers. Their indecision during the winter of 1775–1776 worried commander in chief George Washington as well as pro-independence strategists in the Continental Congress. Part of our tale of 1775 involves the often-bitter backstage battle for political allegiance.

Massachusetts: The Coercive Acts as a Seedbed of Revolution

As the North American rampart of the militant Protestantism so involved in England's two earlier revolutions, New England stood to be—arguably *had* to be—the epicenter of the British imperial crisis of the 1770s. Where King George and his ministers erred was in underestimating the *American* nationalism growing in the other colonies, generated less by Boston's provocative tea dumping than by the Crown's overreaction. To many Patriot leaders, the Coercive Acts—in colonial parlance, the Intolerable Acts— reiterated the prerevolutionary arrogance and practices of Charles I before the English Civil War and of James II before the Glorious Revolution of 1688. But with or without the analogy, the result, as it had been in the previous century, was a growing revolutionary mindset.

On September 12, 1774, the military governor of Massachusetts,

Lieutenant-General Thomas Gage, unnerved by summer militia rallies and huge public demonstrations, shared his foreboding in a letter to the American secretary in London, Lord Dartmouth: "It is needless to trouble your Lordship with daily Publications of determined [local] resolutions not to obey the Late Acts of Parliament . . . The Country People are exercising in Arms in this Province, Connecticut and Rhode Island, and getting Magazines of Arms and Ammunition . . . and such Artillery as they can procure, good or bad . . . People are resorting to this town [Boston] for Protection . . . even [from] Places always esteemed well affected . . . and Sedition flows copiously from the Pulpits. The Commissioners of Customs have thought it no longer safe or prudent to remain at Salem . . . and are amongst others come into the Town [Boston], where I am obliged likewise now to reside on many accounts."[6] Intermittently optimistic in late spring and early summer, Gage now admitted the truth: New England was all but out of control.

The Bay Colony, proud of its early self-government and charters dating back to 1629, had since May been occupied by four additional regiments of British troops sent to enforce the Boston Port Act and the companion Massachusetts Government Act. These two statutes stood out among the five acts urged by George III and enacted by Parliament between March and June 1774.* Designed not just as punishment for December's Boston Tea Party, these measures were also expected to caution and humble the other colonies. Instead, the prevalent response was radicalization.

Although the punishment of Massachusetts included installing army commander Gage as governor, by winter neither office gave him any real punitive reach. The farmers of the colony's interior, less concerned about tea or even the Boston Port Act—this closed Boston harbor to shipping until the dumped tea was paid for—reacted quickly on learning of the colonywide scope of penalties imposed by the Massachusetts Government Act. The Massachusetts Charter of 1691 was eviscerated. Key provisions of the new statute all but eliminated town meetings, ended locally chosen juries, gave the governor sole power to appoint and remove judges, and transferred the selection of the Governor's Council, the upper legislative house, from elected representatives to Crown appointees.

A third new statute, the Justice Act, inflamed matters further by interfering with traditional British concepts of trial by jury. Under this legislation, someone acting under Crown authority—customs officer, naval

*The Quebec Act is included because of its overlapping time frame and the ire its provisions aroused.

captain, soldier, or county sheriff—who was charged with committing a capital crime in performance of his duty could have his trial moved from the province in which the act had been committed. The governor need only decide that no fair trial could be had locally. Concluding that soldiers could shoot and escape punishment, people in Massachusetts called it the "Murder Act," an epithet echoed by George Washington and other conservative Virginians.[7] The fourth statute, another Quartering Act, imposed soldiers on unwilling civilians.

The Quebec Act, unrelated but enacted more or less simultaneously, established the Catholic Church in French Canada, while also extending Quebec's boundaries south to the Ohio River. This was a particular blow to the western territorial claims maintained by Massachusetts, Connecticut, and Virginia under their seventeenth-century charters. Its religious dimension will be examined in Chapter 3; however, the enactment of new constraining and insulting borders was also a frontal challenge to incipient American manifest destiny.

As details crossed the Atlantic in June and July, indignation in Massachusetts deepened into confrontation. From Pittsfield in the western hills to Plymouth in the east, huge crowds in the 3,000-to-5,000-person range rallied in the colony's principal shire towns to shut down what were now seen as corrupted and compromised local governments, courts in particular. In Worcester, the local militia—some arrayed in company formation and led by uniformed officers—paraded in support. Two thousand protesters thronged Worcester Common on August 26, and some 6,000, many armed, assembled on September 6, the day the court was to convene.[8] What stunned Gage was that these were not a city mob but family men—farmers and yeomen. He and his councilors decided it would be too dangerous to send troops; those soldiers, indeed, might be needed to protect Boston. The huge demonstrations, besides closing the county courts, also frightened royal appointees singled out by the people into resigning their offices. Some fled to England. Lexington was still seven months away.

New England: The First Front Line

By October, an aroused Provincial Congress and the Committee of Safety, its executive arm, had taken de facto control throughout the colony save for occupied Boston. Military preparations were barely disguised. For his part, Gage had begun new fortifications. The eighteenth-century city was virtually an island, connected to the mainland only by a thin neck of land, 30 yards wide at high tide. There the British built a fortified gate, emplaced cannon, and constructed minor outerworks. By the time they evacuated eighteen months later, the once-scrawny neck had turned into a miniature fortress.[9] Both sides were ramping up.

Through early 1775, the embattled British general remained able to ferry or march troops within a 30-to-40-mile range. Two schooners were employed in January to send a company of regulars to Marshfield in the old Plymouth Colony. There they protected a fearful assemblage of Tories, to whom Gage had earlier sent arms. Then in February, 240 redcoats under Colonel Alexander Leslie quietly took ship to Marblehead, disembarked, and marched north to capture cannon and munitions stored in Salem, the province's second seaport.

The outcome smacked of comic opera. Once the British column was spotted in Marblehead, Salem residents were warned just in time to move the sought-after cannon. When Leslie neared the town center, he found a drawbridge raised and behind it a considerable body of county militia. A local parson, advising the colonel that the cannon had already been dispersed, arranged an unusual bargain: Leslie agreed that if the bridge was lowered so that he could march across, fulfilling that part of his orders, he would in fact proceed only 50 rods. Then he would look around and march back, which is what he did.

By late March, with war in the unseasonably springlike air, Gage sent out scouting officers in civilian clothes. They reported back that any major expedition—plans had again focused on Worcester, the Patriots' main arms depot 48 miles west of Boston—would be surrounded and overwhelmed, probably meaning war. In any event, hostilities began three weeks later on April 19, when a mixed force of 700 infantry and royal marines marched just sixteen miles west, acting under orders to take or destroy military stores closer at hand in Concord. Instead, after eight militiamen were killed on Lexington Green and a small quantity of stores and powder destroyed in Concord, the redcoats came under attack by thousands of swarming minutemen. They were, as every schoolchild knows, chased back to Boston with heavy casualties. War was beginning.

Little about these great events was altogether spontaneous. Several decades ago General John R. Galvin, former U.S. supreme commander in Europe and a skilled military analyst, published a volume about the Massachusetts forces entitled *The Minutemen*. Dismissing the "mythology" that had "depicted them as a small but courageous band of farmers who responded to a spontaneous call to arms, an untrained and poorly armed rabble," he set out different premises. Fourteen thousand Bay Colony men were "under arms in the militia and Minute Man regiments. They were alerted by organized alarm riders via a system that dated back to the 17th century wars. They had trained intensively for a year and were armed with the same type weapons as the British."[10] One military historian has suggested that Massachusetts had the best-trained militia in British North America.[11]

Within days of Lexington and Concord, 20,000 Patriot militia from Connecticut, New Hampshire, and Rhode Island, as well as Massachusetts, encircled Boston. Then eight weeks later, on June 17, a second encounter, bloodier still, followed on the Charlestown peninsula across from Boston. The fighting actually took place on Breed's Hill, but it was mislabeled for the ages with the name of nearby Bunker Hill, more elevated and slightly farther from Boston. The choice might have been made by Connecticut General Israel Putnam, who in the darkness of the previous night decided to fortify the lower-lying and less-advantageous position. But whether or not the motive of such in-your-face entrenchment was to bait the British into a frontal attack, that is what happened, as General Howe declined the flanking move that might have brought easy victory. With Breed's only 800 yards across the Charles River from the city, large crowds watched from both Beacon Hill and Cobb's Hill, site of the British artillery. Carefully dressed ranks of scarlet-clad infantry, grenadiers, and royal marines paraded uphill into withering fire from New Englanders with muskets and ancient fowling pieces, although not nearly enough gunpowder. After failing twice to overcome well-entrenched rebels, the king's troops prevailed in a third advance only when the colonials ran out of ammunition. Even untouched British soldiers—a minority that day—returned to their boats with gaiters and leggings reddened to the knees by the hillside's gore-spattered tall grass and weeds. Officer deaths, in particular, put grim black edges on survivors' letters home. The number of British officers killed and wounded on June 17 represented a quarter of those officers killed and wounded during the entire Revolutionary War.

True, this is a familiar tale, the outline having long since entered American folklore. What the familiar tale generally omits is how much resentment had been building and over so long a time. Boston had been occupied by British regulars since 1768. As we will see in more detail, New England by 1775 had become a sullen townscape of cannon hidden in hay barns and root cellars half filled with powder kegs. Its coast was a harborscape of sloops and schooners with crews long skilled at smuggling back desirable goods from the French, Spanish, and Dutch West Indies. Now gunpowder, flints, and muskets had replaced tea and taffetas. Town greens, for their part, had become muster grounds for the best-organized trained bands and militia since the men of Oliver Cromwell and England's Eastern Association, many of whose great-great-grandsons and cousins three times removed now lived in New England.

Part of the April 19 legend is that Massachusetts militiamen, not British regulars, fired first on that fateful morning. Even some captured British officers, subsequently deposed for evidence, gave their own side the blame. That part of the legend is probably true, but either way, what exactly happened cannot be recreated. What we do know is that top Revolutionary leaders like Samuel Adams and Joseph Warren, president of the Massachusetts Provincial Congress, quickly implemented a domestic and foreign information-cum-propaganda campaign little short of brilliant.

In retrospect, Samuel Adams was essential to putting Massachusetts at the center of 1775's Revolutionary universe. His fame produced comparisons in other colonies—Christopher Gadsden was the Sam Adams of South Carolina, Cornelius Harnett the Sam Adams of North Carolina, and Charles Thomson of Pennsylvania. Yet there was only one full-fledged arch-manipulator: Sam Adams. Silversmith Paul Revere became horseback herald to this puritan Machiavel and rode into immortality. Between 1773 and 1775, a handful of men coordinated, connected, and unfolded an insurgency that still cries out for an American Shakespeare. In later chapters, we will watch the dramatic sequence of connected acts—the Boston Tea Party, the huge 1774 civil rights demonstrations (for so they were) in the shire towns, that September's great Powder Alarm, the Suffolk Resolves, Revere's ride to Philadelphia, the Resolves' not-so-coincidental embrace by the First Continental Congress, the ensuing mobilization of New England, April's hallowed militiamen, and the immortalization of Lexington and Concord into the shot heard round the world.

It was a triumph of communications as much as Revolutionary ideology. We must remember that the First Continental Congress, during the autumn of 1774, had specified that the other colonies' support for Boston, if and when blows came, would depend on the British being the aggressors and having fired first; Adams and Warren both knew that irrefutable proof would be essential. So within a few days of the shots that had not yet been heard around the other colonies, no less the world, local justices of the peace had taken statements from roughly 100 eyewitnesses, including captured British soldiers. Warren then prefaced and packaged them for maximum effect, and the reins passed to a Massachusetts-to-Georgia chain of couriers and fresh horses. One especially vivid description captured the speed: "The newspapers, all of them weeklies, published their stories, borrowing liberally from each other and embroidering the apocryphal details of atrocities. On the Monday after the battle, accounts were in the Connecticut and New York papers; on Wednesday, in the Pennsylvania papers; on Thursday, in those of Maryland; on Saturday, in Dixon & Hunter's *Virginia Gazette;* and on through to the Carolinas, until the news reached the *Georgia Gazette* in Savannah. Many of the papers, unwilling to wait for their weekly publication date, got out handbills as soon as the news was received."[12] We will come back to the ripple effect of *rage militaire* in a few pages.

The triumph achieved by Patriot propaganda in London was equally spectacular. The hapless Gage contented himself with penning a defensive account of what had taken place on April 19, which he sent off with other official papers on the British ship *Sukey.* His further instructions were only that any mail to the Massachusetts agents in London was to be seized. However, using the British mails was not what Adams and Warren had in mind. Four days after the unimpressive *Sukey* set sail, the fast schooner *Quero,* owned by the Derbys of Salem, left on a single-purpose mission: bringing the first and most persuasive explanation of Lexington and Concord to Britain. Twenty-eight days later, the *Quero* slipped into a quiet English inlet on the Isle of Wight, across from Southampton, and Captain John Derby, making his personal way through Britain's naval heartland, quickly delivered his documents and affidavits to the agents who represented Massachusetts in London. They in turn took them to the office of the (pro-American) Lord Mayor of London and to sympathetic, even friendly newspapers. The *Sukey* took two more weeks to arrive, further embarrassing Gage and the American secretary, Lord Dartmouth.

If *Quero* was no ordinary schooner, John Derby was no ordinary sea captain. The Derbys were the foremost shipowning family in heavily maritime Salem and also the town's leading Patriots, deeply involved with the Sons of Liberty and Salem Committee of Correspondence. During the war years to come, the fast privateer ships built or bonded by the

Derbys—boasting names like the *Oliver Cromwell,* the *Hampden,* and the *Tyrannicide*—were the port's most successful. All told, Derby privateers captured 144 prizes for a profit of almost $1 million, and by the late 1780s, Elias Hasket Derby, John's brother, became the first American millionaire.[13] Samuel Adams had known where to turn.

Distance itself was usually a friend to the Patriot cause. With British ports as much as 5,000 miles away, when distances were lengthened by routes and winds, connections to Boston and New York could be drawn out and erratic. Going east, the average sailing time was four to six weeks, but the westward voyage usually took six to eight weeks. The Derbys could do better, but for the British, official communications were slow, instructions too often out of date, and reinforcements promised by London typically months late.

During 1775 British military logistics also suffered from undependability and overreach. General William Howe, taking command from Gage in October, was kept in Boston for nine months after Bunker Hill by London's inability to provide supplies and the transports needed to evacuate his soldiers. They did not depart for Halifax, Nova Scotia, until March 1776. In the interim, the Boston garrison was penned up—hungry, cold for want of fuel, and with ships of the wrong size to be effective in New England waters. These months, during which British power was all but wasted, provided vital time for the Revolution to deepen its thirteen-colony roots.

Preoccupation with Boston and New England hindered Whitehall's ability to take a larger political and economic view of trouble also unfolding from Chesapeake Bay south to the Savannah River. British historians, in particular, have also paid too little attention to the Continental Association, set up by the Philadelphia Congress in October 1774 to manage and enforce its phased-in suspension of trade with Britain. Close to 1,000 committees of all kinds were launched on the township, city, and county levels between the summer of 1774 and the summer of 1775, and through them Patriot-faction activists gained powerful control over grassroots economic activities and frequently much else.

Many of these associations also became political auxiliaries. Military historians like Walter Millis, John Shy, and Don Higginbotham make a parallel case for a second dimension of 1774–1775 Patriot takeover—the use of provincial congresses and various committees to purge and reconstitute local militias. These served to bind the loyalty of civilians when no countervailing British troops were on hand. In Millis's words, "repeatedly it was the militia which met the critical emergency or, in less formal operations, kept control of the country, cut off foragers, captured British agents, intimidated the war-weary and disaffected, or tarred and feathered the notorious Tories. The patriots' success in infiltrating and capturing the old militia organizations . . . was perhaps as important to the outcome as any of their purely political achievements."[14]

At sea, New England was Britain's first target. The Royal Navy, with some 30 ships on the American station, exasperated by its inability to adequately protect British seaborne supply lines, soon vented frustration by island raiding and town shelling. In September 1775, Vice Admiral Samuel Graves, acting on instructions from home, ordered his ship captains to "proceed along the [New England] Coast, and lay waste, burn and destroy such seaport towns as are accessible to His Majesty's ships."[15] As we will see in Chapter 14, coastal residents were shocked, and in some areas they panicked. During these months, Patriot leaders wisely began to jettison earlier rhetoric that had blamed Parliament's army or the "ministerial navy." Increasingly, they began placing the onus squarely on George III, an unjust king willing to tyrannize his American subjects. In August, King George had proclaimed subjects in the thirteen colonies rebels, tidings that arrived in November more or less at the same time as news of the October bombardment and burning of Falmouth, now Portland, Maine.

The contemporary map reproduced on page 5 shows the tight 1775–1776 patriotic siege lines encircling fortified Boston, itself almost an island. It also shows the multiple islands of Boston Harbor, several garrisoned by British troop detachments. Most have long since been swallowed up by the expanding city, but in 1775, a half dozen—Hog Island, Noddle's, Deer, Snake, Peddock's, and Great Brewster—saw intermittent battles during the four months after April 19. Several of these involved 500 to 1,000 men. As the king's soldiers and sailors searched for sheep, cattle, timber, and firewood, colonial forces sought to remove them from the islands and deny the British occupiers food and forage. Yankee rebels also burned down the old lighthouse on Great Brewster, vital to British nighttime navigation because Boston Harbor was full of tricky shoals, tides, and fog banks.

After Bunker Hill, much of the 1775 fighting in New England took place on coastal waters rather than on land. As a maritime battleground, Massachusetts Bay—the shoal- and inlet-studded crescent from Cape Cod on the south to Cape Ann in the north—favored the rebels. Yankee ship captains and pilots knew its channels and sandbars; the British did not, and few local pilots dared aid them. Moreover, the large 50-, 60-, and 70-gun

British warships were of little use in such shoal-ridden waters. However, small British vessels, more mobile, were also vulnerable to capture. By June, Massachusetts seamen had captured a half dozen British sloops, tenders, and barges. Up and down the Atlantic coast, the most effective American tactics relied on small craft. As we will see in Chapter 23, this universe included canoes, swift and silent enough to scout Castle William, the British island headquarters; New Hampshire gundalows; speed-rigged Chesapeake pilot boats; Pennsylvania row galleys; and small flotillas of 15-to-30-foot whaleboats, oar driven by skilled fishermen and capable of moving 200 to 300 men for a quick strike. September and October also saw a half dozen light (40-to-75-ton) and handy schooners ordered into action against British supply ships by George Washington—unsurprisingly they were nicknamed "Washington's navy."

The other New England provinces were allies of Massachusetts and had also begun their arms buildup in late 1774. After Lexington and Concord, the Connecticut legislature voted 6,000 soldiers to support the siege of Boston, established a provincial navy (July 1), and set up a "War Office" in secure, inland Lebanon, the home town of feisty Governor Jonathan Trumbull. That small frame building, just off the town's huge green, would manage the state's regional and national war effort for eight straight years until peace came in 1783. On April 22, the Rhode Island legislature approved sending 1,500 men to help Massachusetts, and seven weeks later it authorized the war's first provincial navy. On June 18, the provincial sloop *Katy* captured the Royal Navy tender *Diana* in Narragansett Bay. New Hampshire, in turn, had militia drilling by April 23, and on May 17 its Fourth Provincial Congress met to enact legislation for the "common defense," including a standing army of 2,000 men.[16]

By the summer of 1775, in short, mobilization and at least minor confrontation was New England wide. Seaports from the Maine district, then part of Massachusetts, south to New London and New Haven, Connecticut, fortified their approaches. Kittery and Portsmouth put a log boom across the Piscataqua Harbor that the two towns shared and emplaced coastal batteries. Salem, Massachusetts's second city, decided to sink hulks to block the harbor channel and erect forts on Juniper Point and Winter Island.[17] Such precautions were sound. Between May and December, British warships burned Falmouth, torched parts of Newport and Jamestown (R.I.), and shelled six other New England towns. Threats were made against

Portsmouth. New England was indeed the first front line. However, by
August and September, confrontation was spreading.

The South's Revolutionary Summer

The scattered armed encounters of April and May, mostly confined to Massachusetts, including its Maine district, might still have been isolated and
kept from interfering with serious political negotiations. Not so Bunker
Hill on June 17, which hardened attitudes on both sides. Colonial newspapers printed in some detail King George's own warlike assessments,
although it would be November before word arrived of his August proclamation naming the Americans rebels. By August, the Royal Navy was
seizing growing numbers of American vessels under Parliament's spring
Restraining Act, especially in New England waters. Autumn saw colonial
belligerence crystallize over the multiple burnings and bombardments, over
reports of the king hiring mercenaries, and over British ministers' blunt
comments that Americans must be treated like foreign enemies. Lord Dartmouth, a relative moderate, confided to a summer visitor that the government had decided that the same force would be employed "in America as if
the inhabitants were French or Spanish enemies."[18] The Patriots, equally
militant, had expelled royal governors, captured Ticonderoga and Crown
Point, and then pushed on into British-ruled Canada, aiming to take Montreal. Although news was slow to arrive, neither side was leaving much
room for reconciliation.

Confrontation soon spread farther afield. By autumn, ships from New
England, Virginia, and South Carolina together had paid armed visits to
take or seize munitions in four loyal British colonies in the hemisphere:
Bermuda, East Florida, Nova Scotia, and St. John's (now Prince Edward
Island). South Carolina had scrapped a munitions-gathering excursion to
the Bahamas, but the Continental Navy went there for gunpowder and
cannon in early 1776. King George and Parliament could fairly judge in
August 1775 that Britain faced a full-scale thirteen-province rebellion showing unmistakable momentum toward independence. The autumn months
became a turning point for many Americans, although conservatives in the
middle colonies—New York, New Jersey, Delaware, Pennsylvania, and
Maryland—still cherished hopes of reconciliation.

By year's end, a few square miles of Boston represented the sole remaining seat of British occupation, authority, and might—and this applied to the length and breadth of the thirteen colonies.[19] The rapid spread of insurrection in the plantation colonies during the spring and summer of 1775 came as a particular shock to British officials, given their supposedly high ratios of Loyalists. Nevertheless, by late summer, the coast from Chesapeake Bay to Georgia's Sea Islands had become the second theater of armed disaffection. Besides provincial gunpowder magazines, Patriots that summer seized a series of military installations—Fort Charlotte on the Savannah River, Fort Johnston in North Carolina, and Fort Johnson on Charleston Harbor.

In Virginia, most populous of the provinces, the royal governor, John Murray, Earl of Dunmore, shaken by a politically harrowing April and May in the capital of Williamsburg, bolted on June 8 to Yorktown and the protective safety of HMS *Fowey.* Hostilities commenced in August when HMS *Otter,* a naval sloop within Dunmore's command, began raiding plantations. Then in October, a small flotilla led by *Otter* tried to burn the town and port of Hampton but was driven off by Virginia riflemen. November saw Dunmore and British forces occupy the port of Norfolk. However, they withdrew to ships in mid-December after Patriot troops defeated a combined force of British regulars, local Loyalists, and armed black ex-slaves at Great Bridge, fifteen miles to the south. On New Year's Day, Dunmore's small fleet began a bombardment of Norfolk, which caught fire and burned. Patriots, who regarded the seaport as a nest of Loyalists, completed the burning and destruction.

North Carolina's Josiah Martin became the second southern royal governor to run on July 16, 1775, fleeing to the sloop of war *Cruizer* just hours after Patriots captured and burned Fort Johnston near the entrance to the Cape Fear River and Wilmington, the province's principal town. On board *Cruizer,* Martin kept in contact with inland settlements of Loyalist Scottish Highlanders and Piedmont dissidents he had politically befriended. Despite months of planning, the planned Loyalist rising fizzled out in February when a combined force en route to the coast was defeated in battle at Moore's Creek Bridge.

Lord William Campbell, South Carolina's new governor, had just arrived from Britain in June 1775. But on September 15, after Patriot militia followed up their July capture of outlying Fort Charlotte by seizing Fort Johnson, the principal Charleston Harbor installation, Lord William fled. He took refuge in HMS *Tamar,* a "worm-eaten" navy sloop patrolling off the coast. Open hostilities commenced in the autumn, when the South Carolina naval vessel *Defence,* sinking hulks to block the Hog Island Channel near Charleston, exchanged cannon fire with the British sloops *Tamar* and *Cherokee.*[20]

Officials in London had expected better from Georgia. But in mid-1775, the local Patriots took substantial control of government through an extralegal Provincial Congress and Council of Safety. This closely reiterated similar transfers of authority in Virginia, North Carolina, and South Carolina—and by January top officials were in custody. Disdaining house arrest, Governor Sir James Wright fled in February 1776 to HMS *Scarborough.*

Focusing on these facts changes the way we think about these months. Even New England had nothing to match the exodus of the southern royal governors. History had already shown the effects of such action. Back in the early seventeenth century, the so-called Flight of the Earls—the exodus of key Irish Catholic nobles to Spain—was taken on the European continent as signaling the end of Gaelic Ireland. The flight of royal governors from New Hampshire to Georgia augured similarly for embattled British North America.

The breakdown in royal authority was a grievous political wound. It had been replaced by de facto American self-rule through local committees of correspondence and safety, trade-monitoring committees of inspection, oath-swearing associations, militia organizations, and provincial congresses. They began to exercise power twelve to eighteen months before the July 1776 arrival in New York of massive but belated British military might. This Patriot infrastructure, activity, and enforcement represented a governmental and political underpinning of American independence that was never effectively defeated or disassembled.

Despite lack of international legal recognition, the Continental Congress functioned as a de facto war government. By the end of 1775, the United Colonies had also created an army (June 15), a navy (October 13), and even a marine corps (November 10). American regiments were camped in Canada, wooing French *habitants,* occupying Montreal, and finally—too late—besieging the rocky citadel of Quebec. Below New England, from Philadelphia to Sunbury, Georgia, coastal defenses were springing up along key rivers and harbors. Pennsylvania, overcoming Quaker inhibitions, opted to protect Philadelphia with a small fleet of row galleys, river obstacles, and artillery batteries.[21]

To facilitate defense and coordination, Congress separated the colonies into three separate military commands—the Northern Department (Connecticut, Rhode Island, Massachusetts, and New Hampshire), the Southern Department (Virginia, both Carolinas, and Georgia), and the Middle Department (New York, New Jersey, Pennsylvania, Delaware, and Maryland). New England, with its four collaborative provinces, was a sector unto itself. The southern plantation elites were not far behind, but backcountry populations made those colonies less cohesive, and their Revolutionary future would be less secure in 1778–1781, when the British made a more serious southern invasion than the fumbled one of 1775–1776.

Map 1 shows the thirteen colonies and their major cities and rivers. Only half of the provinces conducted censuses in the decade before 1775, so there is no reliable way to include and detail the growth that was becoming such a topic of discussion in North America, Britain, and the European continent.

The Middle Colonies of 1775: The Politics of Ambiguity

The five "middle" provinces represented a third and more complex political geography too often skipped over or ignored in analyses of the early Revolution. Urban radicals in New York and Philadelphia favored independence, but partly as a vehicle for economic and social upheaval. The reverse side of the coin—this in addition to economic, cultural, and religious antagonisms that inhibited middle-colony consensus—was that many wealthy New Yorkers and Pennsylvanians, wary of the Sons of Liberty and organized mechanics, thought they would be safer remaining under British rule. Patriot congresses and committees of safety held a partial, extralegal sway in all five middle colonies, aided by *rage militaire*. The existing institutions of government, however, were divided. As of December 1775, royal governors retained at least toeholds—William Tryon in New York, William Franklin in New Jersey, and Robert Eden in Maryland—and the legislative assemblies in New York and Pennsylvania remained in conservative hands.

Luckily for the Patriots, the extent to which British authorities had focused on Boston during the 1770s left hardly any scarlet-jacketed soldiery in middle-colony barracks. This persisted in late 1775 although New York was the next obvious battleground once British leaders vacated their untenable position in Massachusetts. A Dutch possession until captured by the Duke of York (later James II) in 1664, New York a century later was the strategic and military gateway to the Hudson-Champlain corridor. Regaining full control of its storied eighteenth-century north-south warpath of rivers, portages, and lakes—one army moving north from New York City, another south from Canada—would split the rebellious colonies more or less down the middle. That, of course, had become London's plan by the summer of 1775, but the logistics of implementing it would be difficult.

Having been drawn into war before achieving readiness, Britain lacked transports to move the worn-out troops in Boston to New York before winter's onset. Thus, as the year ended, no British regular unit was stationed in the colonies' swing region. New York's last company of redcoats had marched out of their barracks in July, boarding the nearby 64-gun warship *Asia*—partly, cynics said, to keep them from deserting.[22] Two other British regular units in New York—small detachments stationed at Ticonderoga and Crown Point, the once grand, now decrepit French and Indian War bastions—had been taken captive by New Englanders in May. Gage's tardy April order to General Carleton to reinforce Ticonderoga by sending a regiment from Canada was overtaken by war. In a similar vein, combative instructions from the Cabinet sent in January 1775 by Lord Dartmouth, the American secretary—Gage was finally ordered to start moving aggressively, even at the risk of war—had been delayed initially in Whitehall, then held up by a particularly rough wintertime ocean crossing. Gage's aides did not sign for them until April 14. On the British side, policy making for both Massachusetts and the Hudson-Champlain corridor had taken a costly winter holiday.

New York, in the meantime, was a weak link in the Revolutionary chain. Its timorous Provincial Congress was not even in charge of the May-June buildup in the province's own northern counties. The Continental Congress, along with officers of Massachusetts and Connecticut troops actually on the scene, had most of the say. Back in February 1775, while Gage dawdled, the Massachusetts Committee of Correspondence had sent an agent to Lake Champlain and Canada—John Brown, a Pittsfield lawyer and confidant of Samuel Adams. He reported in late March that "one thing I must mention to be kept as a profound Secret, the Fort at Tyconderogo must be seised as soon as possible should hostilities be committed by the kings Troops. The people on N. Hampshire Grants have ingaged to do this Business and in my opinion they are the most proper Persons for this Jobb."[23]

When the two citadels fell in May to a small force from Connecticut,

Massachusetts, and the so-called Hampshire Grants (Ethan Allen and the Green Mountain Boys), the way to Canada opened wide. Quebec, too, had lost garrisons to reinforce Boston. But despite the spreading Patriot confrontations with British forces in Virginia and Charleston Harbor, violence was held off in the five middle colonies, save for New England–guarded upper New York. The region remained politically ambivalent. John Adams would later argue that a naïve middle-colony desire not to break with Britain had interfered with Congress's invasion of Canada.[24] Most observers counted Loyalist politics and anti-independence sentiment strongest in New York, but caution and lingering hope for reconciliation enjoyed a vocal constituency in all five provinces. As January turned to February and March, avid independence backers like cousins Samuel and John Adams of Massachusetts and the Lee brothers of Virginia fumed at what they saw as delay and obstruction.

To committed Patriots, not least Benjamin Franklin, Pennsylvania was the middle-region linchpin because of its influence. The Quaker colony's relatively powerless governor John Penn, a grandson of founder William Penn, was not much of an obstacle. The important opposition to independence came from Pennsylvania's wealthy Quaker elite and the newer Anglican power axis of merchants and lawyers. Together, the two conservative elements dominated the provincial Assembly, which continued to look to the familiar Penn Charter and reject separation. To heighten the stakes, Pennsylvania was expected to sway two less important neighbors: New Jersey, half of which was the former Quaker stronghold of West Jersey; and Delaware, smaller still, which had long shared a Philadelphia-based governor with Pennsylvania.

Ironically, William Franklin, the royal governor in New Jersey, was the illegitimate son of Benjamin Franklin. Respect for the father kept New Jersey Patriots from arresting his Tory son. In mid-June 1776, however, as sentiment shifted in next-door Pennsylvania, the New Jersey Provincial Convention would declare the younger Franklin "an enemy to the liberties of this country" and order him confined.[25] He was sent to Connecticut for detention.

In the political geography of 1775, then, Pennsylvania stood as the critical domino. Her influence also touched Maryland. If Virginia loomed large over the Chesapeake, Pennsylvania dominated Maryland's northern border and also shipped large quantities of wheat through the burgeoning port of Baltimore. The Adams cousins, Samuel and John, because they expected

New York to support independence once Pennsylvania and its offspring did, in effect had a "keystone" strategy, as we will see in Chapter 19. Pennsylvania's nickname as the Keystone State came from its swing role in the presidential elections of 1796 and 1800.[26] But its pivotal politics were evident a quarter century earlier.

As we will elaborate in Chapter 2, for reasons of history, government, and culture, four provinces—Massachusetts and Connecticut, Virginia and South Carolina—were the most assertive in 1774–1775. By contrast, New York, New Jersey, Pennsylvania, Maryland, and Delaware were the cross-pressured, wavering provinces, further inhibited by local awareness that their region was certain to provide many of the Revolution's early military battlegrounds.

If the absence of a British military presence between the spring of 1775 and the spring of 1776 nurtured an artificial relaxation in the middle colonies, summer's invasion would change that. Indeed, between October and December, erstwhile American confidence slumped as the Continental Army reeled from late-summer and autumn military defeats in and around the city of New York. These drubbings came at the hands of General Howe's 35,000-strong British and mercenary forces, which had assembled in July and August. Disenchantment in the region further deepened following the Americans' inglorious late-autumn retreat across New Jersey into Pennsylvania. Beginning a discussion of the American Revolution in 1776 slides over the middle colonies' vulnerable psychologies and politics.

Americans today can reasonably wonder: If the radical faction had not pushed several independence-leaning resolutions through Congress by clever tactics in May and June, would a further delay have been fatal? What would uncomfortable New York, New Jersey, and Delaware delegates have later decided if the vote on independence actually taken on July 2 had been postponed to unhappy September or perilous October? George Washington summarized the regional gloom in a letter to his brother dated December 18, 1776: "Between you and me, I think our affairs are in a very bad situation; not so much from the apprehension of General Howe's army, as from the defection of New York, Jerseys and Pennsylvania. In short, the Conduct of the Jerseys has been infamous. Instead of turning out to defend their Country and affording aid to our Army, they are making their submissions as fast as they can."[27] Thomas Fleming, the New Jersey historian, has taken December's pattern of middle-colony disenchantment a province farther: "In Delaware, loyalists and anti-independence moderates controlled the legislature and fired Caesar Rodney and Thomas McKean as their delegates to the Continental Congress." The irony, he pointed out, was that "although contemporary Americans celebrate it [1776] as the year of their national birthday . . . for Americans who lived through the revolutionary experience 1775, not 1776, was the year of great patriotic outpouring."[28]

So it was. Events and decisions in 1775 had put the sustaining congresses, associations, conventions, and committees in place. Fortunately for the United States, George Washington's just-in-time military triumphs at Trenton (December 25) and Princeton (January 3, 1777) managed to restore—now in a more experienced, cautious, and sober vein—some of the spirit and hope of the early days, when Virginia burgesses had worn fringed shirts and tomahawks, and virtue had been presumed all-conquering.

The North American Communications Lag

At a certain stage, students of the American Revolution experience a distinct déjà vu in reading for the fourth or fifth time about this or that communications lag. These explain how delay or adverse winds kept instructions from reaching a British general or how slow sea travel during the winter of 1775–1776 kept anxious politicians or members of the Continental Congress three or four months behind in knowing the thoughts of British ministers or parliamentarians. People were on tenterhooks. New Englanders waited for undecided moderates to accept the depth and near-irreversibility of London's war preparations; middle-colony delegates anxiously awaited word of rumored British peace commissioners.

Many scholars have cited individual situations; others have described the particular hazards and delays of winter voyages across the North Atlantic. But a brief overview seems in order.

Consider the months between August 1774 and July 1776, a pressure cooker period during which many Americans made up or changed their minds. Two periods stand out during which the North Atlantic winter held up information—November 1774 to April 1775, then essentially the same calendar of icebergs and adverse winds a year later—thereby slowing down decision making or implementation. British policy makers and military commanders, and American Patriots and Loyalists alike, waited for news or instructions. In retrospect, it seems implausible that cross-pressured colonists could have seen much hope for reconciliation with Britain in early 1776, but they did—and information took three to four months to make a superficial round trip and probably five to six months to sink in and be absorbed.

Britain and the North American colonies had two of the world's best-educated and most literate populations. Besides, many historians view the American insurgency as one of the first—if not *the* first—modern popular revolutions. While the role of public opinion was modernizing, communications between the two sides of the Atlantic, even in the 1770s, were almost premodern, trapped in drawn-out sea crossings not much faster than the seventeenth-century Spanish voyages undertaken just after navigators first understood the circular wind pattern over the Atlantic. In 1775 knowledge and technological improvements were accelerating—the discovery of longitudes in the 1760s, the mapping of the Gulf Stream in the 1770s. (Benjamin Franklin, an early oceanographer, took measurements even while returning from England to America in 1775.) Other breakthroughs were imminent, like the turn-of-the-century fitting of steam engines into vessels and the 1840s invention of the telegraph. None, though, were at hand to permit the American Revolution to unfold at the more rapid decision-making pace of the Civil War. We can only speculate on what might have been different.

1775: Pinpointing the Pivotal Year

Speed-conscious contemporary Americans love nothing more than digital symbols as glib shorthand. Ones commonly employed include discovery-evoking 1492, flag-waving 1776, or Depression-unleashing 1929. Nor is the twelve-month calendar rigid. In 1950, say, the American college "school year" ran from September 1950 to June 1951. Nowadays August through May prevails. The U.S. government starts its fiscal year in October and goes through the following September. And so on.

Historians, too, employ license in helping routine chronology become more evocative. The idea of a "long" nineteenth century stretching from revolutionary 1789 to a shattering 1914 is widely entertained; likewise a "long" eighteenth century, spanning the ferment between 1688 and 1815. Wars and revolutions are usually what justify this century-bending. Years, too, can be stretched. Historian Joseph Ellis, in his book *American Creation,* plausibly contends that "the fifteen months between the shots fired at Lexington and Concord [April 1775] and the adoption of the Declaration of Independence in July of 1776 can justifiably claim to be both the most consequential and the strangest year in American history."[29]

Like the "long" eighteenth and nineteenth centuries, each enlarged to accommodate related wars and revolutions, this book posits a "long" 1775. Our sequence begins in mid-1774—the summer leading up to the First Continental Congress in Philadelphia, which twelve colonies (all save Georgia) had convened in angry response to the Coercive Acts that strong-armed Massachusetts. These British punishments had a reverse watershed effect— turning colonial outrage into a flood in 1775 that crested in the spring of 1776. The early-twentieth-century historian Allen French, in his magnificent volume *The First Year of the American Revolution,* began his own chronology in the April tumult of Lexington and Concord. He ended his saga in the middle of May 1776. This was when Congress intrepidly recommended that laggard colonies set up new forms of republican government because "it is necessary that the exercise of every kind of authority under the said crown should be totally suppressed." Remodeled governance, it was argued, would permit better "defense of their [peoples'] lives, liberties and properties."[30] What Congress actually did was to ax the last bastions of opposition. Indeed, French's reference is to just one of several "little declarations of independence" scholars have identified as anticipating the one in July.

To French, May 15 was conclusive: "[John] Adams himself said that the Gordian knot was cut. For here in fact the sovereignty of Britain was repudiated, and this enactment was used in France to show that America was ready to declare its independence."[31] Still, why use a May cutoff? Even unsigned until August, the July Declaration had a powerful yet rarely elaborated arousal effect. Half of its pages, the ones rarely read or remembered, spelled out two dozen reasons why King George III had betrayed the colonies, the supposed British constitution, and the duties of a worthy king. Some of these indictments were thin, but others resonated; this was a supposed eighteenth-century legal prerequisite for justifiable revolution. The naïveté of blaming ministries while expressing fealty to the monarch was over. In summer's celebrations, as we will see, Americans began to emphasize a personal rejection of King George—tearing down his statue for lead to make bullets, burning his royal coat of arms, banning prayers on the king's behalf, and more. Thus did America solidify commitment to a new and king-free republic.

In contrast to French's volume, then, my "long 1775" continues through

July 1776. It does, however, halt before late summer's British military campaign in and around New York. That was the defining *negative* event of 1776. By contrast, the "long 1775" that came before represents the loyalties, constituencies, and foundations built over many months—almost-forgotten battles in places from Pennsylvania to North Carolina and Georgia, far-flung American raids and invasions, new provincial navies and neglected ship actions. It likewise includes intensive—and surprisingly successful—colonial negotiations with Iroquois, Shawnee, Cherokee, and other Native American tribes along the frontier. This early Revolution also includes a pervasive global munitions-gathering contest spurred by a royal prohibition in 1774. Deny munitions to the thirteen colonies, British officials argued, and there would be no rebellion. Perhaps, but British efforts failed.

This emphasis on arms, mass demonstrations, explosive trade goods, and even mob psychologies puts my pages somewhat at odds with John Adams's famous contention of a more cerebral transformation—the war, he said, was first won in hearts and minds before muskets were lifted. The rotund Massachusetts lawyer, never even a militia officer, conducted his skirmishes and ambushes—and for the most part quite successfully—only in courtrooms, meetinghouses, and legislatures. He misjudged the continuum, the seamlessness, between war and politics that Clausewitz and many others have perceived and explained.

To be sure, a vital transformation in American thinking—the colonists' ballooning New World pride and incipient nationalism, their gradual shift of loyalty away from a once-cherished British monarchy to a new American Congress—did take shape before the serious fighting. Awareness was growing of bonds between different colonies and sections, as well as the immensity of a shared North American opportunity. The scarcely veiled royal disdain apparent by mid-1775 helped to erode old fidelities. Nevertheless, Lexington-Concord, Bunker Hill, and a dozen less-known battles and confrontations were essential catalysts. No chronicler should ignore, but many do, the war mentality that took hold in early 1775. Some of its consequences were perverse, notably the hubris that kept Patriots from learning needed military lessons, and led to massive disillusionment, especially in the middle colonies, when defeats came rapidly in the second half of 1776. However, without that early optimism, the Revolution might not have taken place—at least in the form it did.

For New Englanders, April 1775 was not the beginning; nor was it even close to the beginning. Their Revolution was taking shape in 1774, as we have seen. An argument can be made that war became all but inevitable in the autumn of 1774 after the First Continental Congress.

"I once had considerable Expectations from Congress," said New York Anglican minister Charles Inglis, "but since they adopted the fiery Resolves of Suffolk in Massachusetts almost all hope of good from them vanished."[32] Pennsylvania historian Sydney Fisher, in his 1908 four-volume history *The Struggle for American Independence,* distilled middle-colony frustration: "It is quite obvious that the [Suffolk] resolutions were in effect a declaration of independence by the patriots of Massachusetts, although the word independence was not used. If Congress approved of them, approved of a government set up by the patriots in hostility to the British government, it was certainly committing the rest of the colonies to an open rebellion and war unless England was willing to back down completely," as with the Stamp Act and the Townshend Acts.[33]

Rebellion, then, was much in motion before Lexington and Concord. In South Carolina, Patriots took gunpowder and weapons from arsenals and magazines in Charleston and nearby Hobcaw one night in April 1775, weeks *before* any news had come from Massachusetts. The Commons House of Assembly had fired the night watchmen at both magazines in February.[34] General William Moultrie later recalled that as spring came, "the militia were forming themselves into volunteer uniform companies; drums beating, fifes playing; squads of men exercising on the outskirts of the town; a military spirit pervaded the whole country; and Charleston had the appearance of a garrison town; everything had the face of war; though not one of us had the least idea of its approach."[35] As we will see, South Carolina, like Massachusetts, had been pulling the British Lion's tail for a decade and a half.

Virginia, too, was proactive. Between September 1774 and May or June 1775, 27 different county volunteer independent military companies were organized. On March 14, five weeks before Lexington and Concord, Virginia's governor, Lord Dunmore, wrote to the Earl of Dartmouth, the American secretary, saying that the colony was preparing for war and that the extralegal Provincial Convention had voted to raise troops.[36] Then in the early morning hours of April 21, before news arrived from Massachusetts, 20 marines from HMS *Magdalen,* moored near Williamsburg, entered the town magazine on Dunmore's orders and took fifteen and a half barrels of powder to their vessel, subsequently transferred to the frigate HMS *Fowey.* But when the detachment was discovered, aroused Williamsburg Patriots needed quieting by local leaders. Confrontation, these men advised, would be premature. Irate volunteer companies soon marched on the capital, and on June 8, Dunmore fled.

Two more explanations flesh out vital timing. Military historian Charles Royster, in *A Revolutionary People at War,* was appropriately blunt: "Popular *rage militaire* vanished by the end of 1776 and never returned. Even in 1776 it was a weak echo of its loudest moments in 1775 . . . throughout the war they called for a revival of the spirit of 1775."[37] David Ammerman, an expert on the First Continental Congress, specified that "in attempting to explain the advent of armed conflict in British America, the months between May 1774, when news of the Coercive Acts first arrived in the colonies, and April 1775, when British troops clashed with the provincials at Lexington and Concord, are of crucial importance. Prior to passage of the first of the Coercive Acts a variety of courses lay open to both the British and the colonists; after the engagement at Concord there was almost no possibility of avoiding full-scale civil war."[38] Both assertions ring true.

New England and plantation-colony episodes are rarely interwoven in the history books, which helps to downplay the Revolution's deep roots in the winter of 1774–1775. Even in Quaker-imprinted Pennsylvania, 1774 resolutions condemning Britain's Coercive Acts were numerous in Scotch-Irish and to a lesser extent in German towns and frontier settlements—Hanover (June 4, 1774), Middletown (June 10), Frederickstown (June 11), Lancaster (June 15), and so forth.[39] As we will see, zealous Presbyterian Scotch-Irish constituted the third early leg of Revolutionary sentiment along with Yankee New England and southern tobacco and rice planters.

These pivots and calendars involve more than snappy titles and minor hair splitting. Over the last two centuries, the Revolution has become the defining event—the political touchstone—of national patriotic sentiment and self-portraiture. Every year brings another ten or twenty interpretations, thanks to the efforts of U.S., Canadian, and British historians. Semantics sometimes promote confusion. The "War for American Independence" ended in 1783, but has the broader underlying "American Revolution" ever ended? Many contend it has not, enthusing that the process—and the American Mission—is ongoing.

That argument is one these pages will sidestep. This book's more narrow purpose is to distill and chronicle the new psychologies, beliefs, and antagonisms of 1774 and 1775 that launched the Revolution and to a considerable extent entrenched its existence at the grass roots. It is also about the forces that shaped the emerging republican plurality of the 1770s, so to speak. Whether or not "the American Revolution" continued to manifest itself in Lincoln's Gettysburg Address or in the 2003 overthrow of Saddam Hussein is an entirely separate debate for an altogether different book. But first, this introduction requires one more essential preview.

The Global Competition for Munitions, Weaponry, and Mercenaries, 1774–1776

Despite his mistakes as a ruler, George III hardly overreacted on October 19, 1774, when he characterized Massachusetts as being in a state of rebellion and approved a Privy Council order prohibiting the unauthorized export of war supplies from Britain to America. Nor was it premature that colonial governors were quickly instructed to "take the most effectual Measures for arresting, detaining and securing, any Gunpowder, or any sort of Arms or Ammunition, which may be attempted to be imported into the colonies."[40] These strictures set off the late 1774 and early 1775 expeditions and seizures in New Hampshire, Rhode Island, and Massachusetts, as well as the actions in Virginia and South Carolina that occurred before news of Lexington and Concord. The provincial powder encounters were as much consequences of a widening chasm as causations, and even the trigger status of Lexington and Concord is not unqualified.

The American munitions crisis was already global. The Admiralty, for its part, sent implementing orders to the Royal Navy. The undersecretary of state dispatched candid alerts to British secret agents. *King George's Correspondence,* edited by Sir John Fortescue, a military historian, confirms that agents' reports on gunpowder and munitions smuggling were often forwarded to the king, who was a fascinated reader.[41] He should have been: the trafficking reached from the Baltic to the Bay of Biscay, from Haiti to the West African Slave Coast, where inferior-grade muskets were a staple easily come by. If the global gunpowder confrontation was clearly a prelude to the Revolution, it could also be called a first stage or opening round.

It was just days after October 19 that the Massachusetts Provincial Congress, with no knowledge of the Privy Council order, established a Committee of Safety and a Committee of Supply. The two groups were charged to work with each other, and to cooperate with individual towns across the

Bay Colony in order to monitor British troop movements, suppress Tories, purchase and distribute ordnance and supplies, and prepare a well-armed militia to protect the public safety. A month later the Committee of Safety took a more hurried view, telling agents to buy up what weaponry and munitions they could find anywhere else in New England.[42] The clock on effective preparation for a likely war was already running.

Through the summer of 1775, responsibility for obtaining gunpowder and arms lay with the thirteen colonies and whatever private individuals they might commission. However, between July and October, the Second Continental Congress became active in urging the individual colonies to get into the munitions trade. Then between September and November 1775, the Congress established both a Committee of Secret Correspondence, charged with obtaining and distributing military supplies, and a Secret Committee, which was to employ agents overseas, gather intelligence about ammunition stores, and arrange their purchase through intermediaries (to conceal that Congress was the true buyer). There is no record that the First Continental Congress had taken kindred measures in the autumn of 1774, but it is all too easy to imagine secret discussions and activities.

Philadelphia quickly became the nerve center. To begin with, it played home to Congress—bringing together the key plotters and orchestrators from New England, Philadelphia, Virginia, and the Carolinas. But the Philadelphia of the 1770s had also become North America's leading mercantile city and a major shipbuilding center. Two of its major merchant firms, Willing & Morris and Nesbit & Conyngham, quickly came to the fore in the 1775 munitions trade. Much speculation has also attached to Franklin's own role, even while he was in London during the winter of 1774–1775. To at least one French historian, Franklin was the linchpin.[43] A twentieth-century chronicler mused about the vital wartime role of a "commercial-maritime-diplomatic complex" that has since "dropped out of sight . . . suppressed by the generation which bequeathed to us the Parson Weems attitude."[44] By late 1774, as we have seen, New England's preparations were overt. Thomas Cushing, a Massachusetts delegate to the Continental Congress, wrote to London on December 30, 1774, to tell Benjamin Franklin that Patriots, wise to the Privy Council's "political manoevre," were "therefore adopting the most Effectual Methods to defend themselves against any Hostile invasions of the Enemies to America." He further advised Franklin that in December (after news of the council's order had arrived), both Rhode Islanders and New Hampshiremen, under instructions, had raided royal forts to seize substantial stores of cannon, arms, and munitions.[45]

Secret agents and secret committees proliferated on both sides. Paul Revere, for example, was not just Samuel Adams's bearer of great news—or even "the Winged Mercury of the Revolution." He also led an association of 30 or so Patriots, mostly mechanics and artisans, who kept watch in Boston over the movements of British troops and active Tories.[46] General Gage had his own spies and agents reporting on Patriot weapons, gunpowder purchases, and storage depots.[47] William Eden, the young undersecretary of state who also ran the British Secret Service, began a rise that during the Napoleonic years would put him into the Cabinet and the peerage as Lord Auckland.

Weaponry, we must remember, had become a major item of world commerce. Europe's frequent seventeenth- and eighteenth-century wars had spawned a large continental armaments industry—cannon forged in Liège, powder and small arms from Amsterdam, Rotterdam, and Maastricht, the best fine-milled gunpowder from France, and a wide variety of war matériel from France's military and naval arsenals. Bayonets, for example, took their name from the facility in Bayonne. By 1774, munitions makers in France, Spain, Holland, and the Austrian Netherlands (Belgium) were alert to the potential market opportunities of a major conflict in North America. This runs contrary to the widely held American view that the flow of European munitions and weaponry to the colonies began only in 1776, with the French and Spanish shipments arranged by playwright Caron de Beaumarchais and others working for the Comte de Vergennes, the French foreign minister.

Newspapers in Boston, New York, London, and continental Europe made frequent reference to earlier traffic. During the winter of 1774–1775, British diplomats pressed the governments of France, Spain, Portugal, Denmark, Sweden, and Holland to issue prohibitions against shipping arms to the British colonies.[48] Several did, but pressure from London often went beyond diplomacy. On January 5, 1775, the *New York Journal* reported that to implement the king's October Order in Council prohibiting arms exports, "two [British] men of war were ordered to the Texel in Holland, in order to prevent the transportation of those articles in English bottoms to America."[49]

More common practice, though, was for arms and munitions to travel in French, Spanish, Dutch, and Danish vessels to the Caribbean colonies of those same nations—French Martinique or Cap Français in

Saint-Domingue, Spanish Hispaniola, Dutch St. Eustatius ("Statia," the famous Golden Rock), or Danish St. Croix. All of these ports were familiar to American smugglers; all were entrepôts to which American agents or purchasers now flocked. Sometimes the foreign vessels would clear for those legitimate destinations, but then make instead for some small port or quiet harbor in the rebellious North American provinces. In early 1775, a frustrated Admiralty broadened its stop-and-search instructions to British naval commanders. Now they were also to inspect and seize such foreign ships as approached—or "hovered" near—the thirteen rebellious provinces. On the high seas, however, Royal Navy officers were told to stop and search foreign vessels only based on well-founded information. Neutral nations found such practices infuriating, but the British government correctly understood both the infractions and the stakes.

Such was the backstairs munitions struggle that accompanied and literally enabled the overt war of 1775—Lexington and Concord, the siege of Boston, Bunker Hill, the capture of the Carolina forts, Ninety Six, Lake Champlain, St. John, Montreal, Hampton, Great Bridge, Norfolk, et al. Neither the British nor the colonials were prepared for a shooting war until the possibility became real in the aftermath of the Coercive Acts. The rebels' potentially crippling deficiency lay in lack of muskets, cannon, and powder. Not only had North American gunpowder makers generally shut down after the French and Indian War, but the American Department in London periodically queried royal governors on the supplies at forts, magazines, and storehouses in their respective provinces. By the spring of 1775, these were dangerously low. When George Washington took command of the army besieging Boston in late July, he was told there were 308 barrels of gunpowder. Most of that turned out to have been used at Bunker Hill. In truth, the army was down to 36 barrels.

The situation briefly improved in August, with considerable credit belonging to South Carolina. Official state archives tell the tale. In February 1775, the Secret Committee of the South Carolina Provincial Congress began planning a seizure of the Charleston armory and two powder magazines, carried out on April 21. In June, the South Carolina congressional delegation in Philadelphia reported that powder was badly needed for the siege of Boston. The next eight weeks proved fruitful. Patriots operating out of the port of Beaufort, near Port Royal Sound, teamed up with the Georgia Provincial Congress to seize the *Philippa,* a British ship with 15,000 pounds of powder, just outside of Savannah. Then in August, a South Carolina armed vessel under orders for New Providence in the Bahamas was diverted to capture the *Betsy,* an ordnance brig with 111 barrels, en route to East Florida to supply the British garrison at Fort St. Mark. Much of this was hurried north to Washington's army.[50]

Wealthy Charleston also had the funds and location for large-scale smuggling. According to state annals, "Charlestown's extralegal government was conducting a substantial illicit arms trade with the French and Dutch islands by demanding payment in arms and ammunition for the rice it exported. One such exchange—a transaction with the island of Hispaniola during July [1775]—required three schooners to transport the cargo. Lacking the British military or naval presence they needed to suppress such traffic, the Crown officers in South Carolina could only watch helplessly while the leaders of the Patriot faction turned their colony into a veritable arsenal of revolution."[51] How important Charleston's flow was to Washington's first summer is hard to say, but it could have made the August-September difference.

One must wonder why gunpowder machinations haven't become a prime Revolutionary topic of inquiry. We will see, for example, just how many 1774–1775 Patriot raids, captures of forts, seizures of arsenals and magazines, land battles, and maritime confrontations had as their dominant or supporting motivation the procurement of gunpowder, along with muskets, flints, and cannon. If the Patriot forces at Bunker Hill had possessed adequate powder, they would have hurled back the third British wave of attackers, not just the first two. One commander, Colonel William Prescott, publicly said so and heard no rebuttal.

The king, his Cabinet, the royal governors, and British military commanders manifestly shared this concern well before the Privy Council order. In August 1774, correspondence with Lord Dartmouth, General Gage wrote that he was planning "a series of missions against the arsenals and powderhouses of New England, designed to remove as many munitions as possible—enough to make it impossible for the people of that region to make a determined stand."[52] Both men must have understood the gravity. Even three years later, discussions of General Burgoyne's defeat at Saratoga took note of how French powder, muskets, cannon, and military support were now flowing openly—indeed copiously—to the American rebels.

In a sense, the global munitions contest—on a scale far beyond its conspicuous manifestation at Lexington and Concord—was the opening grand battle of the American Revolution.

PART II

THE REVOLUTION—
PROVOCATIONS,
MOTIVATIONS, AND
ALIGNMENTS

CHAPTER 2

Liberty's Vanguard

The delegates from Virginia were the most violent of any—Those of Mary-land and some of the Carolinians a little less so. These Southern gentlemen exceeded even the New England delegates. They together made a Majority that the Others could have very little Effect upon.

Tory New York lieutenant governor Cadwallader Colden, describing the regional politics of the First Continental Congress, 1774

They had themselves suffered little, if at all, from the English government. Under it, they had prospered and multiplied. It required of this part of the people great intrepidity, wisdom and generosity to join their cause with men already stigmatized as rebels.

Patriot New Jersey governor William Livingston, explaining the Loyalist instincts of the middle colonies, *Memoirs,* 1833

Amid the turbulence of late 1774, even the haughtier among the thirteen colonies came to accept the need for equal voices—one province, one vote—in the deliberations of the new Continental Congress. Any more complicated insistence would have set off a diversionary and possibly dangerous political squabble.

The thirteen were not equal, of course—not remotely. And this was especially true with respect to individual political stature—size, history, reputation, experience in government, and recent prominence in upholding liberty and American rights, all of these critical pre-Revolutionary attributes. So in describing how 1775, the long year, actually unfolded, four provinces move front and center—Virginia, Massachusetts, South Carolina, and Connecticut. Their leadership was vital, at first politically but soon militarily.

The first to be settled (1607), the most populous, and the most widely esteemed, Virginia led the pre-Revolutionary pecking order. When the Old Dominion spoke, younger colonies listened. Committees of correspondence in nearby Delaware and Maryland, wondering in mid-1774 about the wisdom of an all-colony conference to oppose the Coercive Acts, began by seeking their senior neighbor's counsel.[1] Virginia then took the lead. And when that First Continental Congress deliberated in September and October, its central blueprint for exerting political leverage on Britain by suspending imports and exports followed the "Virginia Association." This was the model Virginians had drawn up in August during their own provincial first convention.

Come 1775, more of the actual fighting between British and colonial troops took place in Massachusetts than in Virginia. This upheld the New England colony's more combative history, as well as the British focus on punishing Boston. Second to Virginia in its founding (1629) and third among the thirteen in population circa 1775, the Bay Colony had spent the prior decade out front—provoking military occupation in 1768, pioneering the first major committee of correspondence in 1772 (Samuel Adams's Boston-based system for distributing information to other Massachusetts towns), and daring the Boston Tea Party in late 1773. In March of that year, though, Virginia had issued the first call for each colony to establish a committee of correspondence in order to keep in close touch with the others, a crisis-hour boon to Massachusetts. By 1774, all thirteen were loosely networked.

Despite its prickly and Puritan image, the Massachusetts of mid-1774 enjoyed new stature and sympathy as the victim of Britain's harsh retaliation for the tea being thrown into Boston Harbor. The king and Parliament had badly miscalculated, not realizing that the tea shipments were unpopular almost everywhere. Pennsylvania governor John Penn reported back that "the general Temper of the People, as well here, as in other Parts of America, is very warm. They look upon the Chastisement of Boston to be purposely vigorous, and held up by way of intimidation to all America; and in short that Boston is Suffering in the Common Cause."[2]

Although Massachusetts had always been preeminent in New England, its delegates came to the First Congress on their best behavior to uphold their refurbished credibility. Samuel Adams got off to a shrewd and ecumenical start by suggesting that Philadelphia Anglican rector Jacob Duche give the opening invocation, which Duche did, to wide approval.[3] The Adams cousins were gladdened—possibly even surprised—when the Congress voted a ringing endorsement of Massachusetts's own Suffolk Resolves. Few would have imagined that a month earlier. Part of what sustained the Bay Colony's momentum, as we will see, was rare political talent: two Machiavellis (Samuel Adams and Joseph Warren), a legal scholar (John Adams), and a Winged Mercury (Paul Revere).

That these were the two most important provinces in 1774–1775 is clear. The caveat is that trite telling has brought about oversimplified explanations and unjustifiable omissions. Several other colonies played more forward roles than chroniclers typically note. And even for Virginia and Massachusetts, greater emphasis must go to how vital activity and confrontation reached back through 1775 into the tense and electric months of 1774.

Identifying the 1774–1775 Vanguard

To explain the whys and wherefores of why four colonies were in the vanguard, the most instructive approach is to explain why the other nine were not. The yardsticks are uncomplicated. Most of the thirteen were simply too small, too new, or lacking in some essential pre-Revolutionary mindset, thereby underscoring the four preeminent roles.

Setting aside the early-twenty-first-century attributes and relative importance of the thirteen is essential. What counts is what they were like long ago—their political and cultural quirks and personalities—in the crucible of 1774–1775.

Pennsylvania was fast-growing and prosperous. Three decades of heavy emigration from Europe had made it the second most populous province, displacing Massachusetts. It had the biggest city (burgeoning Philadelphia), the colonies' most central location, and the largest population of several swing ethnic and religious groups: Scotch-Irish, Germans, Quakers, Presbyterians, and Lutherans. If this religious diversity reflected the province's tolerance, it also generated many divisions, which were not conducive to bold politics. Philadelphia was also British North America's center of relative sophistication in matters philosophical, cultural, and scientific.

Also, having been established by royal grant only in 1683, Pennsylvania lagged the independent thinking of the colonies a generation or two older. A further reluctance mirrored the colony's heritage of pacifist-minded Quakerism. On top of which, local politics during the 1760s were kept parochial by fierce infighting over whether to continue proprietary government under the Penn family or become a royal colony. These distractions squelched, rather than encouraged, the larger debate developing in New England, Virginia, and South Carolina.

Pennsylvania would ultimately wield a different weight. For all that the colony had to be coaxed, even shoved, by pro-independence schemers, its late commitment made a powerful wave. Still, we do best to examine Pennsylvania as a key laggard, not vanguard. The heated debates of 1774–1775 involved ink, rhetoric, huge crowds, and printing presses—and the presence of two successive Continental Congresses—but never British bayonets or naval broadsides from the 44-gun frigates probing the Delaware River. London, too, recognized Pennsylvania's indecision.

New York, another fast-growing province, included the colonies' second-largest city, which doubled as British North America's foremost imperial center. Population statistics of that era have major gaps, but as of 1770, the future twentieth-century "Empire State" ranked only fourth, fifth, or sixth (in a three-way demographic horse race with North Carolina and Connecticut). Politically, New York was atypical and cosmopolitan, its Assembly dominated by landed gentry. Several manors doubled as political units. Despite its seventeenth-century Dutch colonial antecedents—a heritage that complicated local Patriot insistence on the "rights of Englishmen"—by the 1770s, most observers ranked the colony first in both loyal sentiment and pride in its British connection. Distrust of next-door New England was rife, just as it had been under Dutch government. "Between New England and the Middle States," later argued historian Henry Adams, "was a gap like that between Scotland and England."[4]

If Massachusetts was rebellious, pre-Revolutionary New York struck many outsiders as indecisive and London clinging. Four counties in the lower section of the province—New York, Richmond, Queens, and Westchester—had an Anglican church establishment, the only such in the northern colonies, making it a center of what critics called ecclesiastical imperialism. New York was also the hub of Britain's North American military administration; and as a royal colony, "New York had little to buffer it from the demands of English politicians who viewed North American affairs primarily as an opportunity to strengthen their influence at home . . . by securing as many provincial appointments (such as governor, attorney general, provincial secretary or naval officer) as they possibly could."[5] The General Committee of South Carolina commiserated by letter to New York Patriots that "we are not ignorant of that crowd of placemen, of contractors, of officers, and needy dependents upon the Crown, who are constantly employed to frustrate your measures."[6]

To one regional historian, "more than Pennsylvania, New York displayed noticeable streaks of Anglophilia."[7] To another, "The social customs of prominent New Yorkers were slavishly copied from London models. New York not only had replicas of the most prominent London entertainment halls but even named its resorts Vauxhall and Ranelagh."[8] In 1775, the best residential districts along Broad Street and from Bowling Green along Broadway to the western end of Wall Street were said to follow "the latest London architectural fashions."[9]

Not a few New Yorkers saw their future on an imperial horizon. Merchants and lawyers looked ahead 50 or 100 years and imagined their city and Philadelphia becoming new hubs of empire, when the center of gravity of English-speaking people moved from the British Isles to North America. No such advancement could be expected by Yankee New England, with its disdain for mother-country corruption, or by the slave-owning southern plantation colonies.

New York, in consequence, was where British strategists aimed to split the not-quite-united colonies. For one thing, the Crown had earlier favored New York's claim to present-day Vermont over New Hampshire's, a boon to New York land investors. In the spring of 1775, Parliament omitted New York from that year's second Restraining Act barring colonial trade with Britain and the West Indies. Alexander Hamilton, then still a college student, had a different concern—that if New York continued to be irresolute with a Loyalist bias, New Englanders might invade and end its autonomy in order to deny the British.[10]

In and around New York City, many elements conspicuous on the Patriot side were groups that conservatives and moderates viewed skeptically: artisans, mechanics, Liberty Boys, seamen, and Anglican-baiting Presbyterians. Not surprisingly, stolid Dutch farmers across the river in Brooklyn were heavily Loyalist. By mid-1775, Loyalist strength meant that Patriots could not rely on militias in lower New York counties like Kings, Queens, Richmond, and Westchester. During those months, Congress had to ask Connecticut and to a lesser extent New Jersey for soldiers to keep order in New York or suppress Tories. In turn, having Connecticut troops in Manhattan only made ambivalent Yorkers more nervous. Right through July 1776, New York was the last colony to support independence. Its profile could be sketched in one word: *reluctance.*

So much for the large swing provinces. In 1775, neither was able to marshal a political consensus, let alone emerge as a driving force. Not a few of New York's prominent Patriot leaders and delegates to Congress—several Livingstons, Philip Schuyler, and James Duane—were moderate conservatives who did not want a vanguard role. A zealot like Isaac Sears wound up moving to Connecticut.

Other colonies could not be pacesetters or influence wielders for want of size or weight. Among the four least populous—New Hampshire, Rhode Island, Delaware, and Georgia—several had strong rebel biases. None, however, bred political leaders of national stature. New Hampshire and Rhode Island, besides being small, lay in the regional shadow of Massachusetts. Tiny Delaware, despite gaining its own Assembly in 1701, was still a three-county appendage of Pennsylvania. Georgia, established in 1733, often depended on South Carolina, its strong-minded neighbor. Georgia's royal governor, Sir James Wright, half joked that his colony would have kept out of the Revolution if only the Savannah River, the boundary with South Carolina, had not been so narrow.[11]

Not that being a nursery of great issues or major national leaders was a blessing. Had Delaware, for example, been a political pivot, its large ratio of vocal Loyalists might have forced a military solution. That was never necessary. And New Hampshire, for its part, was the one state the British Army ignored between 1775 and 1783.

North Carolina, bold enough in 1775, fell short of being a major force. Despite its population trebling in the quarter century before the Revolution, the colony had begun its existence in the 1720s as a minor periphery of the greater "Carolina" headquartered in Charleston. Much poorer than rice-plantation-rich South Carolina, the northern offshoot was also a study in confused identity—its northeast (the Albemarle) grew around an early population spillover from adjacent Virginia, while its southeast (Cape Fear) was settled in the 1720s from next-door South Carolina. Prior to its huge influx, the new province had little political coherence or weight. As of 1775, many of the new settlers in North Carolina's central or Piedmont region had poured in from Pennsylvania and Virginia looking for cheap land and better opportunity. But this was more destabilizing than unifying. Unfocused latter-day population growth produced nothing like the 170-year history and self-confidence of Virginia or the 150-year Puritan battle-consciousness that inspired Massachusetts.

Elsewhere, two midsize colonies, Maryland and New Jersey, while not leaders, were weightier than the minor quartet. But neither had a location or history that lent itself to pre-Revolutionary leadership. Maryland stood out as the only colony among the thirteen launched under a Catholic proprietor, the English Lord Baltimore, in 1634. The proprietorship of the Calvert family (no longer Catholic) still prevailed in 1774, and as in Pennsylvania, that issue confused and parochialized local politics. Maryland's leading Revolutionary statesman was Charles Carroll of Carrollton, a French-educated Catholic member of the Continental Congress. His best-known service came in early 1776 as part of a congressional mission to Catholic Quebec. By 1775, Maryland was largely Protestant, but several older Chesapeake counties—St. Mary's, Calvert, and parts of Anne Arundel and Prince Georges—retained a locally important Catholic gentry.

In agricultural terms, much of southern Maryland was tobacco country, but its leaf production was well below Virginia's. Northern Maryland's principal crop was wheat, as in next-door Pennsylvania. Indeed, the booming port of Baltimore principally served a wheat-growing Pennsylvania hinterland, and Baltimore's Patriot faction had ties to Philadelphia radicals. As we have seen, in 1775 the Continental Congress put Maryland in a military district with the middle colonies—the "bread colonies"—and so will this chapter. Maryland talked tough on preparedness and gunpowder procurement but was cautious with respect to independence. John Adams commented "that this is so eccentric a colony—sometimes so hot, sometimes so cold; now so high, then so low—that I know not what to say about it or to expect from it."[12]

New Jersey represented another awkward piece in the colonial jigsaw puzzle. As of 1702, it combined the two "Jerseys" that had begun separately—West Jersey, the southern half abutting Philadelphia, and East Jersey, the northern section across the Hudson from New York. But their cultural dissimilarity lingered. West Jersey bore a substantial Pennsylvania and Quaker imprint, while East Jersey had a mixed New England, Scottish, New York Dutch, and German population. No nursery of potential national leadership existed. In 1774, New Jersey's royal governor illustrated the province's lack of cohesion by citing how the capital still alternated between Perth Amboy in former East Jersey and Burlington in old West Jersey.[13]

Between 1776 and 1778, New Jersey became just what many New Jerseyans had feared—a venue of battles, from Fort Lee on the Hudson to Trenton, Princeton, and Monmouth. This, too, had inhibited New Jersey forwardness. The colony's best-known political activists—its first governor,

William Livingston, from the New York family, and John Witherspoon, member of the Continental Congress and later president of Princeton University—came to New Jersey with ideas shaped elsewhere. Witherspoon, for example, came to the colonies from the covenanting southwest of Scotland in 1768 at age 45, already Presbyterian, already evangelical, already radical.

These capsules underscore a basic reality: most colonies were followers, not leaders. The process of elimination, by cataloguing smallness, lack of influence, or a dearth of local identity, leaves us with the other two vanguard colonies. South Carolina, chartered in 1667, was only midsize once shorn of North Carolina and Georgia, but it was aggressive, vocal, and wealthy. Connecticut, first chartered in 1635, also aggressive, was until 1770 the fourth most populous province. At this point, we can put population nuances aside. Size certainly counted, but history, achievement, and pride seem to have been the distinguishing characteristics.

The traits shared by the four vanguards clumped around the assertiveness of the early-chartered colonies, all of them established back in the seventeenth century by mainstream English "church" Protestants (as opposed to Catholics or Quaker and Baptist sectarians). These were the provinces grandly launched with pompous, permissive charters that extended their territory to the Pacific and made their early mindsets quasi-imperial. Likewise, the four could boast long continuous periods of something close to self-government. They gloried in their little parliaments (especially Virginia's House of Burgesses and South Carolina's Commons House of Assembly), their overseas military expeditions (to St. Augustine, Port Royal, Louisburg, and Quebec), and their proud New World identities. None of the four were about to accept disinheritance by a Parliament and British political milieu they disdained as corrupt.

Nationalism, territorial expansion, and early versions of manifest destiny highlighted a common drive. The grandiose charters were important psychological enablers. So, too, was each province's 90-to-150-year history of substantial self-government, some of it usurped from royal governors. Such partial autonomy allowed unusual military adventuring and widespread firearms ownership and militia organization, as well as haughty transatlantic imitations of parliament and locally determined church establishments. These privileges and consciousness of charters and rights rule out any superficial political comparison with eighteenth-century British counties of more or less similar size—English Sussex, Devon, or Yorkshire, or even Scottish Ayr or Irish Antrim.

These unusual colonial self-perceptions become still more relevant as the mid- and late-1760s emphasized Britain's own strengthening imperial determination. In 1774 and 1775, the king and Parliament made entirely clear their commitment to reverse a half century of permissive or indecisive rule. This had begun with the more or less "salutary neglect" of 1720–1756, followed by the wartime preoccupations of 1756–1763 and thereafter by the erratic 1760s, during which ministerial provocation alternated with conciliation. For example, passage of the Stamp Act of 1765 was followed by its repeal in 1766; then passage of the Townshend Acts of 1767 was followed by their substantial withdrawal in 1770. London's belated emphasis on imperial discipline had a certain logic. But alas for the king and Parliament, the colonies of 1774 had five times the population and ten times the self-confidence of the fledglings circa 1725.

As we have seen, the mother country's new turn toward harsh restraint, crystallized by British outrage over the Boston Tea Party, reached critical mass through the Coercive Acts. Bluntly restated, the message from King, Privy Council, and Parliament to the other twelve colonies was unsparing: behave, do what we tell you, or you, too—speaking here to Connecticut and Rhode Island—may lose your precious charters and feel the prick of a sharp bayonet. That threat came too late; confrontation was spreading.

Leadership and Confrontation: Virginia, Massachusetts, Connecticut, and South Carolina

In the early 1760s, as the Seven Years War in Europe ended in a surfeit of London self-confidence, all four provinces sought to protect their existing degrees of self-government. The principal tactic, unnecessary in self-governing Connecticut but conspicuous in Virginia, Massachusetts, and South Carolina, required a determined lower house of the legislature. The Virginia House of Burgesses, the Massachusetts House of Representatives, and the South Carolina Commons House of Assembly each maneuvered against British-appointed governors, succeeding through tactics of insistence, provocation, and power grabbing. Eventually, these initial measures gave way to the displacement of established government by extralegal bodies and conventions. Royal executives, sometimes in near fury, usually countered by dissolving or proroguing the offending house. When fighting began in 1775, it had a background of political confrontation going back at least several years.

As later chapters will amplify, the fighting that broke out in 1775 tended to come in provinces where politics had broken down. Initially, this meant New England, some parts of northern New York, and the plantation colonies—Virginia, South Carolina, and sections of North Carolina and Georgia adjacent to South Carolina. Even after Lexington and Concord, the king and his ministers chose not to send soldiers into the less offensive middle colonies. These were either holding back from flat-out confrontation—or in the case of New York, willing to placate the Crown by provisioning nearby warships like HMS *Asia*.

The few violent episodes in the middle colonies were pretty much exceptions that proved the noncombative rule. The bloody beating of a local ship captain by a British naval boarding party off New Castle, Delaware, in March 1775 supposedly prompted the Assembly a week later to unanimously approve the autumn proceedings of the First Continental Congress. In July, with a rumor of British warships coming up the Delaware River, the Pennsylvania Committee of Safety and the New Jersey Provincial Congress cooperated in placing defensive obstacles along the waterway. New Yorkers were frightened on the night of August 23 when the 64-gun *Asia* briefly bombarded Manhattan to halt Patriots' removal of cannon from a nearby fort. Only a handful of injuries resulted, but a large civilian exodus followed. A month later, marines from the *Asia* stopped New Jersey's Perth Amboy stage boat and carried off a Connecticut officer, in American eyes committing a "felonious piratical outrage."[14]

It was in the vanguard provinces that clashes were overt and growing. The 1774–1775 events in Massachusetts, the best chronicled, ranged from full-scale battles like Bunker Hill to island raids in Boston Harbor, British bombardment of coastal towns, and Patriot captures of small British naval vessels as far afield as present-day Machias, Maine. The backdrop to violence in Massachusetts is that Boston's first occupation troops—two regiments—dated back to 1768, having been sent in response to tax- and customs-related riots. Some historians put the roots of 1775 conflict that far back—or even to 1761.[15] In any case, the events in Massachusetts do not lack for historians.

Events in Virginia are less well known. The colony's records, copious and

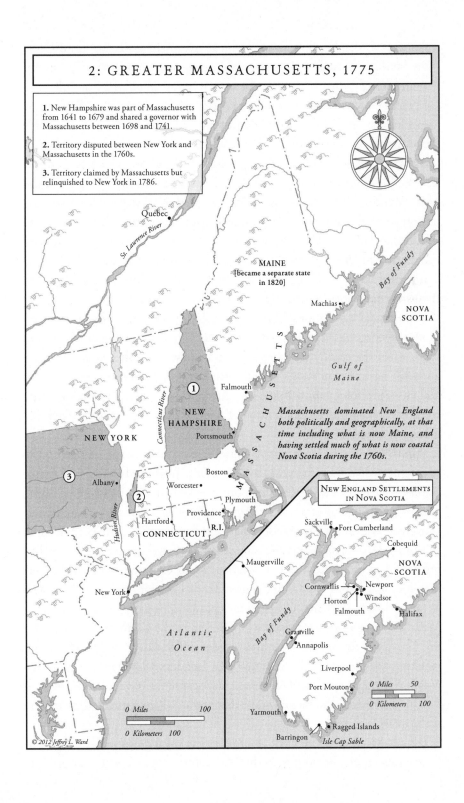

2: GREATER MASSACHUSETTS, 1775

1. New Hampshire was part of Massachusetts from 1641 to 1679 and shared a governor with Massachusetts between 1698 and 1741.

2. Territory disputed between New York and Massachusetts in the 1760s.

3. Territory claimed by Massachusetts but relinquished to New York in 1786.

Quebec

St. Lawrence River

MAINE
[became a separate state in 1820]

Machias

NOVA SCOTIA

Bay of Fundy

Gulf of Maine

Falmouth

NEW HAMPSHIRE

Portsmouth

Connecticut River

NEW YORK

M A S S A C H U S E T T S

Massachusetts dominated New England both politically and geographically, at that time including what is now Maine, and having settled much of what is now coastal Nova Scotia during the 1760s.

Boston

Albany

Worcester

Plymouth

Providence

Hartford

R.I.

CONNECTICUT

Hudson River

New York

Atlantic Ocean

NEW ENGLAND SETTLEMENTS IN NOVA SCOTIA

Sackville
Fort Cumberland

Cobequid

Maugerville

NOVA SCOTIA

Cornwallis
Newport
Horton
Windsor
Falmouth
Halifax

Bay of Fundy

Granville
Annapolis

Liverpool

Port Mouton

Yarmouth

Ragged Islands

Barrington

Isle Cap Sable

0 Miles 50
0 Kilometers 100

0 Miles 100
0 Kilometers 100

© 2012 Jeffrey L. Ward

reasonably available, show cooperation between the governor, Lord Dunmore, and the House of Burgesses beginning souring in 1773. Dunmore, not surprisingly, dissolved the house after it set up an official Committee of Correspondence to keep in touch with the other colonies. He dissolved it again in May 1774, following the burgesses' support for Boston and their recommendation for holding a Continental Congress later that year. That summer, Virginia Patriots embraced the extralegal provincial convention device. The first met in August to elect delegates to the imminent Philadelphia Congress. A Second Convention followed in March 1775 before Lexington and Concord, and a Third Convention sat during July and August, effectively taking over colonywide governmental authority as Dunmore transferred his headquarters to a British warship. May saw independent companies led by Patrick Henry march on Williamsburg, the capital, but they were persuaded to turn back.

Two more Conventions followed in 1775 and 1776. In the meantime, the House of Burgesses kept itself adjourned until finally shutting down in May 1776, when the colony switched over to its newly established government anticipating independence.[16] Fighting in Virginia began in October 1775, and this chronology, punctuated by skirmishes, battles, and ship actions, warrants greater historical attention, if not quite equal place with, events in Massachusetts.

South Carolina's Commons House of Assembly is the belligerent so widely neglected over the years by historians. Indeed, the state has a long tradition of fierce and aggressive politics, thrown into subsequent disrepute—as Massachusetts's recurring combativeness was not—by South Carolina's prominence in starting the Civil War of 1861–1865. The fire-eater spirit of 1860 secession and the 1861 attack on Fort Sumter were arguably previewed in the 1760s and 1770s, when South Carolina aided the United Colonies to become the United States. Confrontation with Britain began as far back as 1762, when Christopher Gadsden, by 1775 a principal leader of the province's radical faction, won election to the Commons House. The royal governor refused to swear him in, meanwhile dissolving the House for violating the Elections Act (a statute that London wanted an excuse to rewrite). Although new elections were held, because the governor and the new Commons House remained at odds, the provincial government did no public business into 1763.

More altercations followed. In 1768, a new royal governor dissolved the Commons House for taking up the Massachusetts Circular Letter protesting the Townshend Acts. Still another dissolution followed in 1769 after the Commons House—gratuitously, and probably unlawfully—ordered the payment of 1,500 pounds sterling to a London fund set up to aid John Wilkes, a British radical jailed for criticizing King George. Over an eighteen-month period, the royal governor, Lord Charles Greville Montagu, dissolved the Commons House four times, and the legislators replied in kind by asking London for Montagu's recall.[17] Candidly put, the South Carolina patriotic elite frequently delighted in out-Bostoning Massachusetts.

In the words of local historian Walter Edgar, "The Wilkes Fund Controversy was as important as parliamentary taxation in convincing the elite that if it wanted to control the political destiny of South Carolina, revolution was the only answer. Imperial officials underestimated the resolve of the South Carolinians. The colony's elite was determined that it would not knuckle under to the 'unjust and unconstitutional measures of an Arbitrary and Oppressive Ministry.' For all practical purposes, royal government in South Carolina ceased in 1771 (the last year any legislation was passed), four years earlier than in other colonies."[18]

Next came the extralegal stage of the province's insurgency. This included the establishment of a mass-based committee in Charleston (1773), the creation of a "General Committee" or shadow government (1774), and the late 1774 action whereby the General Committee created a new body to better represent the backcountry and elect delegates to the Second Continental Congress. This was the Provincial Congress, which met in January 1775 as a formal, if not official assembly. On April 21, as we have seen, a Secret Committee was appointed to put the colony in a state of defense, which included measures to seize munitions and arms. Then on June 14, the Provincial Congress gave executive powers to a Council of Safety, which would work with the congress and act on its behalf during adjournment.[19]

By early 1775, South Carolina's preparations were sufficiently advanced that war supplies were arriving from the West Indies. By autumn, the colony must have exceeded any other in forwarding gunpowder to Washington's army in Massachusetts.[20] Like Virginia, South Carolina saw skirmishes, small battles, and ship actions in 1775. An unsuccessful British southern expedition, planned in 1775, ended in a June 1776 disaster when the Patriot force defending a half-constructed Sullivan's Fort near Charleston fought off—and sorely embarrassed—King George's navy.

Connecticut was another hive of pre-Revolutionary activity. Military

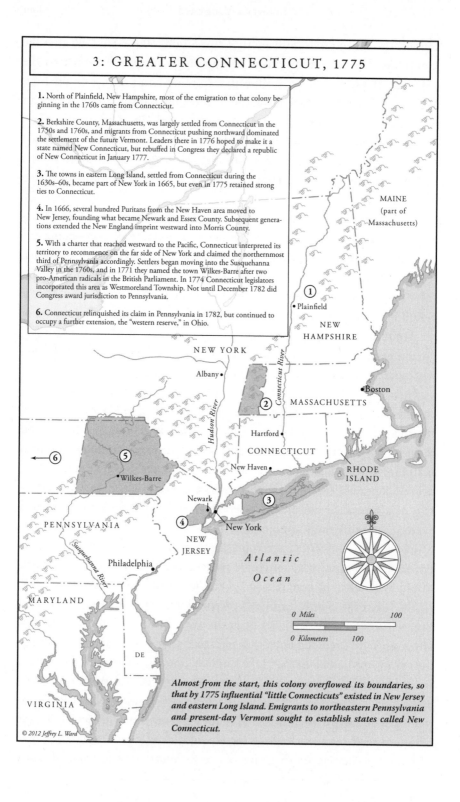

3: GREATER CONNECTICUT, 1775

1. North of Plainfield, New Hampshire, most of the emigration to that colony beginning in the 1760s came from Connecticut.

2. Berkshire County, Massachusetts, was largely settled from Connecticut in the 1750s and 1760s, and migrants from Connecticut pushing northward dominated the settlement of the future Vermont. Leaders there in 1776 hoped to make it a state named New Connecticut, but rebuffed in Congress they declared a republic of New Connecticut in January 1777.

3. The towns in eastern Long Island, settled from Connecticut during the 1630s–60s, became part of New York in 1665, but even in 1775 retained strong ties to Connecticut.

4. In 1666, several hundred Puritans from the New Haven area moved to New Jersey, founding what became Newark and Essex County. Subsequent generations extended the New England imprint westward into Morris County.

5. With a charter that reached westward to the Pacific, Connecticut interpreted its territory to recommence on the far side of New York and claimed the northernmost third of Pennsylvania accordingly. Settlers began moving into the Susquehanna Valley in the 1760s, and in 1771 they named the town Wilkes-Barre after two pro-American radicals in the British Parliament. In 1774 Connecticut legislators incorporated this area as Westmoreland Township. Not until December 1782 did Congress award jurisdiction to Pennsylvania.

6. Connecticut relinquished its claim in Pennsylvania in 1782, but continued to occupy a further extension, the "western reserve," in Ohio.

MAINE
(part of
Massachusetts)

① • Plainfield

NEW
HAMPSHIRE

NEW YORK

Connecticut River

Albany •

② MASSACHUSETTS

• Boston

Hudson River

Hartford •

CONNECTICUT

⑥ ← ⑤

New Haven •

RHODE
ISLAND

• Wilkes-Barre

Newark

③

④ New York

PENNSYLVANIA

NEW
JERSEY

Atlantic

Susquehanna River

• Philadelphia

Ocean

MARYLAND

0 Miles 100

0 Kilometers 100

DE

© 2012 Jeffrey L. Ward

VIRGINIA

Almost from the start, this colony overflowed its boundaries, so that by 1775 influential "little Connecticuts" existed in New Jersey and eastern Long Island. Emigrants to northeastern Pennsylvania and present-day Vermont sought to establish states called New Connecticut.

historians describe the province as slipping into its own eighteen-month *rage militaire* after the September 1774 powder alarm, with preparedness moving forward.[21] Where Connecticut differed completely from Virginia, Massachusetts, and South Carolina was in the collaborative nature of executive-legislative relations. Because of a unique 1662 charter, all but sacrosanct across the province, the "freemen" of Connecticut elected their own governor and legislature and had since the prior century.[22]

So as 1774 lengthened into 1775, no bold or hurried usurpations were necessary—no extralegal assemblages, no huge, outdoor mass embodiments of "the people." The radical, pro-independence governor, Jonathan Trumbull, first chosen in 1769, was returned to office at regular intervals through the war's end in 1783. Sixty-five years old in 1775, he was called the "rebel governor" by the British because his readiness to act was unique. In next-door Rhode Island, Governor Joseph Wanton, although locally elected, had to be removed by the Patriot legislature in 1775 for ambivalent sympathies.[23]

Trumbull's role was unique in yet another way. Having spent many earlier years in the Connecticut House of Representatives, he worked easily and comfortably with both it and the Council. As the Revolution took hold, both bodies delegated much of their military supervisory power to Trumbull, facilitating a highly effective war leadership that extended through 1783. By the time Washington had spent a summer besieging Boston, Trumbull was among the general's closest collaborators. He could make quick decisions, and a well-run Connecticut regime was geographically positioned to speed militia regiments to Boston, New York, Lake Champlain, and eventually Canada.

Back in June 1774, when the Connecticut House had become the first elected North American assembly to urge all the colonies to meet and collaborate against the Coercive Acts, its resolution had also included a call for union.[24] More than in other colonies, authorities in Connecticut, especially Trumbull, looked beyond immediate provincial concerns. This was partly because of a religious precursor of American manifest destiny: Puritan belief in the new nation as the Chosen of the Lord. Even sympathetic biographers admit that Trumbull's biblical language produced snickers in some circles; however, his efficiency was widely respected.

Given the colony's radical politics, during 1774 Connecticut's small *Loyalist* minority, not the Patriot majority, was forced into an extralegal maneuver: the Middletown Convention. Its organizers sought to reverse the colony's commitment to westward expansion, to remove Trumbull, and to change the manner of selecting the Council, but they failed. The governor had no difficulty retaining his office. After news of the Coercive Acts began arriving in the spring and summer, Connecticut emoted with Massachusetts. If the latter's 1691 charter could be torn up, Connecticut's might be next. General Gage and some in the Cabinet hoped as much.[25]

Just like Massachusetts, Connecticut moved early for military preparedness. According to historian Richard Buel, the General Assembly, in its autumn 1774 session, "commissioned two independent military companies, organized two new militia regiments, and ordered an inventory of the colony's artillery." Next, in an even greater break with precedent, "the legislators ordered the militia to train for twelve half-days before May 1, 1775, each non-commissioned officer and private to be paid six shillings for his time. They organized four more militia regiments, provided for a general inventory and repair of weapons, ordered the mounting of cannon at New London, and required the colony's entire armed force to muster at the end of November."[26]

"Connecticut was practically in a state of war in the first months of 1775," noted another historian, "even before the skirmishes at Lexington and Concord plunged America into full-scale hostilities with England."[27] As the winter of 1774–1775 brought war ever closer, authorities concluded that for towns to double their powder and shot as advised would require outside sources of supply. Therefore the Council, acting alone, commissioned Nathaniel Shaw, a Patriot merchant and shipowner of New London, to send fast vessels to friendly West Indian ports.[28] Connecticut men had plenty of the needed smuggling skills.

After April 19, Trumbull and his legislative allies, in an emergency session, ordered 6,000 men, or one fourth of the militia, on immediate service, embargoed any export of the province's food products (to ensure close control), and ordered the purchase of more munitions, including 3,000 stands of arms. Follow-up actions in May included adoption of articles of war for Connecticut soldiers like those drawn up by the Massachusetts Provincial Congress, as well as enactment of a statute promoting the local production of "Fire-Arms and Military Stores." By May's end, six regiments had been formed, each of roughly 1,000 men. Finally, to assist the governor in military management when the legislature was not in session, a Council of Safety was established.[29] This was Trumbull's war cabinet.

The further importance lay in Trumbull's ability to speedily commit

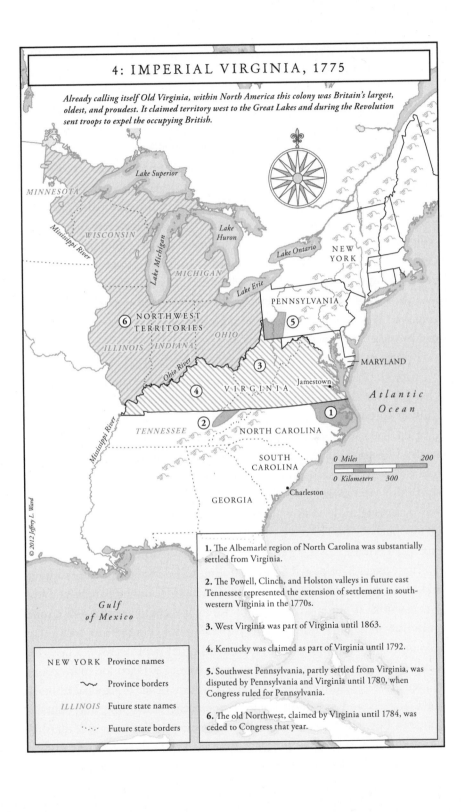

4: IMPERIAL VIRGINIA, 1775

Already calling itself Old Virginia, within North America this colony was Britain's largest, oldest, and proudest. It claimed territory west to the Great Lakes and during the Revolution sent troops to expel the occupying British.

MINNESOTA

Lake Superior

WISCONSIN

Mississippi River

Lake Michigan

Lake Huron

MICHIGAN

Lake Ontario

Lake Erie

NEW YORK

PENNSYLVANIA

⑥ NORTHWEST TERRITORIES

OHIO

ILLINOIS   INDIANA

Ohio River

⑤

MARYLAND

③

④   VIRGINIA   Jamestown

Mississippi River

②

TENNESSEE

①

Atlantic Ocean

NORTH CAROLINA

SOUTH CAROLINA

0 Miles   200

0 Kilometers   300

GEORGIA   Charleston

Gulf of Mexico

© 2012 Jeffrey L. Ward

1. The Albemarle region of North Carolina was substantially settled from Virginia.

2. The Powell, Clinch, and Holston valleys in future east Tennessee represented the extension of settlement in southwestern Virginia in the 1770s.

3. West Virginia was part of Virginia until 1863.

4. Kentucky was claimed as part of Virginia until 1792.

5. Southwest Pennsylvania, partly settled from Virginia, was disputed by Pennsylvania and Virginia until 1780, when Congress ruled for Pennsylvania.

6. The old Northwest, claimed by Virginia until 1784, was ceded to Congress that year.

NEW YORK   Province names

〜   Province borders

ILLINOIS   Future state names

·-·-·   Future state borders

troops. With Massachusetts regiments mostly deployed around Boston, Connecticut became the United Colonies' northeastern reserve armory. By autumn, the province had 2,300 soldiers participating in the siege of Boston, over 1,000 in northern New York garrisoning Ticonderoga or marching to Canada, and three regiments camped in southwestern Connecticut, just over the provincial border from New York. From time to time, men were sent at Washington's request into the next-door province to keep order or suppress Tories.[30]

With British warships based in Rhode Island occasionally prowling Connecticut's adjacent waters, Trumbull told Washington that he was obliged to station a seacoast force to protect New London, Norwich, Groton, and Stonington.[31] By the end of 1775, Connecticut was defending or attacking on four fronts, meanwhile serving as a principal supplier of meat, wheat, and flour for American armies around Boston or heading into Canada.[32] It was an extraordinary dual role, facilitated by Trumbull's prior commissary experience and Connecticut's central geography.

Besides being the only serving governor of 1774–1775 to continue on in wartime, he had been a prominent Connecticut merchant during King George's War and the French and Indian War, holding contracts to supply "flintlocks, cutlasses, cartouchboxes and belts" for a previous invasion of Canada. Later he provisioned provincial troops at Lake George. He also represented Connecticut at intercolonial conferences on war strategy, including meetings with Massachusetts governor William Shirley and Lord Loudon, the British commander in chief. Trumbull's principal weakness as a merchant was that being most of all a political figure, he let too many customers run up too much credit. However, as governor he seems to have been careful with provincial finances, making enemies with high wartime taxes.[33]

These pages have paired South Carolina and Connecticut with Virginia and Massachusetts in terms of 1774–1775 patriotism and preparedness. Now it is essential to note further vanguard colony characteristics—a strong commitment to outward territorial expansion, a willingness to press other colonies with migrations, incursions, and border controversies, a taste for small-scale foreign policy, a record of enthusiastic participation in invasions of French and Spanish colonies, considerable experience in regional military collaboration, and a far-flung circle of mercantile, smuggling, and political contacts. Elites in New York and Pennsylvania might dream of leadership in a future British Empire if North American growth favored the middle colonies, but southern plantation elites and New Englanders had no such illusions. Neither slave owners nor "Oliverian" Puritans could expect any leading role in British metropolitanism. Those two sections needed independence and a self-guided American westward expansion.

The Geography of Power: Territorial, Economic, and Cultural Expansionism

Simple, straightforward maps of the boundaries of the colonies in 1750 or 1775 do little justice to the expansionism of the four—their territoriality, regional settlement outreach, and demographic imperialism. Born out of the Westward Ho! religious, commercial, and cultural legacy of Elizabethan England, these colonies, Puritan and Anglican alike, inherited that drive and expansionist mentality and made it American.[34]

If the four vanguards contained roughly half of the population of the full thirteen and somewhat more of the wealth, their political and cultural influence was more disproportionate. Beyond New England, something like 20 to 25 percent of the population of both New York and New Jersey had Massachusetts or Connecticut ancestry, which showed in their local politics. Emigrants from Virginia spread not just southward and westward but northward into southwestern Pennsylvania. Much of Georgia, as well as the lower Cape Fear section of North Carolina, were commercial and cultural outliers of South Carolina.

These attributes show best on a quartet of portraits—maps 2 to 5—designed to show for each province its charter-based claims to western territory, its earlier out-of-colony migrations and forts, the districts it once included, and its persisting land claims. Virginia and Massachusetts display the farthest outward reach. However, even in 1776 and 1777, settlers of two contested areas that hoped for statehood—one in Vermont, the other in northeastern Pennsylvania—competed for the name "New Connecticut" to display their origins. Neither happened, but New York and Pennsylvania could testify to Yankee territorialism.

Massachusetts, dominant in New England both geographically and culturally, is the place to start. In 1775, its boundaries included most of what is now Maine, which did not manage to separate until 1820. Next-door New Hampshire had shared a governor with Massachusetts from the 1690s to 1740, and the boundary remained ill defined until 1741. Indeed, much of southern New Hampshire had been settled from Massachusetts, and many of its towns took shape under a Boston grant.

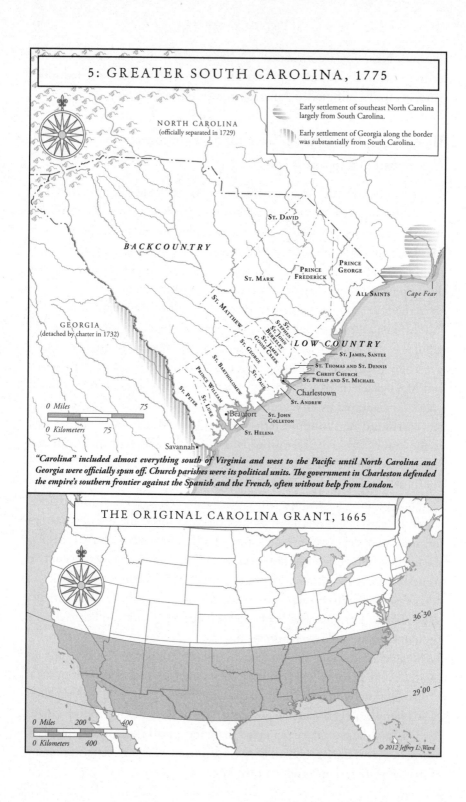

5: GREATER SOUTH CAROLINA, 1775

Early settlement of southeast North Carolina largely from South Carolina.

Early settlement of Georgia along the border was substantially from South Carolina.

NORTH CAROLINA
(officially separated in 1729)

BACKCOUNTRY

St. David

Prince George

Prince Frederick

St. Mark

All Saints

Cape Fear

GEORGIA
(detached by charter in 1732)

St. Matthew

St. Stephen
St. John
Berkeley
St. James
Goose Creek

LOW COUNTRY

St. James, Santee

St. George

St. Thomas and St. Dennis

St. Bartholomew

St. Paul

Christ Church

St. Philip and St. Michael

Prince William

Charlestown

St. Peter

St. Luke

St. Andrew

0 Miles   75

Beaufort

St. John
Colleton

0 Kilometers   75

St. Helena

Savannah

"Carolina" included almost everything south of Virginia and west to the Pacific until North Carolina and Georgia were officially spun off. Church parishes were its political units. The government in Charleston defended the empire's southern frontier against the Spanish and the French, often without help from London.

THE ORIGINAL CAROLINA GRANT, 1665

36°30'

29°00'

0 Miles   200   400

0 Kilometers   400

© 2012 Jeffrey L. Ward

During the Revolution, New Hampshire several times seemed on the verge of coming unglued. If its Merrimack Valley settlements looked south to Massachusetts, scores of townships farther west favored seceding to join nearby towns west of the Connecticut River in what later became Vermont. In 1775, the future Vermont was disputed between New Hampshire, New York, and independent-government advocates, but in May Massachusetts and Connecticut officials made the decisions to attack nearby Fort Ticonderoga.

Through much of the eighteenth century, maritime and fishing-dependent Massachusetts had designs farther northeast than Maine. The several Massachusetts-led military assaults on French-held Nova Scotia between the 1690s and the 1740s partly reflected fishery-related objectives. In the early 1760s, emigrants from Massachusetts by the thousands settled along the western coast of lower Nova Scotia. Until the sixties, a determined Massachusetts—a painted wooden replica of the sacred cod still hangs in the Boston statehouse—looked to what are now Canada's maritime provinces for commercial expansion and British control of North Atlantic fishing rights.

Map 2 shows the geographic and demographic reach of "Greater Massachusetts" in 1775. Some of this represented former glories. Like Boston's earlier lead among American cities, Massachusetts's prospects for northward expansion had peaked. The exception, of course, lay in the tantalizing possibility of a regime change in Canada. Memories of earlier expeditions and captures helped to explain the ongoing interest of Massachusetts leaders in Nova Scotia, the Bay of Fundy, and the Champlain-Hudson corridor, as Chapter 10 will amplify.

Bay Colony settlements in the middle and southern colonies, by contrast, were relatively few—a handful in New York along its border with Massachusetts, and another handful in New Jersey. The latter clumped in the northern section around Morristown and along the southern coast stretching from Greenwich, the site of New Jersey's own December 1774 Presbyterian-led Tea Party, to Cape May and its whaling enterprise. In 1775 some New Jerseyans overestimated half of the population as being of New England stock, but a third of the active Patriots might have been.

Land speculation in the district of Maine by Massachusetts investors continued after the Revolution, as did commitment to the fisheries, but the conquest of Canada never materialized. For Yankees, the post-Revolutionary population movement would be a great westward, rather than northern, advance. Between 1783 and 1830, Massachusetts and the rest of New

England, unable to clip off bits of New York in 1775–1776, sent a vast Yankee settlement wave across its upstate counties, all but submerging the Mohawk Valley Palatines, retired Scottish soldiers, and old Dutch Tories of Kinderhook and Hoosic in a tide of Ebenezers, Jonathans, Abigails, and Patiences. This, of course, did nothing at all to change the politics of 1775. The combativeness of Massachusetts expressed its past glory and pride, its cagey Yankee plotting, and the now-burgeoning millennial belief that God had picked a New England–led America as the next Chosen Nation.

Neighboring Connecticut shared much of the Bay Colony's millennial faith and expansionism. However, its own territorial imperative was westward and southward and only secondarily northward into the Berkshire Hills, the Green Mountains, and the upper Connecticut Valley. In consequence, map 3, with its portrait of Greater Connecticut circa 1775, raises a different set of implications. Four provinces and another future state had hard-charging "little Connecticuts" within their boundaries, whose pushy politics they did not always appreciate.

Self-governing from the 1630s when three early settlements combined, and then given a permissive charter in 1662, Connecticut soon did colonizing of its own. During the 1640s, Puritan emigrants crossed what is now Long Island Sound and put down towns—eleven by 1660—and churches along the eastern end of Long Island. These remained part of Connecticut until 1665. In 1666 thirty families from New Haven planted a settlement that became Newark, New Jersey; others began the town of Shrewsbury. Later emigrants launched Fairfield and Union, New Jersey (first called Connecticut Farms). As for New York, Connecticut officials, encouraged by the sweep of their charter, at various times tried to take parts of Westchester County and western Long Island towns from the Yorkers, but failed.[35]

By 1775, New Jersey's Connecticut settlement had grown to be Essex County, the heartland of the province's pro-independence activists. The catalogue of its leadership is striking, and several years later the town of Connecticut Farms became a revolutionary battlefield.[36] The Yankee settlements of eastern Long Island, in turn, became Suffolk County, New York— also a future hotbed of independence sentiment in a province with relatively few. New York's Tory lieutenant governor Cadwallader Colden understood the connection: "[Suffolk] county in the east end of Long Island . . . was settled from Connecticut and the inhabitants still retain a great similarity of manners and sentiments."[37]

More than Massachusetts, Connecticut admitted to being somewhat "Oliverian." By some accounts, Oliver Cromwell himself had almost emigrated there in the 1630s, and Thomas Hooker, a Connecticut founder, was the brother-in-law of John Pym, a prominent Parliamentary leader in the English Civil War. Historians at Yale are surprised to note that three streets converging near the university—Whalley, Dixwell, and Goffe—are named for regicides who signed the royal death warrant in the 1649 execution of Charles I. All three fled to Boston and then in 1661 to Connecticut, were hidden by sympathizers, remained free, and died in the province many years later. The flagship of Connecticut's Revolutionary state navy would be named the *Oliver Cromwell*. When Governor Trumbull's eldest son visited England in 1764, he went up from London to visit Huntingdon, Cromwell's birthplace.[38] For those of the Crown's strong supporters who damned the American Revolution for its Cromwellian resemblances, Connecticut does provide substantiation.

However, to come back to politically influential Connecticut emigration, it was not limited to nearby New York and New Jersey. Travelers to the coastal Georgia pinelands south of Savannah in our own day are often startled to see a neat white eighteenth-century New England church surrounded by historical markers and the occasional Yankee license plate. This is Midway, in what was once colonial St. John's Parish, in 1777 renamed Liberty County. In 1774, this unusual, substantially New England–settled parish rallied to the support of Boston and elected a delegate, Connecticut-born Lyman Hall, to the First Continental Congress. Hall did not go to Philadelphia with that thin credential, but he went in 1775 as one of two Georgia delegates to the Second Continental Congress and later signed the Declaration of Independence. Sir James Wright, the royal governor, deplored the parish's "strong tincture of . . . Oliverian principles."[39] Thus the anomaly of historians surprised by votes in the Continental Congress that conjoined Georgia with Virginia and New England.[40] Emigrants from Connecticut were not a breed to be taken lightly.

Two other outliers of Greater Connecticut, by contrast, complicated matters for pro-independence strategists. We can begin with the three-way struggle for what became Vermont. In 1775 New York had legal title, based on a ruling by the Crown in 1764 against rival claimant New Hampshire. Even so, many local residents still referred to the "Hampshire Grants." After Lexington and Concord, claimants under New Hampshire deeds presumed that war would vacate the royal adjudication. So did the Green

Mountain Boys, whose Connecticut-born leaders—Ethan and Ira Allen, Remember Baker, and Seth Warner—wanted a separate entity. The name "New Connecticut," chosen by an early 1777 Patriot convention, had to be dropped because Yankees seeking statehood for northeastern Pennsylvania had taken it first.[41]

Irritated New Yorkers thought they saw Connecticut nibblers everywhere: occupying Fort Ticonderoga, gathering on Lake Champlain, inciting Green Mountain separatists, sending troops into Westchester and New York City, and colluding with their Puritan cousins in eastern Long Island. The two, New York and Connecticut, had roughly comparable populations in 1775. In military terms, though, the Yankee province was far better organized.

Meanwhile, Pennsylvanians also saw Connecticut through angry eyes. Under several ambitious land schemes, initially the Delaware Company, then the much bigger Susquehannah Company, Connecticut's Patriot government wound up in 1774 claiming northeastern Pennsylvania—enrolling it as a Connecticut township—based on an expansive reading of its charter. Several armed encounters had already begun what historians named "the Pennamite Wars." Another flared up in late 1775, when a 500-man Pennsylvania force invaded, but soon retreated. Congress eventually stepped in, but things remained legally unresolved through 1782.[42]

Which brings us to Virginia, another military-minded and expansionist province. In 1775, the Old Dominion, too, was trying to bite off a large chunk of territory from Quaker Pennsylvania. The latter had been vague about its boundaries and about what territory it would be responsible for defending. Even relative to Connecticut, plantation-owning Virginia was a colony immersed in land speculation—by the early 1770s, planters looked to offset the increasingly difficult economics of tobacco production.

Before profiling Virginia, a broader generalization is appropriate. All four of these colonies were more than plucky, more than merely willing to stand up for their rights. They could fairly be called *aggressive*. With broadly empowering royal charters, including language that in some cases suggested no superior authority in Britain but the Crown, they resembled the "marches" or counties palatine of England's fifteenth and sixteenth centuries—or so some of their gentry believed. The marches and counties palatine helped hold England's northern and western borders against the Scots and Welsh, and the four North American vanguard provinces by the late eighteenth century had repeatedly held and counterattacked against France in the north and west and Spain in the south. The analogy is only partial, but the aggressive, border-protection aspect fits.

Of the four, early-seventeenth-century Virginians took most seriously the charter language about boundaries reaching not just to the Great Lakes but to the South Sea. From 1626 to 1671, westward expeditions were vigilant—literally. One in 1669 thought the Indian Ocean "does stretch an arm or bay from California as far as the Apalatean mountains." Another two years later reported that "sayles" could be seen from the peaks.[43] By the 1740s and 1750s, when Virginians began to concentrate on the more prosaic westward and northwestward expansion allowed under their charter, the sequence of land companies they organized over three decades sounds like a roll call of future American states: Grand Ohio, Greenbrier, Henderson, Illinois, Illinois-Wabash, Indiana, Loyal, Mississippi, Ohio Company of Virginia, Transylvania, Vandalia, Wabash, and Walpole.[44]

Several companies, to be sure, represented no more than a name change. Others encompassed huge intentions. The Illinois Company, established in 1766, proposed to operate within an area bounded on the east by the Wabash River and on the north by the Wisconsin River. Other names that resonated were those of shareholders destined for political fame: Lee, Randolph, Jefferson, Henry, Washington, Pendleton, even Franklin. After peace came in 1763, every year saw thousands of individual Virginia residents head south down the Great Wagon Road. Organized land speculation, however, looked west and northwest.

So did military leaders. Whereas Connecticut and Massachusetts generally pointed their war making north against French Canada and its Indian allies, Virginia by 1750 directed its military expeditions and banners west and northwest, joining what would be the great Anglo-French contest to rule the Ohio Valley. In 1753, George Washington was present at the beginning of the French and Indian War officially as a Virginia military commander, but also as a member of the extremely interested Ohio Company. He was instructed to tell the French encamped at the Forks of the Ohio that they were trespassing on English territory. This he did, and then returned twice—in 1754, to surrender to the French at Great Meadows, and in 1755, as a colonial officer who performed credibly with General Braddock's ill-fated British army. When Forks of the Ohio became British in 1763, Virginia as well as Pennsylvania had a strong claim.

The Old Dominion's claims got a further boost in 1774 when provincial troops under the royal governor, Lord Dunmore, took the field against

Ohio's Shawnee and Mingo Indians and extracted a treaty that secured another stretch of Virginia-claimed territory already known as Kentucky. In 1775, Kentucky and the part of present-day Pennsylvania around the Forks of the Ohio (Pittsburgh) were both administered from Virginia, despite officials in Philadelphia belatedly labeling the Pittsburgh district as Westmoreland County, *Pennsylvania*. The point here is less about which province got the Forks—eventually, Pennsylvania did—than about the aggressiveness of the two provinces, Connecticut and Virginia, busy trying to detach territory large enough combined to represent 20 to 25 percent of what is now Pennsylvania.

Although land hunger was a prime motive, historians who find little more than economics at work make a mistake. Much grander dreams were involved. Virginians like George Washington and Thomas Jefferson and Connecticut leaders like Jonathan Trumbull thought in terms of a nation being born—of a destiny, be it manifest or biblically millenarian, being fulfilled by every pioneer, town builder, and Conestoga wagon driver moving west. In 1751, Jefferson's father, Peter, drew the first map of Virginia spreading into the Shenandoah and upper Potomac valleys; and George Washington always waxed fulsomely about the westward course of empire in general and his beloved Potomac River in particular.[45]

History lived on almost everywhere in Virginia, just as it did in New England. By 1775, the pride of Virginian leaders was starting to work for independence or its equivalent. George Washington was not alone in seeing hostility or even conspiracy in British treatment of the colonies and Americans. By some accounts, ordinary Virginians had thought along roughly similar lines in 1676, when under the leadership of a small planter named Nathaniel Bacon, they rose against the abuses of Royal Governor Sir William Berkeley. That uprising failed, but a mid-twentieth-century Virginia historian, Thomas Jefferson Wertenbaker, romanticized about its example, concluding that "it gave the English Privy Council a realization of what was to be expected when the Americans were driven to desperation. But after all, the [Bacon] movement was symptomatic, not conclusive. The flight of Berkeley to the Eastern Shore foreshadowed the flight of Dunmore to Norfolk and Gwynn's Island; the burning of Jamestown by the patriots in 1676 had its counterpart in the burning of Norfolk by the patriots in 1776; Bacon's Declaration of the People was the forerunner of the Declaration of Independence."[46]

Fourth of July prose, to be sure. Contemporary chroniclers doubt that

Virginians of 1774–1776 took particular inspiration from Bacon or his rebellion. During the lead-up to the Revolution, too many new provocations were at work—from planter debt levels and British commercial exploitation of tobacco, to the Coercive Acts and London's decision to put the territory north of the Ohio River within Quebec and beyond Virginians' reach. But pride was part of what made Virginia revolution-minded.

Which brings us to South Carolina. If that colony was both wealthier and more politically incendiary than Virginia—in 1775, clearly true—two explanations stand out. First, a pair of highly lucrative crops—low-country rice and indigo—were more profitable than Chesapeake tobacco; and second, a cocksure sort of wealth. South Carolina was the only British North American colony settled from the Caribbean, notably from sugar-rich Barbados, England's original New World plum.

The first proprietors of Carolina—*South* Carolina didn't exist until 1692—were eight prominent royalists, men to whom a restored King Charles II had cause to be grateful. The charter he issued in 1663 swept across the map of North America from the Atlantic to the Pacific, employing two bold latitudes roughly 500 miles apart. The upper followed the southern boundary of Virginia; the lower ran west from what is now Daytona Beach, Florida, to mid-Baja California in Mexico. Plans were even made for a local aristocracy, to be headed by landgraves.

This vast territory was trimmed in 1689 by the tentative separation of what became North Carolina, and then again in 1732 by the creation of Georgia. However, the conveyance had been generous in more than square mileage. Rare powers were granted, most notably the charter's so-called Bishop of Durham or county palatine clause delegating authority normally held only by the monarch. In addition to land, crops and mining, and tax and customs rights, the charter also included "the rights to make war and peace, create towns and ports, grant 'titles of honor,' [and] raise and maintain an army."[47]

In contrast to early Virginians, Carolinians spent little time searching for the South Sea on the other side of the Blue Ridge. They had other things to watch for, notably invading Spaniards. Through the sixteenth-century explorations of Hernando de Soto, Spain had a strong earlier claim to the region and declined to recognize the validity of any English grant. If Massachusetts and Connecticut manned New England's northern frontier against French Canada, South Carolina took on the role of subtropical frontier guard against incursions from Spanish Florida. By the early 1700s, that responsibility had grown to include blocking the commercial and military advance of France into the lower Mississippi and Tennessee river valleys. Here South Carolina remained preeminent even after Georgia became British North America's new southernmost frontier.

The English colonies in the Caribbean already grew exotic crops and worried about Spain, so it is fitting they furnished Carolina's first settlers. According to historian Walter Edgar, "between 1670 and 1690 about 54 percent of the whites who immigrated came from Barbados," although that category often included emigrants from other islands. Another adds that "the Lowndes and Rawlins [came] from St. Kitts, the Lucases and Perrys from Antigua, the Meylers and Whaleys from Jamaica, and the La Mottes from Grenada."[48]

If pride, hot blood, and quick tempers were West Indian attributes, wealth was another: "Virginia might be the Old Dominion and Massachusetts the Bible Commonwealth, but Barbados was something more tangible: the richest colony in English America."[49] In fact, South Carolina managed to do almost as well, despite sugar's inability to thrive in the low country. By the middle of the eighteenth century, two other cultivable crops, rice and indigo, had put the province on the road to riches, and by 1774, the comparative private wealth statistics for major American urban areas were stunning. These are estimates, in pounds sterling, for mean aggregate wealth per inventoried estate: Charleston—£2,338; Philadelphia—£397; Suffolk County, Massachusetts (Boston)—£312; and New York—£278.[50] Even if these figures exaggerate the differences, the comparison remains apt.

In the early eighteenth century, the colony profited from its border watchdog role. "South Carolina legislative committees," noted one historian, "used the Spanish menace as full or partial justifications for [currency and fiscal] policies which otherwise probably would not have passed the scrutiny of British officials."[51] The early military ventures were generally successful—St. Augustine, Pensacola, and other Spanish settlements were taken and burned, and Spanish retaliation against Charleston headed off. The Carolinians also built up Indian alliances and trade networks. Then by the 1750s, the menace shifted to French power, advancing eastward and discomforting South Carolina in Alabama and Tennessee while menacing Virginian interests in the Great Lakes and the Ohio Valley. The South Carolina Commons House of Assembly, with its longtime role in guiding and funding its colony's military expeditions, took a prominent role again during the 1756–1763 war.

For unusual reasons—South Carolina's subtropical, humid climate had a decaying effect on gunpowder and munitions supplies—the House had for years appointed a special gunpowder committee. It oversaw the adequacy of provincial weapons and gunpowder, record keeping with respect to imported gunpowder, and the provisioning of South Carolina troops.[52] This oversight body had a large membership during the French war, which continued in peacetime. We may wonder if the expertise developed by so many legislators might not have guided Charleston's extraordinary 1775 prowess in obtaining gunpowder from all points of the compass. William H. Drayton chaired the province's Secret Committee in 1775, and his son, who edited his memoirs, claimed that it was through this powder "that the American arms penetrated into Canada and the siege of Boston was continued."[53]

Equally to the point, South Carolina's influence extended far beyond her nominal borders. Charleston was the chief port and commercial center for both Georgia and part of North Carolina, notably the subtropical Cape Fear section adjacent to South Carolina and settled from there. As the Revolution approached in 1774 and 1775, Wilmington and the Cape Fear district became the center of patriot activity in the province, as we will pursue in Chapter 25. Georgia, as a new colony in the 1730s, had been tutored by South Carolina, and 1776 saw a movement to unite them, but Georgia ultimately declined.[54]

Less well known, but perhaps just as important, were the ties between New England and South Carolina. Many low-country planters summered in Newport, Rhode Island, an easy trip by sea. Few Charlestonians lived in Boston, but Massachusetts had contributed a substantial contingent of residents to the South Carolina capital. Through much of the eighteenth century, the biggest congregation in Charleston worshiped at the Circular Congregational Church, initially ministered by New Englanders. Architectural guides to Charleston invariably include the Circular Church graveyard, with many works by Massachusetts carvers as part of "the richest repository of eighteenth-century iconic gravestones in the country."[55] One persistent reason why peeved royal governors dissolved the Commons House of Assembly was its members' frequent responsiveness to Boston viewpoints. Royal Lieutenant Governor William Bull, a Charleston insider, once complained of how Carolina minds had been "poisoned with the principles which were imbibed and propagated from Boston and Rhode Island."[56]

A final enigma in the political pathology of pre-Revolutionary South Carolina is this: Why would so wealthy a colonial elite be so willing to jettison the political and social systems, the British markets and government subsidies (for indigo and naval stores), that made it rich? Arguably, from a mixture of West Indian temperament, a rich colony's presumption of invulnerability, and a pique at seeming British lack of respect. West Indian sugar nabobs were admired in London for their wealth, many lived in England, and dozens were members of Parliament. South Carolina rice planters, although many were schooled in England, were not wealthy enough to ignore their plantations and live there. To add further insult, when London filled high positions in Charleston—admiralty judge, councillor, or attorney general—Britons were typically named, not Carolinians. Virginians, including George Washington, had their own pique at Britain, but the anger of the low-country elite seems different.

In 1775, by way of conclusion, the four vanguard provinces had an importance beyond their obvious size and clout. They had half of the population and more than half of the wealth. But in political forwardness, historical gravitas, and overt confrontation, their share of the thirteen-colony total might have been 75 to 80 percent. They provided over three quarters of the soldiers fighting the British that year, largely because of Massachusetts and Connecticut.

Still, if this emphasis is a four-colony tale, the book's overall focus is on six provinces. In addition to the aggressive quartet, we will emphasize the two wavering, skittish battleground colonies of Pennsylvania and New York. Concentrating on these six would be less appropriate in dealing with the entirety of the war, but it encompasses most of the political and military action in 1775. In the next chapter, which deals with the role of ethnicity and religion in launching the Revolution, the four vanguard colonies stand out again for being relatively cohesive. New York and Pennsylvania, with their complicated interplay of ethnicity and religion, turn out to be the slowest to agree to full-fledged independence.

CHAPTER 3

Religion, Ethnicity, and Revolutionary Loyalty

Religious doctrine and rhetoric . . . contributed in a fundamental way to the coming of the American Revolution and its final success. In an age of political moderation, when many colonials hesitated at the brink of civil war, patriotic clergymen told their congregations that failure to oppose British tyranny would be an offense in the sight of Heaven. Where political theory advised caution, religious doctrine demanded action. By turning colonial resistance into a righteous cause, and by carrying the message to all ranks and in all parts of the colonies, ministers did the work of secular radicalism and did it better.

Patricia Bonomi, *Under the Cope of Heaven,* 1990

Where is the man to be found at this day, when we see . . . bishops with indifference, who will believe that the apprehension of Episcopacy contributed fifty years ago, as much as any other cause to arouse the attention, not only of the inquiring mind, but of the common people, and urge them to close thinking on the constitutional authority of parliament over the colonies?

Former president John Adams, 1815

Taken together, religion and ethnicity offer the best yardsticks of how Americans chose sides in the political and military clashes that became the Revolution. That is true from the Carolina backcountry through the middle colonies to the white-steepled towns of New England. Not that adequate detail can always be found.

Besides which, it's often difficult to disentangle which identity was the motivating factor. Was being Scotch-Irish the key or being a staunch

Presbyterian? Sometimes a political or military service choice might reflect both influences.

Ethnicity was a major factor in eighteenth-century military recruitment or service, which provides a useful introduction to the era's tendency to think in such terms. To state the obvious, both individual soldiers and military units taking part in the Revolution were frequently identified by ethnic or national origins. The name-calling could be venomous: pillaged New Jersey farmers cursing Hessian hirelings or British officers damning "black regiments" of somberly clad Yankee Congregational preachers. But some of the labeling was matter-of-fact. If Pennsylvania was to have a German-speaking battalion, it would perform best if everyone spoke or understood German. And when dissident Separate Baptists in Southside Virginia, making a political bargain, enlisted together in a company in which one of their lay preachers would hold frequent services, Revolutionary officials were ready to oblige.[1]

British recruitment for service in North America was consciously ethnic and religious. Because relatively few Englishmen would enlist in the army to fight English-speaking colonials, many of the men raised came from the Celtic fringes of Ireland or Scotland. Many were Catholics, now a prime target for recruiters. More numerous still were the "Hessian" mercenaries hired by the British Crown from a half dozen north German Protestant states allied by treaty or subsidy to George III and the House of Hanover. Patriots commented bitterly on these arrangements.

For an English monarch to use foreign troops to put down English-speaking subjects in the seventeenth or eighteenth century was innately unpopular. When American colonists criticized the king's use of Hessians or Scots Highlanders, they did so within a historical framework shared and pointedly voiced in early 1776 by the pro-American minority in Britain's Parliament. "Is there one of your Lordships," said Lord Camden, "who does not perceive most clearly that the whole [arrangement] is a mere mercenary bargain on one side, and the sale of human blood on the other?"[2] Others in Parliament questioned the cost and the dubious constitutionality of the king's close relationships with Hanover and other German states.[3]

Stuart kings had been attacked for using Irish Catholic soldiers on English soil in the 1640s and 1680s. Criticism also ensued when Hanoverian kings introduced hired German troops into Britain, as in 1745 and 1756.[4] Members of Parliament complained about the monarch's costly web of troop-hire arrangements and subsidies to north German states. Such was the sensitivity that the nineteenth-century English historian W. A. Lecky could write that his country's 1776 conduct "in hiring German mercenaries to subdue the essentially English population beyond the Atlantic, made reconciliation hopeless, and the Declaration of Independence inevitable."[5]

The ethnic makeup of British North America in 1775 also complicated Patriot enlistment and mobilization. Over one third of the colonists taking up arms for "the rights of Englishmen" were German, Dutch, Irish, Scottish, or Scotch-Irish. Some never assumed that they enjoyed the "rights of Englishmen," cherishing instead Old World ties and relationships to Dutch or German state churches (which often made them Loyalists). Ethnic and religious identifications were usually central to colonists' views and loyalties, and they cut in many ways.

Ethnicity and Religion: Germans, Irish, and Scotch-Irish

Although they were only a small minority in New England, Germans, Irish, and Scotch-Irish—inaccurate as those labels might be—probably represented 40 to 50 percent of Patriot enlistments in the middle colonies, which produced frequent epithets and references. In Pennsylvania, the singular prominence of the Scotch-Irish in both the Patriot cause and the American army prompted Quakers and Anglicans to grumble about the Revolution as a Scotch-Irish, Irish, or Presbyterian war. British officers constantly repeated the charge, with one calling the people of the Carolina Waxhaws district "universally Irish and universally disaffected," although they were in fact Scotch-Irish.[6] Even General Charles Lee of the Continental Army openly grumbled about Pennsylvania's political "Mac-ocracy," which he understood to mean Scotch-Irish Presbyterian.

Germans in turn became so unpopular in Pennsylvania, as their immigration peaked in the 1750s, that Benjamin Franklin had wondered, "Why should the Palatine Boors be suffered to swarm into our Settlements . . . Why should Pennsylvania, founded by the English, become a colony of Aliens, who will shortly be so numerous as to Germanize us?"[7] However, as their ranks grew, political criticism trailed off.

By the 1770s, Scots were also unpopular among English Whigs and in the plantation colonies dominated by Americans of English descent. Scots were thought to be pushy, too dominant in the Chesapeake tobacco trade, too politically influential in Virginia and the Carolinas, and too well positioned in London and the empire. Thomas Jefferson openly attacked them in an early draft of the Declaration of Independence—his disdainful reference to "Scotch mercenaries"—although colleagues removed the slight.[8] The simultaneous prominence of Scots on the American side—generals like Hugh Mercer, William Alexander, Lachlan McIntosh, and Arthur St. Clair—kept broader criticism subdued.

As for religion per se, many if not most Americans saw its hand in the run-up to war. Congregational and Presbyterian ministers and theology were thought to incite rebellion, while Anglican clerics and teachings were seen as instilling loyalty and subservience to authority. So we must return to the conundrum: Was *ethnicity* and its politics the key, or was *religion* the more influential yardstick of who took which side?

The ever-growing ranks of German colonists offer a litmus. The Eighth Virginia Continental Regiment, enlisted from the rolling, rich farm country of the Shenandoah Valley, was German-speaking, as were dozens of rebel battalions and companies from Pennsylvania. Such troops were usually best kept together under equally fluent officers and sergeants. Raising German units was an established practice. South Carolina, in fact, had preceded Pennsylvania by fielding a German-speaking regiment during the French and Indian War, raised to defend the Saxe-Gotha frontier settlements from marauding Cherokee. In 1775, although Charleston formed a company, the German Fusiliers, no large-scale recruitment was possible among the Lutheran Germans of the Saxe-Gotha district. They were heavily Loyalist, partly because of the oath to King George II taken by the original immigrants in the 1730s and 1740s. Breaking it, men feared, might cost them their land.

Affection for the Crown among eighteenth-century German colonials had logical enough roots. The first two Hanoverian kings, German born, took an active interest in attracting Protestant Germans to British North America, often settling them in frontier districts exposed to French or French-Indian raids. In New York's Mohawk Valley, the local Palatine Germans, descendants of early-eighteenth-century Protestant refugees from a Rhineland devastated by French invasions, no longer felt indebted to Britain for their transatlantic passages. New respect, however, had grown for the family and heirs of Sir William Johnson (1715–1774), the Mohawk Valley's great man and chief landowner. After marrying a Palatine, Johnson had favored her people. Ethnicity counted. In 1775 and 1776, many Palatines fled to Canada with Johnson's Loyalist son and nephew.

Besides Lutherans and Reformed Church members, Pennsylvania was home to tens of thousands of sectarian or "Peace" Germans—Amish, Mennonites, Dunkers, Moravians, et al. They had been recruited by William Penn and Quaker leaders, pleased to welcome other war-weary refugees. Like the Quakers, the Peace Germans were content with the Crown and Pennsylvania's Quaker-orchestrated Charter of 1702. When the Revolution came, most tried to be neutral. The Moravians turned buildings into hospitals for the American wounded, at considerable cost to their own health. Religion clearly guided their wartime actions.

Even where ethnicity seemed to predominate, an underlying religious context usually applied. The German immigrants invited or attracted to British North America between 1715 and 1775 were almost all Protestants because religious cousinship underpinned mid-eighteenth-century Anglo-German relationships. The Lutheran House of Hanover assumed the British throne in 1715 because of religion, not ethnicity. Under the Succession Act, the Electress Sophia of Hanover was the closest heir who met the all-important criterion: Protestantism. Even after Sophia's son became King George I of Britain, he also remained Elector of Hanover, a substantial north German Protestant principality. High-church Anglicans in England and Scotland—the tenth of the population who retained leanings to the exiled Catholic Stuarts—grumbled constantly. Most were outraged at the British Crown being passed to Hanoverian Lutherans who remained preoccupied by continental politics, German marriages, German religious networks, and costly subsidies to German princely allies.

These Hanoverian biases included planting Protestant Germans in British North America, first as desirable settlers but second as frontier defenders against the soldiers and Indian allies of Catholic France. From Waldoboro in Maine, settled in 1748 by Germans from Brunswick and Saxony, to Ebenezer in the Georgia pinewoods, tens of thousands were brought over, especially during the 1730s and 1740s. Most unhesitatingly swore loyalty to George I or George II, and by 1775 these well-remembered oaths often remained persuasive. The leading Lutheran patriarch in Pennsylvania, Henry Melchior Muhlenberg, a 1742 emigrant, considered himself doubly bound because he hailed from Hanover, the king's own ancestral homeland and also an early center of sixteenth-century Lutheranism. Until 1776, Muhlenberg insisted on including King George III in his prayers.[9] Here ethnicity and Lutheranism blended.

What justifies this detail is the ballooning pre-Revolutionary importance of German settlement. The German inhabitants of British North

America were concentrated in the pivotal middle provinces—Pennsylvania (33 percent German), New Jersey (10 to 15 percent), Maryland (10 to 20 percent), and New York (10 to 15 percent).[10] The Piedmont and valley sections of Virginia, North Carolina, and South Carolina likewise held German-speaking concentrations, as did Georgia. The sects or Peace Germans were a small minority, except in Pennsylvania where two thirds of them lived. Overall, "Church Germans"—mostly Lutherans and adherents of the German Reformed Church—outnumbered the pacifist sects by roughly four to one.

Pennsylvania's Church Germans favored the Patriot side, as did those in Virginia. When North Carolina Patriots needed help winning over local Germans, Pennsylvania Lutheran and Reformed ministers obliged with pastoral letters of support. But the Germans in North Carolina's Piedmont remained divided, as were those in New York, New Jersey, and Maryland.

This is a long, but hopefully effective, way of concluding that the principal wartime yardsticks and decision-making factors for Germans, as for most other colonials, reflected more religion than ethnicity. The latter was frequently interwoven but secondary. Take the Eighth Virginia Continental Regiment, authorized in late 1775. Its first colonel was John Peter Gabriel Muhlenberg, American-born son of Pennsylvania's cross-pressured Lutheran patriarch. Ordained by Lutherans and Anglicans alike in 1772, the younger Muhlenberg had gone to Woodstock in Virginia's Shenandoah Valley to minister to a bilingual Lutheran church, but quickly found himself in politics. In January 1775, the 29-year-old clergyman was elected chairman of his county Committee of Correspondence and Safety. By year's end, he was helping with the Continental regiment to be raised among local Germans, and on January 12, 1776, he received its colonelcy.[11]

Nine days later the young minister made a well-remembered military debut. After preaching his Sunday sermon—and here accounts vary—Pastor Muhlenberg threw off his gown, stood in the pulpit in his blue and buff colonel's regimentals, and supposedly said, "There is a time to pray and a time to fight—this is a time to fight," He then proceeded to enroll large numbers of his congregation.[12] Late-eighteenth-century America, these actions tell us, was still a culture in which clergymen not only proclaimed just wars but sometimes led their parishioners to battle. Pastor Muhlenberg would have led them more as Lutherans than as ethnic Germans, but the line was not easy to draw.

As for the Scots, the Irish, and the Scotch-Irish in British North America, if counted together they would have been more numerous in 1775 than Germans. Both Germans and Scotch-Irish concentrated in the broad interior corridor that ran south from New York to the Carolinas, where their loyalties were pivotal. But just who was Scottish, who was Irish, and who was Scotch-Irish (the largest group) was hard to define and enumerate. Even the first U.S. Census in 1790 stumbled over Celtic breakdowns. And Scotch-Irish political and religious divisions were especially complex and convoluted.

Where religious detail is available, these are the better explicators of Revolutionary loyalty. Unfortunately, the schisms and factions of seventeenth- and eighteenth-century Scottish and Irish Presbyterian church history, together with the inroads during the 1760s and 1770s of keening, emotional, and often illiterate Baptist preachers, can overwhelm even the most committed scholar. In Scottish church history, "Secession" churches pile on other aberrations; nonjurors sneer at established "churchmen." This book will offer details only where absolutely necessary.

In terms of political importance, though, let us recall the premise set forth in Chapter 2: that "the Irish," the Scotch-Irish, and the Presbyterian Church, variously, were the mainstays of the 1775–1776 revolution in all five middle colonies. Anglican and Quaker distaste for them, in turn, helped spur a countermobilization. Were complete population details—town by town, congregation by congregation, offshoot by offshoot, presbytery by presbytery—somehow available for the full kaleidoscope of denominations, sects, and new faiths in the Irish and Scotch-Irish concentrations running south from Pennsylvania to Georgia, that would be revealing. Such information would probably deal with some now-unanswerable questions. Additional religious explanations would emerge for otherwise-insoluble demographic and cultural blurs on a moving frontier.

Despite this interpretive haze along the Appalachian foothills, we can fairly say, based on the patterns of political faction, that religion—though only a collateral *cause* of the Revolution—played a major role in guiding its political alignments and loyalties. This was especially true in 1775, and it is most clearly seen in the trio of provinces that met a set of three criteria: (1) no colonywide church establishment; (2) a drumbeat of church-related issues during the 1765–1775 period; and (3) a vocal antagonism between republican-leaning Presbyterians on one side and Anglicans, Quakers, or both on the other. The middle provinces of Pennsylvania, New York, New Jersey, and Delaware fit best, but the model also makes some sense in Maryland.

However, this middle-colony framework does *not* apply in the very different circumstances of New England, especially the three provinces with dominant Congregational church establishments—Massachusetts, Connecticut, and New Hampshire. In 1774–1775, the Congregationalists quickly overwhelmed the small, often high-church Anglican minorities. Religious politics got sorted out, in part by Anglicans fleeing. Thereafter it was less important.

Nor does the middle-colony model work in Virginia and the Carolinas. Here a controlling elite of plantation-based low-church Anglicans—men who disliked bishops and managed their churches through individual vestries—managed the early stages of the Revolution. Opposition to this leadership was greatest in backcountry regions only recently settled (with mixed Celtic, English, and German populations) and full of itinerant preachers and evangelical enthusiasts. A separate opposition, on ethnic and economic grounds, came from Scottish-born royal officials, merchants, and recent Highland emigrants who were enthusiastic participants in Britain's global empire.

Overall, New England and the plantation South were the centers of 1774–1775 patriotism, and we shall return later to the tricky aspects of their provinces' internal alignments.

The Religious Background of the Revolution

Edmund Burke, the late-eighteenth-century British statesman with a great gift for illuminating the American condition, pointed out to an inattentive Parliament in early 1775 the central part that religion played: a "fierce spirit of liberty is stronger in the English colonies probably than in any other people of the earth." Much of this, Burke said, flowed from their heavy settlement by Protestant refugees and dissenters. "Religion, always a principle of energy, in this new people is no way worn out or impaired . . . The people are Protestants; and of that kind which is most adverse to all implicit submission of mind or opinion. [Worship in] our Northern colonies is a refinement on the principal of resistance."[13]

Made up of Congregationalists, Presbyterians, Lutherans, Reformed Church adherents, Quakers, and Baptists, religious dissenters as the English categorized them in 1775 numbered almost two thirds of America's churched population. In England, dissenters were only 7 percent. This was a sharp decline from the higher ratios that had roiled England during the

Civil War of the 1640s, and emigration to North America accounted for some of the falloff. The New World's many denominations and doctrines included a Calvinist majority (Congregational, Presbyterian, Reformed, and some Baptist groups) in perhaps half of the provinces, further fleshing out Burke's portrait. Calvinism epitomized resistance.

Scholars who cite religion as a prominent cause or even precondition of the American Revolution often emphasize the Great Awakening—the evangelical and democratic wave, inspired by revivalists like George White-field and Jonathan Edwards, that swept much of British North America between the 1720s and the 1750s. Succinctly put, the Awakening's insistence that *individuals* must experience rebirth and achieve a direct, personal, and emotional relationship to God served to elevate the role of ordinary folk and weaken the European principle of divine delegation of authority through a state church or anointed king. This change, in turn, implied broader religious disestablishment, not just of state churches but of the need for priests, bishops, or other learned interpreters or intermediaries.

A third aspect, specific to the New World, proclaimed a millennial belief that God was giving up on a corrupted Europe so that a United Colonies of America would become the new Chosen Nation. The broad support that the Great Awakening provided for the political insurgencies of 1774–1775 has been widely discussed, so this discussion will confine itself to citations.[14]

More attention is warranted, though, to the mobilizing force of belief in the Anglo-American colonies as a chosen people. For believers, instead of being merely *just,* the war for American independence became vital to God's plan. Such language particularly engaged the Puritan provinces, im-bued with faith in New England's leadership role. Some of the muskets pointed on April 19, 1775, had a millennial target as well as a worldly one.

William G. McLoughlin, a prominent twentieth-century U.S. religious historian, expanded the nation's "chosen people" historical mission to include a total of five religious revivals, all of them producing major cultural and political watersheds. "American history," he said, "is thus best under-stood as a millenarian movement."[15] This hypothesis, offered in 1978, seems less apt amid the United States' early-twenty-first-century disillusionments. Nevertheless, the Chosen Nation explanation was a powerful driver in the 1770s. One reason why Connecticut governor Jonathan Trumbull fre-quently placed "the united colonies" or "the country's future" ahead of narrow provincial interests—a boon to both George Washington and Congress—was his religious commitment to America's global mission.

To Ruth Bloch, a twentieth-century historian convinced of religion's huge part in the Revolution, New Englanders by the mid-1770s were shifting away from their former preoccupation with the Puritan past to the uplift of a millennial future. Moreover, her research "on the frequency of millennial statements in printed literature suggests that such ideas may well have been as common among Presbyterian and Baptist patriots in middle and Southern regions as they were among New England Congregationalists."[16]

Martin Marty, a distinguished American theologian, in 1970 hyperbolized the United States as a "righteous empire." In the minds of many Protestants, he added, it had taken flight in 1776 as an "evangelical empire." Culturally, its heritage of mission was English, and Marty reached back to the biblically referenced (Deuteronomy) words of seventeenth-century Massachusetts governor William Bradford, *"May not and ought not the children of these followers rightly say: Our faithers were Englishmen what came over this great ocean, and were ready to perish in this wildernes; but they cried unto the Lord, and he heard their voyce and looked on their adversitie."*[17] Jonathan Edwards, the colonies' greatest mid-eighteenth-century theologian, also heaped importance on the role of British North America, anticipating that it would succeed Britain as "the principal nation of the Reformation."[18] The sustenance that this role gave to the Revolution should not be underestimated.

In *Under the Cope of Heaven: Religion, Society, and Politics in Colonial America,* historian Patricia Bonomi concluded that the last decades of pre-Revolutionary British North America displayed an *increasing* "interpenetration of religion and politics." She described a rising tempo: "Reflexes generated by the schisms of the Great Awakening and by the colonists' denominational rivalries made for a contentiousness that pervaded the entire realm of the provincials' behavior, and eventually the categories in which they framed political and religious issues became almost interchangeable. Indeed, what Clarendon said of England at the time of the Civil War might also be said of the American colonies by the mid-eighteenth century: 'the ecclesiastical and civil state . . . [are so] interwoven together, and in truth so incorporated in each other, that like Hippocrates' twins they cannot but laugh and cry together.'"[19]

Elevating the tie between politics and religion circa 1775 to an equivalency with riven 1640s England is excessive. Whereas the Stuart Church of England was reestablished in the 1660s after the English Civil War, the mid-1770s overthrow of Anglicanism in the six out of thirteen American provinces where it had partial or full establishment was never reversed. The American overthrow stuck because a critical change was under way. Colonial Americans were concluding that even a loose interweaving of the ecclesiastical and civil states should be ended. The bolder argument that the American Revolution was, deep down, a religious war in the manner of the English Revolution likewise stretches too far. Too much of the colonists' motivation in 1774 and 1775 involved a drive for economic and political self-determination conjoined with frustration at being reined in territorially. True, partly related frustrations operated in the 1640s. Some 130 years later, however, nonreligious factors carried greater weight in the motivation of thirteen colonies some 3,000 miles distant from the imperial center, provinces with a history of self-government that were also burgeoning economically and diverging ideologically.

Toward this end, later chapters will amplify some of the continuities between the English Revolution (or English Civil War) of the 1640s and the American Revolution, which also had characteristics of civil war. The role of religion was important in 1775, but less intense than it had been 130 years earlier. My 1999 book *The Cousins' Wars* traced a thread of persisting concern about the interplay of religion and liberty through all three major English-speaking civil wars, with each displaying elements of millennial belief and fears about conspiracy. Each of these eras saw a growth of radical Protestant sects like the one visible in the 1770s. This was no coincidence.

Within the thirteen colonies, the *overall* kaleidoscope of religious belief or denomination explains better than any other single context how Patriots, neutrals, and Loyalists lined up politically or militarily in 1775. Across the pre-Revolutionary American provinces, in an era when much of the printed material was religious, religion probably remained the most important self-identifier, certainly among churchgoers.

The Politics of Religion, 1775: The Congregational, Presbyterian, and Vestry Anglican Coalition

The outlines of Patriot-faction religion are clear enough. Building on Massachusetts, Connecticut, Virginia, and South Carolina, we can easily prepare a "mental map" of the generalized religious constituencies of the Revolution in its opening years. Of the four New England provinces, three had a Congregational Church establishment, while the fourth, Rhode Island, had no establishment but a dominant mix of Baptists and

Congregationalists. Color New England "Congregationalist/Patriot." For the moment, minor denominations, quibbles, and exceptions can be pushed aside.

The five plantation colonies come next, each with an Anglican Church establishment of sorts. Here a Patriot hue can be used for an area that begins with Maryland's Chesapeake tobacco counties, then jumps across the Potomac to the tidewater and Piedmont of Virginia, another tobacco culture. Eastern or tidewater North Carolina is a further extension, originally populated by English settlers from Virginia and South Carolina. Tobacco-growing in the north, North Carolina gave way to rice and naval stores in the lower latitudes.

The subtropical extension, in the South Carolina low country, produced the most lucrative crops, rice and indigo. Southernmost Georgia, raw and sparsely populated, repeated this agriculture in a less affluent fashion. This Chesapeake-to-Georgia coastal swath represents the second great Patriotic leadership concentration circa 1775. It hosted a broadly similar religious establishment: relaxed, low-church Anglicanism, vestry-run by local plantation and commercial elites almost as hostile as New Englanders to bishops or to British religious supervision. Here, too, minor quibbles and exceptions can be pushed aside for now. This area should be mentally colored "Vestry Anglican/Patriot."

The third region of revolution-friendly religion generally follows the foothills of Appalachia from New York's Hudson highlands south through northern New Jersey, eastern and central Pennsylvania and northern Delaware into Maryland and then down into the southern backcountry, following the Great Wagon Road from Philadelphia through western Virginia and the Carolinas. By the 1750s, this area had a distinctive, early-immigration Scotch-Irish overlay. It bristled, almost literally, with a score of Presbyterian churches—Donegal, Octorara, Timber Ridge, Fourth Creek, Thyatira— that became famous in the Indian wars or in the Revolution for fielding fighting men, sometimes right out of Sunday pews and occasionally led by a fighting preacher. In New York and New England, rebel Presbyterians were at loggerheads with minority Anglicans of the high-church Tory variety. However, from Virginia south, the churchgoing Presbyterian Scotch-Irish were allied with the very different vestry Anglican elites who led the Patriot side. It is easier to conceptualize than to neatly map.

Any good mental map must fundamentally differentiate between northern and southern Anglicans. In Virginia and South Carolina, 60 to 80 percent of the vestry Anglicans took the Patriot side. From New England to New Jersey, where only 5 to 10 percent of the population was Anglican, the latter were more high-church than otherwise, and roughly three quarters became Loyalists or neutrals.[20] These ratios blurred in Pennsylvania and Maryland, but it would be impossible to draw a clear border.

The middle colonies have complicated divisions, more easily imagined than reliably drawn. Presbyterians dominated the Patriot coalition, the ranks of the Scotch-Irish augmented by New England Yankees who migrated to New York, New Jersey, and Pennsylvania. They usually wound up as Presbyterians, because New England's established Congregational Church didn't travel well beyond its home region. In any event, by the 1770s the New England Congregationalists and middle-colony Presbyterians were semiofficial allies. They had not been able to achieve the full-fledged merger advocated and worked for in the 1760s by Congregationalist Ezra Stiles and others, but cooperation was close.

Presbyterian ecumenicalism extended to the theologically kindred evangelical wings of the German Reformed and Dutch Reformed churches. Central New Jersey's evangelical Dutch Reformed churches, for example, cooperated with neighboring New Light Presbyterian congregations, and Patriot leader William Livingston urged a working alliance against Anglicanism.[21]

In Pennsylvania and New York, where religious pluralism nurtured rivalry and infighting, political factions developed identifiable denominational characteristics and alliances. Take Philadelphia in the 1760s. Lawyer William Allen, describing 1764 election results to Governor Thomas Penn, recounted church by church: "We had great help from the Lutherans, and Calvinist among the Dutch[;] from the other sects we had great opposition: we had about half of the Church of England and the Presbyterians to a man." The dynamics were well summarized by historian Alan Tully: "When politicians spoke of the electorate in ideal or didactic terms they might talk about freemen, but when they spoke about mobilizing the electorate, it was in terms of the Quaker, Presbyterians, Baptist, or German church interest . . . Religion became the main vehicle by which ethnicity gained political representation."[22]

By the mid-1770s, Pennsylvania's evangelical-leaning Presbyterians, German/Dutch Reformed, and Lutheran churchgoers were more or less on the same side. The opposing conservative or incipient Loyalist bloc, in turn, combined high-church Anglicans with nonevangelical Dutch and Germans, some in churches allied to the Anglicans. It also attracted many Quakers (fearful that their longtime political and religious dominance was eroding). Thomas Barton, a Pennsylvania Anglican rector, bluntly opined that "many of the principal Quakers wish for it [episcopacy, whereby Anglican bishops are sent to America], in hopes it might be a check to the growth of Presbyterianism."[23] Not a few wealthy Quakers, including the Penn family, had already converted to Anglicanism. This reckoning is slightly oversimplified but compatible with the religious coloration of politics in Pennsylvania and New York.[24]

In New York, too, the importance of religion in politics reflected how many legal controversies and political gambits were connected to denominationalism. The basis of friction was the Ministry Act of 1705, which established the Anglican Church in four counties in and around the city of New York. This status, in turn, led to combative proposals: at one extreme for broader Anglican establishment; at the other, for complete disestablishment. It also led to acrimony over petitions for bishops, to bitterness by other Protestants that local authorities would not charter non-Anglican churches and colleges, to fears about civil liberties, and to indignation by Presbyterians in Westchester County or Baptists in Queens about being taxed to support Anglicanism.[25] By the 1770s, New York's DeLancey faction was Anglican-led, and the rival Livingston group Presbyterian-led. Provincial politics in Maryland, Delaware, and New Jersey shared the central tension between Anglicans and Presbyterians.

So to return to our mental map of 1775, the third entry should include an important but imprecise stippling for Presbyterian centers stretching from the Hudson highlands through Pennsylvania to the southern Piedmont and backcountry. Middle-colony Presbyterians by themselves weren't powerful enough to lead their provinces toward independence in the manner of Yankee Congregationalists and vestry Anglican southern planters. But it was a rare Presbyterian concentration—a Scottish church or a quirky splinter group—that wasn't strongly on the Patriot side.

Bishops, Vestries, and Anglican Church Establishments

With London so distant, individual church vestries—governing groups of church elders—became essential to maintaining local control of plantation-colony Anglicanism. In old colonies like Virginia and South Carolina, many became instruments of the local gentry. In a minority of parishes, vestries counted less because the church or its rector was funded from London by the Society for the Propagation of the Gospel (SPG) or was under the thumb of a royal governor or a proprietary family like the Calverts in Maryland. The Patriot bias or incipient Toryism of Anglican congregations often hung on distinctions like these.

These differences are vital to understanding the chasm between low-church, antibishop, plantation-colony Anglicanism and the high-church, please-send-us-a-bishop, northern-colony variety. The first flourished in the old English-settled southern tidewater or coastal low country—from Chesapeake Virginia through the Carolinas. There, for a century or so, Anglican churches were generally controlled by the same local elites who made the decisions in the Virginia House of Burgesses, the North Carolina General Assembly, and the South Carolina Commons House of Assembly.

The development of local control through Virginia's Anglican vestries traced back to a combination of seventeenth-century Puritan influence and eighteenth-century emphasis on decision making by the laity, not by London episcopal authorities.[26] Until the 1740s and 1750s, Virginia had few dissenters, and local elites routinely governed church affairs. No SPG influence came into Virginia. Indeed, in 1771 the House of Burgesses voted overwhelmingly to commend two local ministers "for the wise and well-timed Opposition they have made to the pernicious Project of a few mistaken Clergymen, for introducing an American Bishop; a Measure by which Disturbance, great Anxiety and Apprehension would certainly take place among his Majesty's faithful American people."[27] "In no other colony were the parsons so active and united behind the Patriots' crusade," said historian Bonomi. "In 20 of 60 counties in the colony, the minister of the parish or some resident minister of the church was elected by the people as a member of the County Committee for Safety . . . After the war began, all but one of the 14 army chaplains were ministers of the Anglican church."[28]

In South Carolina, on top of vestry control, ministers' salaries were paid by colonial authorities and parishes had become key units of local government. From the start, dissenters had been much more numerous than in Virginia and "were frequently elected [Anglican] vestrymen and churchwardens." A candid South Carolina Anglican minister wrote in 1720 that his parishioners were "Latitudinarian in Protestantism . . . and do not imagine much real difference in Principle 'twixt Churchmen and Dissenters of all

Denominations."[29] Four decades later another Anglican minister famously commented that it would be positively unsafe for a bishop to set foot in Charleston.[30]

In locally dominated churches, where theology was usually relaxed and low church, sentiment in 1775 was by and large pro-Patriot. The Virginia and South Carolina ratios were lopsided. According to Bonomi, "South Carolina was distinguished for the number of ardent patriots among its Anglican clergy, three-quarters of whom supported the Revolution. A similar proportion of the Anglican rectors resident in Virginia in 1776 favored the American cause."[31]

High-church and probishop Anglican clergy and churchgoers were hardly unusual in the South. But they did not represent the dominant political culture. High-church southern clergy tended to cluster in places where vestries were weak or nonexistent. The bulk were in parishes substantially dependent on funds from the SPG, as in Georgia or much of North Carolina, or in provinces where a proprietor or royal governor controlled parish patronage. Calculations vary, but in Maryland, North Carolina, and Georgia, less than half the local Anglican clergy supported the Revolution.[32]

With Virginia and South Carolina Anglicanism essentially local and Whiggish, the cockpit of what eighteenth-century dissenters and rebels called "ecclesiastical imperialism" lay in the middle colonies. Episcopal historian John Woolverton is candid: "Far more than Boston, Philadelphia or Annapolis, after 1700 New York would be the key to the expansion of the Church of England north of the Potomac."[33] Four counties in southern New York had an Anglican Church establishment, the only one in the North. Examples of militancy ranged from attempts to extend official Anglican establishment to the Manor of Philipseburg to refusal by the heavily Anglican Governor's Council to charter dissenting churches and the predominance of Anglicans given positions in New York government.[34]

Anglican growth in the northern colonies was substantial after 1750, for reasons that ranged from increased support of the established church by royal governors to stepped-up London (SPG) missionary activity at the grass roots. Inroads were also made by Anglican churches that offered traditionalists refuge from the evangelism and religious "enthusiasm" roiling Congregational and Presbyterian ranks. In any event, during the fifteen years after 1760, some one hundred new Anglican churches were built, most in the northern provinces.[35] Of these, the largest number were in Connecticut, especially in the western counties adjacent to New York, but New Jersey and Pennsylvania also showed significant increases. So did inland North Carolina, where royal governor Arthur Dobbs mounted strong support during the 1760s.

Anglican growth in Pennsylvania, New Jersey, and especially New York in the 1760s also fattened on alliances and potential mergers with a handful of ethnic denominations that back in Europe enjoyed national church status or prestige—German Lutheran, Swedish Lutheran, Dutch Reformed, and German Reformed. The Dutch Reformed Church in particular enjoyed English guarantees under the 1664 Articles of Capitulation, through which New Amsterdam had become New York. Swedish Lutheranism had already joined the Church of England in the old Swedish-settled parts of Pennsylvania and New Jersey. Old-line German Lutherans in New York and Pennsylvania—mindful of the dual practice of Britain's Hanoverian royalty—also considered conforming to the Church of England.[36]

Conservative Dutch Reformed congregations extended as far up the Hudson River as Albany, but most of the Old World congregations tied to European church hierarchies and still speaking their ancestral language concentrated in New York, Philadelphia, and the long-settled corridor between those two cities. Collaboration with the established English Church made sense, because the last handful of imperiled French-, Swedish-, and Dutch-speaking churches were also fighting to hold a new generation that spoke English, preferred more democratic church governance, wanted clergy ordained in America, and was probably also more evangelical. Like the Church of England, the Old World churches were also fighting off an American Revolution.

The imperial context was important. In the early 1760s, the government in London was cocky, even arrogant from its huge victory over France and the great territorial gains confirmed in the 1763 peace treaty. International prestige also realigned, and British diplomats now took precedence over their French counterparts in the courts and chancelleries of Europe. The accession of George III in 1760 had put an aggressive Anglican on the throne—a young man, very empire-minded, who chose mostly Tory advisers and friends. By contrast, his German-speaking great-grandfather (George I) and grandfather (George II), Lutheran-born, had been attentive to German politics and had found their English political allies principally among Whigs who were moderate Anglicans and relatively friendly to dissenters.

Patriot leaders, alert to the neoimperial thrust of His Majesty's government visible in taxation, customs enforcement, and curbs on American frontier settlement, had reason to fear Anglican favoritism in religious matters. But imperial preoccupations also pointed in some new directions. A much bigger empire meant more Catholic subjects—in Quebec, Nova Scotia, Florida, the Caribbean, and Mediterranean, and no longer just in beaten-down Ireland. More tolerance was necessary, as we will see shortly. The Church of England was now the state church of the world's leading empire. Gone were the days, just two decades earlier, when a German-speaking George II could half dismiss the church as a ragbag of ex-Jacobites, divine-right believers, Scottish nonjurors, and the like. Now the national church must command respect, and the American colonies, the last strongholds of English-speaking religious dissent, were a good place to start.

Historian Carl Bridenbaugh, in his episcopacy-focused tome *Mitre and Sceptre,* emphasized that "no sooner had the Treaty of Paris been signed than the Archbishop of Canterbury prepared to launch his campaign for an American episcopate." During the 1763 session of Parliament, the archbishop told one correspondent that "we must try our utmost for bishops."[37] Many of the increasingly influential Anglican clergy in the middle colonies and lower New England certainly hoped so. Fanciful rumors in London and Boston newspapers in 1764 had the English Dean of Bristol going to New York with the title Bishop of Albany, and later expectations had bishops going to the West Indies instead. In Quebec, a Roman Catholic bishop had actually arrived in 1766.[38]

Fierce American reaction to the passage of the Stamp Act in 1765 may have nipped aggressive Anglicanism in the bud. Five months earlier, Dr. Samuel Auchmuty, a New York Anglican cleric, had talked about pursuing an act of Parliament to turn that province's counties into parishes, making all inhabitants pay taxes "toward the support of a minister of the Established Church." Among the provisions of the Stamp Act, moreover, was one requiring that revenue stamps be affixed to "all documents" in any "court exercising ecclesiastical jurisdiction within the said colonies."[39] The New England newspapers found that a disturbing hint.

Anticipating a great contest with hostile Congregational and Presbyterian pastors, Anglican clerics began in the mid-1760s holding annual meetings in New York, New Jersey, and Pennsylvania. On the other side, Congregationalist Dr. Ezra Stiles, a future president of Yale, in 1766 formed a loose confederation of dissenters, mostly Congregationalists and Presbyterians, to guard against Anglican encroachments. Meetings were held every year through 1775. Although Massachusetts did not send delegates, to avoid further provocation of London, participants came regularly from Connecticut, New York, New Jersey, Pennsylvania, Delaware, and Maryland. The confederation also added Virginia, both Carolinas, and Georgia as correspondents.[40]

Scholars who call the debate over bishops important in bringing on the Revolution—Bridenbaugh, Bonomi, Ruth Bloch, J.C.D. Clark, James Bell, and others—cite a string of events and publications between 1770 and 1775 that kept the issue alive. These ranged from a Maryland Anglican petition for bishops in 1770 to a 1774 address by New Jersey rector Thomas Bradbury Chandler fulminating against Presbyterians.

Politically, though, there is no evidence that the upper echelons of the British government wanted to send bishops to America in 1775. Ten years earlier perhaps, but not during the immediate pre-Revolutionary period. In our early-twenty-first-century milieu, the idea of bishops and ecclesiastical imperialism being a throbbing issue may seem dubious.*

But protagonists have continued to emerge. To Bridenbaugh, "Anglican bishops became the principal symbol in the American mind of the threatened ecclesiastical tyranny. The American Revolution of 1760-1775 resulted quite as much from a religious as a political change in the minds and hearts of the people." To Bonomi, "the pervasiveness of American anxiety regarding a bishop cannot be denied. The question was hotly discussed in correspondence, and it was perhaps the pivotal issue in the New York assembly elections of 1769."[41] The similarly minded Bell entitled his 2008 book *A War of Religion*.

In 1815, John Adams, looking back after 40 years, leaned in the same direction. At very least, ecclesiastical imperialism and the proposal for American bishops was one of a trio of religious issues that also included Tory embrace of the doctrine of "passive obedience" and widespread colonial arousal over British passage of the Quebec Act in 1774.

---

*We should remember, though, that in 2006 a Religious Right campaign to take over the Republican Party and the government of Ohio became a cause célèbre and was decisively defeated in the general election.

Tory "Passive Obedience" Doctrine Versus "Republican" Religion

Clergy in 1775 could see an old disagreement—and a longtime battle—being rejoined. It went back to the 1630s and 1640s, when Puritan and Parliamentary objections to episcopacy and the divine right of kings helped to bring on the English Civil War.

Debate was more complicated by the late eighteenth century, but Congregational and Presbyterian ministers were at least half right in describing prewar Anglicanism as a belief system that encouraged "passive obedience" to authority and, in some cases, continued to hint fond remembrance for Stuart-era "divine right." Anglican clerics, in turn, were at least half right in calling Congregationalism and Presbyterianism "republican" religions, theologies that almost by nature bred restiveness and antimonarchical sentiments. During the 1760s and 1770s, both sides entered into moral and political combat with zeal, making religion prominent, if not decisive, in the onset of the American Revolution.

Caricature prevailed on both sides. Pennsylvania loyalist Joseph Galloway, in his *Historical and Political Reflections on the Rise and Progress of the American Rebellion* (1780), blamed the conflict on a seditious alliance of Congregationalists and Presbyterians, "whose principles of religion and polity were equally averse to those of the established church and government." Quakers in the same province castigated "blood-thirsty Presbyterians, who cut off King Charles's . . . Head" and who, in both state and church, shaped government "after the Model of a Geneva Republic."[42]

High Anglican clerics in the middle colonies reminded church officials in Britain that the government's "best Security in the Colonies does, and must always arise, from the Principles of Submission and Loyalty taught by the Church," which they "were constantly instilling" into their flocks.[43] The teachings of the church, in short, strengthened the monarchy. Churchmen especially deplored the New Englanders for instituting oppression and refusing to tolerate freedom of speech or religion. There was some evidence, but then criticism shaded into vituperation, attacking the "republican zealots and bigots of New England; whose tender mercies, when they had power in their hands, had ever been cruel."[44]

Among the leading Anglican clerics, Maryland's Jonathan Boucher was especially combative. His 1775 address, delivered from the pulpit of Queen

Anne's parish church in Annapolis, approached seventeenth-century royalist theory: "Government is not of human but divine origin," and "it is with the most perfect propriety that the supreme magistrate, whether consisting of one or many, and whether denominated an emperor, a king, an archon, a dictator, a consul, or a senate, is to be regarded as a vice-regent of God . . . All government, whether lodged in one or many, is, in its nature, absolute and irresistible."[45] Historians trace these ideas to Sir Robert Filmer in his 1680 volume *Patriarcha*. New Jersey Anglican rector Thomas Chandler also praised authority and obedience. In his late 1774 essay "A Friendly Address to All Reasonable Americans," he insisted that "the ill consequences of open disrespect to government are so great that no misconduct of the administration can justify or excuse it."[46]

Samuel Seabury, rector in Westchester, New York, convened an unusually large protest meeting of Loyalists in nearby White Plains in April 1775. He was later arrested and briefly jailed in Connecticut. In 1777, as a chaplain to His Majesty's troop—and presumably expecting a British victory—Seabury orated that "in the empire to which we belong, the supreme Authority is vested in the King, the Lords and the Commons of the Realm, conjunctly called Parliament, and to the Laws of the supreme Authority absolute submission and obedience are due, both upon the principles of religion and of good policy."[47] John Adams and others frequently accused Anglicans of propounding the pernicious doctrine of "passive obedience," and here is Seabury praising "*absolute submission* and obedience" (italics added).

If some high churchmen harked back to seventeenth-century absolutism, Anglican theorists and propagandists had no trouble in tying Congregationalists and Presbyterians to their own seventeenth-century echoes. A leading Boston Congregationalist minister, Jonathan Mayhew, preaching on the one hundredth anniversary of the execution of Charles I, beyond dismissing the doctrine of passive obedience, argued that scripture did not require submission to a bad ruler. On the contrary, disobedience was "a duty, not a crime." The people themselves were the "proper judges."[48]

"The colonial pamphleteers of the 1750s and 1760s," wrote one scholar, "vigorously revisited the memory of Archbishop William Laud's strictures against the Puritans in the late 1620s and 1630s," as well as the abuses of government under Charles I.[49] The "ideology of dissent" that grew up in England and the colonies drew heavily on John Milton's mid-seventeenth-century political rejection of divine right in favor of the counterauthority to depose an unjust king. The excesses of Charles I and James

II showed the interdependence of religious and civil liberties. Others recalled how divine right and nonresistance doctrines had resurfaced in the 1709–1710 controversy over and impeachment of high Tory churchman Henry Sacheverell, stirring them into the 1760s debate. The *Independent Whig* and *Cato's Letters*, widely read in America and widely credited with helping to shape pre-Revolutionary thinking, identified "the High-Church Jacobite clergy of England" and the "ungainly Brats of Passive Obedience [and] the Divine Right of Kings and Bishops" as the greatest threat to liberty.[50]

Although this old debate had cooled in Britain by the 1770s, it remained very real in America, where the pot of dissenter versus Anglican politics was once again boiling. And much of the new heat came over the Coercive Acts and the Quebec Act of 1774 and what they suggested about harsh British attitudes.

The Quebec Act and the American Revolution

In 1775 many Americans, including George Washington and Thomas Jefferson, had a sense of a British conspiracy to deny American liberties. Chapter 7 will look at how these interpretations emerged.

But one specific is appropriate to pursue here: how colonial distrust and apprehension, including perception of a threat to American religious freedom, was fanned in 1774 by the Coercive Acts and the almost-simultaneous Quebec Act. The latter, in establishing Catholicism in Canada and overriding the westward land promises of colonial charters, became an early Rorschach blot—American colonials could see different, sometimes extreme, implications depending on the particular intentions they read into British actions.

From the British standpoint, the act could be described as one to reassure the French in Quebec that the French Civil Code and the Catholic religion would be respected. There would be a governor and a council, but no provincial assembly and no right to trial by jury. Catholics, who had already welcomed a new bishop, would now be eligible for public office. The boundaries of Quebec would be extended south to the Ohio River in order to include settlements of French *habitants* in Vincennes, Kaskaskia, and Cahokia.

For His Majesty's government, that could be interpreted as a sophisticated step, given how Britain had beaten the drums of an anti-Catholic crusade through most of the 1756–1761 fighting in Europe and North America. However, the 1763 peace treaty had further expanded the British Empire, which already included Mediterranean Catholics in Gibraltar and Minorca, French Catholics in Nova Scotia, Catholic Highlanders in Scotland, and a large Catholic population in Ireland, by adding many more. Quebec held 70,000; Caribbean Grenada, a small increment. Newly British West and East Florida counted 10,000 to 20,000 French, Spanish, and Minorcan Catholics. Conciliation was already a policy in Ireland and the Scottish Highlands—the end of the Stuart threat had muted Catholic insurgency—and British strategists wanted to eliminate a potential French fifth column in Canada should the thirteen colonies set North America ablaze.

Had Quebec been a remote French island in the Indian Ocean, British concessions would hardly have mattered. But in the real world of 1774, the Quebec Act touched four or five raw American colonial nerves. Recognizing Catholicism right next door was a provocation in New England and in New York, where men of Huguenot extraction like John Jay were incensed. Bringing a Catholic bishop to Canada was another piece of dubious symbolism. Concern about rights to a jury trial had refocused in New England after the Coercive Acts tampered with Massachusetts procedures. Britain's decision not to allow an assembly in Quebec spread jitters far afield in South Carolina, which suspected that British officials would be happy to eliminate the one in Charleston. The Quebec Act's blunt dismissal of the western territorial claims of Connecticut and Virginia, both charter based, offended beyond persons involved with western lands. Patriots in Connecticut and Rhode Island already feared for their charters—Anglicans in Newport had mounted a serious drive against Rhode Island's charter in 1764.[51]

Whereas the four Coercive Acts fanned political and economic distrust of the mother country, the simultaneous Quebec Act also stirred religious concern, another dimension of conspiracy-consciousness. "In the wake of the Quebec Act, especially" said one historian, "the depiction of Great Britain as Antichrist became frequent throughout the colonies."[52] From a survey of printed material during the period, historian Ruth Bloch concluded that "by the 1760s, both the conflicts of the Great Awakening and the Anti-Catholic crusade of the French and Indian War had re-enforced the inclination of American Calvinists to see themselves engaged in a cosmic battle with Satan . . . The symbolic link forging the connection between Great Britain and the Antichrist was typically the pollution of Roman

Catholicism. In Boston and elsewhere, traditional anti-Catholic Pope Day celebrations became occasions for dramatizing the patriot cause."[53]

To one British historian, London's new twist in grand strategy touched multiple fears: "All land between the Ohio and the Mississippi—subject of furious debate between London and the expansion lobby since 1763—was now incorporated into Quebec. In the eyes of many North Americans, this threatened the encirclement of the thirteen colonies by an absolutist government—a resurrected New France; it restored the pre-1762 threat. If the Act were allowed to stand, the thirteen colonies would be penned into a geopolitical reservation from which they could not escape."[54]

As we will see, Patriot thinking was sufficiently conspiracy-minded by 1774 to intertwine these suspicions. That September, as the First Continental Congress met, Arthur Lee, then one of the Massachusetts agents in London, reacted that "every tie of allegiance is broke by the Quebec Act, which is absolutely a dissolution of this government; the compact between the King and the people is done away with."[55]

Since the nineteenth century, scholars mindful of modernism and its insistences have been careful to explain that the religious intensity of the sixteenth and seventeenth centuries, and to a lesser degree the eighteenth, will seem implausible to contemporary readers. This is true, and it helps to explain why interpretations widely accepted 150 years ago—for example, the importance of theologian John Calvin and his doctrine in explaining the wars fought for liberty in England, Scotland, and America—have been consigned to a Victorian rubbish dustbin. Perhaps the history of religion in American war and politics needs a rebalancing.

Our next chapter will turn to another side of the Revolution—the extent to which it was a quest for economic self-determination across a spectrum of issues from trade, taxes, manufacturing, and currency to trans-Appalachian settlement. But economics, like religion, is only one explanation of the Revolution among several, and it, too, should not be considered all-determining. In Pennsylvania and New York, both principal cockpits of religious influence on politics, we will see how the economic specialties of merchants—smuggling from the West Indies, say, versus importing British dry goods for resale—also played a powerful role in how such men chose sides in 1775. Yet Philadelphia merchants' choices were at least as likely to reflect whether they were Anglicans, Quakers, or Scotch-Irish Presbyterians. A balance always has to be struck.

CHAPTER 4

A Revolution for Economic
Self-Determination

The specific grievances that Americans held against the metropolis [London] reflected economic concerns. Several of the "reforms" introduced by Parliament after mid-century seemed to many colonists designed to reduce current profits and to limit future prospects. Nor was it only Parliament that appeared determined to undermine American prosperity. The rapacious behavior of metropolitan merchants in the 1760s and 1770s threatened the abilities of Americans to engage in new or, in some cases, even traditional pursuits.

John McCusker and Russell Menard,
The Economy of British America, 1607–1789, 1991

The impact of the Currency Act [of 1764] should not be overlooked. Its psychological effects were especially important. It served as a constant reminder that the economic well-being of the colonies was subordinate to the desires of the imperial government at the very time when colonial legislatures were beginning to demand equality for the colonies within the empire. Furthermore, the stubborn refusal of imperial authorities in the late sixties and early seventies to repeal the Currency Act or to relax their rigid interpretation of what constituted legal tender currency persuaded many Americans that British officials either did not understand or were utterly callous to colonial problems.

Jack P. Greene and Richard M. Jellison, "The Currency Act of 1764," 1961

Americans in the 1770s, while prosperous relative to most of the world, were also worried. The perceived threat to that well-being was coming not from some foreign foe but from the mother country, through seeming intentions to cut the colonials down to size, both politically and economically.

Although politics and economics frequently intertwined, this chapter focuses on the latter. Indeed, roughly a dozen economic circumstances and resentments played a significant role in 1774–1775 and the run-up to revolution. Telling that story requires this book's longest chapter, but the dozen elements cannot be neatly disentangled, and they also frame two of the Revolution's principal regional motivations. In addition, as we will see, a catalogue of the war's economic interest groups and constituencies—mercantile, maritime, plantation, professional, speculative, and debt-ridden—puts further emphasis on the Revolution's commercial ingredients.

Full-fledged independence was not a North American colonial ambition in the early 1770s, but support was unmistakably brewing for greater home rule, which included economic self-determination. Through the 1750s, British policy, resting on a basically mercantilist framework, had built a relatively prosperous economy. But by the 1760s, awareness of a population inpouring and rich economic potential encouraged Americans to ask serious new questions about what existing colonial obligations and new signs of imperial harshness meant for future prosperity.

Succinctly put, many New Englanders, Virginians, Carolinians, and others were starting to develop a new, incipiently nationalist "American" outlook. As we will see, analyses of pre-Revolutionary speeches, letters, and newspaper contents document a change in self-perception.

Europeans, too, were attaching more import to British North America. What the Old World called the Seven Years War (1756–1763) had actually begun in 1754 near the forks of the Ohio River, where French and British rivalry converged. By war's end, as many key battles had been fought in North America as in central Europe, a notable first. To newly attentive Austrians, Prussians, and Russians, Britain's empire in North America had become a vital, even critical, prop of her global and maritime predominance.

British ministers and parliamentarians had evidence close at hand. Along the western coast, from Bristol north to Glasgow, a half dozen cities owed their mushrooming growth to trade with the North American colonies. So did industries from textiles to ironware and copperware, as well as Josiah Wedgwood's pottery, Nottingham's stockings, and Sheffield's gleaming steel. By 1774, roughly 40 percent of British manufactured exports went to the American colonies. The many implications were grist for the mills of politicians, publicists, philosophes, and emigration agents alike.

Sounding much the same from Britain or Sweden to the Mediterranean, the word *America* evoked promise. Religious liberty was a beacon for many; economic opportunity, for even more. Enthusiasts ranged from Jean-Jacques Rousseau to preacher John Wesley. Most of the emigration came from Protestant northern Europe, largely British allied. Poor tenants on Scotland's Isle of Skye even had a dance called "America"—couples whirled in a circle till all were in motion, showing how emigration sentiment caught hold.

Between 1700 and 1750, the population of the thirteen contiguous mainland colonies quintupled from 250,000 to 1.2 million. Then between 1750 and 1775, it doubled to between 2.5 and 3 million, exceeding Holland, Denmark, Portugal, or Switzerland. Even Prussia, its population reduced to 4 million in 1763 by wartime devastation, was not far ahead.

Officials in London, by this point, had begun to worry about regional population losses in parts of Britain. Heavy Scotch-Irish emigration from Ulster was seen as ending any chance of a Protestant majority in Ireland; in the Scottish Highlands, clan chieftains gloomed over the depopulation of their islands and glens. In 1763, the British government acted to prohibit British and American settlement west of a line drawn along the peaks of the Appalachian Mountains. Several motivations were at work: to reduce Indian wars and curb military outlays; to discourage further emigration from Britain; and to keep Americans weak enough to be dependent. Mercantile theory applauded population, and the British government didn't want to lose any more of it.

Even English and British identities were in flux. The British historian Linda Colley has written convincingly about how eighteenth-century psychologies knit together English, Welsh, Scots, and some Irish as "Britons."[1] Three thousand miles away, by contrast, diverging interests and a sense of the apartness bred by that great distance were remaking English-speaking colonials into Americans.

Most New Englanders and Virginians, proudly British in 1744, felt less so by 1764. A further decade saw many edging toward open enmity. The term *colonist* was picking up negative connotations, as in "mere colonial." Even future Loyalists, who would shrink back from full independence, typically favored greater self-determination—seeking a separate American parliament or London's pledge not to tax the American colonies without consent. Popular commitment to self-determination had a powerful economic content—concern not only over tax policy but over provincial authority to issue local currency, elimination of customs abuses, the opportunity to manufacture, freer trade among the various colonies, and much more. In the religious sphere, comparable assertiveness opposed Anglican bishops for America and demanded colonial disestablishment of the Church of England. As we have seen, many Dutch and German Reformed congregations sought local, not Old Country, supervision of their churches and preferred American-born or English-speaking pastors.

Few historians would dispute colonial support for greater self-determination. The confusion is over how to label that demand. Politics and constitutional change were necessary means. However, much of the underlying dissatisfaction involved religion, as we have just seen, and economics, to which we now turn.

Many Economic Roads to Revolution

This chapter will identify a dozen serious bones of pre-Revolutionary economic motivation and contention. That there were so many is important in itself. By 1774 and 1775, little about the colonial economy had not been drawn into debate.

It is best to begin at its heart—a money supply kept small, primitive, and usually inadequate by British mercantilist thinking and administrative practice. Much of this was intentional. It was a founding seventeenth-century principle of mercantilism that specie—gold and silver—be drawn back to the mother country. This was accepted subordination: colonies were to *serve,* not to be guided toward maturity and self-fulfillment. Change was beginning, but slowly.

Among the mainland thirteen, with currency often scarce, levels of indebtedness had soared since the 1740s. If money was the first problem, debt was the second. Debt-related lawsuits clogged the colonial courts. In New England and the plantation colonies, debt matters were everyday conversation. An insufficient money supply was tied to another imperial fundamental: that valuable colonial export commodities had to be routed through Britain to profit middlemen there. Return payment often came in overpriced goods.

This reflected a third hinge of friction: the statutory mandate that colonists sell specified commodities only to British merchants. Those affected were spelled out in the mid-seventeenth-century Navigation Acts' "enumerated list," which had further expanded in the eighteenth century and especially since the 1750s. In practical terms, each addition made more American producers British commercial captives, even though enumeration had started out a century earlier by guaranteeing markets. If enumeration, money supply, and debt appear related, they clearly were.

During the 1760s, some restive Americans began to complain that proceeds lost by tobacco growers in particular, because their great crop had to be sent to Britain—and only from there resold profitably all over Europe—amounted to a massive de facto tax. This diversion alone, the critics said, more than compensated the mother country for its protective umbrella. Sometimes overstated but hardly specious, this contention tied into a fourth point of frustration. Parliament, in which the colonies had no representation, therefore had no right—or so some Americans insisted—to impose transatlantic taxes.

London had not directly taxed before the 1760s, but it acted during that decade with a sequence of controversial levies, notably the 1765 stamp tax and the 1767 Townshend taxes (on glass, paints, paper, and tea). Townshend's were repealed in 1770, save for the levy on tea. That was reiterated in 1773, setting Boston's famous tea party in motion. However, after the Coercive Acts took center stage in 1774, the tax issue per se receded.

Here a point should be made. The dozen economic issues, although interrelated, were not constant. They varied in importance. The colonists' contention that unfair enumeration was actually a thinly disguised tax—and therefore constituted a good argument against additional levies—intensified amid the tumult of imperial relations in 1774–1775. Trade moved to the fore.

A sixth altercation of the pre-Revolutionary period involved what several twentieth-century historians labeled "customs racketeering." Much stricter enforcement commenced in the early 1760s with a major strengthening of a British Customs Service that had been locally ineffective. Multiple tightenings between 1762 and 1767 imposed new duties, established an American Board of Customs, specified elaborate and near-punitive loading and bonding requirements, provided for removal of customs-related trials to juryless admiralty courts, and instructed Royal Navy ships and officers to collaborate in aggressive, by-the-book customs enforcement.

People in Massachusetts, Rhode Island, and eastern Connecticut were especially irate. In 1764 British aggressiveness in pursuing molasses smugglers—generally ignored until the sixties—prompted provincial gunners manning Fort George in Newport, Rhode Island, to fire shots at the *St. John,* a naval schooner seizing molasses-carrying vessels in Narragansett Bay. An enthusiastic crowd quickly gathered. When cannoneer Daniel Vaughn, having acted under orders, later reported back to the Council, "they wanted only to know why he had not sunk the schooner."[2] In more or less self-governing Rhode Island, intrusive British warships were becoming enemies.

The limitations that Britain had imposed on colonial manufactures—principally through the Hat Act of 1732, the Woolens Act of 1699, and the Iron Act of 1750—at first drew little complaint. The tax and trade-boycott controversies of the 1760s and 1770s, however, made curbs on what the colonies could produce a more heated topic. With each boycott, Americans devoted more rhetoric to the need to produce or manufacture locally more of what was being imported. We can describe the boycotts of 1765–1766 and 1767–1770 as a seventh confrontation. Rising tensions over manufacturing became arena number eight.

In 1774, when the First Continental Congress called for a strong response to Britain's Coercive Acts, delegates embraced a much bolder trade stoppage, which displaced tax policy as the fulcrum of Patriot strategy. Instead of relying on uncooperative merchants to stop importing specified British goods, Congress put forward a new brand of association: all twelve participating provincial delegations pledged to prohibit *popular consumption* of British goods, commencing that very autumn. Nonexportation of American commodities to Britain, until then never ventured, would follow in the autumn of 1775. This was to allow Virginians the time needed to cure, pack, and ship their 1774 tobacco crop, essential to gaining cash and credits.

Strict enforcement now merged with patriotism. Congress recommended establishing provincial, county, and local committees to monitor compliance, publicize violators, and seize goods and cargoes where necessary.[3] The sweeping extralegal authority and potentially treasonable nature of these organizations quickly became a ninth adversarial dimension. Merchants still played a part, but hard-line activists were coming to the fore.

Throwing down this gauntlet moved the colonies to the brink of economic war. However, before picking up that combat in Chapter 9, these pages will also amplify several other controversial dimensions of how British imperial prescriptions limited American opportunity.

Of course, many imperial constraints barred American economic self-determination. No one pretended otherwise. Yet by the 1770s, British rules and favoritism struck more and more colonials as unacceptable. For example, the right to sell American tobacco in France, made lawful for Scots after the Act of Union in 1707, remained prohibited to Americans. Thomas Jefferson, not a particular admirer of "North Britons," liked to argue that *English* Americans ought to be on an imperial par with *non-English* Scots. Such arguments resonated in tobacco country, where Scottish traders were greatly resented.

The Royal Proclamation of 1763, in turn, barred British subjects from settling beyond the Appalachian Mountains on western lands earlier fulsomely described and conveyed in several seventeenth-century royal charters. Westward vistas had tantalized generations of explorers, surveyors, and investors. However, by the 1770s, British forts in places like Ohio and Illinois had been shut down to uphold a new linkage: no settlers were wanted, and little expensive protection from the Indians would be furnished. A related goal voiced in 1763 and 1764 was to bottle up the thirteen colonies along the East Coast, channeling expansion northward to Nova Scotia and southward into now-British Florida, with its supposed opportunities for tropical agriculture. Westward flow would be blocked. As late as 1767, George Washington dismissed the Proclamation Line as nothing more than "a temporary expedient to quiet the Minds of the Indians." But as we will see, contemporary British explanations and policy pronouncements suggested otherwise.[4] Perceived British hostility to American westward movement became a tenth friction.

While settlers could squat illegally, investors and speculators in the western lands were often stymied. In most colonies, not least Virginia, investors preoccupied with western lands were prominent in supporting the Revolution. After the Proclamation Line had been received angrily, a few adjustments were made. The Quebec Act of 1774, however, stunned British America by placing the lands that would become Ohio, Indiana, Illinois, Michigan, and Wisconsin within the political boundaries and French-sprung legal system of Quebec. Virginians already contemplating their trans-Ohio acreage were told to go fly a fleur-de-lis-shaped kite. The western-lands aspect of the Quebec Act became another grudge.

Last but hardly least, the unfolding events of 1775 made it essential to purchase arms, ammunition, sulfur, and saltpeter in the West Indies or from complicit European merchants. Congress soon modified its nonexportation provisions, and shipping food and tobacco for powder, hitherto encouraged, now became official policy.[5] It marked a transition to open war.

Colonial insistence on economic self-determination, in short, became confrontational well before Lexington and Concord. Within a few months, economic war led to shooting war. But before going on to describe the loyalties and constituencies that emerged in 1775, more must be said about the principal economic conflicts and insoluble disagreements. Matches were being put to a surprisingly short fuse.

The 1764–1774 Economy: Too Little Money, Too Much Debt

Of the various economic roads to revolution, several were more extended pothole than surface. Currency mismanagement, our first focus, may not seem innately war provoking. However, in many provinces, the lack of a regular colonial coinage or reasonably sound, officially authorized paper money was periodically crippling. In the late twentieth century, as monetary historians reevaluated the importance of currency—or of its lack—in pre-Revolutionary America, British neglect of local money supplies drew overdue attention.

Simply put, despite affluence by global standards, British North Americans had to make do with a relative shambles of a currency system and money supply. The credos of eighteenth-century mercantilism—accumulating gold at the seat of power ranked high—encouraged London's offhanded behavior. Consider this candor from the Oxford-based *Blackwell Encyclopedia of the American Revolution*: "The monetary system of the colonies was based on the use of Spanish coins from the mines in Latin America, since Parliament had refused to allow the export of English coins. The colonies supplemented the coinage with paper monies which the 13 assemblies issued independently at various times."[6] Or *didn't* issue, as was often the case, because of the limitations set forth in Britain's Currency Acts of 1751 and 1764. Even royal governors were sometimes appalled by the monetary dearth.

As British North America grew during the first four decades of the eighteenth century, the separate money supplies of the various colonies were subject to the oversight of the government's Board of Trade. No specie—silver or gold coins—could be exported to the colonies from Britain, and minting privileges were also denied. Massachusetts initiated paper money, but London's concurrence was assured only when colonies were raising money for local military purposes that the Crown favored (and did not want to fund itself).

Still, with hard money scarce and most commodities unsuitable for a monetary purpose, paper currency became the principal answer. Military needs were the best justification for issuance. In one scholar's words, "the colonies were at war for thirty-four of the first seventy-four years between the first emission of paper bills by Massachusetts in 1690 and the prohibition of further issues by Parliamentary statute in 1764. On many occasions paper money issues were the only method to obtain the cash needed for military expeditions. Thus, it was both to supply the needs of trade and to meet the demands of war that paper currencies became instruments of finance in eighteenth-century America."[7]

To mid-eighteenth-century Crown officials, the real downside of colonial paper money was that when it became legal tender, people in Boston or Charleston could use it for cheap settlement of debts to British merchants. Colonists who shipped enumerated goods or commodities to Britain—tobacco, rice, pig iron, or tall pines for Royal Navy masts—got paid by bills drawn on London or through goods shipped back in return. Encouraging other enterprise in the colonies (or the money supply to nurture it) was not a priority at the Board of Trade.

Across most of the thirteen colonies money was a crazy quilt of coinage, paper, and commercial confusion. Before we continue on to its pre-Revolutionary significance and politics, a look at the many inadequacies is useful.

Currency necessarily took many forms. Some of the silver Pine Tree shillings minted in seventeenth-century Massachusetts remained in circulation. Provincial authorities sometimes imported chests of Spanish silver or small English copper pieces, to which London had no objection. The popular silver eight-real piece—*thaler* or dollar—used widely in North America was famously adaptable. It could be clipped, "sweated," hollowed, or otherwise reduced in silver content. Divided into two-real portions, it yielded four "two-bit" pieces—the ancestors of latter-day U.S. quarters.

Valuation was often a challenge. "Gold is very scarce here," New York merchant John Watts advised a colleague. "I shall write to my friend Mr. Allen to send you £500 sterling if a Vessel of Force offers. Half Johannes' are the only Gold that can be picked up in any Quantity. They pass at 63/.* Moidores are very rare at 46/; so are guineas at 36/ and pistoles at 29/." Provinces were usually barred from imposing their own parochial values on coins. New York governor Sir Henry Moore in 1769 vetoed a bill making gold coins legal tender at specified local rates because that would have im-

---

*A slash was shorthand for shilling. So 63/ meant 63 shillings. Sometimes it was a slash with a minus sign: 63/-.

properly conflicted with a parliamentary valuation.[8] Even gold and silver transactions could be slow and complicated. By one estimate, some "10 to 15 percent of the money stock had to be weighed and its fineness proved before it could change hands."[9]

Some commodities also served as currencies. The term *buck,* for example, reflected how for many decades deerskins were legal tender in South Carolina and elsewhere. At some point, presumably, one buckskin of quality was worth eight reals in South American silver. Wampum passed in places, as did tobacco in the Chesapeake. Beginning in the 1730s and 1740s, Virginia and Maryland required official inspections of tobacco and established public warehouses. The receipts furnished by warehouses were effectively monetized and could be sold or tendered for settlement of taxes, fees, and debts. Their worth, however, varied with the daily price of tobacco.

Britain continued to drain gold and silver back to her own exchequers. One method was to make taxes, duties, and customs charges or fines payable in specie. Opposition to the Stamp Act in 1765 became even more bitter because the stamps required for taxable transactions—publications, conveyances, mortgages, and many more—had to be paid for with hard money, however difficult to come by in a troubled economy.

Paper money—above and beyond its frequent scarcity—also contributed to the confusion. Each colony's paper money had a different valuation. In 1740, for example, to match £100 sterling would take £160 in the local currencies of New York and New Jersey, £170 in Pennsylvania, and £200 next door in Maryland, but it would require £800 in South Carolina money and £1400 in North Carolina.[10] This necessitated reference guides like the *American Negotiator,* published in London, that provided exchange rates between pounds sterling and the various provincial paper pounds.[11]

During the decade before the Revolution, merchants in Britain did not have to take colonial paper as legal tender. They were, however, free to take it at a substantial (or whopping) discount. Nor did any colony have to take another's paper notes, which made for some interesting diplomacy. New Jersey was betwixt and between. With East Jersey a commercial adjunct of New York and West New Jersey a Pennsylvania outlier, both larger provinces usually took New Jersey notes. But in 1772, New York caused a ruckus by temporarily declining.[12] In 1774 and 1775, after Massachusetts moved to break with Britain and looked to its neighbors for aid, the Bay Colony found it politic to once again let Rhode Island and Connecticut money circulate within Massachusetts.

If valuation was chaotic, it was further complicated by the widespread use of barter and credit arrangements. In Connecticut, shopkeepers had to be ready to price their goods flexibly, adjusting for any payment delay and for whatever commodity might be tendered. As described by one participant, four major possibilities existed: "Pay, money, pay as money, and trusting. *Pay* is grain, pork and beef &c, at the prices set by the General Court that year. *Money* is pieces of eight, rials or Boston or Bay shillings (as they call them) or good hard money as silver coin is termed by them; also wampum, viz. Indian beads, which serve for change. *Pay as money* is provisions, as aforesaid one-third cheaper than the Assembly or General Court sets it. And *trust* is as they and the merchant agree on for time."[13] This did not exactly match Adam Smith's prognoses for a modern economy.

As for credit, its role in cash-short 1767 Virginia was summarized this way: "Even well-to-do growers had to make most of their purchases on credit. Property for sale generally bore two prices: one for cash customers and a significantly higher one for those who bought on credit. The annualized interest incorporated into the credit customer's price ranged as high as 15 percent, triple the legal interest ceiling of 5 percent . . . It was hidden interest charges that explained why British manufactured goods could be obtained far more cheaply in northern seaports than in Virginia." Nor did the economic distortion end there. When debts were called in and currency was not obtainable—as in a money supply dearth—"debtors were often unable to sell property for cash at a decent price," and those who paid obligations with property "had to pay perhaps double what they owed." Sheriff's auctions, in turn, sometimes brought only one fourth of the real value of the assets being sold.[14]

British attitudes toward currency regulation had created some earlier economic and political crises—for early-eighteenth-century South Carolina because of military demands and related issuance of notes, and for Massachusetts in the 1730s because of land banks and military-related printings. However, our pre-Revolutionary focus begins with the Currency Act of 1764, a measure later specifically condemned by the First Continental Congress.

By that act, British ministers and Parliament assumed full direction over what provincial governments could or could not do in terms of currency issuance. The first direct constraint, the Currency Act of 1751, had barred the issuance of paper notes as legal tender in the four New England colonies. Although paper currency could be issued in some forms, essentially for internal purposes, British merchants did not have to take it in payment. Some restraint was justified; too much New England paper money had been issued in the 1740s, albeit much of it for war-related purposes. The basic pattern of military-related issuance repeated during the French and Indian War, especially in Virginia. British authorities went along while the paper was helping to finance the joint war effort. But as soon as peace came in 1763, the Crown's renewed concern with creditors' interests rang a tocsin for remedial legislation.

In extending statutory restraint to the other nine colonies, the 1764 act did not ban paper money; nor did it require any province to immediately recall its paper currency already in circulation. What it did do was to prohibit further legal-tender issuance and to insist that all colonies retire their existing issues on the dates scheduled. This was not small stuff. The result was a further squeeze on provincial economies already experiencing major contractions through the end of wartime stimulus. Virginia and North Carolina had been identified in London as the principal misbehavers, and four plantation colonies—Virginia, the Carolinas, and Georgia—led in protesting to Parliament and the Privy Council.[15]

The pain lay in the double squeeze applied—first, the money-supply shrinkage from the retirement of old notes, and second, the allowance of only a few ways to issue new ones. For a while, in 1766 and 1767, as complaints arose, talk grew on both sides of the Atlantic about repeal. That came to naught when the inflexible Earl of Hillsborough became American secretary in 1768.[16] Upon his departure four years later, Parliament in 1773 passed a modifying act, which made some needed exceptions. In practical terms, though, currency liberalization came only on the heels of the severe British credit crisis of 1772, and after five or six years of constriction, so that concession was both too small and too late.

Currency-deprived and debt-saddled local economies—a description that best fit the tobacco colonies—often bred a corollary system of legal traps and snares for small farmers and became a cornucopia for attorneys, wealthy lenders, and sheriffs (who in some jurisdictions worked for percentages, not salaries). As we will see in Chapter 6, it was this kind of distressed milieu that in the late 1760s incubated the Regulators' movement in North Carolina. Fees on a £4–5 judgment could come to £2–3. Royal Governor

William Tryon acknowledged that his fast-growing but currency-starved province had to make do with one third of the money supply it required.[17]

If these scarcity effects are usually downplayed, the skimpiness and lack of detail on the complexity of that era's currency-and-debt mess is partly responsible. It also takes a punctuation of household anguish, resort to violence, and bitter politics to come alive.

For example, few observers have cared that most colonial paper currency took the form of so-called bills of credit, issued by provincial governments in anticipation of tax revenues. This seems essentially technical. However, for the four or five years beginning in 1765, as colonies adhering to Currency Act mandates used tax revenues to pay off many of these bills and remove them from circulation, some British officials perversely took this as evidence of the lightness of the American tax burden. If the debt taken on during the war could be paid down this easily, it couldn't have been very heavy.

Not exactly. As specified in the act, when tax revenues were used to pay off provincial notes, that simultaneously shrank that province's paper money supply by 15 or 25 percent or whatever share had to be removed from circulation. South Carolinians took complicated actions to circumvent these requirements.[18] Elsewhere, the notes were usually destroyed. Merrill Jensen was almost alone among twentieth-century U.S. historians in explaining the process, which amounted to a hidden but painful levy on economic activity.[19]

Paper money shrinkage cut deepest during the several downturns of the pre-Revolutionary years. Using a generalized North American chronology, these took place between 1761 and 1766 and then again between 1772 and 1774. In some colonies, though, Currency Act crises created a separate local chronology of foreclosures, debt litigation, and hard times.

The economics and politics of money supply shrinkage would become a major national issue again in the United States during the 1870s, 1880s, and 1890s and then again in the 1930s. Its importance during the decade before the American Revolution deserves equal attention. It is probably true, as economic historians have argued, that British North America was one of the world's most prosperous societies. But the same was true of the United States during those later periods.

Estimates have been made of the money-supply contraction occurring in the farm states during the Populist angst of the late nineteenth century and then again during rural crisis periods of the 1920s and 1930s. Alas, no

similar data are available for the colonies between 1764 and 1774. Retrospect-
ive estimates of the thirteen-colony money supply or money stock as of 1775
have indeed been published, but most appear to reflect as much guesswork
as science. In *The Emergence of a National Economy, 1775–1815*, Curtis Nettels noted that the pre-Revolutionary colonies "suffered from an acute
shortage of hard money; all the coin in circulation in 1775 would not have
paid a year's expenses of the Continental Army."[20] Another expert, economic historian John McCusker in *The Economy of British America,
1607-1789*, collected estimates ranging from $30 million in Spanish dollars—
postwar guesswork by Alexander Hamilton—to levels considerably lower.[21]
Estimates of hard and paper currency available per person in British North
America ranged from a stingy £1 to an acceptable £3, more or less the ratio
for the mother country. These definitions raise enough questions that the
proverbial grain of salt has to be more like a pinch.

The angry comments of merchants, land investors, and ordinary
consumers recorded at the time seem more revealing. To be sure, many early-
twentieth-century "Progressive" historians overemphasized—and frequently also oversimplified—economic causations of the Revolution. Their
subsequent critics, the Neo-Whig or Consensus school, erred by all but
omitting economics. Fortunately, the late twentieth century developed an
explanation that yes, paper money was sometimes inflationary, but British
currency policy did indeed favor British creditors while frequently disad-
vantaging the colonies.[22]

The serious politics that surrounded currency matters, however, is generally recognized. Bernhard Knollenberg, in *Growth of the American Revolution: 1766–1775*, ranked the Currency Act of 1764 in second place, behind
only the Stamp Act, as a reason for "continuing discontent" in the
mid-1760s.[23] Others cited 1765 testimony before a committee of the House
of Commons in which Benjamin Franklin had listed the Currency Act,
along with the Stamp Act and restrictions on trade, as the principal reasons
for the colonies' rising dissatisfaction with Parliament. Then in 1774, the
Statement of Rights and Grievances issued by the First Continental Congress named the Currency Act of 1764 as one of the thirteen specific acts of
Parliament that delegates to the Congress found "intolerable."[24]

This bespeaks a deeper popular economic discontent than could ever
have arisen from an abstract focus on imperial relations. John McCusker
and Russell Menard, in what remains the principal text on colonial economic history, rebutted the lingering emphasis on ideology as all-explaining.

Although "the dispute took a constitutional form, it is clear that economic issues played a central role . . . The Currency Act of 1764 portended a limitation of the colonial money supply as well as the disruption of domestic commerce."[25]

Back in 1961, colonial historian Jack P. Greene and colleague Richard M. Jellison, discussing inadequate scholarly exploration of the Currency Act's "impact on the Revolutionary crisis," summarized: "Certainly, the Currency Act was not one of the more explosive issues in the debate between Britain and the American colonies. Still, with the single exception of Delaware, each of the colonies affected considered it a major grievance. Coming during a period when a growing population and an expanding trade were aggravating a chronic shortage of specie, it could scarcely have been more untimely."[26] In *The Currency of the American Colonies, 1700–1764*, the principal survey of colony-by-colony issuance, economic historian Leslie Brock described the Currency Act of 1764 as the British Board of Trade's "crowning blunder."[27]

If too many historians are quoted here, it is to help overturn prior misjudgments. Late-twentieth-century scholars developed more serious assessments, and interpretation of the pre-Revolutionary political economy must catch up. Without these citations, I would feel less free to place the emphasis this chapter does on the role of currency.

As might be expected, the four vanguard colonies were conspicuous in opposing British curbs. Indeed, their currency issuance arose from their disproportionate role in eighteenth-century North American military expeditions and the defense of the empire's southern, western, and northern frontiers, many of which Britain never reimbursed. Overactivity in Massachusetts, Connecticut, Rhode Island, and New Hampshire during the French and Spanish wars of the 1740s prompted the 1751 act, which applied only to New England. British officials had also disliked Massachusetts's land bank, popular among farmers, which Parliament had disallowed in 1741. John Adams later recalled that "the act to destroy the Land bank scheme raised a greater ferment in this province than the Stamp Act did."[28]

Some argue that as the imperial crisis intensified, New Englanders' pioneering role in paper money helped to stimulate the local growth of alternative economic ideology.[29] As we will see, the New England provinces didn't even wait for independence before they turned to paper currency again in 1775.

To the south, Virginia and the Carolinas were the main targets of the

1764 act, although its terms also applied to the middle colonies. Virginia had offended the ministry in London by its large-scale 1755–1762 paper issuance, predicated partly on wartime financial needs that ranged from supporting Braddock's expedition to the Forks of the Ohio in 1755 to raising troops after Spain declared war in 1762. However, the greater offense lay in declaring this grand emission legal tender to satisfy private debts, which made British merchants and creditors howl.[30] North Carolina, the poorest of the southern colonies, was also blamed for issuing paper that rapidly lost value. Even so, by 1768 it had only £60,000 of provincial currency in circulation for a population over 150,000.[31]

South Carolina, active in issuing paper during the first half of the eighteenth century to fund expeditions against Spanish St. Augustine and the Tuscarora and Yamasee Indians, was the other major regional offender. Economic historian Joseph Ernst, in his *Money and Politics in America, 1755-1775,* described the province as "the *bete noire* of the early critics of American paper money."[32] By 1766, Carolinians were again concerned with the impact of currency shrinkage on prosperity. As noted, Virginia, the Carolinas, and Georgia petitioned for the 1764 act's repeal, and the southern colonies reportedly led the push to have the First Continental Congress name the Currency Act as one of Britain's "intolerable" actions.[33]

Twenty-first-century Americans who have seen the U.S. Federal Reserve flood the financial system with money may have trouble appreciating the opposite extreme. However, the citizenry of 1892 or 1932 would have empathized with eighteenth-century sufferers. In Virginia, for example, the total currency outstanding dropped from £230,000 in 1764 to £105,000 in 1771 and £55,000 in 1773.[34] Monetary shrinkage in the early 1930s could have been no worse.

For a fuller overview, it is essential to pair the frequent inadequacy of provincial money supplies with a second, interlocking circumstance: high and disruptive colonial levels of debt. The two fed each other.

At peaks of local indebtedness, Virginians and Marylanders went so far as to torch jails or break prisoners out. The North Carolina Piedmont broke into armed revolt in 1771. Court systems circa 1772–1773 were clogged with recovery actions. Provincial assemblies, for their part, faced a parade of debt-related controversies—legislation regarding debtor recovery, bankruptcy laws, and appropriate judicial venues. Inadequate money supplies, besides intensifying demand for credit, expanded the ranks of debtors.

In situations where currency was scarce or almost nonexistent, creditor lawsuits exposed debtors to unusual peril. As we have seen, in *real* values, two or three times the amount at stake would be taken. Court and attorneys' fees added to the blow. Thus the plea among farmers and planters at such times: *Close the courts.*

The attempts by Charles Beard and other Progressive historians to posit economic explanations of the Revolution had some legitimacy. By the mid-twentieth century, though, their case had lost credibility because of a perceived bias toward economic determinism, as well as an apparent contention that debt evasion rather than patriotism had motivated Virginia planters—not just national icons Washington and Jefferson but hundreds of smallholders. Debt psychologies among the Founding Fathers were considerably more complex.

Nevertheless, the interaction of Chesapeake currency and debt trauma with regional sensitivity to British tobacco policy helped make for explosive politics. Because American producers had to send their crop to British merchants, the latter extended most of the credit necessary to keep the wheels of planter commerce turning. What became intense competition between London and Scottish tobacco merchants during the 1760s and up to the crisis of 1772 worsened matters. It encouraged the overextension of credit that gave way to such a painful bust—in its way, a small preview of Anglo-American bank and credit card company excesses in the 1990s and early 2000s. Chesapeake borrowers, like those centuries later, had let themselves be drawn into a reckless overreliance.

The thirteen-colony total of indebtedness was extraordinary. From a few hundred thousand pounds sterling in 1740, debts owed to Britain by North Americans soared to £4.5 million in the mid-1760s. At the peak in 1772, before the heavy and profitable tobacco sales of 1774–1775 allowed considerable planter debt repayment, the total might have reached £5–6 million, a staggering sum in that era, although nobody really knows. Merchants alone claimed £3 million owed in 1775. By way of context, £4–5 million equaled about half of Britain's annual peacetime budget in the 1760s. There was little likelihood such an amount could be repaid.

Tobacco, Debt, and Land Speculation

The colony-by-colony breakdown of the amount Americans owed to British creditors in 1776 reflects crop geography as much as anything. Virginia's debt was by far the highest, a figure some estimates put as high as £2–3 million sterling.[35] T. H. Breen, a leading scholar of the colonial Chesapeake, noted the political dimension: "An examination of post-revolutionary [British] debt claims reveals that in 1776 at least ten of Virginia's great planters owed £5,000 or more. This was a huge sum. In the £1,000 to £4,999 range appear such familiar names as Jefferson and Washington. According to one historian who has analyzed British Treasury records, 'at least fifty-five of the individuals from whom £500 or more was claimed were members of the House of Burgesses from 1769 to 1774.'"[36]

Serious planter indebtedness to Britain extended to South Carolina (£350,000) and Maryland (£289,000).[37] In 1771, a boom year, imports to the Chesapeake colonies (Virginia and Maryland) from Britain totaled £920,000, while the two colonies' exports reached only £577,000—an unprecedented deficit reflecting commercial exuberance.[38]

As war began, most of the indebtedness to British lenders did indeed concentrate in the plantation provinces. Except for British-oriented merchants in Massachusetts, New Englanders had borrowed relatively little overseas. The substantial amounts of debt run up prior to the Revolution by Connecticut residents were mostly owed to creditors in Boston or New York.[39]

Compared to tobacco-ensnared Virginia, South Carolinian debt to Britons was much less burdensome. Local planters owed more to in-province creditors, and as of 1775, few were clearly overextended.[40] Consider one measurement of comparative affluence: in North Carolina, the annual value in sterling of exports for each white resident was a low £1.17; in Virginia, £2.82; and in South Carolina, a striking £9.13. Tobacco-dependent Virginia was closer to poor North Carolina than to rice-and-indigo-rich South Carolina.[41]

Debt bingeing in the Chesapeake flattered neither side, British or American. Colonists complained that British commercial practice sucked them dry. Their tobacco could be sold nowhere but in Britain, where it brought prices that planters called inadequate relative to the markups London and Glasgow merchants enjoyed when reselling the leaf in France, Holland, and elsewhere. George Washington and Thomas Jefferson both saw insidious enticements and relationships at work. In Washington's words, "Our whole substance does already in a manner flow to Great Britain." To Jefferson, British merchants at first offered good prices and easy credit, but once the client was in their clutches, they cut prices, so that the planters became "a species of property annexed to certain mercantile houses in London."[42]

Beyond this entrapment, planters argued, many of the British merchants were unethical, sending back poor-quality or overpriced goods in payment. This is plausible. The British historian J. H. Plumb, for one, described the crippling debt as "created very largely through the cupidity and dishonesty of the London factors."[43] Fierce competition in the British tobacco industry presumably made corner cutting commonplace. As for the quality and price of goods sent back to American sellers, to cynics it reflected how the colonies were a captive market.[44]

Samuel Adams was especially caustic about colonists' willingness to accept what in 1771 he called "the Baubles of Britain"—laces, fans, ribbons, decorated teapots, and the like.[45] One historian recalled the charges by Virginians and Marylanders that British merchants made the colonies a "dumping ground for shopworn, unsalable merchandise; cheating on weights and measures."[46]

The larger problem lay with planters' tastes for British-manufactured luxuries. In Virginia, Thomas Jefferson's father-in-law John Wayles observed that "within these 25 Years £1000 due to a Merchant was looked upon as a sum imense [sic] and never to be got over. Ten times that sum is now spoke of with Indifference and thought no great burthen on some Estates . . . In 1740, I don't remember to have seen such a thing as a turkey Carpet except a small thing in a bed chamber. Now nothing are so common as Turkey or Wilton Carpetts, the whole Furniture of the Roomes Elegant and every appearance of Opulence." In South Carolina, where newspapers advertised every luxury, eighteenth-century historian David Ramsey later recalled that "it was in the interest of Great Britain to encourage our dissipation and extravagance for the twofold purpose of increasing the sale of her manufactures and of perpetuating our subordination."[47]

The first American boycott in 1765–1766, and even more the follow-up between 1767 and 1770, combined colonial neo-Puritanism and debt frustration into a powerful discontent. Nonimportation became a moral cause, not just a tactic in helping to force Parliament's 1770 repeal of the Townshend duties. Frugality became patriotism, as did eschewing fripperies, gewgaws, and trinkets, lavish funerals and expensive British fashions. The most vehement advocates began counter- "enumerating" British goods—listing what imports would not be accepted. Hundreds of committees and voluntary associations prepared lists of items not to be purchased—and some newspapers then published lists of "enemies of America" who bought them.

British officials were outraged—and helpless. General Thomas Gage wrote in 1769 that "Committees of Merchants at Boston, N. York, and Philadelphia contrive to exercise the Government they have set up to prohibit the importation of British goods, appoint Inspectors, tender Oaths to the Masters of Vessels, and enforce their Prohibitions by coercive Measures. In times less dissolute and licentious, it would be a matter of Astonishment, to hear that British manufactures were prohibited in British provinces, by an illegal Combination of People."[48]

After Parliament largely repealed the Townshend duties, tensions eased. However, the First Continental Congress, in its response to the Coercive Acts, recommended a Continental Association to manage nonimportation, nonconsumption, and nonexportation. Section eleven of the resolution specified that enforcement would lie with a committee "chosen in every county, city, and town, by those who are qualified to vote for representatives in the legislature."[49] Thus were the *elected* foundations of the new revolutionary government put in place.

New England and the plantation provinces displayed the highest profiles of paper currency bickering, and the politics of indebtedness followed essentially the same geography. In Massachusetts, internal creditor-debtor regionalism came to the fore in the summer of 1774, when farmers throughout the province shut down the county courts. So, too, in Connecticut, where an earlier bankruptcy and currency debate during the late 1760s helped to fuel the takeover of the provincial government by Jonathan Trumbull and the radical Patriot faction, whose base was in the debt-burdened eastern counties.[50] In 1766, Connecticut farmers in Wallingford and Windham called on judges to sit less frequently and urged relaxation of the debt laws. Three years earlier the province had enacted New England's most debtor-friendly bankruptcy statute but had to repeal it after eight months.[51]

Predictably, debt-related and court-closing controversies reached their greatest intensity in tobacco country. In 1762, Virginia's House of Burgesses passed bankruptcy legislation somewhat favorable to debtors, only to see it vetoed by the Privy Council at the request of British merchants. In 1765, during the Stamp Act crisis, many of Virginia's local justices, mostly gentlemen and planters, unnerved British creditors and merchants simply by refusing to hear cases. In 1770, the House of Burgesses voted to curb Williamsburg's so-called hustings (borough) court. This tribunal, friendly to merchants and traders, had a unique jurisdiction that allowed creditors to sue any Virginia debtor—not least burgesses and political visitors—who could be caught within the capital's boundaries. When the Privy Council vetoed the change, it was accused by the House of being in collusion with Scottish tobacco merchants.[52]

In early 1774, Patrick Henry and Thomas Jefferson proposed that all payments on Virginia debt should stop; and by mid-1774, most county courts had closed their doors or were about to. According to Virginia historian Woody Holton, "Throughout the war, Virginia courts refused to try creditors' suits against debtors, which prevented debtors from undermining white solidarity by attacking creditors, sheriffs, courthouses and jails."[53]

Planters, lawyers, and officeholders in Maryland had worried about acute debt levels and currency shrinkage in 1765 and did again in 1772–1773, after credit and banking crises in Britain toppled dominoes up and down the Chesapeake. In late 1774, the Provincial Congress voted that "no merchant or factor who violated the Continental Congress's nonimportation directives would be allowed to collect money owed him." By mid-1775, the provincial convention specified that "a creditor desiring to sue for debt had to obtain a license from the local Committee of Observation." In some areas, the militia had to be called in because "debtors openly attacked the jails, freeing persons taken into custody for defaulting on their payments."[54]

To complete the tobacco province roll call, by 1773 debt-related legislation had also become a cause célèbre in North Carolina. The bill extended the so-called foreign attachment clause in order to maintain the ability of Carolinians to attach the property of nonresidents for debts owing to residents. London officials and Governor Josiah Martin, anxious to protect British merchants, sought to repeal the clause. The Assembly, however, preferred a stalemate that closed the courts for a year. Historian Greene underscored the animosity toward British creditors: "Of all the British restrictions in the years after 1763, North Carolinians found this one the most objectionable. Next to parliamentary taxation probably no other issue was so important in promoting the rise of Revolutionary sentiment in that colony."[55]

Having established the centrality of tobacco, we must tie in another friction—the ever-expanding list of commodities that colonial producers were legally obliged to ship to Britain. Here, as in the currency and debt categories, some detail is essential.

In the plantation colonies, Patriots were concerned about the burdens of enumeration—mostly on tobacco, but also on rice. New Englanders were incensed by parliamentary legislation that targeted the so-called Triangular Trade—the selling of fish and provisions in the French West Indies, from which ships could bring back molasses to New England, in order to produce rum, a major Yankee industry. Molasses was only the by-product of an enumerated commodity (sugar), but during the 1760s, as we will see, the British government decided to curb New England's access to its supplies in the West Indies.

The escalating agenda of imperial commodity management over a century tells us a lot about mother-country motivation. The early enumerated list—sugar, tobacco, indigo, dyestuffs, and other tropical and subtropical crops stereotypically associated with empire—was relatively uncontroversial. It had been bluntly stated and was generally accepted in the existing American colonies. So, too, for British insistence, in the name of maritime power, on controlling and receiving North America's output of ships, spars, and naval stores like tar and pitch, as well as the Crown's right to mark and cut "king's trees"—the tallest, straightest, and thickest northern pines needed for masts by the Royal Navy. Copper, hemp, rice, and whale oil were added during the early part of the eighteenth century.

Accepting these prescriptions went to the core of what Britain expected from colonies. Even into 1773–1774, the best-known pro-American voices in Parliament—Pitt's and Burke's, for example—brooked no dissent. In consequence, most American leaders believed that attacking the basic trade laws would only confirm British charges of designs for independence. As late as 1775, Benjamin Franklin suggested that the colonies would be willing to reaffirm the Navigation Acts, because that was not where their complaints lay.[56]

In fact, Franklin's information was out of date. Additions made to the enumerated list in the quarter century after 1750 were generally unpopular. Iron and lumber were enumerated in 1764, as was potash (an essential chemical for textile processing). With respect to iron and lumber, Parliament's motives were dual: to undercut American potential for manufacturing but also to channel more profit through British middlemen. The Revenue Act of 1764 added coffee, pimentos, raw silk, whale fins (used in women's corsets), and more to the list. In several cases, London's motives included preempting the trade in items that colonial Americans sold to pay for goods to be smuggled back from Holland.

Even enumeration of tobacco, the most important North American export, was slowly becoming less acceptable. By the late 1760s, many Virginians were starting to doubt the crop's future and were shifting to wheat. As political realists, most Virginia, Maryland, and North Carolina growers felt that they could not openly oppose enumeration, but that did not bespeak acceptance of Britain's monopoly.

Virginia historian Holton has taken the undercurrent of Chesapeake unhappiness with British treatment of tobacco back to the seventeenth century: "The Navigation Acts and the resulting depression in the tobacco market," he noted, "were repeatedly blamed for social unrest in subsequent decades, especially during Bacon's Rebellion (1676), the largest insurrection in Virginia history, and the 1682 plant-cutting riots. But London's recrimination persuaded tobacco growers that criticism of the Navigation Acts was hopeless."[57]

As early as 1740, the House of Burgesses had petitioned the Privy Council for "free export of their Tobacco to foreign Markets directly," which was denied. By contrast, as Virginians knew, in 1730 Carolina rice growers had been allowed to export directly to southern Europe, although other enumerated exports had to go through Britain. In 1739, the sugar colonies, even better connected in London, had been permitted to export sugar directly to Europe.[58] Tobacco growers felt mistreated, and between 1764 and 1766, indictments of the system's unfairness were voiced by Virginians Richard Bland, Richard Henry Lee, George Mason, and Arthur Lee. In 1774, critical resolves were voted by Fairfax and Albemarle county conventions. Richard Henry Lee pointedly denounced Britain's tobacco policies at the First Constitutional Congress, although the Congress itself took no position. Thomas Jefferson in turn authored the pointed condemnation approved by Virginia's third convention in 1775: that the Crown had failed to offer Virginians "a free trade with all the world."[59]

Until 1774. most tobacco growers confined themselves to indirect complaints. One favored tactic was to emphasize how Parliament's various plans to tax the colonies, besides being unconstitutional, were unjust and unwise because the burdensome trade system already represented a massive burden and de facto tax on American production. Maryland lawyer Daniel Dulany, later a Loyalist, set out the first arithmetic in his famous 1765 pamphlet *Considerations on the Propriety of Imposing Taxes.* "From Virginia and Maryland," said Delany, "are exported *communibus annis* 90,000 hogsheads of tobacco to Great Britain of which it is supposed 60,000 are then exported. But these colonies not being permitted to send their tobacco immediately to foreign markets . . . in proportion to their demands, the re-exported

tobacco pays double freight, double insurance, commission and other shipping charges." To make matters worse, "If the colonies were not restrained
from directly importing foreign commodities they would, it is presumed,
pay less for them, even by 50 percent, than they do at present."[60]

Returning to enumeration, Dulany concluded that tobacco growers
would have received an additional £3 per hogshead (some £180,000) had
they been allowed to ship elsewhere without going through Britain. On
top of which, Britain imposed duties totaling nearly £400,000 a year on
tobacco coming into the kingdom, which planters argued that they paid.[61]
Britain was collecting tobacco-related proceeds through multiple pockets.

Rising concern about the Navigation Acts was not confined to tobacco
growers. South Carolina rice planter Henry Laurens, later president of the
Continental Congress, claimed in 1769 that "the Navigation Acts subjected
him to a much greater tax than any person of equal fortune on the other
side of the Atlantic [paid]." Massachusetts conservative Thomas Hutchinson privately argued against the Stamp Act on the same basis. The Duke of
Grafton in 1766 told the House of Lords that "it is said America is not
taxed. I answer they pay taxes in taking your manufactures.[62] Hector St.
John de Crèvecoeur, the memoir writer and future Tory, called the purchase
of English goods under the mercantilist system "the taxes that we pay." One
historian noted that "in 1766, George Mercer, who had tried unsuccessfully
to enforce the Stamp Act in Virginia, told a parliamentary committee that
even if Virginians had bought the stamped paper, it would have cost them
much less money than the Navigation Acts already did."[63]

So long as Chesapeake growers muted their trade complaints, British
demands for new taxes—the 1764–1773 parade of levies and duties imposed
by Parliament—constituted the prime visible zone of friction. But by 1774,
antitax sloganry like "no taxation without representation" was losing its
centrality. By 1775, few Patriot leaders still saw merit in the idea of North
American representation in a corrupt Parliament 3,000 miles distant. Debate was shifting into a new and broader context: the rearrangement or
breakup of existing economic and imperial relationships.

Molasses, Rum, and Smuggling

A second clutch of resentments, pivoting on British customs policy, maritime regulation, and antismuggling enforcement, had also come to the fore,
principally in New England. A decade earlier, faced with the Royal Navy

being given antismuggling responsibilities, the multiple injuries of the Sugar Act, the rise of admiralty courts, punitive customs enforcement, and suchlike, New Englanders—being more belligerent than genteel Virginians—had replied on occasion with cannon, boarding parties, and boat burnings.

This discord went back to the last years of the French war. American vessels had continued to trade with the French West Indies in the late 1750s and early 1760s, even though the provisions, lumber, and livestock they carried to islands like Saint-Domingue, Guadeloupe, and Martinique in return for French West Indies molasses indirectly supported the French war effort. Ships and merchants from Philadelphia and New York, including many subsequent Loyalists, had participated along with New Englanders. However, as imperial policy toughened, the remedies chosen—writs of assistance in 1761, the Revenue Act of 1762, the Customs Act of 1763, the Sugar Act of 1764, the Stamp Act of 1765, and the Townshend Acts of 1767—struck hardest at New England, particularly Massachusetts and Rhode Island.

Historians specializing in pre-Revolutionary issues like trade, admiralty court, customs, and customs revenue have explained what colonial ire this barrage of legislation produced. Hundreds of pages of detail were involved. Unfortunately, little maritime angst can be captured in a page or two of commercial explanation. We will see in Chapter 7 how some prominent historians argue that even in the 1760s Americans were developing a belief in British ministerial conspiracy. New Englanders could—and many did—take the evolution of customs policy as evidence of manifest hostility.

One maritime scholar has summed up: "In any list of grievances drawn up by the colonies to explain the reasons for that 'open rupture' the operations of the customs service ranked high. An American reading that passage in the Declaration of Independence which denounces the king because he had 'erected a multitude of New Offices, and sent hither swarms of Officers to harass our people, and eat out their substance' would understand this reference to the customs officials." He continued that "more specifically, the complaints in the Declaration that the colonists had been deprived 'in many cases of the benefit of Trial by Jury' and transported 'beyond seas to be tried for pretended offenses' singled out the Admiralty court system, which was a major element in the customs apparatus. And the whole purpose, the basic function, of the customs service was protested in the Declaration when the colonists had complained that the king had 'combined, with others, to subject us to a jurisdiction foreign to our constitution . . . giving his Assent to their acts of pretended legislation . . . For cutting off our Trade with all parts of the world.' " These are the words of Thomas Barrow, author of *Trade and Empire: The British Customs Service in Colonial America.*[64]

Once Parliament in 1762 and 1763 directed naval vessels into the business of suppressing colonial smugglers, argued another historian, "the British navy suddenly became a greater menace to ordinary colonial commerce than were French vessels." This was because "the laws governing seizures at sea are based on where vessels are found and the papers they carry . . . British naval officers were unfamiliar with trade customs and applied the letter of the regulations given to them . . . As the crews received one half the net proceeds, it was profitable for them to seize colonial ships on purely technical grounds. Trials were in the Admiralty courts, the burden of proof of innocence was upon the owner of the seized vessel."[65] In any event, news of the plans for peacetime customs enforcement by the navy was said to have caused "greater alarm" in Massachusetts than the French capture of Fort William Henry in 1757.[66]

The Customs Act of 1763, in turn, led to North American governors being instructed to step up enforcement, and 20 ships of war, mostly sloops and brigs, took up positions off colonial seaports.[67] Their principal target was molasses smuggling. The old Molasses Act of 1733, rarely enforced, was replaced in 1764 by the Sugar Act, which dropped the duty on a gallon of molasses from six pence to three pence. From New England's standpoint, even three pence seemed prohibitive on a product priced at twelve pence a gallon, but now enforcement gained sharp teeth—and not just additional customs officers and the cannon of the Royal Navy. Besides the Sugar Act's six sections on molasses and sugar taxes, another 40 additional sections were devoted to a flood of customs and commerce revisions adding up to "a constitutional revolution in the relations of the colonies to the home country." Documents, clearances, and fees required, and penalties imposed for violations astounded shipowners and mariners.[68]

Until 1764, Parliament had only looked at North America's oceangoing trade. Now it extended regulation—clearances, fees, and potential fines and seizures—to intercolony traffic. Much of this was coastal trade, including the small wood and lumber boats that operated along New England and Carolina coasts far from any customs house. Such was the harassment that a defendant was required to pay the costs of the suit brought even after being proved innocent of the underlying violation. Worse, before an owner whose vessel had been charged could appear in (admiralty) court, he had to post a £60 bond to cover the costs of the suit.[69] Nor did Parliament's reach stop with applying one or two years' worth of legislative minutiae and new bonding requirements to a lengthy list of cargoes, commodities, and destinations. The Stamp Act enacted in 1765, besides taxing court documents, land conveyances, and the like, took even broader aim at maritime transactions—it taxed all clearance papers, cockets (documents), transfer agreements, bonds for categories of goods, and so forth. When the main body of the Stamp Act was repealed in 1766, substantial portions remained in effect. As for the Sugar Act, most of its customs and commerce provisions remained operative even when the per-gallon duty on molasses was reduced to a bearable single penny. This brief detail should be enough to explain why New Englanders, in particular, were so angry.

The last big clump of legislation—the Townshend Acts passed in 1767—is best remembered for a further set of new taxes that were all withdrawn in 1770, save for the ill-fated one on tea. But in 1767, policy makers also mandated a new American Board of Customs Commissioners and unwisely located it in Boston. There the board became a favorite target of Samuel Adams, the waterfront mob, and eagle-eyed practitioners of tarring and feathering who sought out unpopular customs officials. Three times during the next seven years—in 1768, 1770, and 1774—the board was obliged to take hurried sanctuary at midharbor Castle William, safe under the guns of such naval vessels as were not pursuing suspect merchant ships for half shares in prize money.

Here it is useful to note the different impact of customs militancy within the thirteen individual colonies. "New England and Charleston, South Carolina, were the areas of the most intense [customs] warfare against American trade," according to Oliver Dickerson. "North Carolina, Virginia and Maryland were scarcely molested. There were relatively few complaints from Pennsylvania, New Jersey or New York." The relative quiet in the tobacco provinces reflected the tie-in of the largely Scottish merchants there to the ministry back home. The prominent Patriots singled out in New England and South Carolina—John Hancock and Henry Laurens—had commercial ties to English merchants allied with opposition forces in Parliament.[70] On the other hand, this customs celebrity helped both Hancock and Laurens wind up as presidents of the Continental Congress.

The Crown's provocative agenda may also have had a little-discussed ulterior motive. Serious concern was being expressed in the early 1760s that unless the fast-growing American colonies were quickly reined in, they never could be. Timely coercion was already an issue in 1760 when George III became king. By 1763, senior customs and Board of Trade officials were circulating memoranda like one approved by the king's favorite, the Earl of Bute, that said "His Majesties possessions in North America are so many more times extensive than the Islands of Great Britain, that if they were equally well-inhabited, Great Britain could no longer maintain her dominion over them. It is therefore evidently her Policy, to set bounds to the increment of People, and to the extent of the settlement in that Country."[71] Keeping population near the seacoast and controllable was essential. Nathaniel Ware, the comptroller of customs, opined in 1763 that never could there be a "more favorable opportunity than the present" to achieve the colonies' proper subordination before wartime troops were withdrawn. Otherwise, the northern colonies were within "a very few more years to maturity" and departure.[72]

In 1763, the Treasury reported to the king that the colonies' "vast increase in Territory and Population makes the Proper Regulation of their Trade of immediate Necessity, lest the continuance and extent of the dangerous Evils . . . may render all Attempts to remedy them hereafter infinitely more difficult, if not utterly impracticable."[73] Arguably, this objective of demographic, economic, and commercial constraint can be seen in not just one but a series of actions: the Proclamation Line of 1763, the Customs Revenue Act of 1763, the Currency Act of 1764, the Sugar Act of 1764, and the Stamp Act of 1765. These controversies involved much more than mere constitutional disagreement.

Although this punitive dimension gets little attention, it could consume a chapter, not just a few paragraphs. Sometimes the evidence has a tie to a particular province. One local account, for example, quoted a British secretary of state confiding to a South Carolinian: "We must clip your canvas. You increase too fast in shipping. You will soon be too powerful on the water to be governed by the mother country."[74]

What tobacco was to Chesapeake sensitivities, sugar—or rather molasses, its principal by-product—was to coastal New England. Each year hundreds of ships from Salem, Boston, Newport, Providence, New London, and elsewhere carried fish, cheese, barreled beef and pork, lumber, and horses to the French West Indies at considerable profit, returning with great quantities of molasses, from which Yankee factories would distill ordinary rum, that famous elixir of English-speaking seamen. British sugar colonies like Barbados, Jamaica, and St. Kitts also produced molasses, but much less, and because they used it to produce high-quality rum, little was left for New England. Growers in the French West Indies, however, produced greater quantities of sugar and also a larger output of molasses. On top of which, they had little permissible use for it because the home government in Paris prohibited rum making to protect French brandy producers. Massachusetts and Rhode Island found temptation irresistible.

These were the two provinces most intensely involved in smuggling and rum distilling. Most of their ships were locally owned, not British owned. The Bay Colony housed over 100 rum distilleries, tiny Rhode Island fully 30. Molasses was the cornerstone of its provincial economy.[75] Massachusetts was more diversified, albeit particularly committed to its symbolic fisheries. Coastal and West Indies ship carriage, lumber cutting and milling, shipbuilding, fishing, and rum production were the province's major enterprises. All five priorities converged in trading with—and smuggling molasses back from—the French West Indies.

Two thousand miles to the south, the French islands craved New England's lumber, cheap codfish, cheese, beef, and other provisions, less costly than shipments from Bordeaux or Nantes. On the trip back, Yankee captains took mostly molasses. The British West Indies, as indicated, were a much poorer fit for Salem, Boston, Newport, and Providence. The Rhode Island Assembly explained all of this in a 1764 remonstrance to the Crown. Of the 14,000 hogsheads of molasses the colony imported each year, only 2,500 came from the British Caribbean. In fact, all the molasses in the British islands, provincial legislators showed, wouldn't be enough to support Rhode Island alone for a single year.[76] The new British customs policy, they contended, would put Rhode Island half out of business. Rum production was less vital to Massachusetts, but vessels could not profitably sail to the West Indies without a return cargo. This meant that the Bay Colony would lose by far the largest—and essential—market for its lower grades of codfish.

The New England provinces were an uncomfortable fit in the British imperial economy. Masts aside, they produced no strategic crop—by 1775, even naval stores came mostly from the Carolinas. Indeed, New England essentially reiterated Britain's own dominant portrait: maritime carriage, fishing, livestock, grain, and (after independence) manufacturing. Some 30 percent of the British Empire's merchant fleet was built in America, the largest portion of it in New England. Much like Old England, New

England lived by the sea, on the sea, and from the sea. In fairness, the authorities in London had been well aware of this, trying (unsuccessfully) to nurture a New England naval stores industry between 1690 and 1720. By the 1760s and 1770s, they were losing patience.

By the mid-1760s, in short, the effect of the Sugar Act and the heavy-handed new customs practices was to challenge the viability of the New England economy and with it the region's ability to buy large quantities of British manufactures. But if British policy makers were losing patience, so were Boston radicals.

The analogy to the Chesapeake has merit. New England, too, had a vital commerce in which policy resentments mingled with cost pressures to instill a pre-Revolutionary dislike of British practices. Instead of tobacco, currency, and debt being the catalyst, maritime New England's ire involved trade, the mishandled duty on molasses, and malevolent customs enforcement. In the early 1770s, Rhode Island had been the hot spot of Yankee customs conflict. But by 1774, Massachusetts had become the epicenter of a broader crisis.

As with the belated partial liberalization of London's currency regulation, a less intrusive customs enforcement in 1772–1773 was too little too late.[77] In any event, New England and South Carolina ships would soon be bound away for old, familiar West Indian ports to smuggle back the ultimate in prohibited French goods: gunpowder, ordnance, and stands of arms fresh from King Louis's arsenals.

This is not to ignore New England's secondary interest in manufacturing, or for that matter the considerable attention paid by New York, Pennsylvania, and Maryland to British crimping of the fledgling American iron industry. Nor is it to pass over the clash of British land policy and Patriot speculation. These, too, were objects of colonial demand for economic self-determination. But they did not rank with the two great complaints that motivated New England and the tobacco provinces.

The Economic Constituencies and Opponents of Revolution

As the Revolution gathered momentum in 1775, frustrated Loyalists singled out two religious denominations—Congregationalists and Presbyterians—for being rebels and republicans almost by doctrine. They likewise identified three particular groups of economic malcontents: smugglers, evasion-minded debtors, and speculators in western lands.

The religious finger-pointing was logical enough. Across the thirteen colonies, some 70 to 80 percent of Presbyterians took the Patriot side, and New England Congregationalists might have been even more stalwart. The broad economic stereotypes require more clarification. Merchants with a smuggling avocation during the prewar decade took the rebel side overwhelmingly in Massachusetts. Native-born speculators in western lands lopsidedly favored the Revolution, excepting men whose opportunity came from positions under the Crown. As for debtors, although widespread inflammation against creditors helped to breed a *climate* of Revolution, gauging Patriot-versus-Loyalist ratios in so large a group would be guesswork. That being said, economic circumstances, commitments, and vocations were important in guiding loyalties. The bigger the stake or vulnerability, the more heavily it usually weighed—and the more likely economics was to counter religious or ethnic ties.

British placemen and officials—from governors, attorneys general, and justices down to retired army officers and a host of lesser Crown officeholders—were obvious vocational pillars of Loyalism. Appointive positions were well salaried, and in hundreds of cases—in the colonies, as in Britain—one man could hold and be paid for three or even four offices. Judge Edward Winslow of Plymouth, Massachusetts, "was the local customs collector, the registrar of the Court of Probate, the Clerk of the Common Pleas and General Sessions of the Peace, as well as 'first magistrate in the county of Plymouth.'" The ubiquitous Lieutenant Governor Thomas Hutchinson—Patriots nicknamed him Sir Thomas Graspall—was also justice, member of the Council, and captain of Castle William. North Carolina's Edmund Fanning collected pay as town commissioner for Hillsborough, public register, assemblyman for Orange County, and Crown prosecutor.[78] New York, being the Crown's principal administrative center, had a concentration of placemen. South Carolina was notorious for royal appointments—the courts and Governor's Council, in particular—going to Britons at the expense of Carolinians. At one point in the 1760s, the locally born held only two Council seats out of ten. The archetypal placeman was Egerton Leigh, attorney general, admiralty court judge, and Council member.

Notwithstanding Patrick Henry, James Otis, and other Patriotic firebrands, the most prominent lawyers, especially in commercial centers like Philadelphia, New York, and Boston, were drawn to political power and influence, not to the local Sons of Liberty. Later British compensation to displaced American Loyalists identified 55 lawyers and 81 physicians.[79] Doctors, too, had practices centered on the wealthy and influential. Quite a few Church of England clergy—for example, Samuel Seabury and John Sayre in Connecticut—doubled as physicians.[80]

During the 1760s and early 1770s, British officials and royal governors dwelt on enlarging the provincial patronage pool—the civil list, in that era's parlance—and having it funded automatically out of revenues collected in America. Samuel Adams, the Patriot faction's leading Machiavellian, feared that such patronage could dangerously enlarge Crown influence. Indeed, "chains of interest" flourished. Beyond Boston, chains in Massachusetts centered on courthouse and lawyer cliques in the Springfield area—the so-called River Gods—as well as in Marshfield and Plymouth to the southeast.[81] Well-connected Congregationalist as well as Anglican "friends of government" could be drawn in, as in southwestern Connecticut towns like Ridgefield, where Congregational Church friends and relations of influential New Haven Crown prosecutor Jared Ingersoll allied with local Anglicans.

One notable Philadelphia axis—Loyalists who worshipped at the fashionable First Presbyterian Church—grouped around lawyers who shared training at London's Middle Temple, relations and close associates of former Pennsylvania chief justice William Allen, and the well-connected Shippen clan. Members of the city's Second and Third Presbyterian churches, by contrast, were overwhelmingly on the Patriot side.[82] Dozens of other relationships could be found up and down the seaboard, helping to explain seeming religious anomalies.

Certain commercial niches also bred Loyalists. Substantial merchants, especially in the major cities and the fifteen or so towns with populations of 4,000 to 8,000, had beliefs forged since the 1760s in the heat of importation and boycott acrimony. Merchants' loyalties, when not pulled by ethnicity or religion, were often swayed by specialties and by British commercial relationships, to which we will shortly return.

Many people in coastal towns had maritime loyalties. Shipbuilding, along with iron working and rum distillation, were the three enterprises deemed industries by British yardsticks. Two of these, shipbuilding and rum, were at their most important in New England. In that region, maritime vocations made most participants rebels—hostile to British customs agents and regulations, furious at the Royal Navy over impressment, and sympathetic to smugglers, even if they themselves rarely indulged.

As for ordinary seamen, whose sentiments will be examined in the next chapter's urban focus, sweeping political judgments must be somewhat hedged. During the Revolution, thousands served on Tory and Loyalist privateers operating out of New York and lesser occupied seaports. Arch-maritime Nantucket tried to be neutral. However, between 1763 and the outbreak of the Revolution, seamen leaned very much to the Patriot side—participating in waterfront mobs, resisting press-gangs, putting up Liberty poles, or burning revenue boats.

Militiamen, of whom the thirteen colonies mustered some 70,000 in 1775, often took politics from those activities, as we will see. Loyalist-leaning individuals, obliged to serve in the militia in a Patriot-dominated region, if not converted at least learned to keep quiet. Enlisted men in Philadelphia organized themselves into class-conscious associations and played a driving role in radical politics.

Another large group of radicals in Boston, Philadelphia, New York, and Charleston were artisans (many of them middle class), "mechanics," and journeymen. Unskilled laborers were typically put in a different category. The next chapter will have more detail, but in all four cities men in skilled to semiskilled vocations were a major pro-Revolutionary force by 1775. As the big seaports grew between 1750 and 1775, tax and household surveys documented a rising stratification by wealth and income. Artisans—the description then stretched to include architects, newspaper publishers, painters, and musicians—generally lost ground to the richest percentiles and felt buffeted by hard economic times. Whiffs of what later generations would call class consciousness came into play. Artisans and mechanics were drawn to the rebel side by several factors—dislike for the rich merchants who sold imported goods from Britain, self-interest in promoting American manufactures, and enthusiasm for boycotts and other political activities aimed at replacing British-made luxury goods with simpler, less expensive products made locally.

Farmers, small or substantial, pursued the dominant vocation in a late eighteenth century that was still overwhelmingly agricultural. Their politics would have varied widely with community, religion, geography, and relative prosperity. Growers of crops enumerated by Britain—tobacco, indigo, rice, naval stores—will be considered separately. A different set of variables affected unhappy tenants of New York's great landowners or patroons. Some mid–Hudson Valley tenants angry at their great Whig landlords—in Livingston Manor, for example—followed dissatisfaction to the Tory side.

Unhappy tenants of landed Tories like the Philipses, Bayards, and DeLan-
ceys probably reacted the other way. Landowners whose western land speculations were jeopardized by British policies mostly went against the Crown.

Local patterns and market dependence could also persuade. Prosperous,
long-established commercial farming areas adjacent to Manhattan and
Philadelphia were conservative and Tory-leaning in 1775. Partly guided by
distinctive cultures—the Quakers of Greater Philadelphia or the old-line
Dutch-speaking farm communities circling Manhattan—they were content to supply British occupiers.

The hinterland saw other influences. Farmers whose westward migration
had been thwarted or delayed by the Proclamation Line in the 1760s—or
who feared British-led Indian raids a decade later—would mostly have
taken the Patriot side. So-called Peace Germans—Amish, Mennonites,
Moravians, Dunkers, et al. who tilled some of the richest lands in Pennsylvania and central North Carolina—wanted to avoid taking sides. Congregationalist farmers in stony New England would have been rebels. By
contrast, neutralism shading into Loyalism flourished in parts of the Carolina backcountry, where settlers nurtured greater grudges against coastal
plantation elites than against a faraway George III.

The precarious side of farm economics, particularly where tobacco cultivation quickly exhausted the soil, pushed many wealthy landowners and
planters to enlarge their income through land investments. Virginians were
lured into the various companies pursuing large grants in the Ohio Country, Kentucky, Tennessee, Indiana, and even the Great Lakes. Farther
north, others looked elsewhere, but anxious Virginia investors reducing
their dependence on tobacco and hoping to pay off their debts through land
profits outweighed any others politically. George Washington himself explained the emphasis: "the greatest estates we have in this Colony were
made . . . by taking up and purchasing at very low rates the rich back Lands
which were thought nothing of in those days, but are now the most valuable
Lands we possess." By 1775, Washington, Jefferson, Mason, Arthur Lee, and
Patrick Henry were looking and investing beyond the mountains.[83]

Planters living in Virginia's Northern Neck or the adjoining Piedmont
were especially drawn to the Ohio Company and supported its interests,
which contributed to both the French and Indian War and Lord Dunmore's
1774 fight with the Shawnee. One early-twentieth-century Virginia historian went so far as to claim that "for Virginians, the Revolution was in part
a war of agrarian conquest; the British land system was broken down; ter-

ritory to the west was brought again under the control of Virginia, and virgin lands were opened to settlement. So unanimous was the support of the Revolution by the agricultural class in Virginia that scarcely a loyalist was to be found among the planters."[84]

Debt pressure and land hunger drove Virginians into radical rhetoric. Historian Bruce Mann has explained that "the image of debtors as slaves was a common one before the Revolution, although almost exclusively in the tobacco regions of the Chesapeake . . . they [planters] clearly felt enslaved, both by their British creditors, whose duns threatened their personal liberty, and by Parliament, whose duns threatened their political liberties. Hence the spectacle, so anomalous to modern sensibilities as well as to contemporary British observers, of slaveholders denouncing British conspiracies to reduce them to slavery."[85]

Mercantile loyalties varied by specialty. The broad merchant category— participants also edged into ship owning, loan making, store keeping, land speculating, and manufacturing ventures—was among the largest in influence and political involvement. Historian Arthur Schlesinger, Sr., in his *The Colonial Merchants and the American Revolution,* correctly emphasized their 1760s importance but generally made only a twofold distinction. He differentiated between Loyalist-leaning dry-goods importers and Patriot-tending "wet goods" merchants likely to trade with the West Indies and deal in rum, molasses, and smuggled provisions.[86] In general, Progressive historians overlooked the revealing subcategories—importer from Britain, shopkeeper, vendue auctioneer, Scottish factor, goods smuggler from Holland, and so forth—that best explained individual political loyalties.

To begin with, merchants, compared to other economic groups, were so impacted by most of our dozen issues that *not* taking sides would have been difficult. Those in the large seaports, where from 1765 to 1774 imports and protests were constant topics, would have been buffeted by a cross-current of currency, debt, trade regulation, taxes, and customs matters. Most of all, they would have confronted nonimportation, boycotts, and antiluxury drives, and at least in the North, no other vocations would have been as influential or as well represented in town meetings, chambers of commerce, associations, and the like.

Taking the major cities in 1775, Loyalism was significant in Boston's mercantile community and prevalent in New York's. Philadelphia's economic climate was unusual because so many established merchants were Quakers unhappy with the independence movement but hesitant over open

Loyalism (at least prior to the British occupation of 1777–1778). Few generalized statements satisfactorily explain the political behavior of all three merchant communities.

Loyalties in Boston have been well parsed by historian John W. Tyler, whose sophisticated survey of the entire group by politics, religion, wealth, and specialization was further polished through cross-checking with confidential private insurance records. This way he found out who was sailing to what port with what cargo and bringing back what in return. Out of 318, 118 became committed Loyalists, 37 remained "scrupulously neutral," and 163 actively sided with the Patriots.[87] Given the lopsidedly patriotic sentiment in Massachusetts as a whole, these choices were hardly overwhelming.

In New York, a majority of merchants apparently took the Loyalist side. Among members of the New York Chamber of Commerce in 1775, 57 were Loyalists, 21 were neutrals, and only 26 were Whigs. The Committee of Fifty-one, a 1774 association, included 26 Loyalists, 7 neutrals, and 18 Whigs. No breakdown exists of specialties among New York merchants, but one chronicler emphasized two groups taking the Patriot side: persons involved in sugar refining and distilling, and those connected to the West Indies with a reputation for smuggling. By contrast, the most conspicuous Loyalist merchants held official positions (especially on the Council), had thrived on British contracts during the French and Indian War, traded principally with England, Scotland, or Ireland, or managed branches of British firms.[88]

Loyalists and neutrals also outnumbered Patriots in Philadelphia's mercantile community. Religious divisions explained much of the split, according to the principal researcher.[89] Anglican and Quaker merchants had the expensive carriages; less affluent Scotch-Irish Presbyterians led the minority who were Patriots. The long-established Quaker merchant community took a largely neutral or pro-British position.[90] During the late 1760s, the split deepened: "Resonant fear of Presbyterian hegemony was a major factor in the Quaker merchants' view of the Revolutionary movement. They perceived an inexorable logic to the Revolutionary process that had nothing to do with commercial problems, parliamentary taxation or ministerial tyranny. Like their forebears of the seventeenth century, the Presbyterians were evidently using discontent over constitutional issues to seize power for themselves and deny their fellow Christians freedom of conscience."[91]

Unfortunately, the New York or Philadelphia studies do not detail the mercantile community by subcategories as in Boston. More broadly, Patriotic commitment in Boston was greatest (two to one) among the West Indian, southern European, and coastal traders, many of whom smuggled, as well as among rum distillers (who profited from smuggled cheap molasses). These findings do match the similar but looser conclusions for New York. Patriotic views in Boston were also high among the three dozen merchants whose primary activities were hard to define or unknown. Tyler surmised that "involvement with West Indian and southern European ports at the fringes of the mercantile system probably fed gradual realization of how much their interests lay beyond the empire." Boston Loyalism, conversely, was highest among merchants in dry goods, invariably imported from Britain, and among factors (many Scottish) who represented British mercantile firms.[92]

For both Boston and Philadelphia, the experts agreed in emphasizing the role played by the various associations, nonimportation quarrels, and boycotts, especially in the heated climate of 1770. Many moderates who had supported nonimportation in 1765 balked at continuing in 1770, and many of these eventually wound up on the Loyalist side.[93] The divisions of 1770 were prophetic.

Religious and ethnic factors were important enough in all three cities that the commercial cleavages generally illustrate the divisions stressed in Chapter 3. Congregationalist merchants in Boston were Patriots by three to one while Anglicans were Loyalist by more than two to one. In New York, the Loyalist majority of merchants was disproportionately Anglican. In Philadelphia, the Anglican third of the mercantile community tilted Loyalist in 1774 and 1775. In ethnic terms, Boston's Scottish merchants, almost all of them foreign born or representatives of British firms, were overwhelmingly Loyalist.[94]

As a further nuance—an important one, to be sure—Scots, most of them representatives of British concerns, proved heavily Loyalist in every seaport. Philadelphia had relatively few in 1775. However, in 1777, after Virginia's House of Delegates (the renamed House of Burgesses) expelled Scottish merchants unwilling to take a loyalty oath, they flocked to the now-British-held Quaker City. By one account, occupied Philadelphia soon held 115.[95]

Distinguishing between Scottish and Scotch-Irish ethnoreligious patterns is essential in four other southern mercantile centers—Baltimore, Maryland; Norfolk, Virginia; Wilmington, North Carolina, and Charleston, South Carolina. Baltimore's merchant community, little involved with tobacco, was led by Scotch-Irish of the Patriot faction with ties to their coreligionists in Philadelphia.[96] Norfolk's merchants, by contrast, were disproportionately Scots, mostly tobacco-connected, who represented British firms. Of these, many were expelled. Of Virginia's wartime property confiscations, fully one third by value were imposed on the "hated Scotch merchants of Norfolk."[97]

In North Carolina, a majority of merchants seem to have been Loyalist, many of them Scots who exported tobacco and lumber and imported British manufactures. In December 1774, one of them became the first North Carolinian charged for refusing to sign the Association. He was John Hamilton, the province's most important merchant, who at his own expense later raised a Loyalist unit, the Royal North Carolina Regiment.[98] Charleston's merchant community was also significantly Scottish, although less so than Virginia's. Most of the Scots were Loyalists. It is usually imperative to distinguish between Scottish Presbyterians and Scotch-Irish Presbyterians.

Although nineteenth-century and early-twentieth-century historians discussed these relationships openly, that is no longer true. The circa 1775 politics of Scottish tobacco merchants in Maryland, Virginia, and the Carolinas—matched by four or five southern Loyalist regiments formed with substantially Scottish enlistments—is a neglected facet of the Revolution's opening years. Hostility to tobacco traders, factors, and merchants in Virginia and adjacent northeastern Carolina seems to have crystallized around the prominence of Scots. This, however, echoed a similar controversy in England over the success Scots had achieved since the 1750s in commerce, imperial administration, and the British Army. Virginians and Carolinians of English descent, angry at perceived favoritism to Scots, simultaneously seethed over Parliament's disinterest in colonists' proud claims to the "rights of Englishmen." In any event, these nuances may explain why merchants in Virginia and much of North and South Carolina were pushed or cast aside and Whig planters of English descent took control of the Revolution in these locales.

If farming per se was rarely a force in politics and loyalty, a significant personal or community involvement in the production of certain commodities (and manufactures) usually was. Tobacco planters were so lopsidedly on the Patriot side by spring 1776 that even would-be Loyalists like William Byrd III and Thomas, Lord Fairfax, Washington's great early patron, quietly retired to their plantations. Parenthetically, one economic historian concluded that "tobacco-growing regions tended to be more revolutionary than the wheat-growing regions in the same states."[99]

South Carolina's rice planters favored the Patriot side in 1775–1776 by at least two to one, but there was no real nose counting. Greater Loyalism probably prevailed among growers of indigo, the province's second-ranking export behind rice. Indigo was the enumerated crop more dependent on British bounties, and its cultivation in the Carolina low country took off only in the 1740s, when wartime conditions interrupted the usual flow from French and Spanish colonies, indigo being a dyestuff vital to Britain's all-important textile industry. The volume of southern indigo exports, mostly Carolinian, ballooned from 5,000 pounds in 1746 to nearly 1.5 million pounds in 1774.[100] The effects on Carolina cultivator loyalties circa 1775 have received little attention, but concern over losing the British market would have mattered. Moses Kirkland, a Tory leader, had a major indigo plantation, and some fleeing Tories used indigo as currency.[101]

Naval stores—pitch, tar, and resin—principally came to Britain from North Carolina. Much less important than tobacco, rice, and indigo, they seem to have affected few loyalties, even in the Cape Fear section of North Carolina, where North Carolinians got the name "Tar Heels" from the sticky residue. Cape Fear patriots were so militant that in July 1775, when whale-hunting Nantucket tried to become neutral, the local association cut off any export of "all kinds of Provision" to the Massachusetts island.[102]

To the north, the Crown's policy of reserving New England's thickest and tallest white pines—"king's trees"—for the Royal Navy stirred considerable resentment in Massachusetts, New Hampshire, and the District of Maine. Successive eighteenth-century White Pine Acts did not merely specify that marked mast trees (usually over 30 inches in diameter) were untouchable; they interdicted the cutting of *any* white pine tree, except under naval license.[103] Full enforcement, one chronicler noted, could have prevented settlers from clearing land or using even small white pine logs to build a cabin.

Northern New Englanders fumed at the handful of contractors holding mast contracts, but widespread illicit logging and milling took place. The principal specialist concluded that price paid for mercantilism was in "the hardened opposition to British rule nurtured by the forest legislation on that first American frontier. When [former New Hampshire governor] John Wentworth, in 1778, told his superiors what were the shortcomings of the forest legislation, he might have gone further and emphasized the folly of a policy which drove a wedge between the colonists and the Crown."[104]

By contrast, whale oil—enumerated and bountied by Britain—tied its leading producers in coastal New England, the islanders of Nantucket, to their lucrative transatlantic market. Nantucket's 1775 attempt at political neutrality infuriated both Massachusetts and the Continental Congress, but whaling in that era of spermaceti candles and oil lamps was a substantial and lucrative business. "From 1771 to 1775," wrote one chronicler, "Nantucket accounted for 50 percent of colonial whaling ships, and 70 percent of the colonial catch . . . Nantucket whalemen annually sent out 150 ships, totalling 16,075 tons and employing over 2000 seamen." By way of profit, "whale oil accounted for 52.5 percent of all sterling earned by direct exports to Great Britain from New England between 1768 and 1772."[105] Tiny Nantucket represented a prime example of mercantilist dependence.

Another British mandate—the 1764 requirement that pig and bar iron be shipped only to Britain—annoyed ironmasters from New York to Virginia but particularly offended Pennsylvania, the center of colonial iron making. By the mid-1770s, about one seventh of the world's iron production was coming from North America, and two generations of British policy makers had discussed the mother country's best approach. According to Pennsylvania iron historian Arthur Bining, as early as 1729, British forge owners had approached Parliament to draw up legislation "providing that all forges in the colonies should be destroyed, and no new ones set up."[106] However, the colonies' agents in London blocked action. By 1735, British ironware producers followed up with a proposal to suppress all secondary iron manufacture in America. Fifteen years later Parliament hammered out a resolution. This was the Iron Act of 1750, which eliminated duties on colonial iron sent to London but required that after June 1750 the colonies could erect no additional slitting mills, plating forges, and steel furnaces (although existing ones could continue to operate). Provincial governors were instructed to monitor compliance, but Bining suggests much was never reported.[107]

Not a few large iron investors failed. However, those who carried on mostly took the Patriot side, especially in Pennsylvania. Ironmasters George Taylor, James Smith, George Ross, and James Wilson were all signers of the Declaration of Independence, and three other ironmasters were members of the Pennsylvania Constitution Convention.[108] Much of Pennsylvania's pre-Revolutionary iron output was shipped down the Susquehanna to the port of Baltimore, where the Royal Navy kept watch. In 1765, right after iron was enumerated, one local merchant reported to a colleague that British men-of-war would "not suffer our vessels with iron to pass without a regular clearance the expense of which being so heavy the iron will not bear it."[109] Ironmasters, said Bining, stood for the American cause "almost without exception."[110] As for New York, Patriots had a lesser edge among that province's iron makers: "Not all of them supported the Revolution, but few opposed it vehemently. Most ranged politically across a spectrum from passive loyalism and neutralism to Revolutionary commitment. Overall, neutrals predominated, outnumbering the patriots by two to one. The patriots, however, outnumbered the identifiable loyalists by five to three."[111]

Economic constituencies in the American Revolution must weigh in any practical analysis. The very different responses to mercantilism between whale oil producers and irate pig and bar iron makers, for example, suggest less interest in imperial theory than attention to industry-by-industry economics. As for the role of economics in constituency formation, degrees of proof can be found in each of the dozen economic issues that stirred pre-Revolutionary unhappiness. The legal acrimony surrounding "taxation without representation" fell away quickly enough when nonimportation and nonexportation moved to the forefront in 1774; and whether these measures were constitutional seemed to matter hardly at all.

CHAPTER 5

Urban Radicalism and the Tide of Revolution

In Philadelphia . . . 1,682 of the 3,350 taxable males in 1772 were artisans. Their political weight was critical in any contested election in the first two-thirds of the eighteenth century. And in the wake of the Seven Years' War, as the imperial crisis unfolded, they played a dynamic role in the formation of a revolutionary movement in the largest city of British North America.

Gary Nash, *The Origins of American Radicalism*, 1984

The people of the waterfront played a central role in the revolutionary conflict, first as the shock troops of the mobs of the resistance movement, and then as combatants at sea. This participation infused the revolution with an egalitarianism it otherwise would not have had.

Paul A. Gilje, *Liberty on the Waterfront*, 2004

The lower sort [in Philadelphia], committed to both patriotism and egalitarianism, found its instrument of political empowerment in the militia and its political voice in the Committee of Privates.

Steven Rosswurm, *Arms, Country and Class*, 1987

Radicalism can just as easily be rural as urban, as we will see of the American backcountry in 1775. Frontier and tenant-farmer belligerence could match that of the waterfront. Nevertheless, the colonies' principal cities—Boston, New York, Philadelphia, and Charleston—played unique pre-Revolutionary roles as the vortex of communications, opinion molding, ruling elites, political transformation, and incipient nation building. More than other locales, urban economies also reflected the radicalism of angry seamen, the rise of labor, and the increasing polarization within a great empire.

The forces radicalizing Philadelphia between 1774 and 1776 would exercise double influence, swaying not just one province but the climate in which the Continental Congress, meeting there, struggled toward independence and nationhood. Choosing the meetinghouse of the Company of Carpenters as the initial venue, not the grander colonial State House, itself augured a changing of the guard.

Back in 1700 or 1710, the four cities had been less distinguishable from their hinterlands. Boston, then the largest with 8,000 residents, was strongly Puritan and English-sprung, just like the adjacent shores of Massachusetts Bay. Among New York's population of 5,000, roughly half still spoke Dutch, as did many farmers and burghers nearby. Philadelphia was small—less than two decades old in 1700—and soberly Quaker like its trim environs. Charleston held 2,000 people, but its vulnerability to Spanish and French attackers still weighed on its growth.

Urban Political Crucibles

By 1765, the French and Indian War had brought tens of thousands of British soldiers, swollen payrolls, lucrative supply contracts, and much new building. Philadelphia, now boasting 18,000 inhabitants, had vaulted ahead, while Boston (15,000) was still in doldrums that dated back to the 1740s. Too many Boston men had been killed in the various wars, and part of its shipbuilding, cod fishing, and trading had migrated to other, smaller Massachusetts ports. In New York, most of a population enlarged to 15,000 now spoke English, reflecting wartime enrichment and the city's new eminence as the administrative and military center of British North America. Charleston, enlarged from 2,000 people to almost 11,000, was no longer a mainland offshoot of England's Caribbean sugar islands. It had become the maritime and commercial hub of a British lower Atlantic coast that stretched from North Carolina through Georgia to the former Spanish tropical fortress of St. Augustine and the Florida keys.

Not all was well. The wartime boom gave way to a postwar slump in the 1760s, and currency shrinkage imperiled several provincial economies. However, the population increase continued. As the following table shows, Boston lagged. But as 1775 approached, the other three cities were completing eras of geographic and residential expansion.

The Four Major American Cities: Populations 1750–1775[1]

	1750	1760	1770	1775 (or other year)
Boston	15,890	15,631	15,520	16,450 (1771)
New York	13,300	15,000	21,000	25,000 (1775)
Philadelphia	13,926	18,598	26,789	32,073 (1775)
Charleston	8,200	9,700	11,500	12,800 (1774)

Broad forces drove population growth. As the overall thirteen-colony population soared from 500,000 in 1700 to almost 3 million in 1775, the urban centers did no more than keep pace. In fact, their combined growth during that period—from 30,000 to 90,000—represented a *slower* expansion. Many rural districts, especially in the backcountry, were filling in more rapidly.

Immigration directly from Europe also swelled the cities, especially Philadelphia, the center of German and Irish disembarkation. British trade was booming, especially that with North America. Between 1700 and 1774, exports from the thirteen to Britain increased from roughly £300,000 to £1,845,000 while exports from Britain to North America soared from roughly £200,000 to £2,843,000.[2] North America's principal seaports profited handsomely.

At the seat of empire, population growth in England and Wales was much slower—from 5 million in 1700 to perhaps 6.5 million in 1760 and not quite 8 million in 1775. Seaports and manufacturing centers led the British advance. In later centuries, Americans would contend that by 1775 Philadelphia, supposedly home to 35,000, had become the "Second City" of the British Empire behind London. That was an exaggeration; Philadelphia was not second.[3] In Scotland, Edinburgh was larger, and probably Glasgow. In the England of the mid-to-late 1770s, a period of rapid urban growth, Bristol's population had climbed above 50,000; Birmingham, Manchester, and Liverpool were all in the 30,000-to-40,000 range.[4] Outpacing the leading American cities, Birmingham, Manchester, and Liverpool had all trebled or quadrupled their head count during the eighteenth century.

Their upsurge displayed the fullest benefit of Britain's Atlantic empire and its booming trade and manufacturing. Meanwhile, another similarity deserves note—the emergence of British and American urban centers as seedbeds of political, economic, and legal reform.

On both sides of the Atlantic, burgeoning English-speaking cities rode a cultural and economic wave that concentrated its rewards principally among exemplars of the imperial system—great landowners, capitalists, merchants, manufacturers and importers of favored commodities, those in the professions, government officials, and military officers. Tensions rose accordingly. As overall wealth mushroomed, the share enjoyed by tenant farmers, laborers, seamen, spinners, journeymen, and artisans declined, sometimes sharply. The distributions of wealth circa 1775 identified by economic historians for Philadelphia, New York, and Boston were not too divergent from those in London, Bristol, and Liverpool. Moreover, as we will see in Chapter 16, major English urban areas where middle-class voters enjoyed the franchise in 1774–1775 were often those most sympathetic to the angry colonies. Bristol, the great seaport, sent the pro-American Edmund Burke to Parliament. Middlesex, the populous county abutting London, sent the radical John Wilkes, who was generally pro-American. In Norwich, until midcentury England's third city, the pro-American element of the Whig party wore blue and buff—the uniform of the American Continental Line—as local colors.[5]

The English word *radical* took on a new connotation during the nineteenth century that departed from its tamer eighteenth-century association with parliamentary reform. Use of the bolder meanings to characterize the American Revolution can be confusing. To one historian of American radicalism, the impact of English "plebeian culture"—the customs, traditions, and rituals of the laboring populations—was discernible in the American Revolution, for example, in the practice of tarring and feathering. But it was not a source of political radicalism in the future sense.[6]

As for the touchy theme of *class,* Gary Nash, a chronicler of colonial America, allowed that "eighteenth-century society, to be sure, had not yet reached the historical stage of a mature class formation." However, because simply ignoring class would create a different problem, he emphasized new horizontal differentiations rather than vertical divisions in urban society.[7] Differently put, pre-Revolutionary America had many social and economic strains, divisions, and grudges worth attention, even if the use of class terminology is premature.

In discussing what behavior is urban and what is not, this chapter's premise is uncomplicated. Seamen, mariners, artisans, and mechanics were disproportionately concentrated in the major cities. The principal 1774–1775 strategic importance of the militia was Boston centered, and the greatest radicalization of militiamen, marked by proliferation of committees, came in Philadelphia.

The Sons of Neptune

Nothing better confirms the early and provocative participation in the American Revolution by seamen, ex-privateer captains, smugglers, and waterfront mobs than its impact on everyday parlance—the salt-sprayed antecedents of so many important 1774–1776 terms and practices. The gamut runs from hot tar Liberty Jackets to Liberty Poles and briny Tea Parties. Boston was indeed the epicenter. However, "Jack Tar" also left a trail of conflict in New York, Philadelphia, Charleston, and scores of lesser seaports like Falmouth, Salem, Gloucester, Newburyport, Marblehead, Newport, Providence, New Haven, New London, Annapolis, Norfolk, Wilmington, and New Bern.[8]

Tarring and feathering, to begin with, had earlier English origins. King Richard I, bound for the Holy Land in 1189, declared that anyone committing a crime on the ship would be tarred, feathered, and put ashore. Mentions of tarring and feathering are found in *Hakluyt's Voyages* (1589) and *Holinshed's Chronicles* (1587).[9] The practice in America reached its peak of notoriety in the New England colonies between 1768 and 1770 as a communal punishment, then spread elsewhere. A biographer of Samuel Adams vividly evoked the skin-shredding and blistering process: "Pine tar was a familiar commodity in colonial America; it was used to waterproof ships, sails and rigging. A thick, acrid dark brown or black liquid, tar was obtained by roasting mature pine trees over an open-pit fire and distilling the bituminous substance that boiled out. Some victims were fortunate enough to be tarred over their clothes or protected by a frock or sheet. Others were stripped, and the tar was brushed, poured or 'bedawbed' over their bare skin. When heated, tar would blister the skin . . . After the tar came the feathers, also a familiar commodity in British North America."[10]

To add insult to sometimes crippling injury, a victim was often carted through a principal street of his town—very few were women—and subjected to raucous jeering and mockery. Middle-class Whigs found tarring and feathering objectionable, but sailors, in particular, found it appropriate. When Boston customs official John Malcolm was given a Liberty Jacket in

1774 by a crowd "heavy with sailors," they cited not only his brutality and injustice but his "having seized vessels on account of sailors having a bottle or two of [smuggled Dutch] gin on board."[11] Rough payback they counted as fair play.

Liberty Trees or Liberty Poles also had maritime origins, often having been ships' masts. Boston led in 1765 with a famous Liberty Tree, a large 120-year-old elm, identified for the populace by a plaque secured with the large deck nails used by shipyards. It became a favorite rendezvous.[12] Charleston also had a Liberty Tree that served as a meeting place—a giant live oak, the iron-wooded pride of low-country shipbuilders. New York, however, had a succession of Liberty Poles, generally put up by seamen and torn down by British soldiers, rivals with little use for each other. The city's fourth Liberty Pole (58 feet high), erected by seamen in 1767, survived until January 13, 1770. On that date, British regulars from the Sixteenth Regiment split the pole with explosives, brought it down, and sawed it into pieces.[13] This led to what New York historians recall as "the Battle of Golden Hill."

On January 19, atop the crest of nearby John Street, cutlass-wielding and club-carrying seamen and workers, led by Isaac Sears, the former privateer captain who ran the local Sons of Liberty, met bayonet-armed redcoats of the Sixteenth. By one account, "the ensuing battle of Golden Hill—perhaps the first head-on clash between colonists and redcoats of the Revolution—resulted in numerous injuries and one fatality, a seaman who was run through with a bayonet." A second eruption came the next day on Nassau Street, "when a large party of seamen, fed up with the loss of jobs to military personnel and vowing to revenge the death of a fellow Jack Tar the day before, came to blows with some soldiers."[14]

A month later Sears and the Sons of Liberty put up a fifth pole, another great mast (some 80 feet) carried down from an East River shipyard. Well sunk and ironclad at its base, this one survived until October 1776, cut down only after British forces regained Manhattan. Other towns with poles included dozens in Massachusetts, along with seaports like Newport and Savannah. Providence, Rhode Island, like Boston and Charleston, preferred a Liberty Tree.

New York's battle on Golden Hill was followed just weeks later by the Boston Massacre of March 1770. This, too, reflected the growing animosities between British regulars and the waterfront mobs. Part of the ill will involved job competition—how off-duty soldiers took work at rates that undercut local wages, sometimes by as much as 50 percent. Before the Golden Hill fight, seamen had gone around the area, driving away soldiers with clubs and warning employers against rehiring them. John Adams called their mutual animosity such that "they fight as naturally when they meet, as the elephant and Rhinoceros."[15] Revealingly, the "massacre" in Boston, which left five civilians dead, took place just a block from the Customs House and involved another provocative waterfront crowd. Of the five men slain, three had maritime occupations: seaman, ropewalk employee, and caulker.[16] Engravers on the Patriot side preparing propaganda—Paul Revere, for one—drew the redcoats' victims in middle-class clothes and postures. Waterfront mob fatalities commanded less sympathy.

The orchestration of seaport mobs—where they came from and who led them—deserves mention. Well-heeled privateer captains, mostly from the 1756–1763 French and Spanish war like New York's Isaac Sears and Alexander McDougall, could call on old crews and enjoyed credibility with seamen. Tavern owners like Jasper Drake (Isaac Sears's father-in-law) were also influential, because their waterfront premises were both maritime information centers and popular venues where illegally obtained goods changed hands. Men who owned shipyards or had a number of vessels under their control—Boston's John Hancock, for example—were also able to turn out crowds and provide suitable refreshment.

Other mob breeding grounds included ropewalks—sheds sometimes a quarter-mile long and employing dozens or scores of men. In them, spinners "walked" yarns of hemp from wheels and wove them together in the correct manner to make a heavy rope. A close-knit group, spinners worked six twelve-to-fourteen-hour days a week and were paid better than seamen but less than artisans. With each of the large seaports having at least three or four ropewalks, they were a prime source of violence. Rope makers in Boston later prided themselves on having provoked British redcoats into the Boston Massacre.[17]

Next to the Sons of Liberty, the name Sons of Neptune is barely known, but angry seamen and sailors sometimes so identified themselves. In 1765, a letter signed by "The Sons of Neptune" threatened an attack on lower Manhattan's Fort George if the Stamp Act was enforced locally.[18]

Boston's North End Caucus, dominated by Samuel Adams—himself the grandson of a sea captain—had strong ties to the waterfront. One supposition is that the name *caucus* derived from the prominence of attending caulkers and shipwrights.[19] Caulkers were the workers who made boats waterproof by filling their cracks and seams with pitch or oakum. In Boston, many lived on North End streets close to the Green Dragon Tavern where Adams's caucus met.[20] John Adams also later recalled when the caucus met in "the sail loft of Tom Dawes."[21]

The last great pre-Revolutionary confrontation staged by smuggling-prone merchants, caulkers, ropewalkers, and their political leaders was, of course, the Boston Tea Party. It *could* have taken place in New York, Philadelphia, or Charleston—these three ports, as well as Boston, had been picked by British officials to receive the original shipments of East India Company tea. In Philadelphia, the tea ships were turned around and not permitted to land. In New York, the principal ship came late and was ordered back. Another vessel did have some tea dumped into the harbor.[22] In Charleston, after the tea arrived, no one would receive or pay the required duty, so it was seized by Crown officials and stored in the basement of the Exchange. Anonymous radicals had threatened to torch that tea ship, and in 1774, when activists found out a just-arrived vessel, the *Britannia,* had seven chests of tea, "the General Committee [South Carolina's extralegal Patriot authority] forced the consignees to board the ship, smash in the chests, and empty the contents into the Cooper River."[23]

Even so, it was in Boston that the fates converged. Royal Governor Hutchinson refused to let the principal tea ship leave without unloading, so on December 16 several hundred Patriots—spurred by a don't-fail-us letter from Philadelphia—implemented carefully laid plans to dump £18,000 worth of tea into the harbor.[24] History was well served. No other city could have carried off the burdens and military challenges of the next sixteen months so well, which Samuel Adams probably understood.

Further elaboration on the salt air that stiffened the Revolutionary wind is almost unnecessary. However, the 1750s and 1760s saw frequent allusions to the famous but short-lived revolt led in Naples by a fisherman named Masaniello. Thomas Hutchinson in Boston was not the only royal official to tell Patriots, "You are so many Masaniellos." Officials in Maryland, New York, Virginia, and London used the same calumny.[25]

Some Crown officials went so far as to blame the Revolution on maritime Americans. As we have seen, Joseph Galloway, a leading Loyalist, singled out two vocations: smugglers and speculators. In 1765, General Thomas Gage cast his blame for the Stamp Act protests: "This Insurrection is composed of great numbers of Sailors headed by Captains of Privateers."

Other provincial governors also singled out the roles of seamen and former privateersmen in those riots.[26]

Geography and population reinforced the maritime dimension. Of the four seaports, each was substantially waterfront in a spatial and not simply commercial sense, as the four eighteenth-century maps reproduced elsewhere display. Boston was a virtual island, save for a thin neck leading to the mainland; its farthest inland point was only a half mile from water. New York was the water-encircled southernmost portion of Manhattan Island, separated from New Jersey on the west by the Hudson and from Brooklyn by the East River. Philadelphia was bounded by the Schuylkill River on the south, with its waterfront facing east along the Delaware. Charleston, in turn, was a peninsula pointing into its harbor, with the Ashley River to the west and the Cooper River to the east. Both the Boston and Charleston waterfronts were further extended by huge wharves.

Although ordinary seamen could participate in Boston town meetings, most did not meet even the minimal property requirements for voting in any city elections. For many, participating in mobs or riots must have been a political sport they could enjoy right in their own vocational backyards.

Maritime vocations—seamen, sailors, pilots, shipwrights, shippers, caulkers, dockworkers, carters, chandlers, sailmakers, and others—abounded in each seaport. Boston remained the most intensively maritime, even though rival Massachusetts ports like Marblehead, Salem, and Beverly were taking away shipbuilding, trading, and fisheries employment. Boston made some rebound during the 1765–1775 period; its population reached almost 17,000, about where it had been in the 1740s. However, by most maritime measurements, Philadelphia and New York had pulled ahead. What Boston clearly still led in producing between 1750 and 1775 was also relevant: *economic and political frustration.*

Philadelphia, by the 1770s, led the other three seaports in both ship-building and volume of exports. The city had a large commercial hinter-land, and its population had grown more than the others' between 1765 and 1775. In a good year, some 700 to 800 ships visited the Quaker City, more than came to Boston. Between 1750 and 1775, the tonnage of ships regis-tered in Philadelphia by merchants rose from 7,092 to 16,809.[27]

Maritime New York had thrived during the French and Indian War, fattening on British war expenditures, smuggling, and lucrative privateer-ing. The city's merchant fleet had tripled between 1749 and 1762—from 157 vessels to 477 in 1762, and from a tonnage of 6,406 to 19,514.[28] Several thousand privateer crewmen were discharged as the war with France wound down in the early 1760s, and local joblessness remained high. The mob violence of 1768–1770 came easily.

On a per capita basis, Charleston was the most prosperous of the four in 1775. Although this principally reflected rice and indigo, its maritime facade was grand enough take the wind out of even Yankee sails. Huge wharves made its Cooper River waterfront look like a floating market, and wharf construction was just beginning on the Ashley River side. Upon entering Charleston Harbor in 1773, Josiah Quincy, Jr., of Massachusetts commented that "the number of shipping far surpassed all I have seen in Boston. About three hundred and fifty sail lay off the town."[29] Local historian Robert Weir said of Charleston that to "a far greater extent than often realized, it was a seafaring town," and at the height of the shipping season in February and March, more than 1,500 seamen were ashore.[30]

Precision about the numbers of seamen in each of these cities is obviously impossible. Visiting tars, of course, could also riot. According to an estimate by maritime historian Jesse Lemisch, "To those discharged by the navy at the end of the war [1762–1763] and others thrown out of war by the death of privateering were added perhaps twenty thousand more seamen and fishermen who were thought to be direct victims of post-1763 trade regulations."[31] Although these frustrations maximized in New England and New York, they were a factor in dozens of seaports.

In retrospect, the ship has been called the earliest factory, and seamen the first international labor force, with unusually democratic principles. These sentiments were reinforced during the late seventeenth and early eighteenth centuries by the "against all flags" psychologies of pirates and piracy. Blacks also represented 10 to 15 percent of the seamen from New York northward. Labor historians emphasize the uniqueness of these backdrops.[32]

Skeptics of the out-front role played by seamen, sailors, and waterfront mobs in gestating the American Revolution need only consider earlier revolutionary precedents in the Anglo-Dutch world. In Holland, the famous *watergeuzen*—in English, the sea beggars—of the 1560s and 1570s were radical Dutch Protestant corsairs who sailed under letters of marque from William of Orange. Dutch historians generally regard their capture of Brielle and Flushing in 1572 as triggering the general revolt of the Netherlands against Spain. In pre-civil-war England, according to historians Peter Linebaugh and Marcus Rediker, "the mass resistance of sailors began in the

1620s, when they mutinied and rioted over pay and conditions; it reached a new stage when they led the urban mobs of London that inaugurated the revolutionary crisis of 1640–1641."[33]

As American seamen edged toward revolution between 1740 and 1775, worse explosions were brewing in the British Isles. Once peace in 1763 had seen 20,000 sailors discharged, the Royal Navy tightened its discipline, sought further economies, and reduced its material conditions (food and wages). In 1768, sailors and seamen in London "struck"—as in "took down"—their vessels' sails, tying up commerce and giving labor relations a new byword: *strike*. Riots against impressment and press gangs proliferated, and an activist adopting the name Nauticus penned *The Rights of the Sailors Vindicated,* in which he compared the sailor's life to slavery.[34] When another strike in Liverpool in 1775 led to authorities firing on the crowd and killing several, sailors pulled ships' guns to the city center and fired on the Mercantile Exchange, leaving "scarce a whole pane of glass in the neighborhood." On both sides of the Atlantic, sailors were "a vector of revolution." Mutinies and desertions within the Royal Navy grew after 1776, "inspired in part by the battles waged against press-gangs and the king's authority in America." Between 1776 and 1783, "an estimated forty-two thousand of them deserted naval ships."[35]

During the years between 1760 and 1774, a half dozen issues, led by the abuses of British naval impressment, converged to rile American seamen. To describe impressment into the Royal Navy as carrying a fate of death or slavery was only a slight exaggeration. Three out of four men who were pressed died within two years, with only one in five killed in battle.[36] Under the so-called Sixth of Anne statute enacted in 1708, American seamen were not to be impressed. However, British warships frequently ignored that constraint, especially in and around Boston.

The greatest provocation came in 1747, when British Commodore Charles Knowles sent a press-gang through Boston, taking up seamen, including many who had already been paid wages for imminent voyages, as well as artisans and landsmen. As Knowles proceeded, a huge Boston mob, swelling to near 4,000, took as hostage three of the naval officers running the press, obliging Governor William Shirley to intervene. Ultimately, Shirley himself decided to flee to the harbor fortress, Castle William. However, he persuaded Commodore Knowles to free most of the men impressed, and the leadership of the militia escorted the governor safely back to Boston from Castle William.[37] Impressments along the Massachusetts coast surged in 1775, because of local fighting and the needs of so many Royal Navy warships.

New York, too, had vivid experiences with naval impressment. In 1756, when a British expeditionary fleet was short of hands, 3,000 men cordoned off the city at two o'clock in the morning and pressed some 800 men, of whom half were later released. In 1760, when the frigate HMS *Winchester* stopped and sent a press party to the local privateer *Sampson,* its crew fired on the British, killing and wounding several, before escaping into the city. Then in 1764, when four fishermen were seized and taken to a nearby man-of-war, an angry crowd burned the ship's barge in front of city hall, forcing city officials to negotiate for the fishermen's release.[38]

Small vessels also found themselves harassed by punitive customs enforcement. Coasters with two- or three-man crews, under an owner without influence or money, were helpless prey when charged. They could not afford bribes or the expense of going to court over illegal seizures, and many infractions were no more than technical. Customs officers could and did charge owners with "breaking bulk before entry" if they had put any part of their cargo ashore, or shifted portions to make repairs, or even thrown overboard some spoiled fruit. Coastal vessels making only short local trips within Massachusetts or Connecticut waters could be seized for lack of clearances or bonding, even though a higher court would have to dismiss. On top of which were the clearance fees, which even for small craft could be three dollars. "The little fellows," said Oliver Dickerson in *The Navigation Acts and the American Revolution,* "had to endure such treatment as they received. It was cheaper to submit to the illegal exactions than risk seizures and court costs."[39] Magnates like Henry Laurens and John Hancock could fight back against smuggling charges, but not Jonathan Anonymous from Annisquam.

Even individual seafarers were targeted. Despite hard times, crew members were no longer allowed what had traditionally been nonwage compensation—the "venture," or small amounts of goods that crew members had been permitted to put in the ship's hold at no freight charge and then to resell. After the reorganization of 1764, customs officials began to seize these, too.[40] Several of the customs men tarred and feathered in and around Boston earned their Yankee Jacket for such activities.

Economically, fishermen often found themselves in the same boat as smugglers. The molasses trade—the ability to bring it from the French West Indies as a profitable return cargo—was part of a broader commercial relationship in which New Englanders needed to sell low-quality dried fish, lumber, and provisions to the French islands. For Massachusetts, the profitable fish were the high-quality dried cod—those best cut and preserved—shipped for the most part to southern Europeans, especially Italians and Spaniards. Britain permitted those sales to be made directly. The lower-quality scraps, however, also had a market in the French Caribbean, where they were used to feed black slaves in the sugar islands. Without these sales, broader fishing economics became marginal.

The final convergence of maritime resentment came in 1775. In late March, Parliament passed the New England Restraining Act, details of which soon arrived in Boston. Effective July 1, Massachusetts, New Hampshire, Connecticut, and Rhode Island could trade only with the British Isles and the British West Indies. Vessels caught going elsewhere would be seized. Also in July, New England ships (except those from Nantucket) were to be barred from the North American fisheries. By July 1, as things turned out, large numbers of Massachusetts fishermen had enlisted in the provincial army. Before year's end, many others would soon sign up with privateers.

Without the Sons of Neptune, the American Revolution would have been quite different—if, in fact, there had been one.

Artisans, Mechanics, and Manufacturers

Artisans and mechanics, neither a very precise job description, roiled Philadelphia politics between 1774 and 1776, and with Congress assembling there, they also swayed national politics. Their pro-Revolutionary activities mattered less in the other cities—in Boston, because of the 1774–1776 British occupation, and in Manhattan because of the late 1775 and 1776 exodus as invasion threatened.

Philadelphia's particular urban culture has also fascinated historians alert to early glimmerings of manufacturing and labor economics. One study discussed a "Republic of Labor."[41] But a case can also be made for the emergence within the large artisan community of an economic "middle class" politics in the Philadelphia of 1775.

If the four principal urban centers had a combined workforce in the neighborhood of 25,000 men, somewhere between one third and one half were estimated to be artisans and mechanics. The maritime sector was almost as large, but seamen were hard to count, and in any event, the two vocational cultures had a large overlap on wharves, in shipyards, warehouses, ropewalks, sail lofts, ships' chandleries, and distilleries, and in cooperage, portage and hauling, fish processing, tavern keeping, and numerous other pursuits.

In sea-fronting Boston, artisans and mechanics unrelated to maritime enterprise probably totaled under 10 percent of the workforce, fewer than in the other major cities. The maritime coloration dominated, but with the British Army in occupation until General Howe's departure in March 1776, the Patriot population was in any event substantially dispersed or constrained.

New York had 3,000 seamen in 1772, by one estimate. No census of artisans exists, but 300 carpenters were supposedly on hand in 1765 during the Stamp Act riots "to cut down the Fort Gate" if any redcoats fired.[42] Here, too, a considerable portion of the artisans and mechanics would have been marine craftsmen. Skilled craftsmen were prominent in the Sons of Liberty from the 1760s on. Leaders in 1775 included men like John Lamb, an instrument maker, and Marinus Willett, an upholsterer, both of whom became middling figures in New York's Revolution. To city historians, the formation of a Mechanics Committee in 1774 was a milestone. As "a plebeian counterpart to the Chamber of Commerce, it confirmed the growing sophistication of the city's working people. Its leaders over the next few years had hitherto been on the fringes of political affairs. Now they were at the center."[43]

But not for very long. If the influence of the "Body of Mechanics" grew during the second half of 1775 and into 1776, it was partly because many better-off residents were fleeing the city, unnerved by an August 1775 broadside from the 64-gun HMS *Asia* and the expectation of an invasion. As those redcoats arrived in 1776, the mechanics' importance dissipated, and in the words of one chronicler, autumn's actual "British occupation scattered and broke them, and not until the end of 1783 would they be in a position to intervene collectively."[44]

Of the three largest cities, then, Philadelphia is rightly singled out for the economic and political importance of its artisans. Printer Benjamin Franklin became an early spokesman, and from the 1730s to the Revolution, artisans and mechanics in the Quaker City had substantially higher incomes and wealth levels than their urban compatriots elsewhere.[45] The City of Brotherly Love also had distinctly fewer riots, lacking either soldiers barracked locally or naval press-gangs.

In Philadelphia, the terms *artisan, manufacturer,* and *mechanic* were *all* used, if not quite interchangeably. In those days, *manufacturer* referred not just to a capitalist but also to a workman or master—usually in one of the crafts like metalworking, brewing, baking, textiles, and leather making that were moving toward "industry" status.[46] References to manufacturing grew steadily during each of the city's nonimportation controversies: 1765–1766, 1767–1770, and 1774–1775. Interestingly, British General Thomas Gage, no great shakes militarily during his 1774–1775 command in Boston, in an earlier 1768 role had been a sage analyst of comparative urban economies. "During my Stay in Philadelphia," said Gage, "I could not help but be surprized at the great Increase of that City in Buildings, Mechanicks and Manufactures . . . They talk and threaten much in the other Provinces of their Resolutions to lessen the importation of British manufactures; and to manufacture for themselves: but they are by no means able to do it. The People of Pennsylvania lay their plans with more Temper and Judgment, and pursue with more patience and Steadfastness. They don't attempt Impossibilities or talk of what they will do, but are silently stealing in Mechanicks and Manufacturers; and if they go on as they have hitherto done, they will probably within a few years Supply themselves with many necessary articles which they now import from Great Britain."[47]

To colonial historian Carl Bridenbaugh, Philadelphia was "a prime example of a city that had large enterprises requiring substantial outlays of invested capital, which was what Englishmen meant by manufactures rather than the small handicrafts that produced articles used in daily living." Three stood out—flour, iron, and shipbuilding.[48] Leaders in those businesses were capitalists with wealth far beyond artisan levels.

Record keepers, though, clung to the old eighteenth-century categorizations. According to one seasoned Philadelphia watcher, 1,682 of the 3,350 taxable males in 1772—well over 50 percent—were artisans. A second survey of the city's tax lists found that of 3,432 listed property owners in 1774, 30 percent were artisans. Based on the vocations listed in *The Philadelphia Directory* in 1785, a third study reported that more than one third of the household heads were "mechanics." A fourth, based on 1774 tax assessment ledgers, categorized 47 percent of the city's taxables as artisans (and marine crafts were only one subcategory out of seven).[49] Bridenbaugh, who had found artisans constituting 30 percent of 1774 property owners, added that "this figure only represents heads of families, possessing real estate, servants, slaves and domestic animals, and does not even indicate the total number of master craftsmen, let alone journeymen and apprentices."[50] Clearly, they were a large group of taxpayers and voters.

Before continuing with pre-Revolutionary Philadelphia, let us briefly detour to wealthy Charleston, which also had a substantial artisan community. The census of 1790 counted 1,933 (white) heads of families, and listed 429 master craftsmen and mechanics. In 1775, an unusual ratio of the artisans practiced luxury trades—cabinetmakers, upholsterers, silversmiths, painters (limners, painters, and gilders), coach makers, chaise makers, and wheelwrights. Aside from tailors, who imported expensive English fabrics and were more likely to become Tories, a number of luxury-craft artisans were members of the Sons of Liberty and Patriot faction and frequent attendees at the meetings convened by Christopher Gadsden under the Liberty Tree.[51] Each of South Carolina's nonimportation movements—in 1765–1766, 1768–1770, and 1774—saw them in the van of efforts seeking to bar British imports and to promote American manufactures. This made artisans important, albeit subordinate, allies of the planters whose extralegal organizations assumed much of South Carolina's de facto governance in the early 1770s.

Center stage, however, clearly belonged to Philadelphia. Its artisans and mechanics not only reshaped local politics but helped to remold the 1775–1776 ideology of a pivotal province and to influence the national Congress meeting there. Part of the foundation had been laid by Benjamin Franklin, who had nurtured Pennsylvania artisan power and pride constantly from the 1740s forward. His role in supporting the cause of manufacturing and, more important, in turning artisans and mechanics into the core of a politically active volunteer provincial militia, had much to do with the Patriot faction's provincial triumph.

Artisan politics went way back in Philadelphia. The city had been prosperous almost from its founding, and even during the 1720s artisans and mechanics were numerous enough to be courted by an unusual governor, Sir Robert Keith, known for his populist politics. Echoing some of the ideas of English Civil War radicals, he organized a Leather Apron Club and said that instead of favoring the wealthy, "Civil Government ought carefully to protect the poor laborious and industrious Part of Mankind."[52] Keith's ideas lingered into the 1730s, and Franklin in some respects picked up his political baton. Artisans and mechanics began to win some low-level offices during the 1760s, and then came into their own during the 1770s.

Economic conditions in Philadelphia, like those in other cities, boomed during the French and Indian War years, then slipped into a postwar depression in the early 1760s. Then, after gains later in the decade, another downturn began in 1772. Economic historians—and Philadelphia has drawn its share—tend to emphasize how upper-income groups managed in these difficult times far better than ordinary artisans, mechanics, and journeymen. The latter, by this argument, "suffered through a prolonged depression that saw the gains of the past thirty-five years quickly wiped away."[53] Wages dropped even as food prices climbed. Purchasing power shrank.

The effects on different economic strata can be gleaned from public records. As the eighteenth century got under way, middling craftsmen held 17 percent of the city's recorded wealth. By the 1726–1736 decade, that share had dropped to 12 percent, and by the decade before the Revolution, to just 5 percent. A vocational notch down, the share of lesser artisans and unskilled laborers slid to a mere 1 percent. The richest Philadelphians, during the same period, increased their share of citywide wealth from 25 percent to 56 percent.[54] The pre-Revolutionary decade was the one during which ownership of a carriage—and more tellingly, multiple carriage ownership—soared among the same stratum.

Quite a few artisans would have been middle class, and among the 500 taxpayers in the top tenth, perhaps 60, 80, or 100 would have been successful builders, bakers, ironmongers, and master craftsmen. However, most artisans would have been in the middle third; and many of the poorest sort—cordwainers, weavers, and the like—would have been in the lower third, where breadwinners were losing purchasing power. A majority would have lost ground while the "class" tensions of Philadelphia in 1774–1776 heated up.

Historian Richard Ryerson, whose book *The Revolution Is Now Begun: The Radical Committees of Philadelphia, 1765–1776* (1978) is unrivaled for its portraiture of the city's unique committees, divided their rise to power into two main periods. The first ran from roughly 1770 to the summer of 1774, which he labeled "the revolution of the elite." The second, from mid-1774 to 1776, represented "the legitimization of radical politics." It became "the revolution of the middle classes" in early 1776, and Pennsylvania politics reached its truly radical stage that May.[55]

In places, Ryerson's account lists committees, conventions, and associations in an abundance that evokes the English Civil War or even Jacobin France. Yet they have been distilled into clear and revealing portraits of the social upheaval in political decision making occasioned by the changing memberships of six successive citywide "umbrella" committees. Their very names specified their expansion—the Nineteen of May 1774 became the Forty-three of June 1774 and then the Sixty-six of November 1774. The First One Hundred of August 1775 gave way to the Second One Hundred of February 1776. One powerful graph illustrates the religious change: a sharp reduction in Quaker participation. A second displays the pronounced decline in the average wealth of committee members. A third identifies the groups whose inclusion declined—merchants especially, but also professional men—alongside the principal vocation whose inclusion ballooned: *mechanics*. Their membership on the successive committees soared from 5 percent to 40 percent, while merchants dropped from 60 percent to 30 percent.[56]

If this represented a "revolution of the middle class," others have described the final stage in somewhat Marxian terms. Left-leaning historian Steven Rosswurm concluded that "artisan consciousness in Philadelphia far overshadowed that in New York and Boston. A secret ballot provided these mechanics with the means, which their New York counterparts lacked, to assert their interests."[57]

However, his principal emphasis is on the circumstances that abetted the rise of a radical militia. "That Pennsylvania did not have an established militia system created the opening for the lower sort. Since there was no militia to be under gentry domination, the laboring poor did not have to struggle with those above to have their voice heard. Perhaps more important, since militia rules had to be established anew, the laboring poor were able to place their imprint on the association as no other rank and file was able to do during the Revolution . . . the Philadelphia lower sort transformed and politicized the militia and made it, among other things, the institutional embodiment of their growing power."[58] Marxist-sounding, but institutionally descriptive.

The single most important military embodiment was the Committee of Privates, organized in September 1775. Intriguingly, several of its leaders had first come to some prominence six months before, in launching the United Company of Philadelphia for Promoting American Manufactures. This organization, like several others, served "as an entryway into Philadelphia politics for several important ultraradical leaders."[59] Given existing imperial law, propagandizing for manufacturing was almost innately rebellious. Later that autumn the United Company president, Daniel Roberdeau, was elected commander of the Pennsylvania militia and James Cannon, a prominent United Company organizer, became secretary of the

Committee of Privates and later a prominent member of Pennsylvania's 1776 Constitutional Convention.[60]

The rise of Philadelphia's artisans, mechanics, and advocates of new manufactures, influential in itself, was also bound up with the emergence of a radical militia, to which we are about to turn. These developments soon offended middle-class Philadelphia, including prosperous artisans. However, before that countertide, the stages of economic and military radicalization contributed to the transformation of Pennsylvania politics in May 1776, which made it possible for both the colony and the full Congress to swing behind a declaration of independence. Philadelphia radicalism played an important role in tipping the balance.

The Radical Role of the Revolutionary Militias

In 1775, the four vanguard colonies individually prided themselves on what combined into five centuries of military history—local wars against Pequots, Abenaki, Shawnee, Cherokee, Yamasee, and Creeks, vigilant defense against French and Spanish invasions, and participation in foreign expeditions against Quebec, Port Royal, Louisbourg, St. Augustine, Havana, and Cartagena. As colonies, they maintained no regular regiments, but among the thirteen they had the lengthiest annals of militia organization and raising volunteers for expeditions and special units (for example, the "Virginia Regiment" George Washington commanded during the French and Indian War). This background was good preparation for the challenge of 1774–1775, and it was "urban" in the limited sense of being managed in colonial legislatures and capitals: Boston, Hartford, Williamsburg, and Charleston.

At the weakest edge of the preparedness debate, Pennsylvania, because of its Quaker heritage, was the lone North American province in which an assembly had steadily refused to enact legislation establishing an official militia. This fed widespread disgruntlement—a climate in which three decades of frustration over the periodic need to embody a volunteer militia increasingly united the province's expansionist and nationalist elements, most of whom took the Patriot side in 1775. Part of the militia mindset that emerged in 1775–1776 was a bold leveling agenda. Resentful of the Quakers, it demanded not just military democracy but equality of obligation: everyone would have to serve, and those who did not would be fined in proportion to the property they owned.[61]

The province's heated militia politics between 1774 and 1776 has drawn its share of attention. Progressives have seized on examples of how the need to enlist or recruit soldiers from the lower and middle tiers of colonial society obliged the Patriots' gentry leadership to entertain economic incentives and egalitarian commitments. Similar although weaker egalitarian demands arose in Virginia and Maryland, notably in Philadelphia-influenced towns like Baltimore and Annapolis.[62] However, the emergence and political influence of a radical Pennsylvania militia centered on Philadelphia is the prime example.

In many colonies, the militia of 1775 developed a second dimension as a de facto police—active on behalf of local committees of safety and inspection in suppressing Tories, political *banditti,* and potential local insurrections, and in enforcing loyalty and Association oaths. Below the Mason-Dixon Line, the militias also had a historic role of watching out for runaways or conspiracies involving indentured servants and slaves. General histories of the Revolution tend to shy away from these functions and the harsh practices involved. Without these police aspects, though, the Revolution might not have been able to entrench itself in 1775 and 1776.

On a grander strategic plane, some military historians contend that the ability of Congress and the Patriot faction in 1775 and early 1776 to take over local government, including control of the militia, while British forces were all but nonexistent outside of Boston, was critical to the Revolution's ultimate success.[63] This was surely "radical" in an institutional sense, representing the transformation of the seventeenth-century English "trained band" into what twenty-first-century analysts might call a "nation-building" framework—the Revolution's politically potent combination of minutemen, militias, and de facto police.

In the four vanguard provinces, the militias' role was a century or a century and a half in the making. General John R. Galvin, a Massachusetts man and former Supreme Allied Commander in Europe, published a persuasive volume in 1996 entitled *The Minutemen: The First Fight: Myths and Realities of the American Revolution.* He argued, as briefly noted in Chapter 1, that while twentieth-century mythology has portrayed our citizen soldiers, the heroes of Lexington and Concord, as a spontaneous assemblage of untrained farmers, the reality was otherwise. Fourteen thousand Massachusetts colonials were under arms by 1775, to be "alerted by organized alarm riders via a system that dated back to the 17th century wars. They had trained intensively for a year and were armed with the same type of weapons as the British."[64] Massachusetts minutemen dated back to an Indian war in 1645, with instructions updated in 1703 and 1757.

The many British generals of the French and Indian War who took away a disdain for Yankee soldiers were partly mistaken—most confused regular militiamen with the temporary troops raised by bounty payments for out-of-province service. For such instances, Massachusetts, Virginia, and other provinces went outside the militia system to recruit servants, apprentices, and vagabonds—"strollers" in official language. The militia, by contrast, was a more reliable cross-section of each town based on the required service of all males between 16 and 60. One historian who stressed the difference added that "the Massachusetts militia on the eve of the Revolution was probably better prepared for war than any other militia in the colonies."[65]

Considerable credit belonged to Samuel Adams. In 1770, as a member of the provincial House of Representatives, Adams urged the strengthening of what he described as a neglected and poorly armed militia; by 1773, a committee was pursuing the matter. In the spring and summer of 1774, when news of the Coercive Acts arrived in Boston, Adams moved to harness popular furor. By late August, some 2,000 local militiamen—many in company formations led by their officers—joined other thousands demonstrating in Worcester. Planning was ultimately Boston centered. A few days later, when General Gage sent a detachment of soldiers from Boston to remove 200 half barrels of the king's gunpowder from a nearby storehouse, rumors somehow spread inland that British ships were shelling Boston, or that six Americans had been killed. So aroused, some 20,000 armed New Englanders, mostly Massachusetts and Connecticut militiamen, began to march toward ostensibly embattled Boston before messengers brought truer information. Was the rumor entirely an accident? Patriot leaders agreed that it had been good practice.

These reactions made Gage reconsider his notion of sending troops 50 miles to Worcester on September 6 to protect the opening of local courts. On that day, militia companies from most Worcester County towns were on hand, led by their officers, and seemingly prepared to fight. When no redcoats came, belief spread that Gage's bluff had been called. On September 7, the Worcester County Convention called for a reorganization of the militia—all current field officers were asked to resign so that some could be replaced—and, in the old phrase, recommended the establishment of special units ready to march at "a minute's warning." By the time conventions followed in Essex, Suffolk, and Middlesex counties two weeks later, Worcester County reported having incorporated seven regiments of a thousand men each.[66]

The first Massachusetts Provincial Congress, meeting at Concord in early October, seeking to sidestep the provocation of a twenty- or thirty-regiment provincial standing army, opted for a provincewide extension of the minuteman concept. Under the auspices of a nine-man Committee of Safety, all local militia companies would elect new officers. With these as building blocks, new battalions, regiments, and minuteman units would be sorted out. The Provincial Congress adjourned in late October, and the Committee of Safety and the Committee of Supplies took over. Tory colonels and majors unwilling to resign were forced to do so, including Major General William Brattle, the no-longer-acceptable provincial militia commander.

With Patriot leaders aware that time pressed, training continued through the winter—on town greens or in fields, barns, and even taverns. From Cape Ann to the Berkshires, wagons with gunpowder, cannon, lead, muskets, and bayonets headed for the two principal munitions depots in Concord and Worcester. Gage had many spies, so little of this was a secret, but information leaked both ways. When the British commander marched troops to the Charlestown Battery, to remove its cannon before they could be stolen, they had just been spirited away. On March 30, 1775, Brigadier Hugh Percy, one of the British Army's best soldiers, marched a full brigade to Jamaica Plain, five miles south of Boston, and had his men knock down farmers' stone walls at possible ambush sites. Three weeks later the troops retreating from Concord along roads lined with mile after mile of stone walls and ambuscades had no such opportunity, and many died.

Galvin's book is by far and away the best chronicle of how long and how well managed Massachusetts's preparation for Lexington and Concord had been. Conflict was less an accident waiting to happen than an expectation. On March 30 the Provincial Congress had resolved "that whenever the Army under command of General Gage, or any part thereof to the Number of Five Hundred, shall march out of the Town of Boston, with Artillery and Baggage, it ought to be . . . opposed; and therefore the Military Force of the Province ought to be assembled."[67] Had Gage marched two regiments to Worcester in early September, war might have come then, but Patriots profited from having another six months.

Early in September 1774, Gage had written to Lord Dartmouth that

Connecticut was "as furious as they are" in Massachusetts. On September 8, delegates from two eastern Connecticut counties met in Norwich. "Anticipating that they might soon 'be under the disagreeable necessity of defending our Sacred and Invaluable Rights, sword in hand,' they called on their two dozen towns to supply themselves with a full stock of ammunition, and suggested to the General Court that the provincial militia be strengthened by the raising of at least 5,000 soldiers."[68]

Thirty-seven hundred of the militiamen who started for Boston after hearing September's gunpowder alarm came from Connecticut, which relative to its population essentially matched Massachusetts in 1774–1776 militia readiness.[69] Its minuteman concept also dated back to the seventeenth-century Indian wars. Connecticut's eighteenth-century practice, again like that of Massachusetts, had been to raise troops for *out-of-colony* service through bounty payments, a relationship volunteers saw as essentially contractual. With that help, Connecticut had fielded an army of 5,000 during the late 1750s.[70] This bounty approach floundered during the Revolution, but it did enable Connecticut mobilization in 1775–1776 to get off to an important fast start.

After eastern Connecticut's September 1774 convention endorsed mobilization, the provincial House of Representatives agreed to commission new companies and encourage the resignations of a handful of Tory militia officers. In one military historian's words, these actions made the militia "the officially-sanctioned intimidator of the timid and uncertain, and silenced the few men who might have supported increased imperial control."[71] Through the autumn and winter, most Connecticut towns formally adopted the association voted by the First Continental Congress and chose committees to implement it.

In Massachusetts, Tory officeholders had started fleeing the province in 1774, despite the nominal protection of Gage and his soldiers. In Connecticut, though, a charter colony where British rule had almost no reach, the Patriot faction could apply the colony's full authority. A few persecuted or assaulted Tories fled in 1774, but in January and February 1775, small Tory conventions in the western counties of Fairfield and Litchfield attacked Whig politics and affirmed allegiance to "the King, Lords and Commons."[72] Governor Trumbull, who had declined to protect Tories harassed by mobs, now identified them in a March address to legislators as "depraved, Malignant, avaricious and haughty." Whig legislators acted to investigate military officers accused of Toryism and appointed a committee to pursue Tory activity in suspect communities like Newtown and Ridgefield. Several militia units were purged or dissolved.

By the autumn of 1775, even conservative western towns were disarming or jailing local Tories and calling for enactment of a comprehensive, colonywide anti-Tory law. To George Washington's applause, Connecticut in December enacted an anti-Tory statute that, by one description, "made it a crime to be loyal to the empire in word or deed." Adherence to Britain became treason against Connecticut, prompting Tories in Britain and other colonies to damn Trumbull as "the Rebel Governor." Washington, though, had already turned to him to provide troops to help suppress Toryism in several New York counties.[73] In 1775 and 1776 and arguably through most of the war, New York, New Jersey, and Connecticut authorities saw suppressing Loyalism as the militias' most important task.[74] In this, Connecticut arguably pioneered.

Among the plantation colonies, Virginia and South Carolina had long-standing militias but were not trailblazers like the two New England regimes. Even so, by the 1770s, Virginia and South Carolina militias were funded by the House of Burgesses and Commons House of Assembly. Royal governors could do little without legislative collaboration.

The Old Dominion's militia record was unimpressive during 1774 and 1775, despite traditions going back to Virginia's early-seventeenth-century beginnings as a military regime that had sought soldier-settlers.[75] As the eighteenth century opened, the militia's role was minimized by Virginia's great distances. Mounted soldiers "ranged" between the frontier forts— thereby originating the term *ranger*.[76] Over the next half century, the colony was so little menaced by Indians, French, or Spanish "that the militia virtually ceased to exist there."[77] Military effectiveness was greater in more compact, town-centered New England, where militias were part of the culture.

Some Virginia militia came into their own in 1774, fighting the Shawnee in what was named Lord Dunmore's War. Many of the battalion and regimental commanders involved—Andrew Lewis, William Christian, William Preston, and Adam Stephen—would serve together again in the Revolution. The other local military units to emerge in 1774 and proliferate in 1775 were the independent companies organized by Patriot-faction planters, prominently including firebrand Patrick Henry. Unpaid but hard to control, these volunteers were a far cry from a large and reliable soldiery, and plans to reorganize the militia began in July 1775.

Portions of tidewater Virginia verged on anarchy. Governor Dunmore had fled Williamsburg, taking refuge on HMS *Fowey*, promising freedom to slaves who would run away to join his forces, which many soon did. But because Virginia had virtually no funds and tax revenues were in abeyance, preparedness had to be obtained on the cheap. The solution proposed by the Patriot convention in August—a regular body of 1,000 men, plus 8,000 "minutemen" who would be paid only when called up—produced few of the hoped-for enlistees. Meanwhile, Dunmore's unfolding bid to recruit black slaves and white indentured servants stirred a dialogue among lower- and middle-income whites about their own economic frustrations and needs. The upshot, between July and October 1775, was that relatively few minutemen could be enlisted. Too much service was required, at times inconvenient for farmers; slave overseers were excused, which produced resentment; pay disparities between officers and men rankled; and officers were appointed, not elected. Virginia's best troops were those taken on the Continental establishment and paid by Congress.[78]

South Carolina managed better. Its provincial forces and militia had spent much of the previous half century charged with defending the southern borderlands of British North America. Rarely were these expenses reimbursed. By the 1770s, the Commons House of Assembly, which handled the funds, had developed enough micromanagement of military affairs to utilize four relevant committees: Powder Receiver's Account, Armory and Fortifications, Commissary Accounts, and Militia and Town Watch.[79] According to one expert, by "using legislative committees to apply military grants and in exercising the right to nominate military officers, the lower houses in the southern royal colonies wielded greater authority over military affairs in their respective colonies than did the House of Commons in England."[80]

Like Virginians fighting the Shawnee in 1774, South Carolina's soon-to-be-Patriots had the bonding experience of an Indian war, which also disenchanted them with the culture and reliability of British generalship. South Carolinians from Francis Marion and Thomas Sumter to William Moultrie and Christopher Gadsden all served in the Cherokee War of 1761. Militia Colonel Henry Middleton and Colonel James Grant, the British commander, developed enough mutual disdain to fight a duel.

Southern Patriot militias played a vital role in 1775 and early 1776, including that of the new southernmost colony, Georgia. One military historian, looking at Georgia between 1754 and 1776, placed it alongside

Massachusetts, South Carolina, and Virginia as colonies in which the militia played a key role in the coming of the American Revolution.[81]

Later chapters will amplify Whig militia successes in defeating the first Loyalist risings or British incursions into South Carolina, North Carolina, and Virginia. In a nutshell, December 1775 saw South Carolina Whig militiamen under Colonel Richard Richardson crush Loyalists under Patrick Cunningham. The next month Georgia militiamen under Colonel Lachlan McIntosh were ordered to Savannah to repel a British flotilla, which eventually departed with thirteen rice-laden ships rather than attack the city. Then in February, North Carolina militiamen under Colonels Richard Caswell and Alexander Lillington defeated a rising of loyal Scottish Highlanders from upper Cape Fear at the Battle of Moore's Creek Bridge. Virginia militiamen and minutemen did well in October and December 1775 engagements at Hampton and Great Bridge, respectively.

By far the greatest egalitarian and radical militia enterprise unfolded in Pennsylvania. As we have seen, military unpreparedness had become an Achilles' heel of the Quaker government as the population grew and surged westward. This was understood on both sides of the Atlantic. In the early 1740s, during that decade's war with France and Spain, Governor George Thomas told the Board of Trade in London that no military effort could be expected while the Society of Friends controlled the provincial Assembly. Thomas went so far as to suggest that Parliament pass an act excluding Quakers from membership in the legislature.[82] Benjamin Franklin, a transplanted New Englander alert to the usefulness of militia, took a lead in 1747 by organizing a volunteer militia association. He did so after the Assembly refused to act even as enemy privateers hovered near Delaware Bay. Following in the footsteps of Governor Keith, Franklin criticized Quaker obstinacy and urged the "middling people, the Farmers, Shopkeepers and Tradesmen," to sign up. Within days, more than 1,000—over one third of the city's adult white male population—had done so. In all Pennsylvania, some 10,000 enlisted.[83]

Nor did the militia issue go away. It smoldered, and then again burst into flames. In November 1755, with French forts and Indian war dances in Pennsylvania's own backyard, the upper Ohio Valley, some 700 Germans, protesting weak western defenses, marched on Philadelphia. Although still rejecting an official militia, the Assembly passed legislation to authorize a volunteer one. In December, Franklin, now cooperating with the Assembly, organized a general election of militia officers in all ten city wards. Then he paraded his volunteer soldiery. In the words of historian Nash, "the militia struggle politicized nearly every element of Philadelphia society. The proprietary leaders organized an independent militia, recruited five companies of supporters and counterdemonstrated in the streets. Even Franklin's old organization of leather apron men, the Junto, became so obsessed with politics that its Anglican majority harassed supporters of the popular party into resignation. Religious groups split along political lines and clergymen became parapolitical leaders."[84]

In mid-1763, when Pontiac's War once again lit up the West with burning cabins, the defense issue was rejoined, and minimal response from the Assembly rekindled western anger. Furious Scotch-Irish frontiersmen, the Paxton Boys, killed peaceful Conestoga Indians and later marched on Philadelphia, cheered by increasingly sympathetic Germans. Quaker pamphleteers portrayed the march as the "latest installment in a perpetual Presbyterian holy war against the mild and beneficent government of the Kings of England." However, Pastor Henry Muhlenberg, the leader of provincial Lutherans, mocked how "sundry young and old Quakers formed companies, and took up arms to repel the Scotch-Irish." He recalled how "the pious lambs in the long French, Spanish and Indian wars had such tender consciences, and would sooner die than raise a hand in defence against these dangerous enemies, and now at once like Zedekiah, the son of Chenaanah, with iron horns rushing upon a handful of our poor distressed and ruined fellow citizens and inhabitants of the frontiers."[85] Muhlenberg helped to translate anti-Quaker tracts into German.

Such controversy tells us much. It obviously reinforces the arguments in Chapter 3 about how much religion came to count in the politics of pre-Revolutionary Pennsylvania. It also suggests that backcountry Pennsylvanians were just as sensitive to Indian issues and fears as southern backcountry residents, to be discussed in Chapter 6. More immediately, though, the episode underscores the unique political psychology that militia issues could tap among frustrated Pennsylvanians. Without this three-decade frustration, the degree of radicalization that took over the militia movement could not have gestated.

Lexington and Concord further aroused two major Pennsylvania groups to join the new militia "associations": the mechanics of Philadelphia and the hinterland Scotch-Irish and Germans. In the words of one chronicler, they were "the disenfranchised element—the people who had been petitioning for more counties and greater representation; the mechanics and artisans of

Philadelphia who had been denied any share in the government by the ruling aristocracy; the frontiersmen who felt that the Assembly had not given them adequate protection against the Indians."[86] In June 1775, the Committee of the City and the Liberties of Philadelphia petitioned the Assembly to be allowed to equip, train, and drill able-bodied men—and despite substantial caveats, the Assembly could not refuse.

To an extent, the legislators were ratifying a fait accompli. Thirty-one companies of Philadelphia militia had already been organized that spring. However, ideological tremors were just beginning. "By the fall of 1775," said Gary Nash, "the Philadelphia militia had become a school of political education, much in the manner of Cromwell's New Model Army. Organizing their own Committee of Correspondence, the privates began exerting pressure on the assembly to take a more assertive stand on independence. They also made three radical demands for internal change: first, that militiamen be given the right to elect their own officers, rather than only their junior officers, as the assembly had specified in the militia law; second, that the franchise be conferred on all militiamen, regardless of age and economic condition; and third, that the assembly impose a heavy financial penalty, proportionate to the size of his estate, on every man who refused militia service, and use this money to support the families of poor militiamen."[87] During roughly the same autumn months, Virginia officials faced related, but lesser, economic demands in trying to reorganize that colony's military structure.

The evolution of committees in Pennsylvania, however, left Virginia and Maryland far behind. Names like Committee of Privates and Committee of Officers never migrated below the Mason-Dixon Line. Poorer Virginians might have been more deferential, but they also lacked Philadelphia's great urban political crucible.

Thus, events and developments in Pennsylvania provide the principal American Revolutionary parallel—and only a partial one—to the circa 1646–1647 onset of left-radicalism in the victorious English Parliamentary army. During the English Civil War, militia extremism was a late-stage phenomenon, not the early-stage eruption it was under Philadelphia's unique circumstances. As English soldiers' demands for democracy in both church and state grew, moderate schemes to curb or disband them only brought further tumult. Then in 1649, after King Charles I was tried and executed, England more or less became a republic, but within several years, it fell under military rule more authoritarian than left-radical.

In the seventeenth century, too, the most important militias were urban. As the English Civil War opened in 1642–1643, the trained bands, the militia forebears of that era, were rarely a factor. Most declined to leave their counties on behalf of either king or Parliament. The notable exception came in London, where trained bands numbering some 18,000 men moved overwhelmingly into the Parliamentary army. These bands furnished "the reserve on which Parliament relied in every emergency" during 1642 and 1643, much as New Englanders, especially Connecticut troops, would be the vital Patriot reserves of 1775 and 1776.[88]

For better and worse, Patriot leaders in the thirteen colonies were well aware of English Civil War precedents. As they too tried to mold citizen-soldiers into hard-fighting, reliable units, Cromwell's famous 1644–1645 "New Model" success came often to mind. In 1775 Virginia's George Mason sought, somewhat unrealistically, to "new-model the whole militia."[89] That did not happen, although some of the Continental regiments organized in 1775 and 1776 did, in a sense, New Model themselves into strong units.

Arguably, the Patriots' attention to militias and minutemen during 1774 and 1775 was as effective in timing—through its early-stage consolidation of the American Revolution—as the later-stage New Model Army proved to be at Naseby and the other battles during 1645 and 1646 that consolidated Parliament's victory in the English Civil War. Eighteenth-century New England, perhaps wiser from memory, did much of its New Modeling *before* widespread hostilities.

1775: The Militia's Importance as a Foundation of Revolution

Let us conclude with the thesis raised earlier: that by taking control of local government, militia structures, and police power across most of the thirteen-colony landscape in 1774–1775, insurgents established the framework that eventually brought success in the War for Independence. In contrast to the naïveté that citizen-soldiers must prevail through virtue, this policy represented a steely realpolitik.

The American rebels of 1775, unlike most other popular revolutionaries before or since, enjoyed the rare benefit of beginning their war in control of the local armed forces, the colonial militias.[90] To be sure, during the year or so before April 19, that achievement required foresight, purging, and strong-arming. "The colonial militia did not simply slide into the Revolution," according to military historian John Shy. "Military officers, even where they were elected, held royal commissions, and a significant number of them were not enthusiastic about rebellion. Purging and restructuring the militia was an important step toward revolution, one that deserves more attention than it has received."[91]

The Massachusetts Provincial Congress had acted, even before the First Continental Congress announced its Association in October 1774, to specify that local committees be set up to enforce its provisions. "The Association," argued Shy, was the vital link in transforming the colonial militia into a revolutionary organization . . . even where the Association encountered heavy opposition, it effectively dissolved the old military structure and created a new one based on consent, and whose chief purpose was to engineer consent, by force if necessary. The new Revolutionary militia might look very much like the old colonial militia, but it was, in its origins, less a draft board and a reserve training unit than a police force and an instrument of political surveillance."[92] The imprimatur of Congress made such organizations possible, and these multiple pressures forced Americans to commit themselves politically.

Shrewd Loyalists understood the significance of these early consolidations in areas they later sought to bring back under Crown control. After Britain's partial reoccupation of South Carolina in 1780, James Simpson, the Loyalist-named attorney general, concluded that it was from "civil institutions"—the earlier restructuring of government—"that the rebels derive the whole of their strength." Even many who had favored royal government were skeptical that it could be revived.[93] To British military historian Piers Mackesy, "Behind this despair was the rebel militia . . . it was they who subverted royal government at the outset of the rebellion and secured control of the machinery of authority for the rebels; who stifled early threats of counter-revolution; who defended the civil institutions of the revolution throughout the war; and who restored Revolutionary control wherever the British and loyalists had temporarily overthrown it."[94]

The internal police and surveillance function of the Revolutionary militia, visible from the Carolinas north to New England, is one that specialists have emphasized. In a related vein, the militia also fought in many small skirmishes and engagements—the so-called *petit-guerre*—too localized or minor for Continental armies. During the entire 1775–1783 period, for example, the militias participated on their own in 191 engagements in New York, New Jersey, and Connecticut, as opposed to the 485 times they and the Continentals combined. However, specialists seem to agree that the internal security function was paramount.[95] "One of the key contributions of the Whig militia," said one, "was its successful suppression of the Tory element in the states. When the Tories threatened the control of the new Whig governments in the first three years of the war, the state governments turned to their militiamen to locate, apprehend or kill the Tories."[96]

These few pages, more than others, will deliberately cite historians as the literary equivalent of expert witnesses. The pivotal long-term importance to the American Revolution of the civil and military committees, congresses, regiments, and associations set up in 1774–1775 is one of this book's central arguments. So let military historians John Shy, Walter Millis, Piers Mackesy, and the others testify in their own words.

Mackesy, a recognized British military expert on the American Revolution, emphasizes that "the militia, in its role as an internal security force, enabled Washington to keep the Continental army together in the middle colonies and to detach as necessary to meet specific incursions." American Walter Millis, in his classic *Arms and Men,* wrote that "repeatedly it was the militia which met the critical emergency or, in less formal operations, kept control of the country, cut off foragers, captured British agents, intimidated the war weary and disaffected or tarred and feathered the notorious Tories. The patriots' success in infiltrating and capturing the old militia organizations by expelling and replacing officers of Tory sympathies, was perhaps as important to the outcome as any of their purely political achievements."[97]

In short, purging, politicizing, and deploying a powerful internal security force was a critical 1774–1775 achievement with enormous consequences. John Shy's summary is comprehensive: "Once established, the militia became the infrastructure of revolutionary government. It controlled its community, whether through indoctrination or intimidation; it provided on short notice large numbers of armed men for brief periods of emergency service; and it found and persuaded, drafted or bribed, the smaller number of men needed each year to keep the Continental army alive. After the first months of the war, popular enthusiasm and spontaneity could not have sustained the struggle; only a pervasive armed organization, in which almost everyone took some part, kept people constantly, year after year, at the hard task of revolution."[98]

Luckily for the future United States, many British political leaders and generals began the war with a critical, even contemptuous view of the Americans, especially New England militiamen. Benjamin Franklin liked to quote a General Clarke—assumed to be Thomas Clarke, King George's military aide—boasting that with one thousand grenadiers he would cut through America "and geld all the Males, partly by force and partly by a little Coaxing."[99]

Disdainful of the New England bounty seekers and draftees they saw in the Champlain-Hudson corridor during the 1757–1759 campaigns, few British generals comprehended the difference between those hired recruits and regular-serving Yankee militiamen. George Washington himself shared much of the skepticism, being appalled by some of the short-term enlistees he saw in June 1775 on taking command of the army besieging Boston. But despite his doubts about the reliability of militia in major battles—here his skepticism was appropriate—by late 1775 he was applauding Connecticut's laws to restrain and punish Tories and others acting against the public interest. He specifically advised other provinces to follow Connecticut's lead in assigning this responsibility to the militia. By the war's end, he opined that "the Militia of this Country must be considered as the Palladium of our security, and the first effectual resort in case of hostility."[100]

The militia was often harsh in its methods, more so than the regiments of the Continental Line. However, without that political and military backstop, the American Revolution would probably not have survived its many reverses.

CHAPTER 6

Challenge from the Backcountry

After 1760 the increase in immigration [to America] became so great that it constituted a social force in itself, a force that added strain to the established relationship between the colonies and Britain. Even if there had been no political struggle between Britain and America, the relationship between them would have been altered . . . the extraordinary territorial and demographic expansion of the mainland colonies after 1760 presented problems to the British rulers of North America that could not be solved within the limits of the ideas of the time and of the government's administrative capacity.

Bernard Bailyn, Voyagers to the West, 1986

The main purpose of stationing a large body of troops in America [would be] to secure the dependence of the colonies on Great Britain.

William Knox, future undersecretary of the American Department, 1763

For all that British policy makers of the early 1760s had hoped to keep colonial Americans dependent and confined east of the Appalachian crest, they could not. Ironically, British strategists failed to recognize the extent to which the newly populated frontiers and hinterlands also posed dilemmas for would-be rebel governments. Many new settlers were as hostile—or even more so—to their provinces' coastal planters, Hudson Valley aristocrats, or staid Puritan Congregational church dignitaries as to any royal governor or far-off Parliament. Neither the hugeness nor the sentiment of the backcountry was well understood as war broke out.

By the late twentieth century, though, technology had enabled maps of America circa 1775 to present extraordinary detail on population distribution that, had it been possible to assemble and circulate at the time, would have better informed Patriot leaders and London officialdom alike. The Crown had strategic opportunities that went uncomprehended. Indeed, the details of frontier settlement still surprise even the expert.

What map 6 displays is straightforward. The light gray coloring shows the part of New England and New York already populated by 1760. Alongside, marked in dark gray, stretches the great expanse first settled during the 1760–1776 period. The upper swath of dark gray—the northern backcountry, along an arc from Maine to New York—added half again as much territory to the adjacent longer-settled regions. That affected, but did not hugely change, those provinces' politics.

The larger southern backcountry, shown in map 7, was not much smaller than the sections of the four colonies already settled in 1760. As map 7 shows, Virginia's older core still dominated, but the sprawling new population in the fast-changing Carolinas and Georgia gave each royal governor some ground for hope. This is the more famous backcountry—the canebrakes, river bottomland, and baptismal creeks thronged in the aftermath of the French and Indian War by families and opportunity seekers alike. Over the same period, it also changed by a significant in-migration of a different nature: runaways, former convicts, ex-servants, and ne'er-do-wells from London stews, Bridewell cells, Philadelphia servants' attics, debtors' courts, and Irish bogs. Tens of thousands poured south along the Great Wagon Road from Philadelphia to Augusta, Georgia, shaping a 1775 backcountry soon to be further inflamed by rebellion and war.

The Great Expansion: 1760–1775

Watchers had been awed. On the first day in 1769 when it opened for business, the land office at Fort Pitt on the Forks of the Ohio had 2,790 applicants. Three hundred miles to the south, in Salisbury, North Carolina, one observer reported that during the autumn and winter months of 1766, a thousand wagons had passed through heading west. Many more people crossed the Atlantic. From Irish ports alone, between March 1773 and June 1774, some 20,450 emigrants sailed to America.[1] Many of those reaching the backcountry did so within months of arriving in America.

To Frederick Jackson Turner, theorist of how the eighteenth- and nineteenth-century frontier remolded America, the upland South was the "new Pennsylvania," an extension of that state and its early hybrid population. As early as the 1730s and 1740s, rising costs of land in the Quaker

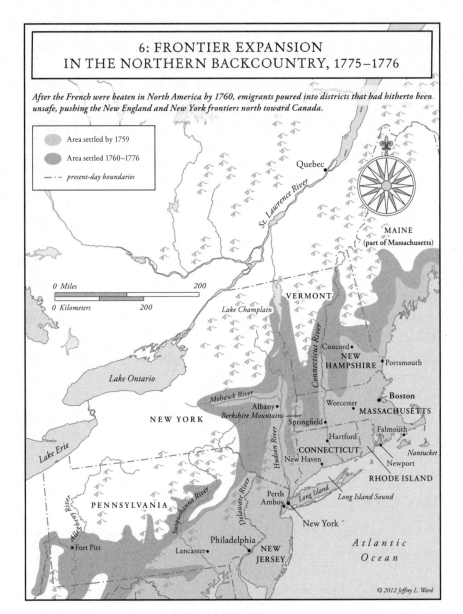

6: FRONTIER EXPANSION
IN THE NORTHERN BACKCOUNTRY, 1775–1776

After the French were beaten in North America by 1760, emigrants poured into districts that had hitherto been unsafe, pushing the New England and New York frontiers north toward Canada.

Area settled by 1759

Area settled 1760–1776

- · - *present-day boundaries*

Quebec

St. Lawrence River

MAINE
(part of Massachusetts)

0 Miles   200

0 Kilometers   200

VERMONT

Lake Champlain

Connecticut River

Concord
NEW
HAMPSHIRE   Portsmouth

Lake Ontario

Mohawk River   Worcester   Boston

Albany   Springfield   MASSACHUSETTS
Berkshire Mountains

NEW YORK

Hudson River   Hartford   Falmouth

CONNECTICUT   Nantucket

New Haven   Newport

Lake Erie   RHODE ISLAND

Allegheny River   *Susquehanna River*   *Delaware River*

Perth   Long Island   *Long Island Sound*
Amboy

PENNSYLVANIA   New York

Atlantic
Ocean

Philadelphia
Fort Pitt   Lancaster   NEW
JERSEY

© 2012 Jeffrey L. Ward

colony pushed new arrivals and younger sons toward more affordable stretches of Virginia and the Carolinas—pressures that only intensified during the 1760s and 1770s. A later chronicler, though, more accurately described the backcountry South as "Greater Pennsylvania."[2] Certainly many of the ethnic and religious migrants to the Carolinas looked back northward for kinship, not eastward to an unfamiliar southern tidewater.

Geographers and historians alike have drawn maps of the southward routes taken by the principal English, German, and Scotch-Irish migrant groups. Millions of amateur genealogists have since retraced those movements. Even twenty-first-century visitors to a trio of contiguous counties in northern South Carolina—Chester, York, and Lancaster, each named for a familiar county back in southeastern Pennsylvania—will spot county seats with a few old streets and buildings more akin to those 500 miles north.

The thesis of Pennsylvania extended can be overdone. A century later, during the siege of Fort Sumter, Yankee sympathy was scarce in upcountry South Carolina. Besides, the pre-Revolutionary routes became a southward and westward funnel for more than Pennsylvanians. These others included convicts from the shiploads Britain sent annually to America, runaway servants, burned-out frontier families fleeing tomahawks (and instantly hostile to southern Indians), former Regulators abandoning North Carolina after their 1771 defeat, rowdy "boys" (Steelboys, Whiteboys, Oakboys, etc.) from gangs in rural Ireland, and the incipient Cracker types that many Georgians, Carolinians, and even the Cherokee initially referred to as "Virginians."[3]

Violence was a backcountry staple. The major preoccupation of British mapmakers in drawing the contours of the southern backcountry was to update the ever-changing "Indian Boundary" from Virginia south. This was more to protect and placate the Indians than to favor settlers or land speculators, not a Crown priority. The controversial Proclamation Line of 1763, more or less following the Appalachian peaks, provided only a rough demarcation. Subsequent boundary adjustment came through an ongoing colony-by-colony process under the aegis of royal governors and John Stuart, Britain's Indian superintendent for the Southern Department. Officials in London had a veto, but for the most part they wanted to uphold the Proclamation Line.

Over the next decade, changes in the Indian Boundary were mostly minor. In Virginia, despite promises of land to French and Indian War veterans and the efforts of the Ohio Company, the Indian Boundary was not moved north or west of the Ohio River. The only major change, following the Fort Stanwix cession in 1768, was to open up eastern Kentucky lands abutting Virginia.[4] As we saw in Chapter 4, the hopes and frustrations of Virginia's land speculators became a driving force for revolution. The Indian Boundary was a related issue.

In North Carolina, a new Indian Boundary was redrawn *east* of the Proclamation Line in 1767 to reassure the Cherokee, even though it put thousands of recent settlers on shaky ground, west of lawful occupancy. According to the principal historian of these twists and turns, "here in the frontier beyond the North Carolina-Cherokee segment of the Southern Indian Boundary Line more than anywhere else along its great length . . . [the] line seemed to play a crucial role in determining the allegiance of a large group of frontiersmen in the Revolution." To another chronicler, the line "did more than anything else to alienate the borderers."[5]

In South Carolina, however, the border agreed on by the Cherokee and provincial officials at the Congress of Augusta in 1763 was slowly but significantly moved back into Cherokee country, which pleased settlers. The colony's two-year war with the Cherokee had ended somewhat equivocally in 1761, and subsequent border conferences between 1766 and 1773 resulted in small additional Cherokee land concessions and further white incursions into Indian hunting grounds.[6]

Circumstances in the border region soon pitted some white Carolinians against others. The firming up of the Indian Boundary, by one analysis, explained the rapid emergence of backcountry's vigilante-type Regulator movement. "The Dividing Line between the Cherokees and North and South Carolina was set between 1765 and 1768, and the South Carolina Regulation began in 1767 . . . once the boundary between the Carolinians and their most threatening external adversary had been fixed, colonial leading men could address enemies within their own society." According to colonial historian Tom Hatley, these included vagrants, *banditti,* horse thieves, runaway servants and slaves, and the like.[7]

From Virginia to Georgia, boundary modifications were major events, affecting frontier residents, surveyors, squatters, land company investors, provincial assemblies, and militia officers alike. At least one of the king's ministers also paid close attention—the Earl of Hillsborough, who served as American secretary between 1768 and 1772. A huge landholder in Protestant northern Ireland, Hillsborough was also a long-standing alarm sounder about emigration to North America, which he wanted to halt. A

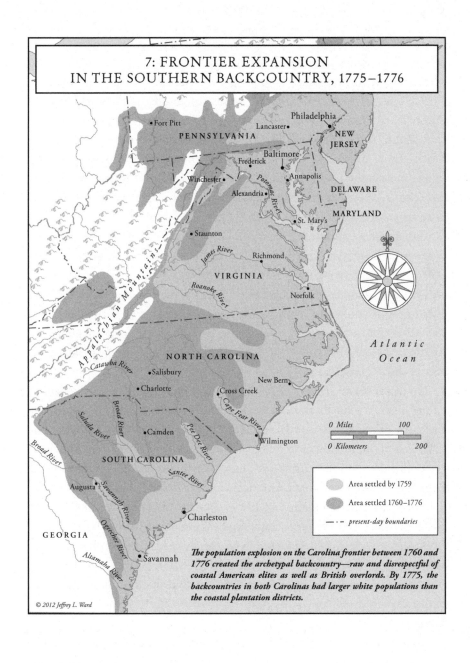

7: FRONTIER EXPANSION
IN THE SOUTHERN BACKCOUNTRY, 1775–1776

Philadelphia
• Fort Pitt
Lancaster•
PENNSYLVANIA
NEW JERSEY
Baltimore•
Frederick•
Winchester•
Annapolis•
Alexandria•
DELAWARE
St. Mary's•
MARYLAND

• Staunton

James River
Richmond•

VIRGINIA

Roanoke River
Norfolk•

Appalachian Mountains

Atlantic Ocean

Catawba River
NORTH CAROLINA
•Salisbury
•Charlotte
New Bern•
Cross Creek•

Cape Fear River

Saluda River
Broad River
•Camden
Pee Dee River
Wilmington•

Broad River

SOUTH CAROLINA
Santee River

Augusta•
Savannah River

Charleston•

GEORGIA

Ogeechee River
•Savannah

Altamaha River

0 Miles 100
0 Kilometers 200

Area settled by 1759

Area settled 1760–1776

— ·· — *present-day boundaries*

The population explosion on the Carolina frontier between 1760 and 1776 created the archetypal backcountry—raw and disrespectful of coastal American elites as well as British overlords. By 1775, the backcountries in both Carolinas had larger white populations than the coastal plantation districts.

© 2012 Jeffrey L. Ward

government report in 1773 estimated that during the prior five years or so, Ulster had "been drained of one fourth of its trading cash and the like proportion of the manufacturing people" by transatlantic emigration.[8]

Back in 1753, Hillsborough had proposed—and Parliament had quickly rejected—a census in Britain to establish a basis for deciding when emigration should be blocked or allowed. Even at that early date, both George Washington and Benjamin Franklin had come to see the Irish peer as a dangerous enemy—Washington noted his "malignant disposition towards Americans."[9] Few issues engaged Washington more than threats to America's westward expansion.

Officials had undertaken just one head count related to the southern backcountry. In 1755, John Stuart's Indian Department had prepared a detailed survey of how many "gun-men"—musket or rifle-bearing warriors—the various Cherokee, Catawba, Creek, Chickasaw, Choctaw, and Alabama tribal groups could put in the field (some 10,000).[10] For various reasons, including the fur trade and minimizing defense costs, government policy implicitly favored the tribes and preferred to keep land-hungry Americans east of the Appalachians.

No record seems to have been kept of the influx of white settlers. Neither camp, British officials nor colonial plotters, had compiled or sought to make use of the frontier settlement detail displayed in map 7. Despite London's fear of population growth, no grand strategic memorandum pondered the political and military implications, which abounded. Could cutting off British emigration to North America succeed? If the frontier could not be held back and the population of British North America reached 5 million by 1790, didn't that argue for some kind of home rule in which the Americans paid for their own defense? Even the British military plan that coalesced in 1775 around reinvading the thirteen colonies from Canada down New York's Champlain-Hudson corridor wound up stumbling almost as badly over out-of-date demographics as over flawed coordination in London.

To the dismay of generals whose images of America were time frozen in 1757 or 1760, large numbers of New England backcountry settlers had pushed farther west. General John Burgoyne's later surrender at Saratoga in October 1777 was previewed months earlier when a major detachment of his force was overwhelmed near current-day Bennington, Vermont, and forced to surrender by flocking New England volunteers and militiamen. In a letter to Lord George Germain, Burgoyne, with verbal flair befitting an amateur dramatist, later acknowledged that the Hampshire Grants had become a wasps' nest: "A country unpeopled and most unknown [in] the last war . . . [it] now abounds in the most active and most rebellious race of the continent, and hangs like a gathering storm upon my left."[11]

By contrast, George Washington and Thomas Jefferson were widely informed, at least about their own colony's vast hinterland. Jefferson's father, a cartographer as well as a planter, had collaborated in the Fry-Jefferson map of 1755, which drew in detail western Virginia's frontier and borderlands.[12] We have seen how Virginia and South Carolina militia leaders gained wartime experience of their frontiers in 1761 and 1774; New Englanders, for their part, had cut military roads and freighted provisions northward for generations.

Of course, many of the seaboard merchants, lawyers, and gentry who led the Revolution in its early stages had only middling acquaintance with the backcountry in their own provinces and knew little about backcountries elsewhere. For example, many of the coastal North Carolinians in the forefront of the 1775–1776 opposition to British policy had also officered in the front ranks of the militia led by Royal Governor William Tryon when he crushed several thousand backcountry insurgents at the Battle of Alamance in May 1771. Not a few beaten farmers remembered the tidewater Whigs as bitterly as they did Tryon.

For all of these reasons, backcountry districts in roughly half of the thirteen colonies presented an internal challenge to Revolutionary leaders in 1775. Historians have focused on the South, but as map 6 makes clear, there was also a northern backcountry, from Maine to the Mohawk Valley. A "middle" backcountry would have centered on Pennsylvania. Portions of its northeast were being contested by Connecticut even as Virginia claimed and occupied western territory around the Forks of the Ohio.

Backcountry discontents varied from colony to colony, reflecting the diverse origins of the migrants as well as their varied reasons for relocating between 1760 and 1775. Building a sense of community took time, and abusive, distant, or corrupt officials made poor relations worse. On top of which, not a few new arrivals were fleeing debt, harsh masters, court orders, or military service.

Especially below the Mason-Dixon Line, description of the inflow as a "stampede" hardly exaggerates. Between 1720 and 1780, about 49,000 square miles of territory west of Virginia's Blue Ridge were settled, and of these, 32,000 square miles were occupied only during the two decades between 1760 and 1780.[13] To Bailyn, this phenomenon represented one of American history's blind spots: "If, as seemed likely in 1771 and 1772, the struggle between Britain and her American colonies had been peacefully resolved and people had been free to concentrate on other major issues of the day, history would have recorded more clearly than it has the importance of a remarkable development of the 1760s and 1770s that was temporarily cut off by the Revolution . . . an extraordinary flood of immigration to British mainland North America, and closely associated with that, a sudden and immense spread of settlement in the backcountry of the coastal colonies and in the trans-Appalachian West." Bailyn's own encyclopedic survey, *Voyagers to the West: A Passage in the Peopling of America on the Eve of Revolution,* has helped to remedy the statistical neglect.[14] The political yeast, however, also warrants attention.

For the Carolinas and Georgia, the great influx obviously affected the choice of loyalties in the pre-Revolutionary era. Lesser effects were felt in Virginia. For that matter, even across the roof of New England— through Maine and upper New Hampshire and the Hampshire Grants that became Vermont—growth ratios resembled the beanstalk effects in the Carolinas. The raw numbers and cultural upheaval were less, though, because northern New England's great population explosion followed the Revolution.

Among all the volatile backcountries, center stage during the early 1770s went to the ballooning hinterlands of the Carolinas, with their attendant mixture of corruption, lawlessness, itinerant evangelists, hardworking families, and so-called Regulators. The warmer piedmont of South Carolina and Georgia beckoned a partly Celtic culture enthused over reports that pigs and even cattle could overwinter out of doors on acorns and grass. Flimsy cabin walls would suffice, and corn liquor was cheap. Generations of college students have absorbed the stereotype-laden portrait in *The Carolina Backcountry on the Eve of the Revolution,* compiled from the journals of Anglican preacher Charles Woodmason.[15]

As Woodmason elaborated, with disdain and sarcasm, this semianarchy extended to religion. Churches were few and far between. Denominational differences, revealing and important, were only loosely mapped. A score of Presbyterian congregations and churches planted in the migrations of the 1730s, 1740s, and 1750s to Virginia's Shenandoah Valley and south into the Carolinas were the rock-hewn and education-conscious oldsters of dissenting religion in the southern backcountry. Located along the Great Wagon

Road from Pennsylvania, some attracted relatively learned ministers. Schools usually followed, and sometimes colleges.

Below Virginia, new Anglican churches in the southern backcountry were few. The small clapboard churches of the evangelical denominations generally lacked settled ministers. Hardly any were on hand to perform marriages or baptisms. Itinerants carried much of the burden. Many districts were unchurched, and denominational loyalties were fluid. Even many Scotch-Irish Presbyterians fell away.

The predominant religious thrust in both backcountries, northern and southern, was insurgent and evangelical—biblically flavored, salvationist, keening, and body shaking. It dissented not simply from the religious establishments of England and Scotland (Presbyterian) but from the churches of educated New England (Congregational) and the Plantation South (elite, unemotional Anglican). Despite having been founded in the seventeenth century by religious refugees, the Puritan meetinghouses of Massachusetts and Connecticut now found that they, in turn, had created refugees from their own middle-class culture and university-educated clergy. Many of the disenchanted fled to "Separate" or revivalist Baptist churches.

From the Green Mountains to the Blue Ridge and beyond, the backcountry revivalism of the 1760s and early 1770s extended the Great Awakening into circumstances that were politically as well as theologically unpredictable. Congregational ranks in New England were riven by the rise of evangelical and enthusiastic factions and breakaways. The movements that became Shakers, Universalists, and Free Will Baptists all established footholds in New England during those years, much as Quakers, Baptists, and Ranters gained traction in the 1640s amid the chaos of the English Civil War. By 1777 and 1778, the Revolution in New England had launched small but wild-eyed sects like the Come-Outers and the Merry Dancers, who blazed a lusty path in inland Maine.[16] In the Hampshire Grants, political unrest and factionalism were abetted by denominational tumult: Anglicans, Baptists, and Dutch claiming under New York land grants, deists like Ethan Allen, Separates of various hues, Congregationalists akin to those elsewhere in New England, Scottish Covenanters, and many more. Where they can be sorted out, confused politics makes a bit more sense.

The emotional and charismatic dimension of the southern backcountry reached far beyond Baptists. Mystical and pacifist German offshoots of Pennsylvania's Dunkers had migrated to the hills of southwestern Virginia and parts of North Carolina. Their behavior in the 1750s discomforted both church Germans and Colonel George Washington, who accused them of consorting with raiding Cherokees.[17] A German Lutheran district in the lower South Carolina backcountry was infected in the late 1750s by a so-called Webber heresy, in which some men believed they were God and others the Devil—and killed each other. The public hanging of Jacob Webber, however, reinforced immigrant German distrust of the Charleston elite and gave local pre-Revolutionary politics a Loyalist coloration.[18]

Other fringe elements of some local significance included the Reformed and Seceder church offshoots of Presbyterianism in the Carolinas. The Methodists were still nominally part of the Church of England, and several of their British-born missionaries in Maryland were expelled for Tory sympathies.

Nevertheless, from the roof of New England to Carolina's Piedmont balcony, the most important apathy toward the Revolution came from enthusiastic and doctrinally militant "Separate" Baptists. Theirs was a religion in which unschooled preachers itinerated, exhorted, shook, and trembled to assert their own direct summons to God. They condemned the constraints imposed on them by civic authorities, state-sanctioned Congregationalists, and vestry Anglicans—the same Patriots who complained about the injustices Parliament and the king's ministers sought to impose. This made for uncomfortable political as well as religious relationships.

Ironically, Baptist fervor was introduced to the southern backcountry by missionary-minded evangelicals from New England. The leader, Shubal Stearns, built a Separate Baptist network in North Carolina. Then disciples of Stearns, moving to upcountry South Carolina, built an outsider culture of itinerancy, "love feasts," female deaconesses, adult immersion, and disdain for learned ministries that was unpopular with local authorities. These practices also put them at odds with the more sedate theology and behavior of other Baptists—the long-established Regular Baptists of Charleston and the Welsh Tract, most of them Patriots, as well as older Baptist associations in Philadelphia and Rhode Island.

However, before we discuss the attributes of religion in the Carolina hinterlands, it is necessary to understand the sometime role of the backcountry as a political subculture or mistreated stepchild of established government. Such circumstances became an understandable nursery of disrespect for civic authority. From the Bay of Fundy to the Savannah River, backcountry residents, most of them new arrivals, had reasons to distrust their provincial governments, complaints that often distanced them from the dominant Patriot-faction elites.

Backcountry Grudges and Ambivalent 1775 Loyalties

In roughly half of the thirteen colonies, official neglect, corruption, or misgovernment of backcountry districts—this in addition to newly settled areas' typical lack of nearby courts, adequate law enforcement, or representation in provincial legislatures—bred serious disaffection among new arrivals. Parts of New Hampshire, the Maine district of Massachusetts, northern New York, Pennsylvania, and both Carolinas are examples.

Little should surprise us about how provinces and counties with exploding populations quickly outgrew twenty-year-old, ten-year-old, or even five-year-old frameworks of government. Or how colonial assemblies, content with familiar arrangements, were slow to reform regional maldistributions of districts and courthouses that by the 1770s had become unacceptable. However, when government facilities remained three to five days distant for fair-sized populations, that went beyond mere inconvenience; so, too, when land sales, record keeping, and sheriff's offices evolved beyond sloth into open corruption. In colonies that made reasonable efforts to keep up standards—this list usually includes Virginia, Massachusetts, and Connecticut—no great alienation was apparent in the expanding hinterlands. However, several provinces let discriminatory practices and corruption breed enough resentment to influence backcountry loyalties as the Revolution approached.

Here squabbles over *external* territory can be set aside. Virginia, Massachusetts, and Connecticut all had unsustainably remote outliers: Virginia soon lost her settlements in western Pennsylvania and in Kentucky (which became a separate state in 1792). Massachusetts had no claim to its settlements on the Bay of Fundy in Nova Scotia, and its noncontiguous Maine district became a separate state in 1820. Connecticut lost its outlier in northeastern Pennsylvania, and Vermont became a separate state in 1791. These claims complicated relations between Virginia and Pennsylvania and between Connecticut and Pennsylvania, but fortunately not in ways that seriously threatened the Revolution.

The internal circumstances of New Hampshire, New York, North Carolina, and South Carolina were more complicated—in several cases, divisive enough to endanger provincial stability. Small to begin with, New

Hampshire almost became smaller. Its western and northern towns in the Connecticut Valley, little tied to the eastern seacoast centers that were New Hampshire's early core, had been largely settled from Connecticut and Massachusetts. They were grossly underrepresented in the New Hampshire legislature under Royal Governor John Wentworth in 1775, and the inequity persisted under the province's new 1776 constitution. Many western townships considered splitting off entirely. According to the principal history of New Hampshire in the Revolutionary period, between 1776 and 1782 "a part or a whole of this [Connecticut Valley] region was independent," and in 1781 thirty-five of those distant towns tried to join up with Vermont.[19]

If northern New England was somewhat unstable and ambivalent during the 1775–1777 period, next-door New York had its own headaches. Back in 1764, King George III had ruled that New York, not New Hampshire, held proper title to the "Grants" west of the Connecticut River. Once empowered, New York, ever at odds with New England, speedily set up its own counties, courthouses, and Anglican Church entitlements. Well-connected Yorkers obtained large land grants in the new territory, while New York officials disallowed titles awarded earlier by New Hampshire. By 1770, this had brought on small-scale border warfare, which pitted the Green Mountain Boys, led by the Connecticut-born Allen brothers and their cousin Seth Warner, against the despised Yorkers attempting to rule the Green Mountains from Albany. In 1771, Ethan Allen and his irregulars faced down and scattered a large New York posse under Albany sheriff Henry Ten Eyck. Although angry New York authorities outlawed Allen, no serious invasion was ever mounted.[20] New York ultimately had to surrender its Green Mountain slice of New England, but Yankee gains might not have ended there.

By 1775, independence-wary New York had stumbled into its own reverse vulnerability. Some Patriots in Connecticut and Massachusetts hoped that amid the chaos of 1775–1776, New York's boundaries could be trimmed for their benefit. Through grants in the 1750s and 1760s, New Hampshire had claimed westward to the Hudson. The Grants took over that claim. Massachusetts and Connecticut also had border disputes with New York. Eastern Long Island, in turn, had once been part of Connecticut. Alexander Hamilton was not the only New Yorker to worry about the possibility of dismemberment.

In a second scenario, had New York factions, Patriot and Crown supporters alike, fallen into civil war in 1775, more Yankee troops might have crossed the border in various places—and stayed.

Pennsylvania was a more remote possibility for dismemberment. For decades, as we have seen, its Quaker-run Assembly had offended popular opinion in three principal ways: (1) antique legislative districts that guaranteed control of the Assembly to the three original Quaker counties while grossly shortchanging the burgeoning half dozen to the west; (2) a persisting refusal to establish a provincial militia to protect western settlers; and (3) enough general nonresponsiveness to bring about a movement during the mid-1760s to end government under the charter given William Penn and remake Pennsylvania into a regular colony. By the winter of 1775–1776, backcountry hostility had firmly set against Philadelphia's conservative Anglican and Quaker elites. Had these conservatives managed to hold control and block independence in May and June 1776, could Pennsylvania have fragmented? Could the Susquehanna and the northeast have gone to Connecticut, and the west to a Patriot-governed Virginia, while greater Philadelphia slipped under militia government? Probably not, but who can be sure?

In short, large backcountry populations were sometimes major destabilizing forces within provinces, and the Carolinas stood out. Their backcountries were the two areas that royal governors told London were certain to rise against coastal Patriot elites. And to an extent, they did.

The coastal Whigs controlling North Carolina's Assembly may have been no more politically devious than the Philadelphia Quakers. However, they had tolerated and sometimes condoned the abusive and corrupt land-related and tax-collection practices that helped to provoke the Regulator movement. That famous insurgency began in 1766 with the founding of the Piedmont-based Sandy Creek Association, and it ended in 1771 after bloody suppression at the so-called Battle of Alamance. As a movement, the hapless insurgents combined an unusual blend of naïve politics, economics, and religion with a generally valid indictment of corrupt land practices and sheriffs.

So compelling were the complaints of corruption and malpractice that the new royal governor arriving in late 1771, Josiah Martin, worked to reposition the Crown as more sympathetic to what Regulators had sought. Convinced that he had struck a popular chord, in 1775 Martin assured London that many ex-Regulators would rally to the king's standard, joining the interior's thousands of loyal Scottish Highlanders. Martin misread the practicalities—many disillusioned ex-Regulators had already headed west to the mountains. However, the coastal plantation elites captaining the Revolution, some of them prominent at Alamance as militia officers, also worried about the enmity still lingering in the Piedmont.

South Carolina's coastal elites, more powerful and much richer than those in North Carolina, had also for some years neglected the province's burgeoning backcountry. Courts, law enforcement, and seats in the legislature were thinly provided, but laws passed to meet some of these needs had been disallowed by the Privy Council, so the Crown lacked clean hands. Even so, a considerable historical confusion—widespread belief that the two Carolina "Regulation" insurgencies were similar—requires a basic reinterpretation.

Except in name, the two were not alike; fundamental differences existed. In North Carolina, that colony's Regulators were predominantly New Light or Inner Light religious believers, partly swayed by radical theology, partly acting out of political naïveté, and generally immature in tactics. Numerous women also participated, unusual in that era, and Regulator ranks included Separate Baptists, disowned and fallen-away Quaker emigrants from Pennsylvania, some pacifist Moravians and Dunkers, and only a small minority of Presbyterians. Significantly, the colony's Presbyterian clergy and Sons of Liberty opposed both the Sandy Creek Association and the local Regulation, and strongly discouraged Presbyterian participation.[21]

Not so in South Carolina. Many of that colony's Regulators were to a considerable degree regional vigilantes and were for the most part tied to the backcountry's white, male power structure. Besides pressing for local courthouses, close-at-hand law enforcement, and new backcountry seats in the South Carolina Assembly House of Commons, these Regulators worked to break up or round up so-called Scovilites or Coffelites—horse thieves, *banditti,* runaway slaves and servants, vagrants, and white hunters who lived with Cherokee women.[22] This was an important distinction. Most of these Regulators were neither politically naïve nor religiously spiritual. Denominationally, they were an ordinary mixture of the unchurched with Presbyterians, Anglicans, Lutherans, and Regular Baptists. As we will see in Chapter 19, they fought overwhelmingly on the Patriot side when backcountry civil war broke out in 1775.

Backcountry unhappiness, then, was less an aberration than a commonplace in the American colonies circa 1775. The catch is that each set of intraprovincial antipathies had local ingredients that only subtle and well-informed British strategy could have maximized. The border situations in Pennsylvania and the Hampshire Grants doubtless swayed some wartime loyalties. But for all that data is thin, the cultural and religious dissonance in the Carolinas was more important. The royal governors of both Carolinas, who told London that backcountry malcontents would support the Crown against the Whig gentry, were overconfident and inept. On the other hand, five years hence in 1780 and 1781, British policy makers brought about a prolonged civil war in the two Carolinas along somewhat similar fault lines.

Tomahawk Patriots: The Frontier and the Indian Threat

Across much of the South, a frontier Indian menace worked wonders for the Patriots of 1775 in subordinating backcountry dissension. The term *menace* is no exaggeration, because roughly a decade after the French and Indian War, and the aftershock of Pontiac's War in 1763–1764, few observers doubted the intensity of ongoing settler fear.[23] The North American colonies had spent two thirds of the years between 1739 and 1764 in French and Spanish wars that included a bloody Indian frontier. The year 1774 alone saw war with two tribes—the Shawnee in western Virginia and the Creeks in Georgia. Many of the tribes, by this point, preferred to resist rather than be pushed back farther by never-ending white-settler incursions.

Through 1774, frontier uncertainties kept some white loyalties conditional: Would King George and his Indian Department officials offer the best protection? Would the Patriots now taking control appoint equally effective Indian agents? George Galphin, who represented both Georgia and South Carolina with the Creek tribe, was one who appeared to fit the bill. Would the Shawnee (or Ohio's Delaware) be neutral? By mid-1775, the Abenaki and some Iroquois factions seemed well disposed, but would they remain so? Prospects remained murky for many months after Lexington and Concord.

New England was no longer on the front line of colonial Indian fighting, save for what is now Vermont. As conflict spread in 1775, the Champlain corridor stood to be a principal British invasion route, renewing the importance of yesteryear's tribal enemies. Patriot envoys were hard at work. Colin Calloway, the principal chronicler of Indian attitudes toward the American Revolution, described the courtship of the formerly French-allied

Western or St. Francis Abenaki: "Before his abortive attack on Montreal, Ethan Allen sent a Stockbridge [Indian] ambassador in May 1775 to win the support of the Caughnawaga, St. Regis, Lake of the Two Mountains, and St. Francis Indians, promising them blankets, tomahawks, knives and paint, and proclaiming his love of Indian peoples and knowledge of their ways. The Seven Nations of Canada declared their intentions not to fight the Yankees, and the Penobscots, Passamaquoddies, Micmacs and St. Johns Indians [of Maine and New Brunswick] displayed pro-American sentiments. In December 1775 the Continental Congress passed a resolution to call upon the Stockbridge, St. Johns, Penobscot and St. Francis Indians 'in case of real necessity.' Caughnawaga became a major center of Indian activity in the opening months of the war as redcoats and Yankees vied for Indian support and the tribes assessed the new state of affairs."[24]

This partial success is typically lost in 1776-centered portraiture. In the autumn of 1775, for example, some 40 Abenaki joined the American invasion of Quebec! Once those expeditions came undone, though, so did the interest of Canadian tribes in an alliance. Indian support for the British reemerged in 1776, although the Penobscot, Passamaquoddys, and Stockbridge of New England remained American allies.

To the west, northern New York's Mohawk Valley also became contested ground. Sir William Johnson, superintendent of the Northern Indian Department, who long kept much of the Iroquois nation loyal to Britain, had died in 1774, leaving shoes no one could fill. His nephew and successor, Colonel Guy Johnson, fled to Canada in 1775 and ran the Northern department from there. Many of the Johnson family's Scottish and Palatine German supporters and tenants took the Crown's side, moving north. Hundreds abandoned their properties to join Loyalist regiments. The valley stayed divided, with many Tories remaining and assisting the British in later invasions.

In July 1775, Patriots also sent emissaries to the embattled Iroquois Confederacy. But of the six tribes, only one wound up on the American side—the Presbyterian-missionary-influenced Oneida. For many months, apprehension that invasion through the Champlain corridor and the Mohawk Valley might restore British control kept some ambivalent New Yorkers on the fence. Only in the autumn of 1777, after two separate British expeditions were defeated at the Battles of Bennington, Oriskany, and Saratoga, did the balance tilt to the American side. Even then, the valley remained torn by a local civil war.

A battleground where loyalties more clearly turned on the Indian threat was central and western Pennsylvania. As we have seen, Quaker policy had been to stay on good terms with the Indians—a relationship that sometimes included selling them hatchets and muskets—rather than extending settlement westward and undertaking major defense outlays. The far west of Pennsylvania, near Pittsburgh and the Forks of the Ohio, was claimed in 1775 by both Pennsylvania and Virginia. By early summer, perceptions as to which side would better protect the region swung on impressions of Virginia's mercurial governor.

By November, Lord Dunmore's plan to bring the Indians down on Virginia had damned him. A largely Indian force was to be led through Ohio and western Virginia by British and Loyalist officers. After traveling down the Potomac, it was to link up with Dunmore in April 1776 at the port of Alexandria. Gage in Boston had at first approved the idea, but public exposure that autumn turned the issue of Indian danger against the British in both colonies, Virginia and Pennsylvania.

For the most part, a different set of tribes menaced the southeastern frontier in the Carolinas and Georgia. Here, too, the question was which side would offer better protection. The British government's Southern Indian Department, under Superintendent Stuart and his key deputies, Alexander Cameron (who dealt with the Cherokee), Charles Stuart (with the Choctaw), David Taitt (the Creeks), and Farquhar Bethune (the Chickasaw), was both Loyalist and Scottish, as were many of the Indian traders in the southeast.[25] By late 1775 and 1776, these relationships suggested that when the frontier burst into flame, the Cherokee and the Creeks would be British allies. Opposing Indian dangers might unite backcountry whites who otherwise would have been more divided politically.

In both Georgia and South Carolina, the Patriot faction initially kept open lines to both Creeks and Cherokee, even working to ensure delivery of the usual annual supplies of arms or ammunition counted on by the tribes. In Georgia, the gunpowder promised to the Creeks during the autumn was not brought until February 1776.[26] In South Carolina, Patriot leaders attempted delivery in late October 1775, sending a wagon loaded with some lead and a thousand pounds of gunpowder for the Cherokee's winter hunt. However, that wagon was waylaid and captured in the backcountry by Tory irregulars, who thereupon cited the supplies as evidence that *Patriots* sought to arm the Cherokee against the Loyalists.[27]

Frontier memories made that explanation too illogical to succeed. South

Carolina's 1759–1761 war with the Cherokee, as we have seen, had been a training ground for many future Patriot military leaders. Many backcountrymen had also been left unhappy over its inconclusive result and distrustful of the British as too attentive to the Cherokee.[28] In consequence, when a South Carolina Patriot militia, in December 1775, defeated several hundred armed Tories, Indian traders, and Scovilites camped across the Indian Line on Cherokee land, they tapped into old frontier and vigilante psychologies. Whig historian David Ramsey, writing a decade later, concluded that "the names of the Scovilites and Regulators were insensibly exchanged for the appellation of Tories and Whigs, or the friends of the old order and the new order of things."[29] This evocation, said historian Tom Hatley, scored a Whig "propaganda victory" by "tapping deep-seated anti-tribal fears among the backcountry farmers."[30]

After deciding on full-scale war during the spring, the Cherokee, in company with hundreds of Indian-connected Loyalists, on July 1 attacked the settlements along a broad front from Virginia to Georgia. After initial shock and white flight, troops from all four colonies counterattacked, in numbers that ultimately reached 6,000 men. This campaign, which broke the strength of the Cherokee nation, produced a great psychological victory. Historian Ramsey wrote that "several who called themselves Tories in 1775 became active Whigs in 1776 and cheerfully took up arms against the Indians, and in the second, against Great Britain, as the instigator of their barbarous devastations."[31]

The Cherokee became a Whig recruiting poster. A chronicler more sympathetic to the British and Indians agreed that "the Cherokee attacks promoted unity among most backcountry inhabitants, regardless of their political persuasion . . . [Loyalist] Robert Cunningham 'would not at first believe that the British Administration were so wicked as to Instigate the Savages to War against us.' When he realized it was true, Cunningham and other Loyalists imprisoned in Charleston offered to serve against the Cherokee and the Council of Safety released them from confinement."[32] Would-be neutrals in the backcountry changed their minds after seeing Loyalists painted like Indians among their attackers, enabling Patriots to consolidate firm political control that lasted almost four years until the British turned south in 1780 and invaded South Carolina in force.

In Georgia, many frontier settlers had at first believed claims by Governor Wright and his friends that British strength and influence would best safeguard them from nearby Creek Indians able to put several thousand "gunmen" in the field. But these Indian-hating "Crackers"—a term Wright himself used—changed their minds after becoming convinced that "their [British] rulers preferred the Indians and the Indian trade to the interests of the settlers." In 1775, these inhabitants came to believe that John Stuart, the Indian superintendent, was planning to bring the Cherokee down on them. In the words of one Georgia historian, "the rumor, false though it was, was the most effective weapon the liberty faction could have used to win over the people of the frontier. Fear of Indians kept the frontier loyal in 1774; fear of Indians would sever that loyalty in 1775."[33]

One irony was that by beating the Cherokee so decisively, troops in both Carolinas reduced their menace to no more than an occasional small raid. Loyalists could no longer easily be tied to Indians when the more serious civil war unfolded in 1780 and 1781.

A few British officials in the southern colonies—Virginia's Dunmore was obviously one—had argued in 1775 it would be best to quickly mobilize the Indians as allies. But Stuart, the superintendent, remembering South Carolina's Cherokee War of 1759–1761, understood better. Unless the Indians operated with British troops and were kept somewhat under their control, he thought, Cherokee or Creek depredations would benefit the rebels.[34]

In this early stage of the war, Patriot victories over the Cherokee between July and October 1776 were anticlimactic. Their defeat in South Carolina had been preordained when the Snow Campaign of December 1775 united the white settlers. As for Virginia, defeat of the Cherokee in the new state's far southwest also came after Dunmore's credibility had been all but lost with his late July evacuation of Gwynn's Island, just off the mouth of the Rappahannock River.

The effect that anti-Indian feeling had on southern backcountry psychologies was not lost on Patriot politicians. Thomas Jefferson had been anti-Indian in 1775, but as governor in 1781, he issued especially harsh instructions to George Rogers Clark and his Virginia troops for dealing with the upper Ohio Indians: "The end proposed should be their extermination, or their removal beyond the [Great] lakes. The same world will scarcely do for them or us."[35] So much for the endowment of all men with inalienable rights.

Religious Refugees and Evangelical Insurgents

Among the migrants to the backcountry were some fleeing war or escaping civic obligation. Others were forsaking state churches and patriotism for a charismatic religion of salvation and oneness with a personal God. Most of the second category were evangelicals, children and grandchildren of the Great Awakening, not a few of whom had little use for a revolution allied with Whig town or county governments and churches with an educated clergy.

The North Carolina backcountry, besides Separate Baptists, had a small but politically combustible admixture of disowned and fallen-away Quakers who had left Pennsylvania. In northern New England, many evangelicals were at religious and political odds with the Puritan cultural hearth of greater Boston. Many were poor and uneducated. While not Tories, they disliked Congregationalism's "God is an American Patriot" military commitment and theology. Some New Lights and "Inner Lights" (Quakers or fallen-away Quakers) believed that God held a different set of priorities. The true role of the American Revolution, or so they explained, would be to disestablish southern and New England state churches, making way for the new direct-relationship creeds through which God truly made himself known.[36]

This was certainly the view of many Baptists. Those in Rhode Island and Connecticut got along reasonably well with their relatively democratic and Baptist-friendly Patriot governments. However, in Massachusetts (including its Maine district) and in New Hampshire, Baptists assailed established Congregationalism and its political allies for denying them religious and tax-related rights akin to those that Americans were insisting on from Britain. In Massachusetts proper, Patriot leaders worked out an arrangement whereby most Baptists supported the Revolution and were willing to bear arms.[37] But across New England's northern roof, where both government power and the war were distant, an emotional immersion in religion—the kiss of charity instead of militia duty—tilted a sizable minority of Separate Baptist preachers and their adherents toward neutralism.[38]

The future Vermont, with no local church establishment, would become a famous seedbed of prophets and sect organizers, including the families of Mormons Joseph Smith and Brigham Young; John Humphrey Noyes, the founder of the Oneida community; and William Miller, the founder of the Adventists. If any part of the northern backcountry matched Maine for sects and religious quirkiness, it was Vermont.[39]

Even so, the most powerful religious yeast of 1775 was bubbling in the southern colonies, where Anglicanism's final, fading decade as a gentry-dominated, established church promised to open a wide door for itinerant-led, emotional religion. To be fair, Virginia Anglicans did a better job than other colonies, organizing dozens of Anglican churches in the backcountry. Lutheran and Presbyterian churches were also allowed, and dozens thrived. Even so, a large vacuum existed, and by the 1760s Separate Baptists had taken particular hold in Southside counties close to the North Carolina border. The years just before the Revolution saw the largest growth. By 1774, Virginia had 54 Separate Baptist churches or chapels, up from 14 in 1771 and just 7 in 1770.[40]

North Carolina's burgeoning hinterland was thinly churched. Although a royal governor made concerted efforts on behalf of the established church during the 1760s, by 1775 only two Anglican churches had been built west of the fall line—in Hillsborough and Salisbury. In Charlotte, the largely Presbyterian community had successfully demonstrated against an Anglican church there.[41] As for Separate Baptists, whereas their seedbed in Virginia circa 1775 involved a half dozen Southside counties, in North Carolina most of the Piedmont was in the grip of dissenting denominations— Baptist, Presbyterian, German Reformed, Quaker, Dunkard, and Moravian. Baptists probably constituted a plurality.

Anglican weakness against a powerful tide was equally obvious in South Carolina, where as of 1775, only three parishes, St. Mark's, St. Matthew's, and St. David's, served the entire backcountry. By 1777, as districts replaced parishes as state political units, a report to the Commons House listed 91 dissenting churches or meetinghouses versus only 25 Anglican churches and chapels.[42] In Georgia, Anglicans had only two major churches—Christ Church in Savannah and St. Paul's in Augusta. In a colony less than 40 years old, most denominations were just getting started.

The vestry Anglican leadership of Virginia and the Carolinas, as we have seen, was generally latitudinarian and rarely high church in theological matters. This was especially true for many prominent Patriots. George Washington, Thomas Jefferson, Patrick Henry, and the Lees in Virginia, along with Christopher Gadsden, William H. Drayton, Henry Laurens, and Charles Cotesworth Pinckney in South Carolina, were all Anglicans who personally supported disestablishment. Others, while less amenable, nevertheless saw disestablishment as political handwriting on the Patriot wall. As war broke out, these flexibilities permitted Patriot outreach to local Presbyterians (easy) and to Baptists (more complicated). Religion, like politics, was evangelizing and democratizing. The only question was how much.

Here is a framework. Of the roughly 250,000 or so migrants, including women and children, who came to the southern backcountry between 1760 and 1776, perhaps 30,000 to 40,000 would have been baptized or nominal Anglicans. Actual church-attending Anglicans would have been many fewer. Another 50,000 to 80,000 of the incomers would have been nominal Presbyterians, Regular Baptists, Lutherans, or German Reformed, but most would have faced difficulty finding a church near enough to attend. At least 100,000—doubtless including a sizable element of ex-convicts, indentured servants and runaways, *banditti,* drifters, as well as lapsed German and Irish Catholics (in a Protestant culture)—would have been essentially unchurched.

Thus the opportunity for the humbler sects and denominations that proselytized through itinerants and scoffed at learning and position. Far more than Presbyterians—and in immediate terms, much more than Methodists—this favored Baptists, especially the low-status Separates. By the mid-1770s, an expanding membership further abetted Baptists' influence both in new-constitution making and in setting conditions for military enlistment. By the end of 1776, all four southern colonies, now states, were moving down the road to disestablishment. The shift was most gradual in Virginia. Its provincial Declaration of Rights, adopted in 1776, recognized religion as a private matter of individual conscience; then a law enacted in 1777 suspended the Act for the Support of the [Anglican] Clergy. Complete disestablishment, however, did not come to Virginia until 1787.[43]

Elsewhere it came more easily. The North Carolina constitution, adopted in 1776, disestablished Anglicanism and called for complete separation of church and state. By 1777, South Carolinians had prepared disestablishment provisions to be included in the 1778 state constitution. Georgia's new legal framework of 1777 provided for free exercise of religion, disestablished the Anglican Church, and replaced the old colonial parish structure (Christ Church, St. Johns, et al.) with new counties.

Baptist civic and military collaboration with the Revolution varied from colony to colony. Patriots in Virginia, by and large favoring disestablishment, were flexible enough that Baptists understood an arrangement could be reached. Besides religious liberalization, agreements were worked out under which Baptists would serve together in individual companies, holding religious services and sometimes having preachers as their captains.[44]

In South Carolina, Baptists split during the 1775 civil war. Regular Baptists in the longer-settled low country were mostly allied with other dissenters and vestry Anglicans in the Patriot coalition. Upcountry South

Carolina, however, had clusters of radical and Tory-leaning Separate Baptists, several of whose leaders had come from the section of North Carolina where radical Baptists and fallen-away Quakers had helped to nurture an unusual politics. In the area between the Saluda and Broad rivers, as we will see, a concentration of Separate Baptist churches was a center of backcountry neutralism and Loyalism.

Separate Baptist Zealots, Presbyterian Radicals, and Methodist Tories

No one can pursue the role of Presbyterian, Baptist, and Methodist splinters and factions in the Chesapeake and southern backcountry during the American Revolution without wading into quicksands of interpretation and political correctness. Nevertheless, because the backcountry itself was so important to the war in 1775–1776 and then again in 1780–1782, some wading is necessary.

In South Carolina, before later chapters examine the local civil war politically and militarily, it is necessary to elaborate the interplay of religions in choosing sides. Likewise, before subsequent pages amplify the failure of the ex-Regulators of North Carolina to rise on the king's behalf in 1775–1776, more attention must be paid to the denominations involved. Fortunately, some revealing detail is within reach.

Through much of the nineteenth century, and up until the 1960s and 1970s (in some cases, even more recently), scholars from the mainstream of Southern Baptist religion and culture—at universities like Furman and Mercer, and at institutions like the Southern Baptist Theological Seminary and the North and South Carolina Baptist Historical Societies—dealt reasonably candidly with the extreme behavior of early Separate Baptist preachers and congregations in the Carolinas.[45] These extremes dated back to the 1760s and 1770s *before* the Separates were drawn into more acceptable conduct by the Baptist church mergers in southern states and related cultural transformations of the late 1780s and 1790s. Southern Baptists are now by far and away the largest religious denomination in the Carolinas, and publications in recent decades have minimized the Separates' initial religious and political behavior. Baptists are hardly unique; other Protestant denominations have also tidied up with respect to the decade of the Revolution.[46]

The newly active Methodists, whom we will revisit in the Chesapeake region, were not a major presence in the northern or southern backcountry.

Their seeming Toryism in eastern Maryland—pro-British missionaries and occasional interference with Patriot militia recruitment—was less of a problem in Virginia.

Separate Baptist activity in the South first unfolded in the North Carolina Piedmont after the arrival in 1755 of New England missionary Shubal Stearns. He and his brother-in-law, Daniel Marshall, established a church at Sandy Creek, east of what is now Greensboro. In just seventeen years, a network of 42 new churches and 125 ministers developed from that small beginning, making the Sandy Creek church "the mother of all Separate Baptists."[47] Separate Baptists, whose beliefs also reflected and bred dislike of civic authority, helped to nurture the North Carolina Regulator movement. This came about through the overlapping Sandy Creek Association, founded in 1766 to confront local corruption and encourage rural political activism.[48] Although not a member, Stearns kept in close touch. Following the Regulators' defeat at the Battle of Alamance, fought just a few miles away in 1771, troops under the order of Governor Tryon devastated this section of the Piedmont. The membership of the Sandy Creek Separate Baptist Church plummeted to 14 from 600 as residents fled. Tryon, who led the reprisals, charged that the majority of rebellious farmers were Baptists and Quakers.[49]

This was probably true, but the interaction of Baptist New Lights and Quaker Inner Lights in the North Carolina backcountry told only part of the tale. The Pennsylvania-fed population of the Piedmont also included two other faiths with mystical and pacifist overtones: Dunkards, Moravians, and loosely affiliated sympathizers of German background. The Regulator movement also bore some of their imprint, according to one of its closest researchers.[50] No group so unusual—or so unmilitary minded—was likely to reassemble to fight under Loyalist auspices.

A hundred-odd miles to the southwest, many of the same population groups—Pennsylvanian and North Carolinian, Scotch-Irish, German and English, Presbyterian and Baptist—had also been pouring into the South Carolina backcountry. Churches were few, and denominational lines were melting. Larger numbers of Scotch-Irish were disaffecting, and here again the influence of Shubal Stearns was at work, albeit through preacher Philip Mulkey, whose preachings went far beyond those of his early mentor.

Just as Stearns seeded a large group of Separate Baptist associations in Piedmont North Carolina, Mulkey did so in South Carolina, beginning in 1759 or 1760. Older histories of South Carolina Baptists identify his Fairforest church as the first in a network of Separate associations that rapidly spread through that province's backcountry.[51] Their locations, collected and marked in one old map, can be shorthanded as the area lying between the Broad and Saluda rivers. It is no coincidence that Revolutionary war buffs use this same shorthand to describe the regional stronghold of Loyalists and would-be neutrals during the South Carolina civil war of 1775.

Distaste for Mulkey was one of the few criticisms voiced by Anglican Woodmason and also by Richard Furman and Oliver Hart, the two leading (but non-Separate) Baptists on the Patriot side in 1775 and 1776. Mulkey was later excommunicated by establishment Baptists, who in 1790 warned against him for adultery, perfidy, and falsehood. It is undisputed that his churches seem to have embraced the more controversial practices usually shunned by Regular Baptists—love feasts, laying on of hands, washing feet, and kisses of charity—and "elderesses and deaconesses" were found.[52] In Woodmason's eyes, Mulkey and his colleague, Joseph Reese, were men of considerable but perverse influence.

Baptist historians have concluded that Mulkey—to whose political activities in 1775 we will later return—"was probably a loyalist or carried non-resistance far."[53] For the moment, though, theology deserves priority. The troublesome aspect of Separate Baptist activity, apparent as the Revolution unfolded in New England and the South, was its occasional tendency to revisit the extremes of previous wartime radical Protestant sects—the Anabaptists of Münster during the German religious wars of the sixteenth century, and the Ranters, early Quakers, familists, and Baptists of the English Civil War years.

These groups' recurrent theological transgression was antinomianism— derived from the Latin *anti,* which means "against," and the Greek *nomos,* which means "law." One form of antinomian excess was belief that those who had received divine grace were absolved from observing normal laws and moral restraints. A second lay in caricature extension of the Protestant concept of the priesthood of all believers. God and Christ, the argument went, were present in all those saved and reborn, and perfection was possible during life. Sin came from the imagination—it was an upper-class plot to suppress the poor—and during the English Civil War, Ranters "defended from the pulpit the view that adultery, drunkenness, swearing, theft, could be as holy and virtuous as prayer."[54]

Clearly, the ex-Revolutionary soldiers who joined the Come-Outers and Merry Dancers in backwoods Maine during the 1770s had an antinomian tint, as did the Separates in remote New Hampshire and Vermont, being conspicuous rebels against civil authority as well as state-supported churches. The American backcountry of the 1770s was the perfect nursery, much like remote northwest England in its earlier role as a radical refuge and breeding ground during the 1640s and 1650s. Was Mulkey's South Carolina backcountry a similar incubator? At first blush it would appear to put the *a* in antinomian, but hardly any Separate Baptist church records remain. Many of these congregations and chapels did not survive the war. In South Carolina, a half dozen minor battles were fought near Baptist chapels—Stevens Creek, Horn's Creek, Mobley's, Belin, and Little River— suggesting that they might have been targets or rallying points.[55]

Sectarian offshoots of Presbyterianism also had a considerable effect on revolutionary politics and loyalty in the backcountries of both Carolinas. Consider the oddly named "Catholic Presbyterian Church," organized in upcountry South Carolina just before the Revolution. Its name did not mean *Catholic* as in "Papist," but *Catholic* as in "universal." The goal of Reverend William Richardson was to unify, or at least keep on speaking terms, the various splinter and seceder groups spawned in the acrimony of eighteenth-century Scotland and Northern Ireland.[56] Fifty miles to the west, Robert and Patrick Cunningham, Loyalists influential in the South Carolina backcountry, came from a family that "had struggled for religious liberty in Scotland before migrating to Virginia in 1769."[57]

But perhaps the most important Presbyterian zealotry in the backcountry, at least with respect to events in 1775, involved the Covenanters of Mecklenburg County, just across the North Carolina border. What their leaders stood for, albeit oversimplified, was a belief that the obligations of the seventeenth-century Scottish League and Covenant passed down through the generations. In their eyes, these old covenants rendered unlawful the subsequent kingship of eighteenth-century British monarchs. Alexander Craighead, the most influential pre-Revolutionary preacher in what is now metropolitan Charlotte, was censured by Pennsylvania Presbyterians in the 1740s for what were seen as near-treasonable views. He then left Pennsylvania and went next to Virginia, and then from 1756 to 1766 built a large Mecklenburg following. These strong-minded Presbyterians, in turn, dominated the Mecklenburg assemblage of May 20, 1775, which passed the famous, but also widely doubted, resolution known as the Mecklenburg Declaration of Independence. We will touch on it again in looking at Congress and the many "near-declarations" that came before the one on July 4.

If the Mecklenburg Declaration is legitimate, rather than partly spurious, then Thomas Jefferson may have paraphrased its language rather than vice versa. Here its radical and peculiar Presbyterian origins are extremely relevant. They support the argument that the Mecklenburg Declaration was real, not faked. But they also suggest the probability that the delegates—who had convened amid the excitement of just hearing news of Lexington and Concord—soon reconsidered their potentially treasonable language. They may have watered it down into the merely belligerent document that appeared eleven days later as the Mecklenburg Resolves. Aroused Scotch-Irish sectarians could have written the first version; and canny Presbyterian lawyers and businessmen could have rethought its wisdom.

Did the renewed civil war in the Carolina backcountry of 1780–1782 have important religious aspects and overtones that continued the enmities of 1775–1776? Almost certainly, but few records survive.

Convicts, Runaway Servants, and Incipient Crackers

Dr. Samuel Johnson, a high Tory, famously called Americans "a race of convicts."[58] Although Johnson grossly exaggerated with respect to the entirety of the thirteen colonies, it is true that roughly 50,000 British convicts were transported to America between 1700 and 1775 and most went to Virginia and Maryland. Both colonies, justifiably indignant, between 1719 and 1772 together passed a half dozen laws to exclude, levy duty on, or interfere with these shipments. All were rejected by the Crown.[59] Benjamin Franklin wished that the colonies could repay Britain appropriately—by shipping back rattlesnakes.

Textbooks rarely publish the relevant estimates, but they are not in great dispute. During the first three quarters of the eighteenth century, roughly 307,400 white immigrants arrived in the thirteen colonies. Of these, some 49.3 percent were free, 33.7 percent were indentured servants, and 17 percent were transported convicts.[60] Redemptioners, most of them Germans, were better off than indentured servants—Germans made contracts as families—and are typically categorized as free migrants.

New England had both the fewest indentured servants and the fewest slaves. "South of New England," said historian Abbot E. Smith in *Colonists in Bondage*, "more than half of all persons who came to the colonies . . . were servants."[61] Had Dr. Johnson described American colonists as "a race of servants and convicts," he would have had better grounds.

Indentured servants were rarely well treated. They could go to court in most colonies, but sometimes their effort only wound up extending the term of their indenture. Like most historians, Smith declined to describe indentured servants in flattering terms. Obscure shopkeepers, schoolteachers, and pioneer farmers were "the best, but there were many more. Men and women who were dirty and lazy, rough ignorant, lewd and often criminal . . . Nor should the fact be forgotten, particularly when dealing with indentured servants, that it was also the last resort of scoundrels. A great many servants went to the colonies simply because, for one reason or another, they wanted to get out of their own country."[62]

Others were shanghaied, kidnapped, rounded up on the roads of Ireland, or recruited from places like Bridewell—the London women's prison. Planters in Virginia, home to many indentured servants and transported convicts, admitted that they did not always distinguish between the two. The convicts were also sold to private owners for seven or fourteen years, for crimes possibly no more serious than minor theft. The historian Gordon Wood reckoned that "in the colonies, servitude was a much harsher, more brutal and more humiliating status than it was in England." Others preferred a Caribbean comparison.[63]

Like the transported convicts, a high percentage of indentured servants were brought to Maryland and Virginia, although through the 1750s Pennsylvania was another favored destination. How large a part former servants and convicts, along with successful runaways, played in shaping the pre-Revolutionary southern backcountry is obviously guesswork, but an estimate can be ventured.

Approximately 250,000 migrants flooded into the southern backcountry between 1760 and 1775, probably two thirds of whom originated in Pennsylvania, Maryland, and Virginia before heading south. It seems reasonable to assume that many of the 24,000 English and Irish convicts put ashore and sold in the Maryland-Virginia region between 1745 and 1775 would have participated.[64] Some would have looked for a new start; runaways would have sought distance and anonymity. Now let us assume that Pennsylvania, Maryland, and Virginia between 1765 and 1775 would have been home to a collective average of 75,000 indentured servants. This suggests a second and larger migration pool: time-finished or runaway ex-servants.

To hypothesize that 50,000 to 75,000 of the 250,000 migrants of all ages might have had such backgrounds seems plausible. Maryland was well known for its high ratio of indentured servants whose bad treatment made them untrustworthy. Several analyses prepared for the British during the Revolutionary period made a similar point: harshly treated servants were a potential fifth column.[65] Irish ex-indentured servants in Philadelphia had a record of deserting from both armies. After their time served, ex-servants' circumstances rarely improved. In the 1740s, according to one survey, nearly three out of four indentured servants had wound up on the public dole.[66] One district of Pennsylvania just over the border was thought to have a sizable concentration of Maryland runaways.

The larger question attaches to Virginia: Why did so many Georgians and Carolinians, to say nothing of Creeks and Cherokee, use the term *Virginian* to describe the poor whites who took the Great Wagon Road south? Flight from the 1750s Indian devastation in the Shenandoah Valley and elsewhere on the province's frontier offers one explanation. Between 1753 and 1758, the population of Augusta County plummeted from 10,000 to 5,000, with most of those leaving heading south.[67] That area also produced a set of rambunctious borderers known as the Augusta Boys—an Old Dominion imitation of Pennsylvania's roistering Scotch-Irish Paxton Boys. White runaways doubtless added to the flow.

Some Virginians had long worried over their convict and indentured-servant ratios. "The inhabitants of our frontiers," wrote Governor Alexander Spotswood in 1717, "are composed generally of such as have been transported hither as Servants, and being out of their time, settle themselves where land is to be taken up and that will produce the necessaries of Life with little Labour."[68] By the 1770s, convicts were being transported west in quantities and sold by "soul dealers" in the hinterlands of Maryland and Virginia. Just after the Revolution, a Loyalist refugee from Georgia observed that "the Southern Colonies are overrun with a swarm of men from the western parts of Virginia and North Carolina, distinguished by the name of Crackers. Many of these people are descended from convicts that were transported from Great Britain to Virginia at different times, and inherit so much profligacy from their ancestors, that they are the most abandoned set of men on earth, few of them having the least sense of religion."[69]

Whether Virginia, the Carolinas, or Georgia bred the first Crackers is a matter for sociologists. What seems indisputable is that the pre-Revolutionary southern backcountry hosted them on a large scale, and that more of those vagrants, *banditti,* and horse thieves would have wound up with the white Tories of the Indian frontier than would have become Whig stalwarts.

Together with the religiously disaffected, they gave neutralism, if not Loyal-ism, a substantial backcountry base.

Across all thirteen colonies, however, one encouraging trend of 1774 and 1775 had less to do with population shifts and more to do with many colo-nists' rising awareness of beliefs and hopes that they shared with people elsewhere in the thirteen. So it is to these sensibilities and their incipient nationalism—to encouraging and rapidly expanding intercolonial ties in communications, commerce, religion, and constitutional argument—that we now turn.

CHAPTER 7

The Ideologies of Revolution

To know whether it be in the interest of the Continent to be independent, we need only ask this simple, easy question: "Is it in the interest of a man to be a boy all his life?"

Thomas Paine, *The Crisis*, 1776

In London for awhile, the American war had been called "the War of Parliament." It might as aptly been called "the war of the two constitutions."

John Philip Reid, *Constitutional History of the American Revolution*, 1993

We are unfailingly drawn by the whys and wherefores of great events. Searching, identifying, discovering, and exploring origins are preoccupations, perhaps even compulsions, of human nature. In the physical world, explorers seek the source of the Nile; scientists, the origin of the species or of life itself; archaeologists, the lost continent of Atlantis.

Economists, historians, and political theorists, although given to remaining indoors, behave similarly. They publish books and studies on the origins of scientific economics, World War I, or the American party system. They identify the social sources of religious denominationalism in the United States, the sources of political instability in Weimar Germany, and so on. But while one can be definitive in locating the source of the White Nile in Uganda's Lake Victoria, it's rarely possible to be precise in dealing with human events.

Generally speaking, the more one-dimensional an explanation of something complex and far-reaching, the greater the grounds for skepticism. And the larger the event, the less likelihood of it having a single cause or origin. With respect to revolutions, bold theses perhaps work best for bloodshed-driven polities like France and Russia. They apply less well to English-speaking countries. And so this is a reluctant chapter—one that will avoid great emphasis on "ideology" (defined as a system or body of ideas). The better explanation of pre-Revolutionary sentiment in America is multiple, combining popular discontents with British rule, an emerging sense of specifically American community, a shared culture of dissenting Protestantism, a fear of hostile conspiracies in London, and a legitimate apprehension that colonial interests were being neglected or throttled by officials 3,000 miles distant.

An important minority of historians argue that the American Revolution was strongest among those populations who had been in the colonies longest. It maximized, they say, in the regions of old seventeenth-century English settlement and heritage: New England and Virginia. Support was generally weaker where more recent European emigrants kept their language and Old World ties and were less engaged by 1775's political debate.[1] Although there were exceptions, time in America counted. Upholding the colonists' perceived rights as Englishmen, a motif of Yankee and Virginian orators, would not necessarily have inspired German Pennsylvanians, Hudson Valley Dutch, the Scotch-Irish influx of 1773–1775, or Carolina's Gaelic-speaking Scots Highlanders. These elements had their own historical sensitivities, group preoccupations with property rights (Teutons especially), or particular desire not to break oaths they had sworn, on arriving in the 1740s or 1750s, to Britain's House of Hanover. In four or five of the thirteen colonies, persons of non-English descent were a majority among whites.

Late-seventeenth- and eighteenth-century England had been the preeminent ally and protector of embattled French, Dutch, German, and Swiss Protestants—and respect and gratitude lingered among emigrants to the colonies from those backgrounds. Even to some Americans of English descent, the Crown was gratefully remembered for favors and assistance. The Quaker William Penn, for example, had received his Pennsylvania charter in 1681 from Charles II. To many Quakers, the last Stuart kings were patrons, not the objects of scorn they were to many Congregationalists and Presbyterians. Nearly a century later the Philadelphia Quaker Annual Meeting of 1775 praised royal rule and deplored sedition. Such are some of the obstacles to overly sweeping abstractions about the origins of the American Revolution.

On top of which, black slaves were about one fifth of the overall thirteen-colony population. Should their ideologies and motivations be set out separately? Perhaps not. But no more than one slave in a hundred would have been interested in the English radical Whig definition of *liberty*. Their focus would have been on their own liberty, as the response of many thousands to Lord Dunmore's proclamation in 1775 showed. Many free blacks in New England, on the other hand, fought on the Patriot side, probably for reasons that substantially overlapped those of their white compatriots-in-arms.

Neighborhood also helped to define *enemy*. Along the frontier, as we have seen, Whig pamphlets took a backseat to a near-at-hand tribal menace. The 1775 relevance of sixty-year-old indictments of English Jacobites and parliamentary corruption reprinted in Williamsburg and Philadelphia newspapers paled alongside searing ten- or fifteen-year-old memories of Huron, Seneca, Shawnee, Cherokee, or Creek raiding parties. Fifty or a hundred would recognize the names of Pontiac, Cornplanter, or Dragging Canoe for every frontier cabin dweller who could identify John Trenchard, Thomas Gordon, or Henry St. John, Viscount Bolingbroke.

Nor, for the moment at least, is it necessary to repeat New England concern over the economics of molasses smuggling or customs harassment or the parallel angst in Maryland, Virginia, and North Carolina over currency shortages, debt suits, and the commercial practices of British tobacco merchants. But any plausible definition of *ideology* must include an emerging sense of economic frustration.

Another very relevant underlying theme is simply this: *The American Revolution was as much a civil war as a revolution.* It did not represent one whole people rising against the overlordship of another. Hundreds of thousands in the thirteen colonies sympathized more with Britain than with Congress, and at least as many in Britain wished the rebels well. Here the Revolution resembled the other two major English-speaking civil wars— the English Civil War of the 1640s and the American Civil War of the 1860s. None reflected a nationwide or popular consensus; to some extent, they pitted region against region; and in places, people of one church opposed those of another. But as internecine conflicts, these wars also pitted brother against brother, and neighbor against neighbor. In divided border areas, many people tried to stay neutral. Ideology was not a day-to-day point of reference.

However, even if 60 percent of the population was actively or passively Patriot, we are still looking at a de facto civil war. Four individual colonies are usually counted in the local-civil-war category—New York, New Jersey, and both Carolinas. Portions of all four were still experiencing that local civil war in 1782. Delaware and Maryland, by contrast, shared a large Loyalist-leaning region on the Delmarva Peninsula but sidestepped all-out civil war. The openness of local bays and rivers to British warships able to land soldiers or marines encouraged Patriot restraint. To avoid sustained fighting, officials on the peninsula spent as much time tolerating Loyalists as actively suppressing them.

Nor was the Revolution a unique period of American internal conflict. Over the centuries, the very heterogeneity of the United States has made going to war a painful process, especially when large populations are un- happy about having to fight the "old country." Doubters should examine the huge swings in county-by-county returns for German areas from Ohio to the Dakotas in 1916 or 1940—or even urban Italian districts in 1940. Yankee New England did not want to fight its own "old country"—Old England—for a second time in 1812, as that section's presidential caucuses made clear. And if these elections sparked internal tensions, deciding on war with a foreign nation was a relative picnic compared with the nation's one other crisis on the eve of *civil war*—the Lincoln-Douglas- Breckenridge-Bell four-way presidential race of 1860. Ethnic, religious, sectional, and economic preoccupations cut across obvious lines—for ex- ample, the 15 to 20 percent backing won by the pro-compromise, antiwar candidate (Constitutional Union nominee John Bell) in several New England districts. Most of these were unhappy at disrupting trade or cotton-manufacturing ties to the South.[2]

The politics of decision making before America makes war is typically painful. Broad consensus is rare. Decision making before a civil war is even more divisive. Which brings us back to 1775. Had it been possible to have a thirteen-colony popular plebiscite on war or independence then or in the spring of 1776, the returns probably would have been as complex as 1860's emotional mirror of sympathies, grudges, kinship, and self-interest. Perhaps war in 1775 would have won no more than the 39 percent of the total vote won by Abraham Lincoln in 1860. American historians have come up with a wide range of estimates. Obviously, this complicates grand ideological pronouncements.

Part of why civil wars are difficult to explain is that so many different reasons are at work in different places. Of course, it is more plausible to single out narrow-gauge ideological origins for the Revolution if one is talking about only a subsection of the population. Conceivably, an important slice of middle-to-upper-class white males of English descent who frequently read the Boston, New York, Philadelphia, or Charleston Patriot press—some 3,000, 4,000, or possibly 5,000 men of Whiggish political sentiment—would, if polled by an eighteenth-century George Gallup, have more or less upheld historian Bernard Bailyn's famous ideological contention. Perhaps they were roused not by "common Lockean generalities" but, as Bailyn argues, by the oft-reprinted writings of the radical publicists and opposition politicians of early-eighteenth-century England. Those publicists' warnings did seem applicable once again, as harsh British policies unfolded in the 1760s and early 1770s.[3]

However, there was a lot more behind proto-Americanism than a small educated cadre who read newspapers. The remaining 96 to 98 percent of the population, little given to reading beyond hymnals, bibles, almanacs, and tavern prices, would have paid more attention to preachers, pocketbooks, folk history, and tribal memories ranging from the siege of Londonderry to Calvinist theology. Even Thomas Paine's fast-paced and highly influential *Common Sense* was more king bashing than elevated discourse.

This being said, there is much to support Bailyn's collateral argument that many Revolutionaries—not least Washington, Adams, and Jefferson—were driven by belief in a British conspiracy to undermine American liberties. Americans' long-standing fascination with conspiracies is such that any reasonable definition of ideology must include that proclivity. The history of Anglo-American political attentiveness to allegations of plots and conspiracies goes far back—indeed, both were mainstays of Plantagenet and Tudor history. This context is examined later in this chapter.

We cannot simply discard ideology, though—far from it. From a broader perspective, it is too parochial to root the American Revolution in the potting soil, however rich, of radical pamphleteering. These pages will argue that the growth of colonial pride, commercial frustration, and incipient nationalism circa 1775 had a much broader and more affirmative "ideological" genesis. A growing national sense of community had begun to interact with other relevant factors—increasing awareness that maturity required economic self-determination; the quirky, colony-by-colony evolution of American "constitutions" and law; and the powerful influence of a dissenting Protestant theology. Wariness of British designs came in part from a more cynical Boston-Philadelphia perception of British policy than Parliament or Whitehall professed. To set the scene for the motivations and actions of 1775, five more or less ideological categories can be shorthanded: Community, Commerce, Constitution, Calvinism, and Conspiracy.

Community: The Growth of American Nationalism

The eighteenth century was a period of massive realignment within the "community" of English-speaking peoples better known as the British Empire. In the home island alone, Scotland was added to a union that transformed English, Welsh, and Scots into Britons. New French speakers were included in Quebec, Acadia (Nova Scotia), Senegal, and the West Indies. Tens of millions of non-English speakers were added in India, and in 1783 3 or so million Americans were subtracted.

Although the change in North America did not come about overnight, the contiguous thirteen colonies developed closer relations with one another as they lost belief in a shared imperial community led from London. Part of what provoked Bostonians in 1773 was that tea policy was made by His Majesty's government to benefit the East India Company, another emerging horizon of empire.

The disillusionment that pervaded the loose confederation of thirteen ex-colonies in 1783, weary after eight long years of war, stood in sharp contrast to the enthusiastic but naïve union and *rage militaire* of those thirteen in 1775. Jefferson and Hamilton were among the Revolutionary leaders who feared for the future, but further into the eighties the uncertainty began to fade. Nor was the United States alone in its political posttrauma syndrome. Britain, too, finished the war gloomily, replacing the imperial hubris of the 1760s with a sense of lost prestige, brutal debt burdens, and concern over other potential falling dominoes from Ireland to the West Indies.

By the 1790s, both nations' fears had relaxed. The United States returned to rapid economic and population growth under a new constitution, while Britain, under a revitalized conservative government led by William Pitt the Younger, regrouped to defeat Napoleon and to make the nineteenth century the first of clear "British" preeminence.

Unfortunately, much of the gestation of American community and then of nationalism in the 1760s and 1770s has been lost in what can be called Fourth of July boosterism. The clumsiness of the American Revolution Bicentennial Commission in stereotyping the Revolution around 1776 only intensified the existing confusion and oversimplification. Belief that almost everything important came together in 1776 ignored the extent to which a

sense of community and incipient nationalism was taking hold in the thirteen colonies many years before the Declaration of Independence. Amid the
approach of the bicentennial, colonial historian Carl Bridenbaugh wrote
regretfully that after nearly a half century of studying the Revolution, he
had never found any satisfactory explanation of what the rank and file of
the colonists were like in 1776 or of their "hopes, fears and kindred emo-
tions." Blaming the date fetishism that surrounded 1776, and its implication
that patriotism sprang to life suddenly in that year, Bridenbaugh subtitled
his book *The Growth of American Patriotism Before Independence.*[4]

By the mid-eighteenth century, colonial interconnectedness was growing like Jack's Beanstalk. Six years after the first postal service was set up in
1692, a post road stretched from Portsmouth, New Hampshire, to New
Castle, Delaware. By 1732, as road traffic grew, a Boston bookseller published *The Vade Mecum for America: Or, a Companion for Traders and Trav-
ellers*. It listed the towns and counties, their principal roads, courts, religious
meetings, and public houses, from the Kennebec River south to the James
River in lower Virginia. Next came detailed maps of New England and the
mid-Atlantic provinces, enabling not just travelers but dreamers to see the
colonies' scope and spread. A revised version of the Fry and Jefferson map
centered on Virginia appeared in 1755 with a new feature: detail of "The
Great Wagon Road from the Yadkin River through Philadelphia, distant
435 miles."[5] A country was taking shape across the coincidental borders of
individual British provinces.

Ferries proliferated, and stagecoaches and packet boats traveled surprisingly far afield. By 1769, passage could be booked from Charleston to Pensacola in what was now British West Florida. Sea travel from Charleston to
Newport, Rhode Island, was short enough to turn Narragansett Bay into a
cool and breezy summer resort favored by rice and indigo planters and their
families. Easy passage the other way brought enough New Englanders to
Charleston to help fill the city's famous Circular Congregational Church.
One governor even complained about seasonal winds deluging South Carolina in sedition-minded visitors and writings from Rhode Island and Massachusetts. Princeton, still at that time the (Presbyterian) College of New
Jersey, attracted young southerners of that faith—and in May 1775, a clique
of them, back home in Charlotte, North Carolina, penned the so-called
Mecklenburg Declaration of Independence.

The major seaports developed commercial hinterlands and markets that
cut across colony borders: Charleston's included Georgia and southeastern

North Carolina as well as all of South Carolina; Philadelphia's drew in northeastern Maryland, Delaware, and western New Jersey as well as most of Pennsylvania; New York's stretched around eastern New Jersey and southwestern Connecticut as well as lower New York. A similar commercial extension often explained paper currency use. South Carolina paper bills circulated beyond the colony's borders. New York and Philadelphia merchants usually found it wise to accept New Jersey money.

The population was even more mobile than the commerce was interconnected. As we have seen, Greater Pennsylvania reached down into South Carolina. Within the thirteen colonies, it is a good bet that one third to one half of the 150 or so counties that existed in 1775 had populations in which "outsiders"—persons born outside the province or with at least one parent born outside—outnumbered "natives." Connecticut had planted emigrant colonies as far south as Georgia, and such people kept in touch. Mid-Atlantic Pennsylvania in particular, but also nearby parts of Maryland and Virginia, tended to overflow southward after the 1720s and 1730s. In 1775, this population flood, much of it along the Great Wagon Road, was recent enough and fresh enough that many ethnic groups—Germans, Welsh, and Scotch-Irish—as well as religious denominations, including Baptists, Quakers, Presbyterians, Lutherans, and German Reformed, looked back to Pennsylvania for clergy, goods, specialized publications, and information from societies, meetings, synods, and associations.

In 1775, North Carolina Patriots enlisted Pennsylvania Presbyterian leaders to write supportive letters to their coreligionists in the politically divided Carolina Piedmont. Within the Dutch Reformed Church, the same sharp differences between the Conferentie and Coetus factions applied in New York as in New Jersey. And for some ten years, Congregationalist minister Ezra Stiles had been hard at work promoting, if not quite achieving, religious mergers—most notably between Congregationalists and Presbyterians, but also between Congregationalists and Baptists in southern New England.[6]

Togetherness born of serving in multicolony military expeditions was also important, especially in the four vanguard provinces. New Englanders had cooperated since early days, having established the United Colonies of New England in 1643 to ensure their common defense amid the descent of Old England into civil war. The famous New England expedition of 1745 that captured the French fortress of Louisbourg had drawn support from Massachusetts, Connecticut, New Hampshire, and Rhode Island alike.

South Carolina authorities, for their part, had not only collaborated with Georgia and North Carolina troops from time to time but journeyed as far afield as the Ohio Valley. A South Carolina company participated in the Virginia expedition against the French in 1754 led by youthful militia colonel George Washington.

This bonding process included a shared sense that emerged during the French wars: frequent disdain for the competence and reliability of British generals and London-based armchair strategists. A huge ratio of colonial troops sickened and died during the bungled British sieges of Cartagena and Havana in the 1740s, arousing indignation in the provinces suffering losses. The Royal Navy's arbitrary impressment of American seamen bred bitterness in New England, as did Britain's decision to return Louisbourg to France after colonial forces had captured it.

Wars also bred provincial community. The prominent role of the locally recruited South Carolina Regiment in the Cherokee War of 1760–1761 imparted not just a distaste for inept British commanders but a fellowship of colonial captains and majors who would become Patriot leaders in the Revolution. The western Virginia regiment organized to fight the Shawnee during Lord Dunmore's War in 1774 also drew officers from prominent families who would serve together in 1775–1776.

Population growth also spread institutions across colonial boundaries. Organizations taking shape around those connections and ambitions began using the term *American*—the American Philosophic Society in 1743, *The Royal American Magazine* in 1741, the American Society for Promoting Useful Knowledge in 1768, the American Medical Society in 1771, and several more in 1773. One historian who searched colonial newspapers to catalogue the explicit symbols of identification used—*American, Great Britain, Virginia, Massachusetts,* and the like—found that "a fairly high degree of community awareness" existed by the French and Indian War. However, the "take-off" point came in the early summer of 1763.[7] This was well before the Stamp Act furor of 1765, and we have noted several probable catalysts. The summer of 1763 was when British politicians started talking about not letting the American colonies spread out or get too big. It was also when news arriving in New England about British naval vessels joining customs officers in a new crackdown on American smuggling produced a level of Yankee apprehension not seen since the fall of Fort William Henry in 1757.

What community the term *British* meant or included was also unclear. Imperial officials and American opinion molders of the 1750s, 1760s, and

1770s employed the description "British Empire" to express markedly different concepts. To British ministers and their advisers, the vital derivation came from the Roman imperium. This concept did not connote specific geography or territory but a vehicle of administration, discipline, authority, and subordination.[8] Colonials in North America or the West Indies, by contrast, generally viewed the British Empire as a geographical or political entity within which they, too, played a vital role and enjoyed the much-belabored rights of Englishmen. In 1751 Benjamin Franklin described the empire as encompassing both sides of the Atlantic—and enthused that in another century "the greatest number of Englishmen would be on this side of the water."[9] Lawyers for the Crown did not share the American interpretation of empire, nor did they welcome such population projections. The American pride of future was by no means confined to future rebels. In the 1750s William Shirley, the royal governor of Massachusetts, had included the colonists within his conception of the empire, urging that they be given representation in Parliament.[10] William Pitt, addressing the House of Commons in 1766 as first minister, identified the profits of trade with the West Indies and North America as "the fund that carried you triumphantly through the last war . . . You owe this to America." North American egos had also swelled with the international comments heard and read about in 1762 and 1763 as France and Britain negotiated an end to the Seven Years War. The chief French negotiator, the Duc de Choiseul, stated what was widely assumed in Amsterdam, Madrid, and St. Petersburg: that "in the present state of Europe it is colonies, trade and in consequence sea power, which must determine the balance on the [European] continent."[11]

If British imperialists had swollen heads in 1763, so did many Americans who knew full well which colonies were being discussed. By 1775, as we have seen, North American population gains had put the mainland thirteen ahead of Holland and Switzerland, close to Denmark and Portugal, and not too far short of Prussia, which had dropped to a population of only 4 million people following severe losses in the Seven Years War.[12] If French and other Continental leaders unhappy with Britain's new supremacy commented openly on the American colonies having shifted the balance of power, their sotto voce speculation was more cynical. Would the revolt of the American colonies humble the British Lion? Was France already encouraging that dissatisfaction and incipient nationalism to become revolution?

Commerce: North Americans' Increasing Rejection
of Economic Subordination

To Louis Hacker, a progressive historian of the mid-twentieth century, "the struggle was not over high-sounding political and constitutional concepts: over the power of taxation and, on the final analysis, over natural rights: but over colonial manufacturing, wild lands and furs, sugar, wine, tea and currency, all of which meant, simply, the survival or collapse of English merchant capitalism within the imperial-colonial framework of the mercantilist system."[13] No other cause or category, he contended, mattered nearly as much.

Economic determinism was then in vogue. Hacker held forth in 1935, when Franklin Roosevelt's New Deal had consummated the triumph of the Progressive School. However, within two or three decades, their overinsistence would be matched by an opposite excess: the thesis of Neo-Whig or Consensus historians that political ideals and constitutional concepts were all-important in explaining the Revolution, while economic causes were peripheral at best.

Almost by nature, intellectuals exaggerate the importance of ideology and doctrine. Nevertheless, the ups and downs of the different schools of American history can be important. It is a cliché that politicians talking about employment, budgets, and spending are often simply regurgitating the ideas of some dead economist. Perhaps, and politicians giving pompous speeches about the United States as the architect of global democracy may be echoing some dead Consensus historian or Fourth of July orator.

Part of what Consensus historians called constitutional debate was economic. Edmund Burke, the eighteenth-century Briton whose views have usually been applied to buttress a constitutional and ideological approach, in this case emphasized an economic underpinning. "The consideration of those great commercial interests [manufacturing and trade]," he argued in 1769, had become the context in which Britons debated and evaluated imperial policy. Thus, "the spirit of an extensive and intricate trading interest pervades the whole, always qualifying, and often controlling, every general idea of constitution and government."[14] A reasonable capsule might be: *economic* motivations, *constitutional* rhetoric.

In 1775, then, an imperial system that was partly constitutional, partly economic, was in dispute between Britain and America. By the late eighteenth century, the two English-speaking peoples brought increasingly different legal cultures into the courtrooms of empire, divergences to which we will turn shortly. However, the stunning growth of British manufacturing and trade during the prior quarter century had seized Britons' imagination. Descriptions of a new "political oeconomy" were being urged on British officials and parliamentarians by a set of thinkers including Sir James Steuart, Josiah Tucker, Joseph Massie, Thomas Mortimer, and Malachy Postlethwayt. But thinking remained in flux, and mercantilist doctrine continued to guide the king and cabinet. Hints of American rejection of mercantilism, in turn, became unmistakable at the First Continental Congress. The extent to which pressure for modification or repudiation was taking hold in 1774 and 1775 is often forgotten, given the *über*-focus on Adam Smith's *The Wealth of Nations,* not published until 1776.

Let Edmund Burke signpost Britain's confidence of the 1760s: "[Our] object is wholly new in the world. It is singular: it is grown up to this magnitude and importance within the memory of man; nothing in history is parallel to it . . . In this new system, a principle of commerce, of artificial commerce, must predominate."[15] Here Burke is glorying in the intersection of mercantilism and empire so triumphant in 1763. If the increasingly shaky Anglo-American framework could be called constitutional, the shifting tectonic plates were economic.

The tremors most discussed in Britain and America—threatened boycotts, free trade, and no more commodity enumeration—provided political seismography for a relationship coming undone. Britain's demand for colonial subservience and the colonies' insistence on self-determination were two sides of the same bright coin of imperial growth. So, in a sense, were the two countries' diverging prescriptions. Policy makers on both sides of the Atlantic were betwixt and between.

Although the evolution of economic ideology in Britain and mainland Europe is beyond our story, British perspectives on the economic changes roiling the English-speaking Atlantic world of 1775 could not be more relevant. American interpretation of the backdrop to Revolution too often neglects Britain's own interests and apprehensions. Great imperial and economic hubris was interspersed with bouts of political and global angst.

The hubris was understandable. During the 1756–1763 war years, Britain achieved military conquest and unprecedented territorial expansion while maintaining rapid trade expansion, a rare combination. Despite near-global conflict, the nation's imports were up 39 percent. By one calculus, during the eighteenth century as a whole, imports grew by over 500 percent while exports, driven by manufactures, rose by some 560 percent.[16] Although the 1780–1800 period saw the biggest spurt, the takeoff between 1750 and 1775 was also momentous. As Burke's comments underscore, these were decades during which commercial priorities came to the fore in Parliament. The importance of merchants and manufactures burgeoned, and notable political figures from Whigs like Pitt, Rockingham, and Shelburne to ministerial stalwarts like George Grenville concurred that manufacturing, trade, and commerce had become the new guideposts for imperial decision making. Their individual affirmations constitute striking testimony.[17]

The related angst was also notable. Perhaps British power had peaked in 1763, so that France and Spain would fare better in a new war. Edward Gibbon's *The Decline and Fall of the Roman Empire,* published in 1776, raised disquieting analogies. And if the population and resources of the North American colonies were essential to Britain—a view shared by European mercantilists and French foreign ministers—how much wealth and power would be lost if a rebellion succeeded?

By 1774, the king's ministers were aware of the dissonance between upholding imperial authority and the periodic concessions needed to stave off transatlantic confrontations. New Englanders and Virginians were beginning to dispute not just Parliament's right to tax but its right to regulate American commerce. The prospect of colonists stepping up their own textile production spurred Parliament in 1774 to prohibit the export of utensils used in cotton and linen manufactures.[18] The Boston-based customs commissioners, on the other hand, advised London against passing any trade law modification until "the Authority of Government" could be restored.[19] We must remember that as 1774 ended, Patriot committees in the major seaports were taking over supervision of shipping.

The Crown's control over land policy in North America was also breaking down, especially in the southern colonies. When restrictive new rules for making land grants and raising quitrents were published in 1774, certain exceptions were allowed, but royal governors doubted they could carry out the instructions. Patriot committees simply scoffed. In January 1775, the "Darien Committee" in St. Andrew's Parish, Georgia, fit most of its outrage into a single paragraph. The committee resolved that "shutting up the land offices, with the intention of raising our quitrents . . . is a principal part of the unjust system of politics adopted by the present ministry, to subject and enslave us, and evidently proceeds from an ungenerous jealousy of the colonies, to prevent as much as possible the population of America, and the relief of the poor and distressed in Britain and elsewhere."[20] Reasoned discussion was lapsing.

Law could no longer bridge the gap, partly because of legal rigidity in Britain but also because of too many varieties of law in America.

Constitutions: Competing British and American Legal Concepts

William Shakespeare has been thought snide for having one character in *Henry VI* say, "The first thing we do, let's kill all the lawyers." However, complaints about excessive legalism have been a staple in English-speaking countries, and the eighteenth century was another such period. The torrent of new law and regulation that began in England during the 1750s produced widespread complaint on both sides of the Atlantic over a lack of coordination and standardization—and especially over the expense and complexity of the judicial process.[21]

With respect to too much lawyering as a bone of contention between Britain and the thirteen colonies in the 1770s, American constitutional historians have argued that the transatlantic quarrel nailed itself into a box by becoming *too* legal—too unremitting and inflexible in interpretation.[22] This rigidity was related to the larger problem, but also distinct from it.

By one critique, Lord Mansfield, the chief justice, and other Crown legal advisers were to blame for being unable to move relations with America beyond a narrow legal interpretation. They were indeed constrained by a doctrine, entrenched over the generations following the Glorious Revolution of 1688, that upholding Parliament's sovereignty within Britain required enforcing the subordination of the colonies to that body.[23] There was no leeway. For them to owe loyalty only through a symbolic king, a simple relationship later posited for Canadian and Australian dominion status, was not a politically acceptable premise in the 1770s. The royal excesses curbed in 1688 were too recent a memory; Parliament had to be upheld.

In the process, though, upholding Parliament became "too legal" in the late 1760s and 1770s. The trap was that "the Americans first had to acknowledge the 'right' before there could be a renunciation of 'the exercise.' " Had the Americans somehow been able to acknowledge an abstract parliamentary supremacy, "Parliament could then have devised a constitutional mechanism to check any threat from the crown should the colonies provide the king with revenue. But the Americans could not acknowledge without risking their constitutional security to the whims and changing politics of some future parliament."[24]

Across the Atlantic, however, the colonies were also "too legal" but in a different way. The thirteen colonies operated under so many varieties and concepts of law that they believed they could deny Parliament, as well as pick and chose from alternative legal theories. A second Shakespeare, had one been at hand, could have written a play mocking lawyers on both sides as launching "the War of the Two Constitutions" and been no more flippant than the character in *Henry VI*. Summarily put, the two English-speaking nations had developed substantially different legal and governmental cultures, resulting in an unbridgeable pre-Revolutionary divergence. It is certainly plausible to discuss the *constitutional* origins of the American Revolution, not merely the supposed *ideological* ones.

The unwritten British Constitution circa 1775 had, in retrospect, become rigidified around the doctrine of complete and unmitigated parliamentary supremacy, an insistence that did indeed go back to the Glorious Revolution. King George III himself swore a coronation oath to uphold Parliament. Since 1707, no monarch had been permitted a veto. Sensible enough in the abstract, by rigid judicial interpretation parliamentary supremacy had already produced some dubious rulings and mandates within Britain. One case held that the king could not even lawfully proclaim a temporary tax in the West Indian island of Grenada lest this somehow restore the dangerous prerogative power. By another determination, the London Common Council could obtain no remedy from the king—the remedy sought was a royal dissolution of Parliament—whatever the alleged arbitrary nature of the legislators' acts.[25] Parliament was now more absolute than a king had ever quite been under common law.

Under Britain's constitution, the onetime common law "rights" of Englishmen, in earlier days invocable against *royal* transgression, no longer applied as against *Parliament*. Most Americans of the Patriot faction, however, still cherished an older—and strictly speaking no longer valid—view rooted in the old common law: that English liberties could be asserted against *any* institutional transgressor. A few British lawyers still agreed with the old interpretation—one was Lord Camden, the former attorney general. Similarly, in America many Tories upheld complete parliamentary sovereignty. But on the whole, the two peoples separated by the Atlantic held different views of the British Constitution and the extent to which it did or did not still enshrine common law verities about tyrants and the rights of Englishmen. If the tyrants were in Parliament, even the rights of Englishmen were no longer assured.

To further complicate matters, British officials, at home with unwritten constitutions, routinely referred to the "constitutions" of Massachusetts or New York, and some would have used the word to describe the legal systems in the other eleven provinces. In fact, individual nuances abounded. Colonies that still retained seventeenth-century charters from the Crown—by 1775, only Connecticut and Rhode Island—regarded their charters' commitments as binding and beyond Parliament's power to suspend or repeal. At that, Parliament essentially laughed. Jurisdictions like Virginia and South Carolina, citing original charters from King James or King Charles that granted boundaries extending to the Pacific, loosely regarded those territorial commitments as persisting in 1775, even though both had since become royal colonies. Here, too, Parliament scoffed. Prominent American leaders like Benjamin Franklin and John Adams, in turn, periodically hypothesized that their provinces were tied to Britain through the king, not Parliament. Under British law, parliamentary supremacy made that impossible, whatever fanciful interpretations might be entertained in America.

Within each American colony, moreover, the relations between the different branches of government had evolved contrary to the mother country's late-eighteenth-century example. George III might no longer be able to veto acts of Parliament, but royal governors sent to America—except Connecticut and Rhode Island, where governors were chosen locally— could and frequently did veto the bills passed by local legislatures. In other ways, though, governors were handicapped. Even if the governor signed a bill and forwarded it to London, the measure could still be vetoed by the Privy Council. By the 1760s, most colonies had developed adversarial relationships that pitted locally elected assemblies against the chief executive appointed by the Crown or the proprietors (as in Pennsylvania and Maryland). Patriot-faction opinion favored the popular and elected branch, which in most colonies was increasing its political and fiscal power.

Some governors were shrewd, agreeable, and popular—men like Thomas Pownall in Massachusetts, James Glenn in South Carolina, and Lord Botetourt and Robert Dinwiddie in Virginia. A larger ratio, however, were hobbled by insufficient stature, questionable judgment, lack of meaningful patronage at their disposal, and complicated instructions from home that limited their room for maneuver and give-and-take. In short, by the 1760s, the rivalry prevalent in most colonies—popular representatives in assemblies (elected by Whig yeomen and elites) confronting governors appointed by the Crown or ministry—bore an apparent, although superficial, resemblance to the seventeenth-century politics of Puritan and Whig legislators arrayed against Stuart kings. The king-and-Parliament entente within the late-eighteenth-century British system did not operate in the American colonies. Thus, if colonial Whigs of the 1760s harked to yesteryear's rhetoric of liberty versus tyranny that revisited the combats and name calling of the 1630–1715 period—and clearly many did—that was because provincial tensions recalled those years.

The informal "constitutions" of the individual North American provinces had other distinguishing legacies. New England stood out. "In [seventeenth-century] New England court records, one reads little about felonies and misdemeanors but a great deal concerning sin, evil, wickedness, filthiness, pollutions and the like . . . [But] this rhetoric is almost entirely absent from the court records of the early Chesapeake colonies."[26] Furthermore, according to one constitutional scholar, eighteenth-century Massachusetts had its own idiosyncratic, locally controlled and interpreted version of the English Common law.[27] With its town meetings and town-based government, the Bay Colony of the 1750s enjoyed an unusual judicial and jury system capable of frustrating imperial policy. One linchpin, so-called civil and criminal "traverse juries," were even allowed to reshape law and not simply interpret evidence.[28]

Despite Loyalist grumbling, the charters allowing self-government were left untouched in Connecticut and Rhode Island. However, even in the Bay Colony, where the existing charter was suspended in 1774 under the Massachusetts Government Act, elements of Patriot governmental authority persisted at the vital town and county level. This enabled Samuel Adams and his allies to shut down the courts, frighten royal officials into resignation, employ county meetings (never mentioned in the 1774 act) to host the political rallies prohibited at the town level, and control a militia organized town by town. Many juries were still under local control. Simply put, the Massachusetts Government Act, by the beginning of 1775, had failed to reassert British control of Massachusetts government.

As for the "constitutions" of Virginia and the Carolinas, these colonies had swung in the direction of locally elected assemblies gaining control over British-appointed provincial governors. By 1774 or early 1775, Patriot factions were able to seize effective colonywide power. They did this by

blurring the lines between lawful assemblies and the new extralegal committees and conventions that just happened to include many or most of the
same elected representatives. When royal governors dissolved or prorogued
the assemblies for commitment to Patriot agendas, these dissolved bodies
more or less reconvened in a new extralegal form as the General Committee
of South Carolina, North Carolina Provincial Congress, or Virginia Convention. And as we saw in Chapter 1, once these bodies took the reins of
power, helpless royal governors eventually fled to nearby British warships.
These accessions were not seamless legal events. Under British law, they
were neither seamless nor legal. However, they were effective.

Thus, and to make a long story short, some nine, ten, or twelve months
before the official Declaration of Independence, Virginia and the Carolinas
had de facto independence in operation under extralegal arrangements that
hinted at (and in 1776 or 1777 would orchestrate) new state constitutions.
Conceptually, these architects of extralegal governance dragged a broad net,
invoking everything from natural rights and natural law to the old common law and the right to resistance, sometimes adding in the Glorious
Revolution and sentences from John Locke or the Magna Carta. They were,
in effect, doing legal clip-and-paste jobs.

From Maine to Georgia, might ultimately made right, and possession of
government provided nine tenths of the lawful origins of the new republic,
however much far-off British legalists disagreed. A disparity of legal concepts and relationships had made the War of the Two Constitutions
unavoidable.

Calvinism: Liberty's Fighting Credo?

Barely remembered in the twenty-first century, after being pushed aside
during the early twentieth, is the longtime political importance of Calvinism. In the 1500s and 1600s, John Calvin's faith was the militant, fighting
arm of Reformation Era European Protestantism—and in 1775 it became
the fighting religion of Whig Revolutionary America.

To a considerable minority of nineteenth-century British and American
historians, the earlier spread of political liberty against the forces of Rome,
Hapsburg Spain, and Louis XIV marched to Calvinist drums. By these
accounts, the rise of Protestant northern and western Europe, to match and
then outmatch the power of the Catholic Mediterranean, consummated a
200-year triumph of French theologian Calvin's heirs on the battlefields and

in the councils of England, Scotland, Ulster, France, Holland, and Germany. The clash in Revolutionary America—at least half Calvinist by denomination, and a promised land for English Puritans, Scotch-Irish Presbyterians, and French Huguenots, as well as Dutch, German, and Swiss Reformed—marked the last great contest, this time for predominance in North America.

This Calvinist portrait seeps—and sometimes sweeps—through the writings of Victorian-era British historians like Thomas Babington Macaulay and James A. Froude, as well as Americans Edward Bancroft, John Fiske, and John Lothrop Motley. Did these men have a better sense of the religiosity of the eighteenth century than more recent chroniclers? Probably. Were they correct in painting a dour, predestination-minded religious culture as a progressive political force? Probably. This is where twentieth- and twenty-first-century Americans balk and find a religious explanation hard to credit.

The old heroes have been crowded off history's current stage: Holland's William the Silent and William of Orange, England's Oliver Cromwell, Scotland's John Knox and the Lords of the Convention, the French Huguenot Admiral Gaspard de Coligny, and lesser-known Germans and Swiss. The devils of that era were principally Spanish—the Duke of Alba, who executed 18,000 Dutch Calvinists as easily as frontier Texans barbecued beef—and Bourbon French: Louis XIV, who in 1688 revoked the Edict of Nantes, under which French Protestants had been protected.

But modern cultural biases cannot wholly rewrite a prior American reality: that the Calvinist denominations central to these old battles—English Puritans and so-called Independents (Congregationalists), Scottish and Ulster Presbyterians, and members of the Dutch, German, and French Reformed churches—bulked larger in the thirteen colonies of the 1770s than in any major European nation. Some came as religious refugees; more were economic opportunity seekers; many were both. Indeed, America's Calvinist ratios began increasing in the early eighteenth century as German, Huguenot, Scottish, and Scotch-Irish arrivals displaced the English predominance of seventeenth-century emigration. The religious Great Awakening of the 1730s and 1740s further increased the Calvinist coloration because so many (but not all) of the Baptists proliferating in the second half of the eighteenth century were Calvinists. The Awakening's leading evangelist, George Whitefield, was one himself. By rough calculations, at least three fifths of American church attenders in the 1770s would have been

Calvinists, with the remainder being mostly Anglican, Lutheran, or Quaker.

This was not lost on British officials, who, as we have seen, sometimes described the Revolution as a Presbyterian and/or Congregationalist war. Edmund Burke's pointed analysis a month before Lexington and Concord is also worth revisiting: that "the [American] people are Protestants, and of that kind which is most adverse to all implicit submission of mind and opinion." So much so, he added, that religion in "our Northern colonies is a refinement on the principle of resistance."[29]

In New England, resistance was principally Calvinist. The *rage militaire* circa 1775 has been described as follows: "When actual fighting began many New England ministers became 'fighting parsons.' Ministers exerted their influence to raise volunteers and sometimes marched away with them, as did Joseph Willard of Beverly, where two companies were raised largely through his influence. At Windsor, Vermont, David Avery, on hearing the news of Lexington, preached a farewell sermon, then called the people to arms and marched away with twenty men, recruiting others as they went. The fiery and sharp-tongued John Cleaveland of Ipswich 'is said to have preached his whole parish into the army and then to have gone himself.' "[30]

The political implications of Calvinism can be easily stated: that a people's embrace of *ecclesiastical* republicanism is followed by a strong urge to reshape *government* along the lines of the Reformed and Presbyterian churches.[31] As the thirteen colonies grew in the 1750s and 1760s, British strategists feared just this relationship and promoted an Anglican counter-reformation. From the Crown's perspective, Calvinism was still an unduly combative creed.

To Edward Bancroft, writing in the nineteenth century, "the Revolution of 1776, so far as it was affected by religion, was a Presbyterian measure. It was the natural outgrowth of the principles which the Presbyterianism of the Old World planted in her sons, the English Puritans, the Scotch Covenanters, the French Huguenots, the Dutch Calvinists and the Presbyterians of Ulster."[32] John Lothrop Motley, best known for his admiring histories of Holland, asserted that "in England the seeds of liberty, wrapped up in Calvinism and hoarded through many trying years, were at last destined to float over land and sea, and to bear the largest harvest of temperate freedom for the great commonwealths that were still unborn . . . To Calvinists, more than any other class of men, the political liberties of England, Holland and America are due."[33]

"Whatever the cause," said James Froude, professor of history at Oxford, "the Calvinists were the only fighting Protestants. It was they whose faith gave them courage to stand up for the Reformation, and but for them, the Reformation would have been lost." To New Englander John Fiske, "it would be hard to overrate the debt which mankind owes to Calvin. The spiritual father of Coligny, of William the Silent, and of Cromwell, must occupy a foremost rank among the champions of modern democracy as one of the longest steps that mankind has ever taken toward personal freedom."[34] Dozens of French, Dutch, German, and even Spanish historians made similar arguments.[35]

Calvinism is hardly forgotten, though it no longer bears a strong sword. Americans celebrated John Calvin's five-hundredth birthday in 2009 at a summer conference, and believers have been delivering Calvin memorial addresses in Europe and the United States for centuries. On the other hand, even in the somber Victorian era, scholars (and political leaders) understood that grave, Satan-fearing, free-will-denying, and supposedly morose Calvinism was a difficult credo to credit, praise, or embrace. American theologian Henry Ward Beecher put the doubts aptly: "It has ever been a mystery to the so-called liberals that the Calvinists, with what they have considered their harshly despotic and rigid views and doctrines, should always have been the staunchest and bravest defenders of freedom. The working for liberty of these severe principles in the minds of those that adopted them has been a puzzle."[36]

Twenty-first-century opinion is no less reluctant. Yet during Calvinism's zenith of influence, from the sixteenth to eighteenth centuries, it was easy to see why its theology-cum-ideology won respect: a record that combined opposition to royal tyranny with credit for encouraging just wars, republican principles, self-government, education, and even separation of church and state. Because of its role in seeding representative institutions, New Englander Fiske looked back on Calvinism as "one of the most effective schools that has ever existed for training men in local self-government."[37] The hostility of a king believing in divine right had been voiced centuries earlier by James I: "Presbytery agreeth as well with the monarchy as God with the devil." At the Revolution's outbreak, the English writer Horace Walpole remarked more lightly that "Cousin America has run off with a Presbyterian parson."

No other creed had so many of its eighteenth-century churches burned by British troops, especially in New Jersey and in the Carolinas, where they were regarded as rebel hornets' nests. Just as Puritans and Presbyterians had interwoven just-war and chosen-nation beliefs into the English Civil War of the 1640s, so they did again in the 1770s, now aided in the middle colonies by Reformed (German and Dutch) clergy.[38]

With respect to individual denominations, historian Ruth Bloch summarized that "the popular support for the American Revolution came overwhelmingly from Congregationalists, Baptists, Presbyterians and Southern lay Anglicans, almost all of whom can loosely be described as Calvinists. To be sure, the Revolution also enlisted the support of a number of religious rationalists, particularly among the urban elite and the Southern gentry, but on a more popular level, the religious faith of American revolutionaries was in the main Calvinist. The non-Calvinist Quakers, Methodists and Northern Anglicans drifted disproportionately towards neutrality and Loyalism, and typically Calvinist pre-occupations underlay much of the development of Revolutionary ideology."[39]

This hardly establishes Calvinism as a principal ideological or theological driver of the American Revolution. But it might have been among the six or eight most important.

Conspiracy: The Irrefutable Undercurrent

Inasmuch as George Washington, John Adams, and Thomas Jefferson all commented from time to time about a deep-seated British conspiracy to deny colonial liberties, the question is not about whether these suspicions were widely held, but *why*—on what grounds, and with what ultimate importance to the American Revolution?

Bernard Bailyn, the distinguished former professor of early American history at Harvard, put it simply back in 1967: "We shall have much disbelief to overcome. For what the leaders of the Revolutionary movement themselves said lay behind the convulsion of the times—what they themselves said was the cause of it all—was nothing less than a deliberate design—a conspiracy—of ministers of state and their underlings to overthrow the British constitution, both in England and in America, and to blot out, or at least seriously reduce, English liberties."[40]

Use of the term *conspiracy* and its sub rosa equivalents grew during the 1760s. Multiple sore points—fear of episcopacy; the Stamp, Sugar, Currency, and Townshend Acts; the Proclamation Line; anger over customs crackdowns and the stationing of so many troops in Boston—all fed the perception of plotting and hostile motivation that seemed beyond coincidence. Among Washington, Adams, and Jefferson, the lawyer from Massachusetts took his own sense of conspiracy back furthest—to the 1760s. Full belief in deliberate British malice only crystallized in May, June, and July 1774 as word arrived of the Coercive Acts: the Boston Port Act, the Massachusetts Government Act, the Administration of Justice Act, the Quartering Act, and the equally objected-to Quebec Act. With these, said Adams, Britain "threw off the mask."

Jefferson agreed. Although "single acts of tyranny may be ascribed to the accidental opinion of a day . . . a series of oppressions, begun at a distinguished period and pursued unalterably through every change of ministers, too plainly prove a deliberate and systematical plan of reducing us to slavery." Washington, in the Fairfax Resolves he penned with George Mason in the summer of 1774, perceived London as "endeavoring by every piece of art and despotism to fix the shackles of slavery upon us." In a private communication, he wrote that "I am as fully convinced as I am of my own existence that there has been a regular, systematic plan to enforce [these measures]."[41]

The extended history of Anglo-Saxon belief in conspiracy is also helpful. Bailyn harks back to the late seventeenth century: "Almost—but not quite—all of the ideas and beliefs that shaped the American Revolutionary mind can be found in the voluminous writings of the Exclusion Crisis [1679–1681] and in the literature of the Glorious Revolution that in effect brought that upheaval to a peaceful conclusion."[42] These last decades of the seventeenth century, and the first three of the next, he says, were the political and literary maturation years of the "Opposition" thinking and pamphleteering led by men like John Trenchard, Thomas Gordon, and the Viscounts Molesworth and Bolingbroke that made such a strong impression in pre-Revolutionary America.[43] "Opposition by its very nature, therefore—by the very structure of the political system—fed the fears of conspiracy," and did so on both sides.[44]

Bailyn identified eighteenth-century England's institutional bogeyman: "the bloated Leviathan of government they [Trenchard, Gordon, et al.] saw developing—it was in this populist cry against what appeared to be a swelling financial-governmental complex fat with corruption, complaisant and power-engrossing . . . that English liberal thought took on the forms that would most specifically determine the outlook and character of the American Revolution and that thereafter in vital respects would shape the course of American history."[45]

These pages, although mindful of shared thinking, are principally concerned with the emergence and scope of belief in conspiracy on the American side. In sharpening colonial outrage, "conspiracy" would have resonated
with more than what Bailyn described as "the abstruse points of constitutional law that . . . did not determine the outcome one way or another," or
"the abstract ideas of Locke" or the "noble" but less than central ideas of the
Enlightenment.[46] Even American sympathizers in Parliament sometimes
blamed backstage machinations. One of them, Lord Camden, spoke about
the ministry having formed a conspiracy against English liberties. On the
other hand, George III, in his October 1775 speech to Parliament condemning the rebellion, accused its American architects of a "desperate conspiracy."[47] It was a shared heritage.

In the late 1960s and early 1970s, when Bailyn wrote his influential
analysis—*The Ideological Origins of the American Revolution* won a Pulitzer
Prize in history—conspiracy notions had again become widespread in
America because of the assassinations of John and Robert Kennedy, the Bay
of Pigs misadventure, Watergate, and accompanying suspicions about
covert activity in institutions like the CIA and the FBI. For the not widely
known Harvard professor to have written books tying the Founding Fathers and the Revolution to belief in conspiracies could have courted attack,
not least from Consensus historians, congressmen from Oklahoma, and
Fourth of July orators. Caution might have been wise.

Historically, though, if American thinking has a rich vein of conspiracy
theory and paranoia, no small part of it bespeaks an English, Welsh, and
Scottish heritage of many centuries. It is misleading to begin with the exclusion crisis of 1679–1681; nor should we start with Henry VIII and the
Reformation, although that upheaval was an accelerator. The fifteenth-
century Wars of the Roses were little more than an extended series of plots
and conspiracies—witness Shakespeare's own historical settings. During
that same century, the relationship between England, Burgundy, and
France was so fraught with secret alliances and betrayals that plot-manic
King Louis XI was known as the "universal spider." After the Welsh House
of Tudor essentially replaced Lancaster in seeking the overthrow of
two Yorkist kings, Edward IV and Richard III, the connivance only intensified. At this point, Wales—personified by Henry Tudor, the future Henry
VII—joined the Scots in plotting with the French to keep the English
embroiled.

Once the Tudors were on the English throne, both Henry VII and

Henry VIII were so concerned about rivals, pretenders, and conspiracies that they executed even remote claimants. The Reformation in England owed more than a little to Henry VIII's quest for a queen able to bear a male heir and his coveting of the riches of the Catholic Church. As religious conflict grew, plotting in western Europe jumped to a new multilevel, with England playing a major role under Catholic Queen Mary and Protestant Queen Elizabeth alike. The plots mounted against (but also by) England can be followed in detail by reading the many books on the Elizabethan secret service under Lord Walsingham.[48]

The early-seventeenth-century Stuart kings, James I and Charles I, were also schemers, sometimes with France and Spain. The Puritans were likewise given to seeing plots everywhere, with the Gunpowder Plot of 1605 being topped in the 1630s by the Antrim Plot, endless Popish plots, and the "army plot" of Charles I in 1641.[49] As serious civil war developed in 1642, both sides saw conspirators behind every corner—and with considerable justification. Parliament had an active secret service under John Thurlow, and royalist counterconspirators collected in the shadows of an organization called the Sealed Knot.

My 1999 book, *The Cousins' Wars,* hypothesized a psychological continuity between the three major English-speaking civil wars. All three eras included a considerable (although decreasing) intensity of conspiracy charges relative to (1) political and Popish plots and fear of Catholicism or Episcopacy; and (2) concern about treason and about tyranny and liberties being at risk. Such charges came from both sides. Obviously, these themes were more important in the English Civil War than in the American version two centuries later. The American Revolution fell in the middle.

In recent decades, complaints have grown over an interpretation of the "ideological" origins of the Revolution so narrow as to exclude religion and economics. In fact, both influences seem irrefutable, if not necessarily dominant. "Conspiracy" might have been a factor in giving ideology a greater than usual relevance and zest.

Divergent Empires of American Minds

In a closing assessment of revolutionary psychologies, one further cleavage should be attributed to diverging imperial visions. To call this ideology seems strained. It has very little to do with statutes or rights but represents different pathways of imagination. On one side were those who looked over the Appalachians to a Mississippi Valley frontier, or westward across a continent sure to be spanned, or toward a distant China trade already much envisioned in Massachusetts. This was the empire of the American mind, and if it was guided by profits expected in Canton, furs to be trapped in the Northwest, the rewards of trans-Ohio land speculations, or the vastness of a Louisiana to be wrested from France or Spain, those vistas had sixteenth- and seventeenth-century English antecedents in the westward ambitions of Richard Hakluyt, Francis Drake, Walter Raleigh, and many others.

Most opinion molders in our four vanguard provinces generally fit this category. Over four, five, or six generations, their forebears had principally looked westward (sometimes northward or southward), fighting Indians, French, and Spanish in Western Hemisphere campaigns that, at least until the 1720s or 1730s, rulers in London found of little interest or were unwilling to fund. If the first two Hanoverian kings, German-born George I and German-born George II, were preoccupied with German states, German wars, German wives, and German mistresses and therefore treated North America with "salutary neglect," to incipient nationalists that was fine.

The major colonies had managed their own expansion and were usually happy to be left to their own devices. If George II had been little known, he was well regarded. The thirteen colonies boasted 40 or 50 counties and towns named for Hanover, Brunswick (Braunschweig), Mecklenburg, Lunenburg, King George, Prince George, (Queen) Caroline, (Queen) Charlotte, (Prince) Frederick, and the like. Salutary neglect had been popular. Most of the Americans who by 1775 could be described as expansionists—upholders of colonial military expeditions, strong militias, local manufactures, smuggling when needed, and aggressive land companies—were Patriots of growing mind to break with an empire realigning its intentions to tax, confine, and police North American aspirations. Several historians have developed the portrait of expansionism, as well as its opposite, nonexpansionism. Many of those opposed took a neutral or Tory stance in 1775, especially if their appointive or commercial interests looked back to the mother country.

A considerable minority did prefer this Atlanticized and Anglicized imperial model. They embraced the grand British Empire that had taken on such size and wealth over the prior quarter century. Within Britain, many of non-English ancestry had been especially happy to pursue its benefits. The Scots had done so with particular enthusiasm, gaining disproportionate roles in imperial government, in Canada and India, and among the officers' corps of the British Army. A majority of Scots in America shared that loyalty. Formerly French seigneurs and Catholic clergy in Canada joined in. Even Catholics in Ireland, especially prosperous ones, found the empire ready to make some economic and religious concessions. In America's northern colonies, including New England, the Anglican Church had grown rapidly during the second half of the eighteenth century, especially among the mercantile, professional, officeholding, and landowning classes. Not a few imagined a new aristocracy tied to British religion, British commerce, Crown patronage, and London fashionability. Because these opportunities related to the existing empire, not the would-be American one, some of these Loyalists chose to flee between 1774 and 1776, as we will see in Chapter 8.

However, support for the existing far-flung British Empire, as opposed to a Patriot regime, had many more foundations than these. The economic basis of Loyalism was discussed in Chapter 4, but its cultural underpinnings were also substantial. Quakers looked to Britain for commerce and protection. Emigrants from German states allied to the House of Hanover had favorable views of Britain; likewise the Dutch Reformed who belonged to the conservative wing of the church that back in Holland was pro-British. Small ethnic and religious groups in the North American colonies often trusted the British Empire more than they did local Puritans and Scotch-Irish Calvinists. Within Massachusetts, the old Plymouth Colony had a higher ratio of Tories than the original Puritan Bay Colony. Black slaves with some education knew that freedom was more likely to come from courts in England than from courts in Virginia or South Carolina.

In short, two different visions of empire competed for American minds, and in sections of the middle colonies, deciding between them would tear local populations apart. In Part II we have examined the pre-Revolutionary circumstances of the thirteen colonies. Now Part III will turn to the major 1774–1775 battlegrounds—politics, commercial confrontation, preparation for war, and the initial theaters of military confrontation on land and at sea.

PART III

1775—THE BATTLEGROUNDS

CHAPTER 8

Fortress New England?

By 1774, civil government [in Massachusetts] was near its end. The courts could no longer administer justice, and the people of New England were arming and training for war. Parliament closed the port of Boston, and General Gage returned to America to combine the offices of Governor of Massachusetts and Commander-in-chief of the troops in North America. Before the end of the year he was warning the government at home that only a great army could end the troubles, and that a bloody crisis was at hand.

Piers Mackesy, *The War for America, 1775–1783,* 1964

Nothing in the early days of the Revolution, not even the promptness with which Massachusetts poured its men into the field, is so admirable, and perhaps so surprising, as the readiness with which men of the neighboring colonies hastened to its aid. No student of the day-by-day history of that time can fail to wonder at the general unity of New England in the face of a natural impulse for each colony to save its own skin.

Allen French, *The First Year of the American Revolution,* 1934

With New England at a boil, little about the confrontation at Lexington and Concord on April 19, 1775, should have been surprising, save perhaps the remarkable success of Patriot leaders in compiling, circulating, and selling their own preemptive tale of what happened. This story—in Henry Wadsworth Longfellow's version, of "how the British regulars fired and fled"—was not beyond dispute.[1] Centuries later, who actually shot first is less clear.

For Massachusetts Patriots, the stakes of fixing blame could not have been higher. Convincing documentation was necessary for Massachusetts to meet the precondition for support set six months earlier by the First

Continental Congress: that first blood in a major confrontation had to be shed by the British. By April 22, the Provincial Congress had an eight-man committee busying itself with eyewitness depositions. But even earlier, on April 20, a veteran post rider, Isaac Bissell, had begun a five-day trip that outdid even Paul Revere. He rode from Watertown outside Boston to Philadelphia, changing horses and history as he delivered his stark message in town after town—British soldiers had fired on Americans and killed some.[2]

British General Gage, waiting in his headquarters during the day's tumult of the nineteenth, had not thought ahead so well. He kept his troops armed and available in their barracks on the chance that a rising might also flare up within Boston—or that the aroused New England militia, after tasting blood, might carry their attack to the city. In other ways, Gage fumbled, not least in the contest for public opinion.[3] On the Patriot side, even in March and early April, "the certainty of fighting" was leading a steady stream of Whig activists to exit Boston. Gage's many informers presumably told him that, too, among their other details on the Patriot munitions supplies at Concord, the Provincial Congress's adoption of war plans, and the possibility being discussed of a New England-wide Army of Observation.[4] By April 19, no major leader remained in the city; the last, Dr. Joseph Warren, had departed that morning.[5] We must assume that Patriot strategists gave advance consideration to how the news would be disseminated.

The "powder alarm" in September 1774, which saw 15,000 to 20,000 militiamen from Connecticut, Rhode Island, and New Hampshire begin marching, aroused by false rumors of fighting in Boston, was an earlier event in which communication outweighed reality. John Adams, hearing the first rumor in Philadelphia during the opening days of the First Continental Congress, had exulted in the delegates' bellicose response. Paul Revere then brought clarification. After the Congress concluded with a belligerent position in October, Connecticut, Rhode island, and New Hampshire all endorsed its combative language. To merchants and shippers, the Continental Association plan for nonimportation and nonexportation took top billing. Political activists, though, probably paid greatest attention to Congress's endorsement of Massachusetts's fiery Suffolk Resolves. War preparations elsewhere in New England went ahead only thinly disguised, as Gage had advised Lord Dartmouth. Before 1774 ended, as we have seen, New Hampshiremen and Rhode Islanders had seized royal forts to obtain ordnance and munitions. Patriots in New London, Connecticut, had removed harborside cannon and trundled them inland.

Historians taken with July 1776 as a pivot tend to ignore how the colonies had essentially opted for war a year or more earlier. In actuality, the thirteen could not "declare war" because Britain was a parent, not a foreign nation. Nor could the mother country declare war on colonists, especially ones who still styled themselves as subjects of the empire. After a progression of trade ultimatums and restraints—winter 1774–1775 months, during which British officials seriously entertained prosecution under treason statutes—both sides let themselves slip beyond imperial commercial disagreements into an increasingly military confrontation. On July 6, 1775, not quite three weeks after the Battle of Bunker Hill, the Second Continental Congress recognized as much by issuing its not very famous *Declaration of the Causes and Necessity of Taking Up Arms,* largely penned by Thomas Jefferson. Those paragraphs, now all but forgotten, justified resort to force by the impossibility of unconditional submission to Great Britain.

By the legal yardsticks of that era, a rebellion had begun in Massachusetts at least ten months earlier. In late September 1774, Lord North told former Massachusetts governor Thomas Hutchinson, now a prominent Loyalist, that "if they [the Colonials] refused to trade with Great Britain, Great Britain would take care they should trade nowhere else." In November, Lord Dartmouth said privately that if the report of the Congress's endorsement of the Suffolk Resolves was true, "they [the Americans] have declared war against us." On November 18, in a letter to Lord North, the king had described the four New England governments as in a state of revolt.[6] As we will see in Chapter 9, during the winter of 1774–1775 the principal British response to the American challenge to empire came in two major parliamentary decisions to restrain trade, first of the four New England colonies and then of New Jersey, Pennsylvania, Maryland, Virginia, and South Carolina, because they, too, had joined the Continental Association and embraced its ultimatum. By April 12, a week before Lexington and Concord, nine colonies had been given their blunt answer to the challenge thrown down in Philadelphia.

The next retribution, applying to all thirteen colonies, came on August 23, 1775, several weeks after news of the fighting at Bunker Hill had reached London. Drawn in much the same language used back in 1745 to proclaim (parts of) Scotland in rebellion under Charles Edward Stuart, all thirteen were now denounced. Like its predecessor, the 1775 proclamation demanded that all good men help to suppress the rebellion and desist from any communication with rebels.[7]

"Milestones of Rebellion," below, lists the critical speeches, denuncia-
tions, proclamations, and milestones of 1774 and 1775 that marked the road
to civil war. The intensification of British anger was steady and unmistakable, but the wintertime lag in communication delayed knowledge on both
sides of what was being decided.

Milestones of Rebellion: Reactions to the American Revolution by British Leaders, September 1774 to December 1775

September 11, 1774	"The dye is now cast. The colonies must either submit or triumph." *King George III*
September 25, 1774	"From present appearances there is no prospect of putting the late [Coercive] Acts in force but by first making a conquest of the New England provinces." *General Thomas Gage*
November 1, 1774	"If these [Suffolk] Resolves of your people are to be depended upon, they have declared war on us." *Lord Dartmouth, American Secretary, to former Governor Thomas Hutchinson*
November 18, 1774	"The New England governments are in a state of rebellion; blows must decide whether they are to be subject to this country or independent." *King George III to Lord North*
November 29, 1774	"Unwarrantable attempts [the Association] have been made to obstruct the commerce of this kingdom by unlawful combinations." *King George III speech to the opening of Parliament*
December 20, 1774	The proceedings of the Congress "exceed all Ideas of Rebellion." *Lord Rochford, Secretary of State, to Lord Sandwich*
February 1775	The House of Commons by a 296–106 vote passed an address moved by Lord North that declared New England in rebellion and asked His Majesty to reduce that area to obedience.
April 1775	Parliament passed two Restraining Acts, one affecting New England, the second Pennsylvania, New Jersey, Maryland, Virginia, and South Carolina, banning these

colonies as of July from the North Atlantic fisheries and from trading anywhere but Great Britain and the British West Indies.

June 10, 1775	Official word is received in Britain (from General Gage) of the April 19 bloodshed at Lexington and Concord and the encirclement of Boston by New England militia.
June 10, 1775	"America must be a colony of England or treated as an enemy." *King George III to Lord Dartmouth*
July 26, 1775	"Lord North submits to His Majesty that the war is now grown to such a height, that it must be treated as a foreign war, and that every expedient which would be used in the latter case should be applied in the former." *Lord North to King George III*
August 23, 1775	The king proclaimed the thirteen colonies in rebellion and called for loyal subjects to rally.
October 26, 1775	"The rebellious war now levied is become more general, and is manifestly carried on for the purpose of establishing an independent empire." *King George III speech to the opening of Parliament*
December 20, 1775	Parliament completed passage of the Prohibitory Act, prohibiting all colonial trade, with all ships and cargoes belonging to the inhabitants of the colonies to be forfeit. Charles Fox, one of the Opposition leaders, observed that this "puts us in a state of complete war with America."

Proclamations of rebellion were no mere political scoldings. Some three decades earlier, many of the Scottish and English rebels captured—not just officers, but enlisted men, pipers, and even three lawyers—had been hung. George Washington, on taking command of the army besieging the king's troops in Boston, presumably knew the name and fate of Lord George Murray, who had commanded Prince Charles's army from 1745 to 1746. Murray had not been among the 120 rebels executed for treason—most of them hung, drawn, and quartered—only because he fled to France, as did other senior Scottish participants. In keeping with medieval precedents, the skulls of some of those killed, spiked above the gates of the cities in which they were executed, "were still grinning down on the streets" even as Washington took up his American command.[8]

The clash that came on April 19 could have come on March 19 or February 19. The situation across much of Massachusetts had already become explosive. Confrontation in Salem had barely been avoided on February 26 when elements of the 64th Regiment withdrew after failing to seize cannon held there. Twenty miles south of Boston, in what had been the old Plymouth Colony, coastal Marshfield, a wealthy, conservative town dominated by *Mayflower* descendants, had organized a Loyalist association in late 1774. In January, after 200 residents had petitioned Gage for protection, he sent two small vessels with 114 redcoats of the King's Own Regiment under a capable captain.[9]

Near the Rhode Island border, Assonet, another venerable Plymouth Colony town, had been Tory enough in 1774 to petition against the Boston Tea Party. In March, Gage requested a conservative officeholder and French and Indian War hero, Colonel Thomas Gilbert, to raise a local Loyalist force. He then sent Gilbert small arms and ammunition. Tensions rose, and on April 9–10, more than one thousand Bristol County Patriot militia mustered, some of whom raided Gilbert's home, broke up a Loyalist assemblage, and took 35 muskets, two case bottles of gunpowder, and a basket of bullets. The colonel himself fled to the nearby British frigate *Rose*.[10] Bristol County Revolutionary War reenactors, interviewed two centuries later, fairly argued that had anyone been killed, that confrontation, not Lexington and Concord a week later, might have triggered war.

Naval officers were also on edge. On April 5, Gage requested Admiral Graves to send a vessel and another detachment from the 64th Regiment to Fort Pownall, on the Penobscot River in the Maine district. Their orders were to dismantle the fort and take the ordnance and ammunition stored there, a job completed on April 15. On April 11, the admiral ordered the 64-gun *Somerset* to take position to block any attack on Boston across the water from Charlestown. Two days later the four large men-of-war in Boston Harbor, already victualed, were ordered to rig "a month sooner than usual."[11]

On April 20, the Lexington and Concord "morning after," Gage remained cautious, but Graves vented, at least briefly. In his journal, he recalled urging "the burning of Charlestown and Roxbury, and the seizing of the Heights of Roxbury and Bunkers Hill." He had also argued that "we ought to act hostilely from this time forward by burning and laying waste the whole country."[12] The admiral's advice regarding Bunker Hill was certainly sound.

On the Patriot side, the Massachusetts Committee of Safety, acting for the Provincial Congress, called out the colony's entire militia; and on the twenty-third, the congress itself, meeting in Watertown, resolved that a 30,000-man New England volunteer army should be raised. Massachusetts would furnish 13,600, and Connecticut, New Hampshire, and Rhode Island were asked to provide the remainder.[13] This resembled the four-colony "Army of Observation" that had been under discussion *before* the shots fired on Lexington Green.[14]

In short, little was truly accidental about Lexington and Concord. Back in October 1774, the king's order in council, issued to stop munitions exports to the colonies, had been a logical twofold escalation: first, in response to the "economic treason" developing at the Continental Congress, and second, in reply to the Yankee search for gunpowder and ordnance already being reported by British embassies, officers, and agents across Europe and the West Indies. A few months later rebels in Virginia and South Carolina had begun vying with royal governors over control of local gunpowder magazines and arms—the April events in Charleston and Williamsburg— *before* any news arrived of fighting in Massachusetts. All four vanguard colonies were well in motion.

But let us return to New England. By late April, all four colonies had soldiers among the more or less 20,000 militia surrounding Boston. At various points, at least 4,000 to 6,000 men went home, and the actual strength of the besieging "army" may have dipped as low as 10,000 to 12,000 militiamen, plus lingering minutemen. Hardly any non–New Englanders were present. The force was Yankee and remained so until the arrival of George Washington and some 600 Virginia, Maryland, and Pennsylvania riflemen in July.[15]

New England: The Hub of Early Congressional Decision Making

With New England as the principal subject of discussion, the period between April 20 and July 6, 1775—a mere ten calendar weeks—was arguably more essential to the unfolding of the American Revolution than the same but much more hullabalooed time frame a year later. If the military commitment undertaken by the New England colonies in late April and early May was unsurprising, the convening of the Second Continental Congress in Philadelphia on May 10 greatly increased the stakes. This was the period during which the Second Congress cooperated in turning a New England–based insurgency into the American Revolution.

Following up on nonimportation and nonexportation plans was the agenda for the new Congress, but the May 10 date set was fortunate. With fighting already under way, additional weeks or months of delay could have been dangerous. As things were, a delegate from Williamsburg, Virginia, say, would not have heard of the fighting in Massachusetts by the time he had to depart. Taverns and delegate receptions along the way to Philadelphia must have hummed with further news and gossip. New Englanders, though, would have had many hours for discussion and political calculation before setting out on what was usually a five-to-eight-day trip. Plans to seize Ticonderoga were already being hatched in Connecticut and Massachusetts by April 30.

Of the four colonies motivated to choose their delegates to the Second Congress before 1774 ended, three were in New England: Massachusetts, Rhode Island, and Connecticut. Their sense of what would be at stake was fulfilled. As of early May, more than half of the major decisions shaping up in Philadelphia principally involved New England and the New England army besieging Boston.

In the meantime, events were already drawing in the non-Yankee provinces to the south and west. Delegates arriving in Philadelphia were hearing about the powder magazine altercations in Virginia and South Carolina. Furthermore, when news had reached Britain between February and April of how Virginia, South Carolina, Maryland, New Jersey, and Pennsylvania endorsed the Association, the Cabinet and Parliament, further aroused, orchestrated a second Restraining Act in early April to include those five colonies. As word of this extension arrived in May, the effect was to broaden congressional support for New England. Britain was clearly not backing down.

One pivot was whether Congress would adopt—as in "assume responsibility for"—the not-very-organized militia and minutemen besieging Boston. The First Congress had promised its support of Massachusetts if the British fired first, but exactly what that support would entail was not spelled out. However, Congress spent its opening days after May 10 both awaiting late-arriving delegates and preparing an elaborate statement, including some twenty sworn eyewitness depositions, to be sent to London as proof of British responsibility.[16]

That documentation was also expected to reassure those delegates in Philadelphia who remained ambivalent. On the other hand, the soldiers bottling up General Gage were virtually all New Englanders, and their commanders were mostly from Massachusetts and Connecticut. This also concerned some middle-colony and southern delegates.

Question two was related: Would Congress be willing, Massachusetts leaders asked, to give advice on how to reconstitute that province's government in the aftermath of the Coercive Acts and the clash at Lexington and Concord? Some Bay Colony Patriots thought it would be politic to constitute a broadly acceptable new civil government able to supervise the troops doing siege duty, whose numbers and loose organization recalled the historic perils of a "standing army." With Gage excluded, Massachusetts had no executive authority. Would Congress advise?

A third decision had to do with the de facto economic declaration of war issued through the Continental Association, together with its bristling political calendar of nonimportation and nonexportation. This experiment in economic coercion is discussed in the next chapter. For the moment, suffice it to say that an outraged Parliament was already counterattacking. As we have seen, retaliation began with the four New England colonies. Under the New England Restraining Act, finalized in March and effective in July, the New England colonies were prohibited from any commerce that was not with Britain or the West Indies, and were also barred from the North Atlantic fisheries. In April, as we have seen, five other colonies were added. But four more, still being courted by London, remained exempt. This was a touchy question.

Procedurally, we must remember that Congress had reassembled because the British government had rejected the Association and offered no redress. These developments now required the delegates in Philadelphia to revisit a whole range of trade-related issues—what changes to make in nonexportation schedules, how to deal with the four colonies still treated benignly by Britain, and how to cope with the punitive enforcement role the Royal Navy would assume in July under the Restraining Acts.

The fourth challenge, first apparent a week after Congress convened, would come in dealing with Canada and the seizure by New Englanders of

Forts Ticonderoga and Crown Point on May 10 and 11. News of the two captures did not arrive in Philadelphia until May 17, but both erstwhile citadels sat on territory belonging to New York, the most equivocal of provinces. Many moderate New Yorkers still favored reconciliation. New England, however, badly needed the hundreds of cannon that the forts held. Massachusetts, Connecticut, and New Hampshire authorities quickly instructed their delegates to argue against giving up the two fortresses or returning the cannon. By late June, Congress had agreed to keep both and was edging toward an incursion into Canada.

In fairness to New Yorkers and others loath to take any bold measures, both General Gage and Admiral Graves remained cautious through most of May.[17] Until Bunker Hill in June, the largest military engagement involved the May 27 fighting on Noddle's Island in Boston Harbor, an American victory in which roughly a thousand New England troops took part and a British schooner was burned and two redcoats killed.

Another issue, this one not specific to New England, was the financial question: How would Congress and the provinces pay for the bold enterprises now being launched—with what emissions of paper money and with what economic relationships between Congress and individual colonies?

To some historians, the decisions made in June and July tilted enough in the direction of independence that elements of a countertrend became apparent in the autumn of 1775.[18] In London, the Crown's legal officers saw the same early-summer indications, and George III declared the thirteen colonies in rebellion on August 23, several weeks after word had come of Bunker Hill but only days after the arrival of the *Declaration of the Causes and Necessity of Taking Up Arms.* Its message meant war, even if many American leaders lived in a cloud of rose-colored illusion in which firmness—proving that angry colonists would fight—had been embraced as the only way to make Britain back down.

Five Patriot Governments in New England

In each New England province, rebel governments either held power in April 1775 or quickly took over, confirming Patriot control of both the military and the local purse strings. Where reorganization of the militia was unfinished, it was completed, sometimes brusquely. Tories were purged from office, disarmed, or in some instances, jailed.

Connecticut, continuing under its cherished charter, with "rebel" governor Jonathan Trumbull and the Patriot Assembly and Council, had to make very few changes. So, too, for the other charter colony, Rhode Island—at least from an *institutional* standpoint. Although Governor Joseph Wanton had been reelected in April, when fighting broke out, he was deemed too pro-British to remain in office, and Assembly leaders refused to administer the oath of office. Nicholas Cooke, a strong Patriot, became deputy governor and then governor.[19]

New Hampshire, by contrast, had for 30 years been administered by royal governors from the influential and native-born Wentworth family. However. since 1774, power had begun to shift to a Patriot-convened Provincial Congress. In April and May 1775 the Third and Fourth Provincial Congresses ordered an army of 2,000 under the auspices of a Committee of Safety and a Committee of Supplies. All males between 16 and 50 were required to serve in an expanded militia.[20] In June, Governor John Wentworth fled to harborside Fort William and Mary and later to a nearby British frigate.

Next door in the old Hampshire Grants, which King George III had ruled to be New York territory in 1764, the future Vermont was a legal and political battleground. De facto control lay with rough-hewn rebels against New York (and British) authority—Ethan Allen's Green Mountain Boys, almost all of them New England born. Less than two weeks after Lexington and Concord, Allen sat down in Bennington's Catamount Tavern with representatives from Massachusetts and Connecticut. All were anxious to seize nearby Fort Ticonderoga, only 60 miles away but clearly within New York territory. Once it was taken, Allen set up a Council of War, hoping that with backing from Connecticut and Massachusetts, the Green Mountain Boys could dispel New York objections and Congress would approve a Patriot-faction government. That was a pipe dream. Although the Boys kept local control, Congress withheld recognition from Vermont because of New York's opposition and continuing territorial claim.

As we have seen, April 19 had left Massachusetts in a governmental quandary. General Gage, although powerless beyond Boston, had officially dissolved the provincial House of Representatives. Outside the occupied city, British authority had collapsed. The only governing body in existence was extralegal: the Provincial Congress, now in its third incarnation since October. Patriots in New Hampshire might be content operating under nothing more than a provincial congress, but Massachusetts had a much greater role and notoriety—and its manner of governance could expect wider and deeper scrutiny.

To lawyers like John Adams, Massachusetts in 1775 was in breach of its own prior charters—those of 1629 and 1691—by not having either an executive or a legislative branch. Like Connecticut and Rhode Island, the Bay Colony took its erstwhile charters seriously. Now it had within its borders a massive, mixed-colony force besieging British-occupied Boston. So Massachusetts proposed to rebuild its government to conform to the accepted framework of the 1691 Charter. Would that do the trick? Could the Continental Congress decide? After all, its call for local committees of inspection back in late 1774 had been widely accepted as having the force of law.

And Congress, in a momentous commitment, did advise: on June 9, just seven weeks after Lexington and Concord, it recommended that Massachusetts elect representatives to an assembly, which in turn should name council members. The two houses were to "exercise the powers of government" until the king might name a governor who agreed to act under the 1691 charter.[21] That might never happen, but the mention was politic.

The new Revolutionary regimes in New England also reflected changed cultural and religious alignments. One powerful sentiment was to replace Anglican "court-party" elites. A second was to relocate government inland—away from the old milieu, but also beyond the range of a British frigate's cannon or raiding redcoats. The two motivations overlapped in New Hampshire, where the Provincial Congress relocated the capital from coastal Portsmouth, the seat of former royal government. The new site was Exeter, slightly inland and historically Congregational and Puritan. In Rhode Island, the existing seat of government, Newport, saw political influence migrate to rival Providence—farther from the coast, more Baptist and Congregationalist, and less influenced by Newport's Anglican and Quaker commercial elite. Besides which, Newport was unmistakably at the mercy of the Royal Navy; its occupation by British forces from late 1776 to 1779, in which Loyalists collaborated, added to its political fall.

In Connecticut, the towns of New Haven and Hartford had split the role of capital, with Hartford dominating. Convenience and wartime safety led to a new "capital" in Lebanon, the eastern Connecticut home of long-time governor Jonathan Trumbull. Known as the rebel governor, and by autumn a relied-upon confidant of George Washington, Trumbull enjoyed extraordinary support from Connecticut's Assembly and Council. In May they essentially delegated control of the colony's military activity to a War Council headed by Trumbull and operating from a "War Office" next to his home. This new Council's usual attendees all hailed from the province's nearby radical eastern counties. No other province allowed a governor so much personal control.

Some 30 miles from the coast, and near the main road from Boston to New York, Lebanon was well placed for communication. Fleet-footed Narragansett ponies stood hitched at the posts and palings to carry orders to Ticonderoga, the Patriot lines around Boston, or the cannon-producing provincial ironworks in Salisbury (under Trumbull's direct control by January 1776). Lebanon was relatively safe from British raids. Even so Trumbull was a prime target of the British and Tories, and a price was put on his head. He was guarded around the clock by a half dozen soldiers, and much of the time also by post riders able to summon help.[22]

Boston, not surprisingly, had such a strong Patriot imprimatur that it resumed its role as the capital of Massachusetts in March 1776 following the British evacuation. No other seaport capital in New England retained that political credibility. Of course, several thousand Boston-area Loyalists went into exile, a huge number relative to those abandoning Newport or Portsmouth.

As for the rebel Hampshire Grants, today's Vermont, its unofficial 1774–1776 capital was mountain-encircled Bennington. The Green Mountain Boys met in the Catamount Tavern, where they had a ceremony of hoisting offending Tories 35 feet up in a chair and then leaving them to dangle for six to eight hours. However, at a mid-1775 convention, Vermonters replaced Ethan Allen, making the capable but softer-spoken Seth Warner colonel of the Green Mountain Regiment.

New England's provincial governments, in short, were Patriot led and politically reliable. However, all four included towns or regions where disloyalty was widespread or where the new regime's authority was rejected. Even New England had some chinks and vulnerabilities.

Vulnerable Frontiers and Dubious Loyalties

Although New England could fairly be called a Patriot "fortress" in 1775, several of its region's frontiers were exposed. Jonathan Trumbull, sitting in his War Office halfway between New York and Boston, had to watch and plan for the participation of Connecticut troops on most of those fronts and theaters of operations.

In the late summer of 1775, Connecticut soldiers manned Fort Ticonderoga, still decrepit. Others marched along Quebec's Richelieu River, started moving up the Kennebec with Benedict Arnold, participated in besieging Boston, manned the somewhat feeble artillery of seacoast batteries or forts from Norwalk to New London, and stood by on the New York border to suppress that province's Tories and otherwise fill in for its unreliable militia. These multiple roles peaked in late 1775 and 1776. Afterward, despite Trumbull's ongoing importance as a war leader, Connecticut's military forces never again played that unique role of representing New England's—and to an extent George Washington's—unofficial reserve depot.

Soldiers from the other New England colonies were less broadly dispersed. Massachusetts furnished over half the manpower for the siege of Boston, fortified and guarded a long seacoast, and manned sections of the Canadian frontier. A few companies were posted near Machias, in the Maine district, near that era's tense boundary between Massachusetts and Nova Scotia. Troops from the Bay Colony played only a small part in the initial invasion of Quebec.

Some of Yankeedom's best troops came from Rhode Island and New Hampshire. Rhode Island deployed two well-trained regiments in the lines around Boston under Brigadier General Nathanael Greene, who years later would become George Washington's top general in the Carolinas. A sprinkling of Rhode Islanders went up the Kennebec with Arnold. Two of New Hampshire's three regiments were fully formed and represented in the siege, and both played a disproportionate and distinguished role at Bunker Hill. New Hampshire also furnished rangers for the Quebec expedition.

As for maritime warfare, the four provinces kept one eye on coastal defenses—Chapter 14 discusses the British attempts during 1775 to bombard and burn Yankee seaports—while the other watched the Yankee vessels engaging small Royal Navy craft (schooners, cutters, barges, and tenders) and intercepting British supply ships and transports. Massachusetts, Rhode Island, and Connecticut all launched small provincial navies before the end of 1775. Autumn's waterborne assault on British supply ships, substantially at George Washington's own urging, is detailed in Chapter 12.

Taken together, these demanding sectors—the Boston theater, the vulnerable seacoast, the Hudson-Champlain and Kennebec-Chaudière war roads into Canada, and the New York Tory districts that Congress and Washington suppressed with Connecticut militia incursions—made New England the front line of the Revolution in 1775. Virginia and the Carolinas were readying to play a large part, but in 1775 theirs was still a supporting role.

Northern New England's mountainous "roof," protected only by militia, was open to invasion anytime the British could muster 6,000 to 10,000 soldiers, as they finally did in 1777. Middling seaports could be devastated by a pair of 20-gun sloops of war. And whenever the Royal Navy wanted to occupy the Narragansett Bay waters surrounding Newport, it could. In general, though, New England displayed lopsided internal support for the Patriot cause, with only a few stipplings of Tory strength.

But these deserve brief note. The two thirds of Massachusetts—its western, central, and northeastern counties—that had made up the arch-Puritan Bay Colony before unification with Plymouth in 1691 was zealous on the Patriot side. These Puritan areas had suppressed, and to a considerable extent forced out, their Loyalist elites in 1774 and 1775. Exile is a fair description, even though many who fled to British-held Boston remained in the province until departing to Halifax with General Howe in March 1776.

Minor insurrections during the early months of 1775 came in the southeastern counties that were originally part of the older, less Puritan Plymouth Colony. Here conservative towns like Assonet, Marshfield, and Scituate were home to *Mayflower* descendants with names like Winslow, Winthrop, and Standish. Parliament recognized Marshfield and Scituate in March by excluding them from its first Restraining Act. Dissidence also centered in residential concentrations of neutrality-seeking Quakers: Barnstable and Sandwich townships on Cape Cod; and whaling-rich Nantucket and Fairhaven, the island's mainland cousin in the candle, lamp oil, and whalebone corset trade.

By the mid-twentieth century, Old Cape Cod had become a popular song and an even more popular tourist attraction. Histories of its towns, succulent oysters, and Yankee folkways abound. However, there exists no one-volume history of the Cape's town-by-town politics during the American Revolution. It would mar some images.

Nantucket, in particular, became a 42-square-mile political and commercial hot potato for Massachusetts political leaders. Located some 30 miles southeast of Cape Cod, the island was wide open to the Royal Navy.

Because of this geography—and also because Britain bought virtually all of Nantucket's lucrative output of whale oil—the island's Quaker leadership hoped to slip into a semiofficial neutrality. Indeed, several hundred Tories from mainland Massachusetts emigrated there to enjoy a more salubrious political climate. However, because Britain had also exempted collaborative Nantucket from the New England Restraining Act, various opportunity-minded merchants and traders flocked in. Several sought to use Nantucket vessels to smuggle supplies and provisions to His Majesty's forces in Boston.

By mid-1775, the island had become notorious. Patriot-controlled seaports from Wilmington, North Carolina, to Philadelphia passed ordinances against exporting provisions there. Finally, the Congress prohibited exports to Nantucket except from neighboring Barnstable County, Massachusetts, where judges would decide what was needed for local—and only local—consumption.[23]

As for New Hampshire, its minor internal disaffection mattered little because that province, alone among the thirteen, was never invaded. Those who declined to sign the Association in 1775—just 6 percent of the eligible population—centered in Anglican locales and places with Wentworth family ties (Portsmouth, Claremont, and several small towns). Some Baptists, especially in newly settled outlying regions, yawned at the Revolution and disliked New Hampshire's new Congregationalist-run government, prompting what one local historian called a "strong tendency during the war to tar Baptists with a Tory brush."[24] At various times, several dozen remote townships in northern and western New Hampshire wanted to secede and join Vermont.

In Rhode Island, too, religion greatly influenced political loyalties. Anglicans concentrated in Newport, where by one account "the members of Trinity Church (the only Anglican church in Newport) supported the loyalist cause overwhelmingly, and a list of both early royalists and later loyalists reads much like Trinity's Register."[25] Because Quakers comprised another 15 percent of the city's population, neutrals and Loyalists constituted a strong force. Baptists had long-standing, influential roles in Rhode Island, so few embraced the antipolitical or neutral sloganry common among their outsider coreligionists farther north.

Like Massachusetts, Connecticut had a troublesome periphery. In contrast to the *über*-patriotism of its evangelical eastern counties, it had a much more conservative western section, abutting New York, where Anglican strength had almost doubled since 1761. By 1775, churchmen—the label given Church of England members in Connecticut—represented about 25 percent of the population west of the Stratford (Housatonic) River.[26] During the course of the war, the western towns, mostly in Fairfield County, provided many hundreds of volunteers for Loyalist regiments, especially the Prince of Wales' American Volunteers and the King's American Regiment.[27]

Politically, western Connecticut Tories arguably caused more trouble in 1775 than those in Massachusetts (where many had already fled to Boston). In March 1774, a conservative convention, drawing from 23 western towns but principally those in Fairfield, had opposed both Connecticut's western expansion and the reelection of Governor Jonathan Trumbull. In January and February 1775, Tories disrupted patriotic conventions in Fairfield and Litchfield counties, insisting that proper authority in the empire lay with "the King, Lords, and Commons," not extralegal committees, conventions, and associations.[28] In March several Fairfield towns, led by the two Anglican hotbeds, Newtown and Ridgefield, voted against the Continental Association and opposed selecting committees to enforce it.[29]

The Connecticut Assembly, besides putting Newtown and Ridgefield under legislative surveillance, took action that spring to disband a militia company in the western town of Waterbury as "inimical." The legislators cashiered disloyal militia officers in Stamford and refused to commission those chosen in Newtown.[30] Bolder than the Assembly, Patriot militia assembled in large numbers between September and December to disarm Tories in North Fairfield, Newtown, Redding, Danbury, Ridgefield, Woodbury, and Derby, the core of western Connecticut Anglicanism. The Anglican rector in Derby, Richard Mansfield, had been foolish enough to write to New York's royal governor, William Tryon, that if a British army could be sent, it would be joined by 4,000 or 5,000 men from Fairfield, New Haven, and Litchfield counties.[31] Mansfield quickly fled to Long Island.

After taking lesser measures, Connecticut legislators struck hard in December 1775 with an act to prohibit enlisting or encouraging enlistment in the British military, serving with Crown forces, providing them with provisions or munitions, helping to pilot a British vessel, or criticizing the laws of Connecticut or Congress. A year later treason was made punishable by death, and a special committee was empowered to visit western towns and interrogate "all inimical persons."[32] In the words even of a sympathetic

Trumbull biographer, "Here then, in Connecticut . . . was a Detective Code and a Detective Police, for the suppression of internal foes—thorough for the purpose intended as was that of the Duke of Otranto's in the days of Napoleon the First."[33]

This is hardly needless detail. Loyal and reliable Connecticut militiamen were essential to backstop the wide-ranging military commitment Trumbull had undertaken on behalf of Congress and George Washington. Connecticut forces were frequently called upon to help suppress Tory activity in New York, and so comparable behavior in western Connecticut was put down harshly.

Indeed, persisting sub rosa recruitment for Loyalist regiments in Fairfield County displayed what future centuries would call a fifth column. Historians have used the term "military loyalism" to describe both the wayward politics or unreliability of the militia in western towns and the high frequency of militia-age males running off to join the British. Not only was Waterbury, for example, singled out by the dissolution of its militia company, but 66 of the town's men ran off to join the British. Disaffection was closely related to the strength of local Anglicanism.[34]

Although it is beyond the time frame of this book, elements of a civil war wracked southwestern Connecticut by late 1776 after British forces had occupied Long Island. Patriots from Yankee eastern Long Island fled redcoat rule by returning to their ancestral Connecticut. Disaffected Connecticut Anglicans, in turn, crossed the sound to relatively welcoming Long Island areas like Brookhaven, Oyster Bay, Huntington Bay, and Hempstead, all now in British hands. For six more years, Patriots and Loyalists raided each other across the sound, establishing and then operating networks for spying, moving refugees, and smuggling alike. Economically and militarily weary as the years passed, Connecticut by 1777 could no longer play its unique early role.[35]

To the north, politics within the future borders of Vermont, in turn, often reflected the origins of people's land grants: Did individuals hold property under title from New Hampshire or from New York? Those who looked to New York—true of many in the present-day Brattleboro area— also tended to be Tory or Loyalist in the larger continental struggle. Annals confined to Vermont alone usually include highly relevant cultural, religious, and land-grant anecdotes and evaluations. By contrast, one-volume histories of the American Revolution often sidestep Vermont's status in 1776 and thereafter. The Continental Congress, responsive to New York, declined to accept the insurgent-controlled territory as a new state. This not only dashed Green Mountain Boys' hopes for a New Connecticut but put their 1776–1783 activity outside the thirteen-state mainstream.

Vermont leaders did send 700 to 800 militia and Green Mountain Boys under Seth Warner to help repel Burgoyne's Bennington expedition in 1777. But after proclaiming the independent Republic of Vermont, they sulked politically. Between 1780 and 1783, one survival tactic was to continue vague talks with General Frederick Haldimand in Canada about a possible Vermont relationship with Britain.[36] Congress also remained recalcitrant. Vermont became the fourteenth state only in 1791, but between 1775 and 1777, it had done yeoman service for the new nation.

New England, Congress, and the Revolutionary Politics of Command

No debate pushed itself to the congressional forefront as powerfully, in the spring of 1775, as that of responding to the military crisis in New England. Even before the Second Congress convened on May 10, Massachusetts had gone a long way to oblige the delegates in Philadelphia to provide military assistance. This was ensured, as we have seen, in part by speeding southward a vivid first account of April 19. Because messenger Bissell reached Manhattan in three days and Philadelphia in five, Patriots in the cross-pressured middle colonies had Boston's side of Lexington and Concord in plenty of time to encourage *rage militaire* as Congress assembled.

First, though, the delegates had to deal with an erroneous rumor. A report arrived on May 11 that the British had rerouted troops bound for Boston in order to put them ashore in New York. Panicked delegates from that colony, led by James Duane, promptly urged Congress to approve sending a defensive army of perhaps 5,000 men. Its purpose would not be to contest the soldiers' landing but to remain outside the city and "overawe and confine" any farther British advance.[37] Not for several weeks did delegates confirm that those four regiments had been routed back to Boston. In the meantime, New York developed more interest in Patriot soldiery.

A different uncertainty followed news that New Englanders had seized Ticonderoga and Crown Point. Conciliation-minded delegates wanted to secure and safeguard the cannon taken to keep them out of New England hands. And because of rumors that the British might be mounting a southward expedition from Canada, some worrywarts even wanted to return the two forts.

No documentation exists of what the delegates told one another during those May days. They met in sworn secrecy, devoid of record keeping—sensible enough, given possible prosecutions for treason. Initial hemming and hawing to justify Ticonderoga's capture portrayed it as the defensive action of nervous locals—"several inhabitants . . . residing in the vicinity of Ticonderoga." Excitable local folk, the argument went, had been motivated by "indubitable evidence that a design was formed by the British ministry to make a cruel invasion from the Province of Quebec."[38] This was far-fetched.

May's misconceptions and mistakes are not worth disentangling. New reports and evidence in hand soon made the seizure of the two forts no longer appear very risky. On May 13, Benedict Arnold had taken small craft up Lake Champlain to Canada and seized the only sizable British vessel on the lake. Dispatches captured at the same time clarified that British forces in Canada were in disarray. No invasion was coming.[39]

Now *rage militaire* could be indulged. As May ended, Congress requested Connecticut's Trumbull to garrison Ticonderoga with one thousand men and to keep the cannon there. The New York Provincial Congress, for its part, was requested to supply foodstuffs to the new garrison. On June 2, Trumbull ordered Colonel Benjamin Lyman and his Connecticut regiment to proceed north. On June 7, Congress decided that an American army should go to Canada—and here was the caveat—but only if Canadians wanted those forces to come. Delegates still preferred a "defensive" Canadian posture in which they were merely helping another colony. As of June, though, New York had still not raised a single regiment, and its weak Provincial Congress understood the importance of outside assistance. New York delegates in Philadelphia were now obliged to cooperate with those from New England.[40]

After a month of hectic activity, Congress had also begun to grapple with two other central questions, both involving Massachusetts. That province, as we have seen, had sought advice on how to restructure its own government, which Congress offered on June 9. The next question was the critical one: Should it "adopt" the New England troops besieging Gage in Boston? The answer came in less straightforward fashion. On June 9 the delegates in Philadelphia asked New York's Provincial Congress to send 5,000 barrels of flour to the "Continental army" in Massachusetts. A day later they urged the New England colonies to supply the army with all the gunpowder they could manage. In both cases, Philadelphia promised to reimburse the cost.[41]

This mixture of decision and equivocation reflected regional quibbles. On one hand, delegates like Roger Sherman of Connecticut and Thomas Cushing and Robert Treat Paine of Massachusetts insisted that New England soldiers would not accept a commanding general from another section.[42] But other members, especially from the southern colonies, specified naming a commander from outside New England as a condition for adopting a Yankee army. John Adams, who backed George Washington, argued persuasively on his behalf; and when Thomas Johnson of Maryland nominated the Virginian on June 15, Washington was chosen unanimously. According to the U.S. Army's Center for Military History, "on or before June 14, the Continental Congress 'secretly adopted' New England forces besieging Boston and New York forces guarding strategic positions; and openly on this day, Congress appointed [a] committee to draft regulations for new Continental Army and authorized addition of 10 companies of riflemen to be drawn from Pennsylvania, Maryland and Virginia."[43]

Whatever the exact sequence, the logjam was broken and Congress turned to further military-related decisions. Below Washington as lieutenant general commanding, four major generals were chosen: Artemas Ward of Massachusetts, Charles Lee of Virginia, Philip Schuyler of New York, and Israel Putnam of Connecticut. The latter had been boosted by his May 27 defeat of the British in the minibattle of Noddle's Island in Boston Harbor. Horatio Gates of Virginia was named adjutant general. Thomas Mifflin and Stephen Moylan, both Pennsylvanians, were named quartermaster general and muster master general, respectively.

As for the eight brigadier generals named, seven came from New England, and their selection was more or less proportional to each colony's contribution of soldiers. However, further complications developed from how the seniority assigned by Congress in the new Continental forces clashed with the provincial seniority and rank assigned during the recent army reorganizations in Massachusetts and Connecticut.[44] Bluntly put, there was Massachusetts and Connecticut deadwood to be pruned: officers no more than well connected politically, too old, or lacking in suitable command experience.

Skepticism also touched the major generals. Artemas Ward had never commanded a large force in battle and drew criticism for lack of involvement on June 17 at Bunker Hill. Israel Putnam, in turn, was seen as over his head in more than a regimental command. Such were the delayed snags of the extensive revamping of the New England militias during late 1774 and early 1775. Parenthetically, the three new British major generals— Howe, Clinton, and Burgoyne—arriving in Boston in May, had never before commanded in that rank, were all members of Parliament as well as serving generals, and were picked partly because of prior views either sympathetic or not hostile to the Americans.[45] Whether the deficiencies on one side balanced those on the other is hard to say.

The annals of the U.S. Army date its founding at June 14, 1775, and by June 30, Congress had approved rules and regulations for governance of the new Continental force.[46] It was a heady experience, and politicians who should have known better made silly boasts. James Warren, now president of the Massachusetts Provincial Congress, enthused to Samuel Adams that "the army of the United Colonies are already superior in valour, and from the most amazingly rapid progress in discipline, we may justly conclude will shortly become the most formidable troops in the world."[47]

On July 6, 1775, then, it was something of an anticlimax for Congress to proclaim the *Declaration of the Causes and Necessity of Taking Up Arms.* Forces of the United Colonies had been "taking up arms" for the past six months and were more than a little giddy about their prospects.

New England Provision and Supply Capacity

In supply and provisioning, the Patriot cause was fortunate that the war began where it did as well as when it did. Since the 1750s, New England had developed a considerable provisioning business, nurtured by British military demand during the French and Indian War and broadly supported by eager markets in the British and French West Indies. Yankee fish and barreled meat, as well as cheese, hides, and livestock, were cheaper in Jamaica or Martinique than similar produce brought in from Britain or France. Fish had been Massachusetts's leading product, just as autumn meat packing constituted Connecticut's largest industry in 1774.

Especially after Britain cut off access to the fisheries, Massachusetts, Connecticut, New Hampshire, and Rhode Island were hardly prepared to supply an intensive war fought over several years. In 1775, though, they were well positioned to provision twelve months of needs in the northern theater principally involving their own soldiers and some from New York. Dried fish kept for at least a year, so large supplies remained available in Massachusetts. Connecticut, in turn, initially provided large quantities of livestock, barreled meat, and cheese. That province even had a "wheat belt"—from western Litchfield County to Hartford and the Connecticut River Valley—that produced well in 1775, despite ranking far behind the larger croplands of Pennsylvania, Maryland, and New York.[48]

Over eight years of war, Connecticut became known as the "provisions state" because of an unusual convergence of circumstances. The colony's governor through 1783, Jonathan Trumbull, was himself a merchant whose background included provisioning colonial troops during the French and Indian War. By rapidly embargoing exports, Trumbull made sure that, beginning in 1775, Connecticut's commercial agricultural surpluses were reserved for Patriot military consumption. The initial exception lay in exporting provisions for arms and gunpowder.

No survey of Connecticut's role in supplying the Revolution would be complete without noting the province's leadership in producing cannon. Local historians have described how the iron-rich hills of northwest Connecticut and adjacent towns in New York and Massachusetts "glowed at night with the glare of furnaces and the dim glow of charcoal burners."[49] The statistics of their rarely noted achievement are nothing less than stunning.

In November 1775, Washington's need for heavy guns to drive the British out of Boston led him to send his chief of artillery, Colonel Henry Knox, to bring back as many as possible of the large cannon, howitzers, and mortars at Fort Ticonderoga. In the meantime, Governor Trumbull prepared to seize and operate the Salisbury Iron Furnace. On January 2, Trumbull ordered Colonel Jedediah Elderkin to confirm the furnace's suitability for casting cannon, and on February 2, the Connecticut Council of Safety voted to establish a provincial cannon foundry. Trumbull, operating from his Lebanon war office, initially also functioned as general superintendent of the foundry and kept express riders busy riding with messages and orders.[50] Not only did the Salisbury Furnace fully meet the needs of Connecticut's army regiments, provincial navy, and privateers, but the Continental armies and navy were also huge beneficiaries. According to one calculation, "the Salisbury Furnace supplied from 35 percent to 42 percent of all the cannon used by the Americans in the Revolution."[51] Connecticut military historian Louis Middlebrook, after doing a study of the forge in the 1920s, estimated that 75 percent of all American cannon were cast at

Salisbury. Middlebrook was probably indulging in localist hyperbole, but the lesser estimate may be close to the mark.[52]

During 1775, the colony's commissaries and purchasing agents—led by Joseph Trumbull, the governor's son, and Hartford's Jeremiah Wadsworth—made impressive enough records to rise into national roles. As one logistical study concluded, "what must be stressed is that during the first five years of the war, Connecticut held a central, vitally important position in the inter-state system of supply organized by the Commissary and Commissary of Purchases departments, with which the state government cordially cooperated."[53]

In 1775 and well into 1776, Connecticut was not only a reserve depot of soldiers but New England's cannon foundry, reserve granary, and packing-house. The region's "fortress" aspect included an important early capacity to self-sustain.

CHAPTER 9

Declaring Economic War

The popular leaders of America won a victory at the First Continental Congress far greater than they could have expected . . . In the Association they achieved the most drastic form of economic coercion ever attempted in America, and it was coercion aimed at the popular leaders in America as well as Britain.

Merrill Jensen, *The Founding of a Nation*, 1968

The Continental Association is one of the most important documents of American colonial history. By authorizing the establishment of local committees to enforce the embargo of trade, it provided the apparatus that would eventually develop into the government of Revolution. By providing for nonimportation and nonexportation as a means of forcing Great Britain to redress colonial grievances, it convinced Parliament that war was inevitable and thus led directly to the engagement at Lexington and Concord.

David Ammerman, *In the Common Cause: American Response to the Coercive Acts of 1774*, 1973

In considering America's place in the transatlantic economy, the colonial leaders of 1775 suffered from an unfortunate but understandable self-importance and overconfidence. Not only did the mainland colonies boast a fast-expanding population and a large agricultural surplus, but their growth and seemingly vital importance to the future of the British Empire was a topic of conversation across the European continent from Paris to Potsdam.

Twice during the decade before 1775, the British government had backed down on taxing the colonies after the latter moved to boycott British manufactured goods. The rising dependence of some British industries on colonial North America was a matter of statistics. Transatlantic buyers took over half of a growing list of exports—wrought iron and copper, beaver hats, cordage, nails, wrought silk, printed cotton and linen. Flannels and worsteds were not far behind. Politically, goods makers from Manchester, Birmingham, and dozens of other towns were ready to petition Parliament at the drop of a colonial order book.

As a result, boycott advocates in North America became convinced of their ability to force Westminster to retreat on unpopular policies. Then in late 1774, push came to shove over Congress's Continental Association and its unprecedented trade ultimatum. Colonial pressures had counted in the retreats of 1766 and 1770. In the former year, the hated Stamp Act had been retracted after colonial buyers' tactics appeared to cause a 15 percent decline in exports to America. In 1770 Parliament scrapped its Townshend levies of 1767—except for the one on tea—after a second display of boycott damage. British exports to the colonies had fallen 38 percent between 1768 and 1769, a shrinkage that Lord North, the first minister, acknowledged in presenting the government's repeal program to the House of Commons. But he down-played responding to colonial pressure, crediting instead the weight of peti-tions from British manufacturers and merchants.[1]

The Patriots of 1774, too ready to consider both pullbacks as proof of the colonies' new stature and commercial muscle, would have done better to pay close attention to the March 1770 parliamentary debates. North had emphasized the need to end a seven-year pattern of inconsistent policy tied to ever-changing ministries and policy makers: "Our conduct has already varied greatly with respect to America. These variations have been the great-est cause of difficulty." George Grenville, the architect of the ill-fated Stamp Act, agreed: officeholders, he thought, had "given way from one step to another, from one idea to another, till we know not upon what ground we stand." To Wedderburn, the solicitor general, even the partial repeal bill they were debating was "a step further in that repeated contradiction which has obtained with America." Such "fluctuations of administration," agreed another Cabinet member, Henry Conway, had sapped government credibil-ity.[2] That was certainly true.

The incessant politics of faction had also contributed. The Whig rivals who had displaced Grenville and come to power in 1766 were younger and inexperienced, as well as relatively pro-American. They had repealed the Stamp Act more readily on both counts. The 15 percent decline in exports to North America was only one factor.

In the 1770 debate, North freely acknowledged that the 1767 Townshend Act levies, the brainchild of an earlier ministry, had been commercially misconceived. Proponents had naïvely sought "American" revenue by placing duties on certain products—paper, lead paints, and glass, for example—principally manufactured in *Britain*. Besides, as some repeal-minded petitions pointed out, such added levies only encouraged the colonists to think about making these items themselves. North's new regime was rectifying another ministry's mistake.[3]

What too few in Boston or Philadelphia appreciated was that although prior colonial boycotts and nonimportation measures had influenced both retractions, by 1770 British domestic politics and a wariness of confusion and inconstancy counted more. Trade boycotts and nonconsumption were not necessarily a proven or reliable weapon. Moreover, with so many British policy makers fuming over previous retreats and conciliation, no softness would be allowed a third time.

As for the far-reaching demands made by the American Congress in 1774 through the Continental Association, the Cabinet could be expected to rule out concessions to any such extralegal body. The Americans who assumed another British retreat were naïfs or worse. Overconfidence is the best explanation of why so many were willing to rely on the Association, to all but declare commercial war, and to wait expectantly for four or five months for word to come back of British acquiescence.

Naïfs of a different sort were plentiful in Whitehall and Westminster. After almost a decade of British vacillation, by early 1774 many policy makers apparently believed that when Britain, the world's greatest empire, did belatedly crack down on its presumptuous colonials, the latter would turn craven. Silly boasts in this vein by generals and colonels have already been recounted. If the Boston Tea Party was a provocation that Parliament could not be expected to bear, the harshness of the Coercive Acts, enacted between three and six months later, may have reflected a bravado akin to the colonists' own.

Simply put, no modern British precedent existed for such a sweeping punishment of a major English-speaking city as the Boston Port Act imposed. The £2,000 fine the Crown had imposed in 1736 on Edinburgh, the Scottish capital, because of the lynching of a town guard captain (who had fired on and killed members of a crowd of customs rioters), bore no parallel. That punishment, cited as an analogy by parliamentary supporters, was piddling alongside the Coercive Acts.[4] Lord Chatham and other opponents called the Port Act "too severe."[5]

In America, as news of Parliament's multiple coercions arrived ship by ship, jolt by jolt, disillusionment by disillusionment, budding rebels coined their own irate description: the *Intolerable* Acts. By late May, several provinces were consulting about responding through unprecedented trade embargoes. By midsummer a Continental Congress had been agreed to for early September. True, the other colonies had put aside Massachusetts's initial plea to retaliate with an *immediate* nonimportation and nonexportation measure. Even so, a half dozen had indicated willingness to support that approach in the near future should a congress endorse it. In England, meanwhile, Parliament had been prorogued on June 22. Many if not most of its members went home for the summer confident that tough measures would now prevail. That belief was misplaced; economic warfare was about to begin.

The Politics of Winter Delay

Before the First Continental Congress left Philadelphia on October 26, 1774, tired delegates had determined that, absent the redress demanded from Britain, a successor should assemble seven months thence on May 10. That delay was expected to allow Parliament and the king time to review Congress's decisions and then respond. As the chronology on pages 228–229 has shown, warlike words were already flowing, and as October ended, elements of mobilization were visible on both sides: Massachusetts arming, Gage fortifying Boston Neck, the king issuing Orders in Council to stop unauthorized westbound shipments of arms and munitions. With faster communications between Britain and America, fighting might well have begun more quickly.

London had no text of Congress's ultimatums until December, but strong hints began arriving in August. To prepare for a crisis, on September 30 the king and Lord North called an October 1774 general election, hoping for an overwhelming majority in the House of Commons ready to support a firm American policy. This they achieved, winning a Gibraltar-like 321 seats. On November 18, King George wrote to Lord North that "the New England Governments were in a State of Rebellion," and "blows must decide." Crown officials discussed prosecutions for treason. But before long, holiday lassitude took over. As one bemused participant noted, "Lord North is gone to Banbury, Ld. Rochford to his seat, and there is the appearance of all the tranquility which might be expected if America was perfectly quiet."[6] On January 25, when the Cabinet finalized a decision to risk war through aggressive action in Massachusetts, dispatches were much delayed in London, and adverse winds slowed passage to America. Gage in Boston, who back in September had urged the government to start hiring mercenaries, did not receive January's actual march-and-subdue instructions until April 14. It was a notable delay even in a winter of notable delays.

October's Patriot guesswork that a British response would take five to seven months proved out. Patriot organizers had most of winter and spring to embody their newly elected and appointed committees and train their reconstituted militias. Members of Congress who had expected even in September to face war—Samuel Adams, John Adams, and Patrick Henry, to name three—clearly understood that a countdown was beginning. When the Congress returned in May, the United Colonies would already have in place a four-to-eight-month-old network of committees of correspondence, observation, and safety. During 1774 eight colonies—New Hampshire, Massachusetts, New Jersey, Pennsylvania, Delaware, Maryland, Virginia, and North Carolina—had also inaugurated extralegal provincial congresses or conventions. Royal governors tried to block these initiatives, but without success. South Carolina had set up a comparable General Committee, which turned into a Provincial Congress. Connecticut and Rhode Island were already effectively self-governing. The principal laggards were New York and Georgia.

In these provincial and local organizations, we can identify the first framework of local government elected under congressional auspices. The hundreds of county, city, or town committees that Congress had recommended to be elected under the Association—as well as the local ones set up earlier by Virginia and North Carolina—soon widened their supervision of commerce and local economies into an assumption of political and police power. Trade supervision had become a framework for redistributing political authority.

The wintertime North Atlantic would keep uncertain moderates and impatient radicals on edge again a year later in 1775–1776. Loyalists hoped, during those months, for reassurance from the mother country; committed radicals bet on further events to intensify popular disenchantment. But the waitful winter hiatus most critical to the future United States was that first one, in 1774–1775.

The New Calendar of Economic Mobilization

Boycotts and local implementing committees were familiar enough. Non-*importation* had been tested in the 1760s; it was nonexportation that had barely gone beyond conversation. The bolder commitment reflected how many Patriot leaders had been discouraged by experiences with merchants and soured by problems of intercolony collaboration. Stalwarts now relied on two new components. First, an unprecedented mandatory boycott of British imports by American *consumers*. A bigger bet would then be placed on the non*exportation* to Britain of the thirteen colonies' most valuable enumerated commodities: tobacco, rice, and indigo. These new strategies would be implemented by Patriot-led enforcement committees able to orchestrate—foes said *coerce*—public compliance and acceptance.

In contrast to the previous boycotts, the Association of 1774 would be much less dependent on the economic interests and uncertain politics of merchants. Many of them had soured on Patriot politics during disagreements over nonimportation policy in 1769 and 1770. Burdensome costs had been part of merchant disillusionment. By 1774, artisans, mechanics, and yeomen itched to play a much greater part, especially in promoting local manufactures. They would be enlisted for more prominent roles. Stunned British officials and American Loyalists who called Congress's measures revolutionary were absolutely right.[7] However, the implications for social as well as economic upheaval took awhile to sink in because the Continental Congress initially projected an image of unity and moderation.

The first colony-level associations, put forward in August by Virginia and North Carolina, had called for local nonimportation to begin in November 1774. In October Congress scheduled commencement in December. However, counties in the Old Dominion, beginning their committee elections in August, had some already in place before the congressional delegates had headed home. Starting dates were adjusted. Eventually, at least 51 of Virginia's 61 counties selected committees.[8]

New England was just as enthusiastic. The Massachusetts Provincial Congress endorsed the proposed Association in December 1774. It tacked on local regulations aimed at Boston's Tory merchants, who were distrusted for allegedly cheating during nonimportation five years earlier and for refusing to support nonimportation in May as a response to the Boston Port Act.[9] The Connecticut Assembly had acted earlier, unanimously approving the proceedings of Congress, including the Association, in November. By year's end, 28 town committees had been appointed.[10] The Rhode Island Assembly approved in December. New Hampshire sidestepped a veto-wielding royal governor, using a Provincial Convention to approve the

Association unanimously in January.[11] In New England, committees and boycotts, like military preparation, were on a fast track.

The near-unanimity that surrounded the Congress's authorship of the Association in October was an extraordinary coup, although it weakened as the measure's implications sank in. It provided several months of vital comity and reassurance, especially helpful in the middle colonies. The New Jersey Assembly approved the Congress's actions and endorsed the Continental Association in January, in the process neatly outmaneuvering Royal Governor William Franklin. Legislators in Delaware agreed in March 1775, despite considerable opposition in the southern part of the colony. Surprisingly, the conservative Pennsylvania Assembly had acted in December to endorse the Congress and ratify the Continental Association.[12] Pennsylvania was especially interested in encouraging American manufactures, which the Association had endorsed in glowing terms.

Moderates grew more skeptical in January, and New York became the prominent naysayer when its Assembly rejected a Patriot-faction attempt to approve the Continental Congress and its trade agenda. The local Committee of Sixty, an extralegal maritime organization on the Patriot side, took the lead in calling a New York provincial convention, which launched a Provincial Congress. This congress then endorsed the Philadelphia agenda and the Continental Association in late April.[13]

Four of New York's thirteen counties—Westchester, Dutchess, Richmond, and Kings—simply disregarded the Association, and others were hostile. Only two counties—Yankee Suffolk in eastern Long Island, and mid-Hudson Ulster, with its Yankee emigrants and Scotch-Irish Presbyterians—displayed enthusiasm and commitment. A third, Albany, endorsed, but with misgivings. This blend of apathy and disdain, however, made New York seem a voice of reason in London. Indeed, by March, views on the Association were fast becoming the operative measurement of colony-by-colony loyalty in the British calculus. Lord Dartmouth cherished any signs of empathy. In consequence, the only provinces to avoid March and April coverage under the Restraining Acts were the four (New York, Delaware, North Carolina, and Georgia) that had registered partial or substantial dissent over the Association.

To underscore the centrality of these issues, in mid-March, after Dartmouth had received a detailed report on the activity in Virginia from Lord Dunmore, he replied as follows: "The steps which have been pursued in the different counties of Virginia to carry into execution the resolutions of the General Congress, are of so extraordinary a nature that I am at a loss to express the criminality of them." He promised to read the letter to Parliament so that Virginia's trade would be interdicted in the manner of Boston's.[14]

The emergence of tobacco as a Patriot weapon particularly incensed Britain. In the summer of 1774, even before the Continental Congress met, the tobacco colonies, Maryland, Virginia, and North Carolina, had led in promoting a new nonexportation policy. Once Congress's deliberations turned to trade issues, Marylanders and Virginians focused on the date when nonexportation would begin. That reflected the drawn-out calendar of the 1774 tobacco crop, which would not be cured and readied for sale until 1775. Nonexportation, growers argued, had to be stretched out accordingly. A year's proceeds were involved. Despite considerable impatience, the delegates had acquiesced. Virginia, being so important, had effective veto power.

Nonexportation, of course, represented the hitherto untried direct assault on Britain's imperial system. We will examine several pages hence the decisions made in 1774 and 1775 with respect to all three major enumerated crops—principally Chesapeake tobacco but also South Carolina rice and indigo. The purpose, for the moment, is simply to place the southern colonies front and center in the great drama that unfolded first at the Congress and then between its adjournment in October and the convening of the new Congress in May 1775. These three enumerated crops, worth roughly £2 million in 1772, were the prime fruit of mercantilism in British North America.

Save for Georgia, the plantation colonies were quick to endorse the First Congress and the Association. With relatively radical Annapolis and Baltimore taking the lead, a Maryland Provincial Congress—not the Assembly, vulnerable to a veto—met in November to approve the Congress's proceedings and to recommend "inviolable obedience" to the Association. Virginia, in turn, simply let the organization of its county committees continue apace, and its Second Provincial Convention in March voted its unanimous approval of what happened in Philadelphia.[15]

Internal divisions complicated matters in North Carolina, where tobacco was an eastern regional interest. In November a meeting of the Patriot-faction elite held in coastal Wilmington called a Provincial Congress for April. Its membership was virtually identical to that of the North

Carolina Assembly. The distinction was that Royal Governor Josiah Martin could not veto the Convention's handiwork: a strong endorsement of both the First Congress and the Association. However, Martin had helped to arrange a counterpoint. Nine counties, most in the backcountry, where the antitidewater Regulator movement still had supporters, sent no delegates to the Convention. Four sent loyal addresses to Martin condemning the Association's "lawless combinations and unwarrantable practices."[16]

South Carolina, also dominated by a low-country Patriot elite, used a January Provincial Congress instead of the Assembly to endorse the Philadelphia proceedings and the Association, but all went smoothly. Circumstances and events in Georgia, slower to develop, were more complicated. Save for St. John's Parish, Yankee-settled and pro-Congress, Georgia had paid little attention in 1774 and had sent no delegate to Philadelphia. By spring, it belatedly played catch-up and sent delegates to the Second Congress.

This is critical history. To underscore the political attention and pressure imposed by the Association and its relentless calendar, the following pages list the various deadlines and start-up dates specified by the First Continental Congress. This calendar ensured that enforcement committees, especially those in seaport towns, would be vitally engaged—their political credibility hanging in the balance—during the six months through May, when the new Congress was expected to convene. If Britain's decision between war and retreat left little choice, the putative United Colonies had put their future on the line. Legal, procedural, and technical as the Association may seem, its significance between late 1774 and the spring of 1775 is hard to overstate.

The Calendar of the Continental Association, 1774–1775

September 22, 1774	Merchants in the colonies were advised to stop ordering British goods because nonimportation would shortly be imposed.
October 1774	Beginning immediately, no sheep were to be exported to anywhere. (Wool was to be retained in the colonies to make clothing.)
December 1, 1774	No importation of *any* merchandise from Britain or Ireland; no East India tea from *anywhere;* no molasses,

sugar, syrups, et al., from the British West Indies; no wine from Madeira; no foreign indigo. For any such cargoes arriving between December 1 and January 31, recipients had three options for disposal: (1) reshipping the goods; (2) storing the goods; and (3) authorizing the local committee to sell the goods.

February 1, 1775   Any cargoes from Britain arriving in the colonies after this date had to be returned to their point of origin; no other option was allowed.

March 1, 1775   No consumption (purchase or use) of tea, or of any merchandise known or suspected to have been imported after December 1, would be allowed, but with certain specified exceptions.

September 10, 1775   No export of any commodity would be allowed to Britain, Ireland, or the British West Indies.

Sources: *Knollenberg, pp. 180–82; Schlesinger, pp. 607–13.*

As we have seen, disparate political figures from Patriot John Dickinson to Tory Joseph Galloway looked beyond the pretense of unity at the First Continental Congress and saw autumn's events as signaling, if not quite declaring, war. The Congress's handiwork can fairly be taken as a triple ultimatum for Britain: to refrain from suppressing Boston militarily; to repeal the Coercive Acts and other parliamentary legislation reaching back into the 1760s that was unacceptable to the colonies; and to make this redress by May 1775 or Congress would implement the nonexportation portion of its trade agenda. In a way, the delegates in Philadelphia, consciously or not, had replied to what they called the Intolerable Acts by drawing up a set of demands that the British government, by its own legal and imperial yardsticks, would find equally intolerable. As early as September 1774, even before London had reports from the first Philadelphia Congress, Lord North began to focus on strategies for retaliation: "If they refused to trade with Great Britain, Great Britain would take care they should trade nowhere else." By early January 1775, Dartmouth, as American secretary, had made some suggestions, and the Cabinet, in what one British historian called "a direct riposte to the Continental Association," thereupon recommended "that a bill be moved for in Parliament to prohibit for a limited time the associated colonies from trading to foreign ports and from carrying on fishing in the American seas."[17]

On February 4, the Cabinet approved temporary legislation to prohibit American trade outside the empire and bar American access to the North Atlantic fisheries, but limited its initial application to the four New England colonies. On March 9, after the trade and fisheries bill—the New England Restraining Act—passed in the House of Commons and was sent on to the House of Lords, Lord North obtained leave in the Commons for a second act to restrain five more colonies—New Jersey, Pennsylvania, Maryland, Virginia, and South Carolina—for assenting to the Association. In the House of Lords, which passed the second bill on April 12, Lord Suffolk, a principal secretary of state, spoke bluntly of an underlying motivation that went beyond trade: "It was intended as a bill of coercion, to oblige the people of New England to submit to the legal and just power of the mother country." Two months earlier, on February 2, Lord North had laid groundwork for the New England Act by saying that there was a rebellion in Massachusetts, countenanced by support elsewhere.[18]

This, in a nutshell, was the war-related sequence that preceded Lexington and Bunker Hill. It was premised on rebellion in Massachusetts or all of New England; and it equated membership in the Continental Association with disloyalty and criminal behavior (Dartmouth), although the Crown's lawyers hesitated over an equation with treason. In 1775, the imperium-cum-mother country moved into a state of war through findings of local rebellion (Massachusetts and New England), imposition of commercial restraint (March–April), and royal declarations that all thirteen colonies were in a state of rebellion (August) and then outlawry (December). Being a colony was in many ways a commercial relationship and subordination.

It would be convoluted, but possible, to follow the calendar of the Continental Association on the previous pages with a calendar of British commercial and naval retaliation. It spans much the same time period, and indeed the captains of British warships patrolling along the Atlantic coast had to deal with almost as many deadlines, technicalities, and starting dates as the members of a Committee of Inspection in Salem, New London, or Annapolis. We will return to this subject matter.

The Remaking of Local Government

Implementation of the Association within the colonies was not uniform. The thirteen were permitted to differ in how they elected or selected their enforcement committees. Colonies also diverged in how many members their subdivisions chose to fill the new supervisory groups. The four vanguards, Massachusetts, Virginia, Connecticut, and South Carolina, were among the most expansive, using oversize committee memberships to broaden and strengthen community support. These four together named roughly half of the participants in all thirteen colonies.

Local enforcement bodies had different names from colony to colony, although most were called committee of observation or committee of inspection. In some cases, previously established committees of correspondence piled these new commercial chores on top of their existing obligations. North Carolina, forming its own local Association in August right after Virginia, designated committees of safety to implement the new rules and kept to that.[19] Tories who groused about government by associations, conventions, and committees had a point. By whatever names, their local activities and responsibilities soon ranged far beyond the initial subject matter—checking ship cargoes, tracking the origins of goods, watching prices charged by merchants, and monitoring local customs houses. Committees in inland areas, lacking any maritime duties, ranged widely in affairs ranging from regulating the practices of merchants to supervising militia organization, saltpeter procurement, and the administration of loyalty oaths.

Within each colony, these new supervisory bodies were usually elected through processes laid down by provincial congresses, conventions, or even committees of correspondence. However, the new committees did not routinely report to these higher authorities. They were *all* "extralegal." Even so, the extent to which residents in most colonies accepted the mandates of these organizations as having the force of law surprised royal governors—William Franklin in New Jersey, Josiah Martin in North Carolina, and Lord Dunmore in Virginia.[20] By late 1774 and early 1775, these and other irritated governors cited the enforcement committees alongside the congresses and conventions in explaining to Lord Dartmouth that they had lost much or almost all of their ability to govern.[21]

New England's committees were invariably elected by township, counties being secondary in Yankee culture. This ensured a large head count, but that was already characteristic of elected assemblies in the four colonies. According to the principal chronicler of these organizations, historian David Ammerman, Massachusetts established at least 160 committees, typically with about ten members each, which suggests a province-wide roster in excess of 1,600. Connecticut, in turn, counted more than 650 committeemen, and New Hampshire at least 400.[22] All three colonies had a town-based Congregational Church establishment, and the new inspectorates would have overlapped with both Congregational elders and existing town boards of selectmen. Rhode Island had no church establishment and fewer townships, but its committees probably included at least 135 persons. Across New England, 300-odd committees toiled amid a winter-spring drumbeat of powder alarms, secret meetings, and militia drills.

Participation was more haphazard in the relatively lukewarm middle colonies. Enforcement at the county level was the norm in Pennsylvania—nine of its eleven elected such committees. A few committees were chosen by towns or districts. That suggested a probable colony-wide total of about 500 committeemen.[23] Philadelphia, the colony's major port, for its part, was inspected and supervised in 1775 under the aegis of the Committee of Sixty-six, increasingly representative of artisans and small entrepreneurs at the expense of the old Quaker mercantile establishment.

New Jersey, mixing county and township members in the Pennsylvania manner, filled more than 500 committee positions. Two of Delaware's three counties, Newcastle and Kent, established Committees of Inspection to enforce the Association, but Tory-leaning Sussex might not have.[24] The conspicuous nose thumbing, as we have seen, came in New York: "Only three of thirteen counties responded favorably to the Association, efforts in three others to adopt it were suppressed, and most devastating of all, seven counties ignored it entirely."[25] Some of these scoffers were responding to rival Loyalist associations, which contrarily put forward the "undoubted right to liberty in eating, drinking, buying, selling."[26]

In the South, county committees were the rule. Meetings in Virginia opened by approving the Association, and then proceeded to elect an enforcement committee. Fifty-one are known to have chosen groups, ranging in size from 6 members to 69. Separate boards were elected in three large towns: Williamsburg, Norfolk, and Fredericksburg. All in all, Virginia had some 1,100 freeholders busy watching local commerce and morality.

Maryland had almost as many inspectors and regulators—900—despite its much smaller population and complement of just 16 counties. The number of Marylanders serving rose sharply during 1775. In part, explained one leader, that represented political outreach: "It would engage ye. Country People more warmly if gratified in a more Numerous Appointmt. among them."[27]

North Carolina's records are less revealing. However, support for the Association and participation in its local enforcement bulked largest in the eastern tidewater region, especially in the tobacco centers and seaport counties, including Edenton, New Bern, and Wilmington, coupled with Piedmont strength in the Scotch-Irish centers of Mecklenburg and Rowan counties.[28] Anyone doubting that the Wilmington-New Hanover Committee of Public Safety, for example, was the effective "governing body" of the lower Cape Fear region between November 1774 and the spring of 1776 has only to read its published minutes.[29] Its functionaries did everything from setting the price of salt to banning trade with Newfoundland and deporting "inimicals"—the old English Civil War term for enemies of the cause.

Only in South Carolina, in January 1775, did a colony-wide Patriot organization opt to appoint the local committees and specify the enforcement guidelines. This made sense because the existing Charleston-based General Committee, eager to broaden Patriot outreach, decided to have its first Provincial Congress elected from new districts that expanded the participation of an alienated backcountry. The new backcountry delegates had no experience with parliamentary procedures—niceties like seconding, amending, and recommitting—but the Patriot leadership wanted to bring them into vital decisions, including the mechanics of implementing nonexportation. Three months earlier the Congress in Philadelphia had made concessions to rice exporters but left out indigo planters. The new Provincial Congress would have to work a compensation arrangement for angry indigo producers, many of them small growers in the backcountry.[30] The political economics of trade policy were pervasive.

However, before we move on to the rapidly crystallizing circumstances of British trade retaliation and Parliament's imposition of the maritime equivalents of outlawry, it is necessary to revisit the still-untested political economics of the nonexportation of crops. In contrast to New England and the middle colonies, plantation Patriots were playing a high-stakes game: a commercial and political gamble on withholding tobacco, rice, and indigo crops from their mandated English markets.

The Export Weapons: Tobacco and Rice

If any of Virginia's leading tobacco planters predicted in 1774 what nonexportation was likely to bring about by 1776 or 1777, their answers have not come down to posterity. But in 1774 tobacco as a crop arguably profited Britain's monopoly more than it profited Old Dominion growers, and it was those circumstances that made cured leaf the colonies' prime trade weapon.

Although the northern and middle colonies produced enumerated commodities that they planned to hold back from Britain—iron, masts for the Royal Navy—none were local economic mainstays. In the southern colonies, by contrast, tobacco—and in the subtropics, rice—were the principal crops. Tobacco alone accounted for 90 percent of the value of combined Virginia and Maryland exports to Britain and represented three quarters of the two colonies' combined worldwide exports. Rice and indigo, taken together, represented fourth fifths of what South Carolina and Georgia shipped across the Atlantic.

During the summer of 1774, and then during the September-October deliberations in Congress, plantation-colony spokesmen had emphasized key points. First, they would be taking a larger risk in the common cause than the other eight colonies. Second, their individual commitments were necessarily interrelated: Maryland and North Carolina would not withhold their own tobacco if Virginia, the principal producer, was not participating. South Carolina would not hold back rice and indigo if the tobacco producers were not keeping back their leaf.

This inevitably gave Virginia, already the largest and most respected of the thirteen, unequaled leverage. The Virginia Convention, in drawing up its own Association in August, had proposed that nonexportation not start until August 10, 1775. Suggestions from other colonies that nonexportation commence immediately, as even some southerners preferred, were simply unacceptable. Tobacco-crop curing and marketing considerations ruled out speed. The crop cut and hung to dry in autumn 1774 would not be ready for delivery until the next spring. Tobacco production required a unique fifteen-month cycle: seeding in January, cutting in September, curing, stripping, and stemming during the autumn, then prizing or packing the tobacco into barrel-like hogsheads, which were moved to the public warehouses and inspected in January. Shipment to Britain came only in the spring, in a seasonal rhythm that had become part of Virginia culture.[31]

The delegates in Philadelphia had acquiesced. Nonexportation to Britain would not commence until September 10, 1775, thereby allowing the tobacco colonies to sell and deliver their all-important 1774 crop. As for rice growers—mostly South Carolinians but also Georgians and a few North Carolinians from Cape Fear—they, too, had until September to ship to Britain. However, as a further concession, Congress authorized rice planters, *after* September, to ship to all of Europe, mostly destinations hitherto barred by the British Acts of Trade and Navigation. Even beyond the effrontery of withholding enumerated commodities, the regulatory props of mercantilism were starting to fall.

Until 1770, the idea of withholding exports to Britain and the British West Indies had been more banter than serious deliberation. Back in 1769, Virginia's George Mason had raised the idea of not exporting tobacco to help pressure Parliament to repeal the Townshend Acts. In 1770, growers in both Maryland and Virginia formed local associations not to sell below a certain price.[32]

The decisive spur to challenge the system came from the British financial crisis of 1772. Its devastating effects, first felt by English and Scottish merchants, soon undercut the price of Chesapeake tobacco. By one calculation, it swooned from 2.4 pence per pound (Virginia currency) in October 1772 to 1.5 pence per pound in June 1773. Because tobacco could be stored, persisting oversupply from bumper crops in 1770, 1771, 1772, and 1773 made matters worse.[33] As we have seen in Chapter 4, one solution discussed by Chesapeake growers was withholding leaf to force the price up. Some smallholders took the storage approach, warehousing their crops for better demand. In 1774, when Britain responded to the Boston Tea Party by passing the Coercive Acts, canny planters saw a new political opportunity: withholding tobacco exports could become part of a plan to force Britain to repeal those punitive measures. Events now put a patriotic gloss on actions to end the tobacco glut and raise prices.[34]

Indebtedness, a fact of commercial life in the plantation colonies, became a second preoccupation. Growers did not want to shut off their tobacco, rice, or indigo shipments to British merchants while local courts still remained open to creditor suits for debt recovery. To backstop nonexportation, then, various degrees of simultaneous court closure would be necessary in Maryland, Virginia, and the Carolinas. Conservatives were wary, but in practice a considerable amount of court closing was achieved, often indirectly through failure to pass judicial enabling legislation or under the

Association by Patriot enforcement committees forbidding most debt-recovery cases.[35]

Through 1775 and into 1776, tobacco nonexportation was a political and financial success. By the eve of Lexington and Concord, prices in Virginia had risen 60 to 80 percent from their 1774 lows, through a convergence of favorable circumstances. Growers unwilling to ship their leaf in many cases could not be sued in closed or unwilling courts. Buyers in Europe pushed up prices, assuming that the shipments in the spring and summer of 1775 would be the last.[36]

But good fortune was only temporary. Circumstances soured as the Restraining Acts of early 1775 were followed by the more sweeping Prohibitory Act at year's end. In 1776, the British naval blockade grew increasingly effective in blocking sales to European buyers. The early prosperity nurtured by the Association—through high tobacco prices, new issuance of paper money, the stimulus of war mobilization, and subsidies to encourage new industries—gave way to growing inflation and disillusionment. In a sense, *rage militaire* and economic self-congratulation wore off together.

The Perils of Treasonomics

The assumption of mercantilist and imperial thinking was that colonies existed to support the political economy of the mother country. Such a viewpoint underpinned the Coercive Acts. Even the best-known American sympathizers in Parliament—William Pitt, Lord Rockingham, and Edmund Burke—accepted the necessarily subordinate nature of the colonial relationship. Whatever new theories Adam Smith might publish in 1776 in *The Wealth of Nations,* the views of George III, Lord North, and the Cabinet in 1774 and 1775 remained old school. The king himself believed that the North American colonies were critical to the British Empire, much as American "domino" theorists of the 1960s believed defeat in Vietnam threatened America's world position.[37]

Against this psychological backdrop, a belligerent Continental Congress was demanding huge and implausible concessions: no British taxation in America, an end to duties on everything from wine and tea to sugar and molasses, repeal of the Quebec Act (and its bar to American westward expansion), and little or no London control over colonial trade save where Americans might consent. Only if these demands were agreed to would Congress drop its agenda of nonimportation, nonconsumption, and nonexportation. To British Cabinet members, this amounted to criminal rejection by Americans of their colonial status. However, Britain being a nation that abided by its own laws, the Crown's legal officers faced recurring difficulty in identifying workable circumstances for individual treason prosecutions. The necessary evidence would be hard to obtain.

Hopeful searches of the law books, however, went back a decade. Prosecutions had been weighed over boycotts against the Stamp Act and Townshend Acts, the attack by Rhode Islanders on the revenue cutter *Gaspee* in 1772, and the Tea Party in 1773.[38] No prosecutions were actually brought, although the Coercive Acts can be regarded as a massive legal as well as economic sanction against Boston.

The actions of the First Continental Congress prompted even greater indignation. First, Massachusetts and New England were declared in rebellion. In December 1774, an informal meeting took place between Lord North and the Crown's chief legal officers, Thurlow and Wedderburn, who deemed the proceedings of Congress "criminal to a great degree" and found the Suffolk Resolves containing "treason and rebellion in every line," but recommended waiting for more information from General Gage before acting.[39] A few months later Parliament passed the Restraining Acts. Finally, in December 1775, Lord North proposed and passed the Prohibitory Act, declaring the colonies outside of royal protection, which could be considered as an economic outlawry or "group treason" statute.

The treason law, under which British law officers failed to bring meaningful action, dated back to Henry VIII and referred to a king.[40] What many Americans were embarking upon in 1774, though, could be thought of as "treasonomics"—a rejection of their subservient colonial role in the imperial economy. This fell short of "waging war against the king." Most of the plotters would have been happy to remain nominally under the king so long as Parliament could be more or less emasculated. Naïve politically, this was fortuitous legally. No British treason statute covered a war colonists might wage against Lord North or Parliament; witness the repeated 1774–1775 expressions of disdain for "ministerial forces" or the "Parliamentary army" occupying Boston.

Even so, Congress's declaration ending American commercial subservience arguably justified a royal decision to vacate the imperial relationship and to name the wayward colonies outlaws. The Association was not just a tougher replay of the colonies' two earlier importation boycotts. To echo the words of historian Merrill Jensen at the beginning of this chapter, the Association was an unprecedented mechanism for economic coercion.

By contrast, during these same months, Patriot spokesmen could not have been declared in rebellion or called outlaw for insisting that Britain had no authority to lay taxes on them. Many Britons, including William Pitt, said the same thing because Americans had no voice in Parliament—their "virtual representation" being a joke. As for London's fury over large-scale smuggling during the French and Indian War, and the consequent treasonlike allegation that American provisions shipped to the French Caribbean islands had prolonged the conflict, an obvious retort existed: Britons themselves had traded illicitly on a large scale with the French during that same war.

Massachusetts and Rhode Island, although agile practitioners, were amateurs alongside the eighteenth-century gangs of smugglers operating along the south coast of England—from Kent on the English Channel to Cornwall and the Scilly Islands. Even in the twenty-first century, this heritage remains so pervasive—the legend of smugglers' inns like the Mermaid in Rye, the sea-facing old stone churches famous for once storing illegal goods—that the British Ordnance Survey has published a guide to "Smugglers' Britain" and "over 250 Haunts and Hideouts From the Great Years of Contraband." According to the author, "In the eighteenth century illegal trade across England's coast mushroomed. A trade that previously existed as simple small-scale evasion of duty turned into an industry of astonishing proportions, syphoning money abroad, and channeling huge volumes of contraband into the southern counties of England. Even by modern standards, the quantities of imported goods were extraordinary. It was not uncommon for a smuggling trip to bring in 3,000 gallons of spirits . . . Illegally imported gin was sometimes so plentiful that the inhabitants of some Kentish villages were said to use it for cleaning their windows. And according to some contemporary estimates, four-fifths of all tea drunk in England had not had duty paid on it."[41]

The four-fifths calculation probably exaggerates. In 1784 the government estimated that duty had not been paid on 7.5 million out of the 13 million pounds of tea consumed during the preceding year. The cost of all smuggling into Britain was estimated at £2 million—relative to a total government revenue of £12.5 million.[42] During the early 1760s crackdown on North American smuggling, by contrast, the revenue at stake was probably no more than £100,000 to £200,000. As for patriotism, British admirals also lamented the daily flow of vital wartime information from English ports and ships to the French enemy across the Channel.

So why were the thirteen colonies, and New England in particular, the designated whipping post during the decade and a half before 1775? Why were 20 or 30 ships of the Royal Navy ordered to collect customs duties off the American coast instead of concentrating their force off smugglers' coves in Kent, Sussex, Dorset, or Cornwall? Was it because British policy makers feared the American colonies—their ballooning population, their ship-building capacity (between one quarter and one third of British ships were American built), their markets, their western lands, their large numbers of skilled seamen, and their growing capacity to manufacture many of Britain's own specialties? No such disaffection-cum-breakaway was possible along England's southern coast, or for that matter in such smuggling centers of the British Caribbean as Jamaica and St. Kitts. London's discriminatory treatment was not misplaced.

The American population, doubling every twenty-five years, was indeed expected to exceed Britain's in two or three generations. Benjamin Franklin had said the Americans could learn to make most of what Britain manufactured in a short time. Edmund Burke had saluted Americans' skill in their pursuit of fisheries. In France, foreign ministers from Choiseul to Vergennes privately discussed how splitting off America and its benefits to the empire was their surest way to dethrone Britain. In 1775 William Pitt, now Lord Chatham, took to the floor of the House of Lords to offer a caustic economic analysis: "the profit from the trade of the colonies, through all its branches, is two millions a year. This is the fund that carried you triumphantly through the last war . . . this is the price that America pays for her protection."[43]

Such calculations encouraged King George's fear of a domino effect should America be lost. If this particular worry was misplaced, the monarch and his ministers were generally correct to believe that the Americans were heading toward "independency." True, most colonials who denied that did so in good faith, but they required the help of multiple illusions.

Besides overconfidence in the political and commercial muscle of non-importation, too many Americans believed that the colonies' importance to Britain would compel the huge concessions demanded. In reality, the more than 300 Commons seats won by supporters of Lord North in the October 1774 elections ensured support for hard-line policies at least through 1775 and 1776. North, much liked by the king, was in little danger of being dropped for another Whig ministry, especially one under the aging Pitt, a royal bête noire.

Back in 1774, when most Americans could contend with personal conviction that independence was not a goal, many moderates and future Loyalists demonstrated a different naïveté. At the First Continental Congress, Pennsylvania's Joseph Galloway had participated and proposed the alternative course of seeking an American Parliament, even though he would later describe Congress's proceedings as "a declaration of war."[44] His belief probably reflected a confidence in the British Empire and an assumption that the king and Parliament would do their best on Americans' behalf if approached reasonably and loyally. Indeed, many hopeful Loyalists went along with the Continental Association to promote an image of American unity in order to support hard economic bargaining—at least until January and February 1775, when escalating skepticism shattered the facade briefly constructed in Philadelphia.

By this point, of course, elements of the British government and much of the Patriot leadership in New England were preparing for combat, however much poor winter communications assured an information lag. When the details of Congress's October slap in the imperial face reached London in December 1774, they quickly ended Cabinet uncertainty, convincing the Crown to reply in kind. To paraphrase Lord North, the American colonies want to cut off commerce with us, so we'll cut off their access to the North Atlantic fisheries and stop their trade outside the empire—and naval enforcement will start in July. More than a few would-be Loyalists were left in the lurch.

In another twelve to eighteen months, British talk of prosecutions for treason had become less topical as both sides realized that the conflict had become a civil war, which demanded a different etiquette. The colonial economic ultimatums that led to British countermeasures had been a new kind of casus belli.

The Vital Role of the Continental Association and Its Committees

Too much of this has been forgotten. Tens of millions of Americans have visited Philadelphia's Carpenters' Hall, the well-maintained and hallowed building where the First Continental Congress met, worked, and voted. But there are few, if any, plaques in Boston, Philadelphia, Charleston, or any other town singling out a room or building occupied in 1774 or 1775 by the local committee of inspection or public safety. These were the first institutions of independent local government in the future United States.

They ought to merit the attentions of political archaeologists, if not official historic preservation commissions.

The scope of their economic activity, already hinted, ranged from clearing ship departures to setting prices, investigating merchants, and deporting malefactors. In many places, regulation of the economy impinged on cultural practices; and elsewhere it edged toward military procurement and munitions management. In decrying purchases of unnecessary luxuries, extravagant clothing, cheap gewgaws, and types of conspicuous ceremony like costly funerals, the Association sought to harness Puritan morality to reduce wasteful spending and debt. George Washington and other supportive Virginians perceived a covert benefit. Patriotic boycotts of luxuries, including expensive clothing, would give debt-burdened gentlemen a face-saving way to cut outlays they could no longer afford. In the new cultural milieu, even planters accepted committee rulings against dancing classes, balls, entertainments, billiards, and their beloved horse races.[45]

Economic regulation overlapped with war preparation, in turn, when committees found themselves inventorying or seizing citizens' muskets, approving saltpeter collections, enjoining harbor or river pilots from aiding the British, setting militia pay, and hiring carpenters to build river obstructions or gun carriages. Local committees often had to call out the militia and direct its local operations.

The most informed assessments of what it all meant have come from the handful of chroniclers who immersed themselves in the subject matter, organization, calendar, and politics of the Continental Association between October 1774 and the winter of 1775–1776. To call this a "hidden history" of the early Revolution is an exaggeration. But that is principally because it is not really hidden, merely too little studied.

Bluntly put, the effectiveness of the new committee structure confirmed the First Continental Congress's positioning of the Continental Association as a "counter-coercive" response to Britain's spring 1774 Coercive Acts, albeit neither friend nor foe used that characterization at the time. One unhappy appreciation came from Virginia's Dunmore, who observed that Virginians gave "the Laws of Congress . . . marks of reverence which they never bestowed on their legal Government, or the laws proceeding from it."[46]

In Pennsylvania, the authoritative study of Revolutionary committees in that city took particular note of two with commercial origins—the Association's enforcement structure in Philadelphia and the United Company of Philadelphia for Promoting American Manufactures. Taken together, the importance of these two suggested that "the role of patriotic commercial associations in the coming of the Revolution may well deserve the attention commonly accorded political clubs and factions."[47]

The long-run importance of the Association, argued historian Ammerman, lay in "the provision calling the election of committees to enforce the trade boycott. Because approval and enforcement of the Association were placed in the hands of local groups rather than provincial assemblies of congresses, these committees became the regulatory agencies of the First Continental Congress."[48] Nor did they have much supervision during the hectic early months of 1775. No common law and no constitution applied. "It was not until after the outbreak of the war," adds another chronicler, "that any serious effort was made to supervise local committees and by then the Association was no longer the central issue."[49]

Almost a century ago, the historian Arthur M. Schlesinger, Sr., dwelt on the post–April 19 shift of many of these enforcement units into what he called a second or "defense" stage. Here the committees displayed an increasingly military preoccupation. Besides loyalty oaths and measures, these functions included military discipline and nonexportation of items needed in wartime. Scores of committees, including those in the major ports, adopted prohibitions against exports to Nova Scotia, Quebec, Newfoundland, and other colonies that were profitably provisioning the British Army in Boston.[50] On July 15 the Second Congress quietly authorized private individuals or firms to export American produce, tobacco, or food—"the non-exportation agreement notwithstanding"—in return for munitions. Although July's decision was not publicized until October, it signaled that trade was now on a wartime basis.[51]

In terms of the unfolding American Revolutionary economy, the year 1775 was a period of fortunate and necessary optimism, yet these hopes were in many ways unjustified. Without that brave confidence, without that clutch of illusions—naïve assumptions based on a supposedly unstoppable North American reservoir of manpower, an expected great surplus of grain and livestock, and a predicted flood of trade and support from Europe despite a British blockade—the ambitious rebels who launched the Revolution in 1774 and 1775 might not have dared. By 1779 and 1780, Britain's naval chokehold together with rampant inflation had left the new nation's economy at a nadir. However, this book is entitled *1775*, not *1780*. The Revolution succeeded, luckily, because several years of economic bravado preceded the era of disillusionment.

CHAPTER 10

Five Roads to Canada

There is an appearance of Great Britain being under a Necessity of coming to blows with the whole Continent, Halifax and Quebec excepted. Many parts indeed of Nova Scotia begin to grow refractory.

British official, Boston, November 1774

It's generally thought here that if the rebels were to push forward a body of four to five thousand men, the Canadians would lay down their arms and not fire a shot.

Captured letter from Quebec, October 1775

F ew aspects of how the Revolution unfolded in the late spring, summer, and autumn of 1775 are more intriguing—and less adequately pursued—than the multiple avenues of attack opening from New England and New York to Canada. By October and November, British governors and generals feared that rebel forces might well succeed in taking the citadel of Quebec.

The shift of intentions in Congress between mid-May and the end of June was a stormy prelude. The psychological drive of the New Englanders is hard to overstate, but when word reached Philadelphia on May 17 that Connecticut, Massachusetts, and Green Mountain irregulars had taken Ticonderoga and Crown Point, the initial reaction of middle-colony moderates, especially New Yorkers, was apprehension, based partly on fear of a British counterattack. Congress hemmed and hawed through the rest of May. But by the end of June, American invasion plans were taking shape, and the weight of evidence was that many French Canadians and some northern Indian tribes were amenable.[1] Although the British government

had built alliances with Quebec's Catholic hierarchy and local French seigneurs, Governor Carleton in Quebec had misread the French peasantry.
They did not want to be under the thumb of the clergy and gentry and were
open to an American incursion.

Some of the northern tribes wanted to join in. As we have seen, during
July and August, chiefs from the Abenaki and Penobscot visited General
Washington outside Boston and promised their assistance. The real question, in late August, as invasion plans went forward, was whether summer
was too far along and the first north country snow and sleet too near at
hand. The great opportunity had been in June and July, when the first proposals came in and alternative routes were put forward.

Of the potential invasion corridors shown on map 8, three were broadly
familiar: the Hudson–Lake Champlain corridor, mainstay for a century of
northward and southward aggressors; the sea routes New Englanders had
long followed to Nova Scotia and the Gulf of St. Lawrence; and the more
recently adopted Mohawk River–Oswego path to and from the Great
Lakes. Other trails included the Kennebec-Chaudière route through Maine
(used by Benedict Arnold to reach Quebec in 1775) and the never-finished
military road belatedly begun to speed the movement of troops from New
England's Connecticut Valley to the Richelieu River forts guarding
Montreal.

The fact that American plans ultimately miscarried should not inhibit
attention to how close they came to success or to how wide open Canada
briefly was. For Britain, meanwhile, the strategic cost in 1775 and early 1776
of having one army bottled up in Boston and other forces obliged to concentrate in Canada was substantial. The Patriot faction, as Chapter 9 detailed, used this grace period to build up a vital grassroots civic and military
infrastructure across the colonies. By mid-1775, British officials could not
even count on many of their northern Indian allies. The Caughnawagas and
Hurons preferred to be neutral so long as His Majesty's forces in North
America remained penned up in enclaves like Boston and Quebec—a hu-
miliation that prevailed through the autumn and winter of 1775–1776.

New Alliances and Old Hostilities

There was a cultural logic to how invading largely French-speaking Canada
became a New England priority within two to three weeks after Lexington
and Concord. In fact, Samuel Adams and a few associates had begun

plotting months earlier. New France had been New England's hereditary enemy, and the provocative Quebec Act of 1774 had revitalized this psychology and woven it into the mentality of the American Revolution.

Memories were powerful. Francis Parkman, the great nineteenth-century chronicler of New England's French wars, explained the traditional animosities in *A Half-Century of Conflict: France and England in America Before the French and Indian War*. "The French of Canada," he said, "often use the name New England as applying to the British colonies in general." The term "les Bastonnais" was applied just as broadly.[2]

Puritan New England more than returned the fixation. For over a century, its leaders had devilized Jesuit priests—the hated "black robes"—who guided birch-bark flotillas of painted savages down the Connecticut and Kennebec rivers to massacre English settlers and carry off their children to be raised as Catholics in some St. Francis or Huron bark hut. Parkman's own books were known to stereotype a priest-ridden Canada scarcely evolved beyond corruption, religious massacres, and medievalism. Nor, as Canadian historians have noted, was it all Puritan imagination. Militant New France did not allow Protestant settlers. As a supplement to French rule, seventeenth-century Jesuits, in one historian's words, arranged for Quebec to "owe an even superior allegiance to the See of Rome. Until very recently [the 1960s], the papal ensign was as common a sight in Quebec as the fleur-de-lis."[3] Boston, in turn, was the last major American city to vilify Catholicism with the annual mockery of "Pope Day."

Canadian forts and citadels like Quebec, Montreal, and Port Royal (Nova Scotia) had been prime New England targets for generations, and the first Yankee attack on Port Royal—five more would follow—harked back to 1654. Amid the chaotic colonial politics of 1774, then, the British government had miscalculated in establishing a seeming second incarnation of French and Indian Quebec as a new buffer state. Much of inland Maine, New Hampshire, and the future Vermont still retained bitter memories. Towns like Adams in Massachusetts, Walpole in New Hampshire, and Hoosic and German Flats in New York had suffered French and Indian raids as late as the 1750s. What hardly anyone, back in 1760, could have imagined—as the British flag rose over a conquered Canada—was that fifteen years later New England's military ire would again turn northward against a seeming new Quebec threat put in place by new imperial strategists. This time those officials would speak English. Small wonder this issue could move so quickly to the fore in the spring of 1775.

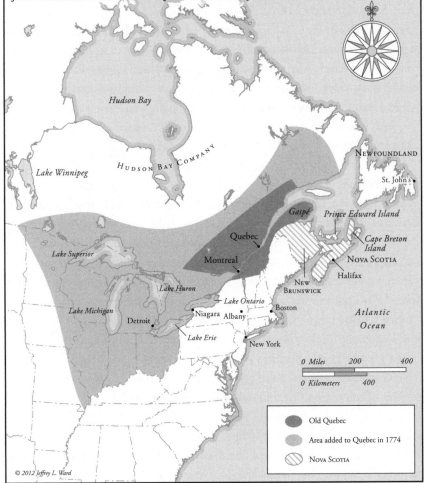

8: QUEBEC, NOVA SCOTIA, AND THE THREAT FROM CANADA

The British Quebec Act of 1774 roughly quadrupled the size of that French-speaking province, and Nova Scotia had already been enlarged to include what is now New Brunswick. Offended colonists from New England south found themselves hemmed in and blocked from western lands they claimed under their charters.

Hudson Bay

NEWFOUNDLAND

Lake Winnipeg

HUDSON BAY COMPANY

St. John's

Gaspé

Prince Edward Island

Quebec

Cape Breton
Island

Lake Superior

Montreal

NOVA SCOTIA

Lake Huron

Halifax

NEW
BRUNSWICK

Lake Michigan

Lake Ontario

Boston

*Atlantic
Ocean*

Detroit

Niagara Albany

Lake Erie

New York

| 0 Miles | 200 | 400 |
| 0 Kilometers | 400 | |

Old Quebec

Area added to Quebec in 1774

NOVA SCOTIA

© 2012 Jeffrey L. Ward

Through the new legislation, imperial Britain had stepped into much of the Canadian footprint loathed by generations of New Englanders. Part of that repositioning, moreover, was intentional. Although the Quebec measure was not designed to supplement the Coercive Acts, its enactment within the same time frame had made many Americans so perceive it. The act did more than recognize the Catholic Church in Quebec, entrench the French seigneurs, establish French civil law rather than English, and deny an elected legislature. It also vastly enlarged Quebec's boundaries, extending them south to the Ohio River. The result was to collect within one presumably hostile jurisdiction many of eastern North America's most warlike Indian tribes while simultaneously blocking and disallowing the western territorial claims of Virginia, Connecticut, and Massachusetts based on their seventeenth-century charters. In terms of ill will, this provocation was *British*.

As to Yankee ambitions for expanded access to the Grand Banks and St. Lawrence fisheries, these were not denied by the Quebec Act per se. However, since 1763, such hopes had been gainsaid by a new British mindset. William Pitt, the former first minister who had urged a Protestant and English-language reorientation of conquered Quebec, had likewise advocated a peace treaty that would have expelled the French from the fisheries. Pitt put great emphasis on the fisheries. Instead, King George III virtually forced Pitt's resignation and also accepted a softer treaty (1763) under which France retained two islands off Newfoundland, St. Pierre and Miquelon, and kept a significant North Atlantic fisheries foothold. In fact, New England's interests and Britain's were steadily diverging.

Control of the fisheries was grand policy. From New England to Labrador, a series of huge shoals or shallow areas off the Atlantic Coast constituted— and still constitute—the world's leading cod fisheries. In the eighteenth century, when France, Spain, Portugal, Britain, and Holland were contesting national access, the waters of the Georges Bank off Massachusetts were among the richest. The Indian word for the region, *Naumkeag,* meant "fishing place," and Cape Cod itself was reasonably named. To take full advantage, New England shipbuilders pioneered the fast, agile schooner—from the Yankee colloquialism *scoon,* "to skim lightly over the water."[4]

By the mid-eighteenth century, New England fishermen looked beyond nearby waters to covet the Grand Banks and the Gulf of St. Lawrence. By the 1760s, though, serious *fischpolitik* compelled New England to reassess its place within the British Empire. Not only did London conceive Nova Scotia in buffer-state terms, but Crown policy also favored two other fisheries: those centered on Newfoundland, and those in England's West Country, based on ports like Plymouth in Devon and Poole in Dorsetshire. Great Britain, too, was a fishing nation, indeed a competitor in North Atlantic waters—and mercantilist enough to close its own markets for fish to American imports. For some British ministers, curbing maritime New England was more than a political or constitutional abstraction.

Britain and New England: Emerging North Atlantic Rivals

In the first half of the eighteenth century, while Boston still remained the major North American city, most New Englanders pursued seaward expansion through the empire. In March 1775, Edmund Burke explained their determination to an ever-less-sympathetic Parliament: "Look at the manner in which the people of New England have of late carried on their fisheries. Whilst we follow them among the tumbling mountains of ice and behold them penetrating into the deepest recesses of Hudson's Bay and Davis Straits . . . we hear that they have pierced in to the opposite [Antarctic] region of polar cold . . . No sea but what is vexed by their fisheries, no climate that is not witness to their toil. Neither the perseverance of Holland, nor the activity of France nor the dexterity and firm sagacity of English enterprise, ever carried this most perilous mode of hearty industry to the extent to which it has been pushed by this recent people."[5]

But by 1774, such praise raised more hackles than pride. In New England, as in Old England, fishing and large-scale smuggling were often interwoven, as we saw in Chapter 9.[6] Even in the 1740s, while Yankee politicians and preachers thundered against both the French Antichrist and the Louisbourg privateers that menaced Massachusetts fishermen, hundreds of Yankee vessels were trading with the French. Then during the 1750s, New Englanders contrabanded on a grand scale in the French West Indies; in the decade before 1775, they traded in a lesser way with the two French fishery islands in the North Atlantic.[7]

As the Royal Navy intensified its 1760s harassment of New England commerce, the French foreign ministry began to see a potential for shifting relationships. In 1765 Americans angry over the Stamp Act were rumored to have sent an agent to Europe to query possible French backing; and in 1768, Du Chatelet, the new French ambassador to London, had proposed to Foreign Minister Choiseul that Paris begin to court the "Nouveaux Angleterriens" with trade opportunities in the French West Indies. Being huge molasses producers, the French islands were a better commercial fit for New England than the British Caribbean islands were. By 1775, it was no huge step for Massachusetts newspapers to make occasional wistful reference to French fleets and assistance.[8]

Massachusetts's commitment to pursuing its interests under a British banner was obviously fading in 1774. To understand the particular reversal represented by the overlapping emergence of Quebec and a newly imperialized Nova Scotia in buffer roles, a revealing picture is worth many more than a thousand words. Map 8 adapted from volume two of the *Oxford History of the British Empire,* shows both the pre-1774 and post-1774 boundaries of Quebec, as well as the new contours of Nova Scotia, which included today's New Brunswick.[9] The newly expanded Quebec, five times the land mass of the old one, abutted the thirteen colonies like the edge of a crude tomahawk, stretching from New England through New York and Pennsylvania south and west as far as the confluence of the Ohio and Mississippi rivers. Within these inflated boundaries—or so many Americans believed and feared—the British Crown was creating the weighty counterforce to English-speaking North America that French kings Louis XIV and Louis XV had never quite managed.

Canadian historians have been more candid than their British or U.S. colleagues. Quebec's first two appointed British governors—James Murray (1763–1765) and Guy Carleton (1765–1780)—both came to admire Canada's seigneurs and Catholic bishops and, more specifically, to see a French Quebec as a better imperial buffer than an Anglicized Canada run by ambitious English speakers: Yankees, Yorkers, and British merchants. "In the authoritarian structure of Quebec society," said one chronicler, Carleton "thought that he discerned a sheet anchor for British power in North America." In 1774 few in the House of Commons paid attention when the radical Charles James Fox had raised a similar point: that "to go at once and establish a perfectly despotic government [in Quebec], contrary to the genius and spirit of the British constitution, carries with it the appearance of a love of despotism, and a settled design to enslave the American people."[10]

In *The Path of Destiny,* a much-acclaimed book of the 1950s, Canadian historian Thomas H. Raddall pictured the act as both mistake and provocation: "By a stroke of the pen it would restore the old menace in the north and west which had kept the American colonists in check for half a century. The ministers assumed with quite false optimism that *habitants* of Canada would be willing to fight, if necessary, to support the British Crown which had granted them this boon; and that merely placing the fierce tribes of the

Middle West under the old auspices of the Chateau St. Louis would hold quiet forever the turbulent American frontiersmen, the best fighting men in the colonies. Thus the Quebec Act lost its original innocence and became a challenge to rebellion, and in America the gifted agitators fell upon it with fury and with glee. All the old passions of the French and Indian wars were dragged out of their dusty cupboards and rubbed hot."[11] Exactly so.

In 1776 and 1777, the British government became willing to signal, in private communications, that parts of the Quebec Act could be repealed and the earlier map restored. However, proclaiming those new boundaries in 1774 had been an irretrievable mistiming—further confirmation that senior officials intended to cut the thirteen colonies back to size by commercial and territorial amputations. Religious liberalization for Quebec, in itself a reasonable Crown concession given the fast-growing number of Catholics within the British Empire, could have been proclaimed within Quebec's pre-1774 boundaries.

Many of the British officials convinced that the Quebec Act would effectively deny rather than infuriate the older North American colonies also indulged a second misconception. To wit: however grand the Crown's 1759–1760 military triumphs in Canada might seem in London, a different view of history prevailed in New England, especially in Boston. There a deeper negative impression had been ingrained over generations by English ineptness and unreliability in prior Canadian campaigns.

This aspect requires a few supporting paragraphs. After 1654, when Bay Colony troops captured Port Royal in French Acadia (now Nova Scotia), English negotiators returned it to France in the Treaty of Breda. What New England thought didn't matter. A generation later, in 1690, Sir William Phips, a Massachusetts-born mariner knighted years earlier for salvaging a gold-filled treasure galleon, led an expedition of New England militia that once again captured Port Royal. But Old England sent no regular garrison, and in 1691 the French took it back.

New Englanders tried again in 1704 and 1707, angered by the success of Port Royal–based privateers in harassing their fishermen. No help came from England, and neither effort succeeded. In 1710, after British naval officers in America declined to aid another expedition planned by Massachusetts, Connecticut, New Hampshire, and Rhode Island, Francis Nicholson, an audacious former governor of Virginia and Maryland, traveled to London and obtained the assistance of 500 Royal Marines. This time the outnumbered French did surrender, and the British 40th Regiment took over as a garrison. Port Royal was renamed Annapolis Royal in honor of the queen and remained British thereafter.[12]

In 1740, however, the French completed a new and much stronger fortress near the northern tip of Cape Breton Island, an ideal location for a French naval base, close to the fisheries, and a safe lair for Gallic privateers. This was the citadel of Louisbourg, soon labeled the Gibraltar of North America for its forbidding 30-feet-high stone walls able to mount 250 cannon. However, it fell in 1745 to a large and highly motivated New England expedition—dozens of vessels, and militiamen from Massachusetts, Connecticut, New Hampshire, and Rhode Island—led by William Pepperrell, a militia colonel from the district of Maine, who soon became Sir William Pepperrell. New England celebrated widely but prematurely. In 1748, by the treaty of Aix-la-Chapelle, Britain returned the great stone bastion to King Louis, in return for the French yielding Madras in India and surrendering fortresses that French armies had captured in Flanders. Time after time Boston and New England had seen Port Royal or Louisbourg handed back or shrugged off because higher priorities—invariably European—had overridden colonists' interests.

Come 1757, the Earl of Loudoun made the first British attempt of that great conflict to regain Louisbourg. However, he dawdled, giving the French time to reinforce their Acadian citadel. Loudoun then decided to give up, and as further luck would have it, a hurricane sank part of the British fleet. Benjamin Franklin described this campaign as "frivolous, expensive and disgraceful to our Nation beyond conception."[13] In 1758, the French held their other great new fortress, Ticonderoga, against a bungled assault by yet another mediocre British commander, James Abercrombie—nicknamed "Nabbycrombie" by Yankee militia—who lost despite commanding a force that outnumbered the French defenders by three to one. Three weeks later the war's second expedition against Louisbourg, this one led by Sir Jeffery Amherst, *did* prevail—carefully following the old plan of landing at Gabarus Bay, by which the New Englanders had triumphed thirteen years earlier.[14]

Amherst's success marked a turning of the tide. Now British forces toppled French forts like dominoes: first Frontenac, then Duquesne, and then Niagara. Finally in September 1759, under General James Wolfe, Quebec itself fell. Giddy Britons celebrated 1759 as the miracle year that raised the empire to global dominance. Colonials in Philadelphia and New York, beneficiaries of massive wartime expenditures (and profits), celebrated almost as enthusiastically. Fewer did so in Boston; arguably its imperial hour had

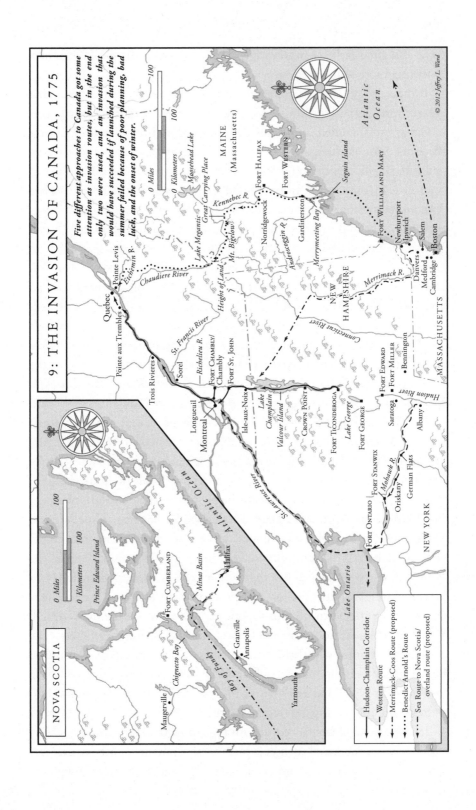

9: THE INVASION OF CANADA, 1775

Five different approaches to Canada got some attention as invasion routes, but in the end only two were used, and an invasion that would have succeeded if launched during the summer failed because of poor planning, bad luck, and the onset of winter.

NOVA SCOTIA

Hudson–Champlain Corridor
Western Route
Merrimack-Coos Route (proposed)
Benedict Arnold's Route
Sea Route to Nova Scotia/
overland route (proposed)

© 2012 Jeffrey L. Ward

come and gone earlier—in 1691, 1710, and 1745—with the mother country hindering more than assisting.

If these pre-1759 annals of hauteur and ineptitude seem repetitious, that is exactly the point. Port Royal and Louisbourg were hardly the only targets in Canada mishandled or casually deprioritized by British authorities over the years. Serious attempts had also been made on Quebec—in 1690, 1709, and 1711. The last two failures left especially sour memories of British non-support or incompetence. In 1709 London "laid aside" its plans for Quebec without telling the supporting New York, Jersey, and New England forces that had moved up to Lake Champlain under Francis Nicholson.[15] In 1711 British ineffectiveness took a different form. A new Tory government in London, out to succeed in Canada where previous Whig ministries had not, sent to Boston the largest expeditionary spectacle North Americans had ever seen—60 ships under Admiral Sir Hovenden Walker and 5,000 redcoats under General John Hill. Just as they had two years earlier, New York and New England militias marched to Lake Champlain in support. However, squalls, fog, and inexpert navigation sunk eight transports on the rocks near the mouth of the St. Lawrence. A skittish Walker sailed back to England, with the concurrence of army commander Hill.[16]

Bostonians were outraged. "Jack Hill" was not a real general; he had never held a command before. His qualification lay in being the court-figure brother of Mrs. Masham, the lady of the bedchamber who had replaced the Duchess of Marlborough as the power behind the throne of the aged Queen Anne. Francis Parkman, in an acid nineteenth-century portrait, observed that Marlborough himself had called Hill good for nothing, while Admiral Walker was "a man whose incompetence was soon to become notorious" after an embarrassed Admiralty sacked him.[17] To make things worse, the Walker-Hill expedition was one that Massachusetts, in particular, had been pressured to assist. Local sailors and pilots were pressed into service; merchants were ordered to furnish supplies at low prices or see them seized. When the colonial troops, assembled at Lake Champlain, heard about the debacle, frustration with British unreliability boiled over, just as it did in Boston. The force commander—Francis Nicholson again—was "so beside himself with rage" that he "tore off his wig, threw it on the ground and stamped upon it, crying out 'roguery! Treachery!'"[18]

In the early eighteenth century, and again in the 1740s, Boston paid a steep social, cultural, and economic price for the mother country's disregard. Still the largest urban and commercial center in North America through the

1740s, the city had poured money and manpower into winning the battle for the North Atlantic. Had France been pushed out of Nova Scotia and denied access to Labrador and Newfoundland, their departure, Bostonians thought or hoped, would leave a maritime opening that Massachusetts could have filled. By 1775, frustration with Britain had become hostility.

Parkman, who rarely dwelt on economics, was blunt: "What with manning the coast-guard vessels, defending the frontier against Indians, and furnishing her contingent to the Canada expedition, more than one in five of her able bodied men were in active service in the summer of 1711. Years passed before she [Massachusetts] recovered from the effects of her financial exhaustion."[19] So, too, in the 1740s. By one account, "the Cartagena and Louisbourg expeditions of 1743–1745, whatever they may have done for Yankee self-esteem, imposed heavy taxes on the middle and lower classes, drained the provincial treasury and left hundreds of families in Boston fatherless and husbandless. Eight years later, Boston's leaders will still be lamenting the staggering burden which the war had imposed."[20]

What Boston economic primacy King George's War (1739–1748) had not dissipated, the 1754–1763 conflict did. Here is colonial historian Carl Bridenbaugh: "The events of the French and Indian War took an extra toll from Boston. Understandably, people were war-weary before the conflict officially broke out . . . Nevertheless, inspired by Governor Shirley, Boston put forth the greatest war effort in money and taxes of all America . . . No testimony to the effect of the war on the city's well-being is more pointed than the bankruptcy notices of twenty-eight merchants, shopkeepers and master craftsmen published in the *Boston Evening Post* at the very time of the second capture of Louisbourg [1759]."[21]

If Bostonians had little confidence in British ministries and army generals, they had even less regard for the Royal Navy, which used maritime Massachusetts as a principal whipping post for both punitive customs policies and the forced impressment of local seamen. During the 90 years before 1775, Philadelphia and New York had only a few riots against impressment, while Boston led with six—in the 1690s, 1702, 1741, 1745, 1747, and 1758. In these years, one must remember, impressment on a ship of the Royal Navy was seen as "approximating a death sentence because of the miserable conditions that prevailed, and according to the [Boston] town meeting in 1746 it was this fear that drove many shipwrights and other artisans to satellite ports."[22] In some years, so many fishermen were pressed that catches and codfish exports plummeted.[23]

Consensus-driven accounts of the Revolution tend to omit or downplay such history and events, which is a mistake. They seeded Boston's unique anger—the waterfront and street mobs, the tarring and feathering of customs officials, the looting and gutting of the mansions of rich officeholders—so visible during the 1760s and 1770s. Depredations in New York and Newport were minor by comparison. The roots of disillusionment ran deep, and in and around Boston one can suggest that the mother country of yesteryear had become a wicked stepmother figure.

New maritime trespasses were on the horizon. In early 1775, after the New England Restraining Act barred the four Yankee provinces from all offshore Atlantic fishing, additional legislation enacted by Parliament subsidized England's migratory cod-fishing industry and allowed mercantile interests in Ireland to take over when American provisions were barred from Newfoundland and other fisheries.[24] Massachusetts was unlikely to ever be back in good graces.

In the spring of 1775, with Boston under siege, both General Gage and Admiral Graves wrote to the governors of Nova Scotia, Quebec, and Newfoundland requesting them to ship provisions to Boston under special license.[25] As recent beneficiaries of favorable policies and subsidies, all three responded avidly, shipping quantities of livestock, beef, mutton, poultry, vegetables, and cheese. Nova Scotia sent so much at such cost that Gage complained about price gouging.[26] Parenthetically, the Canadian colonies had not responded to invitations to attend the Continental Congress. And that body (on May 17), followed by many local committees of inspection, took strong countermeasures, prohibiting exports to Nova Scotia, Quebec, Newfoundland, and other fisheries.[27]

Massachusetts leaders understood that the Crown's relationship with New England had soured, and that regimes in Nova Scotia, Newfoundland, and Quebec were taking the king's side. If the Quebec Act had in some ways scrambled old political, religious, and territorial sensitivities, it had left them cloaked in familiar northern geography: Canada, and how best to invade. By the summer of 1775, the opportunity appeared to be there, with more avenues than ever before.

The Champlain-Hudson Corridor

For Yorkers and New Englanders, this was the old, familiar war road. It ran from Albany north along the Hudson to Lake George, by portage from

Lake George to Lake Champlain, and then north on that lake to Canada's Richelieu River. The Richelieu, in turn, flowed northward for 30 miles until it became a foaming stretch of impassable rapids. After a portage, travelers had a short trip down the rest of the river to the St. Lawrence. From there Montreal was in sight. No ships of any size could go from Lake Champlain to the St. Lawrence. But for the most part, the water and land segments were not difficult for battalions or regiments marching north.

John Brown, an agent sent by Samuel Adams in February 1775, reported back by letter in March. When war comes, Brown said, seize the two gateway fortresses. If the familiar route exercised a strong attraction, so did the 300 cannon at Ticonderoga and Crown Point. New Englanders captured them, but moderates in Congress at first temporized, saying the cannon should not be taken to Boston or Hartford but held for rapprochement with Britain.

Although delays were to be expected, given a new Congress, a new army in formation, and the need to soothe regional squabbles, these wasted weeks were predictive of more to come. Each week lost, in turn, narrowed the summer and early autumn window of plausible invasion. As Chapter 21 will detail, several constraints stood out: indecision in Congress; excessively cautious leadership by the designated commander, General Philip Schuyler of New York; lack of supplies and ammunition; soldiers' short-term enlistments that expired in November and December; and insufficient knowledge by top commanders of northern New England and the alternative routes available.

These pages have already touched on the historical and psychological drive that pushed New Englanders to invade Canada. The issue we must now frame is that of underlying military and political plausibility: Could the Americans hope to succeed? In the summer and autumn of 1775, the answer was yes.

Chronicles wedded to 1776 as the American annus mirabilis say no. Canada, they insist, was too grand a target, too much of a military reach. In addition, the Catholic Church and people of French Canada had been won to the British side by the Quebec Act, a milestone of tolerance, as well as by persisting distrust of their old *Bastonnais* foes. Analyses emphasizing only retrospect are further colored by the Americans' late-winter and early-spring 1776 retreat from Quebec, which developed into a disease-ridden rout.

In 1775, amid that year's American hubris and the near panic in British

Canada, things looked quite different; a timely Hudson-Champlain corridor invasion could have succeeded. The most serious American proposals rightly emphasized speed and seasonality. Even in October and November, both Carleton and Quebec's lieutenant governor, Hector Cramahe, worried that all seemed lost. And as we will shortly see, two centuries later Canadian historian Thomas Raddall made a reasonable case that Nova Scotia held out a greater prospect for American victory than Quebec.

During the weeks after Lexington and Concord, amid one of the earliest-budding springtimes in eighteenth-century North America, premature warmth in New England helped unnerve British generals. Ice broke up early; further snowfall was dismissed. Gage had sent Carleton a belated dispatch in mid-April requesting him to reinforce the tiny garrison in Ticonderoga. Ironically, Arnold and Allen were at Ticonderoga's gates more quickly than Gage's letter reached Quebec.

Not that Carleton could have done much. Two of his four regiments had earlier been sent to Gage; then on April 30, Halifax was stripped of troops to further reinforce Boston. Although several posts in the Great Lakes were still manned by small details, from Montreal east to the new British North Atlantic naval base in Halifax, Canada held only 700 redcoats that summer.[28]

For Britain, the naval situation was little cheerier. Only one vessel was regularly in Halifax. In May, Arnold had captured the one sloop on Lake Champlain, in some accounts called the *King George III*. While not quite "wide open," Canada was extremely vulnerable. Moreover, because the Royal Navy disliked risking the bad weather in the Gulf of St. Lawrence after late September, reinforcements not on hand by October were unlikely to arrive until ice on the river broke up in May.

British vulnerability was also increased by cultural and political discontent in Montreal and the French-speaking rural sections of the St. Lawrence Valley. Official hopes that the Quebec Act had persuaded a sullen peasantry, the *habitants,* to fight for British king and empire proved illusory. Moreover, the mistake had originated at the top, with Governor Guy Carleton, the act's principal architect. He was something of a francophile, and his young wife was an ardent one. Lady Maria was English, the younger daughter of the Earl of Effingham, but she had been educated at the French court in Versailles.[29] Quebec's French-Canadian gentry, the seigneurs, seem to have cherished the faint hint of the Grand Apartment among the hemlocks, snow fences, and ice floes.

In an earlier letter to London, Carleton had enthused that although his regular garrison was small, the *habitants* could "send into the field about eighteen thousand men well able to carry arms; of which number above one half have already served with as much valour, with more zeal, and more military knowledge for America than the regular troops of France that were joined with them."[30] This was altogether unrealistic.

The peasantry, by one account, were overwhelmingly illiterate, content with mere subsistence and suspicious of all foreigners. They were also "devout in their religion while grudging the parish tithes, obedient to the seigneurs while resenting their authority." They had "the peasants' dislike of the corvee, which forced them to work on the roads without pay, and of war, for the militia system of the French regime had demanded the armed service of all able-bodied males from boys of 16 to gray-heads of 60. These two things had put in their hearts a deep hatred of conscription in any form . . . The cold truth was that the Quebec Act, with all its good intentions, had gained for the British the ardent support of the clergy and the *seigneurs,* but no one else. The *habitant* remained unmoved."[31]

Nor were Canada's Indians impressed. Several tribes farther south, from the Passamaquoddy in Maine and Nova Scotia to the Oneida in New York, openly sided with the rebels in 1775, while the more important northern confederations—the Abenaki, Hurons, and Caughnawaga—took generally neutral stands.

Ideological commitment to the rebel cause was thin among the French peasantry, being largely confined to pro-American merchants in Montreal and Quebec City, along with Voltaire-quoting, anticlerical Quebec *Congressistes.* But if few *habitants* were truly pro-American, most were willing to sell food, and some would enlist in their service. Just two criteria had to be met: *Les Bastonnais* must pay in gold and silver, not paper; and the armies of Congress must continue to appear headed for victory in Canada. These circumstances crumbled in 1776, but through 1775 they remained favorable. As we will see, the commanders of both columns advancing that autumn, General Richard Montgomery through the Hudson-Champlain corridor, and Benedict Arnold via backwoods Maine and then Quebec's rock-toothed Chaudière Valley, recruited and enjoyed considerable French-Canadian support.

Only in the spring of 1776 did the *habitants* and Indians tilt back to the British side, as a new set of American failures and weaknesses converged. Once winter set in, the rebels were too weak to capture Quebec. As they ran out of coin, they paid in paper that *habitants* sneered at. Many New England soldiers left in December because of expiring enlistments. And friend and foe alike knew that melting ice on the St. Lawrence would bring the Royal Navy and reinforcements.

But we are getting ahead of ourselves. Could better and quicker decisions between May and August 1775 have brought about American capture of Quebec in November or December, following a September or October occupation of Montreal? Probably, as Chapter 21 will amplify. Could the rebels have held Canada through the war, and then obtained a final cession from Britain in the 1783 peace treaty? That seems less likely.

What can be ventured with very little doubt is that the battle for Canada begun in 1775 was a serious and wide-ranging one, with important ramifications and several lasting benefits.

The Sea Route to Nova Scotia and the St. Lawrence

In October 1774, an *Address to the People of Quebec* sent by the Continental Congress stumbled badly in a sentence alleging that "the injuries of Boston have roused and associated every colony from Nova Scotia to Georgia. Your province is the only link that is wanting to complete the bright, strong chain of union."[32]

This was a major misreading of Nova Scotia, and within nine months a partly New England–settled and somewhat sympathetic place had slipped from expected fourteenth colony to become a declared invasion target of the Massachusetts Provincial Congress. But confusion cut two ways. In the autumn of 1775, Royal Governor Francis Legge was nervous enough to see a rebel behind every lobster trap, and he offended New England–born residents by trying to force them into an unnecessary militia.[33]

Congressional interest in Nova Scotia rekindled several times during the Revolution, and George Washington, after rejecting the first invasion proposal in August 1775, had to do so several times again. For this chapter, suffice it to say that no serious invasion fleet ever sailed—from Newburyport, Machias, or any other Massachusetts seaport. Despite the great familiarity of Bay Colony seamen with Nova Scotia waters and a considerable kinship, the relationship of Massachusetts with its neighbor across the Bay of Fundy might have prompted a modern psychiatrist to use the term love-hate.

Five or six thousand Nova Scotians—perhaps 40 percent of the total population—did share New England ancestry. But what ultimately counted more was not having shared their cousins' intensely political experience of living in Massachusetts during the pre-Revolutionary decade. To many Bay Colony stalwarts, Nova Scotians had become weak and fallen away, a people apparently content to become minions of empire.

For two decades, loyalty had been a focal point of imperial administrators in Nova Scotia. In the mid-1750s, no sooner had war resumed with France than the fearful British government expelled some 6,000 French-speaking Acadians, to be replaced by roughly as many Protestant New Englanders. Promised the same town-government culture they were leaving behind, what the New Englanders actually got was an appearance with very little substance. Towns in Nova Scotia were not self-governing. The Church of England, not the Congregational Church, enjoyed local establishment.

British administrators, understanding fully well what they distrusted about New England—namely, its republican government and religion—simply barred its Canadian reproduction. The other new immigrants brought in—Scots, Germans, Yorkshiremen, and Newfoundlanders—generally accepted imperial sway. Politically, control of the Assembly and Governor's Council rested with a merchant oligarchy tied to interests in the City of London. Executive authority lay with royal appointees in Halifax and the commanders of the all-important naval facilities. Military and naval subsidies kept Nova Scotia, its finances, and its ships afloat.[34]

Massachusetts Patriot leaders seethed in the early summer of 1775, after Nova Scotians sent many cargoes of provisions, lumber, and firewood to British-occupied Boston. That influenced a Massachusetts legislative committee to recommend the summer invasion, which Washington rejected. Plans to invade Canada, while not exactly a dime a dozen in those months, were certainly two-or-three-a-week submissions in the American camp near Boston. Proposals for attacking Nova Scotia usually emphasized the goal of destroying the Royal Naval dockyard in Halifax, and this was the essence of the August submission, also known as the Thomson proposal.

Two centuries later Thomas Raddall concluded that the Thomson proposal had been more feasible than Washington's decision that month to send Arnold through Maine. The Americans, Raddall said, could have landed in force among Yankee-born sympathizers on the Bay of Fundy's Minas Basin. The Royal Navy was always nervous about local fog and tides. After seizing the port of Windsor, an American force of 4,000 to 5,000 men could have marched overland to Halifax, some 40 miles away. Nova Scotia's only British troops were stationed in Halifax that November, but there were just 390—and only 126 were fit for duty.[35]

Noting that roughly 5,000 Americans perished in Canada between November 1775 and June 1776, Raddall argued that had that many been sent to Halifax, they could have held it. Enough timorous ex–New Englanders would have aided their cousins if the Yankees became actual occupiers. He concluded: "With Nova Scotia fixed in American hands the British fleet would have lost its last winter mooring post on the continent north of New York, thus changing the whole face of the war and of the subsequent peace; for the British peace commissioners [in 1782] were in no mood to haggle over an established fourteenth star in the American flag."[36] As a what-might-have-been, Raddall's is on a grand scale.

Angry response to clumsy Royal Governor Legge made Nova Scotians look more rebellion prone in late 1775 than they were. All that came to pass was a small-scale and unofficial invasion from Maine in 1776, which failed to capture Fort Cumberland. Congress never did send a serious expedition to the supposed fourteenth colony.

The Backwoods Route Through Maine

As matters stood in the late summer of 1775, the Kennebec-Chaudière route was not a wise one for a commander to endorse—at least not if the contemplated expedition was (1) setting out well into September, late enough to face snow and sleet en route; (2) starting from coastal Maine and heading north into higher elevations and rugged terrain; (3) relying on a map—drawn back in 1761 by British military engineer John Montresor—that had been edited to omit many details and distances; and (4) including too many men (about 1,150) to avoid scaring off game or to manage the faster time possible for a small party.

This was not the invasion plan drawn up in June by Benedict Arnold, which as we will see was a shrewder variation on the Hudson-Champlain corridor approach. Nevertheless, Arnold chose to accept this route in mid-August, when Washington offered him command of the secondary expedition.

The first American officer to propose the Kennebec route, Massachusetts Colonel Jonathan Brewer, had done so on May 1. This was ten days before Ticonderoga and Crown Point were captured—and more than a month before a skittish Congress would entertain going on the offensive. What Brewer proposed was to take 500 volunteers upstream along Maine's Kennebec River, over a massif called the Height of Land, and then down Quebec's Chaudière River to the St. Lawrence, almost at Quebec City's door.[37] His timing was workable. Had 500 men been ready to go in late July, say, they would have easily completed their trip by late August, a perfectly coordinated diversion if the principal invading army, gathered in the Lake Champlain region, had just crossed into Canada.

Brewer himself was badly wounded at Bunker Hill. And Washington did not sign off on an expedition using the Kennebec-Chaudière back door to Quebec until August. Then he gave that command to Arnold. The main attack through the Hudson-Champlain corridor would be commanded by New York General Philip Schuyler, who had fallen behind schedule.

Since the 1690s, Arnold's route had been a favored war trail for Indians from Quebec raiding the southern Maine settlements in York, Saco, and points east. For these war parties, the south-flowing Kennebec provided a convenient highway. Sometimes colonial forces traveled 50 or 100 miles upstream to retaliate. No British or colonial troops, though, had ever used the full Kennebec-Chaudière route to attack Quebec.

By 1775, English-speaking settlers had pushed 50 miles up the Kennebec. In September, before Arnold's force set off, several local guides and boat builders had scouted the route north to the Dead River and the Height of Land, where major portages would be necessary. Arnold's soldiers would be accompanied, at least to the Dead River, by 20 carpenters who would help with the tiring, grueling portages but also, and more important, maintain and repair the 220 flat-bottomed wooden bateaux. Each weighed 400 pounds empty, and was capable of carrying five or six men equipped with oars, paddles, and poles.[38] Had it left in August, the expedition might have been a grand success.

Instead, cruel weather, excess baggage weight, intermittent low water, flooding, and insufficient food were all problems. The first freezing night came on September 28, the first snow two weeks later. The cruelest condition involved a misconception of distance. Montresor's map, parts of it blanked out, was read by Arnold, his guides, and officers to show lesser distances than in fact existed. By the time the expedition reached the "Great Carrying Place" between the Kennebec and Dead rivers, its men had gone 90 miles and hoped the worst was over; but in fact Quebec City was 270 miles from Fort Western, the jumping-off point.[39] The rear guard of three companies, one third of Arnold's men, eventually turned around and went back to Fort Western.

The saga, obviously, partook of the heroic. Dozens of books have been written about the march to Quebec by Arnold and his remaining 600. They were late, reaching the St. Lawrence only on November 6. Their tattered display was conveyed by one participant: "Our clothes were torn to pieces by the bushes, and hung in strings—few of us had any shoes, but mogga-sons [moccasins] made of raw skins—many of us without hats—and beards long and visages thin and meager. I thought we much resembled the animals which inhabit New-Spain [South America] called the Ourang-Outang."[40]

Even though Arnold was late, the culpable tardiness was that of the main force, first under the sluggish Schuyler, and then under the better (but still slow) Montgomery. Many of the enlistees who had come up the Hudson-Champlain corridor or gone over the mountains were short-term volunteers. Men whose service ended in December—and were committed to going home at that point—should have arrived near Quebec no later than October. Yet there is inspiration in how close they nevertheless came.

The Military Road: From the Coos to St. John

In a letter that George Washington penned to John Hancock in early Au-gust 1775, he raised another route—the possibility of invading through the upper Connecticut Valley. This corridor was well known to Chief Louis of the intermittently pro-American St. Francis Indians. Together with rebel Colonel Jacob Bayley of Newbury (in what would become Vermont), the chief journeyed to visit Washington in late July. Their contention—reiterated by Bayley in several letters—was that the best route to Quebec's Missisquoi Bay or Fort St. John ran northwest from the new settlements on the "Coos," the great oxbow bend of the northern Connecticut River. Troops marching to Montreal from populous central or eastern New En-gland would have a much shorter and faster trip, saving 70 miles. As Wash-ington advised Hancock, the chief had promised that "if an Expedition is meditated against Canada, the Indians in that quarter would give all their assistance."[41]

This alternative, too, could have been useful in 1775 had Washington not opted for the Kennebec-Chaudière route. However, the rough trail was not surveyed until March 1776, and road makers only began work the next

Boston Harbor: A Vital Patriot Battleground of 1775

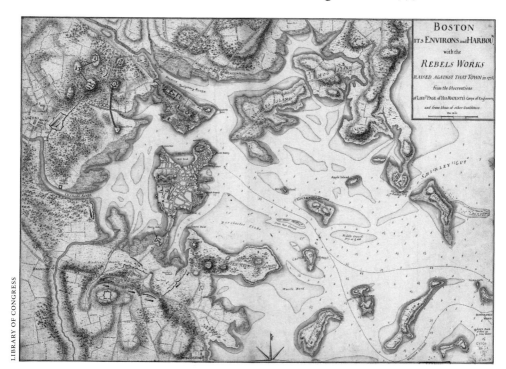

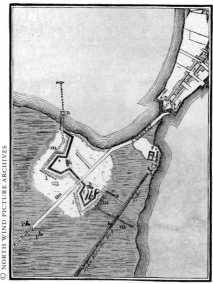

The Boston of 1775 was almost an island, separated from the mainland by only a narrow neck of land. It was an intensely maritime city. By the end of 1775, the British had put up considerable fortifications on Boston Neck, as the lower drawing shows. The islands of Boston Harbor, the easternmost of which are not shown, were impossible for the British to safely occupy because of American raids—the Patriots' so-called whaleboat war. A number of small and midsized encounters took place on Hog Island, Noddle's Island, and Great Brewster Island before the British were forced to vacate Boston in March 1776.

Before Lexington and Concord: The Fortification of Boston Neck and the Confrontation at North Bridge, Salem

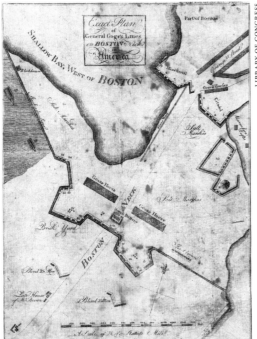

The British fortification on the Neck, begun in late summer 1774, was a set of entrenchments and emplacements to be taken seriously. By December 1775, it appears to have been the only fortification in the thirteen colonies still occupied by British troops.

New England was primed for war by December 1774, the month when patriots seized munitions and ordnance from forts in New Hampshire and Rhode Island. British Colonel Leslie's late February march to Salem to seize cannon, more than six weeks before Lexington and Concord on April 19, could have been the precipitating action. So could the encounters near Assonet on the Rhode Island border on April 9–10. In Boston, meanwhile, the British commander General Gage continued to fortify Boston Neck.

The Maritime Face of Urban America, 1775

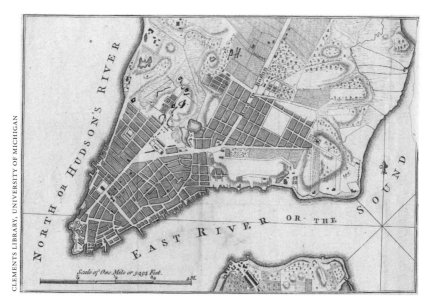

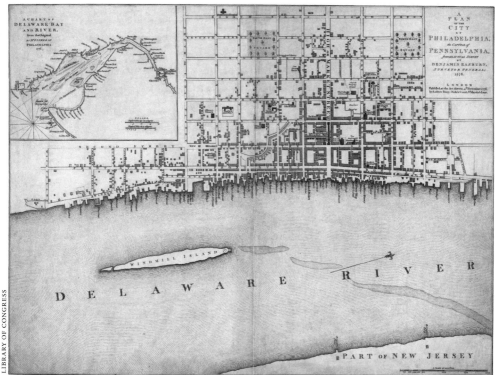

If islandlike Boston was the most maritime of American cities, New York, Philadelphia, and Charleston also had important maritime and shipbuilding enterprises and populations. These maps show how New York City and Philadelphia were dominated by extended waterfronts, which helps explain why seamen figured so prominently in urban political demonstrations and riots.

The Nearness and Psychological Impact of the Battle on Bunker Hill

Engraved for BARNARD's *New Complete & Authentic* HISTORY *of* ENGLAND.

CHARLES TOWN

BOSTON

View *of The* ATTACK *on* BUNKER'S HILL, *with the* Burning *of* CHARLES TOWN, *June 17, 1775.*

Drawn by M.ͬ Millar · *Engraved by Lodge*

The Battle of Bunker Hill was actually fought on Breed's Hill, roughly a third of a mile across the river from watchers in Boston. When Patriots fortified that hill in June in a single night of massive exertion, the result was a such in-your-face challenge to the proud British regiments still smarting from April's ignominious retreat from Concord that they attacked the next day by marching up the hill in formation instead of by a flanking attack. The result was so bloody that one quarter of the British officers killed and wounded during the Revolution met that fate on June 17, 1775. The Patriots retreated only after the third attack, when they ran out of ammunition. General Howe, the British commander, was so moved—all of his aides were killed or wounded around him—that he was wary ever after of attacking entrenched American positions. Not a few of the Patriot civilian onlookers were traumatized by the slaughter. The daughter of the Connecticut governor Jonathan Trumbull, whose husband commanded a Connecticut regiment, sickened and died weeks later after watching the battle.

The Fighting Begins in Virginia

Lord Dunmore, the royal governor, fled to the safety of HMS *Fowey* on June 8, and by summer naval vessels and men under his command began raiding the plantations of Patriots along nearby southeastern Virginia rivers. In September, Patriots acting through Virginia's Third Convention named fiery speechmaker Patrick Henry to command the province's Army of Observation, but most of the fighting would be done by Colonel William Woodford of the Second Regiment. In the defense of Hampton (October) and victory of Great Bridge (December), sharpshooters of the Culpeper County minutemen were especially successful.

The Provincial Navies

COURTESY OF MACHIAS, MAINE, SAVINGS AND LOAN

COURTESY OF CONTINENTAL DISTILLERS

Besides Connecticut and Rhode Island, Massachusetts and Pennsylvania also launched provincial navies that summer. In June, the British schooner *Margaretta* was captured by the American *Unity* near Machias, in what is now Maine. The *Unity*, renamed the *Machias Liberty*, soon became the first vessel in the Massachusetts Provincial Navy. Pennsylvania soon established a provincial navy made up of a dozen row galleys to protect the Delaware River's approaches to Philadelphia.

By the KING,

A PROCLAMATION,

For fuppreffing Rebellion and Sedition.

GEORGE R.

WHEREAS many of Our Subjects in divers Parts of Our Colonies and Plantations in *North America*, misled by dangerous and ill-designing Men, and forgetting the Allegiance which they owe to the Power that has protected and sustained them, after various disorderly Acts committed in Disturbance of the Publick Peace, to the Obstruction of lawful Commerce, and to the Oppression of Our loyal Subjects carrying on the same, have at length proceeded to an open and avowed Rebellion, by arraying themselves in hostile Manner to withstand the Execution of the Law, and traitorously preparing, ordering, and levying War against Us ; And whereas there is Reason to apprehend that such Rebellion hath been much promoted and encouraged by the traitorous Correspondence, Counsels, and Comfort of divers wicked and desperate Persons within this Realm : To the End therefore that none of Our Subjects may neglect or violate their Duty through Ignorance thereof, or through any Doubt of the Protection which the Law will afford to their Loyalty and Zeal ; We have thought fit, by and with the Advice of Our Privy Council, to issue this Our Royal Proclamation, hereby declaring that not only all Our Officers Civil and Military are obliged to exert their utmost Endeavours to suppress such Rebellion, and to bring the Traitors to Justice ; but that all Our Subjects of this Realm and the Dominions thereunto belonging are bound by Law to be aiding and assisting in the Suppression of such Rebellion, and to disclose and make known all traitorous Conspiracies and Attempts against Us, Our Crown and Dignity ; And We do accordingly strictly charge and command all Our Officers as well Civil as Military, and all other Our obedient and loyal Subjects, to use their utmost Endeavours to withstand and suppress such Rebellion, and to disclose and make known all Treasons and traitorous Conspiracies which they shall know to be against Us, Our Crown and Dignity ; and for that Purpose, that they transmit to One of Our Principal Secretaries of State, or other proper Officer, due and full Information of all Persons who shall be found carrying on Correspondence with, or in any Manner or Degree aiding or abetting the Persons now in open Arms and Rebellion against Our Government within any of Our Colonies and Plantations in *North America*, in order to bring to condign Punishment the Authors, Perpetrators and Abettors of such traitorous Designs.

Given at Our Court at St. *James*'s, the Twenty-third Day of *August*, One thousand seven hundred and seventy-five, in the Fifteenth Year of Our Reign.

God save the King.

Even before Lexington and Concord, Parliament had curbed the commerce and fishing rights of the New England colonies, New Jersey, Pennsylvania, Maryland, Virginia, and South Carolina. Then in August, all thirteen colonies were declared in rebellion by royal proclamation.

The Political Cartoon for the Year 1775

A small but important minority in Parliament and the London press favored or often supported the American rebels. This "Political Cartoon for the Year 1775," published in London's *Westminster Magazine*, showed King George in a carriage drawn by Pride and Obstinacy and driven by Scots riding over the Magna Carta and the Constitution into the abyss of conflict with America. Lord North and several Anglican bishops are watching, and First Lord of the Admiralty Sandwich, famous for his lechery, is hiring a young prostitute.

Connecticut, the War Office, and the War

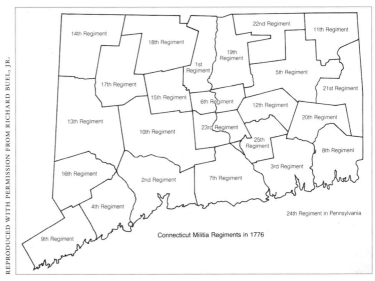

14th Regiment 18th Regiment 22nd Regiment 11th Regiment
19th Regiment
1st Regiment
5th Regiment
17th Regiment 15th Regiment 21st Regiment
6th Regiment 12th Regiment
13th Regiment 10th Regiment 20th Regiment
23rd Regiment
25th Regiment 8th Regiment
16th Regiment 2nd Regiment 7th Regiment 3rd Regiment
4th Regiment 24th Regiment in Pennsylvania
9th Regiment Connecticut Militia Regiments in 1776

When war broke out in 1775, Connecticut's governor, Jonathan Trumbull, had already held his office six years and was infamous in London as the "rebel governor." Not only was Trumbull immediately able to muster the province's full force and treasury on the Patriot side, but Connecticut legislators voted him an unusual authority to conduct the war from a safely located war office on his own property in Lebanon, Connecticut (above, right). During the eight years of war, it was visited by men ranging from George Washington to General Rochambeau, the French commander, and Benjamin Franklin. By 1775, Connecticut's twenty-four army regiments were already organized as shown in the map.

War Along the New England Coast

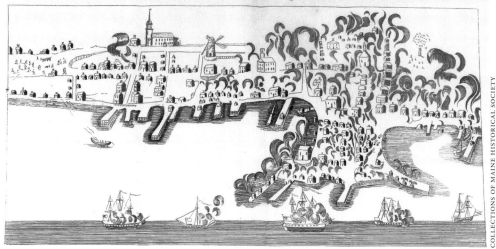

THE TOWN of FALMOUTH, *Burnt by Captain* MOET, Oct.ʰ 18 1775.

By August, the Royal Navy was preparing to burn troublesome New England seaports, and Falmouth (now Portland, Maine) was bombarded and set afire in October. That same month, the British sloop *Nautilus* chased the American schooner *Hannah*, under contract to General Washington and the Continental Army, into the harbor of Beverly, Massachusetts, but was driven off by fire from shore.

Some Soldiers of 1775

In July 1775, George Washington took over command of the Patriot forces besieging Boston from Major General Artemas Ward of Massachussets, shown with him in the painting. The cavalryman pictured above is a trooper of the Philadelphia Light Horse.

The Invasion of Canada

Planning for the invasion of Canada began in Boston well before Lexington and Concord. On May 18, Benedict Arnold briefly seized Canadian fort St. Jean, just north of Lake Champlain, and he simultaneously captured the only British vessel on the lake, making a southward invasion impossible until the British built new ships. The captured vessel, shown above, was named *Enterprise*. Canada could have fallen in November, but Patriot forces were fatally delayed and failed in their December 31 attempt to capture Quebec. The repulse of the Americans at Sault au Matelot was part of the December 31 defeat.

The Patriots' Leading Indian Allies of 1775

Three tribes stood out: the Stockbridge of Massachussets (above, left), who had their own militia company and served in the siege of Boston; the Oneida of central New York, who argued the Patriot cause within the Iroquois confederacy; and the Catawba of South Carolina, who fought alongside regular South Carolina forces in several late-1775 actions. The statue pictured shows Chief Skenandoah of the Oneida with George Washington. The painting of soldiers of South Carolina's 3rd regiment in 1778 shows a Catawba brave and "men of color" who also served.

The First Battles in the South, 1775

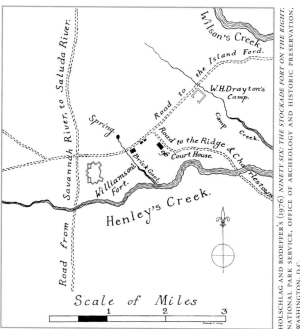

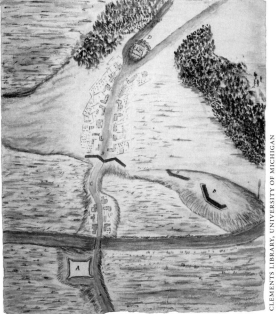

One map located the first battle of Ninety Six (November) in the South Carolina backcountry, where Whig and Tory partisans fought over what history remembers as Williamson's Fort. It was the first battle in South Carolina to involve fatalities. The first land battle in Virginia took place on December 9 at Great Bridge, a dozen miles south of Norfolk. Crown forces, including a company of British regulars, were cut to pieces as they tried to cross the bridge (lower center in the drawing) under fire from frontier riflemen.

Philadelphia: The Navy and Marines Go to Sea

The first recruits for what became the U.S. Marine Corps were recruited in Philadelphia during December 1775, and that same month saw Lieutenant John Paul Jones raise the Continental flag over the *Alfred*, the designated flagship of the new American Navy, also in Philadelphia.

Henry Knox Hauls the Captured Cannon from Ticonderoga and Crown Point over the Mountains to the Siege of Boston

Besides his great need for gunpowder in late 1775, George Washington desperately required large cannon to position on the heights surrounding Boston to drive out the British army. The most obvious were those captured at Fort Ticonderoga and Crown Point back in May, and on October 23, Congress authorized Washington to bring them to Cambridge. His new artillery colonel, Henry Knox, thought he could manage the task. On December 5, Knox reached Ticonderoga, and chose 43 cannon and 16 mortars. Sleds and 160 oxen were to provide the transportation, and the needed blanket of snow—two feet of it—arrived on Christmas Eve. By late January, the ordnance reached Cambridge.

month. In July 1776, they would stop, worried now that such a road might only benefit the British forces poised to march south.

Oswego and Niagara: The Western Route

In New York's Mohawk Valley, Colonel Guy Johnson became superintendent of the Northern Indian Department in July 1774, following the sudden death of his legendary uncle, Sir William Johnson. But less than a year later, burgeoning rebel sentiment in the valley forced Guy Johnson to flee. On May 31, after a warning by General Gage that he was likely to be seized and held, Johnson gathered his closest advisers and several hundred Tories and Mohawk Indians and fled west up the valley.

This was the western route to Canada—along the Mohawk River and some lesser waterways to Lake Ontario, and then north along the St. Lawrence to Montreal and Quebec. In Johnson's case, as circumstances in Canada clouded, he and his principal advisers took ship from Montreal to London.

The western passageways had not been prominent until the 1740s when Anglo-French combat in North America intensified around the Forks of the Ohio and the Great Lakes. But after defeating France, Britain closed many old forts. By the beginning of 1775, only five posts were manned—Oswegatchie (New York), Niagara (New York), Detroit (Michigan), Michilimackinac (Michigan), and Kaskaskia (Illinois). Between them, they housed just eight companies of the Eighth Regiment. In command was Lieutenant Colonel John Caldwell, who had four of these companies stationed with him at Niagara—the old French stone fort where the Niagara River empties into Lake Ontario.[42]

These were not good months for British Canada or for the Northern Indian Department. Johnson's flight had left Colonel Caldwell as the ranking king's officer on the New York and Great Lakes frontier. In late summer, as the rebel armies prepared to cross into Canada, the Indians—including some of the usually pro-British Iroquois—pursued better relations with the colonists and met with Patriot emissaries. With Johnson gone, the Northern Indian Department was a shambles. An apprehensive Caldwell, with only 200 to 300 soldiers, had to keep watch in several different directions.[43]

Just 200 miles from Niagara, the region at the Forks of the Ohio was claimed by both Virginia and Pennsylvania. The collapse of royal authority quickly weakened both Johnson's Indian Department deputy, Alexander

McKee, and Lord Dunmore's local representative, John Connolly. From May 1775 into 1776, power in Pittsburgh rested with a Committee of Safety dominated by Patriot-faction Virginians, who eyed Niagara. In June 1775, Caldwell had conveyed to Carleton his fear of "the Virginians [at Pittsburgh] making an attempt on Fort Erie," an outpost of Fort Niagara on the Lake Erie side of the 30-mile portage and waterway. Later that summer, Caldwell felt obliged to promise support to the Seneca tribe should the Virginians march north.[44]

The Virginians never came, but a second threat to Niagara lay to the east. In November, after General Richard Montgomery's army of New Yorkers and New Englanders had taken Montreal, the general queried which as-yet-uncaptured forts held the largest trove of badly needed cannon and munitions. Quebec led the list, but Niagara was thought to rank next, and he suggested that it might be a worthwhile campaign for Congress's armies.[45] Early in 1776 General Schuyler, the New York theater commander, weighed an attack on Niagara but decided that a march through Iroquois territory would be too risky. The Indian Department now had an agent in Niagara, John Butler, who kept warning the tribes: New England soldiers would come from the east and Virginians from the south to reduce Niagara and "immediately fall upon the Six Nations and extirpate them from the Earth."[46]

Besides Guy Johnson, another important British officer took the western back door to Canada. Colonel Allan Maclean of the Royal Highland Emigrants Regiment reached Montreal in late August by way of Oswego. As we will see, some Canadian historians give Maclean, not Carleton, the credit for keeping Quebec out of American hands.[47]

The American defeat before Quebec in December 1775 did not clearly end the danger to Niagara, but the American retreat from Quebec did represent a watershed. By the summer of 1776, Patriot talk about attacking Niagara, Quebec, or Halifax, if not absurd, would not regain plausibility until the French alliance of 1778 reopened the issue of a Canadian invasion on a new dimension. Chronicles of 1776 can scoff at the initial American attempt, but as Chapter 21 will pursue, the facts and events of 1775 tell a much more complicated tale, in which early British overconcentration in Canada worked against the Crown's victory prospects elsewhere.

CHAPTER II

The Global Munitions Struggle, 1774–1776

What was terrifying [in 1775] was the picture of an America fighting with no weapons . . . the country was as naked and defenseless as a shucked oyster. The colonies were in the nightmare situation of trying to fight the strongest nation in Europe almost barehanded . . . The crying need was for gunpowder. There had been a few powder mills in the country, but they were long out of use.

Helen Augur, *The Secret War of Independence*, 1955

The French government under Louis XVI secretly provided great quantities of critical assistance to the American revolutionaries. They smuggled gunpowder, thousands of muskets and flints, cannon, cannonballs, large quantities of military equipment, boots, medical equipment and even French officers trained in the construction of fortifications . . . Without help from the French, the colonists could not have stood up to the British army.

James M. Potts, *French Covert Action in the American Revolution*, 2005

The wars fought by the United States have been a display case of the nation's ascending capacity for explosives production. The weight of shells fired during the American Civil War set a global record. In World War I, U.S. munitions makers became essential suppliers to Europe. World War II made the United States into "the arsenal of democracy." The atomic megatonnage of Hiroshima crowned American explosive technology. By the twenty-first century, the American military had come to think of itself in war-god-like terms, able to hurl unmatchable thunderbolts.

Not so in 1775. The Revolution began in circumstances remote from Jupiter's realm, better resembling the biblical David clutching his mere slingshot and a few stones. The reality of munitions in Patriot North America that year was one of woeful shortage.

To convince the king and his ministers that the disaffected colonies were willing and able to fight, the potential rebels had to possess cannon and gunpowder in serious quantities. At the time of the Coercive Acts, they did not, as official London knew. In July 1773, Lord Dartmouth had sent a circular letter to North American and West Indian governors requesting information about provincial trade and military supplies on hand.[1]

Few surprises turned up. Ancient muskets and fowling pieces the mainland colonists had aplenty, but these fired every conceivable caliber of bullet—a major handicap for any organized force in a time of war. Some old cannon were on hand in provincial arsenals. So were old "Brown Bess" British Army muskets—named for the unusual hue imparted as their barrels oxidized—left from the French and frontier wars of the 1740s and 1750s. Several thousand specially made rifles, most fashioned by Pennsylvania German craftsmen, gave many Appalachian borderers their reputation for marksmanship. But such weapons were scarce in New England militia units.

As for gunpowder, mainland governors had generally reported little on hand. Powder stocks left from earlier wars had shrunk, not just from usage and spoilage. As popular political unrest mounted in the 1760s, wary royal officials had sold off quantities. Massachusetts had switched to smaller cannon using lesser charges for ceremonial salutes; New Hampshire, by its official count, had only four ounces of powder for each militiaman, and muskets for just one in four.[2]

Most of the cannon, mortars, and ordinary muskets in America, coming from Britain and the European Continent, had been shipped by the Crown during earlier wars. Little gunpowder was produced in the thirteen colonies, and the handful of wartime mills was in ruins. The first contract for North American–made muskets, some 500 during the 1740s, had been fulfilled by Hugh Orr of Bridgewater, Massachusetts, and both the Bay Colony and Connecticut could claim some experience in gunsmithing.[3] In October 1774, the Massachusetts Provincial Congress declared its preference for rearming with locally made muskets. But that pretense dissolved amid the great needs of 1775.

Washington's Gunpowder Crisis

Despite six to eight months of preparation, the ammunition consumed in the Lexington-Concord fighting left Massachusetts authorities with only 82 half barrels in late April. To rebuild its depleted store, the Committee of Safety asked the province's hundred-odd townships for 68 barrels, and some were forthcoming. Even so, by early June, two weeks before Bunker Hill, Artemas Ward, the colony's senior general, worried that Massachusetts would "for want of the means of defense, fall at last a prey to our enemies."[4]

As May's capture of the forts at Ticonderoga and Crown Point escalated into late June's tentative commitment to invade Canada, Patriot focus on gunpowder and small arms only intensified. If on one hand the invasion required arms and ammunition to proceed, by late summer and autumn congressional and military leaders were also viewing major Canadian forts and citadels as potential munitions sources. Washington, after taking command in July, had to guard his own comments lest the army's shortage become common gossip, but by winter he was writing to General Montgomery in Canada "to supply [arms] from the King's Stores in Quebec."[5]

Fears were certainly in order. In late 1774, the future United States had to begin the equivalent of a munitions and armaments race *in utero,* so to speak, in order to survive and emerge politically and legally. Much of the extended year 1775 involves the story of that quest, abetted by French, Spanish, and Dutch officials, diplomats, and merchants.

From the start, the would-be rebels principally depended on shipments from Britain's major political and maritime rivals—nations convinced that a too-arrogant United Kingdom could best be humbled by encouraging the revolt of her North American colonies. Just as mercantilist thinking influenced the British government in squeezing the thirteen colonies, similar tenets encouraged France, Spain, Holland, and others to overestimate the importance of the thirteen. They exaggerated their own chances to profit should the colonies be detached from Britain's commercial and political orbit.

No map or illustration can convey the gunpowder shortage or its importance. However, General Washington's storied speechlessness can help. In early August 1775, when given a drastically reduced figure of powder on hand for the army besieging Boston, he was literally shocked into silence.

Brigadier General John Sullivan of New Hampshire, penning a plea to his province's Committee of Safety to speed 20 barrels, confided that "the General was so struck that he did not utter a word for half an hour."[6]

In July, Washington's first report to Congress had complained, with respect to powder, that "we are so exceedingly destitute that our artillery will be of little use without a supply both large and seasonable. What we have must be reserved for the small arms, and that managed with the utmost frugality." His speechless half hour came after being told that the main magazine in Cambridge held 38 barrels, not 300. Two days later he wrote to John Hancock that the powder in Massachusetts, together with the stocks of New Hampshire, Rhode Island, and Connecticut, totaled only five tons, or roughly nine cartridges per man. By the end of August, although supplies had grown, all of Washington's cannon had gone quiet, except for a small nine-pounder on Prospect Hill, near the new British emplacements west of Bunker Hill.[7]

Despite shipments from Philadelphia, the Chesapeake, and South Carolina, the dearth continued. In December, Washington advised Congress that "our Want of Powder is inconceivable," and in January the army's magazine in Cambridge was all but empty. These months were doubly tense because of a simultaneous crisis of expiring short-term enlistments and the imperative of replacing them with new recruits. In February 1776, he confided to Connecticut governor Trumbull that "I am so restrained in all my Military movements that it is impossible to undertake anything effectual."[8] Lack of powder, for example, kept the general from taking advantage of temperatures bitter enough to offer a firm pathway of thick ice over which the British could be attacked in Boston. In late February, Trumbull sent two tons more, which almost doubled 100 barrels on hand.[9]

Hard as it is to credit that British agents were uniformly gulled, the new commander in Boston, General Howe, never saw—or never took advantage of—any opportunity to attack. Looking back months later, Washington marveled "whether a case similar to ours is to be found: to wit, to maintain a post against the flower of the British troops for six months altogether, without powder, and at the end to have one army disbanded and another raised within the same distance of the reinforced enemy."[10] A fair boast, all in all.

The commanding general masterminded much of the propaganda and disinformation. During that perilous summer of 1775, he leaked word of having 1,800 barrels of powder, insinuating that overabundance explained his order that soldiers stop their random firing because it "elicited the ridicule of the enemy" and disrupted the camp with false alarms."[11] In fact, wasteful firing by citizen soldiers remained a major frustration.

A visitor from Rhode Island who delivered powder to Cambridge in November later recalled another deception. The magazine's supervising officer confided that the barrels were filled with sand to "deceive the enemy should any spy by chance look in."[12] That winter the British intercepted a deceptive "letter" alleging that powder, saltpeter, and small arms were flowing into Washington's camp. Women were finding it "as easy to make Salt Petre as to make soft soap."[13] Somehow, it all succeeded.

Through mid-1775, though, it must be underscored that Congress—convening on May 10 and adjourning on August 2—enjoyed relatively little control over Patriot supplies of powder and arms. The bulk was being captured or imported by individual merchants and by provincial committees of safety. It was not Congress's to allocate. Washington was inhibited by the same slow cobbling together of authority. As one chronicler mused, "There was a tremendous shuttling back and forth of what supplies were available. One colony would lend another a few wagonloads of ammunition to meet an expected danger. Congress would now exact a tribute from a colony in order to supply Washington, and the next day rob Washington to help out a seaport town in great peril."[14]

Fortunately for the future United States, the contest was assuming global dimensions. Patriot regimes or committees in Rhode Island, Connecticut, and South Carolina were among the first to commission private merchant vessels to buy powder in the West Indies or to capture British supply ships. On a grander scale, French, Dutch, and Spanish merchants had begun shipping large quantities of munitions from their own seaports to their Caribbean colonies—French Martinique and Saint-Domingue, Dutch St. Eustatius, and Spanish Santo Domingo—for sale to resident or visiting North American traders and ship captains. In other cases, devious American owners put their vessels under French or Dutch captains with crews and false papers to match in order to thwart the Royal Navy. In mid-1775, Lord Suffolk, one of Britain's principal secretaries of state, commented that "an extensive, illicit and dangerous commerce is carrying on by vessels belong to His Majesty's Colonies under Foreign Colors."[15]

These enterprising Patriots, some with smuggling and privateering skills honed in the French wars, typically retained a sizable amount of powder to arm their own schooners, brigs, and sloops. Local committees of safety, in turn, often insisted that purchased powder and small cannon be brought back to defend threatened home ports and harbors. Of course, where the voyage was entirely private, not a few of the powder barrels were trundled into Yankee, Philadelphia, or Charleston warehouses in anticipation of nothing more patriotic than rising prices. With General Washington obliged to support a large army, this was not an ideal distribution system. Not until September 1775, when the Second Continental Congress set up its Secret Committee and gave it authority and funds to make procurement contracts with reliable merchants, did a better percentage of arms and munitions start flowing directly to Washington's forces.

Want of powder frequently curtailed or denied success on the battlefield. Facing the third British wave on Bunker Hill, running out of ammunition obliged the New England defenders to retreat from their central redoubt. Less obviously, insufficient ammunition forced George Washington to reject most of the propositions made that summer and autumn for tightening the Patriots' tenuous noose around Boston. Inactivity and boredom, in turn, contributed to the encircling army's considerable rate of desertion and soldiers' tendencies to "go home." In August, as New England troops and some New York units collected at the northern end of the Hudson Valley to invade Canada, New York authorities had little ammunition. Only a month earlier their provincial congress had pleaded to Congress: "We have no arms, we have no powder, we have no blankets. For God's sake, send us money, send us arms, send us ammunition."[16]

After the main American army under Montgomery crossed into Canada in early September, the principal British strongpoint blocking its way—Fort St. John on the Richelieu River—held out for eight weeks, causing a near-fatal delay. Cannon and mortars from Ticonderoga and Crown Point, powerful enough to compel its surrender, did not arrive until October 15. Ammunition remained in short supply. Richard Smith, a Massachusetts delegate, described the dispatches Congress received in November: "Arnold is near Quebec, but has not enough men to surround it and his powder so damaged that he has only 5 Rounds apiece."[17] When Arnold arrived before Quebec in November, lack of enough ammunition to confront a rumored sally by British defenders obliged him to retreat toward Montreal and await help and supplies.[18]

By the spring of 1776, as we will see, the arrival of artillery, muskets, and ammunition from France was accelerating, as were sub rosa political commitments from the French foreign ministry. However, insufficient ammunition would undercut Patriot forces, although not critically, in one more major battle: Britain's ill-starred attempt to capture Charleston, South Carolina. On June 28, during the Royal Navy's bombardment of Fort Sullivan, the uncompleted palmetto-wood bastion controlling the entrance to Charleston's harbor, American defenders again almost ran out of powder. At two P.M. the fort's fire slackened, and at three its guns went silent for an hour. All in all, the Americans had used 4,766 pounds of powder, while the attacking Royal Navy had drawn 34,000 pounds from its abundant supply. Colonel Moultrie, commanding the fort, opined that if rebel powder had been adequate, the damaged British ships would have had to strike their colors.[19]

Although both sides made many mistakes during 1774 and 1775, neither underestimated the central role of ammunition. Adapting a term from Christian theology, Samuel Adams candidly proclaimed gunpowder as the *unum necessarium*—the one thing needful. His cousin John may have introduced the cachet in a September 1775 letter that discussed the saltpeter production getting under way in Connecticut, Philadelphia, and Virginia.[20] Irreverent or not, the term was certainly apt.

By the second half of 1775, the stark need for powder had forced decision makers to abandon the previous autumn's abstractions about nonimportation and nonexportation. Exceptions had to be made on both counts. To pay for vital imported munitions, armaments, and medicines (but virtually nothing else), Congress decided to export the commodities and products in the greatest demand—tobacco, indigo, rice, food, barrels, and staves. These arrangements will be amplified shortly.

Harking back in 1776, John Hancock cited the unpreparedness in gunpowder to prove that Americans back in 1775 had not contemplated independence. That was not quite true. Only days before the official British closure of the port of Boston on June 1, 1774, merchant Hancock ordered his own vessels to clear for London. His most trusted captain, James Scott, was sent word to return with a cargo of gunpowder. This Scott did, dropping anchor in Salem on September 30.[21]

By September 1774, Hancock and Captain Scott, as both doubtless knew, were only two players in a game involving hundreds, perhaps thousands.

Europe: The Gunpowder Plots Thicken

That hectic summer of 1774 proved to be the turning point. Upon hearing in May that Parliament was closing down their port, Bostonians urged the other colonies to join a protest by suspending their own trade with Britain. Although such precipitous action was rejected, both maritime New England and the tobacco provinces conducted a broad public debate, filling June, July, and August with generally supportive letters, meetings, and extralegal conventions. Cabals of merchants, smugglers, ship captains, maritime lawyers, rum distillers, and traders to the West Indies and southern Europe—veterans of earlier boycotts prominent among them—doubtless began to plot in taverns, meeting rooms, and exchanges up and down the Atlantic coast. A dozen major New England, New York, and Philadelphia merchant firms already had commercial agents in England, Ireland, Holland, and France and in Iberian ports like Bilbao, San Sebastián, Lisbon, and Cádiz. Gunpowder would have been a frequent topic of discussion.

Benjamin Franklin, in London before heading home in March 1775, was among his several employments the designated London agent of Massachusetts, hardly a low-profile post. He may have made clandestine arrangements with visiting American ship captains, as well as friendly merchants in Amsterdam, Nantes, and Bilbao. Researchers concur that there is no record, either in Franklin's writings or in the documents of various governments. But should we expect documents? During these months, when British officials talked openly of transporting to London for trial such Patriot leaders as Hancock and Samuel Adams, the author of *Poor Richard's Almanac* was already resident in the imperial capital. His home at 36 Craven Street was only a few hundred yards from Whitehall.

Certainly Franklin was both active and careful once back in Philadelphia. Named to the Secret Committee launched by Congress in the autumn of 1775, he left few tracks there. The Continental Congress itself deliberated behind closed doors, and the Secret Committee was even more inscrutable. It routinely withheld information from the parent body and later burned its own records. Indeed, when Franklin sailed back to France in December 1776, there is little record of what he did or said during his visit to Nantes, a seaport front and center in early Patriot gunpowder machinations.

Many years later, as World War I reinvolved Americans with European alliances and the lucre of international trading in armaments and munitions, some historians revisited the events of 1773–1783. These eighteenth-century relationships—and the mixture of motivations guiding both France and America—had become eerily relevant again. Between 1915 and 1935, historians like Edward Corwin, Samuel Flagg Bemis, and Elizabeth S. Kite all penned realpolitik-flavored evaluations, which deserve an explanatory note.[22]

Popular perceptions in America, though, were molded by the Francophile hoopla surrounding the U.S. war entry in 1917. The most famous example was General John J. Pershing's salute "Lafayette, we are here" upon arrival in Paris. In fact, the American Expeditionary Force commander could have more realistically hailed Charles Gravier, Comte de Vergennes. It was he who started a cautious, sophisticated discussion of French aid to America and revenge on Britain mere months after assuming the post of foreign minister in June 1774.

American understanding, though, has been muddled. Just as an idealistic United States supposedly entered the First World War to repay France for its help in 1776 and 1777 (and to make the world safe for democracy), the motivations in France a century and a half earlier are sometimes said to have arisen out of idealism and liberal ideology. The French, if one follows this interpretation, acted on motivations akin to the romantic, pro-American comments voiced by the French playwright Caron de Beaumarchais, whose comedies—*The Barber of Seville* (1775) and *The Marriage of Figaro* (1784)—mocked European aristocracy. Even before he became the public "face" of French arms and ammunition shipments to America, Beaumarchais had enthused over the republican and democratic principles arising in the new world. Vergennes, a subtle diplomat, approved of casting French motivation in the Beaumarchais (and later Lafayette) mold because he understood that Americans would return their deepest gratitude for seeming empathy and admiration.[23]

This is not to doubt Beaumarchais's relative sincerity and great importance. And because 1776 was the launch year of his public orchestration and delivery of French munitions and war stores through the government-sponsored Roderigue Hortalez et Cie, the seeming chronology also permits uncomplicated history. In fact, during 1774 and 1775, the playwright had been an agent for Louis XVI and Vergennes on other projects; his attention to powder and arms questions began in the summer of 1775. Some believe that his munitions machinations began in Flanders in 1774.[24]

The munitions trade was substantial in 1774, its great growth over three centuries a perverse tribute to the steady escalation of European-centered wars, progress in technology, the ballooning African slave trade, and the spread of high-stakes warfare into the Americas. Leading nations generally encouraged gunpowder mills, although the most sophisticated, finest-grained product came from France. The advanced metallurgy essential to casting fine cannon and small arms concentrated in northern and eastern France, the southern part of present-day Germany, the Belgian and Dutch upcountry, and Sweden. Deposits of iron, water power, and forests for charcoal all determined location, as did proximity to Europe's great battlegrounds and warrior nations. No commentator of the period coined a sweeping label like the "merchants of death" tag hung on international arms dealers after World War I. Still, lucrative 300 and 400 percent markups could be had on a 100-barrel powder shipment wending its illicit way from Amsterdam through Martinique or St. Eustatius to a Yankee Doodle welcome in some remote North American estuary.

A few particulars stand out. Traffic between Nantes, the burgeoning French port and slave trade center, and English North America had been rising during the 1770s. More and more commercial agents from the thirteen colonies were taking up posts in western European and Caribbean seaports. And the intensity of French *revanche*—court and ministerial ardor to see England eat humble pie—since 1763 might have been unmatched since the aftermath of Agincourt in 1415.

Seventeen seventy-four furnished two vital catalysts. The first was London's seemingly irretrievable alienation of its North American colonies through spring's Coercive Acts. The second, in France, was the death of King Louis XV and the succession in May of his youthful, inexperienced grandson, Louis XVI. The new ruler quickly named a new foreign minister, Vergennes, who believed that the time for reversing Britain's 1763 gains might be at hand. Opposition Whigs in the British Parliament and insurgents in the American colonies baited Lord North's regime with this same speculation: Do not the French and Spanish already see a unique opportunity to profit from aiding the rebels? Benjamin Franklin, Edmund Burke, and William Pitt, now Lord Chatham, all dwelled on the likelihood.

By the late summer of 1774, French envoys and agents began to report a growing arms traffic to America. British ministers, generals, and admirals were receiving and penning similar accounts, notably including the recently appointed army and navy commanders. General Gage warned London that colonists were "sending to Europe for all kinds of military stores," while Admiral Graves forwarded somewhat greater detail to the Admiralty in four August and September letters.[25]

In early August Sir Joseph Yorke, the British ambassador to the Dutch Republic, reported home that a Massachusetts vessel, the *Polly,* was loading powder in Amsterdam. Three weeks later Yorke put the proposed cargo at 300,000 pounds—150 tons. Besides which, the overall flow of arms and gunpowder from Holland to St. Eustatius and America was increasing rapidly. Between January and September 1774, some 5,000 chests of bohea tea had been shipped to America, with some of the chests assumed to contain gunpowder.[26] The Admiralty sent the sloop *Speedwell* and the cutter *Greyhound* to keep watch off Holland, and Dutch activities were part of what persuaded the Privy Council to act on October 19 and the Admiralty to follow up.

The watch over Amsterdam's seaward access by the two warships kept the *Polly* in Holland that winter and inhibited another locally berthed American sloop, the *Nancy,* with a prior record of carrying powder for New York merchants. The *Speedwell*'s captain further advised his superiors that two Boston agents, Wallace and Dunbar, had spent the winter of 1774–1775 in Amsterdam buying arms and munitions.[27] This quasiblockade by the Royal Navy soon had Dutch merchants opting instead for transshipment through Portugal.

In January, they sent to Lisbon a vessel with 200 barrels of gunpowder and 1,000 muskets. Five hundred chests of arms soon followed. When the brig *Betsy,* Boston owned, arrived in Holland with an illicit shipment of rice, it, too, was routed to Portugal to pick up the desired military stores.[28] British officials had grounds for suspicion. During the first three months of 1774, only 22 British and North American vessels had cleared from Lisbon; during the first three months of 1775, five times as many did so.[29]

Further detail on the routing of Dutch munitions came from New York's acting governor, Cadwallader Colden. In November 1774 he wrote to Lord Dartmouth that "the contraband trade carried on between this place and Holland prevails to an enormous degree, and has in every respect the worst possible effects. The vessels from Holland and St. Eustatia do not come into this port, but anchor at some distance in the numerous bays or creeks that our coast and rivers furnish, from whence the contraband goods are sent up in small boats. Dutch gunpowder has been in use in this colony ever since I came into it. How it was formerly imported I know not. I make no doubt that all we have now is brought in clandestinely."[30]

Even so, some thought the flow of supplies from France was as large or larger. Helen Augur, whose controversial volume *The Secret War of Independence* was an evidentiary breakthrough in 1955, wrote that "by 1774 Vergennes was allowing every sort of illicit trade with the Americans in French ports. But he was such a master of dissimulation that the British embassy in Versailles was kept guessing about the real situation all during that year. At some early period the French ministry also began giving subsidies to French merchants active in smuggling out war supplies for the Americans."[31] Little of this has been precisely documented, but during a period in 1775 in which Lord Stormont, the somewhat gullible British ambassador in France, was absent, his second in charge ventured more candor, estimating that between mid-1774 and mid-1775, France had already furnished the Americans with war supplies worth roughly 32 million livres or 6 million dollars. Some of the matériel had entered through the minor port of York in the district of Maine.[32]

Some observers also questioned the primacy of St. Eustatius, the famed "Golden Rock" of the Caribbean. British Admiral George Rodney, who captured the island in 1781, growled that "this rock . . . has alone supported the infamous American rebellion." However, reports to London from the British embassies in France, Spain, Portugal, and Holland identified more Dutch powder reaching America from French and Spanish ports, at least by 1776. From Amsterdam, it traveled in French holds to Nantes and Bordeaux, and in Dutch vessels to the Spanish ports Bilbao and Santander.[33] Although these ports were where French historian Henri Doniol identified Benjamin Franklin as having secretly made contacts in 1774–1775, dozens of other merchants also had friends and acquaintances there.

Marblehead, for example, had been a dominant supplier of prime codfish to Spanish Bilbao since the late seventeenth century. The American-connected firm in Bilbao was Gardoqui and Company, whose patriarch, Joseph Gardoqui, was a longtime friend of Patriot merchant Jeremiah Lee's, who named one of his vessels for Gardoqui. Lee was also colonel of the Marblehead militia and active with the Massachusetts Committee on Supplies. On February 15, 1775, Gardoqui wrote to Lee pledging support and whatever information came to his attention.[34]

Nantes, for its part, was enough of a commercial and political hotbed to attract both of the Philadelphians who soon dominated the Congress's Secret Committee: Franklin and Robert Morris. The latter named his half brother Thomas as a congressional agent there in 1776, and Franklin inserted his grandnephew Jonathan Williams. In 1774, a Nantes firm bought five brigs from Dutch makers and gave them names including *Boston, Iroquois,* and *L'Américain*.[35] They may well have run war supplies to

York, on a Maine coast that French mariners knew well from mid-eighteenth-century wars.

Not coincidentally, Nantes was a port in which gunpowder and armaments were readily available through a connection at odds with freedom and liberty—the transatlantic slave trade. British slave traders operated from Liverpool, but Nantes played that lucrative role in France. The vessels involved were better armed than most merchantmen, and gunpowder—along with Yankee rum—was one of the most-desired commodities in West African slave ports from Senegal and Gambia south to Angola. Nantes accordingly had large quantities of arms and powders, but the quantities available on the Slave Coast transcended nationality. The Earl of Shelburne believed in 1765 that 150,000 guns had been sent to Africa from Birmingham alone.[36] Muskets of a lesser quality were often shorthanded as "Guinea." During the second half of 1774, an unusual 32 government letters of marque—permitting holders to sail heavily manned and armed—were issued to Nantes ships cleared for Saint-Domingue, France's principal sugar island and slave market.[37] In a new permutation of the Triangular Trade, some probably carried "Guinea" arms to Philadelphia and New England. The traffic was large enough that in the autumn of 1775, three British warships, HMS *Atlanta,* HMS *Pallas,* and HMS *Weazle,* were directed to "range" along the West African coast and seize American ships to prevent them from obtaining arms.[38]

Before 1774 ended, British embassies, agents, and consulates also passed along reports of shipments or possible shipments from Sweden, Denmark, and Hanseatic Hamburg, but these were relatively small potatoes. Belgian historian Marion Huibrechts, with recent research into not just English and French but also Dutch, Flemish, and Austrian archives, has notably enlarged the scope of documentation.[39]

"During the autumn of 1774," wrote Huibrechts, "military supplies for the colonies were on the move in Europe. More and more notices of contraband trade reached London. A vessel from Belfast to Philadelphia stranded near Plymouth (Cornwall) was reported to carry gunpowder. Two ships from London were seized off Gravesend in October 1774 with warlike stores for America. The sloop *John,* David Fenton master, at Hamburg lately from America with rice and logwood, ready to return to New York with chests of tea and barrels, was said to contain ammunition under bills of lading for Saint Eustatius. The *Flora,* Thomas Wilton master, at Hamburg lately from America, presumably on a similar errand. It was common practise for American vessels to carry contraband goods from Europe to the New York Sound." Once they entered successfully at night, "they were safe to land the illicit cargo in one of the many inlets of the sound. Then they proceeded to New York in ballast."⁴⁰ Colden had identified Dutch use of much the same route.

Detailed as this may seem, that is exactly the point. Surprising detail is available for 1774, much more for 1775. We are not talking about one or two ships, one or two European arsenals, or one or two participating nations. This was before the arrangements of Beaumarchais; and hardly anyone in America had ever heard of a young marquis named Lafayette, and no more in Europe knew of a young Virginian named Thomas Jefferson. Both 1774 and 1775 were the little-noticed early stages of a flood—an Old World surge with great implications for New World destiny.

Munitions: A 1775 Preoccupation

If Lexington and Concord were about British hopes to stop a rebellion by seizing American weaponry and munitions, the weeks after Bunker Hill—a Yankee retreat obliged by exhausted ammunition—made New England's challenge equally clear. Huge quantities of powder and other "warlike stores" would have to be obtained. Foreign purchases were essential, but Patriot leaders also expected to meet part of that munitions demand domestically. Modest preparations were under way but soon fell short.

Gunpowder, in retrospect, seems to have transcended its usual wartime role to become a touchstone of American patriotic fulfillment and hoped-for nationhood. In February or March 1774, there had been no such preoccupation, even in tense Massachusetts. In early September, though, the first emergency rallying of Patriot militia powerful enough to cross provincial lines followed the famous "powder alarm"—the false rumors of a British attack on Boston that somehow grew out of General Gage's sending troops to remove the last supply, all "king's powder," from the provincial magazine in Charlestown. The First Continental Congress had just convened, and the overblown "alarm" excited warlike psychologies—"war, war, war was the cry," recalled John Adams, and "if it had been true, you would have heard the thunder of an American Congress."⁴¹

The belligerence coalescing in Philadelphia further supported the Privy Council action of October 19 to curb war matériel exports to America and the British naval and diplomatic implementations that followed. When news of the council's edict reached America in December, New Englanders responded in kind—Patriots in both New Hampshire and Rhode Island broke into royal forts and magazines to take powder, arms, and cannon.

Orders from Lord Dartmouth kept gunpowder front and center. The redcoats obliged to retreat from Lexington and Concord had marched to seize military stores there. In early 1775, the American secretary had told the governors under his department to "take the most effectual measures to arresting, detaining and securing any Gunpowder, or any sort of Arms or Ammunitions which may be attempted to be imported into the province under your government."[42] Like New England, the plantation colonies smelled repression in the air. On April 21, as we have seen, a secret committee of the South Carolina Provincial Congress ordered the seizure of magazines in the Charleston area. A day earlier, Lord Dunmore's nighttime use of a naval landing party to remove local gunpowder stores caused a small riot in Williamsburg. Independent companies in nearby Virginia counties gathered to march on the capital.

Note the confrontational overlap: April 19 in Massachusetts, April 20 in Virginia, and April 21 in South Carolina, with no colony aware of what had taken place in the other two. Chests and bags of unwanted English tea were no longer the focus; barrels and bags of powder were supplanting them.

Less publicized but related events took place elsewhere in the South. Liberty Boys in Savannah took 600 pounds of powder from that town's magazine, while North Carolina Patriots demanded the cannon mounted in front of the governor's palace.[43] On July 10, as we have seen, Georgia and South Carolina colluded to capture a British supply vessel with eight tons of gunpowder, and in August South Carolinians, borrowing a convenient ship, ambushed another British supply ship off St. Augustine in Loyalist East Florida. This yielded another six tons of the *unum necessarium*.

Although munitions alone did not explain the seizure of Ticonderoga and Crown Point, ordnance played a role. As Chapter 21 will amplify, the first plans laid in Hartford and Boston cited cannon in particular. Quebec and Montreal drew related attention. For some weeks, General Washington thought that Quebec might provide the munitions, mortars, and 24-pound and 32-pound cannon he needed to drive the British out of Boston. In addition to Generals Montgomery and Schuyler mentioning the powder stocks at Fort Niagara, Samuel Adams noted in a September letter that the surrender of Fort Chambly near Montreal, a minor post, had resulted in the acquisition of 124 barrels.[44]

Besides Canada, two other early expeditions targeted powder supplies elsewhere in the empire. Patriot sympathizers in Bermuda, which required provisions from America, struck a bargain, and on August 14, 1775, the island's powder magazine was reported "broken into." About 100 barrels of powder were ferried to vessels from Virginia and South Carolina conveniently waiting off shore. As for the Bahamas, after a summer expedition from South Carolina had been postponed, eight vessels of the new American navy under Captain Esek Hopkins of Rhode Island finally reached New Providence on March 1, 1776, and captured 71 cannon, 15 mortars, substantial ordnance equipment, and 24 casks of gunpowder, missing more than 100 casks that Governor Montfort Brown had been able to move.[45]

The efforts by Congress and a half dozen provinces to produce the saltpeter needed for gunpowder were less rewarding. The delegates in Philadelphia during those hectic May and June days, heeding advice from Virginians and Marylanders, sent out printed recommendations that encouraged the retrieval of "nitrous salt" from the earthen floors of buildings and yards where tobacco had been stored. John Adams was more taken with Pennsylvania methods: "Germans and others here have an opinion that every stable, Dove house, Cellar, Vault, etc., is a Mine of Salt Petre . . . The mold under stables, etc., may be boiled into salt Petre it is said. Numbers are about it here."[46]

Massachusetts had begun production in December 1774; Virginia started in March 1775. Then Connecticut began in May, followed in June by New Hampshire, Rhode Island, Pennsylvania, and South Carolina. In the two and a half years after Lexington and Concord, Americans produced some 115,000 pounds of gunpowder from saltpeter extracted locally, or somewhat over 55 tons.[47]

These numbers were not impressive, and so little was produced during the spring and summer of 1775 that the scientifically minded Benjamin Franklin grew discouraged enough to contemplate a resort to bows and arrows.[48] Considering what English longbow men did to advancing French knights and foot soldiers in battles like Crécy and Agincourt, serious damage might have been done to the advancing British at Bunker Hill—albeit not by unskilled Americans who lacked the necessary years of training. Parenthetically, the dearth of bayonets among the rebels at Bunker Hill led to suggestions that they might be issued spears or halberds—medieval pole arms. General Artemas Ward ordered 1,500 spears, and many were kept ready for use in the trenches around Boston. Generals Charles Lee and

Horatio Gates were reported "very fond of a Project for procuring Pikes and Pike Men."[49]

By June and July 1775, impatience to obtain gunpowder (or saltpeter) converged on Congress from every direction. Whatever might eventually be scraped out of Virginia tobacco warehouses or Pennsylvania dovecotes, the Revolution's immediate needs were clear: gunpowder and saltpeter would have to be imported.

By a resolution dated July 15 but not publicized until October, Congress authorized for nine months a partial suspension of the nonexportation agreement hammered out the previous autumn. This was to permit individuals and firms to ship American produce—tobacco, rice, provisions, and the like—to purchase and import munitions. Historians have further interpreted this to authorize any vessel bringing war stores to the United Colonies to take away their worth in prime crops and goods.[50] However, as the munitions crisis worsened during July and August, even bolder measures became necessary. On September 18, 1775, as British-versus-American encounters at sea grew, the Congress established a nineteen-member Committee of Secret Correspondence empowered to import 1 million pounds of powder, 10,000 muskets, and 40 brass six-pounder field pieces, all to be paid for with funds drawn on the Continental treasury.[51] Congress also appointed scores of commercial agents in Europe and the West Indies to drum up trade. Many members of the Secret Committee were merchants, and many of the contracts went to their friends, to relatives—and indeed, to themselves. But within months, gunpowder started to flow in larger quantities.

On October 26, Congress asked the individual colonies to arrange shipments of salable products overseas in exchange for "arms, ammunition, sulphur and salt-petre." Samuel Adams explained the new guidelines to a friend: "No Provisions or Produce is to be exported from any of the united colonies to any part of the World till the first of March [1776] except for the Importation of the *Unum Necessarium* and for supplys from one Colony to another."[52] In fact, some colonies like Maryland and Pennsylvania had already embarked on such activities—sending agents to Nantes and Caribbean ports like Cap Français and St. Eustatius.[53] By 1776, according to one analysis, Virginia had some seven vessels making "powder cruises," North Carolina traded produce for munitions from Bermuda to Martinique, and Massachusetts had 32 ships—some sporting French names—carrying munitions to Europe and the West Indies.[54] Connecticut had begun similar voyages in late 1774 under the aegis of New London merchant Nathaniel Shaw, Jr., who later became the state's naval agent.

The munitions trade was big business. By 1776, the Dutch powder mills in Middleburg and the Zaan industrial district were running at full production to meet the needs of the Americans and orders from France and Spain. British officials vented their frustration over lack of interception by the Royal Navy and ineffectual diplomatic pressures by suggesting innovative pressure tactics. One was to cut off the essential water supplies provided to bone-dry St. Eustatius by nearby British St. Kitts. A second would end the saltpeter exports to Holland from British Bengal.[55]

In France, as a few historians have elaborated, support for America came from many sources and arrangements long before Beaumarchais's overt activities bore fruit in 1776.[56] The firm of Montaudouin in Nantes was especially prominent. It had close relations with Americans, partly through the city's importance in the slave trade. Two other merchants of Nantes, Pierre Penet and Emanuel Pliarne, visited Washington in Cambridge in late 1775 and produced arms by the shipload in 1776. Jean-François Delaville in Nantes was second only to Montaudouin in that seaport's fast-growing American trade.

Two other Frenchmen are mentioned with some frequency. Scholar Jacques Barbeau-Dubourg, a close friend of Franklin's, based in Paris, was in frequent touch with Vergennes in 1774 and 1775 and may have arranged many of Montaudouin's shipments.[57] Donatien Le Rey de Chaumont, also based in Paris, was a principal supplier to the French army and a confidant of Vergennes's. He and Dubourg are the two mostly widely described within France, along with Beaumarchais, as "French Fathers of the American Revolution."

A vital behind-the-scenes contribution was made by Philippe Tronson de Coudray, an artillery officer detailed by the war ministry in 1775 to go through France's ten or so arsenals. His task was to decide what munitions and arms could be earmarked for America if and when the time came.[58] And dozens of individual Frenchmen were enticed by Congress's summer-1775 decision to offer shiploads of American produce to those who brought a shipload of war matériel.

False papers were widely used. Scores of ships from the thirteen colonies put in at French or French colonial ports in 1775, received munitions on board, and then made quick changes of nationality. They took on French masters, who had bills of sale conveying the vessel in question. Sometimes the crews were also French. These practices infuriated British naval officers, and formal complaints were sent to the French governor of Guadeloupe in 1775. The French, in turn, were angered when British warships improperly entered French waters.

Many of these efforts achieved important results well before Beaumarchais's much-noted 1776 success in helping persuade Louis XVI to fund Roderigue, Hortalez et Cie and enlarge the flow of munitions and armaments across the Atlantic. Still, Beaumarchais's 1776–1777 contribution was huge. According to one calculation, by September 1777 he had provided arms and uniforms for 30,000 men, 300,000 muskets (fusils), and 100 tons of powder, as well as 200 brass cannon.[59]

It is appropriate to conclude with a gunpowder statistic. From April 19, 1775, through the autumn of 1777, roughly 90 percent of the 2.35 million pounds of powder available to the American rebels was imported or made from imported saltpeter.[60] By contrast, only 195,000 pounds were either on hand when the Revolution began or were manufactured from internal sources of saltpeter. As we have seen, the thirteen did better during those early years in forging (or capturing) cannon. Small-arms production fell in between. Still, at one point in 1775, Pennsylvania was desperate enough to run newspaper advertising offering to buy muskets.

Few portions of the Revolution have been less saluted, but obtaining gunpowder from European governments and merchants, a global quest that ranged from the Baltic to Africa, from coastal Maine to Spanish New Orleans, was the unsung battle that had to be fought before the Revolution itself could be undertaken and won.

CHAPTER 12

The Supply War at Sea

Every biscuit, man and bullet required by the British forces in America had to be transported across 3000 miles of ocean. Those responsible for formulating British policy, however, failed to come to terms with this, the most basic logistic problem of the war.

David Syrett, *Shipping and the American War, 1775–83*, 1970

The day after the shooting war started at Lexington and Concord, the war for matériel *began . . . the real fight in the New England theater during that first year was a fight not for territory but for* matériel *and that . . . would be fought at sea.*

James L. Nelson, *George Washington's Secret Navy*, 2008

No one [in Britain] foresaw how the army would continue to depend on supplies from home. The distress of the Boston garrison was treated as a temporary difficulty which would end as soon as an adequate foraging area was seized. This was never to happen; and the British army in America rested on lines of communication that were strained to the utmost. Already the shipping shortage was restraining the dispatch of troops, and North predicted that even if more men could be hired on the continent, the transport situation would prevent their deployment in America that year.

Piers Mackesy, *The War in America, 1775–1783*, 1964

Senior British officials generally heeded the autumn 1774 alarm sounded over illicit arms and munitions reaching North America. King George's own avid readership of secret service reports kept his secretaries of state and ambassadors responsive to matters like these. However, no comparable alertness extended to predictable wartime challenges of transport and logistics. Yet the problems in supplying His Majesty's ships and soldiers in a hostile rather than loyal America would be immense, worsening the British disarray so widespread in 1775 and early 1776.

The Crown's undertaking was huge. To some chroniclers, the British ability to send 50,000 soldiers across an ocean would not be equaled again until the twentieth century.[1] But shortages and poor planning were also much in evidence. The Royal Navy of 1775 had an inadequate number of the small frigates, sloops, and schooners needed for effective operations in American waters, especially along the rocky New England coasts, which became graveyards for several unsuitably large men-of-war. Nor were there enough to intercept the American vessels trading for powder and arms in Europe, the West Indies, or along Africa's Slave Coast. A third insufficiency—too few and too poorly protected transports and supply ships—played havoc with the arrival and mobility of British forces in North America. Many provisions ships never reached British troops besieged in Boston, and not enough transports were available to shift those forces to New York in the autumn of 1775. The early war at sea soon became more embarrassment than cakewalk for the world's leading navy.

As we will see, the force that the ministry had expected to converge in the spring of 1776—a New York–centered invasion by British forces and German mercenaries powerful enough to end the war in one campaign—fell far behind schedule and never fully prevailed. To David Syrett, the principal historian of shipping during the Revolution, "the Atlantic Ocean and the inability to think in terms of logistics were two of the most formidable obstacles confronting the British . . . There was during the American War a simple interrelation and interaction between strategy, logistics and shipping which geography imposed on the British effort, but this was not seen in Whitehall, and only dimly perceived at the Navy Office."[2]

Logistics were not yet fashionable. At London's political conference tables, senior commissaries, dockyard officials, paymasters, victuallers, Navy Board functionaries, and ordnance men sat below the salt, if they sat at all. Exceptions could be found—the great influence of a prominent politician like Henry Fox while he served as paymaster of the forces, a non-Cabinet post, or the recognition won by Sir Charles Middleton, comptroller of the navy during the later years of the American Revolution. But Cabinet meetings were an aristocratic milieu; commissaries and logisticians were support personnel.

At the Cabinet level, "most British military efforts during the American

War were planned on the assumption that there would always be enough transports, victuallers and storeships to put any scheme into effect, when in fact the required amount of tonnage was seldom readily available."[3] The staff, in short, would have to make do. John Montagu, Fourth Earl of Sandwich and First Lord of the Admiralty throughout the war, is best remembered for giving his name to a major logistical innovation: the sandwich—meat wrapped in bread for mannerly eating while at a gaming table. Professionally, though, Sandwich paid grains and provisions little attention, and his was a navy that tolerated practices like sound vessels being condemned, given new papers, and sold back to the Admiralty, or written off.[4] Even late in the war, when British supply management had sharpened, the subordinate transport service heard of Cabinet plans to evacuate America only by reading them in the newspapers.

By mid-1775, many of the supply interruptions becoming apparent to London had already bedeviled Thomas Gage. Months before Patriot militia encircled Boston in April, the hapless general had been encircled by Patriot town meetings and committees of inspection able to take control of shipping, commerce, and labor in virtually every Massachusetts seaport. In mid-1774, after the Port Act, these communities had sent provisions, clothing, and fuel to aid needy Bostonians left without economic sustenance. By autumn, they declined to supply Gage. In October, for example, the Committee of Observation in Marblehead collaborated with neighboring towns in detailing the goods and services to be withheld from the occupiers. Included were bricks, lumber, spars, and labor. Carpenters in Salem echoed their Boston compatriots in refusing to build barracks for the soldiers.[5]

Workers in neighboring provinces were also prevailed upon. New York carpenters and mechanics agreed not to work in Boston, and New Hampshire governor John Wentworth was labeled an "enemy of the community" by Portsmouth committeemen for procuring carpenters and sending them to Gage.[6] This was six months *before* Lexington and Concord.

By May 1775, Gage had advised Lord Dartmouth that "very great Pains have been taken to starve the Troops and the Friends of Government in Boston, for no Article Necessary for the support of Life is suffered to be sent from any of the Provinces from New Hampshire to South Carolina, and in most of the sea-Ports persons are appointed to examine everything that is embarked and where it is going."[7] No high policy maker in London thereafter had grounds for surprise.

Maritime New England Strikes Back

Gage must have understood, despite the anger shown by yeomen farmers in the summer of 1774, that the alienation of maritime Massachusetts was older and deeper. Setting aside the disillusionments of much earlier wars, latter-day hostility had been building, layer upon emotional layer, since the first fury over general warrants in 1761, the Customs Enforcement Act of 1763 that enlisted the Royal Navy as a coastal police force, the Sugar Act of 1764 with its procedural harassments, and the stationing of British troops in Boston beginning in 1768. Anger came to a head between May 1774, when news of the Coercive Acts arrived, and spring 1775, when word came of the imminent New England Restraining Act, and Admiral Graves resumed local naval impressment.

Venom was hardly confined to Boston. Twenty-five miles north, Essex County, Massachusetts, played home to the thirteen colonies' leading fisheries. Centered on three adjacent towns—Salem (population 5,300), Marblehead (4,400) and Beverly (2,800)—this seafaring complex had come to rival nearby Boston in size and importance.[8] Weeks before Lexington and Concord, codfish-dependent Essex fumed at word that Parliament was at work on a restraining act that would bar New England vessels from off-shore fishing and trading anywhere but within the empire. Had a war fuse not already been lit, these measures would have done so.

Lord North and his allies described the Restraining Act in Parliament as payback for the Continental Association's own belligerent trade demands. However, parliamentarians sympathetic to America analyzed it in far more negative terms. Lord Camden, a former British attorney general, charged during debate that other previous laws were "by no means so violent in their operations as this." He described the bill as "at once declaring war [against the colonies] and beginning hostilities in Great Britain." In 1776, Lord Rockingham explained the consequences set in motion by the Restraining Act: colonial "seamen and fishermen being indiscriminately prohibited from the peaceable exercise of their occupations, and declared open enemies, must be expected, with a certain assurance, to betake themselves to plunder, and to wreak their revenge on the commerce of Great Britain." The protests of Camden and other Whigs during the February-March debate were published in several colonial newspapers in May 1775, further inciting maritime hostility.[9]

After April 19, Patriots quickly targeted the fuel and provisions required by British troops in Boston. If fuel might seem an exaggerated priority for late spring and summer, firewood was essential for cooking and heating water to wash clothing. Wood was needed to bake bread. Salt pork and beef, from casks often years old, had to be boiled to be made (barely) edible.[10] Expeditions for firewood frequently went as far as Maine and Nova Scotia. Having to be provisioned by sea, Gage and Admiral Graves understood, was an Achilles' heel. The Royal Navy could keep transatlantic sea lanes open, but the New Englanders had the small, fast ships and skilled seamen to harass communications and make occupation duty unpleasant and ill fed.

Maritime capabilities made New England a foe to be taken seriously. By some calculations, America accounted for close to half of the British Empire's worldwide shipbuilding capacity. Between 1700 and 1775, the mainland colonies had expanded their annual output of vessels ninefold, from 4,000 tons a year to 35,000. Roughly one vessel in the British Empire out of three was American built. The North American colonies were also a great nursery of seamen, who numbered 30,000 to 50,000. Thousands in New England were being put ashore as the imminence of Restraining Act enforcement in July closed down the fisheries.

What better place to retaliate than in familiar waters? Maritime New Englanders had led pre-1775 political demonstrations, tarrings and featherings, and riots. In 1775, they would repeat with pistols, cutlasses, and fast twelve-gun schooners. True, North American shipyards had built few large vessels—ones big enough to fight, say, a 36-gun Royal Navy frigate. However, fast 75-ton or 100-ton sloops carrying eight to twelve cannon and 60 men, piloted by local mariners who knew Massachusetts Bay tides, shoals, and estuaries, could easily surprise and capture a virtually unarmed British transport. Dozens of these were en route to Boston, alone or in pairs. For salty Yankee Robin Hoods, Massachusetts Bay promised to be a blue-water Sherwood Forest.

Prior to April's clash, the Treasury in London had been warned by the British Army's principal contractor, the firm of Nesbitt, Drummond, and Franks, that American rebels would try to keep supplies from reaching Boston.[11] Yet the Admiralty made no crisis plans, and Sandwich, generally preoccupied with France, scoffed at Americans. He called them "raw, undisciplined, cowardly men. I wish instead of 40 or 50,000 of these brave fellows, they would produce in the field at least 200,000, the more the better, the easier would be the conquest; if they did not run away, they would starve themselves into compliance."[12]

Of the 30 British warships on the North American station in April 1775, four were line-of-battle behemoths and seven were frigates. Just eighteen were 14-to-20-gun sloops and schooners, or smaller cutters. Of the small craft best suited to watchdog or escort roles, not nearly enough were available in either North American or European waters. Graves acknowledged that some American successes in capturing British supply ships and transports and in running gunpowder and arms from Europe and the Caribbean were to be expected.[13]

It seems extraordinary that the North ministry should proceed from one maritime slap at the thirteen colonies to another—from the Tea Act of 1773 to coercion of Boston in 1774 and then the Restraining Acts of 1775—without mulling potential naval responses: How would the colonies react, and with what stratagems could Britain pursue victory?

After Lexington and Concord, Gage and Graves, who disliked each other, were not good collaborators. They did agree on requesting shiploads of food and fuel from the royal governors of Newfoundland, Nova Scotia, Quebec, and East Florida. By summer, these cargoes were helpful if expensive. And by May, the two commanders also concurred in ordering armed expeditions to seize the tens of thousands of sheep, hogs, and cattle that farmers kept or grazed on the hundreds of islands dotting the coast from Maine to Long Island, but here success was limited. The smoke from burning hay was visible for miles, and British raids drew quick and effective American response. As we will see in Chapter 23, one venture precipitated a fair-sized confrontation—the Battle of Noddle's Island in Boston Harbor on May 27—and there were dozens of smaller encounters.

Several Royal Navy captains, most notably Rhode Island–based James Wallace, obtained provisions after April by threatening to bombard or burn towns that refused to furnish them. During May and June, vulnerable towns that cooperated included Newport, Portsmouth (N.H.), and Marblehead. New Yorkers also obliged HMS *Asia* after that 64-gun behemoth arrived in late May. By year's end, however, few New England towns remained willing to make such arrangements.

Vulnerability at sea cut both ways. By late summer, provisions-carrying vessels of all kinds near Boston were falling into British hands. The Royal

Navy, under orders given by Graves, could seize a wide range of colonial vessels: any found carrying munitions; any approaching ports near Boston with provisions for the besieging rebels; and beginning in July, any violating the multiple provisions of the Restraining Acts. Public opinion in New England frowned on colonials willing to supply the British, but several dodges were used. A Tory merchant in Narragansett Bay, for example, could let his ship be "captured" by the British and minimize opprobrium. As we have seen, Quaker-dominated Nantucket became a problem for Massachusetts authorities in 1775 because some local vessels smuggled supplies to occupied Boston and British Newfoundland.

In need of small vessels, Admiral Graves had bought four local schooners in the summer of 1774 and several more in early 1775. By spring, he could no longer obtain them in a Massachusetts verging on open war. The belief held by many Britons that American ships were cheaply built and of inferior quality, while partly true, was also misleading. The two large warships constructed in New England for the Royal Navy during the previous half century had indeed failed to measure up. Yards in America, unused to building for great size or longevity in service, minimized or simply skipped the expensive process of seasoning wood. Unseasoned wood, of course, rotted more quickly. Slightly built framing, another Yankee practice, was equally unsuitable for major warships. These required sturdiness because of big crews (300 to 800 men) and the weight and recoil of four or five dozen large cannon.[14]

What New England shipyards specialized in were small, handy craft. Schooners were well designed, built for speed, and relatively cheap to construct. In 1774, Graves had recommended the purchase of "three or four good Marblehead schooners" to the Admiralty.[15] The admiral would have been happy to have more in 1775.

As for New England mariners, few had ever wanted to serve in the Royal Navy. Only a handful ever became officers. In wartime, what better suited American masters and seamen alike was the relative informality of provincially commissioned small ships and fast privateering vessels. Throughout 1775, New England mobilized waterborne forces as avidly as army companies and regiments. But the confusing political and legal status of the vessels employed—and of the seamen who manned them—has detracted somewhat from narrative attention.

To simplify, and for a purpose to which we will return, by September 1775 five notable categories of Patriot vessels could be identified: (1) those privately owned (often unexpectedly drawn into action by some local British act); (2) those privately owned but engaged on a provincially authorized mission; (3) those purchased, leased, or operated by a province or by its provincial navy; (4) those privately owned schooners leased by the Continental Army and operated by mariners and seamen serving in George Washington's Boston-area army regiments ("Washington's Navy"); and (5) those privately owned and operated but commissioned either by a province or by Congress to take British merchant ships as prizes. Confusion was rampant.

If these distinctions seem unnecessary, they mattered at the time. The legal status of an American ship or seafarer could, literally, be a matter of life or death. During those months, many British naval officers preferred a simpler, unequivocal term—*pirate*. Furthermore, any captured seaman could be pressed into the Royal Navy, which had a high mortality rate. Striking back was risky business.

On the other side of the ledger, many New England mariners, seamen, and fishermen, angry enough to risk life and limb, brought great skills to a new wartime calling. A smuggler with a decade or two of West Indies experience could outfox the Royal Navy as easily in the waters off St. Kitts or Martinique as in the approaches to Cape Ann or along the Connecticut coast. Yankee fishing vessels, now barred from the Grand Banks fisheries, refitted by the hundreds for commerce raiding. The first six vessels leased by Congress for Washington's own naval force were Marblehead fishing schooners.[16]

Fishermen also fought back by enlisting in the waterborne army—most famously, in Colonel John Glover's "Webbed Regiment" from Marblehead. As recalled by one participant, "Col. Glover's Regiment was stationed as Marine Corps at the Port of Beverly near Salem for the purpose of manning from time to time small vessels of War fitted out . . . to intercept and capture British Ordinance [*sic*] vessels and transports bound to the British Army in Boston."[17] His men would fight far beyond Massachusetts waters. In the predawn hours of August 29, 1776, after Washington's troops had been defeated in the Battle of Brooklyn, the hardy Marbleheaders were on hand to row them a half mile across to Manhattan almost under British noses. Four months later, before joining in combat themselves, Glover's oarsmen ferried Washington's soldiers across the ice-packed Delaware River for the Battle of Trenton. This time, instead of whaleboats, they used Durham boats, the 45-foot carriers utilized at the Durham ironworks fifteen miles upstream. Britain would have been better off allowing the Marble-headers to keep fishing.

The Extent of British Unpreparedness

Some naval historians blame First Lord Sandwich, Admiral Graves, or both for the failures during 1775 and into 1776. The vulnerability of British supply lines, that argument goes, reflected both unpreparedness and weak leadership.

Army officers were among the critics. General John Burgoyne, watching from Boston in 1775, mocked Graves in a letter home. It was difficult, said Burgoyne, to say what the admiral was doing but easier to list what he was not doing: not supplying the army with fresh meat, not defending the islands in Boston Harbor, not preventing the destruction of "King's armed vessels," not using his ships for communications or intelligence gathering. William Eden, the competent British secret service chief, described Graves as "a corrupt Admiral without any shadow of capacity."[18] Sandwich, too, was widely derided. The *Advertiser* of London, for example, noted that Sandwich's mistress, one Martha Ray, was known for raising money for her wardrobe by selling naval commissions.[19]

Experts have criticized the long-standing division of authority over wartime transport within the British military—control was split between the Navy Board, the Treasury (which moved the army), the Victualling Board, and the Ordnance Board. The Navy Board, which played a vital institutional role alongside the Admiralty, lent itself to caricature. Its membership dated back to Henry VIII. One senior member—the clerk of the acts—held an outside position created in 1214, and the titles of his subclerks evoke Chaucer more than Gilbert and Sullivan's *H.M.S. Pinafore*.[20] But mockery seems petty. The clerk of the acts had not gotten in the way of British naval triumphs between 1758 and 1761.

Naval historian Syrett, in his chronicle *Shipping and the American War, 1775–1783*, summed up that Whitehall's "failure to understand the relationship between strategy, logistics and shipping resources permeated almost every aspect of the British conduct of the war."[21] As noted at this chapter's beginning, British military historian Mackesy allowed that strains on shipping curtailed the dispatch of troops.

Blame reached to the apex of British government. An obvious dearth of small sloops, brigs, and schooners, combined with new challenges in provisioning and in managing long-distance transport, was magnified by the confusion and delay of a weak cabinet. Setting aside King George, the War Cabinet—Lord North and five or six others, notably the three secretaries of state, plus Sandwich at the Admiralty—made repeated misjudgments in 1774 and 1775. They continued, one after another: the excesses of the Coercive Acts, the political underestimation of the Continental Congress, the reduction rather than increase of the naval budget as late as December 1774, the steady overconcentration of troops in nonstrategic Boston, the serious miscalculation of British popularity in French Canada, and the adoption and eventual mismanagement of unrealistic timetables for the all-important invasion buildup in New York. The Cabinet further stumbled in letting itself be gulled by French diplomatic reassurances and by counting on Catherine of Russia to provide mercenaries. By the twentieth century, governments had fallen for less.

No marginally prepared navy or transport system, asked to do so much so quickly, could have performed well when further impeded by this sequence of Cabinet-level mistakes and mind changes. North, despite being an acknowledged master of parliamentary politics, freely admitted having no military experience, but the king would not let him resign. Dartmouth, a weak reed in the American Department, was no more experienced in military terms. Lord George Germain, who succeeded Dartmouth in November 1775, had been cashiered from the British Army twenty years earlier. His agenda in office was colored by grudges and factionalism, and he frequently blamed Sandwich—not without justification—for undercutting his military plans by failing to produce transports or warships.[22]

The interaction between grandiose plans and inadequate logistics was costly. During the period between late 1774 and early 1776, Britain lost a geographic control of the thirteen rebelling colonies that she was never able to restore. Especially in the North, regaining those grass roots was beyond reach by 1778 and 1779, when French and Spanish entry signaled the transformation of an American Revolution into a global war. Britons were soon forced into tougher decisions, but their strategic de-emphasis of New England and resurrected prioritization of the plantation South came four or five years too late.

The limitations of British and American naval strategy between mid-1774 and mid-1776 will be touched on again in Chapter 23. For now, it is in order to return to the supply war. An increasingly successful British naval blockade, biting hard by 1777, would put the new United States economy "in irons" through 1780–1781.[23] The British also paid in ships lost to privateers and high insurance rates, but the American economic loss was arguably greater. By contrast, the small-craft river, sea, and harbor wars of 1775 and early 1776—fought by smugglers, gunrunners, and Yankee merchants, and then by government-commissioned schooners and sloops with strange new flags displaying pine trees, palmettos, and rattlesnakes—achieved short-term successes that gave the fledgling government breathing room.

Within weeks of Bunker Hill, Gage and Graves understood that much of the remaining conflict of 1775 would be over provisions, armaments, stores, and how to intercept the other side's vessels at sea. But comprehension in England lagged at the Cabinet level. Senior American officials, by contrast, reflected a bourgeois mindset and instinctively grasped the importance of the supply war. The Massachusetts Provincial Congress had a merchant and seafaring bias. Connecticut and Rhode Island were both governed by longtime merchants, Trumbull and Nicholas Cooke. The Continental Congress met under the presidency of a merchant, John Hancock. And two Philadelphia merchants-cum-politicians, Thomas Willing and Robert Morris (of Willing and Morris), would manage backstage commercial warfare and munitions procurement once Congress launched its Secret Committee in September. Even the supposed landed aristocrats of the United Colonies—Washington, Schuyler, and others—had spent many prewar hours on plantation management, inventories, transport, and storekeeping.

Until Bunker Hill, Graves had avoided aggressive use of the navy. Important commercial and naval enforcement deadlines were at hand, but only a few had gone by. Activity increased in July, reflecting both the aftermath of a bloodbath and the Royal Navy's effective date, under the Restraining Acts, for seizing vessels of the nine cited colonies for trading with *any* ports outside Britain and the British West Indies. That sweeping prohibition included Virginia vessels bringing goods to Maryland or Rhode Island schooners taking rum to South Carolina. In Philadelphia, Congress, too, was slowly but surely shifting its military posture from defensive to a more aggressive mode with respect to Canada.

The relationships between war and commerce were also changing. Congress was beginning to poke holes in the nonexportation program drafted nine months earlier so that tobacco and other highly salable commodities could be shipped to buy desperately needed munitions. From their Boston perch, Gage and Graves were likewise finding the year-old prohibitions of the 1774 Boston Port Act highly inconvenient. That occupied city was now the only British-controlled New England port and had to be opened to prizes taken by British warships and to vessels bringing lumber, fuel, and provisions. So much for the high-flying commitments of 1774.

Confrontation would grow during August and September as British naval activity escalated, the king declared the thirteen colonies in rebellion, and George Washington turned his own eyes seaward to attack British supply lines. American leaders were moving beyond emphasis on protecting their own coasts and trade. To a surprising extent, they would take the offensive on sea as well as land.

George Washington and the Supply-Raiding Origins of the American Navy

No available statistic tells how many American vessels were captured by the British during the transition months of July and August. However, given that the total taken and brought into Boston and Halifax between June 1775 and April 1776 was at least 120, the two-month figure could have been 20 to 30, principally in New England waters.[24] As for British ships taken or emptied by rebels during these months, the number would have been smaller, perhaps eight to ten. That included two British transports carrying powder, the *Philippa* and the ordnance brig *Betsy,* taken by vessels instructed by the South Carolina Council of Safety.[25]

George Washington found himself taking an interest. Upon assuming his new Boston-area command, he had ordered a close watch on the Royal Navy. His general orders of July 9, 1775, specified a daily report "mentioning particularly all Arrivals of Ships and Vessels in the bay; and what changes and alterations are made, in the Stations of the Men of war, Transports and floating batteries &c."[26] It was watchfulness shared up and down coastal New England.

Both in Congress and the individual colonies, the initial concern had been to protect local trade and harbors. On July 18, the delegates in Philadelphia resolved that "each colony, at their own expense, make such provision by armed vessels or otherwise, as their respective assemblies, conventions or committees of safety shall judge expedient and suitable to their circumstances and situation for the *protection* [italics added] of their harbors and navigation on their seacoasts, against all unlawful invasions, attacks, and depredations from cutters and ships of war." A June debate in Massachusetts about arming vessels had also emphasized "the protection of our trade."[27] Rhode Island and Connecticut used similar language.

Even so, bolder rebels like Rhode Island's Cooke and South Carolina's Christopher Gadsden, along with Josiah Quincy and James Warren of Massachusetts, had begun to argue for capturing provisions vessels and store ships. Warren, president of the Provincial Congress, contended on July 11 that "ten very good [sea-]going sloops, from 10 to 16 guns, I am persuaded would clear out our coasts."[28] Washington, after rejecting an aggressive approach in June and July conversations, took a bolder tack in August. He was interested in capturing unescorted and unarmed British transports, as well as in the possibility of recovering some of the Patriot provisions vessels seized by the Royal Navy but then sent to Boston with only small prize crews.[29]

Earlier that month, Washington had asked Cooke whether the Rhode Island provincial sloop *Katy* could voyage to Bermuda to pick up some gunpowder identified by local sympathizers. Cooke took until September arranging for the *Katy* to sail, but by then other Patriot vessels had taken away the promised barrels. Washington had been eager enough to tell Cooke that the expedition would be "at the Continental Expense."[30] During August, the general had also been talking with John Glover, the "webfoot" colonel, about a related project: the hiring by the Continental Army, in Congress's name, of a good schooner, to be manned by the army's Marblehead and Beverly recruits. This would test the plausibility of arming local schooners to go after British supply ships. An agreement was signed on August 25.

The captain Glover recommended, Nicholson Broughton, turned out to be headstrong and a poor choice. However, it is revealing that the instructions Washington gave on September 2 went beyond Congress's July preoccupation with protection. Broughton was ordered to cruise outward from Boston in the schooner *Hannah* and "to take and seize all such Vessels, laden with Soldiers, Arms, Ammunition or provisions for or from said [ministerial army]." He was further ordered to "avoid any Engagement with any armed Vessel of the Enemy . . . the Design of this Enterprise being to intercept the Supplies."[31]

The commanding general, as many have elaborated, may already have visualized the larger force that emerged during September and October—what future writers would nickname "Washington's Navy." It included six to eight schooners varying in size from 40 to 80 tons, each armed with four to ten cannon, mostly four-pounders, and manned by oversize crews of 35 to 60 men. After the slow and disappointing *Hannah* was damaged, another half dozen schooners were obtained and named to woo or flatter a geographic cross-section of congressional and provincial sympathizers: Messrs. Hancock and Warren of Massachusetts, Harrison and Lee of Virginia, Franklin of Pennsylvania, and Lynch of South Carolina. The enlarged franchise for these vessels was set out on October 16, when Broughton was instructed by Congress to take two schooners to the Gulf of St. Lawrence to intercept and capture a pair of British ordnance brigs bound for Quebec with 6,000 stands of arms and a large quantity of gunpowder. He was also to "seize and take (any other transports laden with men, ammunition, clothing, or other stores for use of the Ministerial Army or Navy in America."[32]

Instead, after deciding in November that he had missed the ordnance brigs, Broughton embarrassed himself by raiding inoffensive Charlottetown, Prince Edward Island, and carrying off two provincial officials—both quickly freed and sent home by an irate Washington. The great success was achieved on November 28 by Captain John Manley in the *Lee,* who bagged the *Nancy,* a British supply ship carrying 2,000 muskets and bayonets, 7,000 cannonballs, 53 kegs of flints, a thirteen-inch mortar, seven ammunition wagons, and all kinds of essential hardware.[33] Delighted American generals agreed they could not have drawn up a better cargo list.

October and November brought a seasonal escalation of the increasingly important war at sea. Seventeen seventy-five's final wave of British transports were sailing west to make port, usually Boston, before the fierce North Atlantic winter set in. Colonel Joseph Reed, Washington's military secretary, passed along to Glover the general's urgent request that additional schooners put to sea. Glover was told to lose no time because "a great Number of Transports are hourly expected at Boston from England and elsewhere."[34] The *Nancy* was one, separated from her escorting frigate in bad weather and taken just 20 or 30 miles from Boston and safety.

Lord North and the Cabinet responded to growing American combativeness—the invasion of Canada, escalating arms traffic, naval debates in Congress—by intensifying British replies. On November 20, North initiated parliamentary consideration of the Prohibitory Act, sometimes called the Capture Act, which "banned all trade and intercourse with the . . . colonies . . . during the continuance of the present rebellion." He told Parliament that Britain was now "at war."³⁵ The measure became law before 1775 ended.

In naval history, these are much-commemorated months. The organization of the U.S. Navy is generally dated from October 13, after a convergence of supportive events. On October 3, Rhode Island's delegates had moved in Congress to establish a navy on behalf of the United Colonies, but consideration was put off. Next, on October 5, Congress had received its confidential intelligence that two British brigs laden with munitions would soon reach the St. Lawrence. Then, in a letter dated the sixth, Washington advised Congress that he had begun fitting out and arming vessels at Continental expense. What took place on the thirteenth specifically was that Washington's letter was read to Congress, which shortly thereafter resolved to fit out an armed vessel "to cruise eastward, for intercepting such transports as may be laden with warlike stores for our enemies, and for other such purposes as the Congress shall direct." For good measure, the resolution added that "another vessel be fitted out for the same purpose."³⁶ Thus did Congress, in the first instance as a matter of policy, send ships to sea to attack enemy shipping—and as a result, the United States Navy considers itself born on that day.

Subsequent enactments put flesh on the youthful skeleton. On October 30, Congress authorized a navy of four ships, quickly appropriating the funds on November 2. On November 28, approval was extended to *Rules for the Regulation of the Navy of the United Colonies* drafted by John Adams.³⁷ However, the essential logjam with respect to a navy had been broken on October 13.

Individual colonies, meanwhile, were piercing the sides of schooners and sloops for gun ports and hearing from would-be privateer operators. As we have seen, seven colonies launched provincial navies of various sorts before October 13. Virginia and North Carolina joined them in December.³⁸ Similarly, several colonies—Maryland, Virginia, Pennsylvania, and Connecticut—took a forward role in arranging to trade tobacco, rice, lumber, fish, and other provisions for gunpowder and arms in the West Indies and Europe, sending agents to such ports as Nantes and St. Eustatius. The vessels that plied these routes had many varieties of official papers and a wide variety of prewar commercial origins. A few were also commerce raiders, but most were not.

New England was especially impatient for privateering. On November 2, the two houses of the Massachusetts General Court passed legislation grandly entitled "Act for Encouraging the Fixing Out of Armed Vessells, to defend the Sea Coast of America, and for Erecting a Court to Try and Condemn all Vessells that shall be found infesting the same." Other jurisdictions were not so fast to act, but once Congress in March 1776 passed its own resolution authorizing privateering, many colonies simply used the Continental commissions signed by John Hancock that were sent around in blank.[39]

Here it is important to clarify terms. Properly used, the word *privateer* referred to private armed vessels sailing cargoless and exclusively making war, mostly by taking prizes. However, it was "used at the time, and later, too, with the utmost disregard of its true meaning. Persons with an understanding of maritime affairs constantly spoke of Continental and state cruisers, especially the smaller ones, as privateers. The term was often wrongly used even in official correspondence."[40] Over the full course of the American Revolution, one can speak with confidence of the huge role played by privateers, but references to 1775 and early 1776 must be more guarded.

John Adams, looking back, said of the boats privately fitted out by merchants that "these were my constant and daily topics from the meeting of Congress in the autumn of 1775 through the whole winter and spring of 1776."[41] But this puts him among those who misspoke. One way or another, almost every vessel—from George Washington's navy to Rhode Island's—was fitted out by merchants, either in their own right or in partnership with Congress or with the individual United Colonies.

British Logistical Overreach

Blurred terminology was obviously less important than these vessels' overall effectiveness against British shipping, which was considerable. However, the story of the supply war at sea in 1775—British vulnerability and appreciable American success, at least on a small scale—is clogged with confusions and complications. These ranged from the multiple bureaucracies of the British transport services to the many instructions from the far-off Admiralty or from Graves in North American waters setting out what Americans vessels could be seized under what concern or statute and beginning on what date. Naval officers themselves were confused. The Royal Navy initially had so few ships in American waters that which ports or bays were effectively watched—*blockaded* is descriptive only in New England—varied from month to month. Late in the winter of 1775–1776, the dearth of food in occupied Boston was severe enough that the Royal Navy sailed to Savannah in order to buy or seize rice. The loss of unprotected transports and ordnance brigs, in turn, began a debate about whether to use convoys, station soldiers aboard for protection, or employ large men-of-war with half their guns removed to make room for cargo. No small chapter like this one can attend to these details and differences or fret overly about inevitable imprecision.

In broad terms, the supply war went badly enough for Britain in 1775 and early 1776 that the king and his ministers should have worried about spillover into their larger war-making capacity. How events from the Boston Tea Party to Bunker Hill ultimately trapped both the British Army and Royal Navy in what became a regional debacle is pursued in Chapter 20. First, though, it is useful to look at a second strategic miscalculation of late 1775, this one a southern expedition, that further overextended British transport capacity and logistics.

CHAPTER 13

The First British Southern
Strategy, 1775–1776

The British Southern Strategy was based on the idea of a counterrevolution by Loyalists who, it was argued by British officers in America, comprised the majority of the population in the South.

David K. Wilson, *The Southern Strategy*, 2005

The expedition of seven regiments directed against the southern colonies first mooted in October 1775, culminated in the abortive attempt on Charles Town, South Carolina, on 28 June 1776: undertaken with hopes of speedy success, it dragged on intolerably to achieve nothing.

Eric Robson, *The Expedition to the Southern Colonies, 1775–1776*, 1951

To dismiss the first of the southern regional strategies the British government pursued during the American Revolution as achieving "nothing" was appropriate for Robson, an Englishman. The king himself, in the end, regretted that the ill-fated expedition had ever been attempted.

However, from the Patriot standpoint, this year of wasted British might—kin to the one passed impotently and uncomfortably by His Majesty's army in occupied Boston and the many months frittered away in New England waters by Admiral Graves—was pure gift. It bricked in another vital regional support in the early architecture of American independence.

Early hints of the southern expedition, which over eight months probed and pricked at three colonies—Virginia, North Carolina, and South Carolina—had come in the perceptions of relative colonial Loyalism formed by Lord Dartmouth and his advisers in the American Department during the winter of 1774–1775. Dartmouth was taken with how some colonies hung back from participating in or even accepting the Continental

Association, which by March had infuriated him with its "criminal" behavior. Georgia was apathetic enough to elicit spring criticism from Congress, and several counties in North Carolina had petitioned in support of the Crown. Both colonies, therefore, were left out of the initial Restraining Acts, although by August both were brought within the king's Proclamation of Rebellion.

As we have seen, all four royal governors—Lord Dunmore in Virginia, Josiah Martin in North Carolina, Lord William Campbell in South Carolina, and Sir James Wright in Georgia—had by summer lost control of their provinces, so much so that three took cramped but safe refuge in nearby British naval vessels. From these questionable vantage points, they—Martin most of all—kept up a correspondence with Dartmouth, reiterating prior contentions that most people in each colony were still loyal subjects. If troops were sent, they would rise in the king's support.

By late summer, all four had cited evidence to Dartmouth. Virginia was the most important colony, but Dartmouth had referred to the local population's revolutionary "madness," and the American secretary was also well aware of Lord Dunmore's especially controversial proposals. In May, Dunmore had repeated them in a letter to Dartmouth saying "that if His Majesty should think it proper to add a small Body of Troops to be sent here, a quantity of Arms[,] Ammunition and other requisites for the Service, I would raise such a force from among the Indians[,] Negroes and other persons as would soon reduce the refractory People of this Colony to obedience."[1] These were measures the British government was wary of embracing.

In fact, by October and November, the volatile governor's other aggressive tactics—sending raiding parties up local rivers to pillage opponents' plantations, seizing cannon and munitions, and organizing Loyalist regiments—worried Patriot leaders through their greater than expected success. Parts of southeastern Virginia—the Norfolk region and the lower Eastern Shore—seemed to be coming under Dunmore's control. In early December, he boasted of his success to Dartmouth: "About three thousand have taken that Oath [to the king]" and "I am now endeavoring to raise two regiments, one of white people (called the Queen's Own Loyal Virginia Regiment) the other of Negroes called Lord Dunmore's Ethiopian Regiment."[2]

Dunmore also had more than his share of critics. In any event, news or letters dated October, November, or early December came too late to affect London's autumnal selection of North Carolina as the initial destination. Here, as in so many other circumstances, slow communications would complicate matters.

North Carolina governor Josiah Martin, until 1769 a serving lieutenant colonel in the British Army, particularly emphasized two groups of potential Loyalists. First were the 15,000 to 20,000 or so Scottish Highlanders concentrated in the upper Cape Fear Valley, 4,000 of whom had just arrived in 1774. He was equally optimistic about the ex-Regulators of the Piedmont area, bloodily suppressed in 1771 by previous governor William Tryon at the Battle of Alamance. A considerable number of ex-Regulators continued to equally blame and dislike the tidewater gentry, many of whom now led North Carolina's Patriot movement. Martin had courted the ex-Regulators, expressing sympathy for some of their earlier complaints. He spent three months in the summer of 1772 touring the backcountry, which "hath opened my eyes exceedingly."[3] In 1774, his seeming allies in the Piedmont had responded with petitions against the Continental Congress and its Association.

Governor Campbell of South Carolina, albeit newly arrived, had close ties to that colony's Loyalist community. Being the son of the Duke of Argyll helped with Charleston's considerable Scottish population, and Campbell's wife, the former Sarah Izard, was a South Carolinian from that wealthy conservative family. The governor also counted on the distrust of Charleston's Patriot leaders widespread across the backcountry, especially the restive region between the Broad and Saluda rivers. By mid-1775, a militia regiment there was openly disaffected and leaning toward the king, as Campbell pointed out in a July letter to Lord Dartmouth. Several historians have argued that if the governor had journeyed to the interior and joined Colonel Thomas Fletchall and his men, he might have thwarted the Revolution in South Carolina.[4]

Georgia was less important. Nevertheless, in early 1775 only a few areas were zealous in supporting the Revolution—New England–settled St. John's Parish, and its militant Presbyterian neighbor, St. Andrew's. Several other parishes petitioned against the violent actions in New England, and Georgia's inattention to the Association provoked South Carolina to cut off relations. When the Second Continental Congress convened on May 10, it, too, cut off trade with Georgia.[5]

By the autumn of 1775, Governor Martin probably had more counterrevolutionary irons in the fire than any southern royal governor save the controversial Dunmore. In close touch with the Loyalist Highlanders of the upper Cape Fear, Martin had already tapped into London's well-advanced plans to raise a Royal Highland Emigrants Regiment in North Carolina and New York. Indeed, he had already been allowed to name its principal organizer, Lieutenant Colonel Donald MacDonald, as brigadier general of the North Carolina militia.[6] In November, when another boatload of Scottish immigrants arrived, Martin pointedly had them renew their oaths of allegiance to the Crown before they were granted land.[7] Many other Scottish settlers had already taken such oaths in the old country, some after participating in Prince Charles Edward Stuart's ill-fated 1745 rebellion. Such pledges were taken seriously.

The estimate Martin had conveyed to Lord Dartmouth during the summer was that if a force of 3,000 Highlanders could be embodied and armed by Britain, then under that protective umbrella, close to 20,000 of the province's fighting men—including 5,000 or so ex-Regulators—would rally to the royal standard. The military balance in the southern colonies would shift. Both Carolinas could be retaken, and Virginia would tremble.[8] And he didn't ask for men, just weapons.

Underpinning ministerial optimism was the assumption, shared by the four governors, that majorities in their provinces were either loyal to the Crown or amenable to being pushed in that direction.[9] Although exaggerated, the notion was not silly. But the planning and implementation by the Cabinet and the Admiralty turned out to be inept. When Britain, between 1778 and 1780, shifted a substantial portion of her resources and soldiery southward, this second, better-implemented effort managed to throw the Carolinas and Georgia into bitter civil war, achieving some of what had been contemplated in 1775.

But let us return to the weak first effort. Overt planning began on September 5, not long after the king's Proclamation of Rebellion. Dartmouth instructed William Howe in Boston—the general was about to take over from a departing Gage—that he was to weigh employing some of his forces in a "sudden and unexpected enterprise," which would scare the South and also help to secure provisions for the beleaguered army in Boston.[10] At this stage, the expedition was only proposed, not assured. Within weeks, however, it was pointing just where Martin hoped: toward a landing on North Carolina's Cape Fear, near Wilmington, the colony's leading port.

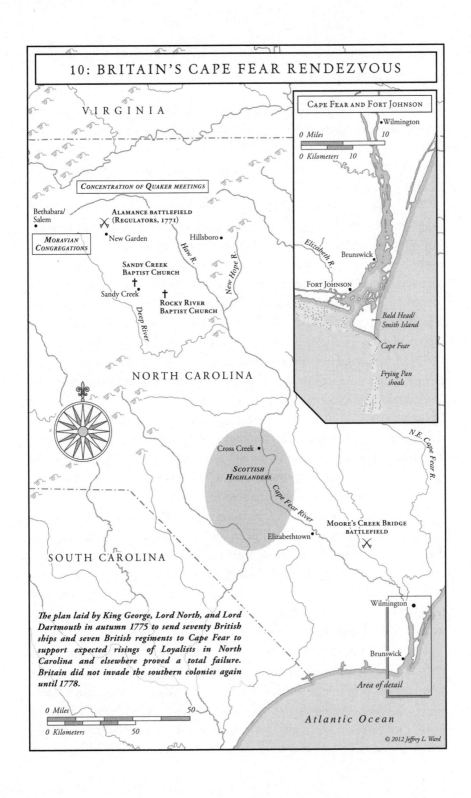

10: BRITAIN'S CAPE FEAR RENDEZVOUS

VIRGINIA

CONCENTRATION OF QUAKER MEETINGS

Bethabara/
Salem

ALAMANCE BATTLEFIELD
✗ (REGULATORS, 1771)

• New Garden   Hillsboro •

**MORAVIAN
CONGREGATIONS**

**SANDY CREEK
BAPTIST CHURCH** ✝

How R.

New Hope R.

Sandy Creek •   ✝ **ROCKY RIVER
BAPTIST CHURCH**

Deep River

NORTH CAROLINA

CAPE FEAR AND FORT JOHNSON

• Wilmington

0 Miles   10

0 Kilometers   10

Elizabeth R.

Brunswick •

FORT JOHNSON
•

*Bald Head/
Smith Island*

Cape Fear

*Frying Pan
shoals*

Cross Creek •

**SCOTTISH
HIGHLANDERS**

Cape Fear River

N.E. Cape Fear R.

MOORE'S CREEK BRIDGE
BATTLEFIELD
✗

Elizabethtown •

SOUTH CAROLINA

Wilmington •

*The plan laid by King George, Lord North, and Lord
Dartmouth in autumn 1775 to send seventy British
ships and seven British regiments to Cape Fear to
support expected risings of Loyalists in North
Carolina and elsewhere proved a total failure.
Britain did not invade the southern colonies again
until 1778.*

Brunswick •

Area of detail

0 Miles   50

0 Kilometers   50

Atlantic Ocean

© 2012 Jeffrey L. Ward

Cape Fear: The Fatal Lure

While hardly ranking alongside the Potomac, the Ohio, or the Mississippi, the Cape Fear is nevertheless North Carolina's longest river, descending 500 miles from its source in the foothills near Winston-Salem to an Atlantic mouth in a very different clime: the pitch pine, rice, and alligator country close to the South Carolina line.

The Cape Fear watershed in 1775 was home to a cultural and political kaleidoscope of recently settled populations, some with little sense of province or community. Quakers and German-speaking Moravians put an otherworldly and pacifist stamp on the hilly north. Former Regulators, in particular Baptists, abounded around the fork—itself close to the Alamance battlefield—where three tributaries, the New Hope, Haw, and Deep rivers, joined to become the Cape Fear. Thousands of Loyalist Scottish Highlanders, largely Gaelic-speaking, predominated within a 30-mile radius of the head of navigation at Cross Creek (present-day Fayetteville). Farther downstream a smaller group of Scotch-Irish imparted a Patriot coloration. The subtropical plantation lowlands, in turn, centered on the ports of Brunswick and Wilmington. These were dominated by Patriots of English descent, akin to their fire-eating cousins in the South Carolina low country. This Brunswick-Wilmingtion axis, scholars seem to agree, constituted the center of the early Revolutionary movement in North Carolina.[11] One suspects the far-off British Cabinet had no inkling of that.

The ministry's initial belief, encouraged by Martin, was that former Regulators in Piedmont counties like Guilford, Anson, Chatham, and Orange would assemble by the thousands and join up with a fearsome Celtic army of clansmen embodied for "King George and broadswords." Together, an unstoppable force of 6,000 or 8,000 men would march to the coast to rendezvous with a British fleet and several regiments of redcoats. Loyalists would restore "lawful government."

If timing went somewhat awry, there was leeway. Late-summer hopes that General Howe would move his army from Boston to New York in October 1775 were falling through. Too few transports were available. In consequence, the general would not be able to leave Boston until March or April. Furthermore, the regiments originally intended to sail from Ireland and England to bolster Howe for the decisive Hudson River campaign in 1776 were also far behind schedule.

As conceived, some of the force from Ireland was to arrive in the Carolinas in March, ideal soldiers' weather for that part of the world. They could perform militarily and then sail north, still in time to meet Howe in New York for a May campaign there. That was the kind of loose Cabinet thinking that sometimes confronted workaday logisticians at the Treasury or Navy Board. On top of which there was also a navigational problem.

Lord Dartmouth and Lord North probably knew little more about the Cape Fear River than John Adams did about the stable favorites British Cabinet members looked forward to racing at Newmarket that spring. Even so, the very label *Cape Fear*—from "the Cape of Feare," named by Sir Richard Grenville in 1585—together with the promontory's wicked hooked shape, visible on any good map, should have stirred caution in Whitehall. It did at the Admiralty. One nineteenth-century North Carolinian has left an apt portrait: "A naked bleak elbow of sand jutting far out into the ocean. Immediately in its front are the Frying Pan shoals pushing out still farther twenty miles to the south. Together they stand for warning and woe."[12]

The Cabinet's initial expectation of enjoying a deepwater port was soon dispelled. Sloops could go up the river, like the eight-gun *Cruizer*, in which Martin had close quarters, but not heavy ships. In early November, Dartmouth had been thrown off stride by word that the fleet's larger vessels—28-gun frigates and up—would be unable to cross the bar at the river's mouth. This would deny the supporting guns of the fleet to any upriver amphibious operation.[13] But no change of plans was made.

On January 10, Martin proclaimed the royal standard raised in North Carolina, sending Loyalist leaders in eight counties authorizations to raise troops, commission officers, and impress necessary provisions and means of transportation. By February 15, the contingents were to meet in Brunswick and rendezvous with the fleet.[14] Their fate will be discussed later, but ultimately only 900 Loyalists, mostly Scots, did battle on February 27, some 25 miles from Brunswick, at Moore's Creek Bridge. In less than an hour, they were cut to pieces by North Carolina Patriot militia.

In Britain, the schedule had fallen apart. The first group of ships, with some 500 soldiers under Henry Clinton, who would command the expedition, arrived from Boston on March 12. However, the main body coming from Ireland—41 transports and warships with 2,500 hundred men from seven regiments—did not make landfall until May 3. They had not even left Cork until February 13.[15] Better they had never sailed, because the expeditions achieved almost nothing during the four weeks the major force spent in the lower Cape Fear region.

Martin, more than any of the other southern governors, exaggerated with his bravado about 20,000 fighting men who would "awe" Virginia and retake the Carolinas. Still, it is fair to say that London's neglect of local geography and navigation, coupled with its inability to transport men in the promised time frame, contributed just as much to the failure. The various components of the 1775–1776 movement southward—several vessels and companies of the Fourteenth Regiment sent to Dunmore in Virginia; May's seven-regiment embarrassment on the Cape Fear; and June's ill-fated joint attack on Charleston Harbor by the army and navy—rarely get comprehensive as opposed to piecemeal attention in Revolutionary accounts. Yet it is the enterprise in its entirety that reflected so poorly on British planning and coordination.

Whitehall 1775: Cabinet-Level Mismanagement

The British government's southern misadventures helped to delay the all-important main attack on New York and to give the Revolution time to consolidate at the grass roots. Far from being inadvertent or accidental, the southern expeditions took form during October as high policy, discussed and approved by King George himself. These were months in which war psychologies notably escalated on both sides of the Atlantic, and impatience might have tempted leaders to dispel boredom with action. George Washington explained his naval ventures in Massachusetts that way in several letters. Perhaps a similar psychology was at work in London.

Although Lord Dartmouth was principally concerned with bolstering the region's Loyalists, he had also been given other arguments. One idea was to open up areas of the southern colonies to supply provisions to British forces; a second was to use southeastern North Carolina as a rear door to nearby South Carolina. In September, Dartmouth ordered the Ordnance Board to begin readying the military supplies Governor Martin had requested. The board began but quickly expressed doubt about sending so much matériel without accompanying British troops. This added dimension obliged senior officials to confer. On October 15, Lord North endorsed the change, advising the king that such an expedition could be mounted quickly and accomplished in time for the soldiers—now four to five regiments—to go north and join Howe in New York by spring. Bolstering

Martin in North Carolina was still the priority, but the prime minister also mentioned the requests for support by Dunmore and Lord William Campbell.[16] King George replied the next day, approving four regiments and giving priority to North Carolina, with Virginia and South Carolina next. High-level instructions for ships to sail from Ireland followed, along with orders for disembarkation in America.[17]

On October 22, with approvals moving rapidly, Dartmouth wrote to General Howe, stating the premise: the expedition should restore order and government in North and South Carolina, Virginia, and Georgia (the latter mentioned for the first time). The main body of troops, to be convoyed by the navy from Ireland, would proceed to the Cape Fear River, "at which place there is good ground to hope they will be immediately joined by the Highland emigrants settled in that area." Inhabitants from four or five back counties were also expected, and "it is these circumstances which have induced the resolution of sending troops to North Carolina." Carolina pilots were to be found to conduct the fleet arriving from Cork into the Cape Fear River.[18] The transports were still expected to leave Ireland at the beginning of December.[19]

On October 24, Lord Sandwich at the Admiralty wrote to Rear Admiral Molyneux Shuldham, who was about to replace Graves as commander in North America. Five regiments would sail from Ireland, and Commodore Sir Peter Parker would command at sea. However, as the Admiralty considered that 28-gun frigates were too large to get up the river, "we shall muster all the small 20-gun ships that can be got ready in time and appropriate them to this service." The transports, being ready, "will probably sail the beginning of December."[20]

By October 25, the list of regiments being sent had grown to seven. Not all were ready or in the right place; the schedule was clearly slipping. Two weeks later, on November 8, Dartmouth—himself now being replaced as American secretary by Lord George Germain—wrote to General Howe that the Cape Fear River was still to be the meeting place. However, because its bar would not admit ships of a large draught and the seven regiments would not have full protection in disembarkation, the army commander accompanying the expedition would have to decide between landing in North Carolina or going on to Charleston.[21] A week later Germain, the new secretary, confirmed these orders.

December 1 came and went, but the expedition did not. In the words of one chronicler, the supposed departure date arrived with "no detailed instructions issued to the commanders, the naval convoy force not ready, the transports not finally fitted, the Ordnance stores still to load, and the composition of the force not finally decided."[22]

Explanations of many kinds were made. Some army units wound up in the wrong place; one frigate had to be dry-docked while others were late; the royal message requesting that Irish regiments be put in service was delayed in reaching the Irish House of Commons; one transport sank in a storm, and others were late; winds were adverse, and the winter weather was awful. Presumably the confusion resembled the circumstances that prompted American troops in World War II to coin the acronym SNAFU.

Germain, operationally in charge, repeatedly blamed "Providence." On January 11, the king, increasingly angry, wrote to Sandwich that "I cannot too strongly inculcate the necessity of setting all forms aside that in the least delay the engaging [of] transports."[23] On March 3, after the main expedition had finally left Ireland in February, a sense of pointlessness was setting in. Germain sent modified instructions to General Clinton, on board the smaller force: If on reaching Cape Fear, the general felt that little or nothing could be achieved, he could proceed northward to join Howe. However, Clinton didn't get that message until the end of May, by which time he had left Cape Fear en route to Charleston. In the meantime, Germain blithely notified Howe that those regiments would be reaching him in time to begin regional operations in New York in May or early June.[24]

If this seems silly, a spaghetti of logistical confusion, that is what it was. However, the larger story also establishes the lower Cape Fear as a scene of unheralded Patriot achievements—a waterway in need of recognition. Here, between late summer 1775 and late spring 1776, the British Cabinet opened a second American front, this time *outside* of New England, and botched it. As we will see, the Patriots of North Carolina's tidewater fortified the lower Cape Fear and Wilmington during the winter, marched militia up the river to defeat the Loyalist Highlanders in February, and then for four weeks in May kept seven regiments of British regulars immobile in steamy riverside camps until General Clinton—unaware that he could have gone to New York—decided to move on to attack Charleston, a worse debacle. Surely there ought to be a monument or two.[25]

Eric Robson, the English historian, researched the relevant documents a half century ago in London's Public Records Office. The materials relating to supply and transports have more recently been grist for other specialists. David Syrett, in his *Shipping and the American War,* devoted two pages to the foibles and failures of the North Carolina expedition. He explained the difficulties the Navy Board, the Treasury, the Ordnance Board, and the Victualling Board had in their competitive management of what was a glaring insufficiency of transports. As for coordination of transport between England, Ireland, the Clyde, Germany, Boston, and the American South, that unprecedented and unmanageable set of demands aroused Sir Hugh Palliser, one of the Admiralty lords: "We are now required to provide (as it were instantly) more transports than the greatest number employed in the last war [1756–1763] which were years growing to the number."[26] It did not help that the several secretaries of state kept changing the plans and confusing the references.

The ships misallocated to Cape Fear could have changed things elsewhere. Had the Cabinet stopped the expedition just before it sailed from Ireland in February, 20 critical transports would have been freed up. And had the southern campaign been ruled out in September instead of being slowly bungled, that could have freed up enough transports by late October 1775 to let Howe evacuate his troops from Boston to New York.[27] That, in turn, might—we can only speculate—have changed the course of the war.

But we are getting ahead of ourselves. If the southern expedition took clumsy shape conceptually and administratively, it became equally as embarrassing to Britain on the battlefield and quarterdeck, as Chapter 25 will detail.

The Southern Mis-strategy

Beginning the day-by-day, blow-by-blow history of the American Revolution in mid-1775 has not tempted British chroniclers, save for the old Whig historians of a century ago, who in any event had little good to say about the king, Lord North, or the Cabinet. In a 1775-centered analysis, King George does not come out too badly. He was correct in feeling that blows must decide, and that whatever New England and Virginia Patriots said, they were aiming at independence. Among the major generals and admirals he appointed in 1774, 1775, and early 1776—Gage, the Howe brothers, Clinton, Burgoyne, Cornwallis—most were moderates, and half had displayed pro-American sentiments in earlier debates as members of Parliament. Whatever Thomas Jefferson wrote in the Declaration, he did not send ogres.

In the few studies of the southern expedition, notably Robson's, George III looks no worse with respect to decision making than North, Dartmouth, Sandwich, and the rest of the Cabinet. He did, of course, share in the general mistake of asking for too many ships too early in the war. Where the king bears responsibility for a larger failure is in the version of government he indulged—a regime headed by a skilled and much-liked political manager, North, who was personally loyal to the king but had no military competence, and a Cabinet for the most part made up of mediocre men whose factional roots were in the generally anti-American Bedford and Grenville factions. In 1775 the Cabinet, besides North as First Lord of the Treasury or prime minister, included the three secretaries of state (Northern, Southern, and American), the First Lord of the Admiralty, the Lord Chancellor, the Lord President of the Council, and sometimes others.

The American secretary (until November 1775) was the Earl of Dartmouth, a moderate who, besides being North's stepbrother, was generally ineffective. The other five were Lords Suffolk, Rochford, Sandwich, Bathurst, and Gower. Footnotes generally mention their Bedfordite or Grenvillite backgrounds and their support for "firmness" against the Americans but make no mention of acumen or competence.[28] Nor was there much military expertise. During the summer of 1775, when war plans were gestating, one member of Parliament—artillery Colonel William Phillips, lieutenant governor of Windsor Castle—wrote to General Clinton that the ministry did "attempt to carry on a War of such magnitude without a serious consultation of any military man" and that the Cabinet members spent most of their time at their country seats.[29] For this inexpert regime, George III was responsible, and he kept it as long as he could, refusing to let North resign until the government finally fell in early 1782 after Cornwallis's surrender at Yorktown.

The southern expedition was a product of these initial Cabinets, but so were many of the other miscalculations of 1774 and 1775. Ironically, the king and North would have had to plan better and more cautiously if they had not won such a large and initially unquestioning majority in the October 1774 general election.

However, it is appropriate to continue in a maritime vein to examine another British policy launched in September 1775: Admiral Samuel Graves's orders to his captains to burn offensive seaports along the New England coast.

CHAPTER 14

Is Falmouth Burning?

Congress having been pleased to appoint us a committee for collecting an account of the hostilities committed by the Ministerial troops and navy in America, since last March, with proper evidence of the truth of the facts related, the number and value of the buildings destroyed, and of the vessels, inward and outward bound seized by them . . . [committees of safety should] furnish us with the necessary materials, sending to us clear, distinct, full and circumstantial details of the hostile and destructive acts, and the captures or seizures and depredations in your colony.

Silas Deane, John Adams, and George Wythe to the committees of safety of all colonies, October 19, 1775

The savage and brutal barbarity of our enemies . . . is a full demonstration that there is not the least remains of virtue, wisdom, or humanity in the British court . . . Therefore, we expect soon to break off all kinds of connections with Britain, and form into a Grand Republic of the American Colonies.

The New England Chronicle, November 1775

Between April 19, 1775, and New Year's Day 1776, British warships bombarded, torched, or attempted to burn over a dozen American cities and towns from Falmouth (now Portland), in the Maine district of Massachusetts, to Norfolk, Virginia, 700 miles south. Another dozen were openly threatened. For some months, this represented a deliberate policy, spelled out by Admiral Graves and reiterated by Lord George Germain. To George Washington, the burning of Falmouth was "an outrage exceeding in Barbarity and cruelty every hostile Act practiced among Civilized nations."[1]

Such burnings, however, were not all on one side. After British cannonades started the fires in Norfolk on January 1, 1776, American soldiers and political leaders opted to keep them burning to destroy what had been a nest of Tories.[2] Were Norfolk to survive, Patriots feared, it could have been rebuilt as a British strongpoint.

Questions also persist about New York. The major conflagration that broke out in British-controlled lower Manhattan on September 21, 1776, has never been fully explained, but many blamed "rebel arsonists." George Washington, watching the blaze from a balcony miles to the north, revealingly commented that "providence, or some good, honest fellow, has done more for us than we were disposed to do for ourselves."[3] In Boston, General Gage stopped letting disaffected Americans leave the occupied city in early summer 1775. He feared that if no one remained save Tories and redcoats, Patriots might set the city ablaze.[4]

To eighteenth-century Americans, fires in major cities were both terrifying and commonplace. Boston led, with eight notable conflagrations. Charleston was plagued by fires and hurricanes alike. Manhattan had only a few, including a bad fire in 1741; Philadelphia, despite a bad one in 1742, was relatively untroubled.[5] Residents relied on flames for both illumination and cooking, so that rows of wooden houses could go up like pine tree shavings. In many cases, the origins of fires were not clear.

Politically, the British suffered from Graves's tactics. In New England, with its fishing and smuggling, and in Chesapeake Bay, with its tobacco dependence, local Revolutionary commitments were well advanced. However, in the middle colonies, where sentiment was more divided, two actions besmirched the British cause during the tense winter of 1775–1776. First came reports that King George was trying to hire Russian and then German mercenaries to suppress American rebels, who insisted that they sought only the rights of Englishmen.

Fence-sitting moderates were also offended by the bombardment and burning of towns, much publicized that winter in Patriot journals. Its menace was palpable. In town after town, even the mere threat of burning or naval bombardment caused a panicked exodus. The actual event, soaring flames or hurtling broadsides, could frighten away 20 to 40 percent of the population. The pathos of panicked refugees became a Patriotic symbol.

Worse for the king's repute, during this period when American colonials were turning against him, was the perception that what was happening reflected his own sentiments and orders. Through burnings and treaties to hire mercenaries, George III—not just Parliament or faceless ministers—was seen violating a monarch's duty to protect his subjects. Both disenchantments encouraged the trend toward rejecting the king pressed that winter by Thomas Paine in *Common Sense*.

Town Burning: Its 1775 Origins

Admiral Graves had first put forward the idea of burning seaports on April 20 in a rambling discourse on how Britain might reestablish control after Lexington and Concord. Before then, such talk had been flippant, like the cock crowing of British generals who promised to whip the colonials with only a few regiments. A month before Lexington, Major John Pitcairn of the Royal Marines had written Lord Sandwich that "one active campaign, a smart action, and burning two or three of their towns, will set everything to rights."[6]

When the first town was torched—Charlestown, Massachusetts, just across the Mystic River from Boston—Pitcairn was there to watch. It went up in flames on the morning of June 17, ignited by red-hot cannonballs from Royal Navy cannon and incendiary "carcasses" from British artillery on the Boston side. This was just hours before British troops were unloaded a half mile away on Moulton's Point for their attack on what became known as Bunker Hill. Rebel sharpshooters had been sniping from some of the vacated Charlestown houses, by the rules of war enough to legitimate the burning.

The fight at Lexington and Concord had not seen any deliberate town burning. Piled-up supplies had been torched in Concord, giving off thick smoke, but the town had not been fired. A few houses had been individually burned in Lexington.[7] British officers, Graves included, had talked of torching Cambridge, a rebel headquarters, but did not. Charlestown in June was the first pyre, and tens of thousands of civilians saw the fire and smoke. Abigail Adams could watch from Braintree. Major Pitcairn died on the slopes just east of Charlestown on June 17, possibly with soot and cinder burns on his uniform. But all was not set to right; the Revolution survived and grew.

Tensions were almost as high in Rhode Island. Angry colonials protesting customs practices had attacked three British vessels during the prior decade: in 1764, provincial gunners fired on the *St. John,* a Royal Navy cutter; five years later, the revenue sloop *Liberty* was seized and burned by a crowd in Newport; and in 1772, the naval cutter *Gaspee* was captured and set afire near Providence. The British government named a commission of Crown-appointed judges from New York, New Jersey, and Massachusetts to investigate the *Gaspee* episode, but public opinion was so inflamed that no witnesses could be found.

In 1774, instead of subjecting troublesome Rhode Island to a smaller version of the Coercive Acts applied next door, the Admiralty sent a no-nonsense Royal Navy captain, James Wallace, to Newport. Presumably the captain had instructions not to spare the rod or cannon. By early 1775, he commanded a small flotilla—his own 20-gun frigate *Rose* and the 20-gun sloop *Swan,* along with five or six smaller schooners and cutters. These were enough to keep a more effective lid on Narragansett Bay than Gage and Graves managed on Boston Harbor.

For a month after April 19, Graves cautioned Wallace to hold back.[8] Through June and July, as rebellion simmered, the captain harassed Newport (located on Aquidneck Island), nearby Conanicut Island (Jamestown), and other bayside stretches. Roughly half of the colony's population lived on islands large or small, which put many thousands within range of Wallace's guns. The result verged on terrorism, but Rhode Island had been extremely provocative.

The captain repeatedly threatened Newport, then the fifth most populous city in the thirteen colonies, with burning if residents let Patriot troops into town; if they declined to provide his vessels with supplies; or if they interfered with his men. Late one night he opened fire, panicking women and children. By one account, "The men of the *Rose* allegedly told the townspeople that they intended to burn down the city the following morning. Wallace did not burn down the city the next day, or the day after that. But he continually threatened to do so, and sporadically fired on the town." Wallace himself summed up: "The Destruction of a Great Town . . . is a serious matter; however something must be done for the King's service."[9] Five months later, the Newport *Mercury* reported that the captain intended to celebrate Christmas by ordering the destruction of Newport. Much of the city, however, had already been destroyed. Minister Ezra Stiles noted in his diary on January 2, 1776, that "more than three-quarters of the Inhabitants are removed."[10]

To fight back, Acting Governor Nicholas Cooke, a strong Patriot, and the General Assembly on June 12 created what became the first provincial navy. Its first vessel, the sloop *Katy,* captained by Abraham Whipple, spent the summer of 1775 in company with her smaller consort *Washington,* playing a game of cat and mouse with Wallace up and down Narragansett Bay, "brazenly removing cattle from islands within sight of the frigate and even recapturing a prize taken by the *Rose.*"[11]

But this barely slowed the British flotilla, and Rhode Island that summer became the first colony to urge the creation of a United Colonies navy.[12] Late August saw Wallace take his vessels to make a brief landing near New London, Connecticut, and then raid Gardiner's, Fisher's, and Block islands for livestock and hay. He concluded by visiting the small Connecticut seaport of Stonington, where the *Rose* for several hours bombarded the long, narrow, and exposed town.

Likewise wary of Wallace, Connecticut in July had become the second colony to set up a provincial navy when legislators authorized the governor and Council to procure, fit out, and employ two vessels to defend the Connecticut seacoast. By October, both were ready for sea—the 108-ton brig *Minerva,* intended to intercept British supply ships, and the 50-ton *Spy,* conceived of as "a spy-vessel, to run and course from place to place, to discover the enemy, and carry intelligence." A third, the brigantine *Defence,* was authorized in December 1775 and ready for sea by April.[13]

Elsewhere in New England, the great Piscataqua Harbor shared by Portsmouth and Newcastle (New Hampshire) and Kittery (Maine) also became a bone of contention. In August a tenuous truce broke down between Patriots in Portsmouth and Captain Andrew Barkley of HMS *Scarborough,* 20 guns, in the harbor. The Portsmouth Committee of Safety cut off supplies to the ship; Barkley cut off all shipping in and out of the port and threatened vengeance on Portsmouth. On August 22, out of provisions, Barkley decided to sail for Boston.[14] Kittery had received some cannon fire, but not Portsmouth.

In what could have been a bloody night in New York but surprisingly proved not to be, the 64-gun line-of-battle ship HMS *Asia,* lying off Wall Street in the East River on August 23, fired a 32-gun broadside of solid shot—9-, 18-, and 24-pound balls—into nearby lower Manhattan. Officers on the *Asia,* seeing rebel John Lamb's artillery company at work removing two dozen cannon from the Grand Battery and dragging them north along Broadway, sent a barge of marines and these exchanged shots with Lamb's men. The *Asia's* captain considered his full broadside, aimed at Fort George, as a warning.[15]

No one was killed, nor was any great damage done. However, as New

York historians point out, thousands of scared residents exited the city during the next few weeks. Merely having to live under the *Asia*'s guns was unnerving. Moravian minister Gustavus Shewkirk wrote on August 28 that "the city looks in some streets as if the plague had been in it, so many houses being shut up."[16]

Just as spring had seen refugees flee from occupied Boston and the potentially devastating firepower of its British men-of-war at anchor, residents in Newport and New York behaved similarly. Historian Bruce Bliven took note by entitling his book about the period *Under the Guns, New York: 1775-1776*.[17] By the end of 1775, over 40 percent of the city's population of 25,000 had departed.[18] In Newport, Patriot leaders recommended evacuation. After an especially menacing threat by Wallace in October, "large numbers of people began the slow journey northward seeking places of refuge. Carts, wagons, chaises and trucks jammed the highways. Streams of people and goods lined the roads in a general migration from the town and off the island. By early November, Moses Brown estimated that more than half of the inhabitants—mostly women and children—had moved out."[19]

Before turning to autumn events, it is appropriate to note earlier Massachusetts bombardment and burning scares affecting a trio of seaports: Weymouth, Marblehead, and Gloucester. The Bay Colony was the prime target.

On May 20, four British vessels sailed from Boston to an island near Weymouth to take on a large quantity of hay, but were repulsed by a gondola full of local residents who burned the supply, giving off great clouds of smoke. The *Providence Gazette* reported that "the Firing and burning of the Hay occasioned an Alarm through the Country and vast Bodies of Provincials were on their March towards Weymouth."[20]

In late April and May, Captain Thomas Bishop of HMS *Lively* used his cannon to obtain provisions from Marblehead and cautioned residents against helping the rebels "upon pain" of their town's destruction. Many fled inland from both Marblehead and Salem.[21] Marblehead was threatened again in December, because of British frustration with its strong artillery battery, which included two eighteen-pound guns. Admiral Graves advised General Howe that he would have to take the town with troops. "Three hundred soldiers with two good frigates," he advised, would be enough to overcome the battery, and the town could then be burned.[22]

Gloucester, the principal port on Cape Ann, north of Boston, was visited several times. Captain John Linzee, in the sloop of war HMS *Falcon*, was instructed by Admiral Graves to cruise in the area, and on August 8 the *Falcon* followed a rebel schooner into Gloucester Harbor, where it had run aground. Two of Linzee's barges tried to pull the potential prize clear, with no success. Thereupon the *Falcon's* six-pounders delivered several broadsides into the town, with little effect. Militiamen and townspeople gathered, shooting back from wharves, rocks, and coves with muskets and employing a pair of swivel guns mounted on carriages. A frustrated Linzee then sent a boat ashore to set fire to the village, but the charge misfired and blew off the hand of the *Falcon's* unlucky boatswain. Next, the hapless captain sent in a captured schooner and a small cutter to try to rescue the two barges and whaleboat he had already sent in. After six hours, all five small British or captured vessels in the harbor surrendered, leaving only the sloop of war, which sailed back to Boston.[23] Two months later, the Royal Navy came back for revenge but decided that the houses were too spread out for effective bombardment.

Beyond these events, New England had experienced what worried officials in late April 1775 had called the "Ipswich Fright"—a panicky willingness on the part of coast dwellers to believe that British regulars had just landed somewhere north of Boston and were burning and killing all before them. According to one local historian, "people's actions in the Newbury area reached fantastic proportions. Roads were filled with masses of people riding horses and vehicles of every description, and crowds of pedestrians, all fleeing northward as speedily as possible."[24]

Coastal defense became a priority in all four New England colonies. In August, when talk had the British leaving Boston for New York, Washington agreed to Connecticut governor Trumbull keeping one regiment for protection of that colony's lengthy coast.[25] Massachusetts, the principal target, faced the greatest challenge. On June 28, the Massachusetts Provincial Congress passed a resolution to establish guard "companies on the seacoast." Thirty-five such units, each with 50 men, were recruited locally to protect port towns stretching from Plymouth County north to Cumberland County in the district of Maine. In December and January, near the peak of seaport burnings, this force, the nation's first coast guard, was enlarged to 2,650 men.[26]

Threatened burning or bombardment was not confined to the northern colonies. Summer events also worsened relations between coastal Virginians and South Carolinians and patrolling British naval vessels. The South Carolina Council of Safety had been active during the summer in sending vessels to capture or transport gunpowder, but the first actual combat in Charleston Harbor came in early November. The Council ordered the provincial armed sloop *Defence* to escort and then scuttle six hulks in the ship channel, blocking British warships from a New England–style bombardment of the city. The sloops-of-war *Tamar* and *Cherokee* sought to stop the *Defence,* and cannon fire was exchanged on November 11 and 12. Patriots hailed this skirmish as the first battle of the Revolution in South Carolina.[27]

In Virginia, British Captain George Montagu of the *Fowey* had threatened in early May to open fire on York, soon to become famous as Yorktown.[28] Governor Dunmore several times threatened to burn or bombard Williamsburg. In late October, the nearby port of Hampton—best known for the Civil War naval battle at Hampton Roads, nine decades later— became the first Virginia town to come under actual bombardment. In November, Captain Montagu fired on Jamestown.[29]

Graves: "I purpose to lay Waste such Seaport Towns . . ."

In choosing towns that deserved a broadside of carcasses—the incendiary shells of that era—Admiral Graves drew up a purely New England list. By late August, his May and June caution had given way to more of the belligerence he had briefly voiced in April: "We ought to act hostilely from this time forward by burning and laying waste the whole country."[30]

On August 26, he noted in his journal how he had hoped for—and had proposed in "secret Confidential letters"—a "policy of making Descents within the New England Governments and destroying the towns on the Seacoasts and the Shipping in the Harbours and Rivers" with the help of "800 or 1000 Marines or Soldiers."[31] On September 1, he told General Gage that "I purpose to lay Waste such Seaport Towns in the New England Governments as not likely to be useful to His Majesty's Stores and to destroy all the Vessels within the Harbours."[32]

To this end, he added that he would also need soldiers, artillery, and a refitting of the armed transports *Symmetry* and *Spitfire* so that they could receive howitzers and mortars. Gage agreed in part on September 4, and the refitting of the two transports began.[33]

Here again a brief chronological reminder is in order. Political and commercial relations between Britain and the thirteen insurgent colonies were deteriorating rapidly in midsummer. In July, the British begin implementation of the Restraining Acts, which included a specific prohibition of (coastal) trade between colonies, even adjacent ones. A Rhode Island schooner could be seized for bringing goods to Connecticut. Meanwhile, effective July 18, the Continental Congress had urged the individual colonies to send vessels to the West Indies to trade for gunpowder. Few lawyers could keep up with the flow of deadlines, authorizations, and variable interpretations, and presumably the same was true of Royal Navy officers and Yankee ship captains. But clearly the matériel war was getting more serious every day.

September brought word that King George had gone before Parliament in August and declared all thirteen colonies in rebellion. September 10, in turn, marked the official date—now losing its practical meaning—that the United Colonies would cut off exports to the mother country. On September 18, as we have seen, Congress established a Committee of Secret Correspondence with authority and funds to commission American ships to trade wherever necessary to bring back powder, muskets, and field pieces. Dozens sailed within a few months. As for the invasion of Canada by Yankee and New York rebels aiming for Montreal and Quebec, it, too, had begun in September.

Admiral Graves, in short, was hardly precipitous in taking a strong line in September. Even so, his orders still had not listed specific towns to be burned. That came in early October. On the sixth, he ordered Lieutenant Henry Mowat, in command of the six-gun armed vessel *Canceaux,* in company with the schooner *Halifax* and the newly refitted and better-armed transports *Symmetry* and *Spitfire,* to go to Cape Ann Harbor (Gloucester). There they were to "burn, destroy and lay waste the said Town together with all Vessels and Craft in the Harbour."[34] Here was payback for Gloucester's rough handling of Captain Linzee and the *Falcon* in August.

Once Cape Ann had been bloodied, Mowat was to head north to bombard other rebellious seaports. "My design," said Graves, "is to chastize Marblehead, Salem, Newbury Port, Cape Ann Harbour, Portsmouth, Ipswich, Saco, Falmouth in Casco Bay, and particularly Mechias, where the *Margueritta* was taken, the Officer commanding her killed, and the People made Prisoners, and where the Diligent Schooner was seized."[35]

Unfortunately for Mowat, when he reached Cape Ann, the artillery officer assigned to the expedition saw limited prospects. For a bombardment from the sea to be successful, he said, houses had to be densely clustered. Those in Cape Ann Harbor were too scattered.[36]

The expedition continued north, but instead of heading for Machias, the admiral's second priority, Mowat turned for Falmouth, where he felt he had been personally insulted in May. Back then, after being ordered to Falmouth in the *Canceaux* to safeguard a cargo, he had been captured while ashore by local radicals. Town leaders, however, returned Mowat to his ship under parole—for which he had expressed his gratitude—and he sailed back to Boston.[37] For this, Falmouth would be pounded five months later by the *Symmetry* and the *Spitfire*.

In Newport, the belligerent Captain Wallace only grew bolder. On August 7, six weeks after bombardment of Stonington, he brought his growing squadron—the *Rose, Swan,* and *Glasgow,* a bomb ketch, and twelve other smaller craft—to bombard the port of Bristol, on the Rhode Island mainland 20 miles north of Newport, until its residents complied with his demand for livestock.[38] In the words of one Patriot who was on hand, "The night was dark and rainy and people ran in terror and confusion. For an hour 120 cannon and cascades [mortars firing incendiary rounds] were discharged on us [and] kept up constant fire on the people."[39] Forty sheep were provided, and Wallace sailed away.

On October 11, residents of Beverly, Massachusetts, were surprised when a locally based schooner, the *Hannah,* under lease to Washington and the Continental Army, ran for safety into their harbor with the sixteen-gun British sloop of war *Nautilus* two miles behind. Normally, Beverly's twisted harbor channel discouraged British warships, but the *Nautilus* under Captain John Collins did not flinch. When the *Hannah* went aground near the shore, Collins seemed to have won his bet. The *Hannah*'s crew had to abandon her. But Beverly townspeople and militiamen, hurriedly assembling, had enough time to carry the *Hannah*'s four-pound guns ashore and set them up. The British sloop continued to attack but came under return fire from muskets, swivel guns, and finally four-pound cannon from both Beverly and Salem across a narrow channel. The *Nautilus* fired back, and buildings were damaged in the center of town. Women and children began evacuating. However, when a cable snapped, the *Nautilus* ran aground, with many of its guns no longer able to bear. The sloop remained under fire for four long hours until freed by a changing tide. Collins escaped, partly because of inexpert Yankee marksmanship. There was no mistaking the almost reckless hostility of local populations that British warships faced in New England seaports.[40]

On October 17, having given up on Gloucester, Lieutenant Mowat appeared in Casco Bay with his new, augmented force and cited orders "to execute a just Punishment on the Town of Falmouth." He gave the population there two hours to evacuate the town, at which time "a Red Pendant will be hoisted at the Maintopgallant Masthead."[41] In fact, the negotiations were more drawn out. However, by the morning of October 18—after a night of panic—the townspeople had not acceded to Mowat's demand to surrender all weapons and take oaths of allegiance. Most local residents then evacuated, and Mowat's five vessels, including a bomb ketch, began a bombardment at 9:30 A.M. that lasted until six o'clock in the evening, when a British landing party went ashore to torch several specific buildings and complete the conflagration. All told, 130 houses were destroyed, along with the new courthouse, the fire station, and the public library. Of thirteen American vessels in the harbor, Mowat took two and sank the others.[42]

The destruction of Falmouth sparked a furor on the Patriot side. That anger, in turn, encouraged Washington to publicly announce his own efforts to arm schooners and also influenced Congress to take its late-October and early-November actions respecting naval construction. On November 1, partly in response to the burning of Falmouth, the Massachusetts Provincial Congress passed its own legislation to commission privateers, although a number were already sailing unofficially.[43]

After Gloucester, Beverly, and Falmouth, the fourth town targeted or attacked in October was Hampton, Virginia. On October 25, under Lord Dunmore's orders, five vessels, led by Royal Navy Captain Matthew Squire in the *Otter,* brought up before the town expecting to burn it, but they were blocked by sunken vessels in the channel. The next day, in a confrontation some enthusiastic Virginians have called the Lexington of the South, the British hacked through the sunken barricade and burned a farmhouse, but were routed when Patriot Colonel William Woodford arrived with a company of riflemen. These poured such heavy and accurate fire on the British vessels—sailors couldn't remain on deck long enough to fire their cannon—that Squire had to retreat, losing one of his tenders and ten men captured.[44]

November now became the month during which the Congress moved decisively toward building an American navy, and during it, perhaps ironically, no towns were bombarded or burned. However, on December 10, Wallace and the *Rose* struck again. Royal Marines under his command burned parts of Jamestown, Rhode Island, torching houses along the road from the Jamestown-Newport ferry.[45]

The other great bombardment-cum-burning came on New Year's Day. The city of Norfolk, Virginia's leading port, was also, as we have seen, a stronghold of Scottish merchants and the principal concentration of Tories in a strongly Whig province. During late December, British forces consolidating after their defeat at Great Bridge, 20 miles to the south, decided to vacate Norfolk and instead go aboard the considerable fleet that also served Dunmore as a floating headquarters. As the British took ship, American forces entered the city on December 29, and riflemen periodically sniped at British soldiers and sailors on the closest vessels. In the middle of the afternoon of January 1, as American forces paraded, somewhat tauntingly, Dunmore's half dozen warships, led by the 28-gun frigate *Liverpool,* commenced firing and continued until ten o'clock at night. Some landing parties came ashore, and fighting persisted in the dock area until the British withdrew, by which time fires were widespread.

Some annals tell that tale and little more. However, as investigators ascertained several years later, although British gunfire had started the fires, Americans fanned them and let them continue. The truth is more than a little embarrassing. As the center of Loyalist strength in the colony, Norfolk had become an anathema. Colonel Robert Howe of North Carolina, the ranking Patriot officer, did not believe that Norfolk could be held without naval control. Thomas Jefferson, in turn, saw it as the entryway to Virginia and urged that the seaport be leveled to keep it from becoming a British rallying point. Updating the Roman statesman Cato's comment that Carthage must be destroyed (*delenda*) to save the empire, Jefferson had written in October to a fellow Patriot that *Delenda est Norfolk.*[46] The American-led destruction of Norfolk took place over a considerable period of days, although on January 21, the British warships *Liverpool* and *Otter* also delivered a further cannonading.[47]

Somewhat later, a commission established by the Virginia Convention concluded that most of the burning had been done by American soldiers. To be specific, the British had destroyed 32 houses on November 30, 19 on January 1, and 3 others on January 21. By contrast, Virginia soldiers had destroyed 863 houses before January 15, and another 416 were leveled in February on the orders of the Convention. In the words of one chronicler, "the report was so potentially politically damaging that it was immediately suppressed. If word leaked out that the Americans themselves were responsible for so much of the burning of Norfolk, it might undermine the cause of revolution." Indeed, it was not made public until 1836.[48]

The other burner, the hapless Samuel Graves, had been recalled months earlier, and he sailed for home in January. His replacement was a colorless rear admiral, Molyneux Shuldham, on station for only a few months. Shuldham is scarcely remembered, but then maritime Massachusetts was all but frozen in place that winter. There is no evidence that Graves was replaced for excessive zeal in burning rebel seaports. Wallace, just as zealous, won a knighthood. Besides, Gage, as military governor, approved Graves's September 1 letter, even to the point of saying that it might have been done earlier.[49]

Lord George Germain, who in November had replaced Dartmouth as American secretary, himself had a distinctly Gravesian view of how to treat troublesome seaports. He later advised the Royal Navy's senior officers in North America to keep "the coasts of the enemy constantly alarmed" through raids and bombardment.[50] He repeatedly asked Admiral Richard Howe to harass the coasts, but the admiral was disinclined—and had the stature to prevail.

As 1776 began, both Gage and Graves had handed their North American batons to two more conciliatory officers, Lieutenant General William Howe and his older brother, Vice Admiral Richard Lord Howe, fourth viscount of that title, who did not actually arrive until July. Their mother, the dowager viscountess, was an illegitimate daughter of George I. Their older brother, Brigadier George Augustus Howe, the third viscount, had been killed by the French near Lake George in 1758. The leading light of his family, apparently hero worshipped by his brothers, he had also been the pride of the British Army assembled before Ticonderoga and also, quite uniquely for a British general, the hero of the army's New England militia regiments. Indeed, the General Court of Massachusetts so regarded George Augustus Howe—who several times had campaigned with New England troops—that a decade earlier it had placed a memorial tablet in Westminster Abbey. Neither Richard nor William Howe was happy to be fighting Americans, and both assumed a tricky dual role: peace commissioners as well as military commanders.

After General Howe vacated Boston for Halifax in March 1776, the Bay Colony was no longer a major battleground. For several months, a half dozen British warships kept watch on the coast, but sweeping orders to burn the province's seaports were no longer issued. Neither of the Howes would want to take such measures against the province that had honored their brother.

Of course, the various peace missions between 1776 and 1778 did not succeed. The Howes returned home to England with more than a little explaining to do. Germain remained in office as American secretary. In 1777 and more conspicuously in 1778, the burning and bombardment of New England towns resumed. By 1781, Fairfield, Norwalk, New Haven, and New London in Connecticut had been added to the list, as well as New Bedford in Massachusetts.

In those later years, Lord North and the king's Cabinet had given up on conquering or holding New England. The locus of battle shifted to the South, where the British government's second "southern strategy" achieved somewhat more success than the first. The bombardments and burnings between 1777 and 1781 were more diversion than pursuit of serious geopolitical designs. By comparison, the burnings back in 1775 were retaliatory and malice driven, a tribute of sorts to the towns that had worked hardest and longest for revolution.

CHAPTER 15

Red, White, and Black

Instead of being cowed by the threat of a British armed liberation of their blacks, the slaveholding population mobilized to resist . . . The news that British troops would liberate their blacks, then give them weapons and their blessings to use them on their masters, persuaded many into thinking that perhaps the militant Patriots were right and that the British government in tearing up the bonds of civil society (as Washington had put it) might be capable of any iniquity.

Simon Schama, *Rough Crossings*, 2008

How is it that we hear the loudest yelps for liberty among the drivers of negroes?

Dr. Samuel Johnson, 1775

Whatever he penned in the Declaration of Independence, in practice Thomas Jefferson did not believe that liberty, equality, and inalienable rights were for everyone. Indians, for example, were in the way of western expansion. In mid-1776, he wrote to a friend that "nothing will reduce those wretches so soon as pushing the war into the heart of their country," and later he was more vituperative in a letter to George Rogers Clark: "the end proposed [for upper Ohio Indians] should be their extermination or their removal beyond the Illinois River . . . the same world will scarcely do for them and us."[1] Fortunately for the United Colonies, however, 1775 was a year during which a cautious Congress emphasized negotiations and peace with Indians, although wars would bloody the backcountry again by 1777.

In the South, wariness of slave revolts also ran high. From Maryland to Georgia, black populations were large enough that militia units often had a second role as slave patrols. One respected historian saw the colonies in "a panic, after 1772, about the imminence of a slave insurrection in regions where blacks already outnumbered whites. This was not idle speculation. Three ferocious and bloody rebellions were already underway, in Surinam, St. Vincent and Jamaica, and all were widely and apocalyptically reported in the North American press."[2] In racial matters, the year 1775 unfolded on tenterhooks.

In parts of the Chesapeake region, white indentured servants were equally suspect. George Washington, for one, worried continually about recapturing his dozen or so if they ran away, which some did. His plantation manager wrote in December 1775 of both blacks and whites that "there is not a man among them but would leave us if they believ'd they could make there [sic] escape . . . Liberty is sweet."[3] The general did not favor liberty for white indentured servants; they were property under Virginia law and had been paid for.

Officials in Britain counted multiple opportunities. Disaffection could be encouraged, and military alliances or enlistments could be obtained from each group: the roughly 200,000 Native Americans living east of the Mississippi River; the 50,000 to 75,000 present and former white convicts and indentured servants; and perhaps most rewardingly, the nearly 500,000 black slaves.

Incitement had to be tempting. With the free white population of British North America numbering only 2.1 million or so, roughly 750,000 others whose attitudes ranged from restive to enslaved and hostile could tilt the political and military balance in some areas. Patriot leaders, many of them prominent militia officers, employers, or slave owners, understood that potential vulnerabilities outweighed the limited opportunities. For British strategists, the reverse applied. By spring and early summer 1775, Jefferson and Washington knew that one ranking Briton, Virginia's Dunmore, was advancing plans to enlist black slaves and white indentured servants. He also counted on Great Lakes Indians to attack the Ohio and Virginia frontier. No other royal governor was so free in his discussions, and Britain paid for his candor.

Most colonies had one or two of these vulnerabilities, and Virginia, uniquely, had all three. Save for Rhode Island and Delaware, each colony had at least a small Indian frontier. Two had fought minor Indian wars in 1774—Virginians with the Shawnee, Georgians against the Creeks. Settlers in northern New England uneasily watched the Canadian Caughnawaga and Abenaki, New Yorkers the vaunted Iroquois, North and South Carolinians the nearby Cherokee. For nearly a century, most tribes of the Great Lakes and Appalachian interior had raided the westward-moving white settlements—now the United Colonies—in loose alliance with the friendlier European power (hitherto France, now Britain) that purchased their furs, sold them trade goods, and encouraged their attacks from a perch in thinly settled Canada.

A less obvious possibility—that the sizable indentured servant populations in Virginia, Maryland, and Pennsylvania were disaffected enough to furnish a fifth column—had gained attention during the French and Indian War. Representatives of the French government later asserted that servants in several colonies—Catholics especially—had in fact been ripe for a revolt against their English and colonial masters.[4]

Black slave uprisings had been feared during the French wars, and two additional decades had enlarged the dangers. Between 1750 and 1775, the combined slave population in Maryland and Virginia had doubled, climbing from 150,000 to nearly 300,000. The numbers in South Carolina had almost tripled. Further roiling the waters, a limited but influential antislavery movement was gaining headway in England and, to a lesser extent, in the American colonies. Emancipation talk grew after June 1772, when Lord Mansfield, Britain's former attorney general, now chief justice of the Court of the King's Bench, held in the famous *Somerset* decision that a slave in England could not be held captive by his master. That ruling, somewhat hedged, said nothing about North America or the West Indies. Indeed, another 61 years would pass before Parliament emancipated the slaves in the West Indies. Nevertheless, the British government in the early 1770s remained supreme and entitled to invalidate any legislation enacted in America. Dozens of newspapers held forth on what the *Somerset* case might mean. Conceivably, British officials could interfere with slavery in the thirteen colonies.[5]

Belief in help from Britain was certainly spreading among slaves in America. "Uncle Sommerset" was a presence on the grapevine.[6] In late November 1774, James Madison, the future president, voiced white fear: "If America and Britain should come to a hostile rupture I am afraid an Insurrection among the slaves may and will be promoted."[7] He also noted that some blacks were choosing captains to lead them to the king's army when it came. Many slaves were psychologically prepared for what they soon heard from Dunmore.

Of all the North American colonists, those in plantation country were most at risk—and those in Virginia perhaps most of all.

1775: A Serious Contest for Native American Loyalties

Much of eastern North America was still Indian country, and borders could be fluid. Visiting Iroquois, Cherokee, and Pamunkey or Nottoway tribesmen were common on the streets of Albany, Charleston, and Williamsburg. In parts of New England and upper New York, white and native American settlements overlapped. Some Iroquois villages were surprisingly prosperous. In 1775, by one account, the Fort Hunter Mohawks lived "much better than most of the Mohawk River farmers," and some Oneida Indians "cooked in metal kettles and frying pans, ate with spoons from pewter plates at meals illuminated by candlesticks." Voters in biracial Stockbridge, Massachusetts, for some years elected both Yankee and Indian selectmen (from the Mohican, Wappinger, Nipmuck, and Tunxis tribes).[8]

Toward the Great Lakes, Shawnee, Mingos, Wyandots, Hurons, Ottawas, and other tribes had until 1760 or so been allies of the French. By the 1770s, they were more aroused than ever before against encroaching white colonial settlers. Even so, they retained doubts about the still-unfamiliar British. Could King George's chiefs continue to provide gifts, trade goods, and protection as the French had for so long? If the king's men were strong enough to subdue their wayward colonists, as they insisted, why in recent years had the red-coated soldiers abandoned so many of their old forts in western Pennsylvania and Ohio—as well as others recently taken from the French, like several on the Great Lakes and Fort Chartres in Illinois (vacated in 1772)? And how had England's soldiers been penned up on Boston's small peninsula? If the two English-speaking peoples fought, perhaps the Indian peoples should remain neutral.

The outbreak of war in April 1775 generated bewilderment and uncertainty among most tribes, not ochre face paint and eager war dances. If any tribesmen reacted to the fighting at Lexington and Concord by quickly taking up muskets and hatchets, it was the "Stockbridge" Indians of Massachusetts. During the winter of 1774–1775, although just 300 strong, they had formed their own minuteman company, winning praise from the Massachusetts Provincial Congress. The Wappingers in their ranks had quit New York's Hudson Valley in the 1760s after difficulties with Sir William Johnson and Tory landowners, which gave them old scores to settle. When hostilities began in April, seventeen Stockbridge volunteers marched off to join the Patriot forces at Cambridge. In the words of chronicler Colin Calloway, "while the Shawnees and Delawares, the supposed terrors of the Ohio frontier, clung to a precarious neutrality, the Christian Stockbridges preached war and presented the western tribes with a war belt and tomahawk."[9]

The Stockbridges drew attention, arguably too much. Peeved English officers opined that the tribesmen had been brought to Boston especially to mock the Royal Navy: "On purpose to insult them, and were taught, by turning up their backsides, to express their defiance of them." General Gage soon contended that the Americans had been the first to employ Indians. In a September letter to John Stuart, the British Indian superintendent in the South, he argued that "the Rebells have themselves open'd the Door; they have brought down all the savages they could against us here, who with their Rifle men are continually firing on our advanced sentries."[10] In fact, Gage had already made several proposals of his own for British employment of Indians.

As noted in Chapter 6, New Englanders got off to a fast start with the local tribes in 1775, enlisting Pigwacket, Penobscot, and Passamaquoddy in the north and Mohegan and Pequot in the South. George Washington personally welcomed a half dozen chiefs to his camp in Cambridge that summer, most prominently Chief Swashan and Chief Louis of the Abenaki.[11] Both Abenaki leaders promised to help if the Americans decided to invade Canada.

Circumstances in New York were less auspicious. In July, both the Continental Congress and the New York body named General Philip Schuyler to deal with the six Iroquois tribes. An Albany merchant, he had decades of trading experience and some credibility, particularly with the pro-American Oneida. However, because of Mohawk and Seneca commitment, the overall Iroquois tilt to the British was unbudgeable. Schuyler's negotiations with the "Iroquois" in the summer of 1775 had limited scope, so that the resultant Treaty of Albany reflected the views of Oneida, Tuscarora, and a few other pro-American minorities. While adherents pledged only neutrality, not support, for some even that stance would not continue past 1776.[12]

Guy Johnson, appointed in 1774 to succeed his uncle, Sir William, as head of the British Northern Indian Department, sacrificed influence by fleeing the Mohawk Valley in June 1775. But he largely regained that loss by the summer of 1776 as American forces retreated from Canada in disarray.

Still, the Iroquois had mounted only one substantial attack during 1775—in September, within sight of Fort St. John near Montreal. A contingent of 100 or so painted Mohawks and Mohawk Valley Tories attacked a wing of the invading American force. When a heavy bombardment from the fort revealed unexpected British strength, General Schuyler—never much of a field commander—withdrew 30 miles southward. The Mohawks justifiably crowed.[13]

In general, Congress's woodlands diplomacy was sober and effective. If keeping the Iroquois, Shawnee, and Canadian Indians neutral through the war verged on impossibility, even its temporary accomplishment in 1775 and well into 1776 was impressive. On July 12, 1775, just as George Washington took command of the new army, the Congress had established Middle and Southern Indian departments, as well as the Northern given to Schuyler. It was hoped that they would be counterweights to the British Northern and Southern Indian departments under Johnson and John Stuart. Much credit belonged to Charles Thomson, the secretary of Congress selected in 1774. Besides displaying backstage skills, for which he was called the Samuel Adams of Pennsylvania, Thomson had also, over a quarter century, earned the confidence of the province's Delaware Indians. In a solemn ceremony, they had likewise given him a name: Wegh-wu-law-mo-end, "The Man Who Talks the Truth."[14] Few Pennsylvania Scotch-Irish were so favored.

The Middle Department, in which Thomson took a particular interest, dealt with the Appalachian and Ohio Valley Indian frontiers of both Pennsylvania and Virginia. Here the key tribes were the Shawnee, Delaware, and Mingo. To complicate relations, a dispute existed between the two provinces over title to Pittsburgh and the Forks of the Ohio River. To officials in Williamsburg, the district was West Augusta County, Virginia; to frontier watchers in Philadelphia, it was Westmoreland County, Pennsylvania. After Dunmore's brief war with the Shawnee in October 1774, Virginia had occupied the contested area. Dunmore left a 75-man garrison in Fort Pitt (renamed Fort Dunmore) under Major John Connolly, as well as small detachments in two other new posts: Fort Fincastle (Wheeling) and Fort Blair (Point Pleasant). After obtaining land concessions from the defeated Shawnee in a preliminary agreement, the ambitious governor intended to follow up with a major Indian conference and peace treaty in the spring of 1775.

War clouds rained on that possibility. News of Lexington and Concord reached Williamsburg on April 29, nine days after Dunmore had inflamed local opinion by having British marines remove gunpowder from the provincial magazine. As relations with the governor went from bad to worse, several of the senior Virginia militia officers who had managed the October 10 defeat of the Shawnee at Point Pleasant—Dunmore himself had been miles from the fighting—began hypothesizing a 1774 plot: Had the ever-cagey Scot kept Virginia troops divided so that the Shawnee could overwhelm the southern force? Commanded by Patriot Andrew Lewis, its ranks included a number of officers who would go on to become Revolutionary colonels and generals.[15]

This seems unlikely. Dunmore, like many Virginians, was caught up in north-of-the-Ohio land speculation and flush with great ambitions, which probably explained his expedition.* On the other hand, new plans may have been afoot by February, when Major Connolly visited Williamsburg and came away with instructions for rallying the Indians to the king's cause once he had returned to Pittsburgh.

Whatever Dunmore's 1774 motivations, by May and June his thoughts had turned to holding Virginia for a certain-to-be-grateful King George— and doing so with the help of enslaved blacks, indentured servants, and Ohio Valley and Great Lakes tribesmen. His first written reference to raising the Indians came in a May letter to Lord Dartmouth.[16] However, in May anti-Dunmore Virginians on the West Augusta (Pittsburgh) Committee of Safety, distrusting the governor, took control in support of Patriot interests. By July, the Pennsylvania and Virginia congressional delegates in Philadelphia sent off a joint letter to Pittsburgh-area residents asking them to keep territorial claims from getting in the way of patriotic collaboration.[17]

Dunmore, though, could still open a few back doors to invasion. One of his last official acts in June was to announce the abandonment of Forts Dunmore (Pitt), Fincastle, and Blair. In July, Major Connolly, now openly taking London's side, disbanded the Pittsburgh garrison. In August he joined Dunmore on board HMS *Fowey* near Williamsburg. After approving Connolly's invasion scheme, the governor authorized him to take it to Boston for approval by Gage.[18]

---

*The oversize ego of John Murray, fourth Earl of Dunmore, was also displayed in his naming or renaming of the Ohio Valley forts. Not only did Fort Pitt become Fort Dunmore, but a second stockade was named Fincastle (after the governor's second title, Viscount Fincastle) and another called Fort Blair (after yet another subordinate title, Baron of Blair). What is now Shenandoah County had been named Dunmore County in 1772.

Gage did agree, but these ambitions soon came to naught. In November Connolly was caught by militia in western Maryland before he could reach Detroit, the invasion's proposed departure point. Meanwhile, in September and October 1775, Virginians and Pennsylvanians working with the Middle Indian Department held a series of conferences, the Fort Pitt treaty councils, in which the Delaware, Shawnee, Mingo, and Wyandot pledged their neutrality, and a great belt of wampum symbolizing the American peace proposal was given.[19] There had been a few transgressions—Indians had crossed the Ohio River during the summer and burned Fort Blair to the ground—but the so-called Treaty of Fort Pitt was signed in October, and then it was loosely renewed at a 1776 meeting held by congressional agent George Morgan. The agreement came altogether undone only in 1777 after Cornstalk, the leading Shawnee chief, was murdered by American militia.[20] Absent Morgan's accomplishment, had an Indian war flamed along the Pennsylvania and Virginia frontier in late 1776 while Washington was being defeated in New York and retreating across New Jersey, the need to split the few available American forces might have doomed a wobbly Revolution.

To supervise the Southern Indian Department, Congress had named multiple commissioners. Within this region, four tribes commanded attention—Cherokee, Creek, Choctaw, and Chickasaw—just as they did in Britain's parallel Southern Indian Department. South Carolina, permitted to name three of the five commissioners, was the hub. The key player was George Galphin, a longtime trader (married to a Creek woman) who had property and interests in both South Carolina and Georgia. War with the Cherokee looked inevitable in 1775 and proved so in 1776. However, Galphin kept a second front from developing in Georgia under Creek auspices. Kenneth Coleman, author of *The American Revolution in Georgia,* gave credit to one man: "The Creeks tended to be mainly pro-British, but there was always a Galphin party in the nation."[21]

By the summer of 1775, the South had several conflict zones. Foremost was the lengthy Cherokee frontier, stretching from far southwestern Virginia to northern Georgia. The second was the controversial Watauga settlement, in what is now eastern Tennessee. The third involved the Creek frontier in Georgia. Invasive white settlements were everywhere the critical provocation, but Patriot political management coped. As we have seen in Chapter 6, Whig strategists in the Carolinas turned the Cherokee threat into a white rallying point in the late 1775 "Snow Campaign" and again through sweeping military victories in 1776. Farther north, Dunmore's machinations also went for naught. In sum, British plans for raising the tribes along the Appalachian and southern frontiers were stymied—first by Patriot negotiators like Morgan and Galphin, but also by militia hammer blows against the Cherokee.

Blood eventually drenched the frontier in 1777 and 1778, but relatively little was shed in 1775, a year of quiet achievement.

Convicts and Indentured Servants: The Threat That Never Quite Materialized

Portions of North America were long-standing human dumping grounds. During the century before the Revolution, indentured servants, along with convicts—felons transported to the colonies from Britain—constituted a slight majority of the 300,000 emigrants to America. Such data, little known, are not a staple of genealogy shelves. However, of that surprising 51 percent, indentured servants made up two thirds, convicts one third.[22]

In 1775, moreover, both groups still represented a significant workforce element, disproportionately numerous in Virginia, Maryland, and Pennsylvania. Because somewhere between 25,000 and 35,000 men were involved, many of them seriously disaffected, their geographic distribution became a strategic concern to Patriots and British strategists. This was especially true in the Chesapeake, where George Washington and John Murray, Lord Dunmore, represented two important poles of sensitivity.

Virginia's Northern Neck, the territory between the Potomac and Rappahannock Rivers, was home to both Washington's Mount Vernon plantation and the tobacco colony's highest ratio of indentured servants. Washington himself owned a dozen, and he worried about their flight.[23] Dunmore, shrewd as well as blustery, held out freedom to both indentured servants and black slaves who would run away and enlist with the British. Among the servants who did was a housepainter indentured to Washington, who was injured skirmishing with Patriot forces in September 1775 and jailed in Williamsburg.[24]

To call indentured servants merely "disaffected" is probably an understatement. In most American colonies, their legal status was chattel—"property." Even their unexpired terms were property, willable to heirs. Indeed, this definition persisted during the Revolution, because most courts tried to keep a "property" label on enlisted servants, to uphold owners' rights to reimbursement for loss of services.[25]

In practical terms, purchasers often treated white indentured servants and convicts more or less similarly. After all, both were "bought" for specific terms of labor. Convicts were costlier, but they also owed a longer period of labor. Records in Baltimore, for example, showed convicts were 25 to 29 percent more expensive, but their terms of servitude were typically twice the average servant's indenture.[26] The labor ranged from demanding to brutal.

The case for most indentured servants and convicts disliking their owners and being ready to run requires blunt explanation. Treatment was typically bad from the start. According to one scholar, "many experienced unrelieved horror from the time they boarded the vessel to the completion of their terms of indenture." Often they were "sold in the same manner as horses or cows in our market or fair." Sometimes, to find buyers, sellers drove the indentured through the country "like a parcel of sheep until they can sell them to advantage."[27] By one British official's estimate, 50 percent of convict servants were dead inside seven years.[28] According to Pennsylvania historian David Waldstreicher in *Runaway America,* "much available evidence suggests that the risks to and possibilities for profit drove masters to treat their bondsmen with a cruelty and lack of care more often associated with the slave societies of the Caribbean and early South."[29]

Ironically, black slaves, selling for roughly three times as much, often got better treatment because they were a lifetime investment. With indentured servants, an employer's optimal return lay in obtaining as much sweat and output as possible over four, five, or seven years.[30] Social historian Gary Nash persuasively notes that "most depictions of early America as a garden of opportunity airbrush indentured servants out of the picture while focusing on the minority who arrived free."[31]

Upon finishing their terms, the 80 to 90 percent of indentured servants who had not managed to run away nevertheless became hard to track. By one account, three quarters eventually wound up on public support; another expert concluded that most of them, four out of five, simply did not amount to much.[32] Victims of a harsh environment or not, many or most would have been resentful individuals. The convict and ex-convict element had more interesting origins. Some were political. Still, between 1718 and 1769, two thirds of all Old Bailey felons went to America, and convicts may have represented as much as a quarter of British emigrants.[33]

Commerce, not politics, explained most of why white indentured servants and transported convicts wound up in Maryland, Virginia, and Pennsylvania. We can begin with the convicts. Between 1718 and 1775, roughly

50,000 were sentenced by judges to transportation to North America from England, Scotland, and Ireland. The British government thereupon turned them over to profit-seeking private merchants. These men arranged the convicts' shipment, usually to ports in Maryland and Virginia. Although provincial authorities in Williamsburg and Annapolis protested angrily and repeatedly, the Crown disallowed any kind of local interference. Benjamin Franklin famously suggested that in return Britain should be sent American rattlesnakes.[34]

In fact, willing purchasers abounded. Demand was high in the region for skilled and semiskilled white labor, even of the convict variety, and ships returning to Britain from the Chesapeake could count on a large volume of tobacco and grain exports from both colonies. The return cargo was the bigger lure. "Here they [merchants] may barter [servants] for tobacco," one observer explained, "upon which they have an immense return of profit."[35] As for the 15,000 or so convicts arriving from Ireland, many seem to have wound up in Philadelphia. Thus the concentration in the three colonies.

Indentured servants were distributed somewhat more widely. Even so, about 70 percent departing from England in the early 1770s went to Pennsylvania, Maryland, and Virginia. According to historian Bernard Bailyn, "Both demand and supply seemed to rise constantly, especially after 1765 and particularly in Maryland, where there was a building boom in the early 1770s."[36]

A combined head count can be ventured. As of 1775, the North American colonies may have had some 15,000 convicts, former convicts, and runaway convicts. Of these, the two Chesapeake colonies and Pennsylvania probably held 12,000. Present or former indentured servants were more numerous—40,000 or so—and Pennsylvania, Virginia, and Maryland likely accounted for 25,000 to 30,000. A combined three-colony total of 35,000 to 40,000 males and females seems plausible.[37]

Two thirds to three quarters of the combined head count—25,000 or more—would have been males of military age, which is the nubbin. Unusually large numbers of indentured servants seem to have emigrated from Britain between late 1773 and early 1776. Probably because of the hard times in Britain in 1773 and 1774, young men from all over, unable to find work, gravitated to London, with many eventually signing indentures. According to Bailyn, "One well-informed merchant guessed that 6,000 were sold in Baltimore alone in 1773–1774; according to another, there were more servant arrivals in Philadelphia than in any one year since the founding of the colony . . . No one in fact knew precisely how many servants were arriving, being sold, and being absorbed into the colonial communities."[38] It is easy to imagine many of the men arriving in 1774 or 1775 being caught up in a vocational vortex: first, escape from an employer; then military enlistment, followed by desertion or capture; reenlistment in the other side' s army; and so on. Sheer opportunism would have been common.

In 1775, Virginia's Third Convention had forbidden the military to recruit servants without a master's permission. However, by mid-1777, General Washington believed that Virginia Continental regiments were full of convict servants *sold* to recruiters.[39] When recruitment was difficult, servants and deserters provided an easy solution. In Maryland, one colonel later explained to Patriot Governor Johnson that "so general a desertion prevails among the servants enlisted into our Army that I have ordered my officers to forbear enlisting any more of them, seeing that it was only recruiting for the enemy not for us."[40] The British, too, had problems with desertions from the Volunteers of Ireland, and the Philadelphia-raised Roman Catholic Volunteers were disbanded after a few years.

By 1774 and 1775, more and more of the demand for servants in the middle colonies lay outside the cities, "in the innumerable country villages of Pennsylvania, Maryland and Virginia," and especially in burgeoning industries: iron, with its blast furnaces, forges, and slitting mills; and construction, with its carpenters, masons, bricklayers, and millwrights.[41] Politically, both of these booming vocations were Patriot dominated—iron working, as we saw in Chapter 4; and construction, which thrived not just on residential building but on the westward land emphasis of the Patriot gentry. George Washington, for one, bought indentured servants to work on his Ohio River properties. Britain's huge transatlantic slave trade might be in the hands of Liverpool Tories, but North American "Soul Drivers"— the men who managed and implemented the trade in white indentured servants—were in many cases prominent Virginia, Maryland, and Pennsylvania Whigs and Patriots. Thus their concern about being targeted.

Master craftsmen in the building trades, who constructed Philadelphia's Carpenters' Hall, were mostly Patriots and large-scale employers of indentured servants. So, too, the Pennsylvania and Maryland iron makers, whose work gangs faced some of the most grueling conditions of the preindustrial era. Charles Ridgely, whose family owned the Hampton-Northampton ironworks, was a leader in Baltimore's radical Patriot faction. Rhetoric about freedom did not stop the Ridgelys from buying 300 or so white servants, mostly convicts, and putting them to work with black slaves, mining and hauling ore, feeding the furnaces, and working the forge. One of Ridgely's escapees was advertised as wearing an iron collar. The family even sometimes speculated in indentures—buying and selling white servants for quick two-month profits.[42] As Chapter 17 will amplify, the ironworks in the Baltimore and Annapolis areas were singled out in a 1775 memorandum by Anglican cleric Jonathan Boucher as prime targets for a British "indentured servant" strategy.[43] As for the servant-heavy Northern Neck of Virginia, George Washington worried in 1775 about Mount Vernon being a Dunmore target.

Although no accessible study exists of "Indentured Servants in the American Revolution" or some such, one would surely be informative. How many servants fled to Dunmore in Virginia? What potential did exist for British recruitment in Pennsylvania districts along the Maryland border reputed for high ratios of runaway servants? Despite concern, white servile insurrections did not occur; servants did not band together to seize plantations. But the apparent destabilization of recruitment and of entire regiments in both armies seems to have been a considerable effect.

1775: The Initial Response of Black Slaves and Free Blacks

Fortunately for the colonists, the run-or-stay choices made by hundreds of thousands of black slaves, as word spread of Dunmore's promise, were more complicated than his lordship might have hoped—or, for that matter, than many a prominent Virginia or South Carolina Patriot might have feared. Even more telling, though, was the extent to which the American rebels saw white psychologies turning in their favor.

Simply put, the loose British notion in 1775 of using white colonial fears of black slave insurgencies to scare southerners away from confronting Britain was poorly thought out. On top of which, Patriot racial psychologies were not the same in Connecticut or Rhode Island as in the plantation colonies, an important divergence.

Save in the overconfident months of 1775 and early 1776, New Englanders generally favored allowing black enrollment in the militia and enlistment by free blacks in the newly authorized Continental regiments. Black military service was well established on land and sea. Scores had served on April 19 and then again on Bunker Hill. However, during the spring and summer, *rage militaire*—cockiness about beating the British—diminished the importance of black enlistments. Self-perceived Patriot civic and military virtue need not stoop to arming slaves and ex-slaves. New York General Philip Schuyler was still making this argument before the Battle of Saratoga.[44] In the South, arousal against Britain's supposed intentions in 1775 made white southerners broadly oppose any black role in the United Colonies' military.

In general, plantation colony indignation over supposed British slave-insurrection plans whetted local anger at the king and North's ministry and drove undecided whites toward the Patriot position. Shrewd British officials understood that from the start. John Stuart noted that "nothing can be more alarming to the Carolinas than the idea of an attack from Indians and Negroes."[45]

Nevertheless, the Patriot calculus began to shift in December. George Washington, who in July 1775 had agreed to a ban on black enlistments, underwent a timely change of mind at year's end. Wariness of Dunmore was a factor, along with a sense that if the Patriots did not enlist blacks, the British would. By allowing this to happen, the American side might have sacrificed 5 to 10 percent of its eventual manpower. On December 31, Washington sent a letter to the Continental Congress urging that black enlistments be reinstated. The larger tide of opinion began shifting in 1776, and by 1779 Congress had moved far enough to recommend that South Carolina and Georgia "take measures immediately for raising three thousand able-bodied negroes."[46] These two states never did, but the number of blacks serving in New England and New York units rose steadily through the war.

Blacks constituted 10 percent of those enlisted in some New York regiments, and more in several from Connecticut and Rhode Island. One such, the First Rhode Island, passed in review after the victory at Yorktown in 1781, and Baron Ludwig von Closen, aide to General Jean-Baptiste Rochambeau, the French commander, observed that "three quarters of the Rhode Island regiment consists of Negroes, and that regiment is the most neatly dressed, the best under arms, and the most precise in its manuevers."[47] In another 1781 visit to the American army at White Plains, New York, Closen estimated that blacks were a quarter of its force.[48]

Advances in information technology have facilitated greater cataloguing and retrieval of what British officials were saying or doing in 1774 and 1775—plans and activities that included discussions in Parliament of emancipation and slave recruitment, tacit acceptance of black enlistment by officials from Lord North in the Cabinet to General Gage in Boston, and most vividly, the repeated pronouncements by Dunmore in Virginia. These various plans and pursuits left a contemporary trail of partial information and rumor, which many slaves took as British rescue intentions. They built hopes accordingly, and then in 1775 fled toward British camps and ships by the thousands.

Whites in the South, however, took British words, court rulings, and actions, inflamed by Patriot-faction overstatement, as evidence that North and his ministers, some British generals, and governors like Dunmore were plotting slave conspiracies, insurrections, and mass escapes. Although this was exaggerated, it was not baseless. Sylvia Frey, a British historian who remarked on "the moral absurdity of a society of slaveholders proclaiming the concepts of natural rights, equality and liberty," also assembled a sweeping documentation of open and covert British activities in her book *Water from the Rock: Black Resistance in a Revolutionary Age.*[49]

"In the end," Frey concluded, "the British strategy of manipulating conflict between the races became a rallying cry for white southern unity and impelled the South toward independence."[50] To whites, it was not credible when some British denied what others of their countrymen were actually doing, saying, and putting in writing.

For blacks, the wide attention given to the *Somerset* case in 1772 and thereafter provided a milieu for hope. James Somerset's name entered black folklore, and not a few slaves talked about somehow getting to England. In 1773 General Gage was presented by Boston slaves with three petitions for their freedom; a year later he received two more from blacks offering to fight if he would arm them and promise freedom.[51]

In 1775, Gage advised the secretary at war, Lord Barrington, that "we must avail ourselves of every resource, even to raise the Negros [*sic*] in our cause."[52] Lord Dartmouth, in turn, had a letter from Lord Dunmore in May about the latter's plan to raise black troops. In July he responded by hoping that the governor had succeeded "among the Indians, Negroes & other persons." Gage sent Dunmore some additional officers.[53]

In early 1775, word came to America from England that a proposal calling for the general emancipation of slaves had been discussed—not introduced—in the House of Commons. It was aimed at "the high aristocratic spirit of Virginia and the southern colonies," and the effort was dismissed by Edmund Burke as diversionary in a speech on March 22, 1775.[54] This was not a single event. On October 26, 1775, William Henry Lyttleton, an ally of North and a former royal governor of South Carolina, introduced into the House of Commons "something like a proposal for encouraging the negroes in that part of America to rise against their masters, and for sending some regiments to support and encourage them, in carrying the design into execution." So backed, said Lyttleton, "the negroes would rise and embrue their hands in the blood of their masters." After eliciting broad disapproval among government supporters, Lyttleton's motion failed by a vote of 278 to 108.[55]

Intriguingly, this proposal appeared during the week when the ministry was developing its plan for a southern invasion—detailed in Chapter 13— and escalating the number of regiments to be employed from five to seven. To Frey, "even without access [by historians] to interministerial discussions," racial issues "were precipitating factors in the shaping of Britain's Southern strategy."[56] Indeed, North had told the king that "we all know the perilous situation of three of them [colonies] from the great number of their Negro slaves, and the small proportion of white inhabitants."[57]

Just how many servile risings actually took place below the Mason-Dixon Line in 1775 and early 1776 is unclear. Not very many. In Maryland, Dorchester County Patriots disarmed local blacks, taking "80 guns, some bayonets, swords," but no whites were attacked. Maryland's royal governor, Robert Eden, advised Lord George Germain that Marylanders were "extremely agitated by Lord Dunmore's proclamation giving freedom to the slaves in Virginia; our proximity to which colony, and our similar circumstances with respect to Negroes augmenting the general alarm."[58]

As for Virginia, despite the thousands of black slaves who ran to the British—a single planter, John Willoughby in Norfolk County, alone lost 87—no slave insurrection in the usual sense of the word occurred. Freedom-minded flight substituted for insurrection.

North Carolina had one panic and one rising. In the summer of 1775, Wilmington's Committee of Safety disarmed local blacks and put the town under martial law. Revolutionaries charged that Captain John Collet, the British commander at Fort Johnston, "had given Encouragement to Negroes to Elope from their masters & they [the British] promised to protect them." Questions were also raised about Governor Josiah Martin.[59] The uprising was partly carried out in July 1775 in the eastern New Bern-Pamlico Sound area. Several hundred blacks had gathered, and 40 were jailed.[60]

Low-country South Carolina, with a black majority, had its great scare in June 1775. Drums sounded, night patrols were mounted, and Patriot leaders orated that the possibility of a British invasion or a slave uprising demanded strong defensive measures. However, the evidence of an actual plot or insurrection was unconvincing. Not so with July's planned uprising in St. Bartholomew's Parish near Charleston. Plotters there confessed to planning "to take the Country by killing the whites." The impetus came from black preachers who talked about how the Old King had received a book from the Lord about freeing the blacks, but he had not. Now the Young King (George III) was about to do so.[61] One slave was charged as a principal instigator and executed.

That southern Patriots achieved political gains from blaming reported or rumored slave insurrections on British encouragement or actions is beyond doubt. Dunmore was an easy target because of his own boasts. His influence also carried into North Carolina. In November 1775, when Patriot Colonel Robert Howe marched to assist Virginia troops in Norfolk, the route chosen had a dual purpose: to block any southward move by Dunmore, but also to keep the black slaves in two northeastern North Carolina counties from seeking liberation under Dunmore's banner.[62] One historian familiar with Governor Martin's correspondence said he "did not entirely dismiss the idea of arming slaves," pointing out to Dartmouth that black populations would "facilitate exceedingly the Reduction" of the plantation colonies.[63]

In May 1775, slaves in South Carolina were aroused by a rumor—begun by American William Lee in a letter from London—that they were to be set free in June when the new governor, Lord William Campbell, arrived.[64] The vessel bringing him was said to have 14,000 stands of weapons, which was untrue. White Charlestonians were quick to perceive a plot and an intended insurrection. A free black named Thomas Jeremiah was charged on weak evidence and executed. To one chronicler, Charleston acted out a kind of collective neurosis, but to others, the public was overinterpreting a considerable array of real knowledge. Southern colonial governors from Martin in North Carolina to Wright in Georgia all complained about false accusations.[65] On the other hand, Eden in Maryland put some of the blame on Dunmore's verbosity, and others may also have complained privately.

Stirred by Dunmore, thousands of blacks ran away from masters during 1775. In Virginia, Frey estimated 800 reached Dunmore, but many more must have reached some form of British protection. Three hundred or so joined Dunmore's new Royal Ethiopian Regiment, which fought credibly at Kemp's Mill in November. A month later 35 of its soldiers were taken prisoner after the British defeat at Great Bridge and sold as slaves in the West Indies or Bay of Honduras.[66]

Runaway slaves in South Carolina and Georgia, lacking the equivalent of an Ethiopian Regiment in which to enlist, made their way to little-populated coastal islands—Sullivan's in Charleston Harbor and Tybee downriver from Savannah—where hundreds found military protection extended by the British. In November information that parties of blacks and British sailors from Sullivan's were landing nightly on the South Carolina mainland to take provisions from local plantations prompted the Provincial Congress to send a company of rangers, apparently including friendly Catawba Indians, to patrol the coast. On the nineteenth of December, 54 Rangers landed on the island, killing several black slaves and capturing others, along with sailors from the British sloop *Cherokee* who were leaving in boats. Other runaways had already been taken to North Carolina in a second vessel, HMS *Scorpion*. At this point, 200 soldiers of the First South Carolina Regiment threw up a battery of eighteen-pounders to control the island, and Sullivan's was no longer a workable refuge.[67]

Frustrated by South Carolina's limited success, Georgia thought to take stronger measures in March 1776. Several hundred runaways had gathered on Tybee Island, but on March 25, a Georgia raiding party found no one on Tybee but a wood and water detail from HMS *Symmetry,* several of whom were killed or captured. The runaways had already been taken away by British transports and merchant ships.[68]

For the British, the net military consequences of Dunmore's activity in 1775 and early 1776 were negative. True, dozens of plantations near the coast were raided or thrown into disarray as slaves fled. In addition, Virginians also found it harder to reorganize their militia because poor whites were angered by special concessions to nervous slave owners. The December 1775 ordinance, which exempted overseers on plantations from service, also became controversial because planters were allowed to designate one overseer for every four slaves, a loophole for gentry families to avoid military service.[69]

Still, the larger effect of racial issues was to unite white southerners behind the Revolution. For example, before Dunmore's waterborne raids, southerners in Congress were less interested than New Englanders in organizing an American navy. By October and November 1775, stung by Dunmore's river and bay shore activity, they had become increasingly supportive. The British expedition to the southern colonies planned in 1775 ultimately failed everywhere.

Among the northern provinces, New Jersey was the only one where black recruits favored the British. In New England, free blacks were not notably wooed away from their town-level militia roles or from their sore memories of British maritime policy. Most remained on the Patriot side. During the war's later years, legislative assemblies in Maryland, Connecticut, New York, and Massachusetts entertained or approved proposals for black regiments.[70] As for blacks serving on privateers or vessels of provincial and then state navies, participation was widespread even in Maryland, Virginia, and the Carolinas, another inadequately told story of the Revolution.

Historians have mounted a small debate over George Washington's change of position on black military service during 1775. A few have gone so far as to tie his decision making during those winter months to the threat to his family and plantation that he perceived in the policies of Lord Dunmore.[71] Tapping black manpower for the Patriot side may have seemed like a wise countermove.

Slavery, Servitude, and Eighteenth-Century Political Semantics

Dr. Johnson's much-quoted observation about the loudest yelps for liberty coming from southern slave owners was not the devastating dismissal of American hypocrisy that twenty-first-century readers might imagine. During the seventeenth and eighteenth centuries, "slavery" had become an intolerable status routinely cited by political thinkers, pamphleteers, and ordinary folk in the English-speaking world. One stanza of "Rule Britannia," penned in 1740, proudly asserted "Britons never, ever, shall be slaves." If slavery was a fate principally associated with blacks, that sentence would have made no sense.

Through the seventeenth century and much of the eighteenth century, however, slavery was *not* the fate of one race alone. That was true even in North America circa 1775. If whites held 450,000 blacks in slavery, another 40,000 or so white indentured servants were likewise "property." White masters sometimes treated them worse than slaves, representing as they did a lifetime investment.

According to a pair of prizewinning evaluations, several North American Indian tribes were also large-scale slave owners and slave traders: the Cherokee were prominent in the East, and the Comanche even more sweepingly in their empire on the southwestern plains. In his book *The Indian Slave Trade,* historian Alan Galley establishes a chronology: "For the most part, slavery was not a moral issue to southern [American] peoples of the late seventeenth century. Europeans, Africans and Native Americans all understood enslavement as a legitimate fate for particular individuals or groups. All accepted that 'others' could or should have that status." Then the concept of race caught hold in the mid-eighteenth century.[72]

Meanwhile, "the Comanche built the largest slave economy in the colonial southwest," according to historian Pekka Hämäläinen.[73] In his revisionist history, the Comanche in that part of North America represented a more potent empire than that of colonial Spain. They took Indian captives, black captives, and Hispanic captives from what is now New Mexico. In the 1770s, their raiding zones extended from western Colorado south to Laredo, Texas. By the early nineteenth century, they were taking white captives in Texas and selling black slaves from one Indian tribe to another.[74]

True, white or Hispanic slaves in Indian Country never amounted to more than a thousand or two. But in the 1770s, a much larger number of European slaves could be found in Morocco, Algiers, and several other parts of North Africa. Reports by the East India Company also mentioned small numbers held in Muslim seaports along the Indian Ocean. The white slaves held in Barbary as of 1730 numbered somewhere between 30,000 and 50,000. Any figure for 1775 would have been considerably lower, because between 1757 and 1767, the sultan of Morocco finally signed treaties with Denmark, Britain, Holland, Venice, France, and Spain.[75] These agreements reduced the inflow of captives, although conclusive action did not come until 1816, when a British squadron under Sir Edward Pellew pounded Algiers to rubble and burned the corsair fleet.

Memories would have remained strong, though, in southern England and New England. The captive-hunting "Sallee" pirates—they hailed from Sale, near present-day Rabat, on the Moroccan coast—did more than capture vessels and passengers in European waters or en route to North America. Although towns in Spain and Portugal were the prime seventeenth-century targets, the corsairs sometimes attacked English and Irish villages, carrying off the captives to North Africa. Many voyagers to Virginia and Massachusetts were among those captured, and well into the eighteenth century, the white slaves taken to North Africa were part of a memory that, more distantly, included English and Scots—the Presbyterian minister John Knox was one—chained as galley slaves by the French and Spanish.

In consequence, for Englishmen or American colonials in the 1750s and 1760s to routinely use "slavery" as an invidious political image does not suggest hypocrisy, even for someone owning a slave or indentured servant. The political usage was well established. Still, new perceptions were in the air. The burgeoning mid-eighteenth-century slave trade had intensified race emphasis in the American South to match that in the Caribbean. Quakers in North America were freeing their slaves, and emancipation was gaining momentum in Britain. The French had ended galley slavery earlier in the century, and the sultan of Morocco thought it wise to stop seizing European slaves.

By 1775, plantation-owning Americans who bemoaned "slavery" could be mocked by British commentators, but Britons were about to stumble over a kindred reassessment. Britain's practice of manning armies with mercenaries—a military version of indentured servitude—was about to make His Majesty's government a butt of criticism among philosophes and other European standard-bearers of the Enlightenment.

CHAPTER 16

Divided National Opinion and Britain's Need to Hire Mercenaries

The American war was clearly a divisive issue in British and Irish politics. At times opponents and supporters of the coercion of the colonists took their differences to the point of violence. And if the merits of the conflict were hotly debated, the process of mobilization of manpower to fight the war was also bitterly contested. [British] divisions over the extent and form of military and naval participation reflected and deepened the divisions over the justice and efficacy of the war itself.

Stephen Conway, *The British Isles and the War of American Independence*, 2000

The conduct of England in hiring German mercenaries to subdue the essentially English population beyond the Atlantic made reconciliation hopeless, and the Declaration of Independence inevitable. It was idle for the Americans to have any further scruples about calling in foreigners to assist them when England herself set the example.

W. F. Lecky, *A History of England in the Eighteenth Century*, 1890

Partly through inability to enlist or conscript a largely unmilitary population of seven million in England and Wales, the British government had too small an army to reconquer over 2 million rebellious English-speaking colonials 3,000 miles away. The 1688 revolution against the excesses of seventeenth-century Stuart kings had left England a people and culture distrustful of standing armies. Thus, the British Empire of the eighteenth century, rich through trade, reshaped itself to minimize any such need, becoming what one historian aptly called Europe's first fiscal-military state.[1] Instead of conscripting unwilling Englishmen, the king and Parliament used British lucre and global financial prowess to hire foreign troops as needed.

This alternative worked satisfactorily for wars fought on the European continent. Britain's peacetime army remained small enough—36,000 in 1774—that embroilment in a Continental war obliged the Crown to greatly expand or even to double its military manpower by contracting for German or Russian troops.[2] In one instance, in 1755 George II had procured 55,000 Russian soldiers to fight for him in Germany, but relations between Russia and Prussia blocked the arrangement's implementation.[3]

The usual British practice was to hire mercenaries from princely states in the Protestant north of Germany—Hesse-Cassel, Brunswick, Waldeck, Anspach-Bayreuth, and others. Kings George I and George II were bound to these rulers through Hanoverian politics and a web of British treaties, subsidies, and royal marriages. These continental embroilments, though, were an annoyance and a provocation to many in Parliament. Public opinion bridled at any hint of German troops being employed in Britain. They had been brought over only twice—first in 1745, when Hessian mercenaries were imported to help put down that year's Scottish rising, and again in 1756, when Hessian and Hanoverian soldiers were hired to help defend England against a threatened French invasion.[4] That kind of employment was acceptable. In neither case had the German troops been used against Englishmen.

That was about to change. In the autumn of 1774, General Gage, confined in Boston, had already anticipated Britain's use of Hessians and Hanoverians in North America. Lord North and the Cabinet, surprisingly, never seem to have pondered the psychological bridges certain to be burned by employing German or Russian mercenaries to subjugate English speakers in New England or New Jersey. Lecky's pronouncement, in the epigraph above, was to the point. The opposition in Parliament, perceiving a distasteful innovation, blistered the government as the engagement of mercenaries—*Soldatenhandel*—moved from planning in 1775 to actual treaties in early 1776.

1775: Divided British Opinions on America

During much of the twentieth century, British historians took the view that English opinion in 1775 had strongly supported coercion in America. That misreading was the mirror image of American insistence that the colonists overwhelmingly favored a revolution, with dissenting Loyalists few and far between. In reality, important divisions existed on both sides of the Atlantic, as documentation since the 1970s has shown.[5]

Earlier British interpretation often erred through preoccupation with a smaller "political nation." Only this elite counted—broadly, the 100,000 or so Britons who voted for Parliament or in municipalities, but especially its core: some 10,000 to 15,000 nobles and gentry, members of Parliament, government officeholders, military officers, Church of England clergy, and substantial lawyers, merchants, bankers, and manufacturers. Clerks, shop keepers, and artisans did not count.

Public opinion, then, was not a great concern. The popular Methodist preacher John Wesley, a war supporter, could aver to Lord Dartmouth in the autumn of 1775 that "the people in general, all over the nation, are so far from being well-satisfied that they are far more deeply dissatisfied than they appear to have been before the Great Rebellion [the 1640s] . . . and nineteen out of twenty to whom I speak in defense of the King seem never to have heard a word spoken for him before."[6] Ironically, the Marquess of Rockingham, a leading American sympathizer, was finding the opposite: that "the generality of the people of England are now led away by the representations and arts of the ministry, the court and their abettors; so that the violent measures towards America are freely adopted and countenanced by a majority of individuals of all ranks, professions or occupations in this country."[7] No Gallup poll or its ilk would exist for another 150 years.

In recent decades, though, it has become clear that significant divisions on coercing or conciliating North America existed even within the "political nation," as well as among the 200,000 to 300,000 persons just outside. This broader group would have included, for example, men not eligible to vote for Parliament but able to participate in associations and to sign petitions in many municipalities and boroughs. Likewise for lower-middle- and middle-class Britons in industrial cities like Manchester and Birmingham that still lacked representation in Parliament.

By 1775, the acceptably small "political nation" approved by conservatives was losing acquiescence among middle-class Britons. The Englishmen pressing hardest against these closed Old World doors would have qualified for the franchise in many of the North American colonies, which may have encouraged some transatlantic empathy.

In sharp contrast to New Englanders or Virginians, *rage militaire*—the desire to shoulder muskets—was rare in workaday Englishmen. No such enthusiasm appeared until 1778, when French entry into the war made immediate the threat of invasion. New artillery emplacements in Cornwall and distant views of French warships off Devon or Sussex did the trick. In 1775, though, early Loyalist refugees arriving in England were "acutely dismayed to find that the home country was not united in support of the American war. The war was very unpopular in many quarters, especially lower down the social scale."[8]

These divisions in British opinion provide an essential context for recruitment and enlistment issues.[9] Within England, support for the colonies was generally strongest in the major cities and in the eastern and southern counties—revealingly, an approximate geographic reiteration of where English Civil War support had been strongest for Parliament and Cromwell against King Charles.

Seventeen seventy-five found London and other major centers like Bristol, Newcastle, and Norwich generally on the side of conciliation. Nine out of twelve London-area parliamentary seats had elected members who were generally pro-American, including the flamboyant radical John Wilkes, who also served as Lord Mayor of London. To John Sainsbury, a British historian and expert on the period, "by denying to the king and Lord North's administration the national unanimity that they sought in the face of colonial rebellion, the pro-Americans [of London] justified their own assertion that the American War of Independence was in fact a civil war."[10] Edmund Burke represented maritime Bristol in Parliament, and the considerable American sympathies of Newcastle and Norwich have been well established.[11]

Unsurprisingly, the southern and eastern English countryside most sympathetic to the colonies had been in the forefront of their initial seventeenth-century settlement. East Anglia—the right thumb (including Essex, Suffolk, Norfolk, Cambridge, and Middlesex) that juts out northeast of London—had been New England's principal ancestral seedbed. Dozens of replicated East Anglian place-names leap out from a map of eastern Massachusetts. In 1775, on the heels of King George's proclamation declaring the colonies in rebellion, five East Anglian counties and towns opposed coercion or petitioned the Crown for conciliation.[12] By one account, East Anglia circa 1775 was as nearly "monolithic" for conciliation as Scotland was for king and coercion.[13] Just west of London, Hampshire and Berkshire were as active as East Anglia.

Nonconforming Protestants—Presbyterians, Baptists, Independents (Congregationalists), Quakers, and others—made up just 5 to 7 percent of the English population in the 1770s. Even so, towns and districts where they concentrated were especially likely to display American sympathies. Dissenters were conspicuous in initiating conciliatory petitions in 1775.[14]

Studies of the procoercion addresses and proconciliation petitions sent to

London in 1775 also confirm clear economic and vocational differences. Whereas the belligerent addresses were signed by Anglican churchmen, government contractors and officials, lawyers, doctors, esquires, and gentry, sympathetic petitions typically attracted support from nonconformist clergy and laymen, artisans, shopkeepers and skilled craftsmen, tavern keepers, and coffeehouse owners, and the radicals among gentry and lawyers.[15]

One has to be careful describing Anglicans as particularly inclined to support coercion. Virtually all of the pro-Americans in Parliament were themselves Anglican simply because conforming to the Church of England was a precondition of holding office. Nevertheless, as described by one British specialist, "there was no doubt where the inclination of the Anglican clergy lay, and they made no secret of their desires to stoke the fires of anti-Americanism. In many parts of the country, the pulpit reinforced a national political campaign for the first time in many years."[16]

Within England as a whole, support for coercion was greatest in the old Tory and Jacobite centers. Backing for the Crown, wrote American religious historian James Bradley, maximized in Lancashire, where residents sought to banish suspicions of their loyalty left from the days of Bonnie Prince Charlie, and in the West Midlands, "a traditional Tory stronghold and a prominent center of the Forty Five."[17]

Political leaders in Scotland, committed to expunging North Britain's erstwhile treason of 1745–1746 through militant enthusiasm for the war and the House of Hanover, brooked little opposition. No Scottish parliament existed, and a mere 3,000 voters chose the men that Scotland sent to Westminster. The principal power broker, Henry Dundas, managed the eighteenth-century equivalent of a machine—Chicago city hall in kilts. English Whigs harped on Scotland as incurably autocratic, but the larger Scottish motivation lay in the fast-flowing benefits and patronage of empire. Braw lads raised on cold oatmeal were now spooning sturgeon eggs. The imperial realm in general—and North America in particular—had become a cornucopia for Scottish soldiers, adventurers, lawyers, overseas administrators, merchants, tobacco factors, and bankers. The details are striking.[18]

Support in Scotland for the American cause was limited to a small fringe—some intellectuals, radicals bred in the tradition of Scotland's Covenanter southwest, and adherents of the Popular Party of the Church of Scotland (admired in America but dismissed as "the wilds" by Edinburgh social arbiters). To raise Highland regiments to fight in America represented a coming of age for Scottish leadership.

The divisions in Ireland were more complicated. Enthusiasm for the thirteen colonies maximized among the 15 to 20 percent of Irish who were Protestants, but particularly among the 10 percent who were Presbyterians. Widely signed petitions for conciliation were sent to the king in 1775 by these communities of Dublin and Belfast. The Church of Ireland—transplanted Anglicanism, replete with bishops and British officialdom ("Dublin Castle") as communicants—overwhelmingly sided with the king. But Ulster Presbyterians, the Scotch-Irish of the Old World, were more numerous and pro-Patriot. Even the English Lord Lieutenant, Earl Harcourt, described them as "in their hearts Americans."[19] Meanwhile, the Catholic nobility and gentry, together with a rising Catholic merchant and professional class in Cork and Dublin, somewhat paralleled their Gaelic cousins in Scotland by seeing and pursuing new commercial and military opportunities in the British Empire. Nor did Stuart claimants to the British throne continue to divert Catholic loyalties. In 1766, the Holy See had cut the cord, ending the Stuarts' voice in the appointment of Irish bishops and senior clergy. Elements of the Irish Catholic hierarchy now dismissed the American Patriots as Calvinists, Presbyterians, and republicans. Since the 1970s, Irish historians have acknowledged the details.[20]

The willingness of George III to turn to Gaelic-speaking regions in military recruitment and enlistment did smack of Stuart-era predilections, even though the "autocratic" ideology visible in 1775 differed by *upholding* Parliament rather than dismissing or suspending it. Still, Rockingham, Shelburne, or a chronicler like Horace Walpole could have cited a famous mid-seventeenth-century portrait of Charles I. That monarch, too, was shown being prepared for the Battle of Worcester against the Puritans by an allegory of Scotland presenting a pistol and Ireland adjusting his armor.[21]

The Political and Ethnic Context of Britain's 1775–1776 Mobilization

The dissimilar attitudes toward the war within the British Isles can be roughly framed: greater reluctance and disagreement in England; self-serving ardor in Scotland; and a duality in Ireland—the era's prize turf for military recruitment—that substantially reflected religious divisions.

Within England, sheriffs and magistrates offering convicted criminals the alternative of joining the army were among the few successful recruiting officers. In Hampshire, one local magistrate took pride in enabling the enlistment of a hundred convicts between December 1775 and June 1776. Just after Christmas, the Privy Council had also ordered local authorities to issue warrants for impressing vagrants.[22] Enlistment in 1775, said one prominent historian, moved "almost imperceptibly in England, where hardly any enthusiasm for the war existed among the classes from whom soldiers were drawn."[23] A later scholar, detailing Scottish martial enthusiasm, counted England "almost comically barren as a recruiting ground." Adjutant General Edward Harvey complained in December 1775 of "sad work everywhere in recruiting."[24]

King George and Parliament could find pro-American views near at hand. The Radical Whigs who controlled municipal government in London openly withheld support from the war effort, and the wounded soldiers, orphans, and widows for whom Londoners first took up collections were *Americans*.[25] Berkshire's county seat, Abingdon, was not far from Windsor Castle; the Earl of Abingdon opposed the war, and the town petitioned for conciliation.

In Nottingham, a Whig textile center represented in Parliament by William Howe, ministerial supporters complained that local authorities "do all in their power to hinder the service by preventing as much as possible the enlistment of soldiers." Historian Edward Gibbon, only months from publishing his monumental *Decline and Fall of the Roman Empire*, criticized dissenters in England and Ireland for impeding the army's growth.[26] Supporters of conciliation in Hampshire mocked the number of Anglican clerics (30) signing the county's coercive address: Was the Church, they asked, planning to organize its own grenadier company?[27]

No new army regiments were organized in England in either 1775 or 1776, partly because King George preferred to concentrate on filling the many empty places in the existing units.[28] This, as we will see, could best be accomplished by sending recruiting officers to Ireland and Germany. Logically enough, enrollment in England seems to have been concentrated in the North and the West Midlands, further confirming the judgment of British and American historians that Crown recruiters emphasized the old Jacobite and Stuart constituencies.[29]

Ineffective recruiting in most of England compelled these alternatives. Although the 7 million people in England and Wales dominated Britain's population, their contribution to the army was small. In 1774, the scantily manned British standing army had only 35,000 officers and men, probably two thirds English.[30] Between September 1775 and September 1777, only 18,000 more were added to the British establishment [army], and of these, a majority came from Scotland and Ireland.[31]

As for Englishmen and Welshmen, even in mid-1776, the British Army may well have contained only 25,000 or so, including its fresh sprinkling of convicts and vagrants. Such was the legacy of the Glorious Revolution of 1688. By contrast, the German state of Hesse-Cassel, as of 1776, had squeezed an army of 22,000 from a population of just 400,000. By one calculation, had England and Wales raised a comparable ratio, 400,000 men would have been called to the colors.[32]

In Parliament's February 1776 debates, the Earl of Shelburne, another prominent American sympathizer, offered a further contrast. During the 1756–1763 war, he said, the British government had drawn a total of 400,000 Britons to fight in both the army and the navy. The current regime, amid an unpopular conflict, was unable to raise one fifth of that number of natives without running to paltry German principalities for salvation.[33] With Parliament still compliant, Lord North handily carried the vote on the treaties by nearly three to one in the House of Commons. If the German arrangements were obviously necessary, they also reflected outdated assumptions. In a war that many Englishmen shunned, using Continental mercenaries to suppress Whig colonists was an unwise undertaking.

The ministry's decision to vastly increase its recruitment from the Scottish Highlands, by contrast, was imperially shrewd. A Scotland no longer swayable by Stuarts or Pretenders was a manpower tap waiting to be turned. Inverness-shire, the heartland of the 1745 rising, was calculated to have 12,000 "military effectives" ready to bear arms.[34] King George did not favor raising new regiments in Sussex or Surrey, but he consented for Glen More and Glen Spean, where Simon Fraser, son of the Lord Lovat executed after the Forty Five, was eager to regain the family estates and titles. Thus, the one new British regiment authorized in 1775 was the 71st Foot: the Fraser Highlanders. Its company commanders represented a former-Jacobite muster roll: MacLeod of MacLeod, Chisholm, Cameron of Lochiel. By 1780, nine more Scottish regiments had been formed, led by the MacLeod, Argyll, MacDonnell, Athol, Seaforth, and Aberdeen Highlanders.[35]

Because a considerable minority of the new recruits were from Catholic glens and braes, Parliament's Scottish Catholic Relief Act of 1778 was designed in part to maintain the flow. The Popular Party of the Church of Scotland, however, helped to defeat the proposal by arguing that its motivation was to raise Catholic troops for use against fellow Protestants in America.[36]

The North ministry's military and logistical courtship of Ireland was on a larger scale. Catholic disabilities were eased, Irish trade favored, and military contracts in Ireland expanded. Cork circa 1775 was playing a prominent new role as a British naval base; and its agricultural hinterland became a principal source of beef, bacon, and butter for the British Army and Royal Navy.[37] Until 1771, the British Army had done little recruiting in Ireland, not least because Catholic enlistment was barred by the Irish Penal Code. In 1775, however, *connive* became the new byword. Recruiters were to "connive" in matters relating to oath taking and the Penal Code. From his perch in Dublin Castle, Lord Harcourt giddily envisioned not the 12,000 potential "military effectives" of Inverness-shire but "two millions of loyal, faithful and affectionate hearts and hands." In the more sober words of British historian Stephen Conway, London had set its sights on "the great mass of under-exploited Catholic manpower in Ireland."[38]

In July 1775, a score of British recruiting parties were active in Ireland, but with only slight success. Then Irish Catholic nobles, gentry, and prospering merchants stepped forward to help. In Dublin, influential Catholics advised authorities of their support and offered to encourage Catholic enlistment even though it was nominally barred, and the Catholics of Limerick put up half a guinea per volunteer for the first 200 to enlist.[39] The Roman Catholic hierarchy went so far as to urge local clergy to preach fast-day sermons on behalf of the British war effort.[40] Recruits were also given to expect that they would receive land in America when the rebels were beaten. One Catholic spokesman, Charles O'Connor, looked forward to British victory paving the way for restoring Maryland to Catholic rule as in the seventeenth century. Then it could "act as a bridle here-after on the Republican provinces north and south of them."[41]

At first, no new regiments were formed in Ireland, so that existing units could recruit and "top off." As a result, supposedly "English" regiments became 30 to 40 percent Irish and Scottish. One such, the 48th, with a county tie to Northamptonshire, within a few years turned out to be 29 percent Scottish and 31 percent Irish.[42] Few of the Catholic Irish enlistees liked Britain much better than they had a decade earlier, and desertions were common. However, the thinned ranks of many regiments had been filled out.

British War Planners Turn to the Continent

The king's grandfather, George II, had sent both Scottish Highlanders and German soldiers to America during the French and Indian War—the Black Watch and Montgomerie Highlanders and Hanoverians in the 60th (Royal American) Regiment. Both fought Indians and French, winning colonists' plaudits. By contrast, little but enmity was forthcoming in 1776 and 1777 when Hessians and Highlanders marched, marauded, stole, and battled through New Jersey counties named for Essex, Middlesex, Somerset, and Monmouth.

That was when New Jersey, in circumstances often chaotic, became the military "cockpit" of the Revolution. In late 1776, as Washington retreated in disarray, lines of command broke down, as did regard for the rules of European-style war. Hessians bore the brunt of criticism. British officers, Loyalists, and aides on General Howe's staff concurred with some of the Patriot protests. Major Stephen Kemble, the British deputy adjutant general, called the Hessians "outrageously cruel and licentious to a degree." Pennsylvania Tory Joseph Galloway described Hessian behavior at the Battle of Trenton as "more attentive to the safety of their plunder than to their duty."[43] However, British, Loyalist, and Patriot forces, who also behaved poorly on occasion, had the advantage of blaming Hessians in a common language. It was not surprising that European soldiers, unused to being fired upon by nonuniformed peasants, reacted brutally. English speakers in general, but American Patriots in particular, won what was an important propaganda war.

The British government's resort to European auxiliary and mercenary soldiers for American coercion may date back to 1774. Gage advised hiring them that autumn, around the time when George III banned the export of munitions from Britain to the restive American colonies. Perhaps sensing that the mercenary business was about to heat up again, Hesse sent an official to London in October to press for a payment still owed from 1756–1763. Countering belief that actual negotiations with Hesse had not begun, one historian contends that "reports of the French envoy Grais make it clear that secret preliminary negotiations began at Hofgeismar during the winter of 1774–1775," with remaining details being resolved during the weeks after Bunker Hill.[44]

In any event, bloodstains were barely gone from June's Massachusetts battlefield before Lord North and his colleagues had multiple mercenary irons in the fire. They had no choice. In 1775, Dutch authorities were approached to see if the "Scottish Brigade," in Holland's service for almost two centuries, could be returned to Britain. That July, Colonel Albrecht von Scheither of the army of Hanover was commissioned to recruit several thousand soldiers in Germany to fill empty places in British regiments in America. King George, in his other role as Elector of Hanover, also began ordering battalions from the Electorate to take over from British units stationed in places like Gibraltar and Minorca, freeing those redcoats for service in North America. And most grandly, in that summer of 1775, Sir Robert Gunning, the British ambassador in St. Petersburg, who counted himself influential with Catherine the Great, began assuring his superiors in London that next year would see 20,000 Russian soldiers sail for Canada and New York.[45]

The notion of sending soldiers to America who could not speak English struck a chord in Whitehall. Unlike privates and corporals from Hertford or Hampshire, they would not respond to shared political values or to colonial insistence about seeking nothing more than the rights of Englishmen. One British captain wrote home that Russians would not be "seduced by the artifice and intrigue of these holy hypocrits [sic]." General Henry Clinton preferred Russians as unable to communicate or desert.[46]

Holland's "Scottish Brigade" was more a mixture of Dutch and soldiers of fortune, albeit with many officers of Scottish descent. When George III requested in 1775 to borrow the brigade, the Dutch prince, Stadtholder William IV, agreed. However, the commercially preoccupied province of Holland objected, preferring complete neutrality that would maintain Amsterdam's American trade. The Revolution also tapped a central split in Dutch politics between the reform-minded Dutch "Patriot" faction and the pro-British Orangists allied with the stadtholder. One major Patriot leader, Baron Johan van der Capellen, took up the colonies' cause, and in November 1775, the States-General resolved the issue. The brigade could be made available, but only if it would not be sent out of Europe. Lord North understood that to be a polite rejection.

Hanoverian Colonel Scheither, London's German recruiter, also came up short. Beginning in September 1775, by mid-1776 he had enlisted only 1,800 men and declined further efforts. Hapsburg officials in Austria, a former British ally now on the French side, opposed Scheither's activities. Clearly, the Austrians said, George III could recruit in his Hanoverian domain. In the empire's other states and free cities, Britain's king had no more right to recruit than a Spanish or Russian ruler would have.[47]

St. Petersburg also held back. In contrast to 1755, when then-empress

Elizabeth of Russia had agreed to provide a large contingent to fight for Britain in central Europe, Empress Catherine proved uncollaborative. After chilling Ambassador Gunning's hopes in September, the German-born czarina followed the counsel of Prussia's Frederick the Great. She sent the British monarch a letter saying that she thought it improper to send Russian troops to another hemisphere to serve a foreign government; better that his majesty put down his own American rebellion. An offended George III complained to Lord North that "she has not had the civility to answer in her own hand, and has thrown out some expressions that may be civil to a Russian ear, but not to more civilized ones."[48]

The more coercion minded in Lord North's Cabinet had welcomed summer's belief that Russian troops, freed up by the end of the so-called Pugatcheff rebellion in 1774, would ere long do their saber dancing in New York. As we have seen, the Earl of Suffolk was delighted. General Clinton spoke of "my friends the Russians." Gibbon, the historian of Rome conversant with decadent empires turning to brutish tribes for defense, talked with friends of visiting a barbarian camp should the Russians stop in Britain en route. Edmund Burke deplored any Russian arrangement: "I cannot, at my ease, see Russian barbarism let loose to waste the most beautiful object that ever appeared on this globe."[49] Horace Walpole acidly remarked on the dismissive reply King George got from "Sister Kitty."

It was more than an amusing episode or simple rebuke to British power. As we will see, Britain faced some degree of backlash against "royal slave-drivers" and the commerce in mercenaries and auxiliaries hitherto broadly accepted across Europe. British finger-pointers had enjoyed some success in 1772 and 1773 comparing Chief Justice Mansfield's decision ending slavery in England with unrepentant American slaveholding. Now American publicists, including Benjamin Franklin, could impugn Hesse-Cassel and the United Kingdom.

The British market for indentured soldiers—*Soldatenhandel,* which included blood money to rulers in compensation for those slain or maimed—evoked new analogies to slavery, lacking only some *mittel europäisch* Harriet Beecher Stowe to pen *Uncle Hans's Barracks.* The French dramatist Mirabeau authored *Avis aux Hessois,* in which he roused Hessians—"you betrayed people, oppressed, sold, humiliated by your fate"—to turn and instead defend America. The philosopher Voltaire, in correspondence with Frederick the Great, found the Prussian monarch deploring how the Landgrave of Hesse had "sold his subjects to the English as one sells cattle to be dragged to the slaughter." Among German thinkers, Friedrich Schiller, Johann Herder, and Immanuel Kant criticized princely practices and greed.[50] In his 1784 tragedy *Kabale und Liebe,* Schiller lamented the selling of German youth into foreign military servitude.[51]

The opposition in Parliament made similar points. During a 1775 debate in the House of Commons, Frederick Bull, a pro-American MP from London, said, "Let not the historian be obliged to say that the Russian and German slave was hired to subdue the sons of Englishmen and freedom."[52] Lord Camden, a former attorney general, told the House of Lords in early 1776 that the so-called treaties with the German states were "a mere bargain for the hire of troops on one side, and the sale of human blood on the other."[53] Benjamin Franklin, the probable author of an incendiary missive (the so-called *Uriasbrief*) imputing blood money practice to Hesse, did make a mistake; those provisions were not in the Hessian treaty. Reimbursements for death and maiming were only included in the troop-hire treaties Britain negotiated with Brunswick, Waldeck, and Hesse-Hanau.[54]

Moreover, these *Menschhandel* and "slavery" comparisons were confined to the army. An equal or perhaps better indictment can be attached to the impressment practiced by the Royal Navy on a scale far beyond any other. The French used chained galley slaves until the middle of the eighteenth century, and British impressment, although chainless, was so unhealthy for those pressed, as we saw in Chapter 5, that three out of four men pressed supposedly died within two years, with just one in five killed in battle. Some of the Royal Navy's most abusive practices came in New England waters, where impressment took place on a large scale despite its apparent prohibition in America under the so-called Statute of Anne.

To return to Hessians and Brunswickers, Ambrose Serle, the principal secretary to Admiral Lord Howe, voiced the frustration felt by conciliation-minded British officials. It would have been better, Serle wrote, "if the Rebellion could have been reduced without any foreign troops at all, for I fear our Employment of these upon this service will tend to irritate and inflame the Americans . . . It is a misfortune we ever had such a dirty, cowardly set of contemptible miscreants." Many Hessian officers, however, felt that it was the British whose misbehavior had embittered the country people.[55] Inasmuch as both Admiral and General Howe were simultaneously peace commissioners in 1776, their discomfort was understandable. The king's decision to hire mercenaries ranked alongside the burning of coastal towns on Admiral Graves's orders in swaying colonist opinion during the winter of 1775–1776.

No compendium details American press reaction to the various mid-1775 and late-1775 stages of British mercenary recruitment. How quickly did the newspapers react to the Russian refusal or to the first agreement negotiated with Brunswick? We do not know. But Virginians had heard about the Russian possibility by midsummer. In his July 28 issue of the *Virginia Gazette,* printer Alexander Purdy published portions of letters written in London in May. The czarina had "promised the ministry her assistance to reduce (what they call) the rebellious Americans, for which purpose she has 40,000 *Russian bears* at their service, to tear us to pieces." Purdie added that it was dreadful news if true, but possibly just a scare tactic.[56]

Later analyses of wartime propaganda revisited the mercenary furor. One twentieth-century commentary judged that "the British, not content with their own brutalities, called to their aid the most vicious and savage allies"—the Hessians. But the author did cite a later partial rebuttal by George Washington: "One thing I must remark in favor of the Hessians, and that is, that our people, who have been prisoners, generally agree that they received much kinder treatment from them, than from the British officers and soldiers. The barbarities at Princeton were all committed by the British, there being no Hessians there."[57]

If the Hessians have been overabused, Lord Suffolk and his colleagues in the Cabinet's caustic and belligerent old guard probably deserve their opprobrium. Back in 1769, the Cabinet's so-called Bedford faction had voted down Pitt supporters by five to four, thereby continuing rather than ending the tea tax that had provided such incitement four years later.[58] Heavy-handedness was a Bedfordite characteristic, foolish when they didn't have the regiments, ships, logistical awareness, and strategic capacity to back it up.

A Military Mismatch: *Soldatenhandel* in an Era of Popular Revolution

Bloody-mindedness aside, Britain circa 1775 had no choice but to hire mercenaries. After the Glorious Revolution, William and Mary and then Queen Anne took part in the major European wars of 1689–1713, which required London's increasing resort to German auxiliaries. Prior to this involvement, large-scale English military activity on the Continent had ended in the fifteenth century with the Anglo-French Hundred Years War.

The Prince of Orange led the reversal, and the House of Hanover followed. Dutch Prince William, on becoming King William III of England, indulged and enlarged his personal war with Louis XIV of France. Then, beginning in 1715, the first two monarchs from the House of Hanover, George I and George II, both German born, escalated Britain's involvement in central European politics, alliances, and German subsidies. During the wars of the 1740s and 1750s, the employment of Hessians and Brunswickers ballooned. Although many English members of Parliament deplored these commitments and costs, presumably they would have been angrier still to see Englishmen forced to fill a large standing army to pursue Hanoverian interests on Palatine or Pomeranian battlefields.

Whatever its merits, the heavy reliance on mercenaries was expensive. A considerable portion of the huge 1756–1763 expenses that drove postwar British Cabinets to demand more revenue from America involved outlays for *Soldatenhandel*. The 90,000-man "British Army in Germany" of 1760, for example, included 37,800 Hanoverians, 24,400 Hessians, 9,500 Bruns-wickers, and only 22,000 British.[59]

Throughout much of 1775, the secretary at war, Lord Barrington, had been admitting to members of Parliament and foreign diplomats alike that Britain would require 40,000 to 50,000 soldiers for its planned grand cam-paign in America, but had only 18,000 rank and file without mercenaries.[60] Barrington didn't expect the army to succeed, and he favored relying on the navy. He also kept sending in his resignation, but George III would not accept it. Nor did Lord North want Barrington to leave. In September 1775, North told an adviser who complained of the secretary at war that he "may perhaps not be so active in promoting measures which he does not approve as we could wish. I do not know that we have any particular neglect to lay to his charge, and without that I am sure that no application for removing him will succeed. The reasons must be very cogent which can carry that point: I speak from knowledge."[61] North, too, freely admitting his lack of military expertise, also periodically approached the king about resigning. Presumably that was part of the knowledge from which he spoke.

Did having to turn to mercenaries and auxiliaries in 1775 cost Britain victory? It is hard to make that specific case with any assuredness. Still, hiring them cost too much—the treaties and pay scales were exorbitant, as opposing members of Parliament detailed at length. Furthermore, moving the Germans from their individual principalities to embarkation points and thence to North America became part of the logistical nightmare profiled in Chapter 12. Ordering up 6,000 Hessians to be marched 80 miles to Ulm or Hanover in 1756 was a cakewalk next to arranging enough transports, escorts, victualling orders, and suchlike to move 20,000 of them, as well as 10,000 British troops 3,000 or 4,000 miles.

Drawn-out German negotiations added to the delay. Too few ships were available, half a dozen seaports and fleet rendezvous locations were involved, and schedules kept slipping. Instead of reaching New York by spring, as early plans had assumed, the main body of Germans—Hessians—were delivered in the summer. The Brunswickers, first to sail, left Europe in February and arrived in Quebec City on June 1.

In addition, some of the Hessian and Brunswicker units were of poor quality or commanded by officers who did not speak or understand English. Some did not comprehend North American warfare, as key 1776 and 1777 battles like Trenton, Bennington, and Saratoga generally confirmed. The British need to rely on mercenaries and auxiliaries had been disdained by France and Spain as early as December 1775, presumably encouraging their support of the Americans.[62] As we will see in Chapter 24, by 1780 and 1781, the British government had barely an ally left in Europe.

Would a less-smug Britain have been able to suppress the American Revolution? Perhaps, if that difference had reflected the sort of political change and somewhat more democratic directions finally achieved by the Reform Act of 1832. Such a Britain would not have had to mobilize Englishmen to fight Englishmen; it would have been able to work out self-government for the United Colonies somewhat akin to that laid out for Canada by the Durham Report in 1839. In the unreformed Britain of 1775, such thinking was not possible.

What may be fair to suggest, though, is that the early-eighteenth-century British "fiscal-military state" with its dependence on foreign "subsidy" troops to fight *ancien régime* conflicts in a still–*ancien régime* Europe was already outdated as the crisis of the 1770s widened. Yesteryear's reliance was not enough to win a new kind of major war (1) arising thousands of miles from Hesse, Brunswick, and the *Soldatenhandel;* (2) putting a global strain on eighteenth-century logistics; and (3) combining an unprecedented English colonial popular upheaval with considerable empathy for their cause even within England. When these new circumstances could not be understood and acted on in 1775, flawed decisions were inevitable. The fact that some of the new methods pursued so desperately (like rights for Catholics and large-scale Irish and Scottish recruitment) would later underpin a nineteenth-century imperial success is another story. However appropriate to the Second British Empire, they were not well suited to the First British Empire, which succumbed in North America.

CHAPTER 17

The Chesapeake—America's Vulnerable Estuary

The most feasible way of ending the rebellion was by cutting off the resources by which the enemy could continue war, these being principally drawn from Virginia, and principally tobacco.

Commodore Sir George Collier, *Royal Navy,* 1779

Cash and credit to pay for munitions would soon run dry without exports to pay the way. Chesapeake grain and tobacco abundantly answered the purpose if they could be shipped out. Tobacco, in fact, became America's chief currency overseas and greatly contributed to sustaining the war.

Ernest Eller, *Chesapeake Bay in the American Revolution,* 1981

With the exception of New York's Hudson-Champlain corridor, no other body of water in the thirteen colonies matched Chesapeake Bay and its over 100 riverine extensions as a potential conduit of invasion—a giant passageway through which an aggressive British deployment might have divided the northern provinces from those to the south. Two hundred miles in length, the bay is an estuary, where salt water and fresh water meet. It remains the largest of 130 estuaries within the boundaries of the United States. Including its tidal tributaries, the bay covers 4,500 square miles as the centerpiece of a watershed that sprawls over 64,000 square miles.

In terms of reach, the bay's arms point in every direction. Wide and lengthy navigable stretches of rivers like the James, York, Rappahannock, Patuxent, Potomac, Elk, Chester, Choptank, Nanticoke, and Pocomoke greatly expanded the potential range of warships and substantial landing parties. Dunmore in Virginia conceived of the Potomac as a water descent, by which an invading force of Great Lakes Indians could meet near Alexandria with a British flotilla sailing upriver from Chesapeake Bay. On the Eastern Shore of Maryland, the wide Nanticoke River was navigable to Seaford, Delaware. Map 11 shows the great bay's sprawling contours and major ports, together with its 1775 battlefields, river defenses, and burned or bombarded towns.

Employed instead as a loose geopolitical noun, the *Chesapeake* of 1775 included most of two colonies, Maryland and Virginia, as well as adjacent portions of two more, lower Delaware and a bit of northeastern North Carolina. South-central Pennsylvania had close ties to the Chesapeake through its rich wheatlands. These sent enough grain and flour south for export to make Baltimore the bay's leading port early in the Revolution. Despite this centrality, the region was a relatively neglected venue in early British thinking. This was doubly a boon for the Patriots, because the Chesapeake lent itself to a number of British actions, especially innovative use of naval power. But as we have seen in several chapters, innovation was not a feature of naval thinking in 1775, either at the Admiralty under Lord Sandwich or on the part of Admiral Graves, who commanded the Royal Navy in North America from an embattled flagship in Boston Harbor. Even when Lord Howe, a much more competent commander, took over in mid-1776, he was so preoccupied with the invasion of New York that "the Delaware and Chesapeake were left unguarded . . . and there was not a single cruiser between the Delaware and the St. Marys [Georgia]."¹ Fortunately for the United Colonies, senior British officers familiar with North America from the previous war had mostly fought French and Indians based in Canada and the Great Lakes. The impressive bodies of water they kept in salutary memory alongside the great victories of 1758–1760 ranged from the St. Lawrence and Hudson rivers to the Forks of the Ohio, a distinct detriment by 1775. The deeper comprehension of Chesapeake opportunities gained by British commanders between 1777 and 1781 came several years too late for timely action. On a smaller scale, seizing control of Delmarva— latter-day shorthand for the peninsula shared by portions of Delaware, Maryland, and Virginia—was usually feasible, potentially rewarding, and never ventured.

Nor was the Chesapeake important only as a venue for battles and invasions. Trade was frequently pivotal. Chesapeake tobacco, and to a lesser extent local grain, served the Patriot side as an essential wartime currency. Three times in 1775 Congress urged the individual colonies, emphasizing those along the Chesapeake, to ship their most salable produce only to

11: CHESAPEAKE BAY: THE MISSED BRITISH INVASION OPPORTUNITY

Chesapeake Bay offered a series of water invasion routes by which Britain might have divided the northern colonies from those in the south. However, British officials understood too late and did not embrace a Chesapeake strategy until the War of 1812, when they burned Washington.

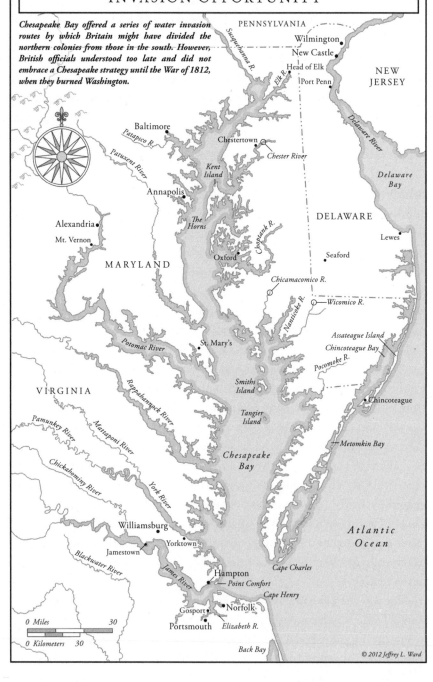

PENNSYLVANIA

Susquehanna R.

Wilmington
New Castle
Head of Elk
Port Penn

NEW JERSEY

Baltimore
Patapsco R.

Chestertown
Chester River

Delaware River

Kent Island

Delaware Bay

DELAWARE

Annapolis

The Horns

Lewes

Alexandria
Mt. Vernon

MARYLAND

Oxford

Choptank R.

Seaford

Chicamacomico R.

Wicomico R.

Nanticoke R.

Potomac River

St. Mary's

Assateague Island
Chincoteague Bay

Pocomoke R.

VIRGINIA

Rappahannock River

Smiths Island

Pamunkey River
Mataponi River

Tangier Island

Chincoteague

Chickahominy River

Chesapeake Bay

Metomkin Bay

York River

Atlantic Ocean

Williamsburg

Blackwater River
Jamestown
Yorktown

James River

Hampton
Point Comfort

Cape Charles

Cape Henry

Gosport
Norfolk

0 Miles   30

Portsmouth
Elizabeth R.

0 Kilometers   30

Back Bay

© 2012 Jeffrey L. Ward

buyers committed to paying with utter necessities: munitions, weaponry, medicine, and salt. Paper money was distinctly less welcome in payment. The foreign sellers having the most gunpowder and arms available—France and Holland—were precisely those anxious for tobacco in return.

Tobacco: The 1775 Currency of Revolution

The considerable price increases in 1774 and much of 1775 reflected British and European anticipation that Virginia, Maryland, and North Carolina growers would hold back shipments once nonexportation began in September 1775. Smuggling, of course, was another avenue. Even in 1770, over 20 percent of merchantable Chesapeake leaf never cleared customs, presumably reaching buyers by unlawful means.[2]

That variety of trade doubtless grew in 1775, although many hogsheads still went to English and Scottish firms. However, American shippers requiring payment in Dutch gunpowder or French muskets conveniently declared surplus by King Louis's arsenals began sending their tobacco to Amsterdam, Dunkerque, and Nantes or, nearer home, to West Indian entrepôts like Martinique and St. Eustatius. Patriots in Maryland and Virginia handled part of this commerce through vessels of their own, but many ships also sailed from Philadelphia under the aegis of politically active and tobacco-wise firms like Willing and Morris and Cunningham and Nesbitt. The former also partnered with Virginia firms like Norton and Beall of Williamsburg in obtaining powder for that market.[3] By 1776, in one calculation, Willing and Morris had 20 ships trading in war supplies for Congress's Secret Committee.[4] Robert Morris, although British born, had grown up in Oxford, Maryland, where his father had been a pioneering tobacco merchant in the 1740s.

During the spring of 1775, as control over provincial gunpowder supplies preoccupied Patriots from Boston to Savannah, Chesapeake rebels did their share. In March, irate Marylanders had tarred and feathered a customs officer who had confiscated smuggled powder. On April 27, local Patriots pressured Royal Governor Robert Eden into delivering up some arms and ammunition that Marylanders demanded, ostensibly "to keep the servants and negroes in order."[5]

Merchants and shippers in Maryland chose the Patriotic side in higher ratios than did those in Virginia, so many of whom were Scottish Loyalists. In both Baltimore and Annapolis, Scotch-Irish merchants with ties to colleagues in Philadelphia matched tobacco growers in their influence over Maryland's Revolutionary movement.[6]

In early December 1775, as Congress again encouraged trade for war necessities, the Maryland Convention named Richard Harrison, a young Virginia merchant, as its agent in Martinique. Tobacco and wheat would be shipped to neutral Caribbean warehouses, then sold by Harrison for arms and ammunition.[7] He teamed with Baltimorean Abraham Van Bibber, and the two jointly represented Maryland and Virginia in both Dutch St. Eustatius and French Martinique. Van Bibber, a Dutch speaker, was an old hand. Traffic had so expanded by January 1775, "there were already *daily* [italics added] consignments from the ports of the Netherlands by way of St. Eustatius—cargoes of gunpowder and other munitions, tea and liquor." After the arrival of a new Dutch governor in 1775, Van Bibber assured associates that "we are as well fixed with him as we were with the former."[8]

The pair were busy men. Between May and July 1776, they reportedly shipped 20 tons of gunpowder to Virginia and somewhat less to Maryland.[9] No records compare Virginia's overall volume to Maryland's, but clearly the gunpowder trade was a priority in both provinces.

Royal Navy ships in Chesapeake Bay did not start seizing every American ship as a prize until March 1, 1776, pursuant to the Prohibitory Act passed by Parliament in December.[10] Until September 1775, outbound vessels might well have been carrying lawful cargoes of tobacco (or something else) bound for Britain. As confrontations between Dunmore and Virginia Patriots increased in the autumn of 1775, few warships would have been available to keep watch at the Virginia Capes, the ten-mile-wide gap through which the lower bay empties into the Atlantic. Revealingly, in 1777, when Britain did have enough vessels on station to make the blockade work, shipping into and out of the bay declined by roughly three quarters.[11] Had the Admiralty in early 1775 thought to find and employ four or five more large sloops and small frigates to blockade the entrances to the Chesapeake and the Delaware River, much more tobacco could have been kept from being sold for vital munitions.

Effective blockade or not, Patriots needing to move goods did have alternative routes. Produce could be sent by river or wagon 40 miles across the Delmarva Peninsula to one of the small, unblockaded ports on Virginia's Atlantic side, often Chincoteague. A second route, which involved a twelve-to-fifteen-mile wagon trip, traversed the peninsula's narrow northern isthmus to reach Delaware Bay, and thence goods went by boat to

Philadelphia. Flour, pork, and beef shipments for the American army normally took this route and avoided the Virginia Capes.

In 1775 and much of 1776, though, Patriot vessels could often slip past the few British guards, especially when captained by local men able to use the creeks and inlets for ducking enemy patrols. One way or another, Chesapeake tobacco and grain got through in sufficient quantity.

Chesapeake Patriots Prepare for War

South of New England, Virginia was the colony that moved most quickly toward a shooting war. Dunmore's belligerence was matched on the Patriot side by Patrick Henry, Richard Henry Lee, Thomas Jefferson, and many more.

Maryland, for its part, had been unusually bold in 1774, endorsing nonexportation of tobacco, then embracing incendiary behavior in mid-October when radical Patriots torched the British tea ship *Peggy Stewart* near Annapolis. This aggressive mindset continued in December at the Provincial Convention, which advised all the counties to organize militia forces and to publish the names of individuals reluctant to serve. In January 1775, radical Patriots in the Annapolis area pronounced that anyone refusing to aid "the purchase of arms and ammunition is and ought to be esteemed an enemy of America."[12] The Convention had suggested county-by-county outlays that totaled £10,000.[13]

Overall, though, the Maryland Convention's military bite was weaker than its bark. Tories openly worked to break up militia musters in Anne Arundel, Frederick, Caroline, and Kent counties during 1775.[14] In December 1775, the Convention authorized 1,444 troops and in June 1776 raised the number to 3,405.[15] On the Eastern Shore in particular, though, many of those enrolled were unreliable. On top of which, militia units in the Patriot-minded Baltimore and Annapolis areas were roiled by radical demands akin to those being voiced in Pennsylvania and Virginia. Some militiamen, angry over the requirement of property to vote, threatened to quit if officials barred their ballots for delegates to the Constitutional Convention. As that voting approached in the summer of 1776, the Anne Arundel (Annapolis) County militia proposed a democratic and popular version of government resembling the program being implemented that summer in Pennsylvania.[16] In Maryland, though, conservatives wound up drafting the new constitution, which foreclosed Philadelphia-style radicalism. Militia dissatisfaction continued, with some men refusing to muster, others grousing about elite-minded officers (and seeking to elect new ones), and still others threatening to lay down their arms unless the fines supposed to be levied on nonenrollers were collected.[17]

Popular reluctance to enlist was also a dilemma in Virginia. In March 1775, the Second Provincial Convention had recommended that each of the 60-odd counties enroll at least one company of infantry and one troop of cavalry to prepare for any emergency. Two to three regiments were expected. Then during the summer, the Third Convention called for raising 3,000 men to defend the tidewater region, with another 425 men to man the western forts and "watch the motions of the Indians." Each county was also told to gather and train companies of minutemen.[18] Paper money totaling £300,000 was voted in support. Burgesses still wore hunting shirts, and *rage militaire* still filled the air.

But it cooled in autumn. The minuteman scheme did not work out in many areas, and late 1775 enlistments fell short. As we saw in Chapter 6, the Old Dominion's militia reorganization bogged down in inadequate public funds and squabbling over conditions of service. Substantial black slave flight to the British now focused Virginia leaders on guarding and protecting plantations, but this priority soured poor and middle-class whites. In late October and November, as fighting began in Princess Anne and Norfolk counties and in nearby Hampton, Virginia's self-defense posture was less than muscular. During this period, Dunmore seemed to be gaining strength with his several companies of redcoats, his 300-member Ethiopian Regiment, and his hundreds of Norfolk-area enlistees in the Queen's Loyal Virginia Regiment. Hundreds of erstwhile Patriot militiamen took British loyalty oaths. By early December, as rebel Colonel William Woodford advanced on the Norfolk area at the head of one of Virginia's (two) regular regiments, augmented by Culpeper sharpshooters, he accepted just one militia company, a unit from Smithfield, 30 miles west. Woodford thought it better not to rely on local militia.[19]

Besides militia reliability, Chesapeake Patriots also began to think about provincial navies. As Dunmore's threat became serious, Virginia's naval weakness also pushed to the fore. From August to November, Royal Navy sloops like *Otter* and *Kingfisher,* with a half dozen small schooners and pilot ships as tenders, were able to maraud at will along the rivers near Norfolk and Portsmouth. Back in May, Dunmore had asked Admiral Graves for a large man-of-war, pointing out—quite accurately—that the Chesapeake's tidal rivers had great depth "even very high up," and that a powerful ship "would strike Awe over the whole Country." He added that more well-armed and well-manned tenders could stop ammunition running at the mouths of the major rivers.[20] Luckily for the Americans, the Chesapeake was not a British priority; no large frigate arrived until February.

During the late autumn of 1775, what was called "Dunmore's navy" dominated not just 40 to 50 miles of coast but 15 to 20 miles inland from Norfolk. Moreover some 20 miles across the bay, residents in the colony's two Eastern Shore counties, already half Tory by inclination, were cowed by the distantly visible mast tops and spread sails of British naval power. Tenders commanded by squeaky-voiced midshipmen or gruff petty officers visited the peninsula at will, often to demand (but also usually pay for) provisions. Eastern Shore residents expected a Dunmore-led or inspired invasion. As for local militia units, Patriot officers doubted their reliability. On top of which, a half million bushels of newly harvested wheat—the peninsula, too, was a famous granary—also had to be kept out of British hands.

The British never seized their Eastern Shore opportunity. Only 400 Patriot militiamen having been raised by November, Northampton County officials sought help from the Philadelphia Congress. Two companies of reliable Maryland minutemen from the upper bay marched down in February and bolstered tenuous Patriot authority.[21]

On the Patriot side, turning small merchant vessels into small warships could be accomplished in a month or two. Thus the relatively rapid calendar of Patriot navy building: "The [Third] Virginia Convention authorized the Committee on Safety, on 24 August 1775, 'to appoint a sufficient number of look-outs and advice boats,' but did not try to organize armed vessels into a navy." The Fourth Convention moved to rectify that omission in December, debating and then approving a resolution to create a navy "for the protection of the several rivers in this colony." The Committee of Safety now had authority to fit out armed vessels.[22]

In fact, the Committee, including such prominent leaders as Edmund Pendleton, George Mason, John Page, and Richard Bland, had already started. By December, two brothers, James Barron in *Liberty* and Richard Barron in *Patriot,* were operating from Hampton as captains of a pair of 60-ton pilot-boat schooners armed with swivel guns. The *Patriot,* procured by Patrick Henry on December 19, 1775, is generally recognized as the Virginia Navy's first vessel.[23] On December 1, Richard Barron, under the orders of the feisty Hampton–Elizabeth City Committee, had stopped the Loyalist sloop *Christian,* outward bound from Norfolk to Britain, and seized important letters. Hampton's aggressive committee was the archfoe of Captain Matthew Squire of HMS *Otter,* who had already been repulsed attacking the town in October. After the *Christian,* some ten other suspected Loyalist vessels were also stopped or seized. On December 23, the Convention expressed approval of the Barron brothers' activities.[24]

Maryland more or less kept pace. On December 8, the Baltimore Committee, acting under provincial orders, began to refit a local merchantman, the *Sidney.* Renamed the *Defence,* it became the colony's first warship. By mid-1776, Maryland would have several more. The *Defence* made its naval debut in March, being hurriedly completed and armed with fourteen six-pounders just in time to face the *Otter.* Captain Squire's sloop had come to the upper bay, accompanied by two tenders, to capture or sink a pair of new Continental vessels, the *Wasp* and *Hornet.* No fight ever took place between *Defence* and *Otter,* though, because both commanders had orders to be cautious.[25] But when *Otter* returned south and was deemed to be retreating, Captain James Nicholson of *Defence* became a hero.

To the north, Philadelphia, having legislated the creation of the Continental Navy, now became the principal locus of its construction. Back in October, Congress had authorized four vessels. Through November and into December, workmen at Philadelphia's Wharton and Humphrey shipyard labored to finish overhauling a 300-ton merchantman, the *Black Prince,* chosen to become flagship of the new Continental fleet under the lackluster name *Alfred.** Baltimore's supporting role in naval construction reflected its emergence as a Patriot-faction stronghold.

In early December, Congress's Naval Committee engaged Baltimorean Captain William Stone and his merchant sloop *Falcon* for a new plan to thwart "the cutters and armed vessels in Chesapeake Bay, under Lord Dunmore." A naval agent arrived in Baltimore with instructions to "act in conjunction with the delegates of that colony to this Congress . . . to procure, with all possible despatch, on Continental charge, two or three armed vessels to proceed immediately to cruize on, take or destroy as many of the armed vessels, cutters and ships of war of the enemy as possible."[26] If that phraseology appears too pompous for a minor maritime enterprise, the ac-

---

*In honor of Alfred the Great, the ninth-century English king credited with beginning the island's first navy. But realistically, how many knew the name?

tivities did not remain minor. These are hallowed months in the history of the U.S. Navy.

The little *Falcon* took new guise as the *Hornet,* mounting ten six- or nine-pounders. A second vessel, the schooner *Scorpion,* became the *Wasp,* boasting—if that word is suitable—eight two-pounders. A third vessel, the brigantine *Wild Duck,* purchased in St. Eustatius by Maryland agent Abraham Van Bibber, arrived in Philadelphia on March 9 with a cargo of gunpowder. Somewhat larger, she was brought into the Continental service to sail under the name *Lexington,* carrying fourteen four-pounders and two six-pounders. One hundred and seventy years later, in the World War II Pacific, the namesakes of the three vessels spoke with more impressive thunder. The aircraft carrier *Wasp* was the eighth naval vessel to bear its name, and so was the carrier *Hornet.* Planes from the latter shot down a wartime total of 1,410 Japanese aircraft. The third carrier, the *Lexington,* had followed four other vessels honoring the same distant forebear. In 1775, what rebel could have imagined the succession?

In January 1776, the original *Wasp* and *Hornet,* their makeovers finished, escorted a group of small Patriot vessels south through the Virginia Capes. On February 14, they joined the rest of the fledgling Continental fleet in Delaware Bay. The Naval Committee's early January orders, assuming winds and weather permitted, were for them to sail to Chesapeake Bay and to destroy Dunmore's flotilla, if its strength, upon investigation, was "not greatly superiour to your own." In fact, Dunmore was strengthened in February by Captain Hamond's 44-gun *Roebuck.* With or without that knowledge, the little fleet—minus the *Hornet*—sailed instead for the Bahamas, where it captured cannon and some ammunition. Dunmore's hold on lower Chesapeake Bay would continue for several additional months.

River Fortification and Green River Navies

Despite the wishful belief of many Loyalists that Britain would negotiate an acceptable peace, the eight months after Lexington and Concord witnessed a steadily escalating American commitment to war, including river and harbor fortification. Despite its shortage of frigates and sloops, the Royal Navy represented a potential threat to keeping major rivers open.

The Continental Congress had voiced almost immediate concern over the Hudson, and in June the New York Provincial Congress chose a committee to inspect the Hudson highlands. A site for fortifications was agreed to, and by summer, construction was under way, even if the site changed. That same month, worry over Portsmouth, New Hampshire, prompted George Washington to send General John Sullivan back home, where he quickly constructed a chained boom—raised and lowered by windlasses—across the mouth of the Piscataqua River. Fire ships and rafts with masses of combustibles waited above the boom as further protection.[27]

To protect Philadelphia and the Delaware River (as well as Congress), initial steps in September included constructing small warships—armed galleys—and emplacing a triple row of iron-barbed timbers named chevaux-de-frise, after their late-seventeenth-century origins in the Frisian province of the Netherlands. In October, officials agreed to site an artillery battery on Mud Island, at the confluence of the Delaware and Schuylkill rivers, which eventually became Fort Mifflin.[28]

Chesapeake Bay represented a unique defensive challenge, given its size and 3,600-mile shoreline. The name itself comes from *K'che-sepiack,* Algonquin for "the Great Salt Water," although only the lower bay was briny. Beyond its relative immensity, the bay's several dozen islands and scores of navigable rivers lent themselves to effective operations by small naval craft—sloops, schooners, galleys, and pilot boats, a type of local schooner specially rigged for speed. Privateers and pirates (picaroons) also thrived on its waters during the Revolution. If British plans were only starting to unfold during the summer and autumn of 1775, little more could be said of Patriot activity.

The terrain surrounding the bay was mostly flat, especially below Annapolis and Easton. As the bay widened, its waters had an increasingly southern feel, accentuated by cypresses, green salt marshes, muskrats, dugouts called bugeyes, barge-riding bandits, and rivers with names like Chicamacomico that conjured up Georgia, Alabama, or Florida Indians. These lower reaches had the major islands, most notably Tangier and Smith. What is more, in sharp contrast to coastal New England, many of its shoremen and fishermen had Tory inclinations.[29] Local poor white watermen, being ill disposed toward the Patriot gentry, generally threw in with the British. In Tory hands during most of the war, Tangier and Smith, along with nearby Hog Island, were used by the British and by Loyalist privateers through 1782. Had the king's forces kept control of Norfolk, the islands would have meshed into a strong lower Chesapeake defense.

Not surprisingly, the language employed by December's Virginia Convention in authoring a provincial navy had emphasized river protection, so the new force had more origins in so-called green-water strategy than in blue-water thinking. Blocking the principal river channels and locating cannon at key points had been among the first measures considered. On the mainland side of Hampton Roads, local authorities sank derelict vessels in the channel of the Hampton River to block or slow down British incursions.[30] During October, as Dunmore's river raids escalated, Virginia's delegates to Congress suggested to the provincial Committee of Safety that cannon could be positioned on particular heights along the James, York, and Rappahannock rivers.[31] But after several months of deliberation, war vessels became the protection of choice.

In the upper bay, Marylanders were initially complacent about the Patuxent and Patapsco rivers. However, when Captain Squire took his infamous *Otter* toward Baltimore in March 1776, defenses were rushed. Depth-marker trees along the Patapsco were replaced by cannon and chains. Worn-out craft were ordered down to Whetstone Point—the later site of Fort McHenry—to be sunk as a channel barrier, and a battery was emplaced at Fell's Point.[32]

However, the greatest spur to river protection in the Chesapeake region involved the strategic but vulnerable Potomac. When Virginians and Marylanders met during the autumn of 1775 to plan defenses where the river narrows, near George Washington's plantation at Mount Vernon, they ruefully discovered that width and depth made obstacles impractical.[33] Next, the Maryland Council of Safety approved the idea of placing warning beacons (to be lit) every five miles from the river's mouth upstream to Alexandria. On foggy or misty days, lookout boats were to take over. But this proposal also went unimplemented.

The Alexandria (Virginia) Committee of Safety took charge because of invasion fears. One town history explained: "Rumor was rife in [October] 1775 that Governor Dunmore had dispatched an expedition of warships up the Potomac to 'lay waste the towns and the country, capture Mrs. Washington and burn Mount Vernon.' Martha Washington remained calm, and though finally persuaded by Colonel [George] Mason to leave home, she stayed away one night only." Fears rekindled in January 1776, when General Washington's plantation manager wrote that "Alexandria is much alarmed and indeed the whole neighborhood. The women and children are leaving the town and stowing themselves in every hut they can find, out of reach of the enemy's cannon. Every wagon, cart and pack horse they can get is employed."[34]

Partly as a result, Virginia decided in January 1776 to organize a squadron to protect the Potomac. The flagship—a 110-ton sloop named the *American Congress*—carried fourteen guns and 96 seamen and marines. Two row galleys were each to mount eighteen-pounder cannon. However, with the Old Dominion bearing full responsibility for defending the James, York, and Rappahannock rivers, Virginians asked Maryland authorities for Potomac region help. They supplied ten barrels of powder to the Potomac fleet's flagship and helped the Virginians purchase the two eighteen-pound cannon from a Maryland ironmaster.[35] In addition, a dozen schooners, sloops, and row galleys were bought or built to protect the other three rivers, and Virginia also funded two galleys to protect North Carolina's Ocracoke Inlet. That entryway provided a back door to Norfolk and the Chesapeake via the Blackwater River.

Captain Hamond of the Royal Navy, who reached Norfolk in February in his 44-gun frigate *Roebuck*, quickly grasped the larger British opportunity: "On account of the navigable rivers of this Country, there is no part of the continent where ships can assist land operations more than this." A small flotilla and a thousand men, he amplified, could "distress the colonies of Maryland & Virginia to the greatest degree, and employ more than ten times their number to watch them."[36] Dunmore had made almost the same argument for an aggressive naval strategy. However, the king, Lord North, and the Cabinet had aimed their southern expedition at North Carolina, and unlike Captain Hamond, the Admiralty may have lacked the acumen—or possibly even suitable maps—to picture the Chesapeake as the potential invasion highway that it was.

1775: Many Potential Loyalists, Few British Reinforcements

Demographically, too, the region could have been an invasion highway. Virginia far surpassed North Carolina in wealth, political influence, and strategic importance. But Chapter 13 has explained how during the autumn of 1775, senior British officials accepted a poorly informed strategy for securing the southern provinces through a rendezvous off Cape Fear to support a Loyalist rising. When a small part of the Cape Fear force under General Clinton, the overall commander, stopped in Virginia in February en route from Boston, a frustrated Dunmore voiced his "inexpressible mortification." He protested to the American secretary, now Lord George Germain, that North Carolina was a "most insignificant province," while Virginia, "the first colony on the continent, both in its riches and power, is totally neglected."[37]

Dunmore was generally correct. The British did not perceive Virginia's or the Chesapeake's importance until it was too late. One Virginia historian elaborated: "If there had been towns of any size in Virginia [after Norfolk was burned], with royal forces to occupy them, or if there had been at Norfolk a fifth part of the army Howe wasted at idleness at Boston in the winter of 1775–76, the history of the Revolution in Virginia and of the Revolution in general, might have been different."[38]

The many ships and seven regiments bound for Cape Fear that winter from Ireland and Boston might have made that difference. With Virginia and Maryland lagging in their military preparedness, a middling British fleet on the Chesapeake with three or four regiments might have sailed up-river to Alexandria, bombarded Baltimore, cut off much of the tobacco-for-ammunition trade, and turned an overawed Delmarva Peninsula into a recruiting ground for Loyalist regiments. Admiral Graves in Boston could have been bypassed.

Instead, by late December, when Dunmore abandoned Norfolk, he had received only 140 redcoats, mostly from the Fourteenth Regiment stationed in St. Augustine (70 arrived in August, 70 more in October). Considering the alarm and anxiety spread in southeastern Virginia by the 1,000 or so men he commanded at his November zenith of local influence, another 500 to 1,000 soldiers might have consolidated a British regional occupation. Despite intimations that autumn that Dunmore might receive the other companies from the Fourteenth, he never got them.

Despite his earl's rank, unusual for a provincial governor, Dunmore's bombast worked against him. As we have seen, he had strutted about his prospects for raising black and Loyalist units, telling Lord Dartmouth several times that "with a few hundred more with Arms, Ammunition and the other requisites of War, and with full power to Act I could in a few Months reduce this Colony to perfect Submission." Gage in Boston had credited enough of Dunmore's boasting to send seven officers, who arrived in August expecting to take up Virginia Loyalist commands, still nonexistent. In addition, Gage had approved the Connolly-Dunmore plan for mounting an invasion from the Great Lakes down the Potomac to Alexandria. This was to include a company of redcoats to be taken from Illinois.[39] That scheme fell apart in November after Major Connolly was captured traveling through Maryland. Dunmore could not say that his ideas had been ignored.

For a waterborne force, Dunmore had begun the summer of 1775 with three warships and five or six tenders. His one or two sloops were effective in the rivers as well as in the bay. A single small frigate was also on hand—initially the *Fowey* (24 guns), replaced in July by the *Mercury* (20), and followed late in the year by the *Liverpool* (28). Occasionally, two frigates were present at one time. Dunmore also procured and partly refitted two merchant vessels: the *William*, which became his floating headquarters, and the *Eilbeck*, renamed the *Dunmore*. Both carried cannon, but not to the extent of a purpose-built warship. The *Roebuck* did not come until February. For purposes of comparison, Royal Navy Captain James Wallace had almost the same mid-1775 strength in Newport to patrol Rhode Island waters and the eastern end of Long Island Sound. Winning the Chesapeake would have been a greater prize.

Loyalists were relatively abundant. Although Virginia had a smaller ratio than North Carolina, from a British standpoint those in the Old Dominion were much more opportunely located. Whereas North Carolina's emigrant Scottish Highlanders clustered 75 miles inland, Virginia's Loyalists concentrated near the seacoast—in Norfolk and its environs, as well as across the bay in what both Virginians and Marylanders called Eastern Shore counties. Between late October and early December, when Dunmore seemed to be solidifying his control of Norfolk and nearby towns, thousands of formerly neutral or Patriot-minded residents put on red cloth badges and swore British allegiance. In fairness, the British Cabinet could not have learned of these inroads until December or January, and the slow-traveling news from Governor Martin in North Carolina also remained encouraging.

Among the Virginia Scottish merchants loyal to the Crown was Andrew Sprowle, proprietor of the colony's biggest shipyard, at Gosport. Extending along a half mile of waterfront, Sprowle's facility included a group of large stone warehouses, a smithy, wharves, and a large iron crane. His executor later noted that British ships usually lay there "in the winter months for the convenience of watering and other necessities, and occasionally careened, refitted, or repaired."[40] Even in 1775 this complex represented a prime naval resource; in later years it would grow into Norfolk Navy Yard.

Delmarva was a particular opportunity. Even without actual British military occupation during 1775 and 1776, the peninsula's lower counties leaned toward Loyalism. Historians usually identify six: Sussex (Delaware); Dorchester, Somerset, and Worcester (Maryland); and Accomack and

Northampton (Virginia).[41] According to one historian, "In the lower counties of Somerset and Worcester, Tories outnumbered Patriots possibly by as much as two or three to one, and, overall, one scholar has claimed that 'with the possible exception of western Long Island, the Chesapeake peninsula had the highest proportion of Loyalists in the colonies.' "[42]

In these counties, tobacco was a lesser crop and generally of an inferior grade. Wheat was Delmarva's mainstay. Patriot nonexportation beginning in September 1775 was also locally unpopular for interfering with a considerable volume of lumber exports (barrels, staves, and the like) to Britain and the West Indies.[43] The interior of the Eastern Shore was poor land, the last part of the peninsula to be settled. High debt levels and uncertain livelihoods aggravated local frustration. Plausibly enough, poor whites saw little reason to fight for the wealthy tobacco planters or the Patriot-faction commercial elite in Baltimore and Annapolis.

Beyond poor whites, some other groups looked to the British: indentured servants; black slaves; and several religious minorities and evangelical movements of local importance. Of the latter, the Chesapeake had more than its share.

As Chapter 15 has discussed, the thirteen colonies' greatest numbers of indentured servants and runaways were in the Chesapeake—in the Baltimore-Annapolis section, the Northern Neck of Virginia, and some Pennsylvania locales along the Maryland border reputed to house many runaways. In November 1775, Jonathan Boucher, a Maryland Anglican clergyman, citing servants' "ill-humor," offered advice in a letter to Undersecretary of State William Knox in London. Five hundred recruits might well be enrolled in Baltimore; "it is certain the richest Harvest of Them may be gleaned there, at Elk Ridge, the Iron-works and Annapolis." He also recommended sending parties in armed vessels to the heads of rivers in Pennsylvania, Maryland, and Virginia to spread word "to the back Settlements where most of these people have been carried."[44]

The Northern Neck of Virginia, home to the Washington, Carter, Ball, and Lee families, had a comparable indentured servant population. According to one historian, "In the convict- and indentured-servant-rich Northern Neck counties, for example, many whites tried to escape to Dunmore, and more plotted their escape and waited for the right moment. Indeed, in some quarters, like George Washington's own estate, Mount Vernon, discontented and rebellious white servants caused almost as much anxiety as enslaved blacks."[45] In the autumn of 1775, the general and his cousin Lund, the estate manager, were especially uneasy about the white servants and black slaves collaborating. "I think if there was no white Servts in this family I shoud [*sic*] be under no apprehension [*sic*] about the Slaves," Lund advised.[46] Washington, as we will see, feared that Dunmore might raid Mount Vernon.

As for black slaves, planters in both Virginia and Maryland worried about uprisings. By December 1775, Dunmore's defeats at Great Bridge and then in Norfolk eased the immediate threat. However, in 1780 and 1781, when the British returned to Virginia in larger numbers, employing the rivers as invasion routes, one chronicler noted that slaves "flocked to the Enemy from all quarters even from very remote parts."[47] It was an ongoing vulnerability.

From the British standpoint, a further Chesapeake opportunity in 1775 and 1776 came from religious preferences. To begin with, poor-white Anglican Loyalism was strong in the lower counties of Delmarva. In contrast to mainland Virginia's largely Patriot-minded Anglican clergy, those in Delmarva took the British side by two to one. Anglican Loyalism also thrived on the peninsular rivalry between Anglicans and the Patriot-leaning Presbyterians.[48]

Irish and German Catholics, many of them indentured servants, were a potential British recruitment pool. Philadelphia's prosperous Irish Catholic merchants—the Moylans, Fitzsimons, Meases, and Meades—were prominent Patriots, as were most of the long-established Catholic tobacco gentry in southern Maryland. By contrast, indentured workers from the Philadelphia construction trades and the Pennsylvania and Maryland ironworks, as well as runaway servants, were ripe for picking. Britain's short-lived Roman Catholic Volunteers Regiment had 180 men at its peak, most of them from Delaware, Maryland, and Pennsylvania. Potential Catholic Loyalism was also apparent in Pennsylvania's iron-producing regions. One British officer, housed locally as a prisoner, reported "something very extraordinary but most of the Roman Catholics are friends to the [British] government."[49] The threat was underscored by periodic talk in 1777 and thereafter about potential risings. If the British landed an army near Baltimore and moved north, they would be joined by thousands of Pennsylvania Loyalists on reaching the areas around York and Lancaster; alternatively, if the Pennsylvanians rose, a British army could march to join them.[50]

Evangelical missionaries had already launched efforts that would turn the Delmarva Peninsula into "the Garden of American Methodism." And in 1775, Methodist leader John Wesley unexpectedly took a strong pro-Tory position in his *Calm Address to the American Colonies*. His Loyalism complicated the Methodists' colonial missionary efforts, concentrated in Pennsylvania, Virginia, Delaware, and Maryland. But Patriots fumed over the message and behavior of the region's principal Methodist missionaries: Thomas Rankin, Martin Rodda, and Thomas Webb, all British by birth and loyalty. Over several years, Rodda was arrested for helping to lead a rebellion on the Eastern Shore, and Webb, a former British Army captain, was jailed for spying and furnishing information to the British.[51]

What further angered Patriot leaders was the repeated interference by Methodist missionaries and itinerants with recruitment and militia musters. In 1777, Colonel Nathaniel Potter, an Eastern Shore militia leader, wrote to the governor that "the spirit of Methodism reigns so much among us that few or no men will be raised for the war. It is a general practice . . . when there is any call for raising men for their preachers to be continually attending their different posts day and night which I am fully persuaded is the greatest stroke the British Ministry ever struck amongst us." In Delaware that year, Patriot leader Caesar Rodney believed that Methodist preachers were recruiting a Loyalist unit in the area along the Maryland border.[52]

Taken together, Delmarva Anglicans, Irish and German Catholics, and Methodists represented a significant population of British sympathizers and potential recruits. Although this chapter has skimmed over the religious factor, we have seen it appear again and again as a major factor in choosing sides for the Revolution. In the Chesapeake, Loyalist numbers augmented the topographic, naval, and economic factors that invited British attentions to the region.

Between 1777 and 1781, when the British—wiser every year—had renewed attention to the Chesapeake, they did tap more of these possibilities, and the wide array of proposals and strategic memoranda, submitted to generals Clinton and Cornwallis in particular, elaborate the opportunity never realized.

An Overview of Lost Chesapeake Opportunities

Six years after the sloop HMS *Otter* failed in its attack on the small Virginia town of Hampton, two great British defeats in the Chesapeake region finally cost them the American war. On September 5, 1781, a French fleet under the Comte de Grasse defeated the Royal Navy at the Battle of the (Virginia) Capes; and on October 19, Lord Cornwallis, no longer able to expect relief, was obliged to surrender his 10,000-man army at Yorktown. Over those six years, British and Loyalist thinkers had left few strategic stones unturned in making the case for greater attention to the region.

In terms of the naval opportunities neglected, what Dunmore pointed out in 1775, and Captain Hamond restated in February 1776, was voiced again by Commodore Sir George Collier, who commanded British naval forces during the brief but effective reinvasion of 1779. The commodore opposed withdrawal because southeastern Virginia was too critical as a base.

The great bay, he said, was a key to victory. "The most feasible way of ending the rebellion was by cutting off the resources by which the enemy could continue war, these being principally drawn from Virginia, and principally tobacco." Toward this end, "an attack and the putting up and shutting up of the navigation of the Chesapeake would probably answer very considerable purposes . . . especially as [their] army was constantly supplied by provisions sent by water through the Chesapeake."[53]

Others advised that Britain should either occupy the entire Delmarva Peninsula or neutralize it more cheaply by garrisoning and fortifying a line between Port Penn on Delaware Bay and the port of Oxford, Maryland, 60 miles away on the Chesapeake side. Map 11 illustrates the geography. Furthermore, had the British seized Delmarva, they would have controlled most of the American coast from Long Island south to North Carolina.

There is no need to repeat the groups that might have been supportive or sympathetic, from slaves and indentured servants to poor-white Anglicans and German and Irish Catholics.

Last but not least, the memo writers and other frustrated Loyalists dwelled on what could be called economic warfare: the importance of seizing or destroying the tobacco so important as a Revolutionary currency and of cutting off the grain, flour, and bread so vital to the American armies. Capturing or destroying tobacco became a major British objective during Collier's brief invasion. As for the importance and opportunity of cutting off Patriot supplies of wheat, flour, and bread, that was drummed repeatedly by Maryland Loyalists like James Chambers and Robert Alexander.

In 1780 and 1781, as British strategy moved toward a showdown on the Chesapeake, even senior generals like Sir Henry Clinton and Lord Cornwallis began to grasp the region's centrality. In April 1781, Clinton advised a fellow general of a new option that could be "solidly decisive" in the war: "Virginia has been in general looked upon as universally hostile; Maryland has not been as yet tried, but it is supposed to be not quite so much so: but the inhabitants of Pennsylvania on both sides of the Susquehannah, York, Lancaster, Chester and the Peninsula between Chesapeak [*sic*] and Delaware, are represented to me to be friendly. There or thereabouts, I think this experiment should now be tried, but it cannot be done fairly until we have a force sufficient not only to go there, but to retain a respectable hold of the country afterwards."[54]

Even in Clinton's musing, one finds neither coherent overall strategy nor firm plan. And Cornwallis's decisive surrender at Yorktown was only six months away.

The hour for a Chesapeake blueprint had passed.

CHAPTER 18

The American Revolution
as a Civil War

The nature of the Revolution [was] a religious and civil war on both sides of the Atlantic. Traditions of political thought and action were carried within and articulated by the mosaic of religious denominations which made up the British Isles and, still more, the American colonies.

J.C.D. Clark, *The Language of Liberty*, 1994

*The orthodox version of the republic's history . . . maintained, of course, that there really had not been any Loyalists, that the Revolution had been a glorious united uprising for the ideals of the Declaration of Independence . . . against a tyrannous Britain. Despite its colonial roots, the American republic claimed to have started unanimously and from scratch in 1776—*Annuit coeptis novus ordo seclorum, *as the one-dollar bill puts it.*

Wallace Brown, *The Good Americans: The Loyalists in the American Revolution*, 1969

From the London City Council to the House of Burgesses in Williamsburg, from John Adams to Edmund Burke, and from Quaker meetinghouses to the Philadelphia Synod of the Presbyterian Church, the conflict boiling up in 1775 brought a stir of related apprehensions. The English-speaking peoples, some observers feared, were on the brink of another civil war, potentially as bitter as the one that had rent the British Isles during the 1640s.

Of the thirteen colonies, those with proud seventeenth-century roots, especially the four vanguards, were home to the elites most conscious of some historical continuity. Massachusetts and Connecticut, with their Puritan antecedents, were proud of how Parliament had stood up to King

Charles in support of English political, religious, and economic liberty. Many of their leaders and preachers circa 1775 considered New Englanders a chosen people who would continue that fight in North America.

Virginia's ties to the English Civil War were mixed. There was both a royalist or Cavalier heritage from English emigration in the 1640s and a Puritan and parliamentarian legacy left by Bacon's Rebellion in the 1670s. Thomas Jefferson was especially mindful of the latter side, avidly researching precedents from the 1640s to support a Fast Day in 1774. But in no sense was Virginia circa 1775 wracked by seventeenth-century memory.

Although the Carolinas had grown out of a charter granted to prominent royalists in the 1660s, that counted little by 1775. What did matter was that both Carolinas, south and north, looked to be badly divided, culturally and regionally. War in the Carolinas would be more fratricidal than in New England or Virginia. In January 1775, the South Carolina Provincial Congress called for prayer "to avert from them [the people] the impending calamities of civil war." Five months later, that body regretted that the king had been misled into measures, which if persisted in "must inevitably involve America in all the calamities of Civil War." By August, the Charleston Council of Safety "viewed with horror the spectacle of a civil war" already in the making.[1]

Ardent war supporters on both sides, frequently cocksure, generally predicted neat and favorable outcomes. Bellicose Tories in England pictured a simple rebellion that would be easily suppressed. Militant American colonials believed that their resort to war would force Britain to compromise. But if not, virtue would triumph in a patriotic war for liberty.

The predictions of deeper pain and civil war trauma proved more accurate, especially in the Carolinas. Local feuds wove themselves into the larger hostilities. Families often divided. Fratricide led into what Winston Churchill later described for South Carolina circa 1780: "Here the fierce civil war in progress between Patriots and Loyalists—or Whigs and Tories as they were locally called—was darkened by midnight raids, seizure of cattle, murderous ambushes, and atrocities such as we have known in our own day in Ireland. [General Nathanael] Greene himself wrote: 'The animosities between the Whigs and Tories of this state renders their situation truly deplorable. There is not a day passes but there are more or less who fall a sacrifice to their savage disposition. The Whigs seem determined to extirpate the Tories and the Tories the Whigs. Some thousands have fallen in this way in this quarter, and the evil rages with more violence than ever. If

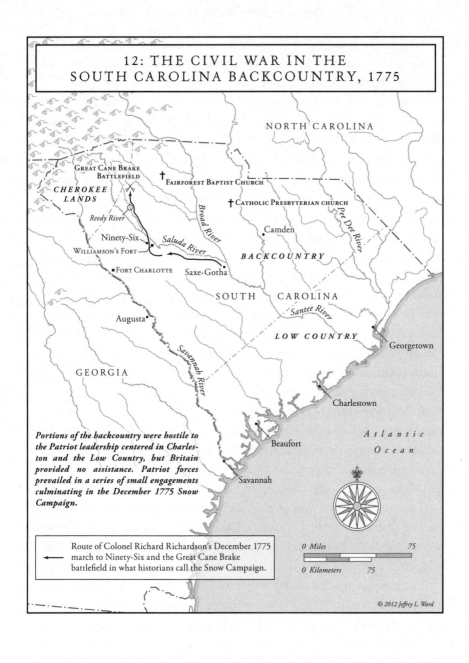

12: THE CIVIL WAR IN THE
SOUTH CAROLINA BACKCOUNTRY, 1775

NORTH CAROLINA

GREAT CANE BRAKE
BATTLEFIELD
† FAIRFOREST BAPTIST CHURCH

CHEROKEE
LANDS
† CATHOLIC PRESBYTERIAN CHURCH

Reedy River

Ninety-Six
WILLIAMSON'S FORT
Saluda River

■ FORT CHARLOTTE   Saxe-Gotha

Broad River

• Camden

Pee Dee River

BACKCOUNTRY

SOUTH   CAROLINA

Santee River

LOW COUNTRY

Augusta•

Georgetown

GEORGIA

Savannah River

Charlestown

Beaufort

*Atlantic
Ocean*

Savannah

*Portions of the backcountry were hostile to
the Patriot leadership centered in Charleston and the Low Country, but Britain
provided no assistance. Patriot forces
prevailed in a series of small engagements
culminating in the December 1775 Snow
Campaign.*

← Route of Colonel Richard Richardson's December 1775
march to Ninety-Six and the Great Cane Brake
battlefield in what historians call the Snow Campaign.

0 Miles   75

0 Kilometers   75

© 2012 Jeffrey L. Ward

a stop cannot be put to these massacres, the country will be depopulated in a few months more, and neither Whig nor Tory can live.'"[2]

Similar mentalities drove the brutality, internecine war, and devastation in New York's Westchester County "neutral ground," New Jersey's Hackensack Valley, and North Carolina's ravaged Piedmont. By one account, bad blood among the New Jersey Dutch who had sided with the Presbyterian wing of the Dutch Reformed Church and those whose forebears in the Conferentie camp had fought in the green Tory uniforms of Van Buskirk's Volunteers, lingered into the twentieth century.[3]

Such bitterness was the darkest face of civil war during the Revolution. On a larger historical dimension, the conflict did indeed reiterate a number of the cleavages, frustrations, and polarities prominent in the 1640s. In a grand sense, stepping around the enmity, gore, and destruction, the English-speaking peoples' three principal civil wars—the English Revolution (or English Civil War), the American Revolution, and the American Civil War—can be acclaimed and exalted. Their cumulative transformation can be likened to a three-century historical ladder, up which the two leading nations climbed and in doing so sorted out their respective populations, ideologies, and economics in a way that ultimately produced *two* successive global hegemonies.

Not only did family-type resemblances usually recur in these great conflicts, but most of the English-speaking world was affected. The English Civil War, although principally English and fought largely on that soil, quickly drew in Scotland, Ireland, Barbados, and even British North America (at that point Virginia, Maryland, Massachusetts, Connecticut, and Rhode Island). Seventeenth-century North America, still unimportant, was more a locale of tension and bickering than of pitched combat, but there were several battles.[4]

During the 1770s, that earlier geography reversed. The military confrontation concentrated in North America, not in the British Isles. Ramifications in the latter rarely rose above name-calling or angry demonstrations, accompanied by the British Army's difficulty in enlisting Englishmen to fight their colonial cousins.

The turnabout in the second cousins' war also extended to relative wealth and power. Back in the seventeenth century, the king's opponents in Parliament, commerce, and the cities commanded a larger share of England's resources. It was the embattled Stuart kings, high church in religion, who had to seek money and assistance from France or Spain. In 1775, the monarch and Parliament, now politically joined at the hip, were the wealthy side, and it was the colonials who had to pursue aid from Catholic France and Spain. They did so, despite being staunch dissenting Protestants.

Any reader looking for a simple, convenient definition of what differentiates a civil war from a rebellion will not find one in weighing the three cousins' wars. Indeed, each of the three was also widely referred to as a rebellion or revolution. Terms applied in the 1640s included the Great Rebellion and the English Revolution. In the 1770s, Britons often referred to the Rebellion or the American Rebellion. And during the early 1860s, the description "War of the Rebellion" was commonly used in the North.

For the American Revolution, suffice it to say its grander dimensions coexisted with internecine warfare. By September 1775, substantial districts of several provinces—New York, New Jersey, the Delmarva Peninsula, and both North and South Carolina—were displaying militant Loyalism. Jefferson's insistence in 1776 that a whole "people" was rising to escape tyranny was greatly overstated. Civil wars are never that simple, and neither were the Great Rebellion and the War of the (Southern) Rebellion.

Where Loyalism was strongest, civil war was either visible or incipient by late 1775. Patriots in New York, for example, could not rely on the militia in most of the same counties that had been unwilling to accept (or even to consider) the Continental Association in late 1774—Queens, Kings, Richmond, Westchester, Dutchess, and Tryon. In New Jersey, Patriot strength lay in New England-settled and Presbyterian areas, and among Dutch Reformed congregations of the Coetus faction. In New Jersey's Anglican, Quaker, and Dutch Tory locales, Patriots could rely on neither militia nor elections. Along the Delmarva Peninsula, as Chapter 17 has described, six adjoining counties in Maryland, Delaware, and Virginia leaned to the Loyalist side, and during 1775 Tories disrupted militia musters in most of them. Two other provinces had at least one populous county inclined to Loyalism—Quaker Bucks County in eastern Pennsylvania and Fairfield County (one-third Anglican) along Connecticut's New York border.

Open war came more quickly in the Carolinas. Within weeks of Lexington and Concord, North Carolina's governor, Josiah Martin, was advising Lord Dartmouth about potential support in both the former Regulator counties of the Piedmont and the Highland Scottish settlements along the Cape Fear. If Martin exaggerated the prospects, his rough geography was correct. In South Carolina, the new governor arriving in June, Lord William Campbell, could see the outline of a backcountry insurrection and began plotting with local Tories.

Over the many years of a drawn-out war, New York, New Jersey, the Carolinas, and to a limited extent Delmarva did in fact become the cockpits most notable for intermittent civil or guerrilla warfare. As we will see, Patriot militias and Loyalists fought repeatedly, even when no Continental troops or regular British units were on hand to pursue structured wartime objectives. During the entire war, the American militia participated on its own in 191 engagements in Connecticut, New York, and New Jersey and did likewise on 194 occasions in the Carolinas and Georgia.[5]

This now gives us two dimensions on which the American Revolution in some colonies may be viewed as a civil war. The most elevated displays the three wars as the grand seventeenth-to-nineteenth-century forge of the English-speaking peoples' separation and success. The second or workaday face of civil war largely reflected the fundamental Patriot versus Tory polarizations in a half dozen colonies. Suspicion and bad blood were easily aroused, because New York, New Jersey, and Pennsylvania were all "melting pot" colonies with distinctive ethnic populations—principally English, Scotch-Irish, Irish, Dutch, and German—and a distrustful mix of religions: principally Presbyterian, Lutheran, Anglican, German Reformed, Dutch Reformed, and Quaker.

In those days, the American melting pot had yet to do much melting. As we have seen in Chapter 3, politics in the three provinces—and also in the Delmarva Peninsula—was substantially influenced by religion and ethnicity. Pastor Henry M. Muhlenberg made no bones about describing the Pennsylvania election of 1764 as having "the English and German Quakers, the Herrnhuters, the Mennonites, and Schwenkfelders" in one party and "the English of the High Church, the Presbyterian Church, the German Lutheran and German Reformed" on the other side.[6] Thus, although demands for political and economic self-determination did much to precipitate the Revolution, in 1775 religion and ethnicity still furnished much of the attitudinal framework through which communities and individuals chose sides. Bloody civil war came as easily to parts of the middle colonies and the Carolinas as it had to England, Ireland, and Scotland in the seventeenth century and to much of Germany during both the sixteenth and seventeenth centuries.

In many respects, the backcountries of South and North Carolina resembled each other. As we have seen in Chapter 6, large sections of both were extensions of a "Greater Pennsylvania." The bulk of Carolina Loyalists and Tories were not locally born but migrants from Pennsylvania or from stopping places on the Great Wagon Road southward from the Quaker colony. The principal exception involved heavily Loyalist Scottish merchants, and North Carolina's Highlanders, most of them recent emigrants from Scotland.

However, before pursuing these two "civil war" complexions of the American Revolution, it is also necessary to cite a third. Petty rather than grand, this typically came from local quarrels and resentments important enough to shoulder their way into people's early-stage choice of wartime loyalties. If the Hatfields choose one side, the ever-hostile McCoys must take the other. Or in circa 1775 Pennsylvania, if the Susquehannah Company Yankee settlers were staunch Patriots, the local Dutch and German-sprung "Pennamites," pushed aside by Yankee machinations, joined Tory ranger units. In the South Carolina backcountry, serious rivalries within militia units, contests over rank or commissions, were sometimes enough to make the loser switch loyalty.

Local grudges and issues didn't usually trump economic, religious, ethnic, and political considerations in choosing sides, but they did play a role.

Local Causations, Minority Consciousness, and Personal Grudges

Jonathan Boucher, the Maryland Anglican clergyman and Loyalist, contended in his later *Reminiscences* that many American Whigs were motivated by personal considerations—"private grudges give raise to public measures." Such matters, Boucher felt, "lie beneath the reach of ordinary historians."[7] If the Tory clergyman was referring to personal debts, land speculation, or planters' sour relationships with British tobacco merchants, twentieth- or twenty-first-century thinking would chalk up such widely felt and shared motivations as economic.

British historians have displayed a taste for explanations that dwell on localism. One of them, Sir Lewis Namier, enjoyed a mid-twentieth-century vogue for his thesis that local issues and interests, not ideology, guided Parliament during the 1760s and 1770s, although that argument has since faded. Several British historians have set out a related explanation of the

English Civil War. Counties like Kent supposedly marched to their own parochial drummer, not to the staccato of national themes and causes.[8] However, the more recent trend in Britain—where English Civil War minutiae commands attention among war buffs and reenactors comparable to that Americans accord their Civil War—is to assess the loyalties of the 1640s as indeed shaped most by religion and secondarily by politics and economics.[9]

On the American side of the Atlantic, "localism" clearly mattered in the 1770s. Still, such grudges and issues were only a minor factor in choosing sides—and this was true even though identification with individual colonies shaped American political consciousness circa 1775 more than the individual circumstances of counties or shires, even identity-proud ones, had shaped the loyalties of Englishmen 130 years earlier.

Part of the impact of "localism" in the America of 1775 came from how many individuals, especially in the backcountry, found themselves in a cultural milieu that was new, raw, and lawless. Take Pennsylvania: in its northeastern Susquehanna territory occupied by claimants from Connecticut, and to a lesser extent in the western districts peopled from Virginia, grudges born of local clashes and rival land claims certainly counted. Tories in western Pennsylvania tended to cluster in tracts settled under Dunmore's grants. To the east, one careful analyst found Susquehanna Loyalism concentrated in two districts where largely Dutch and German drifters and squatters, after being run out by Yankees between 1773 and 1776, took their revenge by joining Butler's Tory Rangers.[10] To another Pennsylvania historian, "Loyalists prove to be largely minority groups; their loyalism was in the main a reflection of looking to Britain to maintain or restore an internal balance of power . . . In every feud-ridden neighborhood they were one of the two local parties; for irrelevant disputes were not generally abandoned at the onset of war: instead they quickly took on, almost at random, the larger enmities of Whig and Tory."[11] Pennsylvania's Patriot chief justice, Thomas McKean, described the circumstances of 1776–1779 by saying that "Pennsylvania was not a nation at war with another nation, but a country in a state of civil war."[12]

Upper New York was similarly riven. Tenants of some of the feudal landholding patroons on the Patriot side—principally the Livingstons—let dissatisfaction draw them into Tory allegiance. In the vast Mohawk Valley lands held by the family and lieutenants of the late Sir William Johnson, the Palatine German population split, and Johnson's Scottish Highlanders began fleeing to Canada in 1775. Old enmities persisted through the war. Nor, as we have seen, could Yorkers maintain their control in the former Hampshire Grants, assigned to New York by the king in 1764. The New England–born Green Mountain Boys took over much of the disputed territory well before the Revolution, and sides chosen often pitted New Englanders against those who held land or office under New York. On March 13, 1775, a sheriff holding royal office by New York appointment ordered his men to fire on a Yankee crowd that had seized a courthouse at Westminster on the Connecticut River. After one Yankee was killed, Yorker appointees were quickly jailed or expelled by the Green Mountain Boys.[13]

In the Carolinas, two thirds of the white population of 1775 had arrived over the previous two decades, many of them coming directly from Pennsylvania or arriving after brief stays elsewhere. No good statistics exist, but we can surmise that these two provinces, along with Georgia, included especially high percentages of white residents born in another colony. North and South Carolina both had "little Pennsylvanias," and just as the parent colony was an ethnic and religious kaleidoscope, so were the backcountries of both Carolinas. As in Pennsylvania, church-centered Presbyterians were mostly ardent rebels. But other upcountry settlements reflected more confusing in-migrations—Regular and Separate Baptists; fallen-away Pennsylvania Quakers; and Moravians, Dunkers, and other German pacifists. Still other migrants included Presbyterians from small breakaway sects who were Loyalists or king haters for doctrinal reasons that even Scottish encyclopedias still have difficulty explaining. Malcontents must have abounded. Backcountry men in general suspected or disliked the vestry Anglican plantation elites who ruled both Carolinas from coastal towns like Edenton, New Bern, Wilmington, Georgetown, Charleston, and Beaufort.

Ironically, when Carolina civil war threatened in 1775, Patriots in Pennsylvania were called to send letters and dispatch preachers who might be able to soothe backcountry disaffection. Patriot leaders in South Carolina organized a mission that included Presbyterian William Tennent of Charleston's Independent Church, and Oliver Hart, the Regular faction pastor of Charleston's First Baptist Church. Both ministers were originally from Pennsylvania. However, their effectiveness in the backcountry was limited. If Pennsylvania had its own incipient civil wars, how much more could have been expected from its southward migrants, with their considerable admixture of failures, runaways, and quirky religious zealots?

1775: The Carolinas and Civil War

When the American Revolution ended in 1783, bitter memories of local civil war remained fresh in New York and New Jersey, about which much has been written. The ill will had been visible in 1775—reliable Connecticut troops were time after time sent into unreliable districts of New York—but little shooting occurred, save in the Champlain region. Not until 1776 were New Yorkers and New Jerseyans busy organizing the surprising disproportion of American Loyalist regiments for which they became famous or infamous.[14]

In the Carolinas, however, open civil warfare began in 1775, just not on a large scale. Potential backcountry Loyalist strength in both colonies was already prompting the calculations of royal governors—and, through their overenthusiasm, the plans of the king and his ministers.

The coming of civil war in the South Carolina backcountry—a grittier stage of confrontation than Patriots seizing Charleston forts and sinking hulks in harbor channels—only began in midsummer. Lack of meaningful local government across most of the interior had made backcountry militia colonels powerful men within their districts, and not all supported the Revolution. The colony's 10,000 to 14,000 militiamen were divided among twelve district-based regiments. In July, as tensions grew, Charleston-based Patriot leaders began to question the reliability and leadership of several units and commanding officers.

The principal dissatisfaction, as generations of South Carolina historians have reiterated, concentrated in the Delaware-sized stretch of land between the Broad River on the east and the Saluda River in the west. This was the district of the Upper Saluda Regiment, commanded by Colonel Thomas Fletchall of Fairforest, a wealthy landowner privately critical of the new regime. Even as a letter was on its way asking him to sign the Patriot faction's Association, Fletchall assembled 1,500 men—most of his own regiment, along with other militiamen—and read them the rebel Association, which they refused to sign. They thereupon endorsed a "counter-association" that reaffirmed loyalty to the king and expressed a hope to live in peace with their neighbors. This alarmed the Council of Safety, as did a further development. With the connivance of an erstwhile Patriot officer, Moses Kirkland, 200 of Fletchall's Loyalist militia had recaptured the Patriot powder supplies, taken some days earlier on July 12 when South Carolina militia had captured Fort Charlotte on the Savannah River. The seeds of civil war were starting to sprout.[15]

The Council of Safety's next move was to send a political and religious mission to the backcountry. Headed by Patriot firebrand William H. Drayton, then chairman of the Secret Committee of the Provincial Congress, it also included New Light Presbyterian Tennent and Regular Baptist Hart. The dissident area between the Broad and the Saluda held the colony's principal concentration of Separate Baptist congregations—many were part of a network centered on Loyalist Reverend Philip Mulkey's Fairforest church—together with some Presbyterians and unchurched Scotch-Irish. The Patriot mission had some success in Presbyterian portions of the interior, but little in the area where Fletchall held sway. Tennent reported to the Council: "We soon found the unchangeable malignity of their minds and . . . bitterness against the gentlemen as they are called . . . [They] believe no man that comes from below."[16]

Drayton seems to have been radicalized by this August setback, as well as by Royal Governor Campbell's collusion with Fletchall, Kirkland, and other backcountry loyalists.* He ordered some of the more reliable militia units to keep pressure on Fletchall and to counter Kirkland's rumored plan to retake Fort Charlotte. The firmness succeeded. Kirkland left for Charleston, and some of the other Loyalist leaders fled the province. Fletchall, increasingly a weak reed, met with Drayton in mid-September and negotiated a neutrality agreement, nicknamed the "Treaty of Ninety Six" after the upcountry town where they met.

In mid-September, confrontation shifted to Charleston, where Patriots seized Fort Johnson, with artillery that controlled part of the harbor. The backcountry, meanwhile, remained relatively quiet until late October, when Patriot forces, on a slim pretext, arrested and jailed Captain Robert Cunningham, the leader of a family about to make a name for bold and stalwart Loyalism. On November 6, his brother Captain Patrick Cunningham, with 150 men, retaliated by seizing 1,000 pounds of gunpowder that the Patriot Council of Safety was sending to the Cherokee as part of a regular seasonal shipment. This was a supply the tribe depended on, had come to expect, and would be angry to see held back. Stunned Patriot leaders moved to placate

---

*Kirkland, apparently persuasive among other qualities, came up with a plan of his own to retake the southern colonies if the British would send arms, munitions, and some officers to help lead the 4,000 Loyalists he would recruit. Governor Campbell took it seriously enough to send the Tory leader to Boston to put the plan before General Gage. However, Kirkland's ship was captured, and he was jailed.[17]

the Cherokee, sending word that the annual shipment was still coming. But now Cunningham made a too-clever move. Together with a prominent white Indian trader, who provided an affidavit, he identified the gunpowder as evidence that the Charleston Patriots were arming the Cherokee to fall on the upcountry Loyalists. Their professed neutrality, Cunningham argued, was just a sham.[18]

After the Loyalists' tactic produced a furor, the Provincial Congress replied with its own "declaration." The notion that it was raising the Indians against the frontier Loyalists was absurd: how could raiding Cherokee know Patriots from Loyalists? The Congress further authorized a large call-up of Patriot-leaning militia to resolve the matter. Several units linked up at the town of Ninety Six, scene of September's unsustained promises, and 500-odd Patriots threw up a stockade.

By November 19, this force was surrounded by roughly 1,900 Loyalists under Patrick Cunningham and several other backcountry Tories. During a three-day siege, one Patriot defender and a larger number of Loyalists were killed in intermittent fighting. On November 22, the two sides signed an agreement that amounted to little more than a prolonged truce. The defenders had been low on ammunition, while the besiegers knew that more Patriot militia was coming. Colonel Richard Richardson, who commanded that reinforcement of 1,500 men, quickly decided he was not bound by the truce negotiated by a subordinate at Ninety Six. However questionable, his interpretation swung the balance of power. As Richardson marched north to the Saluda in early December, his army swelled to 3,000, as Patriots sensed a decisive moment. The assembled Loyalist army, not surprisingly, in two weeks dwindled to 400, and key officers, including Fletchall, were captured or gave themselves up. In touch with the Patriot leadership in Charleston, Richardson granted lenient terms: "mercy, and protection" in return for laying down arms and promising neutrality.[19]

November's First Battle of Ninety Six—all civil war, because South Carolinians were fighting South Carolinians—was something less than a major engagement. Even so, it is proudly recalled locally as "the second battle of the Revolution in South Carolina and the first that involved bloodshed."[20] With the arrival of Richardson's overwhelming force, only a few hundred bitter-end Loyalists held out under Patrick Cunningham. Retreating into Indian country, they camped at the Great Cane Brake on the Reedy River, southeast of present-day Greenville, and sought help from the Cherokee, which was not forthcoming.

On December 21, the Tories were overtaken by 1,300 men under Colonel William Thomson, a senior Ranger officer, whose attack the next morning achieved almost complete surprise. Cunningham escaped but was soon captured. Some of those surprised were killed, but 130 were taken and sent to Charleston as prisoners. As Richardson had done, Thomson opted for leniency, and that policy succeeded. The Loyalist threat of 1775 was over. When the Cherokee war broke out six months later, many erstwhile Loyalists were part of the Carolina armies that routed them.[21]

The day after the Battle of the Great Cane Brake, as Richardson, Thomson, and their men started home, a snowfall began that lasted 30 hours and left two feet on the roads and trails. Local historians still call the expedition the Snow Campaign. But although backcountry civil war ended, embers remained. Four years hence, the area burst into flame again, and a Second Battle of Ninety Six would be fought in April 1781.

As to the civil war in North Carolina, its beginning is harder to date. Royal Governor Martin, whose letters did so much to fuel British expectations of Loyalist uprisings, had become attentive to both the Highland Scots and the former Regulators shortly after taking office in late 1771. In the summer of 1772, a year after the backcountry insurgents of the Regulation had been defeated at the Battle of Alamance, Martin visited the Piedmont and came away convinced that they had been mistreated and wronged. He reported to London that "the farmers had been provoked by insolence and cruel advantage taken of the people's ignorance by mercenary, tricking attornies, clerks and other little Officers."[22]

By the summer of 1775, as we have seen, Martin had sent London a plan for a Loyalist rising involving greater numbers than any proposed by Virginia's Dunmore. Much of its appeal lay in extraordinary enlistment estimates. Martin did not ask for troops, just supplies and equipment for his 10,000 or 20,000 friends and putative allies in plaids, homespun, and buckskin who would march down to Wilmington to meet arriving British ships and regiments.

The North Carolina of 1775, which very few in British politics had ever visited, seemed to be doubling its population every decade—from 70,000 in 1750 to as many as 250,000 in 1775. High-range predictions could not be dismissed. The Highland Scots, for their part, also bathed in an Old World aura of suddenly available military manpower. If the bens and braes of Inverness-shire had a soldier potential of 12,000, the burgeoning upper Cape Fear Valley—with its large influx of McDonalds and McLeods—

might be a New World competitor. General Gage, also enlistment minded, had sent two Scottish officers to North Carolina in July to recruit for a proposed Royal Highland Emigrants regiment. And John Stuart, the southern Indian superintendent, agreed that the greater ratio of frontier North Carolinians leaned toward the Crown.[23]

Wilmington Patriots, in the crosshairs of British calculation, had been as forward as New Englanders since forming a Committee of Safety in November 1774. Besides regulating local commerce and shipping, they undertook defense and loyalty measures. They surveyed the amount of gunpowder in the city and then forbade any sales. In March 1775, the Committee had endorsed the Test provision of the Continental Association, and as the year progressed, the Test oaths were escalated to impose ever greater standards of adherence. Concerned about Loyalist activity among the Scots upriver, in July the Wilmington Committee sent a letter to that area's Committee of Safety recommending loyalty oaths, but Whigs there were outnumbered.

On July 18, 800 Patriot militiamen burned Fort Johnston, near the entrance to the Cape Fear River, after its small garrison had fled. By early autumn, apprehensive Patriots had partially fortified the lower river. In November, the Wilmington Committee of Safety, after leaving each white man with one musket, collected the rest for the 300 men of the North Carolina First Regiment camped just outside the town. On November 16 all white male residents of the area were told to assemble at the courthouse in four days to form militia companies, and several vessels were chained and sunk in the harbor to reduce hostile access.[24]

Royal Governor Martin, still a refugee aboard HMS *Cruzier,* wrote to his principal agent in the Scottish settlements, telling him to begin assembling men. However, although in touch with Loyalist leaders, ex-Regulators, and Scottish recruiting officers, Martin could not raise the king's standard without orders.

Patriot leaders, by contrast, heard on a regular basis from the Provincial Congress or authorities in Wilmington. Besides the preparation to defend Wilmington and Brunswick, firm measures were taken between December and February to suppress Loyalists in the districts where the governor expected assistance. Settlers in the Yadkin Valley who expressed support for George III were forced from their homes, fleeing into the forest and gaining the name "outlyers." Tories in Surry County were easily dispersed. Larger numbers attempted to muster in Guilford County, parts of which had been

Regulator strongholds, but in February, seven local Loyalist leaders were arrested and jailed, and their followers lost heart.[25] Presbyterian ministers sent in November to woo the Highlanders to the Revolutionary cause had gotten nowhere—partly, one assumes, because they did not speak Gaelic. But outside the Scottish settlements, Patriot countermeasures appear to have been generally successful.

Back in the autumn, Martin had ventured that 20,000 men might rise. But prospects shrank daily in late January and early February, as the time came for Highlanders and onetime Regulators to assemble at Cross Creek, the future Fayetteville. The 2,000 or 3,000 Loyalists once predicted just from Brunswick and Wilmington became a pipe dream. Patriot musters there were ongoing; martial law had been imposed, and 20 known Tories were jailed. Weeks earlier the governor's advisers had thought the Scottish Highlander army could reach 6,000 men, but in mid-February only 1,000 or so mustered. Leaders of the ex-Regulators had talked as late as February 5 of marshaling 3,000 or even 5,000 men, but eventually only a few hundred showed up. As in the Forty Five, the Highlanders, with their kilts and claymores, were the romantic figures. The North Carolina Whigs, like the Hanoverians, won the day with methodical suppression.

One circumstance should be underscored. Like the enmity and confrontation in South Carolina, the mobilization and marching to battle in North Carolina during the autumn and winter of 1775–1776 was in the nature of a civil war. This was true even though some of the Scottish Loyalists were only recently arrived from the old country. The only two serving British soldiers involved were Lieutenant Colonel Donald MacDonald and Captain Donald McLeod.

The late February defeat of the poorly led Highlanders at the Battle of Moore's Creek Bridge, to which we will return in Chapter 25, in contrast to the Snow Campaign in South Carolina, did not even temporarily mark the end of local civil war. Whig militia continued to suppress the Scots and other identifiable Loyalists, and small confrontations persisted. And not surprisingly, when civil war returned to both Carolinas in 1779–1780, it repeated on a larger and bloodier scale, following much of the political geography of 1775.

The Cousins' Wars: Civil War on a Grand Scale

In 1775, on both sides of the Atlantic, well-read Whigs and Tories were aware that a new civil war seemed to be arising, at least in part, from the ideological, religious, and even regional footprints of the old one—the English Civil War of the 1640s. Pro-Americans in English politics, as we have seen, remarked that the enthusiastic high-church Anglicans of 1775 seemed to be reprising the royalist fervor of high churchmen prominent in the 1630s and 1640s. Avid Tories, for their part, enjoyed hurling the epithet "Oliverian."

As we have seen, nothing better introduces the scope and intensity of the three great English-speaking civil conflicts than widespread disagreement even over their names. People in the seventeenth and eighteenth centuries also called the English Civil War the Great Rebellion. In the early twentieth century, an Englishman, Henry Belcher, published a book relabeling the Revolution as *The First American Civil War*.[26]

In a way, it was. But obviously, the name has not stuck; nor have historians been obliged to consider the fighting between 1861 and 1865 the Second American Civil War. However, that conflict has been given many other names, including the War Between the States and the War for Southern Independence. Persons mindful of the links among the great civil wars have tried to impose grander appellations on the 1861–1865 period, with practically no acceptance. Examples include the Second American Revolution and the Second War for Independence.[27]

A second important link among the three wars lies in their complex and tangled origins. All three had roots in a combination of politics, constitutional controversy, economic interests, and intense religious belief and disagreement. Amid such input, I would not try to allocate percentages. Religion remained important throughout but played less of a role in the 1860s than it had in the 1640s, with the American Revolution falling in between. By way of quick oversimplification, one can identify common economic threads in which entrepreneurialism, commerce, and opportunity for manufacturing triumphed, with agrarian interests and mercantilism generally losing.[28]

A third bond involves the sort of conspiracy-mindedness displayed by Washington, Adams, and Jefferson in their indictments of King George and British policy toward America in the 1760s and 1770s, as well as their fear of Catholic links to tyranny and absolutism. Such interpretations had also been staples of Parliamentary thinking in the 1630s and 1640s. During the lead-up to the American Civil War, in turn, both sides repeatedly emphasized conspiracies against liberty, whether by the southern "slaveocracy" or "Black Republicans" trying to void the constitutional compact of 1787.

The Cousins' Wars wouldn't be the Cousins' Wars without this ongoing conspiracy chain.[29]

Let us close with a different war-related irony. Despite the fact that the American secretary, Lord Dartmouth, and his stepbrother, Lord North, must have been reasonably acquainted with the divisions in America, neither man—at least in 1775—seems to have internalized a consciousness of the unfolding Revolution as a civil war that divided the English-speaking people. The international law of that era did not approve of foreign intervention in a civil war, and Thomas Jefferson's legally inspired insistence in the Declaration of Independence about one "people" dissolving the bonds that tied them to another people simply didn't comport with demographic and cultural realities of what was in many places a widespread fratricidal conflict. A strong British counterargument could have been made.

But the legend of the Declaration has far outstripped its reality, and it is to these political carryovers from 1775 that we now turn.

CHAPTER 19

The Declaration of Independence—a Stitch in Time?

Within the context of Philadelphia in the summer of 1776, the writing of the Declaration of Independence did not seem nearly so important as other priorities, including the constitution-making of the states and the prospect of foreign alliances with France or Spain. The golden haze around the Declaration had not yet formed.

Joseph Ellis, *American Sphinx: The Character of Thomas Jefferson*, 1996

Urgent international pressures had compelled Congress to issue a declaration in the early summer of 1776. Accordingly, the Declaration reflected a range of concerns about security, defense, commerce, and immigration . . . "Self-evident truths"; "all men created equal"; "unalienable rights," "Life, Liberty and the Pursuit of Happiness": these are ringing words and noble sentiments, to be sure, but they are not in fact what the Declaration proclaimed in 1776.

David Armitage, *The Declaration of Independence*, 2007

Several times in late 1775 and early 1776, a frustrated John Adams mused how much better things would have been with some kind of declaration of independence already in effect. In September he gloomed that Americans, behind schedule, should already "have completely modeled a constitution; to have raised a naval power, and opened all our Ports wide."[1] As late as July 3, more reasonably, he complained that "we might before this Hour, have formed alliances with foreign states. We should have mastered Quebec and been in possession of Canada."[2]

Adams overstated what was possible. For much of 1775, the future United States had what Thomas Jefferson called de facto independence.

Except in Boston, British troops had left or been expelled. Governance was in American hands. David Armitage, a Declaration scholar, has contended that "for almost two years before making the Declaration, Congress had been exercising most of the rights claimed in that document."[3] Congress, after basic nation framing and army building between June and November, thereafter took a number of actions that clearly moved toward "independence," labels that Adams chortled with satisfaction in applying. What the United Colonies did not have was de jure or legally established independence. In part, this was because moderates in the middle colonies, who had experienced no fighting, were hanging back and nursing vague, unrealistic hopes of reconciliation with Britain.

Backstage Patriot strategy regarding independence during the early months of 1776 had practically nothing to do with equality, natural law, or the pursuit of happiness. Its preoccupation was with completing unfinished business, pressuring middle-colony delegates, and getting approval for a Declaration—actual signatures could wait—before the transports and warships arriving in New York could disembark enough professional soldiers to frighten that province and New Jersey back into the arms of King George. The Patriots in Congress succeeded, but not without some heavy-handed tactics and nervous moments. And with very little time to spare.

Declaring de jure independence earlier had not been feasible. Certain preconditions had to be met. Political sentiment and loyalty in America had to metamorphose from condemnation of an evil Parliament to putting blame on a tyrannical George III, and from pursuing only home rule and basic self-determination to cutting the last legal ties with the British Empire. Although the middle colonies were slowest to make the leap, by midwinter their reluctance was being worn down by repeated disillusionment with the mother country—by the burning of American towns; by December's Prohibitory Act, which expelled Americans from the protection of the Crown; by the king's hiring of mercenaries; and by London's unwillingness to send official negotiators or emissaries. Reluctant moderates and conservatives had waited for some kind of reassuring word or hope from England. In the spring, as weather and communications improved, the word from England was belligerent rather than conciliatory.

However, it still remained for Congress to deal with a set of procedural handcuffs. Between November and January, assemblies or provincial congresses in four of the five middle colonies had voted to bind their delegates in Philadelphia to oppose outright independence. New York had done so earlier, during the summer of 1775. Sentiment was changing, but these manacles first had to be removed.

It was also true that opportunities had been lost. Jefferson, in the notes he kept, cited the view of one delegate that had America been independent that winter, the French, readier to be bold, might have prevented the petty German princes from hiring out their troops to Britain.[4]

Fortune smiled on May 8 when the British frigate *Roebuck,* cruising up the Delaware toward Philadelphia, was repulsed by the fire of a dozen Patriot row galleys. No broadside ever fell on Independence Hall. Yet all of the middle colonies remained bound by instructions that seemed out of date. Their eventual decision for de jure independence can be approached in four stages: May 10–15, June 7–11, June 23, and July 1–2. The fourth of July itself was not pivotal because the Declaration, agreed to on July 2, appears not to have been signed by delegates until August, and the last few signatures were only added in November.[5]

But before explaining, it is useful to jump ahead. On June 7, Richard Henry Lee of Virginia, in his colony's name, put a momentous resolution before Congress: "That these United Colonies are, and of right ought to be, free and independent States, that they are absolved from all allegiance to the British Crown, and that all political connection between them and the State of Great Britain is, and ought to be, totally dissolved." A further sentence declared "That it is expedient forthwith to take the most effectual measures for forming foreign alliances." These two propositions stated the essence of what was being sought between May and July.

Lee's resolution could have been passed then, but only by a narrow margin, which would have been foolish and probably disastrous. So a decision by Congress was postponed for three weeks to accommodate the middle colonies in removing their handcuffs and to further the all-important hope of unanimity. After the final vote for independence on July 2, the full verbiage of the Declaration—beyond Lee's vital statements, now inserted into the text—was something of an anticlimax. Nevertheless, the story is worth retelling to emphasize the Declaration's limited meaning *at the time* in 1776, the portentous interpretations having been added by later publicists and generations.

The Limited Role of the Declaration of Independence

Historians generally agree that Jefferson was picked to draft the Declaration of Independence principally because of his writing skills, but also because the more prominent men in this endgame, John Adams and R. H. Lee, had seemingly greater tasks to perform—for Adams, planning foreign treaties and plotting for the new governments needed in many colonies; in Lee's case, taking the lead in proindependence speech making and legislative management. Over the previous two years, Jefferson had developed a unique expertise in setting forth the supposed tyrannical behavior and usurpations of the British government in general and then, by spring 1776, of King George III in particular.

The youthful Virginian had begun this specialization in 1774, penning much of the *Summary View of the Rights of British America,* adopted by that summer's First Virginia Convention. In a year when other Patriots harped on the misbehavior and abuses of Parliament, Jefferson had put a finger on royal responsibility and ventured a bold aside: "Let not the name of George III be a blot in the page of history."[6] Come 1775, he was the principal drafter—this time in Philadelphia by request of Congress—of the *Declaration of the Causes and Necessity of Taking Up Arms,* published on July 6. Once again, British transgressions were the focus, mostly on Parliament's part, but with the addition of Generals Gage and Carleton as military miscreants.[7]

In the spring of 1776, Jefferson was again drawn to Virginia, which was about to draft a constitution to guide its independent and republican future. Here his "black Catalogue of unprovoked injuries" moved center stage, because the king had to be made tyrant enough to justify revolution.[8] Jefferson's sixteen-point list of royal malfeasance dominated the preamble of the Old Dominion's new constitution, adopted in June, and much of the indictment quickly reappeared in his Philadelphia drafts of the Declaration of Independence.

Once such a declaration by the United Colonies was placed on Congress's calendar—the eventual document would devote 60 percent of its space to the abuses of George III—Jefferson was the only plausible wordsmith. By now, he had it all in his head. If Patrick Henry was Virginia's leading rhetorical king basher, Jefferson dominated the literary hatchet work. Indeed, another Virginia lawyer-cum-politician, Edmund Pendleton, congratulated Jefferson over the Declaration for expanding his litany: "I expected you had . . . exhausted the Subject of Complaint against Geo. 3d and was at a loss to discover what Congress would do for one to their Declaration of Independence without copying, but find that you have acquitted yourself very well on that score."[9]

Decades later, with controversy growing over the Declaration and how it had come together—the question of who had really penned what—Jefferson offered several compelling explanations. In 1822, reacting to a comment by Adams that "there is not an idea in it but what had been hackneyed in Congress for two years before," the Virginian did not disagree. He replied that the argument "that it contained no new ideas, that it is a commonplace compilation, its sentiments hacknied in Congress for two years before may all be true. Of that, I am not to be the judge. Richard H. Lee charged it as copied from Locke's treatise on government . . . I know only that I turned to neither book nor pamphlet while writing it. I did not consider it as any part of my charge to invent new ideas altogether and to offer no sentiment which had ever been expressed before."[10]

In 1825, a year before his death, Jefferson was slightly more forthright: "An appeal to the tribunal of the world was deemed proper for our justification. This was the object of the Declaration of Independence. Not to find out new principles, or new arguments never before thought of."[11]

In the press of a busy Congress, where the truly capable one third of the 50-odd members were grossly overworked, the notion of plagiarism is hard to take seriously. This is doubly so because what Jefferson called "commonplacing"—the copying over and rough memorization of great works, thoughts, and phrases—was an accepted skill, and in 1776 the Virginian and his colleagues were intending to blend and express widely held views.[12] Of course they were on the lookout for ideas that were common wisdom and phrases that were well turned or felicitous; obviously they were inclined to borrow.

If Adams was reasonable in saying that most of the ideas and language in the Declaration were "hackneyed," Jefferson was correct in essentially replying "So what?' The imitation of past great documents was overt. In 1775, for example, *The Declaration of the Causes and Necessity of Taking Up Arms* imitated the very similarly titled declaration made by Parliamentary rebels in 1642 with respect to taking up arms against King Charles and that era's abuses-cum-tyranny. The American Declaration of Independence, in turn, drew notably on Virginia's Declaration of Rights of June 12, 1776, which was itself inspired by the English Declaration of Rights published in 1689, after the Glorious Revolution that dethroned King James II. Such imitation was not merely convenient; it was also politically credentialing.

As one piece of evidence, the two short columns below compare Jefferson's draft second paragraph in the Philadelphia Declaration with George Mason's just-written draft of the Virginia Declaration.

Mason (June 1776)	Jefferson (June 1776)
All men are born equally free and independent, and have certain inherent natural rights, of which they cannot, by any compact, deprive or divest their posterity; among which are the enjoyment of life and liberty, with the means of acquiring and possessing property, and pursuing and obtaining happiness and safety.	All men are created equal and independent, that from that equal creation they derive rights inherent and inalienable, among which are the preservation of life, and liberty, and the pursuit of happiness.

Source: Stephen E. Lucas, "Justifying America," in Thomas W. Benson, American Rhetoric: Context and Criticism *(Carbondale: Southern Illinois University Press, 1989), pp. 67–130.*

To the reader who applies twenty-first-century yardsticks, Jefferson plagiarized Mason, whose words had appeared first. Amid the practices of the 1770s, though, Jefferson was doing his job. His words were neither inspired nor original. British commentators essentially ignored them in order to concentrate on the "black catalogue" laid out to justify revolution against tyranny. The indictment of a list of tyrannies was needed to overcome the legal handicap to the Americans of staging mere civil war. Tyranny was a required just cause for seeking independence. And as Samuel Adams explained, "No foreign Power can consistently yield Comfort to Rebels, or enter into any kind of Treaty with these Colonies until they declare themselves free and independent."[13]

Jefferson performed well and with literary flair, accomplishing an important but somewhat cut-and-paste task. Luckily, most of the ill-judged phrases, paragraphs, and themes in his drafts were changed or dropped by his colleagues. The current term *boilerplate*—used to describe standard legal forms or typical, routine thoughts—clearly does not fit because of Jefferson's manifest writing skills. However, as a political document for 1776, the Declaration was "deliberately unexceptional," in the apt words of historian Pauline Maier.[14] As such, it is not unfair to consider much of the text as historical boilerplate of an elevated sort.

"One of the problems with the early history of the Declaration is that there is so little of it," said author Garry Wills in *Inventing America*.[15] Minimal attention was paid to who had authored the document or its key parts until Jefferson was seeking the presidency in 1796.[16] Thereafter party politics and rhetoric gilded Jefferson's role, although in 1819, 1822, and 1825, he was put somewhat on the defensive by plagiarism charges. This is the period during which he emphasized trying *not* to be original.

During these years, Jefferson mounted a propaganda campaign of his own, seeking to be remembered for authoring the Declaration rather than for his controversial tenures as governor of Virginia and later as president. His 1824 celebratory visit to Monticello in company with the Marquis de Lafayette was a particular zenith of mythmaking and iconography.[17] It was 1826, though, when the Declaration began to assume its quasi-religious status, after Jefferson and Adams both died on the same day, July 4, 1826, the supposed fiftieth anniversary of the signing. To Abraham Lincoln, orating a generation later, that had been a religious sign.

Understanding what the document was—and more important, what it was not—is vital to understanding what happened during the spring of 1776. By doing so, we can move beyond the worshipful preoccupation with the Declaration and the year 1776, which has distorted the study and memory of the early stage of the American Revolution.

The Two-Year Wait: June 1774 to June 1776

Simply put, the Patriotic faction's objective during May and June 1776 was to finish building a new governmental structure to replace the colonial-era regimes, while pressuring the middle colonies to support full-fledged independence. Succeeding before the invasion came was vital. The colonies had to be out of the empire and accepted internationally before the huge British Army, as of July reaching New York in almost daily increments, could mount its grand invasion.

Springtime public opinion in the middle colonies had clearly been moving toward independence. However, no one can ever know how regional sentiment might have been cooling or turning timid in late June and July as the scarlet-clad British and blue-uniformed Hessians disembarked on bucolic, harborside Staten Island. That locale, officially Richmond County, was one of New York's most stalwart Tory jurisdictions. Much of its population welcomed the king's soldiers as liberators.

Staten Island's position at the entrance to New York Harbor also put it right next mainland to New Jersey, which must have shivered politically and militarily. New Jersey had one of the North's largest slave populations, and as ships filled the horizon, hundreds of runaways, maybe thousands, sought the British lines. Tories in Richmond County soon organized their own Loyalist regiment. Even Pennsylvania was only 30 miles from Staten Island's western tip.

Had those British and German regiments been able to land and bivouac by April or May, as originally planned and expected, the psychological impact could have been disastrous. Fence-sitting political moderates in New York, New Jersey, Pennsylvania, Delaware, and Maryland would probably have reaffirmed the late 1775 instructions that ordered their congressional delegates to oppose any measures for independence.

Instead, the troops' tardy arrival gave Patriots in Congress and elsewhere two to three vital months to maneuver. Leaders who might have faced treason charges—at very least opprobrium—took full advantage. Three pressures would have guided their arguments and actions.

To begin with, the Revolution was beyond backtracking or temporizing. As of June 1776, a full two years had passed since the initial American crisis of replying to the Coercive Acts, fourteen months since Lexington and Concord, a year since Congress had authorized the Continental Army, and ten months since the king had proclaimed the thirteen colonies in rebellion. This prolonged chronology had drawn the delegates in Philadelphia into strong commitments and governmental decision making that already smacked of de facto independence and its exercise.

By late 1775, the basic framework of the United Colonies was in place, and bolder amplifications were under way. On November 25, it was resolved that all valuables and cargo on captured British ships were to become the property of the United Colonies. On January 2, Congress recommended that provinces disarm and imprison their Tories. On January 12, a proposal to open American ports as of March 1 was postponed for later consideration. On March 14, Congress ordered the disarming of disaffected persons and nonassociators. March 23 saw the issuance of letters of marque and reprisal to American privateers. On April 6, Congress took up the discussion it had earlier postponed, voting to open ports of the United Colonies to ships of every nation but Great Britain. In all of the measures, independence was an unstated subtext.

Among the individual colonies, extralegal institutions were also gaining age and popular acceptance. Connecticut and Rhode Island, with their existing self-government, had not needed them, but the other eleven had. Extralegal groups played their most important role below the new line Messrs. Mason and Dixon had surveyed a few years earlier. They could not be stuffed back into Pandora's box.

Surprisingly, these have not been catalogued. Virginia Patriots used extralegal conventions—the First Convention, the Second, and so forth—to control the province. The First began in August 1774, and the Fifth ended in June 1776, with the implementation of the Old Dominion's new constitution. Maryland also held five Provincial Conventions, beginning in June 1774 and ending in June 1776. Of the five Provincial Congresses held in North Carolina, the first got under way in August 1774, and the last in November 1776. South Carolina had only two, in 1775 and 1776, because local Patriots employed other extralegal bodies in earlier years. Georgia came late to the game with a provincial congress in July 1775.

Both New England provinces with royal governors initially sidestepped their executive veto through provincial congresses—Massachusetts held three, beginning in 1774 but ending in 1775, when the General Court resumed. And New Hampshire employed five, beginning in 1774. New York, New Jersey, Pennsylvania, and Delaware all had one or more provincial congresses, but these did not play the same early and powerful role chronicled in the plantation colonies.

On the national and provincial levels alike, this was hardly the institutional profile of an insurgency about to, or even able to, shut itself down. On the contrary, by the spring of 1776, the lives and fortunes, and indeed the sacred honor, of too many influential and powerful colonial leaders were already irretrievably committed. The war had to be fought.

Pressure number two came from the ticking clock of practical politics. As of early May, instructions from home still reined in the five middle-colony delegations. And whatever the progress of public opinion in Perth Amboy or Annapolis, those procedural handcuffs were still in place on June 1. This is why Congress was obliged on June 7 to postpone consideration of Richard Henry Lee's independence resolution. To act on the basis of favorable votes from just seven colonies was unthinkable. But letting the handcuffs stay on was just as unthinkable.

The third peril lay in the increasing nearness of the British transports, troopships, and escorting warships en route to New York Harbor. De jure independence had to be declared before their 1,000 or so menacing naval guns and their 30 or 40 regiments of professional soldiers swung the psychological balance. May was a month of mostly rumor, but June was more tense. Ships were already arriving in New York from Ireland and Canada. In midmonth, Washington received word that General Howe had sailed from Canada (Halifax) on June 9. Then on June 29, three white flags flapping on the heights of Staten Island signaled that the British invasion fleet had been sighted, and by the next morning, 130 warships were in New York Harbor.[18] Time had almost run out.

Congressional Realpolitik, May 1776–July 1776

Congress was between a rock and a hard place, but John Adams perceived an auspicious trend. Amid his periodic comments of "if only we had . . . ," the delegate from Massachusetts regularly pronounced in early 1776 that this or that action by Congress or Parliament represented a virtual or practical declaration of independence. In March, for example, responding to Parliament's December Prohibitory Act, Adams characterized it as "the piratical act, or plundering act, or Act of Independency . . . It is a complete dismemberment of the British Empire."[19]

On April 6, after Congress opened American ports to the trade of the non-British world, he enthused that "as to declarations of independency, read our privateering laws and our commercial laws. What signifies a word?"[20]

On May 15, the voluble Massachusetts lawyer succeeded in attaching a Revolutionary preamble to an already-radical congressional resolution that demanded new governments in provinces that still operated under British authority and auspices. Adams's preamble, cutting to the political quick, further called for total suppression of the exercise of any kind of authority under the Crown. This meant governments like the ones still operating in New York, New Jersey, Pennsylvania, Delaware, and Maryland.

Not surprisingly, it barely carried. According to one report, six or seven colonies were in favor—New England, Virginia, and one or two from the South—four were opposed, and one or two abstained. Practically speaking, as Adams wrote to his Abigail in Braintree, the preface and resolution together represented "a total, absolute Independence" from Parliament and Crown alike, although a formal declaration would have to follow.[21] To historian Joseph Ellis, it was "a de facto declaration of independence, adopted only after a fierce debate occasioned by the clear realization of all the delegates that, with its passage, the die was cast."[22]

For all that wishes had mothered many of Adams's earlier thoughts, this time he was correct. The contrast between the de facto governance that Congress had increasingly undertaken and its seeming inability to take the final legal step was more than embarrassing. European newspapers carried report after report of British and mercenary troops leaving English, Irish, and German ports. Commercial suppliers, diplomats, and potential European allies alike could fairly query: Are the colonists losing political cohesion? Are they frightened? Are they about to shrink from the final break?

After the decision on June 7 to postpone voting on the pivotal Lee resolution for another three weeks, leaders in Congress stepped up the pressure. To begin with, they appointed a committee to pull together an actual declaration. Adams, Franklin, and Jefferson were named on June 11, along with Roger Sherman and Robert R. Livingston; Jefferson inevitably became the penman. Book after book has described the conditions—location, desk, temperature and summer humidity, the pressure of events, and his preference to be back in Virginia—under which Jefferson wrote. Suffice it to say that he had a first draft in a few days; Adams and Franklin suggested changes, which were generally made; and the committee presented its draft to the full Congress on June 28.

The instructions from home that constrained the middle colonies were not so easily dealt with, and in the meantime South Carolina delegates also put that colony's decision into the uncertain category. As of late June, Charleston was about to be attacked by a powerful British fleet and army—the supposed consummation of the Crown's confused southern expedition—and news of its repulse on June 28 in a stunning Patriot victory did not reach Philadelphia in time to be a factor. With six colonies opposed or undecided on independence—much the same cleavage reported on May 15—canceling the middle colonies' instructions became pivotal.

Back in May, Pennsylvania had been considered the linchpin, partly on the assumption that Delaware and New Jersey would follow its lead. On May 15, the die truly was cast when Congress passed a resolution under which Pennsylvania's existing government was among those to be suppressed as representing royal authority. No guillotines went up on Market Street, but what independence supporters in Congress had done, albeit indirectly, was to hand provincial political power to Pennsylvania's Radical faction. On June 8, the Pennsylvania Assembly, in its institutional death throes, tried to stave off fate by authorizing the delegates in Philadelphia to take any measures necessary, although independence was not specifically mentioned. The Assembly met for the last time on June 14.

The old order had been overthrown. Four days later the province's extralegal Conference of Committees, reflecting a radical Patriot consensus, called a constitutional convention to be held in July. On June 24, members of the Conference unanimously expressed "willingness to concur in a vote of the Congress declaring the United Colonies free and independent states."[23]

For many moderates, that did not resolve matters. However, when the final vote on the Lee resolution came on July 2, two reluctant Pennsylvania delegates, Robert Morris and John Dickinson, abstained. Their actions allowed a three-to-two plurality finally to put the province behind independence.

New Jersey, also required by the May 15 measure to rid itself of Crown-empowered government, in mid-June performed what amounted to a revolutionary two-step: the legislature arrested Royal Governor William Franklin and voted to form a new state government. Then on June 22, its delegates to Congress were told to act as necessary "in declaring the United Colonies independent of Great Britain."[24]

As for Delaware, the Assembly ended its existence on June 15, authorizing its delegates in Philadelphia to concur with Congress in taking necessary measures, but not using the word *independence*. In practical terms, the balance within the three-man delegation swung in favor of independence on July 2, when Caesar Rodney's arrival broke a one-one tie.

The Maryland Patriot faction rallied during June, with county after county sending petitions or instructions to the Provincial Convention asking that body to abandon its previous policy and support independence. On June 28, it did just that.

New York was the weakest link. By June, with a British invasion looming, many of the leading radicals had left the city, and leadership of the Patriot faction was in the hands of relative conservatives like John Jay, James Duane, Gouverneur Morris, and Philip Livingston. Enthusiasm for implementing Congress's May 15 resolution was minimal. The Third Provincial Congress, deciding that it did not have authority to act, on May 31 handed off responsibility to a Fourth Provincial Congress that was to be elected in late June and convene in July. Until it met, New York's congressional delegates continued to be bound by their year-old instructions. Accordingly, they abstained in both the July 1 and July 2 votes on the Lee resolution. And so it was on July 2 that the balloting for independence was twelve colonies in favor and one abstaining. Pennsylvania, Delaware, and South Carolina, opposed a day earlier, took supportive positions on July 2. The deed was done, even as battalion after battalion of redcoats began to disembark in New York after wearying May-June journeys of their own.

The wording of the Declaration was also moving toward acceptance. During several days of debate, Congress removed roughly a quarter of Jefferson's language, deleting quirky notions and rough edges. However, the language that really mattered on July 1 and July 2 was the legal and commercial phraseology Lee had put forward in June. Back then, he had explained the legal necessity: "No state in Europe will either Treat or Trade with us for so long as we consider ourselves subjects of G[reat] B[ritain]. Honor, dignity and the custom of states forbid them until we rank as an independant people."[25] France could aid the colonies illicitly but had to deny that relationship formally.

Scholars of the Declaration have for the most part affirmed the primacy of those international and commercial objectives.[26] In January 1776, Thomas Paine had said as much in *Common Sense:* if independence is not declared, "we must in the eyes of foreign nations be considered as Rebels."

By April and May, mere awareness of these needs was hardening into a sense of priority. That spring, noted chronicler Wills, North Carolina paired the two goals as a recommendation: "declaring independency and forming foreign alliances." Virginia favored independence as part of "the assent by this colony to such declaration and to whatever measures may be thought proper and necessary by the Congress for forming foreign alliances and a confederation of the colonies." New Jersey also came out for "declaring the United Colonies independent of Great Britain, entering into a confederacy for union and for common defense, making treaties with foreign nations for commerce and assistance, and to take such other measures as necessary."[27]

In a different vein, to rebut a potential legal weakness in the United Colonies' position, Jefferson's first draft attempted to define the Americans and the British as two separate peoples. This was important, in one scholar's words, "to re-inforce the perception that the conflict was not a civil war . . . If America and Great Britain were seen as one people, Congress could not justify revolution against the British government, for the simple reason that the body of the people (of which Americans would be only one part) did not support the American cause."[28] As put by another, "although they [the Americans] were now rebels in the eyes of the British king and Parliament, they were not yet legitimate belligerents in the view of the rest of the world. In order to turn a civil war within the British Empire into a war between states outside the empire, it was necessary to create legitimate bodies of combatants—that is, states—out of individual rebels and traitors."[29]

Possibly because Jefferson's notion of two peoples cried out for rebuttal, Congress deleted this phraseology in favor of a broader reference to one people dissolving the bonds that had connected them with another. That still left the argument that what was going on was actually civil war, but it never prompted much debate. British legalists, committed to defining the

Americans as rebels, may have regarded "civil war" as too respectful a description. On the other side, by early 1776 quite a few Americans, not least in Virginia and Maryland, had begun to see independence not as an ideal but as the only alternative to governmental chaos or submission to Britain.[30] They may have had no more taste for legal quibbling.

Because of the hazards facing Patriot leaders should July bring no Declaration, a few historians have cast the sharp practices in Philadelphia between mid-May and July 1–2 as a thinly disguised seizure of power.[31] Military historian John Shy, like others in his profession mindful of the weight of the imminent British attack, called the timing of the Declaration "in part, a Congressional coup intended to foreclose serious negotiations which the British seemed ready to undertake."[32] It is a plausible argument.

Trumpeting the Declaration that summer likewise had a collateral purpose. In various July and August meetings and parades, participants enthusiastically cast George III as tyrant and ogre. His name had already been stripped out of oaths, forms, and procedures in some colonies. The Rhode Island Assembly had done so as early as May 6, when its members renounced the colony's allegiance.[33] But during the summer, the disavowal turned physical. On July 9, demonstrators in New York famously toppled the king's equestrian statue and sent the lead to Connecticut to make bullets. In Boston, said one report, "after dinner, the King's Arms were taken down from the State House, and every vestige of him from every place in which it appeared, and burnt." In Huntington, New York, an effigy of George III was "hung on a gallows, exploded and burnt to ashes." Enthusiasts in Savannah, Georgia, staged a funeral procession and the interment of "George the Third" in front of the courthouse.[34] These actions can also be seen as a celebration-cum-endorsement of Jefferson's blistering case against George III, which took up more than half of the Declaration.

Once read to the soldiers and other crowds, the Declaration, while not forgotten, seems to have receded in importance. Only in the 1790s did interest grow in who had actually written what—Jefferson was running for president—and everyone knows how the legend developed during the nineteenth century. One thing, though, can be said with certainty about the events in Philadelphia on July 1 and 2: the British in New York were only days from disembarkation; Hancock, Lee, Adams, and Jefferson were just in time.

PART IV

CONSEQUENCES AND

RAMIFICATIONS

The Battle of Boston: A Great American Victory

With the beginning of fighting in America, the army at Boston became a strategic liability to the British. The town could not be evacuated owing to a shortage of transports, nor could it be defended against a determined attack, because it was dominated by heights that the British did not have the manpower to occupy. Moreover, Boston was thought to be unfit as a base for an offensive land campaign because it was besieged by an army of Americans in extremely strong natural defensive positions. Boston, though militarily worthless, severely strained the resources of the Royal Navy in American waters.

David Syrett, *The Royal Navy in American Waters, 1775–1783*, 1989

From Gage down all acknowledged that the army was helpless in Boston. April 19 and Bunker Hill had taught the impossibility of conquering the New Englanders, fighting by their chosen methods in that country of rolling hills, winding roads, stone walls, and much cover.

Allen French, *The First Year of the American Revolution*, 1934

I wish this Cursed place [Boston] was burned.

General Thomas Gage to Lord Barrington, June 1775

A s William Howe replaced Thomas Gage as the British commander in North America in early October 1775, the two generals concurred on one imperative: to get the army out of Boston, move it to New York, and utilize that more strategic city as the base from which to regain control of the rebellious colonies. Boston, and beyond it Massachusetts, and perhaps all of New England, was a trap.

A year and a half earlier, a confident Cabinet and Parliament had perceived the port of Boston and the province of Massachusetts as a radical, troublemaking, and vulnerable fringe of British North America. Teaching it a lesson would chasten the other colonies and get them back in line. The Coercive Acts were passed to close down the port, supplant the Massachusetts Charter of 1691, and make local government more subservient. Four additional regiments were added to the Boston garrison. However, the ensuing Battle of Boston—an appropriate way to clump the events between June 1774 and June 1775—was a five-step Patriot ladder to victory.

First came the more-than-expected rallying round of the other colonies, aiding Boston with food and funds. Next, in October, a surprising First Continental Congress tentatively embraced the maverick seaport. Spring 1775 brought Lexington and Concord. Then in June, the Second Continental Congress adopted the New England army besieging British-occupied Boston. A week later, 2,200 redcoated soldiers marched up a grassy hillside, and half were killed or wounded. That day's disillusionment prompted Gage to write to Secretary at War Barrington on June 25 that "the loss we have Sustained, is greater than we can bear. Small Army's cant afford such losses."[1]

Summer brought the occupiers little comfort. Congress issued its *Declaration of the Causes and Necessity of Taking Up Arms*. The besieged troops in Boston suffered from lack of food. And while raiding islands along the New England coast for cattle, sheep, and hay was necessary, failure was frequent.

Gage sent several realistic evaluations to Lord Dartmouth. The rebels, he said, made strong stands behind cover, entrenched quickly and effectively, and took good advantage of the hilly New England terrain. They also benefited from a dense population, committed enough to keep provincial militiamen on hand for a lengthy siege. He saw better prospects in regions with more favorable terrain and more loyal subjects.[2]

General Howe, after replacing Gage, wrote to the adjutant general in London that he had too few troops to attack fortified rebel positions at great cost. He favored simply holding Boston until the men could be moved elsewhere. "To attack the Rebels from Boston would be hazardous," he advised Lord Dartmouth on October 9.[3]

The other British generals in Boston more or less concurred. Burgoyne described New England topography as natural fortification.[4] Clinton concluded that "the disadvantages of our staying here [Boston] are many and great . . . Distemper has already seized us. Confinement is hard duty, and want of fresh meat will increase it, and we shall in the course of a long winter, moulder away to nothing."[5]

The Royal Navy shared the discontent with Boston. Gage commented in June that "the only use is its Harbour, which may be said to be Material; but in all other respects its the worst place either to act Offensively from, or defensively."[6] Admiral Graves, headquartered on HMS *Preston,* was unable even to control the harbor and was recalled shortly after Gage.

The navy had its own stages of embarrassment and defeat. From the start, Graves was unable to establish control over the many islands in Boston Harbor, so that rebel small craft moved with near impunity. The besieged army was desperate for meat and forage, although in peacetime livestock and hay had abounded on the offshore islands. The Royal Navy brought back so little that General Burgoyne, an amateur playwright, wrote letters mocking the admiral's ineffectiveness. Of the 35 transports and supply ships sent to Boston during 1775, only eight arrived there.[7] Come autumn, George Washington, manning a half dozen armed schooners with army personnel (from regiments full of Massachusetts fishermen), took some important prizes. The biggest catch, the munitions-laden *Nancy,* was taken almost within sight of Boston Harbor. Nor could the world's foremost navy deal with fast Yankee whaleboats rowed by mariners able to strike where and when clumsy British men-of-war were unable to sail. As Chapter 23 will pursue, Graves at one point feared that 20 to 30 large whaleboats (carrying 400 to 500 men) might capture the 70-gun ship *Boyne,* its crew having been reduced to only 325 men. By summer, several huge two-deckers had been sent elsewhere.

Boston had become the center of British military activity in North America. The army command was there. And once the Port Act went into effect, Boston became the Royal Navy's North American headquarters. The number of vessels under Graves's command grew from 25 in February 1775 to 29 in late June and 51 by year's end.[8] The city was no more a sideshow for the Royal Navy than it was for a half dozen crack army regiments, including the King's Own and the Royal Welch Fusiliers.

Army officers regularly bemoaned unfavorable military geography: hills, heights, twisting roads, and stone walls perfect for lurking marksmen. However, naval officers could match them with the drawbacks of Boston Harbor and Massachusetts Bay: difficult channels, shoals, confusing tides, and too many inlets through which the harbor could be entered. Even the climate seemed to conspire: fog and gales, and a brutal winter. In the words of one British officer, "The running ropes freeze in the Blocks; the sails are stiff like Sheets of Tin; and the men cannot expose their Hands long enough to the cold to do their duty aloft."[9]

According to early-twentieth-century historian Allen French, Gage began mentioning departure for New York to Lord Dartmouth on June 12, returning to the possibility on July 24 and August 20.[10] By August, a consensus seemed to be at hand.

Moving had obvious benefits. The city of New York sat astride the Hudson-Champlain corridor, dominion over which could split New England from the other colonies. The city's deepwater harbor was wide open to naval might. Provisioning would be much easier. And New York had a reputation as the colony most inclined to loyalism. But as summer turned to autumn, transportation became an obstacle, yielding a reluctant decision: no move until spring. Howe, taking command, was told that too few transports were available to relocate the army, together with the supplies needed, and the several thousand Massachusetts Loyalists who could not be abandoned.[11]

As Chapter 12 discussed, logistics were a weakness in initial British military preparedness. Unfortunately for Howe, the shortfall of transports in autumn 1775 recurred in March 1776. His request was made on minimal notice, after Washington received heavy artillery brought overland from Fort Ticonderoga and quickly positioned those cannon on Dorchester Heights overlooking Boston Harbor. Once the batteries were reinforced, Howe was obliged to evacuate. But too few transports and escorts were available to carry the army and dependent Loyalists for a landing in New York against potentially strong American opposition. Instead, a course had to be set for Halifax, Nova Scotia, a town of 5,000 whose bleak remoteness only accentuated the forced departure. This British embarrassment offered a welcome counterpoint for Americans about to be chased from a Canada they had expected to claim months earlier.

Not every Royal Navy ship left Massachusetts Bay in late March with Howe. Captain Banks of the *Renown*, 50 guns, was left with four other ships to keep watch off Nantasket Roads in Boston Harbor. He was to intercept and send to Halifax transports headed to Boston without knowledge of Howe's departure. But Banks's force left in June after Massachusetts artillerymen constructed a new battery on Long Island. Three more arriving transports thereupon fell into rebel hands.[12] By and large, British strategists were finished with Massachusetts. There would be raids and burnings: Nantucket had British visitors from time to time; and for several years between 1779 and 1782, British forces occupied Maine's lower Penobscot Valley. But broadly speaking, the state of Massachusetts was left alone.

A question rarely posed, but suggested by the sequence of mounting British frustration, is this: How did Parliament, the Cabinet, and King George so misjudge Boston, Massachusetts, and North America, and how did that misjudgment affect the first years of the American Revolution?

Samuel Adams: A Massachusetts Machiavel?

In the pantheon of Revolutionary Ascetics, a remembrance of influential true believers from Citizen Robespierre to Comrade Lenin, Samuel Adams is one of the few qualified Americans. James Rivington, the Loyalist New York printer, unflatteringly likened him to Machiavelli, as did Adams's Massachusetts archfoe, Royal Governor Thomas Hutchinson.[13] To Thomas Jefferson, the elder of the two Adams cousins was "truly the *Man of the Revolution*." In the Europe of the mid- and late 1770s, it was the elder cousin, not the younger one, who was *le fameux Adams*, the principal mover of Revolutionary America. In London, reported Josiah Quincy, Samuel Adams was considered "the first politician in the world."[14]

So was this Yankee Machiavelli responsible for more of the Revolution taking place in Boston than might have otherwise occurred? Did he bait the British into a strategic trap that their generals only belatedly understood? Maybe so—we will consider the arguments—but there will never be proof (or for that matter, disproof).

Over the years, American historians have delivered widely divergent judgments on the elder Adams. He gains approval from most of those willing to describe the events of 1775–1783 in bold revolutionary terms but draws criticism from conservatives eager to portray a gentry-led War of American Independence and loath to hail a shabby backroom political operator.[15] In fact, Adams combined undoubted backroom capabilities with rarely acknowledged scholarship, having returned to Harvard after the usual four years to add a master of arts degree in 1743. His subject, appropriately, was applied political theory. After framing the issue—"Whether it be lawful to resist the Supreme Magistrate, if the Commonwealth cannot be otherwise preserved?"—Adams answered as vehemently as he would in his later prime.[16]

Let us be in no doubt that Adams often manipulated public opinion, employing sharp elbows and manufacturing public frustration above and beyond what already existed. In 1936, historian John C. Miller published a volume entitled *Sam Adams: Pioneer in Propaganda,* arguing that Adams sometimes misrepresented opponents' views, breached political ethics, and sometimes used his position to expunge embarrassing insistences and details from the legislative record.[17] But this critique largely omits how Adams orchestrated great events and outcomes, going far beyond mere propaganda. Proof of this larger accomplishment is limited, though, because the careful Bostonian destroyed many of his papers.

We can begin in 1768, a year when popular restiveness in Massachusetts first provoked the British military occupations that would continue right up through Evacuation Day in 1776. Adams, a member of the state House of Representatives but more powerful in a second role as its clerk, pushed through a so-called Circular Letter to the other colonies, which acquainted them with the abuses of Parliament's Townshend duties and hinted the need for a Congress. When the British government formally demanded the letter's retraction, the House refused by a 91 to 17 vote. This stark refusal, and some rioting, led to four army regiments being ordered to Boston. A popular convention was called, but Adams joined the moderates and cooled any confrontation just before the troops landed.[18] If Tories mocked him for backsliding, he now had his issue—public arousal over military coercion. Both Governor Francis Bernard and conservative leader Thomas Hutchinson acknowledged the year's unprecedented lurch toward extralegal institutions and revolution.[19] Adams's fingerprints were everywhere.

The Boston Massacre of 1770, in which British soldiers fired into an unruly mob, killing five, brought out Adams's Machiavellian side. On one hand, he led the Patriotic faction calling for the soldiers' removal from the city. However, to ensure that the soldiers' trial struck a balance and did not present Boston in an unfavorable light, he enlisted his lawyer cousin to handle their defense.[20]

That same year Adams also took the lead in urging his fellow legislators to improve and strengthen the militia. He understood that in any future emergency or confrontation, it would side with the people, because only a few ranking officers were Loyalists.[21]

In 1770, the many-fingered Adams had also considered a scheme for organizing committees of correspondence in America to inform and coordinate resistance. At that time he put it aside. But in October 1772, with even some political allies skeptical, he launched the Boston Committee of

Correspondence. Its nominal task was to communicate and exchange views with the Bay Colony's several hundred other towns. Three thousand miles away, Solicitor General Alexander Wedderburn accused Adams of telling New Englanders of "a hundred rights of which they had never heard before and a hundred grievances which they never before had felt." But the network caught on, with Plymouth, Cambridge, and Marblehead first to join. By 1774, most Massachusetts towns had committees. According to chronicler Miller, Adams and his associates "proceeded to make the committee of correspondence the most formidable revolutionary machine that was created during the American Revolution."[22]

The Virginia House of Burgesses followed suit in 1773, inaugurating its own committee of correspondence to keep in touch with the other colonies. Not coincidentally, two of the chief Virginia architects, Richard Henry Lee and Patrick Henry, were part of Adams's radical network.[23] In practical terms, Massachusetts's town-by-town communications system aided the radicals to take control of the province in mid-1774 following the Coercive Acts, while Virginia's colony-to-colony structure played a vital part in encouraging support for a Continental Congress and promoting approval of Boston and the fire-breathing Suffolk Resolves. Sam Adams was hardly alone. Related key roles in Massachusetts were played by Dr. Joseph Warren, Adams's principal associate, and Paul Revere, who ran a major caucus and surveillance group in Boston, in addition to his important express riding.

A second essential prop of Boston's move to the forefront in 1774 was local Patriots' willingness in December 1773 to gamble on the political sagacity of dumping £13,000 worth of tea into Boston Harbor. Tea strategy, by this point, was dominating the rivalry between the radical factions in Boston, Philadelphia, and New York over who could take the boldest positions. However, Samuel Adams wanted Boston out front for larger reasons. Not for nothing did foes like Governor Hutchinson disparage him as the Chief or Great Incendiary; now greatness required Boston, not Philadelphia or New York, to host the political fireworks.

Here a bit of comparison is in order. Philadelphia Patriots, also in December, turned back the local tea ships before they landed any tea, although they coupled this action with a strong endorsement of Boston's tea party. This was law-abiding enough not to stir any notable retribution by the conservative Pennsylvania Assembly or Philadelphia's ambivalent commercial elites. New York's tea ships came late, in mid-April 1775. One was turned back, and the second had some of its tea dumped by "Mohawks," but five months after the Boston Tea Party, local authorities looked the other way.[24]

Patriots in Boston, by contrast, enjoyed the waterfront equivalent of Shakespeare's Globe Theatre. The city was their playhouse. If the legal issues surrounding the principal Boston tea ship were complex—which they certainly were—Adams's associates could opt for a splashy extralegal solution. The Patriot faction controlled the provincial House of Representatives, the Boston Town Meeting, most of the local press, the local jury system, and the all-important Boston waterfront. Hostile conservatives were institutionally weaker than in New York or Philadelphia. Because of Boston's reputation, any serious provocation—dumping and destroying a large quantity of tea, say, versus simply turning back tea ships—could easily ignite British desire to teach the city a huge lesson. Parliament might even grasp the chance to rescind the privileges in the Massachusetts Charter of 1691. No other port city could dare such a notable conflagration—or so the Great Incendiary himself might have reasoned.

On December 16, the tea was dumped. From January through April 1774, Adams and his waiting, wary associates acted confidently rather than cautiously. They observed March's fourth anniversary of the Boston Massacre with a strong speech delivered by John Hancock but largely written by Samuel Adams. It called for a Congress of all the colonies, applauded a well-ordered militia, and told Massachusetts to be ready to fight.[25] For several months, the Patriot faction even ventured a second inflammatory gambit as the provincial House of Representatives voted to impeach a royal appointee, Chief Justice Peter Oliver, albeit maneuvers by Governor Hutchinson blocked its implementation.[26] Then in May, details of the reported Boston Port Act finally arrived.

Despite initially unnerving many maritime Bostonians, the Port Act was a political overreaction that played into Patriot hands. As we have seen in Chapter 9, Opposition speakers during the debate in Parliament pointed out that no other English city had been so sweepingly punished. In North America, sympathy mushroomed from Maine to Georgia—literally. Maine sent firewood, fish, potatoes, and some sheep; and Georgia's principal help took the form of £50 and 160 barrels of rice from Yankee-settled St. John's Parish.[27] Activists in the other major seaports were especially supportive.

Looking back five months later, Samuel Adams could write that reaction to the Port Act "wrought a Union of the Colonies which could not be brought about by the Industry of years in reasoning on the necessity of it for the Common Safety."[28] By then, however, he had fanned a lot of dull embers, and Paul Revere had made an extraordinary five-day ride from Boston to Philadelphia with a copy of yet another fiery Massachusetts document, the Suffolk Resolves. The British Cabinet and its military commanders in America didn't yet understand, but they were already being trapped in a Patriot-encircled Boston.

After May 1774, with its news of the Port Act and first hints of a Congress—to which Adams would be sent as a Massachusetts delegate—the Great Incendiary shifted more of his machinations to what later generations would call the national stage. And here is where his dual role as an orchestrator in both Boston and Philadelphia becomes difficult to track.

John Adams left a written portrait of his 52-year-old cousin in Philadelphia burning bundles of correspondence or, in summer's temperatures, scissoring documents into strings and confetti. Congressional sessions were held in secrecy, prosecutions for treason remained possible, and the older Adams explained that "whatever becomes of me, my friends will never suffer by my negligence." Later tampering may have further thinned the surviving documentation. William Wells, an Adams descendent who authored Samuel's first biography in 1865, wrote that "there is . . . reason to believe that letters were abstracted early in the present [nineteenth] century by persons interested in their suppression."[29]

In August, as he was about to leave for Philadelphia, Samuel Adams and his closest colleagues were monitoring several bubbling political cauldrons. Disgruntlement in Massachusetts's central and western hinterland over Britain's new Massachusetts Government Act brought out huge crowds of 4,000 and 5,000 protesters in shire towns like Springfield and Worcester. Not only did they shut down the courts, but the mere weight of their presence persuaded many objected-to Crown appointees to resign. Rural Massachusetts had become as radical as Boston. In the east, General Gage, fearing rising militancy, laid plans to march several battalions to Worcester, where Patriot weapons were stored. Arrangements were also made to remove His Majesty's powder from the provincial powderhouse just outside Boston.

Four hundred miles to the south, Patriots in the Chesapeake provinces, readying themselves for the Continental Congress, prepared to wield tobacco as a political weapon. In doing so, they were embracing the nonexportation strategy Adams had long favored. In Philadelphia, the First Continental Congress was to convene on September 5, and some delegates were already arriving. The topic was the Coercive Acts and how to rectify Britain's treatment of Massachusetts. In all of these venues, Adams had associates and allies: across Massachusetts, fellow legislators, activists, and committees of correspondence; in Virginia, Patrick Henry and Richard Henry Lee; and in Philadelphia, activists like Charles Thomson, a local tea party strategist who in early September was elected secretary of the First Continental Congress. Thomson's capacity for backstage politics was about to win him the ultimate accolade: "the Samuel Adams of Pennsylvania."

As August became September, these several political worlds converged, and we can only surmise the plots and machinations lost to history by Sam Adams's scissors or in his fireplace. On September 1, early in the Massachusetts morning, 250 redcoats sent by Gage removed the powder from the provincial powderhouse. However, with tensions building, he soon abandoned his planned march to Worcester. Over the next few days, as delegates gathered in Philadelphia, the hapless British general also moved to fortify Boston Neck: on September 2 the guard was doubled, and the next day four cannon were emplaced; a year later, it had become a substantial complex.[30]

The departure of Sam Adams for Philadelphia some weeks earlier had left Joseph Warren, a kindred spirit, chairing the Boston Committee of Correspondence and handling intelligence gathering and express rider scheduling. "Correspondence," already hectic and prolific, doubtless surged on September 1. As redcoats bore away the gunpowder, rumors buzzed about soldiers on the march, and comments spread about the British fortifying Boston Neck. We know that dispatches were sent west toward Springfield, north into New Hampshire, and southwest to Connecticut.[31] By the evening of September 1 and through the next day, reports began to circulate that Boston had been bombarded and six men killed.[32] Patriot discussion became mobilization as militiamen and others began to march.

Warren, Revere, and other activists had undoubtedly kept messages flowing over what Gage had done and might yet be up to. Fear of military coercion had been a provincial staple since 1768. But as reports came of huge numbers of men heading for Boston—as many as 20,000, some from as far away as Connecticut and New Hampshire—many Patriot leaders, including Warren, sought to quell the exaggerations and turn back the marchers. A large-scale confrontation or an attack on the British in Boston would have been counterproductive.[33] By September 2–3, the flow had stopped, and Gage by then had abandoned his proposed Worcester march. However, he continued to mount cannon and fortify Boston Neck. Perhaps the dispatches sent out were exaggerated; perhaps the dispatchers simply counted on rumor mills to grind as usual.

By September 9 and 10, reports based on the unfounded rumors—the supposed bombardments and multiple fatalities—reached the newly convened delegates in Philadelphia. As we saw in Chapter 8, the impact was electric. John Adams described the word *war* as being on everyone's lips. In the meantime, Warren had taken over in Boston. On August 16, carefully circumventing the Massachusetts Government Act, he had scheduled an early September Suffolk County Convention in lieu of a special Boston Town Meeting, these now prohibited. He began work on an agenda. On September 9, the county convention issued the soon-to-be-famous Suffolk Resolves. They called for disobedience to the Coercive Acts and Gage's appointees, endorsed nonexportation, denounced Gage's fortification of Boston Neck, and advised Massachusetts to prepare for defensive war.

Paul Revere, Adams's and Warren's winged messenger, took horse for Philadelphia and arrived on September 16. He confirmed that the earlier reports had been excessive, but to a crowd still caught up in the possibility of war, he held out a literary sword—the bellicose Suffolk Resolves. With Samuel Adams and Charles Thomson at work, the Congress approved the resolves on September 17.[34] Conservatives soon lost hope, and when Congress adjourned in October, a commercial war had been declared against Britain, and Massachusetts had been promised support against any British aggression.

If congressional embrace of the Suffolk Resolves was not quite a political coup, it came close—and Sam Adams and his associates dealt in just such Machiavellian accomplishment. Besides which, an even more important orchestration can be glimpsed, if hardly documented, seven months later in Sam Adams's nighttime presence and apparent advice giving in Lexington as the minutemen gathered for morning's historic encounter, then in the Patriot achievement in taking witnesses' depositions that the British fired first, and finally in making sure that evidence and explanations got around the thirteen colonies and also over to England in record time. These details have already been discussed on pages 12–13, but it may well be that the last two weeks in April 1775 were when Samuel Adams orchestrated the triumphant consummation of his life's work.

Bunker Hill and British Military Discouragement

The two-year victory of Massachusetts was stunning. In 1774, Thomas Gage had been prophetic, although disbelieved, in warning his superiors at home about the deep-seated hostility that Britain faced in Massachusetts and New

England. But after Lexington and Concord and Bunker Hill, the general became bitter and concluded that Massachusetts had been implacable and conspiratorial. In July 1775, Gage argued to Lord Dartmouth that Boston was where "the arch-rebels formed their scheme long ago. This circumstance brought the troops first here which is the most disadvantageous place for all operations."[35] Parenthetically, Joseph Galloway, the Pennsylvanian Loyalist and former Assembly speaker, came to the same conclusion, recalling in his memoirs that through Congress's adoption of the Suffolk Resolves, "the foundation of military resistance throughout America was effectually laid."[36]

Nine days after Bunker Hill, in a letter to an old friend, Lord Barrington at the War Office in London, Gage—perhaps even then looking out the window at Boston—summed up with a confession: "I wish this Cursed place was burned."[37] Nor was Gage alone in being affected. General Howe, who came through battle on June 19 without a physical wound, is thought by some to have suffered an important psychological one. The aides accompanying him all died or were wounded on the slopes, and he himself returned with his white gaiters reddened by the bloody grass. Some military historians have concluded that after Bunker Hill, Howe was usually reluctant to attack entrenched American positions.

However, a second psychology may also have been at work. Howe succeeded to the army command in North America (excluding Canada) when Gage sailed for England in October 1775. Early in 1776, his brother, Admiral Richard, Viscount Howe, was given the North American naval command. This joinder was unusual enough, but on the admiral's arrival, the two brothers both assumed a second duty: as peace commissioners authorized to treat with the Americans. Both took that responsibility seriously. General William Howe was also the member of Parliament for Nottingham, a textile town with a large population of Protestant dissenters. In late 1774, he had promised that constituency not to take up arms against the Americans. Admiral Howe had held private negotiations with Benjamin Franklin in London for four weeks beginning on Christmas Day in 1774. He had hoped then that the ministry would appoint a peace commission on which he and Franklin could both serve, but by March the idea had come to naught.[38]

As we saw in Chapter 14, their older brother, Brigadier George Augustus Howe, killed at Lake George in 1758, had become famous among the American troops, admired for his empathy, his openness to new tactics, and his willingness to campaign alongside the New England troops. After his death, Massachusetts paid for a commemorative tablet in Westminster Abbey, and Richard and William Howe, who had greatly admired their elder brother, probably took up their peace commissioner duties in that spirit. By spring 1776, their official instructions-cum-conditions—that for any colony to receive peace, it had to dissolve all congresses, conventions, and associations, and to disband all soldiers armed, arrayed, and paid by the illegal organizations—were outdated and not plausible for discussion even before July's vote for independence. After July, the Howe brothers marched to their own peace-minded drummer: a willingness to win the war only by victories that promoted reconciliation, politically drained the rebellion, or wearied the Americans into giving up. Indeed, before and after the two brothers returned to Britain in 1778, they were accused of neglecting one military opportunity after another. The Howe family papers burned in later years, foreclosing any explanation, but possibly the scars of Bunker Hill and memories of the tablet Massachusetts legislators put in Westminster Abbey had combined in some way that will never be explained.

The Effects of British Confinement and Delay in Boston

Belief that Massachusetts radicals were responsible for leading otherwise loyal colonies astray, and that cutting off the vipers' heads in Boston would end the Revolution, was one of British officialdom's most costly self-deceptions. During 1774 and 1775, as so much emphasis was placed on sending regiments to Boston, Canada was left open to invasion, and at the end of 1775, twelve of the thirteen colonies had no British regulars stationed within their boundaries to command fear or even respect.

Obviously, the king and his Cabinet hardly planned anything like this. If critics are to be believed, relatively little was seriously planned. However, if we date the Revolution from 1774 and 1775, that period's overconcentration of British forces in Boston and its damage to alternative military options—in the middle colonies, along the Hudson-Champlain corridor, or in a more sophisticated southern expedition—jumps right out. Not only did the rebels build a new political infrastructure in much of the abandoned territory—thousands of associations, committees, conventions, and new militia structures—but it was Patriot leaders who effectively determined where the Revolution's major early battles were fought: in the Boston area and along several of the war routes into Quebec.

But British commanders regarded Boston as strategically useless and an awful place to spend the winter of 1775–1776. Had Britain operated the eighteenth-century equivalent of naval and army war colleges, nobody could conceivably have drawn up the strategy Lord North and the Cabinet stumbled into. In fact, North knew he was militarily unqualified and several times asked the king for permission to resign.

The Patriots who knew best what they were about during the period that this chapter has styled the Battle of Boston were a handful of bold political strategists—most notably, Samuel Adams and Joseph Warren—and one commanding general, George Washington. Still, the credit Washington deserves for generalship between July 1775 and March 1776, and also for naval acumen and for his handling of munitions, certainly did not include the original politics of entrapment that lured British ministers and parliamentarians into the Yankee spider's web.

Not a few historians have said of Sam Adams, and to a lesser extent of Joseph Warren and Paul Revere, that during the period from 1773 to 1775, they always seemed to be around when something was happening. However, it has long been unfashionable to renew the popular accolades that Adams and Warren enjoyed in the 1770s and 1780s, when they were two of the Revolution's best-known heroes—*le fameux Adams* and the greatly admired Warren, who died at Bunker Hill fighting as a private soldier because his commission as a major general had not yet arrived. It is unfortunate that this praise has ebbed.

Central importance to the Revolution should no longer be confined to the handful of men who made their names in 1776 through involvement with the Declaration of Independence. Greater attention is in order to the leading politicians, agitators, and propagandists—Adams and Warren fit all three descriptions—who turned Boston and the Bay Colony into the ill-mannered backwoods bobcat that the haughty British Lion had to corner and destroy before anything else, but never could.

Nor was Boston the only strategic miscalculation that preoccupied, misled, and delayed the British in 1775. The American attack on Canada, besides almost succeeding, forced Britain into a northern military emphasis and buildup. This in turn dictated much of the route followed by the grand invasion that the king and Parliament counted on to finish the war in one campaign. We now turn to that flawed strategy.

CHAPTER 21

Canada: Defeat or Victory?

In a short time, we have reason to hope, the delegates of Canada will join us in Congress and complete the American union as far as we wish to have it completed.

Thomas Jefferson, November 29, 1775

The weather is already set in severe and if some unforeseen assistance does not speedily arrive I am afraid thus City and Province will soon be in the Hands of the Rebels.

Captain John Hamilton, Royal Navy, at Quebec City, November 10, 1775

The garrison at Fort St. Jean put up a spirited and valiant struggle against the American forces . . . By delaying the American troops at Fort St. Jean for forty-five days, [Major] Preston and his forces were successful in exhausting and weakening Montgomery's troops. The long siege ultimately delayed the American invasion of Quebec City until winter, which would prove fatal for Montgomery and the Americans.

Inscription, Musée du Fort St. Jean-sur-Richelieu, Quebec

Among the decisions made by the Second Continental Congress between early May and late July 1775—ten weeks that matched or exceeded the gravity of that same period in 1776—the invasion of Canada was among the most influential, with repercussions felt throughout the war. Yet it probably wouldn't have taken place without mid-May's provocative Yankee expeditions that seized Forts Ticonderoga and Crown Point and raided St. John across the Quebec border. These, in turn, might not have taken place without the machinations of Samuel Adams or the north country knowledge of Benedict Arnold, then a captain of Connecticut Foot Guards.

The general verdict of historians, at least until recently, has been to label the invasion a failure and to concede American overambition in trying to make Canada into a future state. However, not only did the northward incursions almost prevail, but they furthered less obvious goals: thwarting and delaying the British use of Canada as a base for an invasion of New York; stalling support for the Crown among the Canadian Indian tribes; minimizing the prospect of British raids on western New England to pull Yankee militia away from the siege of Boston; and seizing some of British North America's remaining supplies of gunpowder, cannon, and mortars.

Ultimate American success, achieved at the Battle of Saratoga in 1777, although hardly a conscious strategy two years earlier, flowed from British officialdom's forced reliance on a substantially Canadian-based grand invasion to put down rebellion in a string of provinces that had their population center near Philadelphia. We have seen how London had overcommitted to a political and military focus on Boston to cut off that Medusa's head of sedition. Then the American invasion obliged an overconcentration in Canada. The ensuing British master plan to split New England from more reconciliation-minded New York consequently required two of its three expeditions to be launched from Canada—the larger taking the familiar Champlain-Hudson warpath southward, the second coming from the St. Lawrence and Lake Ontario and sweeping eastward down the Mohawk Valley toward Albany. This was backward looking because the old French invasion routes, while imprinted on British minds, had never enabled the French to prevail as far as Albany, and this shortfall occurred in decades when the English-speaking districts en route had been only sparsely settled.

By 1775, the population of northern New England had ballooned, and its hostility would prove crippling, as General John Burgoyne reported home with such frustration in 1777. With Whitehall trapped in a geographic time warp, the stakes rose with each year of strategic persistence. The fatal postponement of the Champlain-Hudson and Mohawk Valley expeditions into the summer and autumn of 1777, instead of the autumn of 1776, was an indirect consequence of British forces in Boston coming late to New York and Benedict Arnold's timely October 1776 delaying action on Lake Champlain in the Battle of Valcour Bay. The latter's unusual military capacities included land and sea alike. In June 1775, General Carleton in Quebec had prophetically said of Arnold that he "is well acquainted with every avenue to it [Quebec]."[1]

The muses have ignored how close the American invasion of Canada in 1775 came to success. The vaunted Quebec Act was disliked rather than appreciated by the French-Canadian peasantry—and without their support, Carleton and his advisers were dubious, through much of October and November, about Quebec holding out against the rebels.

For some weeks, the doubt verged on panic. Ships and cargoes were sent back to Britain lest they be captured when Montreal and Quebec fell. Had the incomplete British fortifications just south of Montreal at St. John—present-day St. Jean-sur-Richelieu—fallen in two or three weeks instead of withstanding a siege for 45 days, the American gamble would have succeeded. The main invasion force from Lake Champlain would have secured Montreal in October and then taken Quebec in late October or early November, when its garrison was minimal and its gates wide open.

New York: Insufficient Mid-1775 Invasion Commitment

June and July's gradual hardening of congressional willingness to invade Canada was not matched by a parallel buildup of men, munitions, and martial enthusiasm in the staging grounds near Lake George and Lake Champlain. This was New York territory. Philip Schuyler of New York, appointed in June as one of Congress's four new major generals, was shortly thereafter named to command the invading army. However, New York was not prepared—not militarily and perhaps not psychologically. As its Provincial Congress conceded in a mid-July letter to Schuyler, "Our troops can be of no service to you; they have no arms, clothes, blankets or ammunition; the officers no commissions; our treasury no money; ourselves in debt. It is in vain to complain; we will remove difficulties as fast as we can, and send you soldiers, whenever the men we have raised are entitled to the name."[2]

These were dire constraints, because the invasion clock was ticking ominously. July would have been the optimal month; August was critical. New Englanders knew; so did George Washington. But Congress was in charge and had put Schuyler in command. As of July, the regiments garrisoning Ticonderoga and Crown Point were New England units, and they could have invaded with a few weeks' notice.

To complicate matters, Yorkers and New Englanders were mutually suspicious. As Chapter 2 has noted, some New Yorkers—Alexander Hamilton was one—worried that New England radicals had ambitions to annex border regions of New York, especially if the province continued to equivocate or became caught up in civil war. According to one Connecticut historian, in late spring "New York's inability to man her own posts in this crisis raised the suspicion that she pursued a policy not of involvement but of neutrality, a suspicion fed by subsequent events."[3] That summer, Connecticut units were sent to the city of New York and Fort Ticonderoga at New York's request, and the Yankee province's soldiers also crossed the border to suppress Toryism on Long Island and the mid-Hudson Valley.

However, not wanting to provoke New York into further Loyalism, Massachusetts and Connecticut accepted the northern command going to Schuyler, with Richard Montgomery as his second in command. In politics, though, both generals represented the same conservative, landholding wing of the Patriotic movement in New York. Schuyler's mother was a Van Cortlandt, his wife a Van Rensselaer. Montgomery, the son of a British baronet, was married to a Livingston. Indeed, Schuyler's wife and Montgomery's were cousins. Not surprisingly, both men disliked the egalitarian views, behavior, and discipline of the New Englanders and thought little better of New York's initial Patriot formation, the First Regiment. Commanded at first by Colonel Alexander McDougall, a prominent city radical, it was heavy with members of the Sons of Liberty. Montgomery would later describe that unit as "the sweepings of the New York streets."[4]

Like many officers from the southern and middle colonies, Schuyler and Montgomery looked askance at Yankee majors who were tavern keepers and at captains who were shoemakers. Such criticism was often valid from a disciplinary perspective; Yankee troops were known for insubordination. The Yankees had their own Yorker jokes, not least about the scarcity of New York rank and file. Connecticut Colonel Benjamin Hinman, commanding at Ticonderoga, remarked that although New York abounded with officers, his curiosity had not yet been gratified by the sight of one private.[5]

Also to the point, the Yankees did not care for the pretensions of New York officers. The chaplain of Hinman's regiment wrote bemusedly to his wife back in Connecticut that Schuyler, "somewhat haughty and overbearing," would not heed advice from persons without "some wealth and rank."

The general, he recounted, had only listened to a blacksmith "after I had explained to him that the man was well-descended and only a blacksmith by reason that his grandfather's English estates had been forfeited to the Crown."[6]

Schuyler, though, was hardly the colonial equivalent of a third marquess or fifth viscount. He was principally a businessman, operating both timber mills and shipbuilding enterprises while managing his large landholdings. His earlier military role during the French and Indian War involved not combat but supply, logistics, and shipbuilding. Here his skills were acknowledged. With soldiers having such varied muskets, he was shrewd enough to keep insisting on bullet molds of different sizes. He knew how to build ships. In 1777, Schuyler's program of felling trees, diverting streams, and moving boulders onto roadways seriously delayed General John Burgoyne's southward advance from Ticonderoga to Saratoga.

But in invasion-minded 1775, he was doubly miscast. To begin with, he was not a battlefield commander, for which he had neither qualification nor experience. On top of which, he was no warrior but a reconciliation-minded conservative reluctant to wage all-out war against the Crown. Even Montgomery wondered "but has he strong nerves?"[7]

John Adams later blamed the congressional reconciliationists for the loss in Canada because they "impeded and paralyzed all our enterprises . . . If every measure for the service in Canada, from the first projection of it to the final loss of the province, had not been opposed and obstinately disputed by the same party . . ."[8] Although Adams singled out John Dickinson of Pennsylvania and James Duane of New York, that delegation included others so inclined. Among the conservative wing of the New York Patriotic movement, symbolized by men like Duane, John Alsop, Lewis and Gouverneur Morris, John Jay, and several of the Livingstons, as of mid-1775 probably half had reconciliationist hopes or tendencies. Such sentiments could have conflicted with an aggressive military posture.

Schuyler might have been reticent, and New Englanders criticized him repeatedly: in 1775 for slowness; in 1776 for abandoning Crown Point; and in 1777 for partial culpability in the abandonment of Ticonderoga. His embarrassment peaked in 1778 when British Major John Acland, one of Burgoyne's officers, who had become close to Schuyler during his captivity after the Battle of Saratoga, reported to British generals that the New Yorker had not favored the break with Britain.[9]

Why Quebec Almost Fell but Did Not

Unfortunately for the Patriot cause, delay came in many forms—provincial, political, and military. All were at work in the second half of 1775 as opportunity after opportunity was missed.

In *The War of American Independence,* military historian Don Higginbotham blistered Schuyler as "vastly deficient in assembling and training an offensive army" and lamented his "dilatory tactics."[10] In late July, the general advised the Continental Congress of his easygoing intentions: he would be "going to St. John's with a respectable body, giving the Canadians to understand, when we arrive there, that we mean nothing more than to prevent the regular troops from getting a naval strength and interrupting the friendly intercourse that has subsisted between them and us."[11] The more soldierly Montgomery began the Canadian incursion "with no intention of pressing down upon Quebec just then, but planned to spend the winter at Montreal."[12] That relaxed time frame seems to have lingered. In late October, to quell unrest among his men, he promised that those who continued on with him to Montreal could depart for home. In late August, though, Washington had told Schuyler that Benedict Arnold would be marching to Quebec through Maine.

By early September, as Schuyler and Montgomery moved their 1,500 men into Quebec, the St. John entrenchments had become the designated British strongpoint to block the American advance. Map 8 shows the essential locations and distances. Of the 700 redcoats then stationed in Canada, 200 were in Montreal, 80 were at Fort Chambly, and 400 were concentrated at St. John. These entrenchments on the Richelieu River were not a full, purpose-built fort; they should have fallen in a few weeks, given the cannon and mortars available at Ticonderoga and Crown Point.

The initial approaches to St. John, carried out with Schuyler in command on September 5–6 and on September 10–11, were muddles, as historians generally agree. The first was stung by an Indian ambush, followed by the American commander's gullible acceptance of supposedly friendly advice to retreat. He was told of the fort's completion—untrue—and of potential bombardment by the sixteen-gun schooner *Royal Savage* (which in fact lacked room to maneuver on the river). Schuyler quickly retreated ten miles south, disheartening his inexperienced troops.[13]

The September 10–11 effort, likewise riddled with mismanagement and again demoralizing, resulted in a second retreat back to the Isle de Noix. The hapless Schuyler, whose health problems seem to have been aggravated by military stress, thereupon went home for rest and care. Montgomery, left in command, advanced to St. John and on September 18 undertook a siege and river blockade.

Montgomery's generalship, although muscular alongside Schuyler's, had shortcomings. Not only did he lack artillery experience, but according to one British military history "the American blockade was also extremely lax—Preston [Major Charles Preston, the British commander at St. John] communicated regularly with Carleton and on October 4, two Canadian officers rounded up eight cattle from nearby fields and brought them into the fort."[14] Food supplies were only belatedly cut off.

Neither Schuyler nor Montgomery seems to have understood the need to pound St. John into quick submission in order to reach Quebec by late October or early November. Both men were initially reconciliation minded, and neither initially demanded siege artillery. Indeed, Schuyler retained some of his colony's earlier reluctance to use the cannon and mortars captured at Ticonderoga and Crown Point. In July, he had referred to making use of the field pieces "in the State House Yard at Philadelphia."[15] Historian Allen French dismissed Schuyler's knowledge of gunnery as "strangely vague" in light of his July request for "an assortment of articles in the artillery way."[16] At any rate, when the siege of St. John began on September 18, the encircling Americans were outgunned by the cannon of the British defenders.[17]

Montgomery, no artillerist, may have deplored the very notion of pounding the British into submission as incompatible with reconciliation. He had been a British Army captain himself until 1772. Indeed, although the thirteen-inch mortar nicknamed "the Sow" belatedly arrived from Ticonderoga on October 5, its initial use was apparently ineffective. Details from a diary kept during the siege by the Reverend Benjamin Trumbull, another Connecticut chaplain, noted that by mid-October, officers of the besieging army, New Englanders, New Yorkers, and allied Canadians, were on the verge of mutiny over Montgomery's ineffective placements of artillery. In a council of war, Montgomery reluctantly consented to the new placements insisted upon. Work quickly got under way. Diarist Trumbull's explanation is revealing: the new battery "entirely answered the Expectations of the Army. In a Day or two, it sunk the Enemy's Schooner and opened a more safe passage by the Forts down the Lake [Richelieu River]. Besides, it greatly annoyed the Enemy, and seemed to prepare the Way for all the future Success of the Army. It is remarkable however that General Montgomery never gave any General Orders to erect, man or in any way to maintain or Support this Battery from first to last, nor would he ever own it to be his."[18]

The belatedly intensified bombardment destroyed buildings, walls, vessels, and provisions—the garrison had to sleep in cellars—on a scale that obliged Major Preston to surrender St. John on November 3. Despite commanding scarcely more than "two low-lying small redoubts connected by palisades," Preston had held out against what could have been an American victory won in two to four weeks, and he pointedly noted in his journal that "we may thank our Enemy . . . for leaving us in such slight field Works the credit of having been only reduced by Famine."[19]

Several Canadian historians have come to the same conclusion. One of them, Jacques Castonguay, wrote that "if Quebec has saved Canada from the American Revolution, it seems fair to say that it is St. John that saved Quebec. If Arnold and Montgomery could not take Quebec December 31, 1775, that is primarily due to the small army of Major Preston, in garrison at Fort St. John. The Americans had hoped to take over Canada in early fall 1775, but their plan was thwarted and rendered impossible by the fierce resistance they met on the Richelieu."[20]

Fort Chambly, a less important outlier of Montreal, had surrendered on October 18. Thus St. John's capture in early November meant that nearly 500 of Canada's 700 redcoats were now American prisoners. Montgomery entered Montreal on November 13, but in the meantime Governor Carleton escaped downriver toward Quebec by disguising himself as a poor *habitant*. These weeks of British despondency confirmed the Patriot opportunity. Quebec now lay wide open, and on November 8, Benedict Arnold, leading his remaining 600 down the Chaudière River to the St. Lawrence, could see the great citadel in the distance.

Carleton was especially bitter over French peasant disaffection and widespread refusal to serve in his militia. He told London officials that his defense of the province would have succeeded "had not this wretched people been blind to honour, duty, and their own interest." He also lamented the state of affairs in Quebec: "We have not one soldier in the town and the lower sort are not more loyal than here [Montreal]." As for the Indians, "they are as easily dejected as the Canadian peasantry, and like them chose to be of the strongest side."[21] Although George Washington did not take up the Abenaki chiefs on their promise to join the Americans in invading

Canada, Benedict Arnold enlisted 40 St. Francis Abenaki and ten Penobscot.

As we saw in Chapter 10, British apprehension extended to Niagara in the west and Nova Scotia in the east. General Gage in Boston, on hearing September reports of Arnold's small fleet carrying troops to cross Maine, first surmised they were a Nova Scotia–bound invasion force.[22] In October and November, some 20 ships in Montreal and Quebec sailed for Britain carrying valuable goods, munitions, and government papers. Lieutenant Governor Hector Cramahe, in charge during Carleton's absence, wrote to Lord Dartmouth on November 9 that "two battalions in the spring might have saved the province," but now "I doubt whether twenty would regain it."[23] As late as November 12, legend has Quebec City's St. John's Gate remaining open.

British fortune brightened somewhat when Arnold's troops, reaching the St. Lawrence on November 9, were obliged by weather to wait several days to cross in canoes—and even then only 350 managed to cross by November 13. The remaining 150 were still on the eastern shore. These were the days during which the gates were supposedly open, and even the exhausted 350 men might have taken Quebec. On November 20, a frustrated Arnold wrote to George Washington that "had I been ten days sooner, Quebec must inevitably have fallen into our hands, as there was not a man there to oppose us."[24]

Further optimism followed the arrival of ships, officers, and reinforcements between November 4 and November 19. The first reinforcement arrived by ship on November 4—90 recruits, mostly Irish, from Newfoundland. On November 5, the 28-gun British frigate *Lizard,* which had escorted two powder ships up the St. Lawrence, arrived with a small complement of marines, as well as some 150 naval personnel. These became the core of a 400-man "Marine Battalion" organized from seamen on the various vessels. November 12 brought the arrival of the British officer widely credited with December's successful defense of Quebec—Lieutenant Colonel Allan MacLean of the Royal Highland Emigrants.

Ordered to help defend Montreal, MacLean had left Quebec back in September with 120 of his men, adding 60 fusiliers from the Seventh Regiment as well as several hundred French militia. Blocked near Montreal by American troops, his militia fled, and he hurried back, reaching Quebec by November 12 just before Arnold managed to cross the St. Lawrence. MacLean quickly took over command from a relieved Cramahe, organized the men, inspected the walls, and mounted cannon to best effect. Between the end of October and November 15, the men on hand to defend the city doubled from essentially militia strength to a more impressive 1,800, although the reliability of the 540 Quebecois militia remained suspect.[25]

Montgomery's dawdling also aided the defenders. He had entered Montreal on November 13 but took weeks to move on. After causing a near-mutiny in October by reluctance to pound the British in St. John, he again soured his officers through his supposed cosseting of the British officers captured at St. John and Chambly. Stung by these criticisms, Montgomery resigned. Then he spent another day to work out partial retractions of their slights so that he could honorably withdraw his resignation and resume the campaign. With several vital days wasted, Montgomery wrote apologetically to Washington: "I am ashamed of staying here so long and not getting to Arnold's assistance."[26] So many soldiers had taken advantage of Montgomery's October promise of being able to go home if they stayed to reach Montreal that after leaving a garrison in Montreal, he approached Quebec on December 1 with only 300 men.

As for Arnold, with just 350 men on the Quebec City side of the St. Lawrence, November's new British arrivals soon worried him. A full inspection of his arms and ammunition found so much powder deteriorated or lost that only five rounds per man remained—too little should MacLean decide to sally and attack, as was rumored. Thus on November 18 Arnold had decided to leave Quebec City and move 30 miles south to Pointe-aux-Trembles, where he could safely wait for a Montgomery now far behind schedule. Montgomery's delay meant that the whole surprise and benefit of the grueling march through Maine had been lost. The 1,150 selected volunteers Arnold had started with could just as well have come up the Champlain-Hudson corridor. Had they done so, the combined force could have moved more powerfully and quickly than Montgomery did.

By the time Montgomery arrived on December 1, the days and weeks dissipated during September, October, and November had dimmed the once-bright prospect of victory. Had Montgomery taken St. John and Montreal in October and brought a 1,000-man army to Quebec's walls as November began, the surprise of Arnold's additional 600 arriving shortly thereafter would probably have caused Quebec to surrender. One British official had heard that residents had already drawn up articles of capitulation.[27]

Now fortune favored the British. After MacLean returned to Quebec on

November 12, Governor Carleton made his way back by November 19. By December, the citadel's heavy cannon were fully in position, and by Christmas, some 1,850 defenders outnumbered 1,000 or so attackers. Worse, the enlistment terms of many of the remaining New England soldiers expired on December 31. As the month drew to a close, Montgomery and Arnold had no option. They had to attack, which the British knew—and for which they were prepared.

Montgomery dying in the attack and Arnold being wounded, mainstream American history has somewhat romanticized the actual battle for Quebec and its citadel, turning it into a fight the colonial forces nearly won despite a snowstorm and two-to-one odds in favor of the defenders. Several moments of possible American nearness to victory have become frequent citations: the potential opportunity once through the barricades on the Sault-au-Matelot; the strong position at the abandoned British battery thrown away by Colonel Campbell's muddled retreat after Montgomery's death; and Daniel Morgan's delay and consequential lost opportunity to break through into Quebec's Lower Town.[28]

Perhaps. But the nearness of overall victory on December 31 seems dubious. The Citadel of Quebec had never been taken by enemy attack. The British had won in 1759 because the Marquis de Montcalm, a chevalier, foolishly marched his soldiers onto the Plains of Abraham to do battle, when he could have safely forted up for the winter. Carleton had no such romantic notions, and although Montgomery and Arnold made a gallant attempt on December 31, the genuine American opportunity to force Quebec into surrender ended in November. The portrait of a heroic Montgomery and an almost-victory in that desperate attack has substituted for a reality in which much was unnecessarily lost and wasted.

Benedict Arnold: The Indispensable Man of 1775?

Indispensable is a fair description, but later treason has tainted and shadowed his extraordinary early Revolutionary achievements. Among Arnold's 1775 assets, as a former Connecticut merchant and shipmaster, was knowing his way around the north country. He had sailed to both Canada and the West Indies, and as a merchant he had good contacts and relations with the politically active English-speaking communities in Montreal and Quebec.

When the capture of Fort Ticonderoga and his expedition to St. John several days later brought Arnold's name to the attention of Guy Carleton in Quebec, the latter's June acknowledgment of Arnold's Canadian expertise must have been grudging. No other Yankee colonel had comparable qualifications. But a second part of what pointed Arnold toward Ticonderoga and Crown Point was his knowledge of the two posts' cannon, mortars, and military supplies.

As Captain Arnold of the Connecticut Foot Guards, he had been leading his men toward Boston on April 25 when he met Connecticut Colonel Samuel Holden Parsons in Hartford, beginning a conversation that would prove important to both colonies. When Parsons mentioned the Boston Patriots' shortage of cannon, Arnold cited Ticonderoga as having "a great number of brass cannon." Parsons passed this information to Connecticut leaders, who promptly drew £300 from the provincial treasury for an expedition. On April 29, Arnold arrived in Cambridge and arranged quarters for his troops. The next day, he met with Joseph Warren of the Massachusetts Committee of Safety, pointing out that Ticonderoga, with as many as 130 pieces of artillery, was in such ruinous condition that it could be captured easily. On May 2, Massachusetts made Arnold a colonel on "secret" service and "commander in chief over a body of men not exceeding four hundred" for the purpose of capturing Ticonderoga. He was then to "take possession of the cannon, mortars, stores etc. upon the lake" and return to Cambridge with all the "serviceable" weaponry.[29]

After Ticonderoga and Crown Point fell, both Arnold and the Provincial Congress were unable to arrange for the ordnance to be taken to Massachusetts as Warren had hoped. But while the cannon sat, mid-May found Arnold busy making an inventory, increasing his detailed knowledge of the captured ordnance, munitions, and supplies so that even George Washington tapped it when Arnold visited Cambridge in August. The commanding general quickly requisitioned some of the lead his visitor mentioned for bullets.[30]

May also gave Arnold a chance to display his seamanship. Just days after Ticonderoga and Crown Point were taken, a longtime Arnold associate, Eleazer Oswald, informed him that a few miles to the south, his Patriot force had captured a small schooner from Philip Skene, a retired British officer and large landowner. After arming the schooner with six cannon and four swivels and renaming it the *Liberty,* Arnold sailed north to St. John, as yet minimally fortified. There he surprised and captured the small British garrison, further seizing the king's 70-ton sloop, the only vessel of any size on Lake Champlain. Along with nine bateaux, the captured British sloop was taken south to Crown Point and renamed the *Enterprise*. Until the British constructed another vessel or two, they had no way to move soldiers south on the lake. This barred, for the near term, any retaliatory invasion. Benedict Arnold, until April a part-time captain in the Connecticut Foot, had at least temporarily secured Ticonderoga, Crown Point, and Lake Champlain for Congress.

As befit his new stature, Arnold drafted and in mid-June sent off a long letter and a set of recommendations to the Continental Congress. After describing Carleton's failure to recruit either the French population or the northern Indians, he added that the Canadians had been expecting an American visit and were becoming "very impatient of our delay."[31] What he recommended was both bold and feasible—an invasion plan that called for a small army of 2,000 men and the necessary train of artillery, to depart as soon as possible. The entire force would move north to St. John and nearby Fort Chambly. On arrival, half would be left to besiege those two forts, while the other half headed for Montreal and ultimately Quebec. His argument, based on knowledge and contacts in both cities, was that the gates of Montreal, "on our arrival at that place, will be opened by our friends there, in consequence of a plan for that purpose already entered into."[32] Two thousand men—necessarily New Englanders, because New York was unprepared—would suffice. Speed was essential; there was no need to wait for any larger force.

His timing was politically unfortunate because Congress in mid-June was still caught up in adopting the army besieging Boston, naming Washington to command, and squabbling over the appointment of major generals and brigadiers. The delegates had signaled their willingness to keep Ticonderoga and Crown Point on May 31, but actual orders to invade Canada were not issued until June 27. New Yorker Schuyler was put in command, not Arnold. No relatively unknown New England colonel could have been named. But in the spring and summer of 1776, when painful retrospect was in order, it was clear that Arnold's plan had been by far the best.

One Massachusetts historian summed up: "If two thousand men, well equipped, well supported, could at that juncture [June] have been thrown against Carleton, the result would have been a great success. Arnold's information of the friendliness of the Canadian peasants, and the Indians, was quite correct . . . he could have crushed Carleton."[33]

Both Philip Schuyler and George Washington took Arnold's capacities seriously indeed. In July Schuyler wanted him as his adjutant general but had to appoint a New Yorker. Then in August Washington chose Arnold to command the secondary expedition to Quebec that he had just decided upon, which would traverse Maine's little-traveled high country. There, of course, Arnold distinguished himself with a performance that was likened to those of Hannibal and Xenophon. As for the main expedition, Schuyler fell short of hopes, and Montgomery's performance largely escaped critical scrutiny because of his gallant death on December 31.

Nor did Arnold's spectacular achievements in the north country finish in 1775. On October 11, 1776, months after bedraggled American forces had left Canada, Arnold—now commanding a flotilla of fifteen gundalows and galleys—fought General Carleton and a naval force of 25 vessels under Commodore Thomas Pringle near Valcour Island in Lake Champlain. Because the broadsides fired by the British fleet outweighed Arnold's by two to one, most of the American squadron was sunk. But Arnold had delayed Carleton long enough that the British commander decided to return to Canada. In doing so, he postponed any invasion through New York from Canada until 1777. For that reason, the famed naval historian Alfred T. Mahan rated the Battle of Valcour Island as one of the war's most important American successes: "When Benedict Arnold on Lake Champlain by vigorous use of small means obtained a year's delay for the colonists, he compassed the surrender of Burgoyne in 1777. The surrender of Burgoyne, justly estimated as the decisive event of the war, was due to Arnold's previous action."[34]

A year later Arnold commanded during the decisive American victory in the extended Battle of Saratoga, overshadowing the army's nominal commander, General Horatio Gates. But as in 1775 and 1776, Arnold did not receive the recognition that he expected and deserved. Over the subsequent two centuries, unwillingness to praise a man who later turned traitor doubtless worked to narrow Americans' attention to the invasion of Canada. It is jarring to read about an Arnold whose accomplishments were second only to those of George Washington.

The Invasion of Canada: Victory or Defeat?

Neither description really fits. No true victory could have ended in the ignominious retreat of American armies in June and July 1776. But neither can the term *defeat* be used to describe Arnold's wilderness march, or the many times during October and November when an American victory had been within reach. Overall, in strategic terms, the invasion of Canada achieved most of its secondary goals: the inevitable British invasion southward through New York's Champlain-Hudson corridor was delayed and ultimately thwarted; the Canadian Indians, traditionally hostile to New England, were neutralized during 1775 and early 1776; no attack on the New England frontier was launched from Canada during that period to draw Yankee militia away from the siege of Boston; and a fair amount of vital artillery and gunpowder was captured in Canada, although not the Quebec ordnance and munitions that tantalized George Washington.

British military historians have admitted that the North ministry was stunned on December 23 when a frigate arrived from Quebec with news that the British forces in Montreal had been shattered while another band of rebels had burst from the wilderness near Quebec City, putting the latter under siege.[35] But to one American chronicler, British sangfroid had to accept a new script: "This news forced the government to alter radically its plans for the forthcoming campaign in America. The relief of Quebec and the reconquest of Canada now had to take priority over the invasion of New York." The first and third divisions of transports were assigned for Canada.[36]

The fact that the invasion of Canada ended in retreat produced the predictable historical blurring and intercolony name-calling. New Yorkers blamed the New Englanders who left before December 31 because their enlistments were up. New Englanders criticized Schuyler and blamed the New Yorkers for tardy commitment and supplies. John Adams, bitter at the lost opportunity, blamed the naïve reconciliation wing in the Second Continental Congress led by John Dickinson and James Duane, and some New England historians have concurred.[37]

What should not be debated was whether the invasion was a sound idea. Arnold's June 1775 proposal—a masterful assessment—seems to have been conceptually embraced by Washington even after Congress's rejection. When Montgomery didn't simultaneously put St. John under siege and bombardment while moving part of his force on to Montreal, the commanding general asked why.[38] When Schuyler and Montgomery seemed to procrastinate, Washington worried about Arnold being left out on a limb. Had the latter been named brigadier general, put in command of 2,000 men, and ordered to implement his own invasion blueprint during the summer of 1775, he would have won. His fame might have become second only to Washington, who would deservedly have shared in any Canadian laurels.

In the longer term, any such victory might have been surprisingly complicated. Most historians believe that whatever happened in 1775, Britain would have regained Quebec and Canada within a few years. On the other hand, at least one Canadian chronicler has contended that if the Americans had taken Canada, they could have kept it in the final peace negotiations.[39] Perhaps the most intriguing caveat is that if the Americans had taken Quebec and Canada in 1775, Foreign Minister Vergennes and Louis XVI could have made Canada's return to France a precondition of the essential aid that that nation extended in 1776 and 1777. That could have made the invasion of 1775 seem less wise.

But the actual results, as we have seen, threw the British into a confusion that played havoc with their early war plan. This embarrassment was not confined to Boston and Canada. In Virginia, the early British response to the Revolution miscarried in the hands of a royal governor, John Murray, Earl of Dunmore, whose flashes of strategic acumen were brought to naught by delusions of personal and military grandeur.

CHAPTER 22

Lord Dunmore's Second War

If . . . that man [Lord Dunmore] is not crushed before spring, he will be-
come the most formidable enemy America has; his strength will increase as
a snowball by rolling; and faster if some expedient cannot be hit upon to
convince the slaves and servants of the impotency of his designs . . . I do not
think that forcing his Lordship on shipboard is sufficient; nothing less than
depriving him of life or liberty will secure peace to Virginia.

George Washington, December 1775

Lord Dunmore's unparalleled conduct in Virginia has, a few Scotch ex-
cepted, united every man in that colony. If [the king's ministers] had
searched through the world for a person the best-fitted to ruin their cause,
and procure union and success for these Colonies, they could not have found
a more complete Agent than Lord Dunmore.

Richard Henry Lee, November 1775

That George Washington and Richard Henry Lee, within only a few weeks of each other, could differ so much on the prospects of Virginia's royal governor testifies to Dunmore's important but odd place in the early American Revolution. His brief leadership against the American cause crossed the Virginia skies with an almost cometlike trajectory. More than any other North American governor, he merged his idiosyncrasies and controversial views into the nature of the war in his colony until, like a shooting star, he fell from sight in the summer of 1776. Never again would he return to Virginia.

John Murray, fourth Earl of Dunmore, had been governor of New York for a short time before London moved him to the Old Dominion as governor in 1771. The principal preoccupations he displayed while in New York—

finding opportunities to acquire land—continued to motivate him in Williamsburg. He had come to America, he acknowledged, to make his fortune.[1]

As for broader repute, Dunmore first made his mark in 1774 by getting militia from Virginia's western counties to march north for a short but successful October war against Ohio tribes, the Shawnee, Mingo, and Delaware. These Indians were in the way of westward expansion. Under its seventeenth-century charter, as we have seen, Virginia claimed what is now Ohio and much of the Great Lakes. Land hunger was a Virginian trait, and Dunmore issued numerous patents. King George did not approve of his appointee's encroachment on tribal lands, and in September, Lord Dartmouth cautioned Dunmore that his practices were "a dishonor to the Crown." Further encroachments, he wrote, would not be forgiven.[2] However, before Dartmouth's chastening letter arrived, the western Virginia regiments, on October 10, 1774, after hard fighting, defeated the Indians in the Battle of Point Pleasant.

Although not himself in the battle, Dunmore quickly met with Indian leaders who agreed to peace terms. Besides returning white captives, the Shawnee chiefs were required to deed to Virginia all land east of the Ohio River. This included part of what is now western Pennsylvania and, more important, all of present-day Kentucky.[3] Contrary to western Virginian hopes, no demand was made for settlement north of the Ohio River. Nevertheless, tidewater Virginia leaders were pleased enough that the House of Burgesses congratulated the governor for what annals still call "Lord Dunmore's War." That military success went to his head.

Come spring 1775, Dunmore was too caught up in Williamsburg's new Revolutionary stirrings to meet Ohio tribal leaders in Pittsburgh for a follow-up peace conference. Still, he must have believed that mild peace terms and six months of private words from his chief western representative, John Connolly, were turning October's foes into potential allies against the Virginia frontier. His Lordship was already invoking the Indian threat in intemperate private conversations.

The principal controversies engaging Dunmore between late April and early June had to do with arms and munitions. On April 21, marines from HMS *Magdalen* had carried off the gunpowder from Williamsburg's public magazine and taken it to their vessel. For the next week, the governor misled local officials that he still had the powder near at hand, although in fact it had been taken downriver on HMS *Fowey*. By early May, an edgy

Dunmore was fortifying the governor's palace. His aide, Captain Foy, told those who would listen of supposedly parallel actions by King Charles XII of Sweden. He explained that Dunmore, like the famous Swedish monarch, "has fortified his Home, with Swivel guns at their Windowes, Cut loop holes in the Palace, and has plenty of small arms."[4]

Tension continued. On June 4, when scions of respectable Williamsburg families trespassed and broke into the magazine, three were injured by a spring gun set as a trap. Enraged citizens converged on the magazine and carried away more weapons. The House of Burgesses then ordered the city volunteers to mount a guard at the magazine until further notice.[5] At two o'clock in the morning of June 8, Dunmore and his family fled to the protection of the Royal Navy, the governor insisting that their lives were in danger.[6]

Local apprehensions also reflected the rumors of slave plots and imminent uprisings. Southern white fears fed on talk of local plots, few genuine, and more broadly on reports of supposed British interest in slave emancipation and plans to use blacks in the military.

In Maryland and South Carolina, Patriot-faction insistence on taking control of local gunpowder magazines and supplies openly invoked prospective slave revolts and alleged British encouragement. Historian Woody Holton has documented the concern in Virginia, citing mid-April reports of slave plots in four James River counties near Williamsburg. Virginia attorney general John Randolph, a Loyalist, acknowledged that blacks had approached Dunmore offering their services.[7] Edmund Randolph, a Patriot, later argued that Dunmore "designed, by disarming the people, to weaken the means of opposing an insurrection of the slaves . . . for a protection against whom in part the magazine was at first built."[8]

No other royal governor did more than hint, but Dunmore was blunt in threatening to raise the slaves. On April 22, he told a Williamsburg town councilor, William Pasteur, that should any senior British official be harmed, he "would declare freedom to the slaves and reduce the City of Williamsburg to ashes." On April 28, he amplified that his threat would be implemented if the colony's independent military companies came any closer than Ruffin's ferry, 30 miles from the capital. On May 3, Dunmore issued a proclamation reminding Virginians of their "internal weakness"— the potential for slave revolts and Indian attacks. He added that he would "avail himself of any means" to maintain the authority of the Crown.[9]

What also made Dunmore unique among the royal governors, besides his candor and rank—being an earl whereas most were untitled—was an unusual mix of personal attributes. On one hand, he showed considerable strategic awareness; on the other hand, critics believed that his volatile, egotistical personality bespoke instability or worse.

Dunmore: A Personality to Ruin a Cause

Like many other short men in history, Dunmore was combative and touchy, given to making enemies unnecessarily. Some of these were fellow governors. Several held high office in England. Still others—a category that included both George Washington and Thomas Jefferson—were angry Virginians fearful that Dunmore was capable of sending a raiding party to seize their wives.

In Scotland, Dunmore had been an earl with a manor and a park, but without a castle or family pride. His father, the third earl, had been put under arrest for treason in the Forty Five, but the son was allowed to inherit the title in 1750. The future governor, as a teenager, had been a page boy to Bonnie Prince Charlie and remained sensitive about his family's past. In late September 1775, a Norfolk newspaper laid out the governor's father's role and hinted at Catholicism in the family. Dunmore lost his temper and retaliated by sending a boatload of soldiers to seize the printing press of the *Norfolk Intelligencer* and carry off two of its printers. His high-handedness became a Virginia cause célèbre, damaging not only Dunmore's reputation among Patriots but Norfolk's, this because a crowd of several hundred stood around and let it happen.[10]

Lacking the huge acres of Scotland's grander dukes and earls, Dunmore seems to have regarded his two American governorships as opportunities to amass in upper New York or Virginia's west the territory his branch of the Murrays had been unable to gain in Stirlingshire or Perthshire. As a substitute for other listings, consider the bill for losses in the Revolution he filed with the British government in 1784. He claimed for a house and lot in Williamsburg; his plantation in York County; over 3,400 acres in what is now West Virginia; 51,000 acres on Otter Creek, on the eastern shore of Lake Champlain; and "3,700,000 acres representing his share of the Illinois-Wabash Company's claim on the Wabash River in modern Indiana."[11] The Crown disallowed only the Indiana claim, and Dunmore had amassed this property in just five years.

No other royal governor circa 1775 could match Dunmore's reputation for impolitic behavior and arrogance. The king had been offended by Dunmore's giving land patents beyond "the line specified by His Majesty's authority." Besides which, Dartmouth had also disliked Dunmore's slowness in taking up his Virginia appointment. The governor's further request for home leave produced the tart response that if he returned to Britain, please report immediately so that a replacement could be sent out.[12] Dunmore also angered the American Department, as well as Pennsylvania governor John Penn, by contesting that colony's western boundaries. Dartmouth reproached the combative Scot that "your Proclamation . . . implies too strongly the necessity for exerting a Military Force, & breathes too much spirit of Hostility that ought not to be encouraged in Matters of Civil Dispute between the Subjects of the same State."[13]

During the autumn of 1775, Dunmore's continual demands to be sent more companies from the Fourteenth Regiment stationed in St. Augustine angered Governor Patrick Tonyn of British East Florida, who complained that these subtractions left his colony exposed to France and Spain. During the summer, General Gage in Boston had sent Dunmore officers for Loyalist regiments. They turned out not to be needed because no such units had been organized. In June, when the governor commandeered the armed schooner HMS *Magdalen* to carry his wife and family back to Britain, he countermanded Admiral Graves's orders assigning the vessel to Delaware Bay.[14] In a July tantrum, Dunmore asked that Captain John McCartney of the frigate *Mercury* be removed for consorting with Americans and refusing to harbor escaped slaves without prior legal determinations. The charges against McCartney were dropped, and the tone of Graves's report to London suggested that "the governor had become a bit of nuisance."[15]

Dunmore was also given to naming forts after himself. Three posts in the Ohio forks region were named for three of his hereditary titles—Dunmore, Fincastle, and Blair. The ill-fated stockade he built south of Norfolk was grandly called Fort Murray. The merchant ship *Eilbeck,* which he had taken during the summer of 1775 to become his floating headquarters, was rechristened the *Dunmore.* The only rough parallel that comes to mind is President Lyndon B. Johnson, who named his daughters Lynda Bird and Lucy Baines and his dog Little Beagle—and whose oversize ego led to grandiosity and American frustration in Vietnam.

August and September saw controversial raids carried out by Dunmore's sloops and tenders against Virginia Patriots whose tidewater plantations could be reached along rivers like the James, the York, and their tributaries.

Slaves were carried off or turned loose; houses and barns were plundered.* George Washington believed in late 1775 that Dunmore might sail up the Potomac and raid Mount Vernon. His "greatest fear," said one chronicler, "was that the British would take his wife, Martha, hostage. Washington had left Mount Vernon on May 4, 1775, and had not been back." To his estate manager, the general wrote that "I can hardly think that Lord Dunmore can act so low, and unmanly a part as to think of seizing Mrs Washington by way of revenge on me."[16] Thomas Jefferson had a comparable concern about his wife, another Martha. In November 1775, when she and their daughter were away from Monticello visiting her parents' plantation near the James River, Jefferson told his brother-in-law that he had sent her a letter telling her "to keep yourselves at a distance from the alarms of Ld. Dunmore." Mrs. Jefferson soon returned to Monticello.[17] Some views of Dunmore verged on demonization.

Many Virginia historians have ventured short attempts at characterizing Dunmore's behavior. Some of the words and phrases include "intemperate, arrogant," "lack of self-control," "frantic," and "in a state bordering on what would appear to have been frenzied desperation."[18]

One unintended consequence might have been that in September and October, when King George, Lord North, and Lord Dartmouth were considering the destination of the southern expedition ultimately sent to North Carolina, the colony of Virginia—despite its obvious size and importance—remained in third place behind the two Carolinas. In addition to Dunmore's summer and autumn crowing that with a few hundred more soldiers he could bring Virginia to submission, the king and Dartmouth had too many examples of his unreliability and inattention to instructions. A less controversial governor might have won Virginia a higher priority in the ministry's late 1775 counterrevolutionary planning.

Lord Dunmore's Personal Counterrevolution

Dunmore had not the slightest sympathy with the Revolution. His political connections were with the anti-American Bedfordite wing of Lord North's coalition. His brother-in-law, Earl Gower, was in North's Cabinet as Lord President of the Council. And notwithstanding his bluster, the 45-year-old

---

*Many British historians simply omit Dunmore. He cannot be found in the index of Piers Mackesy's *The War for America 1775–1783*, and the appropriate volume of the *Oxford History of England* has only a paragraph that ends with reference to his "private marauding campaign along the coast of Virginia" (p. 202).

Scot had shrewd perceptions. He understood that slaves, servants, and Indians represented crucial components of Patriot vulnerability. He appreciated Norfolk's importance to British naval supremacy in Chesapeake Bay, as well as the unusual opportunity for raiding offered by Virginia's wide rivers, many navigable by frigates for 20 to 40 miles into the interior. He was especially mindful of the Potomac as a military corridor to and from the interior and well aware of Loyalist strength not only in the Norfolk area but across the bay on the Eastern Shore. These insights might have achieved much, implemented carefully by a sober governor with credibility and stature in London, but Dunmore had offsetting weaknesses.

The trajectory of Dunmore's twelve-month rise and fall can be broken down into stages. For a month or so after his June 8 flight to safety on HMS *Fowey,* he did relatively little. Instead of the open war that seemed to threaten in May, the result was "only a breaking off of communications between a fled chief magistrate and decamping burgesses . . . based on years of irritation festering into hatred and scorn."[19]

In mid-July, he led his small flotilla to Sprowle's shipyard in Portsmouth. From this convenient location, his captains escalated their August raids on the lower Chesapeake and up nearby rivers, bringing away slaves and plunder. Even so, Virginia's Third Convention, meeting between July 17 and August 26, devoted most of its attention to military reorganization rather than to their governor's depredations.

Late August brought more raids by the two Royal Navy sloops and their tenders. Townspeople in Hampton, after an early September hurricane, found one of the British sloop *Otter*'s tenders driven ashore and promptly burned it. The eight-man crew was captured, but Captain Matthew Squire, also on board, managed to escape. Squire and the *Otter* were hated for what the *Virginia Gazette* called his trade of "negro-catching, pillaging the farms and plantations of their stock and poultry, and other illustrious actions highly becoming a Squire in the king's navy."[20] It was a boatload of soldiers and marines from the *Otter* who seized the *Norfolk Intelligencer*'s printing press and equipment on September 30. Dunmore's next move, however, was a sound one—a mostly successful series of raids aimed at capturing rebel ordnance and gunpowder supplies.

He wrote on October 5 to advise Lord Dartmouth that the Americans were mounting captured cannon on field carriages in Williamsburg and that three of his flotilla's tenders had been sent to look for inbound rebel ammunition ships.[21] Over the next three weeks, small forces of 100 to 250 redcoats and Loyalist troops went out to capture or destroy Patriot cannon, muskets, and gunpowder. Dunmore himself accompanied at least one of the expeditions. Their commander, Captain Leslie of the Fourteenth Infantry Regiment, estimated that his men seized or destroyed at least 77 pieces of ordnance.[22] The *Otter* also captured one member of a well-known Virginia shipowning clan, the Goodriches, smuggling in gunpowder, and Dunmore used this leverage to compel the family to shift its loyalty to the Crown. After these measures, Loyalist morale had "risen considerably."[23]

Stung by the governor's munitions seizures, the Committee of Safety decided to escalate. On October 23, it ordered Colonel William Woodford of Virginia's Second Regiment to ready that unit and five companies of Culpeper minutemen, many of them sharpshooters, for an advance on "Norfolk or Portsmouth."[24] Patriot leaders were also looking for a Virginia equivalent to the catalyst six months earlier at Lexington. On October 25, they sent a company of Culpeper riflemen under Colonel Woodford to help the town of Hampton defend itself against a small British naval force—a large schooner, two sloops, and two pilot boats—commanded by the detested Matthew Squire. At high water on the morning of October 26, the five vessels drew abreast of the town and began firing their small cannon and swivel guns. But to their surprise, the individually aimed shots of the Culpeper sharpshooters forced the British sailors to abandon not only their cannon but their helms and any activity aloft. One British vessel went aground, and the others sailed off. The *Virginia Gazette,* exulting that one rifleman had killed from a distance of 400 yards, warned, "Take care, ministerial troops."[25]

Overall, November favored Dunmore—and marked his personal and military zenith. Thousands of hitherto undecided residents and some fainthearted rebels in Norfolk and nearby Princess Anne County took a loyalty oath offered by the governor. Three hundred black slaves enlisted in "Lord Dunmore's Ethiopian Regiment," and somewhat fewer white Loyalists joined the Queen's Loyal Virginia Regiment, headed by planter Jacob Ellegood, former commander of the Princess Anne militia. Dunmore began fortifying Norfolk against eventual attack. And on November 14, he led a force of 109 redcoats and some local militia against a reported 300 to 400 rebels at Kemp's Landing, eight miles south of Norfolk. On seeing the redcoats, many of the American militia ran away. As in Ohio a year earlier, Dunmore fancied himself a conqueror. Accordingly, he raised the king's

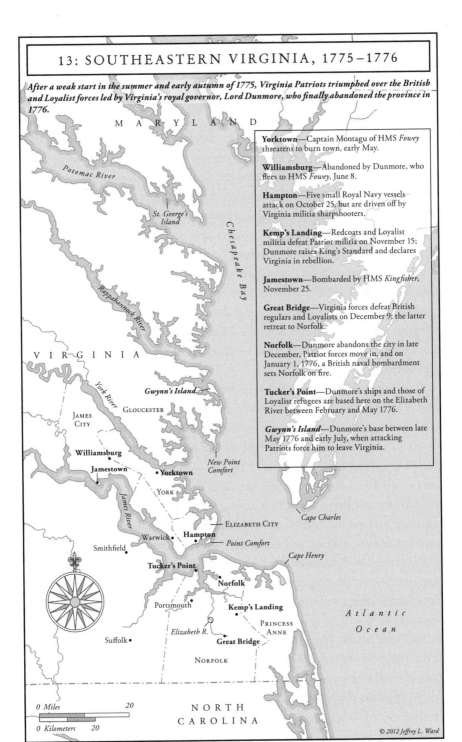

13: SOUTHEASTERN VIRGINIA, 1775–1776

After a weak start in the summer and early autumn of 1775, Virginia Patriots triumphed over the British and Loyalist forces led by Virginia's royal governor, Lord Dunmore, who finally abandoned the province in 1776.

M A R Y L A N D

Potomac River

St. George's Island

Chesapeake Bay

Rappahannock River

V I R G I N I A

York River

Gwynn's Island

JAMES CITY

GLOUCESTER

Williamsburg

Jamestown

James River

Yorktown

YORK

New Point Comfort

Smithfield

Warwick

Hampton

ELIZABETH CITY

Point Comfort

Cape Charles

Cape Henry

Tucker's Point

Norfolk

Portsmouth

Elizabeth R.

Kemp's Landing

PRINCESS ANNE

Suffolk

Great Bridge

NORFOLK

A t l a n t i c O c e a n

Yorktown—Captain Montagu of HMS *Fowey* threatens to burn town, early May.

Williamsburg—Abandoned by Dunmore, who flees to HMS *Fowey*, June 8.

Hampton—Five small Royal Navy vessels attack on October 25, but are driven off by Virginia militia sharpshooters.

Kemp's Landing—Redcoats and Loyalist militia defeat Patriot militia on November 15; Dunmore raises King's Standard and declares Virginia in rebellion.

Jamestown—Bombarded by HMS *Kingfisher*, November 25.

Great Bridge—Virginia forces defeat British regulars and Loyalists on December 9; the latter retreat to Norfolk.

Norfolk—Dunmore abandons the city in late December, Patriot forces move in, and on January 1, 1776, a British naval bombardment sets Norfolk on fire.

Tucker's Point—Dunmore's ships and those of Loyalist refugees are based here on the Elizabeth River between February and May 1776.

Gwynn's Island—Dunmore's base between late May 1776 and early July, when attacking Patriots force him to leave Virginia.

0 Miles 20
0 Kilometers 20

N O R T H C A R O L I N A

© 2012 Jeffrey L. Ward

standard—figuratively, because he did not actually have one—and read a proclamation that declared martial law. He then added: "I do further declare all indentured servants, negroes or others (appertaining to rebels) free, that are able and willing to bear arms, they joining his Majesty's troops as soon as may be."

What had been uttered privately in the spring had now been officially declared. If Richard Henry Lee exaggerated in saying that Dunmore's actions had united all of Virginia save the Scots in opposition, his impolitic November proclamation quickly aided the American cause. "All over Virginia," explains one historian, "observers noted that the governor's freedom offer turned neutrals and even loyalists into patriots."[26] Two members of Dunmore's Executive Council, Robert Carter and William Byrd III, shifted to the rebel camp. Byrd, who had commanded a regiment during the French and Indian War, volunteered his services.[27] Nor was Dunmore's gamble limited to freeing and arming slaves. November was also the month when his scheme to bring the Great Lakes Indians down on Virginia was publicly exposed after the capture in Maryland of John Connolly, his principal lieutenant.

December brought the Patriots' breakthrough. Militia and regulars from Virginia's First and Second regiments now began to move in larger numbers through the colony's southeast—the Norfolk-Jamestown-Williamsburg region—even as Dunmore pulled back and set to work fortifying Norfolk itself. On December 2, Colonel William Woodford of the Second Regiment, with about 350 men, reached Great Bridge, on the southern branch of the Elizabeth River. The town, though only a bridge and a small cluster of homes, was twelve miles south of Norfolk on the principal road to North Carolina. It now held a small stockade—Fort Murray—and some outposts. By December 9, these were expanded and manned by 150 British regulars from the Fourteenth Regiment, some navy gunners, 60 Tory volunteers, and 300 or so ex-slaves now in Dunmore's Ethiopian Regiment, for a total of almost 700.[28]

The Americans, some 800 to 900 strong, included men from Woodford's regiment, some militia, and sharpshooting Culpeper minutemen. They erected breastworks and entrenched to the south of the bridge. The British regulars, Loyalists, and ex-slaves held Fort Murray to its north, in the direction of Norfolk. Under orders presumed to have come from Dunmore, on the morning of December 9 the British formed up and advanced down the causeway, wheeling cannon to the bridge. In front came an advance guard, followed by the grenadier company of the Fourteenth, seven feet tall with their bearskin hats. They crossed the bridge, and behind them trailed 300 Tories and blacks ready to support the expected breakthrough.

Instead, the rout was of the British and Loyalists, further bloody testimony to the shooting abilities of backcountry yeomen who had grown up with firearms. When the grenadiers' captain fell from fourteen bullets—the same number of riflemen had been told to bring him down—and dozens more redcoats had fallen, the British force retreated. Roughly 100 Culpeper riflemen left their entrenchments and started picking off Tories and blacks on the bridge. With the remaining redcoats returning to the stockade, Woodford decided against a counterattack. That night the senior British officer quietly vacated the fort, loaded his wounded on wagons and carts, and headed back to Norfolk. There the redcoats embarked on naval vessels beyond Dunmore's authority. Compared to one wounded Virginian, the enemy loss totaled 102 killed and wounded.[29]

Great Bridge is not a famous name, but its consequences were considerable. Dunmore blamed the officers of the Fourteenth, who had worse to say about the governor's own temper and strategic incapacity. Things would have been well, insisted Dunmore, had he been able to complete his planned breastworks outside Norfolk. Critics scoffed that his barely begun fortifications would have required 5,000 men to man them.[30] Parenthetically, later in the 1780s, when Dunmore was governor of the Bahamas, he again embarked on vast fortifications that cost eight times the planned amount. One historian found a parallel: "the lack of proportion that Dunmore revealed in Norfolk led in Nassau [Bahamas] to a raging controversy over building grandiose fortifications that once again he did not have enough troops to man. That cost virtually bankrupted the colony, and the expenditures generated charges of corruption."[31]

Politically, "news of the turn of events at the Great Bridge threw the loyalists into panic," and "all who were friends to Government took refuge aboard the Ships [in the harbor]."[32] What had been 30 or 40 private vessels in Dunmore's fleet, mostly small, now swelled to about 70. In coming months, it would become less a fleet than a waterborne refugee camp, with many of the refugee families needing British seamen to handle their boats.

Over the next week, Woodford's Second Regiment, together with 300 men from the First Virginia and various units of Virginia militiamen and minutemen, closed in on Norfolk. Three hundred and fifty North Carolina soldiers arrived on December 13, and command passed to a new ranking officer, Colonel Robert Howe of the First North Carolina Continentals. Other units were posted at Great Bridge and Kemp's Landing, where only a month earlier Dunmore had raised the royal standard. By Christmas, there were about 2,500 Patriot soldiers in and around Norfolk.[33]

However, for all that Americans now controlled the city, a new debate had begun among local army commanders and the political leaders assembled in Williamsburg for Virginia's Fourth Convention. The issue was simple: Should Norfolk be strongly fortified and heavily garrisoned, or might it be a better option to destroy the city? That way the British could not seize and rebuild it as a bastion and as a potentially Chesapeake-dominating seaport. Thomas Jefferson was prominent among those favoring its destruction. Indeed, although Dunmore and the British began the fires on January 1 through a bombardment, Virginians actively continued the torching and were later deemed responsible for 80 percent of the fire damage, albeit this was not acknowledged at the time.

Harder to fathom is why Dunmore let himself be trapped into delivering an ultimatum that if the British were not allowed to gather food, Norfolk would be burned. When that access to food was not granted, Dunmore's ships began a cannonade of several hours that set warehouses full of tar, pitch, and molasses ablaze. Many Loyalists on the British ships were appalled, urging that the cannon fire be limited.[34] Equally surprising was that Dunmore, who seemed to realize that Patriots had set many of the fires, never seriously tried to turn that culpability into pro-British propaganda.[35]

The next several months were not kind to the governor. General Clinton, arriving during February en route to North Carolina, later recalled that "we found his Lordship on board a Ship in Hampton Road, driven from the Shore and the whole Country in arms against him . . . I could not see the Use of his Lordship's remaining longer there, especially after the failure of his Attack on the Rebel Post at the Great Bridge."[36]

February's arrival of the 44-gun frigate *Roebuck,* commanded by Captain Andrew Hamond, did give Dunmore new firepower, although *Roebuck* was also under orders to patrol Delaware Bay. Between late February and late May, the governor based his unusual flotilla at Tucker's Point, a promontory in the Elizabeth River some miles west of Norfolk. The once-feisty Scot was relatively inactive, probably because the buildup of Virginia Patriot regiments was ongoing, and both May and June were dominated by the Virginia Convention's conspicuous preparations for independence. Dunmore's sun was beginning to set.

By late May, the Patriots were close to unleashing a new weapon against the embattled governor: fireships on the Elizabeth River, which were to be bought downstream, set alight, and steered into Dunmore's fleet, now numbering some 90 vessels. Captain Hamond, sent for by Dunmore, advised him to withdraw from Tucker's Point. In addition to departing before any fireships came, Dunmore had to flee before the Virginians could put cannon downstream to bottle up his assemblage. Hamond succeeded in extricating Dunmore through a clever stratagem. Beating both the fireships and the not-yet-emplaced cannon, the Royal Navy captain assembled the seaworthy vessels, guided them out of the river, feinted toward the Chesapeake's great exit at the Virginia Capes, and then managed to lead the convoy 40 miles north to Gwynn's Island, where it arrived on May 27.[37]

Dunmore's decline was now in its terminal stage. Although Patriot leaders worried that the British high command might try to reinforce the embattled governor, that never happened. Dunmore's recruitment of Tories on the Eastern Shore for the Queen's Own Loyal Regiment did no more than offset the loss of existing black and white Loyalists to rampant disease. By early July, the Virginia commander, Brigadier General Andrew Lewis, decided that he could safely concentrate Patriot forces to tackle the assembled British and Loyalist forces on Gwynn's Island without leaving Williamsburg vulnerable. On July 8, with units from the First and Second regiments, as well as 1,300 militia, Lewis marched for the island.

It was something less than a bristling fortress. By one description, "at the nearest point the island was only 200 yards from the mainland across a channel that could be forded at low tide. Smallpox had left only 150 to 200 effective troops to defend its three or four square miles, and Hamond had to lend some of his sailors to throw up entrenchments."[38] Where the British had a clear advantage was in warships—the frigate *Roebuck* (44 guns), the frigate *Fowey* (20), the sloop *Otter* (14), and the converted merchantman *Dunmore,* although the frigates could not go into shallows. The Virginians, however, had the heavier artillery: two eighteen-pounders, two twelve-pounders, five nine-pounders, three six-pounders, and six field guns. The British artillery battery on the island had nothing larger than six-pounders.[39]

On the morning of July 9, when Lewis was ready to attack, the *Otter,* the *Dunmore,* and a number of tenders positioned themselves to repel a Virginian amphibious attack relying on rowboats, canoes, and rafts. What took the British by surprise was bombardment from the two eighteen-pounders, which the American gunners had been able to mount unobserved. The *Dunmore* was hit a dozen times before it could be towed out of range, the *Otter* was seriously damaged, and a half dozen tenders were burned or captured. The British artillery was also silenced. However, because the Americans had not yet collected many small boats, Lewis's troops were not in a position to reach the island, and Dunmore was able to withdraw with his vessels that night.[40]

When the Virginians came ashore, they were appalled. Dunmore's force had left some 300 graves at their Tucker Point facility, but Gwynn's mortalities caused more shock. Andrew Lewis recorded that "on our arrival, we found the enemy had evacuated the place with the greatest precipitation, and were struck with horrour at the number of dead bodies in a state of putrefaction, strewed all the way from their battery to Cherry point, about two miles in length, without a shovelful of earth upon them."[41] Another American officer recounted that "it is supposed that they buried 500 Negroes on the island."[42]

Disease was the excuse Lord Dunmore conveyed to Lord George Germain and the American Department. Illnesses had wiped out "an incredible number of our People, especially the Blacks." Without "this horrid disorder, I am satisfied I would have had two thousand Blacks, with whom I should have had no doubt of penetrating into the heart of this Colony."[43]

From Gwynn's Island, Dunmore and Hamond headed up the bay to St. George's Island at the mouth of the Potomac. From here, the governor took a few warships and foraged upriver for food, until driven back by Virginia militia. But on August 4, back in the bay, he heard that General Clinton, having failed at Charleston, was heading back to New York. Now Dunmore's flotilla broke up. About half, escorted by the sloop *Otter,* sailed for St. Augustine, and a smaller group, including Dunmore, headed for New York. Lord Dunmore's second war—the all-important British counterrevolution in Virginia—finished in failure.

Dunmore: The Geopolitics of Personality

In the end, both Richard Henry Lee and George Washington were substantially correct in their assessments of Dunmore. As Lee thought, most Virginians did unite against his policies and personal behavior. Washington, writing from his command post near Boston, was correct about the need to crush the governor before he could attract more followers. However, December proved to be a greater turning point than Washington could have known.

Could another royal governor of Virginia have done better? Probably not. Lacking Dunmore's bold streak, his earl's rank, and his partial success in catering to Virginians' intense land hunger, a more conventional royal governor in Williamsburg might have been marginalized and forced out more quickly. In Maryland and Georgia, for example, Governors Robert Eden and James Wright, while locally respected and reasonably popular, could not straddle the difference between what London required and what a plurality of Marylanders and Georgians wanted. Both men had left their provinces before Dunmore vacated Gwynn's Island and Virginia.

As we have seen, some historians have argued that had two or three more regiments of British regulars been sent to Virginia in October or November 1775, that force might have tipped the balance toward the Crown even with Dunmore as governor. On the other hand, some of Dunmore's military judgment was poor—starting the cannonade that burned Norfolk, for example—and one naval historian has identified the need to detach several vessels to Dunmore as an important reason for the Royal Navy's ineffectiveness in blockading Chesapeake Bay and Delaware Bay during 1775 and the first half of 1776.[44] This ineffectiveness, of course, was felt in the many American vessels that were able to reach Europe and the West Indies with tobacco and other cargoes that they exchanged for arms and munitions.

On a larger dimension, Dunmore's quirkiness might have worked to minimize the importance of what had occurred in the large and populous colony of Virginia. In Quebec, which had only one tenth of Virginia's population, the rebels had to give up the winter siege of Quebec City, and the American retreat during the spring and early summer has been described, fairly enough, as a cavalcade of retreat, misjudgment, disease (smallpox), and death. Dunmore's failure in Virginia likewise involved failure and the abandonment of a strategic city (Norfolk), a critical December 31–January 1 defeat, a gradual retreat, and ultimately, a late-spring and early-summer ignominy marked by smallpox and dead soldiers. But the analogy is never drawn.

It is understandable that British historians may not care to mention Lord Dunmore. Americans, on the other hand, have reason to be grateful that the counterrevolution in Virginia was led by a man with so much egotism and so little eventual success.

Whaleboats, Row Galleys, Schooners, and Submarines: The Small-Ship Origins of the U.S. Navy

The day after the shooting war started at Lexington and Concord, the war for matériel *began . . . [This was] prior to Washington's arrival, and it continued for months, growing increasingly more violent, before Washington became aware of it.*

James L. Nelson, *George Washington's Secret Navy,* 2008

It is probably safe to say that Congress's saltwater navy did not have any significant effect on the overall outcome of the Revolution . . . But what might be said of the deep-water navy cannot be applied to its freshwater counterpart that operated in the remote areas of upstate New York and Vermont along the Hudson River–Lake Champlain corridor. Here an American fleet played a vital role in what was perhaps the most important campaign of the Revolution [the Battle of Valcour Island].

William M. Fowler, Jr., *Rebels Under Sail,* 1976

The silent Yankee canoes that scouted Castle William, the British Army's island headquarters in Boston Harbor, a day after Lexington and Concord, may count as the first vessels in the American navy. A nervous Admiral Graves took their presence seriously enough to station two guard vessels.[1]

Somewhat larger craft are more plausible contenders, including the schooner that in mid-May 1775 led Benedict Arnold's original tiny "navy" on Lake Champlain—as distinct from the larger flotilla he later commanded at Valcour Island. Whether or not Arnold's *Liberty* can be called the first vessel in the United Colonies Navy, the taking of St. Jean and the sloop *George III* represented the first American amphibious operation.

Whaleboats were unusually conspicuous in the early fighting. In the words of one naval historian, "By late May and early June the Americans were waging a vigorous whaleboat war in Boston Harbor. Having scoured all the nearby creeks, inlets and beaches, the Americans had gathered several hundred of these open boats. Of shoal draft and fast over short distances with a few good men at the oars, these boats proved to be a great annoyance to the British. Darting out so quickly that the British barely had time to respond, they attacked the lighthouses in the harbor and landed on the islands to carry off foodstuffs and livestock."[2]

Graves had reason to worry. As we will see, he imagined the ultimate professional ignominy for a British admiral: that 20 to 30 whaleboats, carrying 400 or 500 men, might sneak up on and capture one of his clumsy and undermanned 60- or 70-gun ships of the line. Three years earlier, eight fast whaleboats in Narragansett Bay had captured the more nimble revenue cutter *Gaspee* and then burned it. On May 27, whaleboats sent to remove livestock and forage from several Boston Harbor islands figured in the Battle of Noddle's Island, where Massachusetts forces, after outmaneuvering British longboats and fleet tenders, wound up burning a Royal Navy schooner, the *Diana,* that had run aground. They did not technically capture it, which as we will see is relevant.

Vessels in a few localities became involved inadvertently. On May 12, off Dartmouth, Captain John Linzee of the sloop of war HMS *Falcon,* fourteen guns, took an American merchant vessel just arrived from the West Indies. Putting on a prize crew, he sent it off for Boston with the *Falcon*'s small tender as escort. However, local Patriots, employing "a rag-tag squadron of small craft," caught the tender and its captive near Martha's Vineyard. Fourteen captured British seamen were sent to Taunton Gaol as prisoners.[3]

1775: The Historic Firsts of American Naval History

Americans being a people enamored of records and record setting, even maritime and naval histories pay close attention to the war's unfolding firsts. The episode near Martha's Vineyard, because it antedated the *Liberty*'s May 16 taking of St. John and the sloop *George III* on Lake Champlain, can be called "the first naval action of the Revolution." However, as a case of smugglers versus the Royal Navy—a commonplace in eighteenth-century American waters—it may not properly belong in a naval history.[4]

By Massachusetts yardsticks, "the undisputed honor of being the first to attack and take a vessel of the Royal Navy" goes to the Patriots of Machias, far down east in the Maine district. In early June, two small merchant sloops, *Unity* and *Polly,* escorted by a modest Royal Navy schooner, the *Margaretta,* came looking for firewood and lumber to be carried back to Boston for British barracks. The people of Machias were to be paid in provisions needed by the community, but the political conditions attached became contentious. To make a long story short, after the youthful midshipman commanding the *Margaretta* threatened to fire on the town if its Liberty Pole was not taken down, the aroused Patriot faction seized both accompanying sloops. When the British schooner stood out to sea, several dozen Machias men used the two sloops to follow. The *Unity,* under local fire-eater Jeremiah O'Brien, overhauled, boarded, and captured the *Margaretta,* making her "the first vessel of the Royal Navy to surrender to an American force." James Fenimore Cooper, in his *History of the Navy of the United States of America,* later described the encounter as "The Lexington of the sea."[5]

Some weeks later two other small British naval vessels, the cutter *Diligent,* eight guns, and its tender the *Tatamagouche,* entered Machias still unaware of hostilities and were likewise captured. In August, weeks before Massachusetts officially launched a provincial navy, the *Margaretta,* the *Diligent,* and the *Unity* (proudly renamed the *Machias Liberty*) were taken into provincial service as a down-east Maine guard force. O'Brien was put in command.[6] Here as elsewhere, Yankees made do with what they had: small vessels.

Many brigs and schooners voyaged for gunpowder during late 1774 or 1775 under orders from provincial regimes in Connecticut, Rhode Island, Virginia, Maryland, and South Carolina, for the most part purchasing munitions commercially in European or West Indian ports. However, several were specifically commissioned to capture British supply vessels or seize their cargoes.

Few Patriot organizations could match the South Carolina Council of Safety, military arm of the Provincial Congress, for its spring and summer attentiveness to the United Colonies' gunpowder crisis. Its leaders—men like William Henry Drayton and Arthur Middleton—went far afield for purchases, bargains, or seizures. Whereas New England looked north and west to Lake Champlain and the Crown's major Canadian posts, the Charlestonians pointed south and east to the Bahamas, Bermuda, British

East Florida, and next-door Georgia. In June, their Secret Committee heard of British munitions vessels on their way to Savannah and St. Augustine.[7]

The entrance to the Savannah River, called Tybee Bar, became the Patriot rendezvous. In early July, two barges of seamen and militia from Beaufort, South Carolina, took the Inland Passage to Bloody Point, on their side of the river. Meanwhile, the Georgia Provincial Congress, encouraged by Carolina allies, commandeered and armed a local merchant schooner, the *Elizabeth,* promptly renamed the *Liberty.* This vessel, with its ten carriage guns, apparently inspired the more lightly armed Royal Navy schooner *St. John* to head for the Bahamas. On July 8, the powder-laden British merchantman *Philippa* arrived and was easily seized by the *Liberty* and taken to Cockspur Island in the Savannah River. There the South Carolinians and Georgians evenly divided the powder, each getting some 5,000 pounds.[8]

By July 25, the Patriot leaders in Charleston borrowed—as in commandeered—a local sloop, the *Commerce,* and began refitting it for a raid on the British powder magazines on the island of New Providence. But two days later, word came that a British ordnance brig, the *Betsy,* was en route to St. Augustine with a cargo of military stores. When the *Betsy* was sighted off St. Augustine on August 7, the more lightly armed *Commerce,* with 21 white and five black sailors, took her by a clever ruse. According to South Carolina historians, Captain Clement Lempriere "apparently posted his black sailors conspicuously on deck, kept the rest of the hands below, and deceived the British crew into thinking the *Commerce* was simply a harmless country vessel manned by slaves. The British crew suspected nothing until the sloop pulled alongside the brig and sent over a boarding party armed with swords, pistols, muskets and bayonets." Lempriere paid £1000 sterling for the between 12,000 and 14,000 pounds of powder he took, escaping a British sloop that chased the *Commerce* until giving up in the Inland Passage to Port Royal Sound.[9] If the former *Elizabeth,* now the *Liberty,* arguably founded the Georgia Provincial Navy, the *Commerce* played the same role for South Carolina.

As concern over defenses extended to vulnerable rivers, row galleys gained favor. The Americans invading Canada in September 1775 also used them for aggressive and patrolling purposes on the Richelieu River, and Rhode Island added two to its provincial navy. But the principal innovator was Pennsylvania, which during the summer of 1775 paired a squadron of thirteen row galleys with its iron-toothed chevaux-de-frise as obstacles to British penetration of the Delaware River.[10]

By the end of August, provincial navies were established in six colonies: Connecticut, Rhode Island, Massachusetts (for the Machias region only), Pennsylvania, South Carolina, and Georgia. The scale was small, and except along the Delaware, schooners and sloops dominated. Maryland, Virginia, and North Carolina added local navies in December.

Privateers and privateering had been so popular and financially rewarding during the French wars that proposals quickly reemerged in 1775. Massachusetts led on November 1, passing "An Act for Encouraging the Fixing Out of Armed Vessells, to defend the Sea Coast of America, and for Erecting a Court to Try and Condemn all Vessells that shall be found infesting the same."[11]

George Washington opted for schooners in late August and September, employing the Massachusetts-built *Hannah* as America's first regularly commissioned warship. In a sense, these schooners were quasiprivateers or government privateers because the arrangements gave the crews a share of the booty. The *Hannah* turned out to be slow and disappointing, but several of the other schooners in what has been labeled "Washington's Navy" turned in impressive performances, especially in capturing transports carrying munitions.[12]

Not all of the small craft favored by Americans moved on the water's surface. Early 1775 found David Bushnell, about to graduate from Yale, already at work in Connecticut on what he called a "submarine" and that he hoped to employ against the British men-of-war in Boston Harbor. By August, his associates were already in touch with Benjamin Franklin and Patriot pastor Ezra Stiles. That month, Stiles was informed that "the machine is so constructed that it can move rapidly 20 or more feet under water and attach to the hull of a ship two thousand pounds of gunpowder."[13] But no submerged attack took place until the following summer.

To return to politics, October's British burning of Portland accelerated congressional interest. A few southern members of Congress, like South Carolina's Christopher Gadsden, had been navalists from the start but more were enlisted as conflict spread to Charleston Harbor and the Virginia rivers were raided and plundered by forces under Lord Dunmore. As we have seen, the months of October, November, and December contain the momentous dates in the early history of the U.S. Navy: October 13 and October 30. On December 3, Lieutenant John Paul Jones ran up the United Colonies flag on the Continental Navy's new flagship, the *Alfred*. Then on December 13, in a pretentious move doubted by George Washington and others, Congress voted to build thirteen frigates for the new navy.[14]

Perhaps the number thirteen brought the bad luck, but collectively, these ships compiled what can only be called a disappointing record. As they were completed and commissioned in 1776 and 1777, the increased number of ships and greater professionalism of the Royal Navy regained the North American reputation it had briefly lost in 1775. Half of the new American frigates were destroyed in their shipyards or quickly captured. The water-borne portion of the American Revolution took its laurels just as 1775 had hinted: from the achievements of relatively small vessels, and in later years from the growing importance of privateers.

The Whaleboat Warriors

Their capacity for a quick strike was widely appreciated. Whaleboats had been used in Rhode Islanders' famous attack on the British revenue cutter *Gaspee* in 1772, and from late 1776 on, they played a prominent role in the ferocious raids across Long Island Sound mounted by both Connecticut Patriots and New York Tories. New Jersey Patriots took whaleboats down rivers like the Raritan and attacked locations around New York Harbor.

In 1775, though, Massachusetts was the epicenter. Just weeks after Lexington and Concord, the Massachusetts Committee of Safety was ordering the collection of both boats and oars.[15] The first whaleboat success came in Vineyard Sound in late April, when a single large boat of Naushon Islanders under Captain Nathan Smith, against considerable odds, captured the armed schooner *Volante,* tender to the British frigate *Scarborough.*[16] Six weeks later sailors from the British sloop *Falcon* stove in all of Naushon's whaleboats.

Whaleboats made a mark in the Battle of Noddle's Island in Boston Harbor on May 27. In this drawn-out confrontation, Patriots using them to remove livestock and hay from Noddle's and Hog islands were set upon by British vessels and a marine detachment. Although estimates vary, the British force eventually included 700 or so marines, and the American force under Israel Putnam numbered between 1,000 and 2,000 soldiers, with several field pieces. Most of the livestock and hay were saved, and the Americans also disabled a British sloop and burned the armed schooner *Diana*— with fourteen four-pounders, the largest schooner in Britain's North American Squadron. It was no more than a minor victory, but Congress was cheered enough to make a Continental major general out of Putnam for the part he played.[17]

Follow-up whaleboat expeditions to Pettick's and Deer islands on May 31 and June 2 netted 1,300 sheep and at least 30 cattle. Again, the British could do little to stop the removals, and one man-of-war's barge was taken with four or five prisoners.[18] On July 11, another American raid with 136 men in whaleboats went to Long Island and burned the forage that British soldiers had bundled to bring back to Boston for army horses. An angry Admiral Graves noted in his journal that he did not have men or vessels enough to "secure all the Islands from Depredation." Besides, "the rebels' excursions were always conducted with such Secrecy and Dispatch that the Flames were generally the first notice of their intentions."[19]

Soon after George Washington took command, he reported to Congress on July 20 that "I have ordered all the Whale Boats for many miles along the coast to be collected, and some of them are employed every Night to watch the notion of the enemy by water, in order to guard as much as possible against any surprize."[20] Now Patriots turned to destroying the lighthouses vital to British navigation in the tricky waters of Massachusetts Bay. The Cape Ann lighthouse was destroyed first, and then on July 21, a force of whaleboats under Major Joseph Vose raided Little Brewster Island, site of the Boston Lighthouse. After driving off the British guards, his men burned the wooden parts of the lighthouse and confiscated lamps, oil, and boats.[21]

Major Benjamin Tupper, now emerging as the army's harbor raid commander, took 200 men in 25 whaleboats back to Brewster Island on July 31 to finish the job. They killed or captured 32 redcoats defending the island and took prisoner the ten carpenters doing the rebuilding. This time the lighthouse was burned and destroyed.[22]

By this point, captains of British ships in Boston had become fearful that the Patriots' assemblage of nearly 300 whaleboats—Graves's estimate as of July 24—might be aimed at their own captures. On July 31, John Tollemache, captain of the sloop HMS *Scorpion,* which Graves had stationed near the lighthouse, wrote to tell the admiral it seemed "certain" that he would be attacked. Worse, because his decks had no cover, the *Scorpion* might be taken by small arms alone.[23] That very night a nervous Graves ordered Captain John Robinson of the man-of-war *Preston* to take nine barges of seamen and marines from his ship, as well as from *Boyne* and *Somerset.* They were to burn the 200 or 300 whaleboats reported to be in nearby woods along the Germantown River. However, the American pilots pressed into service refused to give directions, and Robinson turned back, as Graves noted in his journal, because it was deemed "unadvisable to risque so many men and boats in a River totally unknown to all."[24] This happened on the same day that the lighthouse was being destroyed; whaleboats became the talk of the Royal Navy in Boston.

On August 4, Captain Edward LeCras, R.N., and Captain Broderick Hartwell, R.N., commanding officers of the *Somerset* and *Boyne,* respectively, wrote to Graves about their "very weak state of Defence" and potential vulnerability to the whaleboats and to rumored fireships. Hartwell thought it "far from being improbable" that the rebels would endeavor to burn the *Boyne.*[25] Another British officer mocked Graves: "instead of sending his squadron to protect the store-ships and transports from England, [he] has, with the utmost prudence, ordered the ships of war in this harbour to be secured with booms all round, to prevent their being boarded and taken by the Rebel whaleboats."[26]

Whaleboat warfare in the American Revolution was far from finished in August 1775. But in Boston Harbor at least, its great days were winding down.

Row Galleys in the Rivers

Naval attention to row galleys was visible in major rivers like the Delaware, the Hudson, the Piscataqua, and Virginia's four largest waterways—the Potomac, Rappahannock, James, and York. In July 1775, Massachusetts's Josiah Quincy proposed to John Adams that Congress should build a fleet of row galleys along the coasts. They would be small, open oar-driven boats, mounting cannon to fight off British raiders. Congress that month had urged each colony to provide "armed vessels or otherwise . . . for the protection of their harbors and navigation on their coasts."[27]

A few row galleys were indeed used for coasts, most notably along Rhode Island's Narragansett Bay. However, Pennsylvania grabbed attention in the summer of 1775 by launching a provincial navy that soon included fourteen row galleys stationed on the Delaware River to protect Philadelphia. They were 80 to 100 feet in length, propelled by 20 oars, and also carrying two short masts rigged for lateen (triangular) sails. Each mounted an 18- or 24-pounder in its bow, save for a few with 32-pounders. Two swivel guns were also normal. Five of the galleys were named for leading American politicians (Washington, Dickinson, Franklin, Warren, and Hancock), but four were called after pro-Americans in Parliament (Chatham, Effingham, Burke, and Camden).[28]

John Adams of Congress's Naval Committee was duly impressed after they turned back a frigate attack.[29] In May 1776, the galleys, by then numbering thirteen, acquitted themselves surprisingly well against Captain Andrew Hamond's *Roebuck* and its consort, the 28-gun frigate *Liverpool*. Men on the two frigates, heading northward up Delaware Bay under instructions to test Philadelphia's defenses, must have been surprised to see the thirteen galleys approaching with the advantage of both wind and tide. The Patriots had been alerted by an elaborate signals system.

In terms of weaponry, the two frigates mounted 64 cannon to the galleys' thirteen, and the British seamen were experienced where the Pennsylvanians were not. That day, though, the galleys had the weather gauge—they could choose at what distance to engage. Because they had the heavier cannon—the leading galley, the *Washington,* mounted a 32-pounder—they chose distance, a full mile. The galleys' related advantage was that being low in the water, they were hard to hit, whereas the frigates, downwind and sitting high, were much easier targets.[30]

After two and a half hours of dueling, the *Roebuck* ran aground and stuck in soft mud. Luckily for the British, the galleys, about to run out of powder and shot, had to break off. That night, as one chronicler elaborated, was foggy enough that with a combined whaleboat and galley attack, the Pennsylvanians could probably have overwhelmed the still-mired *Roebuck*. Alas, they had not trained in offensive tactics. Captain Hamond later agreed that "if the commanders of the galleys had acted with as much judgment as they did courage, they would have taken or destroyed [the] ship."[31] Although the public's reaction was to cheer the galleys, military leaders remained skeptical.

As we saw in Chapter 17, river-focused defense dictated the late-1775 organization of the Virginia Provincial Navy. The Virginia Convention had authorized eight shallow-draft vessels carrying about 40 men each—two for each major river—but carrying lighter cannon than those in Pennsylvania. The *Norfolk Revenge* and the *Hero* were not quite completed in the spring of 1776, or they might have been sent to attack Lord Dunmore's mixed flotilla upstream on the Elizabeth River.[32] In New York, when the Royal Navy ventured up the Hudson in the summer of 1776, the Patriots deployed row galleys on that river as well, and two of them—the *Washington* and the *Spitfire*—were borrowed from the Rhode Island Navy, which had put them into service on Narragansett Bay in 1775. Before reaching New York, the Rhode Island pair had recaptured two American vessels, the brigantine

Georgia Packet and the sloop *Speedwell,* from the care of the frigate HMS *Scarborough.* In July, as thousands watched in Manhattan, *Washington* and *Spitfire,* with several other row galleys, fought credibly against a small British flotilla including the frigates *Rose* and *Phoenix,* albeit it was the Americans who broke off.[33]

Fighting Schooners

If large row galleys could mount 24-pounders and 32-pounders, the distinctive attribute of schooners was speed. As the war began, no one admired their qualities more than Samuel Graves.

In 1774 he had advised the Admiralty that "three or four good Marblehead schooners would do considerable service in the present weak State of the Squadron," and by October 1775, schooners accounted for five of the 35 British warships keeping watch on the North American coast.[34] From Graves's standpoint, the American schooners, although carrying only four-pounder guns, derived their advantage from nimbleness and from being light vessels drawing little water. They can, he said, "lie under the Land, and, upon observing a Vessel or two unguarded, dart upon them suddenly, and carry them off even in sight of the King's Ships."[35]

George Washington must have had similar views. In August 1775, when he quietly began sending small Massachusetts vessels to sea in pursuit of British supply ships and transports, the craft selected were Marblehead and Beverly schooners. At first, the idea seemed doubtful—the first schooner sent out, the *Hannah,* was too slow—but he persevered, and ultimately the commanding general's vessels took 35 British prizes before Washington left for New York. When Admiral Molyneux Shuldham arrived to replace Graves, he reported to the Admiralty that "I was much concerned on my arrival to hear of the Number of small Arm'd vessels fitted out by the Rebels, and which had taken many unarmed Ones of Ours bringing stores and supplies to this place."[36]

As we have seen, the word *schooner* came into use in early-eighteenth-century Massachusetts, from the local colloquialism *to scoon* or "skim lightly along the water."[37] Schooner-rigged vessels were ideal for local fishermen, handling better in changeable coastal winds.

Chesapeake Bay mariners, searching for similar attributes, developed their own vessels during the 1730s. These pilot boats, as they were called, featured simpler fore-and-aft rigging that facilitated speed and maneuverability and permitted smaller crews than regular schooners. These fast bay-craft came of age during the Revolution, when Maryland's Council of Safety noted "the impracticality of square-sail vessels escaping the bay; that small sharp-rigged vessels would more probably meet with success."[38] After the *Defence,* the three vessels owned or leased by the Maryland Council of Safety were pilot boats—*Dolphin, Plater,* and *Chatham.*

The Virginia Provincial Navy, in turn, began in December 1775 with the pilot boats *Liberty* and *Patriot.* Commodore James Barron soon headed a flotilla of pilot boats and gunboats, with the original two being the best known. *Liberty* served throughout the war, capturing the *Oxford,* a British transport carrying 200 soldiers, and defeating the *Fortunatus,* a British na-val tender twice the *Liberty's* size.*[39] The colonies' most innovative small craft, however, while hardly matching schooners for speed represented an extraordinary breakthrough in stealth.

Connecticut's Experimental Submarine

Given the whaleboat-centered apprehensions of the captains of three great men-of-war in Boston Harbor that summer—*Boyne, Somerset,* and *Preston*—one can only imagine the effect of a credible mid-1775 report about the arrival of the Yankees' underwater torpedo boat. In April 1775, David Bushnell had been building his vessel for almost two years, and by one surmise, "the hull would have been nearly complete."[40] By that summer, John Lewis, a tutor at Yale familiar with the project, wrote to Ezra Stiles in Rhode Island that Bushnell's machine "is almost perfected for the destruc-tion of the fleet in the harbor of Boston."[41]

Bushnell's principal collaborator, Benjamin Gale, had already explained the machine to Benjamin Franklin, who met with Gale in October. The British, too, had heard of the work in progress, and in December New York governor William Tryon wrote to Admiral Shuldham that "it is conjectur'd that an Attempt was made on the *Asia* [formerly in Boston but then in New York], but proved unsuccessful. Returned to New Haven in order to get a Pump of a new construction which will soon be completed."[42]

For all his credibility with Franklin and also Connecticut governor

---

*The careful reader may already be struck by the many warships named *Liberty* during 1775. Benedict Arnold named one on Lake Champlain; another was the first vessel in the Georgia Provincial Navy; the *Machias Liberty* was an early presence in the Massachusetts Provincial Navy; and the *Liberty* that became the first warship in the Virginia Navy had a record to more than match the others.

Trumbull, Bushnell was falling behind schedule. By late 1775, he was losing any chance to strike in Boston. Indeed, the wooden behemoths he hoped to strike had been driven out of Boston by a combination of circumstances: unsuitability, weather, and apprehensions of danger. Now the attack would have to be made in New York Harbor, and Bushnell's team of pilots would not be adequately trained and ready until early September. By this date, British invaders had taken almost complete control of the harbor. Bushnell could no longer delay, and he—or one of his pilots—had to strike quickly. Early on the morning of September 7, the attack on HMS *Eagle*, a 64-gun man-of-war, failed because the screw attaching the explosives wouldn't engage. The pilot—not the most qualified one—guided the *Turtle* clear and, on being seen, set the mine's clockwork in motion and jettisoned it. As he was being picked up by colleagues some distance away, the mine went off "with a tremendous explosion throwing up large bodies of water to an immense height."[43] Had it been attached, that would have been the end of HMS *Eagle*.

Was Bushnell's submarine worthy of success? Almost certainly. But for this chapter, the message could not be more relevant. In the words of Royal Navy Commodore John Symons, "The ingenuity of these people is singular in their secret modes of mischief."[44]

The Semantics of Privateering

If American seamen in general could be expected to choose privateering over the disciplines of naval service, that inclination was most emphatic in New England. Not only did Yankees have a long tradition of manning privateers, but they had an unmatched hostility to the Royal Navy. This was based on its role in punitive customs enforcement of the 1760s, its part in shutting down New England access to the fisheries, and most of all its insistence on making New England the particular 1775 target of naval press-gangs and activities. New England seamen would seek revenge through the easier discipline and better remuneration of the privateers.

But here further caution is in order on use of the word *privateer*. New England was indeed in the forefront. Massachusetts authorities had passed the first colony-level authorization on November 1. The thing is, these "privateers" were not really privateers in the full scope the Revolution later allowed. Washington's schooner fleet was not empowered to capture ordinary British merchantmen, and the commissions given by the Massachusetts

General Court in 1775 permitted only actions against British naval vessels and merchant ships bringing goods to occupied Boston.[45]

Full-fledged commerce raiding—the all-out variety that gave much fuller rein to private profit—took hold in the spring of 1776. Only then did Congress define *privateering* to allow the taking of "all ships and other vessels, their tackle, apparel and furniture, and all goods, wares and merchandises, belonging to any inhabitant or inhabitants of Great Britain."[46] This meant the gloves had been taken off, and John Adams was certainly correct to call this measure a Declaration of Independence in everything but name.

Privateering was the form of maritime warfare to which eighteenth-century Americans were best suited, but the number of actual privateers grew slowly. It only soared in later years when privateering totally overshadowed the fledgling navy in employment and importance.

A Genius for Small and Fast Ships

Like the British and Dutch before them, the seafaring American rebel drew on maritime traditions that had begun by running rings around the wooden walls of earlier institutionalized naval power. The Dutch had declared their independence around a maritime insurgency symbolized by the famous late-sixteenth-century Sea Beggars, who were adventurers, privateers, pirates, and patriots all in one. England's naval coming-of-age might have been at its most glorious against the Spanish Armada and under the Francis Drakes and Henry Morgans, men who represented a kindred blurring of naval, privateer, and piratical identities. The American maritime spirit of 1775 bore some resemblance.

As suggested in the epigraph on page 492, the saltwater or official U.S. Navy of 1775–1783, despite some proud moments, was hardly critical to the outcome of the American Revolution. What *did* play a major role in the outcome were the many instruments of maritime insurgency—Benedict Arnold's freshwater sloops and gundalows on Lake Champlain, the Pennsylvania row galleys that turned back the *Roebuck,* John Glover's Marblehead whaleboat warriors, Washington's schooner captains who captured storeships like the *Nancy,* the "powder cruise" mariners who took tobacco to fetch gunpowder and armaments in St. Eustatius or Martinique, John Derby's fast-scooning *Quero* that got the American description of Lexington and Concord to London two weeks ahead of the official British version, and the 2,000 or so American privateers who captured so many British merchant ships that Lloyd's insurance rates from time to time went through the roof. Submariner Bushnell, too, can be thought of as an underwater David trying a new approach to felling the British Goliath.

Several of the American officers who deserve naval accolades actually held army commissions: amphibious warfare experts like Arnold, Glover, and perhaps most of all, George Washington. The latter's attention to maritime warfare in Massachusetts and his effective use of small-scale amphibious movements both in his retreat from Long Island and in his surprise attack on Trenton three months later epitomized a genius for small ships. Where the new United States did less well during the Revolution was in pretentiously building frigates and foolishly venturing fleet actions like the Penobscot Bay battle in 1779. Jonathan Sewall, a former Massachusetts attorney general departing for Britain in 1776, cut to the quick by pronouncing it disgraceful for Admiral Graves to "tamely and supinely . . . [view] Fishing Schooners, Whaleboats and Canoes riding triumphantly under the Muzzles of his Guns, & carrying off every Supply."[47] Sewall's words were not intended as a compliment to the rebels, but they were a sound appreciation of rebel success in Boston Harbor, at least.

By then, the Boston part of the Revolution was largely finished. If shrewd employment of small vessels had been a key to Patriot success in the Revolution's first year, later yardsticks would be more painful. As the Royal Navy's presence in American waters grew, so did the economic pressure of the British blockade, which, in the phrase of historian Richard Buel, helped to put the fledgling U.S. economy "in irons"—headed directly into the winds and unable to make way—between 1777 and 1780. And in 1781, when Lord Cornwallis's resort to entrenching his tired army on the Yorktown Peninsula offered a chance for a conclusive American victory, that result could be secured only by the traditional battle-fleet supremacy briefly gained over Britain by America's Bourbon Compact allies, France and Spain.

CHAPTER 24

Europe, the Bourbon Compact, and the American Revolution

The dominating British discourse to emerge from the triumphs of the Seven Years War was not merely . . . hubristic, it was also naval, colonial and isolationist . . . As Britain limbered up to fight the colonists in 1775, she had been isolated in Europe for more than ten years . . . Britain went to war in America, and later in Europe, more isolated than she has ever been in her history, before or after, 1940 not excepted.

British historian Brendan Simms, *Three Victories and a Defeat,* 2007

The War with the Americans is memorable as being the only war in which the English were ever defeated, and it was unfair because the Americans had the Allies on their side.

British historians W. C. Sellar and R. J. Yeatman, *1066 and All That,* 1930

How the American Revolution was fought not just in the thirteen colonies but around the world is a familiar tale, told most often with nods to French aid and the contributions of Frenchmen named Lafayette, Rochambeau, de Grasse, and d'Estaing. Once France went to war with Britain in early 1778, a few months after word of the British surrender at Saratoga, the Allies' battleground stretched from the Caribbean to the Indian Ocean.

French gunpowder and arms had been reaching the rebels through Caribbean ports since the winter of 1774–1775, and the greater quantities arriving by 1777 had been vital to success at Saratoga. In 1781, a French fleet under the Comte de Grasse defeated a British fleet at the Battle of the Virginia Capes, setting the scene for Yorktown and Cornwallis's entrapment and surrender. And there the story usually ends, with broader European involvements and circumstances ignored.

France was the most important European power affronted by the British but hardly the only one. Between 1763 and 1775, a Continental version of the imperial hauteur that many unhappy Americans perceived in the behavior of their mother country had given Britain ill-wishers from Seville to St. Petersburg. Monarchs and their foreign ministries viewed the island kingdom as insular and arrogant but also highly vulnerable should the restive North American colonies break into rebellion. Spain, almost as revenge minded as France, had gained importance since the Bourbon Compact of 1761 that strengthened the family and political link between the French and Spanish crowns. As Britain lost old friends and allies, a chance to improve the European balance of power lured the Bourbon entente toward the opportunity of underwriting rebellion in British North America.

The evidence of 1775, as we have seen, showed that much of Europe and the Caribbean and even bits of Africa were *already* abetting that upheaval. Gunpowder and munitions in considerable quantities were crossing the Atlantic from Sweden, Hamburg, Holland, the Austrian Netherlands, France, Spain, Portugal, and West Africa's Slave Coast. Besides French and Spanish annoyance, Austria resented King George's intrusions in German politics and Prussia vented Frederick the Great's personal pique over perceived British insults. The Dutch, ever commercial, mostly disliked British interference with their trade and shipping. But during the heady early 1760s, hubristic British policy makers often seemed not to care.

A few British critics cautioned against overconfidence. The philosopher David Hume worried in 1764 about Britain being tempted by the Roman "spirit of conquest" and lulled by smug certainty about London's wealth and fiscal prowess.[1] As if to substantiate Hume, Lord Sandwich, then a principal secretary of state, commented grandly in 1764 that while Britain would be slow to form new alliances, it would "renew our old ones when proper attention was paid to us by those whose interest it is to be united with us."[2] Bow twice to London, or take your chances. To the playwright Oliver Goldsmith in 1763, "Great Britain is stronger, fighting by herself and for herself, than if half Europe were her allies."[3] But in the 1770s, it would become painfully clear that Britain had almost no allies.

In late 1775, as push came to shove over Britain's quest for mercenaries, the Dutch declined to let Britain borrow Holland's so-called Scots Brigade to serve in America. Catherine of Russia decided against letting the British contract for 20,000 Russian soldiers. Frederick of Prussia, still angry, not only encouraged Catherine's refusal but worked to undercut British

Soldatenpolitik among the German princes.[4] Austrian officials, taking a cue from anti-English coregent Joseph II, sought to block George III from using his dual role as Elector of Hanover to recruit soldiers within the German (Holy Roman) Empire. Indeed, King George manipulated Hanover when, in his capacity as elector, he sent Hanoverian troops to Gibraltar and Minorca in order to release British units there to be sent to America.

During 1775 at least four empires—France, Spain, the Netherlands, and Austria—favored or tolerated their merchants' covert selling of arms to the American rebels. An overlapping foursome—the Netherlands, Russia, Prussia, and Austria—either turned down or interfered with King George's efforts to procure mercenaries. One British historian has found predictions that British hauteur toward allies "would leave her without one single friend in Europe" dating back to the late 1750s.[5]

The existing Spanish and French settlements in North America included numerous rebel sympathizers. Spanish colonial administrators looked the other way as local merchants shipped munitions to American Patriots through Charleston and New Orleans.[6] Not a few French speakers in what until 1763 had been King Louis's colonies—*habitants* in Quebec and Louisiana, Acadians in present-day New Brunswick—preferred joining the American rebels to soldiering under the British flag. The Acadians sourly remembered their ethnic expulsion from Nova Scotia at British hands in 1755. In Louisiana and New Orleans, Frenchmen serving in Spanish militia units became American allies once Madrid declared war in 1779. Many would fight against the British in a succession of Spanish victories from Pensacola, Florida, to St. Joseph on the distant shores of Lake Michigan. In 1778 and 1779, many settlers of French descent in Illinois and Indiana allied with George Rogers Clark to capture British forts at Kaskaskia and Vincennes.

On America's far-off North Pacific coast, the early 1770s saw a convergence and clash of Spanish, Russian, and British ambitions. A new arena was in the making. The extent to which Spain was thinking imperially again had much to do with her reawakening plans for North America.

French, Spanish, and Russian North America in 1775

The continent of 1775 had already become a geopolitical chessboard of global consequence, and most European governments had some interest. Perceptions of North America's booming population, wealth, and prospects between 1750 and 1775 had convinced many of Britain's European rivals and ill wishers that a successful rebellion there would be the best way to cripple Albion Perfide. King George himself worried about that possibility.

The vulnerability of Britain in North America is easily overstated. Certainly no plausible colonial revolt or global war could drive her off the continent. While seventeenth- and eighteenth-century France had built a power base along the St. Lawrence River, the Great Lakes, and the Mississippi Valley, England had carved out a huge fur-trading empire in the far north, centered on Hudson's Bay. In 1775, these tracts—governed by the Hudson's Bay Company—stretched from Labrador in the east across the huge bay and then west to Saskatchewan. This Arctic-fronting domain had nothing to do with Massachusetts or Virginia; it was safely British, although the French did capture one Hudson's Bay post in 1782. Vergennes, the French foreign minister, speculated from time to time about some degree of Gallic restoration in Canada. France would like to have regained the Newfoundland fisheries. But in the continent's far north, Britain was entrenched.

Fortunately for the English-speaking rebels, though, Spain in 1763 had become Britain's principal foe in North America. Spanish king Carlos III, being obliged by the peace treaty to yield Florida (then also including much of Mississippi and Alabama) to the victorious British, was richly compensated by his French ally. King Louis XV deeded over Louisiana, essentially the western half of the Mississippi Valley, together with the port of New Orleans. Combined with already-Spanish Texas, the Southwest, and California, Madrid's power base in North America now included most of the present-day United States west of the Mississippi (excluding Hawaii, Alaska, and the Pacific Northwest). By 1775, moreover, after a decade of domestic reform and rejuvenation, imperially minded Spaniards had great hopes.

Back in the mid-1600s, two centuries of Spanish preeminence in Europe had collapsed following the Thirty Years War (1618–1648). Confirmation came in the Treaty of the Pyrenees in 1659, which passed political, economic, and military leadership to France. However, Philip of Bourbon took the throne of Spain in 1700, effectively allying the two nations in the so-called Bourbon Compact. This was reaffirmed and updated in 1761, and coincided with a period in which Spain modernized her economy, trade, and colonial administration.[7] Succinctly put, Spain, together with France, might again be a force. What had not changed, though, was traditional Spanish hostility toward Britain; if anything, it had intensified. By the 1770s, Madrid began to entertain far-ranging ambitions—not just to curb illicit British trade in Central America and to expand north from Spanish California, but also to recover both Florida and Gibraltar from Britain.

With this new bravura, a Spanish military force from Buenos Aires in June 1770 ejected the small British garrison in Port Egmont, in the Falkland Islands. For Britain, the Falklands were a staging post for a drive into the Pacific. Still, when hawks in the British Parliament shrilled for war, the Madrid government allowed the irate British back into the Falklands.

In moments of reverie, Spanish officials doubtless imagined a new geopolitical opportunity. The nation's earlier military supremacy had been lost in European defeats, but North America was now becoming an important enough battleground that Spanish success there could trump near-irrelevance in yesteryear's European theaters. Perhaps an empire defeated in Germany and the Low Countries could recoup militarily in the Mississippi Valley or along the Gulf of Mexico.

Russian contemplation of a growing world role was more soundly based. To the west, her imperialists sought a naval presence in the Mediterranean. To the east, they gazed across Siberia to Kamchatka, Russia's peninsula on the Pacific. Beyond lay the Aleutian Islands and North America. Several years after taking the throne in 1762, Catherine the Great ordered the resumption of the earlier Great Northern Expeditions, which in 1741-1742 had reached the Aleutians.[8] By 1768, new voyages from Kamchatka had explored well down the latter-day Alaska Coast to the Dixon Entrance, in the southern part of the Alaskan Panhandle.[9]

Here is where the reenergizing of Spain mattered. Officials in Mexico and California felt menaced by rumors of Russian settlements pushing south in the wake of naval exploration.[10] Under the leadership of José de Gálvez, minister of the Indies, Madrid responded by establishing a new naval base in Mexico to support northward exploration, and by colonizing San Diego and Monterrey.[11] In 1773, the viceroy in Mexico City ordered expeditions to sail farther north and assert Spain's territorial claim. The second of these voyages, in 1775, included three vessels under the command of one Bruno de Hezeta. Departing in March from the new San Blas naval base, they got as far north as upper Vancouver Island. Together, the three crews found what became San Francisco's Golden Gate and sailed past the mouth of the Columbia River well before its recognized discovery in 1793.[12]

The British, besides renewing their own efforts to find the Northwest Passage, began planning for Captain James Cook to make a third exploratory voyage, this time to the North Pacific and the Bering Strait. As for the Russians, scholars once convinced that they were principally pursuing geographic knowledge have contended in recent years that their real mission was "to extend Russian sovereignty into northwestern America with the eventual aim of exploiting its natural resources."[13] Thousands of miles to the south, Spanish, Russian, and British explorations were also converging in the waters near the Hawaiian Islands.

No one can say how much such Pacific rivalries shaped broader Spanish or Russian strategy in the mid-1770s. Even so, Madrid's agitation over Russia's supposed southward thrust toward California must be taken as an indicator of resurgent Spanish self-importance and geopolitical ambition. For the thirteen United Colonies, these stirrings could not have come at a better time.

With respect to Catherine's interest in asserting Russian claims in North America or in thwarting British naval power, there is no obvious tie to her impolite refusal of King George's request to hire 20,000 troops. However, Alaska historian Lydia Black, author of *Russians in Alaska: 1732–1867*, described the czarina as involved from the start with Russia's claims in America, adding that "the empress's personal interest in America did not abate until the end of Catherine's reign [in 1796]."[14]

Because the future United States was still decades away from flexing even youthful muscles in these regions, general American histories pay almost no attention to events along the Pacific Coast in 1775. What seems clear, though, is that during Spain's brief quarter century of imperial rejuvenation, resurgent ambitions led her to make significant, if generally unrecognized, contributions to the American Revolution.

Spain and the American Revolution

Madrid paid close attention. As the Revolution began, high Spanish officials, especially the principal minister of state, the Marques de Grimaldi, voiced periodic qualms about the large number of soldiers Britain was sending to America to subdue its rebellious colonists. Should that fighting finish quickly, Grimaldi reasoned, might not the British redeploy these troops to attack Spain's possessions in the West Indies? A belligerent faction in Parliament had urged war with Spain in 1772 following the Falklands incident, although the Spanish Embassy in London played down the threat.[15]

Which leads to the crux. By the 1770s, it was Spain, not France, with whom Britain essentially shared North America. The two confronted each

other along an already trouble-prone border that ran from present-day Minnesota down the Mississippi River past St. Louis to New Orleans. Like
France, Spain wanted revenge—in Madrid's case, a sweeping enough recovery of territory to roll back a century of losses, encroachments, and British
incursions. That kind of war would necessarily involve a large military and
economic commitment.

During the dozen years between 1763 and 1775, Spain's relevant reforms
and modernization plans ran the gamut from a reorganization of public
finance and expulsion of the Jesuits to a rejuvenation of Madrid, reforms in
colonial administration, changes in the colonial trade system, and freer
trade in the Spanish Caribbean.[16] Many of the gains were minor or tenuous,
soon vanishing in the tumult of the Revolutionary and Napoleonic periods.
But the mid-1770s were a time when Spanish officialdom took renewal
seriously.

To return to those years, the expansion of both Bourbon Compact navies had put their combined numbers of ships of the line ahead of Britain's,
the British Admiralty's worst-case scenario. Back in 1765, British naval tonnage still exceeded that of France and Spain combined; by 1770, the Bourbon powers were definitely ahead, and with respect to 1775, historians
appear to disagree. There is also an obvious caveat: what counted more were
ships actually ready to do battle. If King George, Lord North, and the British Cabinet of 1774–1775 were foolish in failing to take seriously the Americans' drift toward war and the rebels' considerable capacity for maritime
annoyance, the various British Cabinets of the 1760s and early 1770s could
be faulted at least as harshly for misjudging or discounting French and
Spanish naval intentions and capabilities.

As successive leading world powers in the nineteenth and twentieth centuries, neither Britain nor the United States respected Spain in a military
sense, and an eighteenth-century precursor of this disregard may help to
explain latter-day U.S. reluctance to acknowledge the considerable Spanish
role in the American Revolution. In addition to one respected earlier Spanish account—*España ante la independencia de los Estados Unidos,* published
in 1925—there have been several recent Spanish and American volumes, but
attention remains inadequate.[17]

"During 1775," according to one specialist, "the Spanish king and his
advisers could not decide on the diplomatic response they wanted to make
to Lexington and Concord." Spain's ambassador to France, the Conde de
Aranda, a respected former president of the Council of Castile and leader

of a major faction at court, was the principal hawk. He favored "joining the conflict immediately, with the combined forces of France and Spain attacking Great Britain as soon as events warranted." Aranda even "went so far as to send Madrid a plan outlining the methods whereby the two Bourbon courts could join their naval forces to cut Great Britain's supply lines and disrupt its commerce."[18]

The Marques de Grimaldi, who advocated neutrality and noninvolvement, was restrained by fear of a sudden British attack. With Grimaldi cautious, discussions between France and Spain did not yield "a unified plan of action. In mid-1775, Charles [Carlos III] and his ministers settled for inertia, deciding to continue normal relations with Great Britain and to profess neutrality until events in North America recommended doing otherwise." This posture was occasionally strained, as in October 1775, when two Spanish ships from central America brought gunpowder to Charleston, provoking an official British complaint.[19]

With Grimaldi continuing to tell both King Carlos and French foreign minister Vergennes that Britain might attack Spain in the West Indies, in late 1775 the Spanish minister of war sent additional troops to Cuba and Puerto Rico. In addition, "Grimaldi decided to expand the observation responsibilities of the Captain General of Cuba to include the monitoring of all events relating to the Revolution, even those not directly threatening to the Spanish colonies. He notified the French court in early 1776 that Spain would be creating a network of observers in North America to provide regular intelligence."[20] In December 1775, supervision in the hemisphere also began passing to a new and active minister of the Indies, José de Gálvez. He and Grimaldi agreed that in the event of war with Britain, Cuba and Louisiana should become the first line of defense.[21]

In 1776, despite ostensible neutrality, Carlos III gave France's agent, Caron de Beaumarchais, one million livres with which to arm the Americans.[22] In late summer, the governor of Louisiana, Luis de Unzaga, delivered 98 kegs of gunpowder from the king's stores to Virginians in New Orleans, who paid and took it upriver to Pittsburgh. Late that year officials including the governors in Havana and Louisiana were instructed by a royal order to supply the Americans with available gunpowder and *fusiles*.[23]

Spain's principal aspirations were territorial. Policy makers sought to regain the Floridas, to capture both Jamaica and the Bahamas, and to eliminate the lucrative British enclaves for cutting logwood (for dyestuffs) along the east coast of Central America. In Europe, the top Spanish priority was to recover Gibraltar, taken by Britain in 1713, and secondarily to regain the western Mediterranean island of Minorca. Achieving most of these objectives would constitute a grand reversal of the losses suffered since the mid-seventeenth century, which helps to explain the years of planning and the expenses undertaken. The American Revolution offered a potentially unique opportunity.[24]

Spain's carefully timed declaration of war in 1779 was quickly followed up by a string of Spanish victories in the Mississippi Valley and along the Gulf of Mexico, mainly owed to the generalship of the capable Bernardo de Gálvez, who was also well supported. His father was General Mathias de Gálvez, soon to become viceroy of New Spain, and his uncle José de Gálvez, Spanish-based minister for the Indies, both sympathetic to the American enterprise.[25] In more or less chronological order, Bernardo de Gálvez's military successes included the capture of British forts in Manchac, Natchez, and Baton Rouge (September to October 1779), the taking of Mobile (March 1780), the successful defense of St. Louis (May 1780), the capture of Fort St. Joseph in Michigan (February 1781), and the capture of Pensacola (May 1781). Then in May 1782, after a combined Spanish and American expedition took New Providence in the Bahamas, the agreement of capitulation turned over all of the Bahama Islands to Spain. In Central American fighting over a set of British trade concessions, General Mathias de Gálvez won most of the battles in Nicaragua, Honduras, and along the Mosquito Coast. However, although their access was narrowed, Britons kept their Central American toeholds.[26]

Logwood concessions or minor battles along the Mosquito Coast are not the point. Simply put, without Spain's 1775–1782 role as an early source of munitions and financial aid, and then as an open American ally, the Revolution would have been less successful. For example, as Chapter 25 will pursue, a revealing chronological overlap can be seen. The second British invasion of the American South, relatively successful in 1779 and 1780, started to falter in 1781. Even before Yorktown, those were the months when Lord Cornwallis's loss of irreplaceable men in the Carolinas through costly battles like King's Mountain, Cowpens, Guilford Courthouse, and Eutaw Springs was aggravated by the string of Spanish victories that culminated in their May 1781 capture of Pensacola, where 1,113 British prisoners were taken.[27]

It is also clear that Spain played an important role—perhaps even a decisive one—in arranging for Admiral de Grasse and the French fleet to put aside other agendas and provide a September-October naval umbrella as arriving forces under George Washington and French General Rochambeau combined in Virginia to trap Cornwallis on the Yorktown Peninsula. Because the Spanish had agreed to protect several French Caribbean islands with their navy while de Grasse was gone, and also to finance part of the Chesapeake expedition, the French admiral, with 26 ships of the line, arrived off the Virginia Capes on August 31 and stayed through October. On September 5, de Grasse repulsed British Admiral Thomas Graves—a different Graves, not the one who failed earlier in Boston—whose 19 ships were unable to break through the 24 men-of-war de Grasse now deployed. This was classic line-of-battle warfare, in which American skills with fast schooners or whaleboats were an irrelevance. With the French fleet blocking relief, Cornwallis had to surrender on October 19.

The French and Spanish navies had put the Royal Navy in a two-ocean squeeze. During August and early September, they massed a combined fleet of 49 ships of the line—disproportionately Spanish—not far from England's southwestern coast, and the British Cabinet's priority need to protect the home islands meant that no naval reinforcements could be spared for North America, which doomed Cornwallis. For this chapter's purpose, the Spanish role requires particular emphasis. Historian Jonathan Dull, in his book *The French Navy and American Independence,* explained that de Grasse must share his laurels for sailing to the Chesapeake with "two extraordinary young Spaniards, Bernardo de Gálvez and Francisco de Saavedra. Gálvez (1746–1786) was acting governor of Louisiana . . . It was in his power as senior military commander in the theater to request part of de Grasses's fleet. Not only did he release all of de Grasse's ships, but also the corps at St. Domingue which had been placed in Spanish service. To coordinate plans with de Grasse he sent his principal aide to Cape Francois aboard Montiel's flagship. This aide, Francisco de Saavedra (1746–1819), was actually a representative of the Colonial Ministry, which was headed by Gálvez' uncle, Jose de Gálvez. In his extraordinary career, Saavedra would become finance minister of Spain and an organizer of the resistance to Napoleon; for his role in de Grasse's campaign alone he merits serious historical attention."[28]

Indeed, Saavedra put some of that financial acumen to immediate use. In July, after the French could not raise funds locally, the future Spanish finance minister arranged for citizens of Spanish Havana, in a single day, to contribute 5 million livres for the North American expedition. Supposedly they were grateful for shipments of American wheat.[29]

Even after Yorktown's surrender in October 1781, British troops continued to occupy Savannah and Charleston through much of 1782. However, the Spanish victory at Pensacola and the subsequent joint Spanish-American capture of the Bahamas in May 1782 effectively ensured that Britain would have to return East and West Florida to Spain at the peace tables. This unwelcome political geography more or less extinguished British hopes of holding on to Georgia and the Carolinas, which meant that London's carefully undertaken second "southern strategy" had been in vain.

Unfortunately for Spain's own hoped-for *reconquista,* that nation's overall military results fell short of what Gálvez managed individually. Despite Spanish victories at Pensacola and in the Bahamas, and some successes in Central America, Britain held on to Jamaica. Several invasions of that island were jointly planned by the French and Spanish between 1780 and 1782, but none were ever mounted. To an extent, that reflected the priority given the American Revolution. The last chance vanished in April 1782 with British Admiral Rodney's victory over a French and Spanish fleet at the Îles des Saintes off Guadeloupe. In Europe, Gibraltar was besieged off and on for two years but never fell, and Spain's recapture of Minorca was a small consolation prize.

By 1783, even the archhawk, the Conde de Aranda, had concluded that Spain should not have supported the French lead in a war in the Americas "opposed to our own [Spanish] interests." The independent North American colonies would now threaten more "grief and fear" inasmuch as their success would inspire convulsions in Spain's own colonies.[30] This proved true. Tensions with yesteryear's ally grew along the Louisiana and Florida frontiers, and several prominent Americans—Aaron Burr and James Wilkinson—lost their reputations for conspiring with Spain.

Politically and territorially, the United States was the only real winner. However, by the early twentieth century, Hispanic Americans and French Americans had gained a different kind of recognition. Up and down the Mississippi Valley, and west to Arizona and California, Spain's 1779–1782 mobilization and war effort has been increasingly treated as the American Revolution in state after state. Historical reviews cover as "their" revolution Spanish engagements from Lake Michigan to the Gulf of Mexico. Organizations like the Sons and Daughters of the American Revolution extend membership to persons descended from Spanish soldiers.

In Louisiana, for example, the ethnic outreach of the Daughters of the American Revolution began in the 1920s. Visitors to the town of

St. Martinville in Louisiana's Lafayette Parish will see a 1974 DAR monument to the (largely French) Attakapas Militia for their service in Gálvez's capture of Baton Rouge and Manchac in September 1779.

In Texas, an organization called the Granaderos (grenadiers) de Gálvez encourages awareness of the Spanish role in the Revolution. The principal Texas connection lies in the Texas Longhorn cattle drives initiated by Gálvez in 1779 to feed the Spanish and Allied armies in the Mississippi Valley. As a young lieutenant, he had led Spanish troops against the Apache, going as far east as the Pecos River, and he remembered the cattle in Texas's Bexar-La Bahía region. At that time, they could not be exported to other provinces and were worth little. But in 1779 Gálvez secured authorization, and through 1782, 9,000 head were driven east to Louisiana, guarded by soldiers and militia from Bexar, La Bahía, and El Fuerte del Cibola.[31]

In 1976, a statue of Bernardo de Gálvez was dedicated in Washington, D.C., at Virginia Avenue and 22nd Street, where it sits near statues of Simon Bolívar, Benito Juárez, and other Latin American liberators. The various Daughters and Sons have much the better understanding. Gálvez fought his battles in what is now the United States and has become a hero of the *American* Revolution.

Britain and the Alienation of Two Continents, 1775–1783

Early in the Revolution, when Virginia burgesses wore tomahawks and fringed hunting shirts to empathize with republican virtue, Patriot leaders often glibly referred to "the Continent." Many were speaking of the Continental Congress, although it was not in fact Continental, lacking any representatives from Quebec, Hudson's Bay, Nova Scotia, the Bahamas, Florida, Louisiana, Texas, California, or the rest of New Spain. Thomas Paine, for one, referred to "the Continent" as if that entity were interchangeable with the thirteen United Colonies. Had that been true—had the conflict in North America not also involved provinces and colonies of Continental Europe—the results might have been less favorable for the English-speaking rebels.

Once Spain declared war in 1779, and Hispanic *vaqueros* began driving Texas longhorns east to feed Spanish soldiers in Louisiana and Virginia riflemen in Illinois, while French-speaking militia marched on Mobile in Spanish uniforms, the notion of a North American continent aroused against Britain became more plausible. What started in Massachusetts and

Virginia had, in a sense, spread to Bayou Teche, San Antonio de Bexar, and Alta California.

Even so, it was another alienated continent, Europe, that truly cost Britain her rebellious North American colonies. Since late in the Seven Years War, Britain had offended almost every nation in Europe, although Portugal remained London's ally and George III had cousins or in-laws in virtually every North German Protestant principality. The evidence that Britain had dangerously alienated most of the Continent is detailed and surprising.

To many influential Britons, trade, wealth, and empire, particularly in burgeoning North America, were what had made Britain strong—powerful enough to win her war in 1759 and 1760, and confident enough to crow during the 1760s that a rich island did not need Continental allies. Many of the king's most reliable supporters in Parliament—the Scots and the old Bedford, Grenville, and Sandwich factions—heartily subscribed to a dual mercantilist and navalist explanation of British success. Lord Sandwich, as secretary of state in 1764, remarked that Britain's influence depended on "making a proper use of its power as an island." In 1765, Thomas Whately, secretary to the treasury, had further amplified: "The trade from whence [Britain's] greatest wealth is derived, and upon which its maritime power is principally founded, depends on a wise and proper use of the colonies."[32]

However, the imperialist and navalist Britons who emphasized the economic importance of North America usually put strong emphasis on those colonies' political subservience. Most advocated the sort of hard-line agenda that the colonists especially resented—tea policies to uphold East India Company interests, naval implementation that made customs enforcement the commercial equivalent of martial law, additions to the enumerated list of commodities that colonial growers could ship only to Britain, crippling regulation of American coastal shipping, prohibition of settlement beyond the Appalachians, restraint of colonial manufactures, and more. Imperialists of this harsher school often urged speedy discipline before population growth made America too strong. Politicians who put the greatest stock in mercantile theory were often especially fearful of a British global unraveling should the American colonies be lost. The king himself worried in 1779 that should America succeed, "the West Indies must follow them . . . Ireland would soon follow the same plan and be a separate state, then this island would be reduced to itself, and soon would be a poor island indeed, for reduced in her trade merchants would retire in their wealth to climates more to their advantage, and shoals of manufacturers would leave this country for the New Empire."[33]

When it came to foreign affairs, British proponents of keeping Americans on a tight rein were often the same navalists and insulars most eager to turn their backs on the old European balance-of-power strategies and German entanglements of the first two Hanoverian monarchs. By contrast, the pro-American old Whig element in Parliament generally deplored this abandonment of the old Continental alliance building so victorious for three decades under George II. Two pillars, they said, had girded the empire—benign treatment of the North American colonies and productive anti-French alliances pivoting on Protestant German states and the Dutch Republic. Brendan Simms and other British revisionists have detailed the policy pronouncements of such leading American sympathizers as Pitt, Burke, Conway, Lords Shelburne and Camden, and the Dukes of Richmond and Manchester. These men saw little but danger in mistreatment of old European allies and American colonials alike, arguing that it played into Bourbon hands. As Burke cautioned in 1772, "He who shall advise hostilities against the Bourbon Compact, till a compact shall take place between Great Britain and her colonies is a foe or a driveller."[34] For this chapter's limited purposes, however, we must note one central failure: by 1775, Britain had alienated most of the continent, including her former friends.

The Duke of Newcastle, a former first minister, had anticipated the drift in 1766. He strove to improve relations with Prussia, he said, so "that His Majesty might have one ally in Europe." But Frederick of Prussia wasn't having it: England "is not interested in anything but naval dominance and her possessions in America."[35] A few years later Joseph II of Austria dismissed Britain as "isolated and almost without allies."[36] By 1772, Lord Rochford, secretary of state for southern Europe, saw France "forming such connections in the north which may make them as formidable there as they have for some time been by their alliance in the south, whilst we have not a single friendly power or ally to boast of."[37]

For almost a decade prior to 1775, Britain had watched European developments that either assumed British inability to respond, confirmed French reassertion, or did both. In 1766, France reannexed the province of Lorraine. In 1768, Genoa ceded Corsica to France after the latter helped Genoa by suppressing a Corsican revolt. Seventeen seventy-two, in turn, saw the partition of Poland among Austria, Prussia, and Russia, and a coup d'état in Sweden with the French on the winning side. Britain was conspicuous by her lack of influence. With respect to Poland, Horace Walpole acidly witticized that the British fleet, "being so formidable will, I suppose, be towed overland to Warsaw and restore the Polish constitution and their King to his full rights—how frightened the King of Prussia must be."[38]

No more than a handful of Americans—Benjamin Franklin, for one—would have followed these events. Yet the changes clearly signaled both the decline of British influence and the rising prospect of Europe's major powers either aiding an American rebellion or declining to provide mercenaries for its suppression. Even Admiral Graves in Boston, with his finger far from the pulse of European connivance, reported four times to the Admiralty during August and September 1774 that American ships were loading tea and gunpowder in northern European ports.[39]

Cockiness among London's insular thinkers dissipated as the mere munitions suppliers of 1774–1776 threw off their neutral camouflage and declared war: France in 1778 and Spain in 1779. Then in February 1780, Russia issued her famous Proclamation of Armed Neutrality, aimed at Britain, which specified principles for the protection of neutral commerce in wartime. Prussia, Sweden, Denmark, and Austria all concurred. Later that year, Britain maneuvered the Netherlands into war out of belief that a neutral Holland, under the new rules, would have been a greater threat transporting munitions and naval stores to France and Spain.[40] Now British concern over lack of allies became acute.

Henry Conway, a former secretary of state, told Parliament in 1780 that Britain was now "at war with America, with France and Spain, without a single power our friend . . . every one of the foreign powers, great as well as small, [is] acting either directly or indirectly in a manner inimical to our interests: even the little Lubeckers, the Danzigers, and the town of Hamburg [are] against us." By 1781, Sandwich at the Admiralty, no longer singing the merits of insularity, admitted that "if Russia declares against us, we shall then literally speaking be in actual war with the whole world."[41]

The cracks in British confidence yawned ever wider, and three months after word was received in London of Cornwallis's October surrender, Lord North resigned. However, despite widespread gloom, the economic disaster predicted by the mercantilists, based on their now-obsolescent doctrine, never came to pass. France and Spain had detached Britain's prime colonies but won only a limited victory; America yielded them no economic benefits. Gibraltar and Jamaica were never captured, and the Royal Navy's defeat of the French Navy in April 1782 ensured that the damage to Britain in any new treaty would be much less than watchers had earlier predicted. The new United States was awarded a western border on the Mississippi, but the Bourbon powers won little—Spain only East and West Florida, along with Minorca, and France some piddling islands. In a few years, it would be clear that the war's huge costs had helped lay economic foundations for a radical upheaval in France. The Bourbon Compact, in 1781 on the cusp of a great victory, would not survive into the new century.

The emergence of the United States, then, was owed to two Old World illusions: the French and Spanish reverie that revolt in America would usher in a new Bourbon era, and the hubristic belief of post-1763 Whitehall and Parliament that isolation, navalism, and fiscal prowess could suppress the thirteen colonies even in a global war that Britain might have to fight without allies. Taken together, the two mistakes enabled a new nation.

CHAPTER 25

The Southern Expedition of 1775 and the Limitations of British Power

I hoped to have been able to send your Lordship a more pleasing account of our Southern expedition than in the enclosed precis.

William Knox, undersecretary of state, to Lord Dartmouth, August 1776

Perhaps I should have been as well pleased if it had not been attempted.

King George III, 1776

The southern expedition planned by King George, Lord North, and Lord Dartmouth in late summer and autumn 1775 ultimately expired in three stages of mishap and embarrassment. First came the defeat in late February 1776 of Loyalist Scottish Highlanders by North Carolina militia at the Battle of Moore's Creek Bridge. Following that was May's month-long inability of seven regiments of British regulars and some 70 warships and transports to conduct meaningful amphibious operations along North Carolina's Cape Fear River. The final failure occurred in late June, when those same ill-fated ships and regiments were bloodily repulsed seeking to force the entrance to Charleston Harbor in South Carolina.

It was all a great travesty. The Crown's only success came in leaving such a muddled trail and confused chronology that the oneness of the operation has been lost, dissipating the attention of historians. The sole British chronicler to profile the expedition in its entirety, Eric Robson in the 1950s, reached a damning conclusion: "In its lack of coordination, its changes of character and objectives, its delays and its misapprehension of the position of the loyalists, it typifies many of the military expeditions of the American War of Independence, and reveals how ill-suited for the conduct of war was the eighteenth century system of government in Great Britain."[1]

The final rebuff in Charleston Harbor is invariably described as a British defeat, but not on a major scale. For the most part, though, the battle has been examined on a stand-alone basis. This sidesteps the larger, longer context of British incapacity. June's debacle did not stand alone. The strains on British logistics deepened, and winter's abandoned schedules and deadlines echoed further into 1776 and 1777. Generals and commodores hoping to claim a late-hour vocational fig leaf only added mistakes. Intelligence, in the scouting sense of the term, went from bad to worse. After Charleston, the British government left the South more or less alone for two and a half years before returning for a second try.

Chapter 13 has already discussed the British Cabinet's amateur assessments and the transport malcoordination that was set in motion in autumn 1775. Repetition seems unnecessary, beyond a reminder as to delay: the expedition's main force, supposed to depart in December 1775, did not leave Ireland until February 13, more or less when it was originally to have arrived off Cape Fear. Obviously, this had serious consequences in the Carolinas. The prospect of Loyalist risings lost credibility. Worse, the transports and troops diverted to the South were among the elements that held up the all-important two-pronged invasion of New York, postponing it from spring 1776 to late summer. Then, because summer's movement south from Canada was not completed by October, General Carleton returned to Quebec. The British had to begin again along Lake Champlain in the spring of 1777.

Extending the interpretations of Boston and Canada set forth several chapters back, these pages contend that the British war machine of the Revolutionary decade was not strong enough in 1775—nor would it be again five years later—to successfully suppress the northern colonies *and* the southern colonies at the same time. Although this became clear by 1781, the failure of the southern expedition of 1775–1776 indicates that simultaneous war in both regions was beyond British achievement in the early years as well. The caution initially voiced by senior officials like Lord Barrington, the secretary at war, and Edward Harvey, the army's adjutant general, that the army was not strong enough to subdue all of America, was usually interwoven with an argument for reliance on the Royal Navy. However, the outcomes also supported a narrower conclusion: that Britain could not manage full-scale northern and southern invasions simultaneously.

Through 1775 and 1776, the British Cabinet was so preoccupied with the northern campaigns and the cul-de-sacs into which the rebels had drawn them that little troop strength remained for the South. The diversion to the Carolinas of the seven regiments under General Clinton and accompanying warships and transports was large enough to strain overall British logistics, but it was too minimal to bludgeon either North or South Carolina. Where it tipped scales was in helping to deny General Howe the transports he needed to shift his soldiers from Boston to New York in October 1775 and again in March 1776. With too few transports and escorts available to sustain an opposed landing in rebel-held New York, Howe had to settle, in the first instance, for overwintering in Boston and, in the second, for being taken to Halifax, Nova Scotia.

February-through-July embarrassment in the Carolinas, coupled with Lord Dunmore's ignominious mid-1776 expulsion from Virginia, doubtless influenced British leaders to concentrate their forces in the northern provinces. Only after Burgoyne's surrender at Saratoga in October 1777 punctured any hope of reconquering New York and New England by a powerful thrust from Canada did the British begin withdrawing from several northern areas of occupation. Philadelphia was vacated in June 1778, then Newport, Rhode Island, in 1779. To military historians, the Battle of Monmouth, New Jersey, fought by Washington in June 1778 against the British troops marching from Philadelphia back to New York, was "the last major engagement of war in [the] North."[2] Thereafter Britain's war in the northern colonies, beyond its headquarters in and around New York City, was generally confined to raids, brief local occupations, and town burnings.*

The turn southward in 1779 was emphatic. One set of arguments had emphasized the pointlessness of keeping New England relative to the importance of the plantation colonies. Charles Jenkinson, the shrewd undersecretary at war, began making this case in 1775. Now it became more persuasive.[3] In late December 1778, Savannah became the first southern city to fall. In December 1779, General Clinton, with 8,700 men, moved against Charleston, which surrendered in May 1780. The second British "southern strategy" was under way, achieving considerable success through 1780 but starting to lose momentum in mid-1781. It imploded after Lord Cornwallis's October 19 surrender at Yorktown, even though civil war persisted in the Carolinas.

Further evidence of British inability to maintain coexisting full-scale campaigns both north and south of the Potomac River can be drawn from

---

*The principal exception, not very significant, is the occupation by the British of the mouth of Maine's Penobscot River (near present-day Castine) between 1779 and 1783.

the war chronology of 1778–1779 and the complaints and insights of British generals. The king's forces were never strong enough to grind down opposition in both regions. Obviously French and Spanish entry into the war in 1778 and 1779 added to Britain's later southern difficulties, but that had been predictable enough in the earlier years to require a higher standard of realpolitik. William Eden, the secret service chief, later recalled that "the malevolent intentions of France and Spain . . . were written in legible characters on every line of all foreign intelligence, and upon every foreign transaction official and extra-official."[4]

The original southern expedition itself warrants more attention. Not only were its campaigns inept, but in North Carolina the anti-British backlash became a major spur to independence.[5] Dunmore's tactics in Virginia had a similar effect, and Charleston shed any genuine or tactical ambivalence on June 29 as citizens watched the British fleet limp away, leaving HMS *Acteon* abandoned and burning on Middle Ground Shoal.

Bagpipes, Broadswords, Mosquitoes, and Palmettos

Bagpipes and broadswords exemplify the romanticized failure of the Scots Highlanders at Moore's Creek Bridge on February 27. Mosquitoes in turn symbolize how seven regiments of the regular British Army on the Cape Fear River were stung by insects and sharpshooters alike during four hot May weeks of strategic frustration. Palmettos, nicknamed "cabbage trees" by the redcoats on the Cape Fear, would soon prove that a Charleston Harbor fort built of their spongy wood and sand could beat off the Royal Navy. It was an inglorious five months.

The degree to which Lord North and his Cabinet could mislead themselves about what Loyalist military support could accomplish in the Carolinas rested on more than the assurances of the Earl of Dartmouth and southern royal governors. Lord George Germain, tougher minded by far, had replaced Dartmouth as American secretary in November 1775, and a few weeks later he echoed the same geography: "An armament consisting of seven regiments, with a fleet of frigates and small ships, is now in readiness to proceed to the southern Colonies, in order to attempt the restoration of legal Government in that part of America. It will proceed, in the first place, to North Carolina, and from thence either to South-Carolina or Virginia, as circumstances of greater or less advantage shall point out."[6]

Not only was the armada not "in readiness" that December, but the belief in Loyalists ready to rise en masse was a widely shared fallacy. This was later summed up by Sir John Fortescue, the British military historian: "It was therefore concluded that the mere presence of British troops in certain quarters would be sufficient to rally the entire population to the royal standard; and it was resolved in effect to base the military operations on the presumed support of a section of the inhabitants. Of all the foundations whereon to build the conduct of a campaign this is the loosest . . . Yet, as shall be seen in the years before us, there is none that has been in more favour with British ministers, with the invariable consequence of failure and disaster."[7] In late 1775, however, policy makers in London were still believers, and they also looked forward to taking control of Charleston Harbor, widely deemed the second objective.

Strictly speaking, Virginia—where the early Revolution, described in Chapter 22, was substantially of Lord Dunmore's shaping—was never drawn into the southern expedition. Clinton, the expeditionary commander, did briefly stop there on his way south in February 1776, but his instructions were for North Carolina. And as we have seen, Dunmore had just been pushed out of Norfolk, and Clinton thought little of his remaining prospects. Nor was Georgia an objective. Several British vessels had arrived off Savannah in January, in belated response to Governor Wright's summer request, but as things turned out, the governor had to take refuge on one of them. A second small British flotilla arrived in March, principally to seize rice boats to feed Boston's hungry garrison. The expedition's only destinations were Carolinian—Cape Fear, and then on to Charleston.

Two varieties of North Carolina Loyalism received the most attention. Such was the circa-1775 recruitment glamour already attached to Scottish Highlanders that London had approved raising a regiment of Royal Highland Emigrants from settlers in North Carolina and northern New York. Predictions that about 3,000 to 5,000 Carolina Highlanders would rally to the king's standard were excessive, but it was reasonable to assume a core of 500 to 1,000 Highlanders, many veterans of the Forty Five or of the recent French war. Three to four hundred had already been recruited for the Emigrants. Nothing so reassuring could be said about former Regulators. Chapter 6 has noted how membership in the Sandy Creek Separate Baptist Church, one of the Regulation's principal seedbeds, plummeted from 600 to 14 as members fled after the fighting at Alamance. Most were not military-minded people. Former governor William Tryon, who in 1771 had identified the participants as mostly Baptists and Quakers, seems not to have been queried by Dartmouth. Many Regulators had fled west into the mountains after the battle, and few of those remaining in the Piedmont had real followings.

As an ex-military man, Governor Martin probably should have doubted London's assurances of timely December sailing and February arrival. In fact, that winter's North Atlantic weather turned out to be especially disruptive. However, the governor had strong personal hopes involved, and in January the various Loyalists were told that they were to assemble in Cross Creek and to meet the British fleet on the Cape Fear River by February 15. With no transports from Britain yet sighted, the senior Scottish officers were cautious. Indeed, at a meeting on February 5 they argued for not assembling their forces until March 1, when the fleet should have arrived. It was the strutting handful of ex-Regulators present who scoffed, saying they had 500 men already organized and expected to field about 5,000, mostly American born, and they "insisted on taking up Arms immediately." The Scots said that under those circumstances, they could only raise "above six or seven hundred men."[8]

Over the next three weeks, ex-Regulator participation withered and shriveled. Despite the boast of 5,000, even the 500 already gathered melted away after hearing of a Whig force closing in. As the combined Loyalists gathered on February 20, the number of ex-Regulators on hand was probably 200 to 400, alongside some 900 to 1,000 Scots, for a total of 1,100 to 1,400. Some went home when Martin turned out not to be on hand with 1,000 redcoats as had been rumored. By the time battle was joined on February 27, only 700 to 900 Loyalists were engaged, of whom only 100 to 200 were ex-Regulators. Historians, local experts, and others use varying figures; they also disagree on whether 30 to 50 Loyalists or as many as 70 were killed and wounded. Everyone agrees that only two Americans were killed or wounded.[9] The number of Patriots in the battle depends on whether only those on the battlefield are counted (1,050) or whether one includes other forces not far away (1,900).[10]

Precision seems unnecessary. The portrait of a Highlanders' gallant last hurrah, although overdrawn, has some truth. Flora MacDonald, famous for saving Bonnie Prince Charlie in 1746, who moved to North Carolina in 1774, apparently reviewed the clansmen sitting sidesaddle on a white horse. Just half had muskets, with the result that 75 men armed only with broadswords were the first to charge. Many died crossing the famous bridge from which Patriots had removed the planking. Not a few fell before the Patriots' two small artillery pieces—a Dutch three-pounder named Old Mother Covington, which fired canister, and a swivel gun called Mother Covington's Daughter. One Whig militiaman recalled his first sight of the enemy: "officers well dressed in gay regimentals, banners and plumes waving in the breeze, and all marching in good order, but with a quick step, to the sound of their pibrochs."[11] Surprisingly, the clash has not been made into an even more inaccurate movie.

British historians who prefer to ignore Moore's Creek can fairly describe it as a small engagement not involving British regulars. However, almost all ignore the ignominious and uncomfortable month subsequently passed on the Cape Fear River by seven proud regiments of British regulars who ducked sharpshooters and staged their handful of raids at night so as to avoid the American riflemen who lined the river's many elevated banks. With no Loyalist army coming, the redcoats had no real purpose.

The British ships originally scheduled to arrive in February dropped anchor between March and May. General Clinton, with a frigate, sloop, and three transports holding two companies of infantry, arrived on March 12. Most days he exercised his men on Battery Island, a small place easily protected by his two warships and beyond sharpshooter range from the shore.[12] But he could attempt little until the 60-odd other ships and seven regiments, commanded by Commodore Sir Peter Parker and Major General the Earl Cornwallis, dropped anchor between April 18 and May 3. The main fleet was so far behind schedule that even their arrival with Clinton on March 12 wouldn't have mattered.

But for a moment, let us suppose that the British war machine had delivered Clinton and Cornwallis in early February, so that the Loyalists gathering in the hinterland could be reassured that transports had just arrived with the 15th, 28th, 33rd, 37th, 46th, 54th, and 57th regiments. It would have sufficed for two or three officers and 25 redcoats to accompany Governor Martin to Cross Creek on February 15. If so, one can imagine some 3,000 Loyalists moving down the Cape Fear to Brunswick and Wilmington—a powerful army, once merged with the seven British regiments. In the words of one North Carolina historian, "The Moore's Creek Bridge Campaign, viewed from a perspective of nearly two hundred years, assumes greater importance than in 1776. Had the loyalists reached the sea, it is not unreasonable to suppose that their ranks would have been swelled considerably by the Tories of the coastal areas. If a junction had been made with Governor Martin, and arms in sufficient number acquired, large numbers of loyalists and Regulators would have flocked to the royal standard."[13]

Reality, as we saw in Chapters 12 and 13, was that the British Army and Royal Navy of late 1775 were overextended administratively and logistically. The Cape Fear expedition was further undercut by several major miscalculations and intelligence failures. Whether or not Loyalists ever fought their way to the seacoast, large warships and transports in the area were handicapped. They could not go up the river to Wilmington; only smaller ships and sloops could do that. The catch was that sloops like HMS *Cruizer,* even if they got past river obstacles, were not heavily enough armed; the batteries of six- and nine-pounders at Wilmington could drive them back.

What's more, the banks and bluffs up to 70 feet high that lined parts of the river favored Patriot riflemen. The initial British assumption was that to be safe, vessels had to keep 200 yards from shore, but it soon became clear that 400 yards were needed for safety against sharpshooters. The redcoats' only accomplishments came from frustrated commanders' indulgences: burning or pillaging the plantations and homes of leading Patriots, including Robert Howe and William Hooper. On May 1, General Clinton ordered the destruction of what was left of Fort Johnston because it had become a haven for American riflemen. The next day, Clinton landed ten companies of redcoats to capture the 50 to 60 sharpshooters, but all that could be found were horses' tracks. The riflemen were back the next day.[14] On May 3, Clinton wrote to Germain that his army was unlikely to achieve much. No water routes beckoned; the weather was bad and soon to become intolerable; there were no horses for his artillery.[15] In addition, Loyalists, being jailed and suppressed, could not be enlisted; by contrast, rebel troops were massing.

In late May, probably after he and Parker and Cornwallis had made a decision to move on to Charleston, Clinton relocated most of his troops to the environs of the old fort, where they kept pine trees burning during the night for illumination to keep the sharpshooters from getting too close.[16] From time to time, rumors circulated about British intent to burn Wilmington, and Patriot commanders feared an attack.[17] In fact, Clinton and Cornwallis had both had enough of North Carolina. On May 31, the fleet sailed for Charleston.

For the British, an underlying and little-recognized problem was that as of late 1775, Wilmington, Brunswick, and the southeastern counties—Brunswick, New Hanover, Onslow, Craven, and Duplin—were the principal muster ground of the Revolution in North Carolina. This region had bred a disproportion of the Revolutionary leadership, and in April 1776, when General Clinton promised a pardon to all who would come in and swear allegiance, the two men he excluded—Cornelius Harnett and Robert Howe—were both from Cape Fear.[18] From the autumn of 1775, when talk began to grow of a British southern expedition that would invade North Carolina through Cape Fear, the local Patriot leadership had busied itself preparing to meet such a force.

More than any other part of the province, the southeastern counties embraced military mobilization. In August 1775, the Provincial Congress had authorized two Continental regiments and minutemen. At Moore's Creek Bridge, the Patriot forces were made up of Craven County (New Bern) militia, New Hanover (Wilmington) militia and minutemen, and smaller contingents from nearby Duplin, Onslow, and Bladen counties. In April 1776, the Provincial Congress sought to counter the additional British regiments expected by establishing four new Continental regiments in addition to the existing pair.[19] In December, Robert Howe had taken one regiment of North Carolina Continentals to help the Virginians beat Lord Dunmore in Great Bridge and Norfolk; and in June, as soon as Commodore Parker had sailed for Charleston, portions of several North Carolina Continental regiments marched south to help in the defense of Charleston. Arousing eastern North Carolina was a British mistake.

Leaving North Carolina, many British officers expected to take control of Charleston's great harbor easily, but it turned out to be another inauspicious battleground.

The Mismanaged Battle for Charleston Harbor

Like the contest for Cape Fear, the jockeying for control of Charleston Harbor—its maritime environs, not the town, constituted the actual target—had started back in the autumn of 1775. Six months later, the port of Charleston was among the most heavily fortified in the new world, and its channels were a risky, ever-changing maze for all but knowledgeable local pilots. Here, too, the Royal Navy would underestimate its task.

Very small craft could use a back door, but for a ship of any size, entry was tedious. Depending on a vessel's draft, it had to choose among six channels, through which it might take seven hours to reach the main docks. The channels, for their part, dictated where major fortifications had been or soon would be placed. Fort Johnson, dating back to 1708, overlooked the southern passage. The main ship channel, in turn, went near Sullivan's Island, soon to be fortified. The northern route crossed a large anchorage near Haddrell's Point, also given a battery of cannon. Preparation for attack between the summer of 1775 and the following spring emphasized both constructing or strengthening forts and blocking channels, usually by sinking old or derelict vessels. In August, Patriots began by removing a beacon on Lighthouse Island and chopping down landmark trees used by pilots crossing the Charleston bar (sandbar).[20]

Patriot militia had already taken Fort Charlotte on the Savannah River in July, and on the night of September 15, three companies of South Carolina infantry, commanded by Colonel Isaac Motte, under orders from the Council of Safety, boarded a packet boat at Charleston's Gadsden Wharf to occupy Fort Johnson, the harbor's main bastion. But the British, hearing of the imminent raid, had dismounted the cannon and then abandoned the installation. The Patriots, in turn, acted after learning of a letter in which Lord Dartmouth mentioned a British attack on Charleston.[21] Governor Campbell quickly fled to HMS *Tamar;* the Patriots remounted Fort Johnson's guns; and war inched closer.

On October 19, after rejecting a more sweeping plan to close the harbor, Patriots decided instead to block two of the northern entryways—the Marsh and Hog island channels. Either might get the Royal Navy close enough to the Cooper River waterfront to bombard the warehouse district with its combustible stores of tar, pitch, and turpentine. Scuttling six old schooners was calculated to provide adequate obstruction, and on November 9, the Provincial Congress assigned escort duty to the South Carolina Provincial Navy schooner *Defence.* Thirty seamen were detailed from the colony's two regiments, and 35 infantrymen were assigned as marines.[22] On November 11, after the expedition set off down Hog Island Creek, the decrepit *Tamar* was perceived to be attacking, and the *Defence* fired back. South Carolina officers were too distracted to sink more than three of the hulks. However, Patriot leader William Drayton got what he really wanted: a definitive confrontation. After pressure from Royal Governor Campbell, both British sloops, the *Tamar* and the *Cherokee,* appeared the next morning and opened fire on the *Defence,* although with practically no effect.[23]

Historians consider this November 11–12 skirmish as the opening battle of the Revolution in South Carolina—in part because Patriot leaders Drayton and Colonel William Moultrie wanted it to assume that role. With popular attention now directed to the Hog Island Channel and Sullivan's Island, this portion of the harbor became the central focus of defense planning. The Provincial Congress had discussed putting a fort there some weeks earlier. In late December, a company of South Carolina Rangers, including a number of Catawba Indians, cleared Sullivan's of its last few British seamen and runaway slaves. Within days, 200 men from South Carolina's First Regiment marched into Haddrell's Point, just to the north, and quickly emplaced a battery of eighteen-pounders.[24]

For *Tamar* and *Cherokee,* this boded poorly. Bad enough that in December, Patriots had cut off local supplies of provisions, water, and fuel. Now rebel eighteen-pounders controlled much of the harbor. On January 6, the king's two sloops and their supporting vessels, no longer able to maintain station, sailed for Savannah. No longer would Charleston's fort builders have to worry about cannonades from the sloops' six-pounders. The Committee of Safety recommended that work begin on a strong fort and battery on Sullivan's Island, which it did.

As we will see, the March-June prelude to the eventual battle is a tale of two preparations. South Carolinians, not always certain the British were coming, worked fortification magic with shilling-each palmetto logs. The British fleet and regiments off Cape Fear, not completely assembled until early May, finally set sail for Charleston on May 31 based on several pieces of misinformation that helped to underpin yet another British military disaster. From the Patriot perspective, the confrontation at Sullivan's Fort is a book in its own right—more than half a dozen have been published. However, this chapter's narrower emphasis is on the British mistakes and misconceptions that made the inept Charleston campaign a fitting conclusion to the southern expedition.

To begin with, the underlying priority was dubious. General Clinton and Commodore Parker left Cape Fear for South Carolina well aware that their army of 2,500 men was insufficient to capture Charleston itself. The plan, as recalled by Clinton, was this: Commodore "Sir Peter Parker having in the mean time procured Intelligence from whence it appeared the Rebel Work on Sullivans Island (the Key to Rebellion Road and Charles Town) was in so unfinished a state as to be open to a Coup de Main & that it might be afterwards held by a small Force under Cover of a Frigate or two . . . I thought Sullivans Island, if it could be seized without much loss of time, might prove a very important acquisition and greatly facilitate any Subsequent Move we should be in a Condition to make in Proper Season

14: CHARLES TOWN AND ITS HARBOR, 1775–1776

Local Patriots began preparing for a British naval attack in the late summer of 1775 when they seized Fort Johnson. During the autumn, they began blocking harbor channels and siting artillery. That winter, work began on Fort Sullivan, with its walls of spongy palmetto wood, which withstood the Royal Navy when it finally attacked in June.

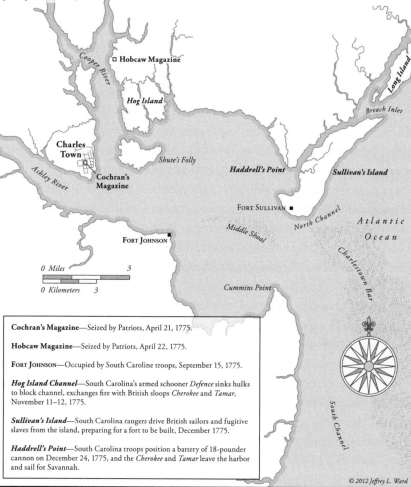

Cooper River

□ **Hobcaw Magazine**

Long Island

Hog Island

Breach Inlet

Charles Town

Shute's Folly

Haddrell's Point

Sullivan's Island

Ashley River

Cochran's Magazine

FORT SULLIVAN ■

North Channel

Atlantic Ocean

Middle Shoal

Charlestown Bar

FORT JOHNSON ■

0 Miles   3

0 Kilometers   3

Cummins Point

South Channel

Cochran's Magazine—Seized by Patriots, April 21, 1775.

Hobcaw Magazine—Seized by Patriots, April 22, 1775.

FORT JOHNSON—Occupied by South Caroline troops, September 15, 1775.

Hog Island Channel—South Carolina's armed schooner *Defence* sinks hulks to block channel, exchanges fire with British sloops *Cherokee* and *Tamar*, November 11–12, 1775.

Sullivan's Island—South Carolina rangers drive British sailors and fugitive slaves from the island, preparing for a fort to be built, December 1775.

Haddrell's Point—South Carolina troops position a battery of 18-pounder cannon on December 24, 1775, and the *Cherokee* and *Tamar* leave the harbor and sail for Savannah.

© 2012 Jeffrey L. Ward

against that Capital [the city of Charleston]."[25] Getting the troops back to New York for the upcoming invasion should have been more compelling, but Clinton needed to return with some battle laurel.

As for the low-built, harbor-facing fort on Sullivan's west shore, it was indeed unfinished—its walls were low, and only two of its four sides were completed, an open back door for a land attack. Until the Royal Navy's bombardment was into its second or third hour, many British officers and some on the American side had assumed the new fort could never withstand such massive firepower, but it seemed to be unhurt.[26]

It was no ordinary fortification. The Committee of Safety had armored the harbor's most vital defenses—Fort Johnson and Sullivan's alike—with cheap and readily available palmetto wood, known for a spongy, difficult-to-break quality. Two thousand palmetto logs had been floated across the harbor in October to strengthen Fort Johnson's walls.[27] Thousands more were used on Sullivan's for a palmetto log fort with sixteen feet of heavy sand and marsh clay packed between its outer and inner walls.[28] Palmetto had been chosen as resistant to both shock and splintering; the wood's unusual texture allowed cannon balls to sink in without fragmentation. Indeed, palmetto forts remained effective as late as the American Civil War. Ironically, the Royal Navy should have been alert, being acquainted with South Carolina's unusual subtropical woods. In the early 1770s, the Admiralty had experimented with South Carolina live oak because of its ironlike hardness and resistance to rot.

It seems, however, that Commodore Parker entered Charleston Harbor with a dangerous dearth of local expertise: "Through an oversight, the British naval bureaucracy had failed to give Parker a single officer with knowledge of the harbor, though, as one dumbfounded Charlestown loyalist observed afterwards, 'this was no obscure place but well known, to many Gentlemen of the Navy.' Even more astonishing was Parker's failure to enlist the aid of Lieutenant John Fergusson and the crew of the sometime Royal Navy ship *Cherokee*, whose firsthand knowledge of Sullivans Island lay at his command a few hours away in Savannah, Georgia. Ultimately, these omissions left the execution of the commodore's battle plan dependent on the reliability of a handful of black pilots, who either had been seized from coastal shipping or had been spirited out of Charleston."[29]

The spring tides had just changed, increasing the dangers from the harbor's many sandbars. The black pilots, unhappy, refused to follow British orders. The *Bristol*'s guide would not take the flagship close to the fort, and the pilot on the 50-gun *Experiment* followed suit. Three smaller frigates, poorly advised by the single pilot they shared, ran aground on the sandbar called the Lower Middle Ground.[30] Most histories give no more detail, but it may be significant that as pilots refused orders, Patriot prospects brightened.[31]

By way of context, no body of men was more important to Patriot committees in the waterscapes including Boston, Philadelphia, coastal Virginia, Cape Fear, and Charleston than harbor pilots and river pilots. Their vocational "treason"—exactly how Patriots felt about willingness to guide British ships—could bring about critical defeats. We have seen in Chapter 23 how pilots in the Boston area, taken on board British vessels for one hurried expedition in July 1775, simply refused to provide directions. As described by Admiral Graves, "Rewards or Threatenings were alike ineffectual. They continued in a manner petrified." Indeed, even before Lexington and Concord, Graves had notified the Admiralty that it had become "almost unpardonable for Pilots to take charge of the Kings Ships and Vessels, several have been driven from their homes and threatened with death for assisting his Majesty's Fleet."[32] On August 21, the Rhode Island Assembly provided criminal penalties for anyone piloting armed vessels save those of the colonies.[33]

On September 16, the Pennsylvania Committee of Safety resolved that river and bay pilots should stay ashore. Anyone who let himself be taken on board a British armed vessel, the committee said, would be deemed an enemy to American liberty. By contrast, Delaware River pilots with already established loyalties were brought into Patriot confidence respecting the location of river obstructions and played a vital role in the local war effort.[34]

Patriots took similar precautions in the two regions visited by the king's southern expedition—the lower Cape Fear and Charleston Harbor. In the former, in January 1776, when the British sloop *Scorpion* required assistance from one local pilot, the Wilmington–New Hanover Committee of Safety took over control and specified what would be expected of each individual pilot.[35] In Charleston, where a prominent free black pilot, Thomas Jeremiah, was executed in August 1775 for supposedly encouraging a slave insurrection, most historians identify racial motives. However, on June 8, Henry Laurens of the Committee of Safety had written to his son in London that "we have ordered the pilots not to board or bring in any Man of War on Transport Ship."[36] Many of Charleston's harbor pilots were black, and Jeremiah's execution may have also been a maritime warning.

As for the Charleston pilots' actions in refusing British requests on June 28, we cannot reconstruct their motivation. Scores of blacks served in the

South Carolina Navy during the Revolution, but it is also possible that black pilots compelled to help the British in the great harbor battle were as petrified as the white Boston pilots had been in July 1775.

The final British mistake in deciding to strike at Charleston Harbor returns us to the mind of Henry Clinton. An additional reason—beyond the fort's presumed vulnerability—for expecting the campaign to be quick and easy lay in an ill-advised belief that his 2,200 men could cross to Sullivan's from nearby Long Island at Breach Inlet, so called, simply by wading across waters only eighteen to 24 inches deep at low tide. Then, after marching a few miles, they could overrun the fort through its open back door— the uncompleted southwestern and northeastern sides. Instead, the water in question turned out to be seven feet deep, not two. According to one officer involved, Captain Sir James Murray, "so much was the general prepossessed with the idea of this infernal ford, that several days and nights were spent in search of it," adding that the crossing should have been abandoned "upon the first discovery of our mistake."[37] Instead, Clinton shifted to a plan in which Breach Inlet eventually had to be crossed by Britons in boats, against a Patriot position now well manned by North and South Carolina riflemen with grapeshot-firing artillery. This attack had to be called off after heavy casualties. The bitter remarks about Clinton that began among officers on the scene continued into the pages of hostile British newspapers.

Simply put, the British defeat on June 28 was a rout. Besides the casualties at Breach Inlet, the navy took a drubbing. Of the three frigates that went aground, one, the *Acteon,* could not be rescued and had to be blown up. Sullivan's fort concentrated its fire on the two major warships, the *Bristol,* 50 guns, and the *Experiment,* 50 guns. Both were shot almost to pieces and would have been sunk had the Americans enough powder for continual firing. Instead, the American gunners had to pause for long intervals, sometimes awaiting more deliveries. In the end, the fort fired only 4,766 pounds of gunpowder to the ships' 34,000 pounds.[38] Even so, the ratio of officers and men killed on *Bristol* and *Experiment* was high, almost Bunker Hill– like. Both captains died, and Commodore Parker literally had the seat of his pants shot off. Only twelve Americans were killed, most having remained safe behind the palmetto walls.

As we have seen, King George stiffened his upper lip and acknowledged that he "should have been as well pleased if it had not been attempted." Indeed, he was less to blame than some of his Cabinet members, colonial governors, and generals.

The American Revolution and the Limits of British Power

It would be hard to find a less impressive trio of British military achievements than the February-June cavalcade of pipes and broadswords at Moore's Creek Bridge, the evening pine fires of seven regular regiments immobilized by Carolina sharpshooters, and the shared failure of the army and navy in the attack on what became Fort Moultrie. It is a cliché of military historians that British wars often get off to a poor start but finish strongly. Not in this war. When Lord North heard in December about Cornwallis's October 1781 surrender, his first words—"My God, it is all over"—were a succinct political as well as military summary. He resigned in April 1782.

The long-term implications of the American Revolution for Britain's future world role did not suffer the damage that many Britons had feared in late 1781 and early 1782. However, the strategic predicament that British strategists never fully confronted was that with the rebellion in America spread over so large a territory, only one major region could be managed at a time.

By 1778, for example, it is fair to say that Britain was losing interest in expending blood and resources to keep control of the old Puritan, smuggling-driven, and innately hostile southern core of New England— Massachusetts, Connecticut, and Rhode Island. British strategists remained interested in peripheries like semi-independent Vermont and the Penobscot district of Maine, but principally as buffer zones for a future Canada. British undersecretaries like William Knox and Charles Jenkinson had already popularized the economic and political argument against Britain trying to keep New England. The region would remain a lucrative market for British goods simply because of their price. Virginia was well worth keeping because of its tobacco, but the best approach to reconquering plantation country, Knox argued, would be to first invade Georgia and South Carolina, the states farthest from northern military reinforcements.[39]

Britain's new logic did indeed point south. However, much of Whitehall was insufficiently mindful of another vital nuance. When Spain declared war in 1779, General Bernardo de Gálvez, the highly capable governor of Louisiana, put his own "southern strategy" to work. As we have seen, between 1779 and 1781, Gálvez captured one British fort or Gulf Coast strongpoint after another: Manchac, Natchez, Baton Rouge, Mobile, and Pensacola; and in 1782, a joint Spanish and American expedition, with the frigate *South Carolina* as its flagship, captured the Bahamas. That loss suggested that Britain would have to recover the latter by giving East and West Florida back to Spain at the peace tables. In such a case, Georgia and South Carolina would no longer be important chess pieces.

Besides which, Clinton and Cornwallis, the two British generals with the longest experience in the South—not least, with unhappy memories of Carolina snipers and palmetto log forts—had their doubts about Britain's second southern strategy even before Cornwallis's eventual surrender. Clinton, as we have seen, doubted the ultimate success of a British strategy in the South that consolidated in South Carolina and Georgia and then built northward. For a while, at least, as noted in Chapter 17, the mercurial general favored a Chesapeake-focused approach.

As the second southern strategy took hold in 1780–1781, British soldiers had been withdrawn from most of the North save for the large headquarters concentration New York City and its environs. Even so, Cornwallis doubted that the force in the South was adequate. In April 1781, he wrote to a fellow general that "if we mean an offensive war in America, we must abandon New York and put our whole force into Virginia . . . If our plan is defensive, mixed with desultory expeditions, let us quit the Carolinas (which cannot be held defensively while Virginia can be so easily armed against us) and stick to our salt pork in New York, sending now and then a detachment to steal tobacco."[40] His capitulation in October, of course, left no real options.

Obviously, Britain did not *conclusively* lose America in 1775. However, it may be fair to say that Britain lost in the end because of circumstances that started to be apparent in 1775. These ranged from too few British troops to subdue North and South at the same time to the Patriots' fierce suppression of Loyalists, the obvious intentions of France and Spain, the dislike of Britain across Europe, the considerable support for America within Britain, and in a more personal vein, the 1775–1778 reluctance of the Howe brothers to crush the Patriots and the Howe family's preference for trying to win in a way that kept the thirteen colonies' attachment.

And so we turn to our final chapter: the opportunity of 1775 and the long-term implications of the Revolution's powerful beginnings.

CHAPTER 26

1775: A Good Year for Revolution

As 1775 drew to a close, both the United Kingdom of Great Britain and Ireland and the self-styled United Colonies of North America were trying something altogether new. Never before had a large mass of European colonists of a major European empire tried to break away and become semi-independent or independent. There were no meaningful guidelines, which explains some of the missteps on both sides. Neither British law nor what passed for international law had clear, easy answers.

The great gamble undertaken by colonial Americans in 1775 succeeded because its timing was plausible and its political, military, and international assumptions were generally valid. Britain never did regain most of the territory vacated in 1775; nor did British power ever overthrow the great bulk of the new local committees, associations, congresses, and de facto governments set up across the land during that year. Europe kept shipping munitions, and France, Spain, and Holland eventually became American allies. The gamble succeeded.

If the timing was not perfect, conflict had become unavoidable. Mid-October 1774 was a critical month when the king's Privy Council prohibited arms shipments from Britain to North America and the Continental Congress delivered its belligerent ultimatum on trade. Absent huge concessions, the colonies intended to withhold tobacco and other exports. For a colony to suspend its role as a supplier of commodities and materials was a rejection of imperial authority. The king's lawyers thought it added up to treason. That made 1774 the Revolution's threshold year. Neither side backed down, and the colonists would have been fools to delay and give Britain more time to bring its economic and military power to bear. Seventeen seventy-five was when opportunity beckoned and confrontation escalated.

The faulty element of what had been put in motion—it became obvious enough in two or three years—was principally *economic*. The king, his ministers, and Parliament refused to bow to the colonial boycotts so grandly announced in late 1774. The British government instead replied with restraints, prohibitions, naval blockades, and the commercial equivalent of outlawry. This had not been expected by the delegates in Philadelphia, most of whom assumed that Britain would back down or compromise as in 1766 and 1770. It was not a fatal miscalculation. But it came close.

Of the four states that had been the vanguard colonies of 1774 and 1775, Virginia and Massachusetts retained national leadership after peace came in 1783. Of the first six American presidents, four hailed from Virginia and two from Massachusetts. However, the sectional emphasis that so influenced British war strategy had its effect, leaving the despoiled lower South the poorest part of the new confederation. Sectionalism was baked into the cake of American independence. By the late 1820s, when the six Virginia and Massachusetts presidents had ended their tenures in office, South Carolina, ever combative, had moved to the forefront of a new cause: nullification and eventually secession. Connecticut retained respect but never regained its centrality in those early years when Jonathan Trumbull was the United Colonies' most dedicated and experienced governor. Because of Trumbull's political influence, the colony's many regiments of militia, its cannon, and its strategic location between Boston, Lake Champlain, and New York City, Connecticut played a disproportionate role. Without the temporary coalescence of the vanguard colonies, there might not have been a Revolution.

The 1775 Framework: Politics, Military Success, and Foreign Support

The implication that the United States sprang miraculously into nationhood in 1776—trumpeted, for example, by the phrase *Annuit coeptis novus ordo seclorum* ("announcing the birth of the new world order") on the one-dollar bill—has discouraged attention to our unusual national foundations built in 1774 and 1775. The vital importance and consequences of the victories and achievements during those years have been left untended. My contention is that between the summer of 1774 and the spring of 1776, the Americans won a number of battles and campaigns and achieved a de facto independence that put slow-moving British counterrevolutionary intentions at a distinct disadvantage from which they never recovered. The Declaration of Independence was a milestone, but only one among several.

The first great battle won by the United Colonies of 1775 might be called the expulsion of British authority. Of the ten appointed royal governors, Gage had been besieged in Boston in 1774, and four others, as we have seen, fled to British warships during the summer of 1775. In October 1775, New York governor William Tryon removed himself to the comfortable merchant ship *Dutchess of Gordon* in New York off Manhattan. In Georgia, Governor James Wright fled to HMS *Scarborough* in February 1776. Patriots delayed taking William Franklin of New Jersey into custody until spring 1776 largely because he was Benjamin Franklin's son. Governor John Penn of the proprietary family retired to his country home after Pennsylvania abolished his office in mid-1776, but he had been a figurehead. During the spring, the Maryland Convention voted to expel Governor Robert Eden, although he had been liked personally. Scores of lesser officials also left or fled.

British redcoats, too, were nowhere to be seen. Those in upper New York had surrendered in May. The last few companies of redcoats in New York City were marched onto HMS *Asia* during the summer, partly to keep them from deserting. Naval historian David Syrett summed up that "by midsummer of 1775, the ships of the Royal Navy and the enclave at Boston were all that remained of the British empire in America," by which he meant the thirteen colonies.[1] The same collapse elicited parliamentary notice in October 1775, when opposition spokesmen noted somewhat flamboyantly that neither Caesar nor Alexander the Great had conquered so much territory in their wars as Lord North had lost in six months.[2]

The Patriot faction in 1775 also won the battle to impose new institutions at the grass roots to implement most of what the founders in Philadelphia recommended. The local committees called for in 1774 by the First Continental Congress were elected or appointed rapidly in provinces, save for New York and Georgia. New Englanders elected several hundred town committees, and together with the organizations in more than 100 counties across the middle and southern provinces, these bodies imposed new hands-on political regimes that quickly assumed authority beyond imports, exports, and maritime regulation. By mid-1775, credible local governments were administering no-nonsense loyalty oaths and exercising control of the local militia.

On the provincial level, self-governing Connecticut and Rhode Island did not require structural changes. Elsewhere, local assemblies put themselves into limbo, taking new form as provincial congresses or conventions. In Massachusetts, New Hampshire, Virginia, and the Carolinas, the new provincial congresses and conventions of 1775 had many of the same members as the old assemblies. However, even before royal governors were obliged to flee, these new bodies had sidestepped their veto and dissolution powers.

One British military historian, Piers Mackesy, offered a broader, if reluctant, salute. The Revolution's successful endurance, he argued, lay in how "before the conflict had become an armed rebellion, the dissidents had seized control of the organs of government." Among other things, they used this control to politicize and wield the militia. The latter, in turn, "secured control of the machinery of authority for the rebels; who stifled early threats of counter-revolution; who defended the civil institutions of the revolution throughout the war; and who restored revolutionary control wherever the British had temporarily overthrown it."[3]

A third early campaign absolutely vital to Patriot success involved bringing sufficient gunpowder and arms to America to support a revolution. Here battle lines had been drawn by late 1774; indeed, most of the early confrontations of 1775 pitted Patriots who were trying to import gunpowder and arms, or to capture them from provincial forts and magazines, against British governors and military commanders who were trying to stop them or working to seize Patriot supplies. The Royal Navy went far afield—virtually blockading the Dutch coast and patrolling West Africa's slave ports—to stop shipments. But Britain failed. By late 1775, Admiral Samuel Graves admitted that he had been able to stop only a small portion of what was being shipped, and naval historians generally concur.

Encouraged by Congress and its secret committees, colonies like Massachusetts, Connecticut, Rhode Island, Maryland, Virginia, and South Carolina were commissioning shipowners and merchants to trade any commodity available—fish, provisions, wheat, rice, but especially tobacco—for war matériel. It remained true, as late as December, that George Washington was looking to a surrendered Quebec for a treasure trove of powder and large cannon to drive the British out of Boston. But in European, Caribbean, and American waters alike, the Royal Navy had too few of the small vessels needed to catch the merchant sloops and schooners transporting munitions to America or to such tropical entrepôts as St. Eustatius, Cap Français, or Martinique.

A fourth campaign, albeit closely connected with the third, required the Patriot faction to cultivate and maintain enough support and influence in Europe to keep the arms and munitions flowing, to interfere with King George's plans to hire mercenaries (as in Holland and Russia), and to keep both the French and the Spanish hooked on the idea of trying to weaken Britain by promoting a revolution in her North American colonies. Eventually, or so men like Benjamin Franklin and John Adams believed, such relations would ripen into alliances. They did.

These battles had to be begun in 1775; waiting was not an option. But for the most part, the four campaigns—the four triumphs—have not been described in the language of shooting wars and battles.

Within the thirteen colonies, however, many more such developments took place in 1775 than believers in *annuit coeptis novus ordo seclorum* like to admit. Chapter 20 employed the term *Battle of Boston* to describe the two years of fierce antagonism that began in the spring of 1774 when the British government confidently imposed the Coercive Acts. Two years later, in March 1776, that same government had to scramble to find transport to Halifax, Nova Scotia, for a bedraggled British army forced out of Boston by new rebel artillery emplacements! That the Battle of Boston was an American victory is beyond dispute. The question is whether it represented something more unusual.

Thomas Gage clearly thought so. In a July 1775 letter to the Earl of Dartmouth, the general had argued that Boston was where "the arch-rebels formed their scheme long ago. This circumstance brought the troops first here which is the most disadvantageous place for all operations . . . Was this army in New York, that province might to all appearances be more easily reduced."[4] Gage, of course, was not the only one to scent conspiracy. Washington, Adams, and Jefferson all thought that British ministries had conspired against the rights of the colonies. It is entirely conceivable that Samuel Adams was thinking and planning for war. If Samuel Adams planned to trap the British in Boston, he probably began in 1773 or 1774, which would make any such plot one of the best-planned and best-sprung political and military traps of the eighteenth century.

New Englanders were clever to push for an invasion of Canada in 1775, in part because it kept the British military there too busy to mount a back-door attack on the American army besieging Boston. Beginning in 1775, the British were forced to overconcentrate forces in Canada. This ensured that the main invasion of the thirteen colonies would be launched from Canada—and that focus remained until the invasion army under Burgoyne was defeated in October 1775.

Two other British political and military miscalculations made in 1775 worked in the colonies' long-term favor. Lord Dartmouth and his colleagues at least passively agreed to Virginia governor Dunmore's strategy of bringing down the Indians on the colonists and enlisting slaves who would run away to join the British Army. However, distaste for Dunmore pushed Virginians toward the Patriot faction and independence. So did the failure of the southern expedition, which alienated the Carolinas and played a role in delaying the invasion of New York.

In short, 1775 was a good year politically and militarily. It was a good year to launch the Revolution, although the forces set in motion during 1774 left little choice.

The Revolutionary Economy: Grave 1775 Miscalculations

Here American assumptions were more mistaken than shrewd. In particular, the Patriots were naïve to embrace the mercantilist assessment of the thirteen colonies being so important that the king and Parliament would have no choice but to accede to the First Continental Congress's far-reaching political, commercial, and economic demands. But earlier nonimportation boycotts had not been that decisive in the British policy retreats of 1765 and 1770.

Back in the autumn of 1774, then, Congress had been foolish to expect that King George and his ministers would back down in early 1775 after eleven of the thirteen colonies endorsed the nonimportation and nonexportation calendar and mechanisms set out in the Continental Association. Even Lord Dartmouth, the relatively conciliatory American secretary, pronounced its intentions "criminal." The British government's anger led to a series of harsh responses—the Restraining Acts of March and April 1775, the king's August Proclamation of Rebellion, and the Prohibitory Act in late December, which declared that as of March 1, 1776, all vessels entering or exiting Americans ports would be subject to seizure.

As trade shrank late in 1775, after the last large export shipments of wheat and tobacco had made the September cutoff, rebels hoped that the ensuing dearth of trade was injuring Britain more. For the most part, though, that was illusory. Nonexportation had become a snare for Patriots, not a laurel wreath. To remedy the mistake, Congress had recommended, and a half dozen provinces soon implemented, activity by local merchants and shipowners to export salable commodities like tobacco and wheat in return for munitions and other necessities like salt and medicines. Foreigners who brought war matériel to American ports were promised similar desirable cargoes. Beyond these exceptions, trade was shrinking, and little resurgence was apparent in April 1776, when Congress finally opened all American ports to non-British vessels and trade.

In the weeks after Lexington and Concord, few were surprised by the economic pain starting to be felt in maritime New England. The Royal Navy in those waters was initially authorized by the Crown to seize vessels carrying munitions or supplies for the army encircling Boston, and within a few months local fishermen were obliged to beach their vessels as Restraining Act prohibitions went into effect. Beginning in July, the Royal Navy was authorized to seize New England merchant vessels bound for any port save a British or West Indian one.

However, because a second Restraining Act also extended the July deadline to three middle colonies and two in the South, trade in these ports also fell off sharply. Little data is available, but figures for vessels arriving in Philadelphia charted a precipitous decline. Between September 6, 1775, and March 1, 1776, the tonnage of shipping entering at Philadelphia was down by two thirds from the usual prewar level, Between March 1776 and August 1776, those already-depressed levels experienced another two-thirds shrinkage.[5]

The strategists who promoted the import and export ultimatums in late 1774 had not anticipated these developments, which also put some of their other optimism at risk. Patriots spoke with confidence about America's great manpower resources—about how the colonies could put as many as 200,000 men in the field. Provisioning them would also be easy, it was felt, because meat and grain production (wheat, corn, rice) exceeded domestic demand. Instead, by late 1776 and 1777, as the Revolutionary economy weakened, expected manpower surpluses turned into troop shortages.

Historians who cast doubt on the effectiveness of Britain's naval blockade were correct with respect to the early days in Boston, and with respect to how much war matériel, especially gunpowder, got through in 1774, 1775, and beyond. However, the Royal Navy did have a large enough presence to discourage and chill an important percentage of ordinary American waterborne trade. Commerce in New York, Philadelphia, New Jersey, and elsewhere was badly disrupted by the effects of British invasions and occupations on the particular area, and by the effects of Royal Navy concentrations in areas of landings or blockades. In some places, large-scale American troop mobilization—like the call-up of the Connecticut militia in mid-1776—also sapped the local economy.

With fewer goods being produced and traded, the wartime economy of the new United States suffered further injury from excessive emissions of paper currency at both the national and state levels. Congress's initial printing was necessary—$5 million by the end of 1775, rising to $15 million in mid-1776—and the money held its value reasonably well until the defeats of George Washington and the Continental Army in the August and September battles in and around New York City. By the end of 1777, as issuance got out of hand, the total of congressional and state currency reached some $72 million.[6] If trade had been thriving, and if products had been widely available, the inflationary effects would not have been so severe, but too much money was chasing too few goods, and inflation soared.

This is not to undertake an economic history of the Revolution, but only to explain the miscarriage of the economic proposals and expectations voiced in 1774 and 1775. After showing strains and inflationary signs in 1776, the Revolutionary economy dipped in 1777, worsened in 1778 and 1779, and probably bottomed in 1780. This failure undermined the Revolution psychologically as well as economically, and many erstwhile Patriots lost faith. The southern states, reinvaded between late 1778 and 1780, suffered more than others and came out of the Revolution in 1783 in the worst economic shape. By some calculations, the economy of what became the United States did not recover to prewar levels until the 1790s.

Between 1778 and 1780, hundreds of thousands of Americans must have wondered, and with reason, whether they would have done better to remain British colonials. The larger answer, though, is clearly no, and not just because economic self-determination had to be pursued sooner or later. Had policy makers of 1775 better understood the economic strains and damages to follow from fighting the mother country, they might not have wanted to gamble. But 1775 was the year to do so, with the political, global, and military stars in alignment; it was the critical year for an American Revolution. No other would have proved so fruitful.

Acknowledgments

No volume this size reaches fruition without incurring some debts and requiring some acknowledgments.

To begin with, my wife, Martha, in addition to putting up with a second round of American Revolution–centered research and trips, shared driving and logistical duties from the Mohawk Valley and the Carolina backcountry to Flanders. She also did the photography in museums, libraries, and archives.

This is my fourth book at Viking edited by Wendy Wolf, and it is hard to imagine working with any other editor. Her assistant, Maggie Riggs, also helped.

As I began *1775*, in the spring of 2009, I had some guidance from Ronald Hoffman, director of the Omohundro Institute for Early American History and Culture in Williamsburg, Virginia. Few scholars have such a broad knowledge of the Revolutionary era. I also owe a debt to the specialists who detailed the particular importance of late 1774 and 1775 in the vanguard colonies of Massachusetts, Connecticut, Virginia, and South Carolina. So too for those who emphasized the importance of the provincial militia reorganizations and political purges during that same period, as well as those who catalogued the organization and scope of the committees set up by the colonies in response to the Continental Association voted by the First Continental Congress in October 1774. These wide-ranging committees—there were nearly a thousand—became vital mechanisms of local control as Patriot government replaced King George's crumbling authority.

My pages have also cited the scholars who have explained that the real American *rage militaire* came in 1775, not 1776, as well as those who have pointed out the various months and episodes prior to the summer of 1776 in which de facto American independence became increasingly clear.

Several other appreciations are in order. In Chapter 4, which identified economic self-determination as a major force behind the Revolution, I cited a dozen or so historians who explained the provocations of British currency laws and regulation. In the early twenty-first century, attention to the nation's money supply has become a staple of discussion and press coverage. However, I would have been more reluctant to emphasize its importance in the 1770s without so many specialists' agreement.

In two cases, foreign historians have pursued directions less attended to by their American colleagues. The critical role played during late 1774 and 1775 by American colonists' global struggle for gunpowder and munitions—and British attempts to halt or intercept those supplies—was spotlighted in 2009 in the doctoral dissertation of a Belgian, Marion Huibrechts. Meanwhile, Canadian historians have gone where most U.S. historians have not in underscoring how near the 1775 American invasion of Canada came to success. I am indebted to Eric Ruel, conservateur of the Musée du Fort St.-Jean, for Quebec historians' arguments that without the drawn-out resistance of that fort's outnumbered British defenders, American forces would have been able to reach Quebec City in November, at which time the great citadel could not have held out.

The frequent inattentiveness to 1775 events carries over into a too-limited range of prints, paintings, and commemorations with the principal exception of Massachusetts. Historians in Virginia and the Carolinas occasionally lament that the early Revolution in New England gets excessive attention, but too few have commemorated their own early battles—like the First Battle of Ninety Six in South Carolina and the defense of Hampton and the fighting at Great Bridge in Virginia.

In terms of prints, maps, and paintings, my thanks goes to libarian Peter Drummey and his staff at the Massachusetts Historical Society, and to the Beverly, Massachusetts, Historical Society and to the Beverly Public Library for permission to photograph their painting of HMS *Nautilus* chasing the colonial schooner *Hannah* into Beverly Harbor. In Machias, Maine, the Machias Savings Bank permitted the reproduction of their painting of the local *Unity* capturing the British armed schooner *Margaretta*. In Connecticut, state archivist Mark Jones and the town of Lebanon Historical Society gave permission to reproduce a painting of Governor Jonathan Trumbull. Professor Richard Buel was kind enough to let me reproduce the map of militia regimental districts in his book *Dear Liberty: Connecticut's Mobilization for the Revolutionary War.*

Representatives of the Army, Navy, and Marine Corps helpfully provided high-resolution images of several paintings. Thanks to Michael Knapp, deputy director of Army museums, and Major Michael Gambone of the U.S. Army Center of Military History for *The Soldiers of 1775*, a representation of George Washington, the commanding general, and Major General Artemas Ward of the Massachusetts forces. Art curator Joan Thomas of the National Museum of the Marine Corps furnished the image of their painting of *The First Recruits, December 1775*.

Below the Mason-Dixon Line, the Culpeper, Virginia, Historical Society provided a portrait of John Murray. In South Carolina, The Charleston Library Society helped with maritime images, and Charles Baxley of the organization Southern Campaigns of the American Revolution assisted in locating several maps and paintings. With respect to Williamson's Fort and the First Battle of Ninety Six, the National Park Service provided vital assistance. At the Ninety Six National Historic Site interpretative ranger Sarah Cunningham was a fount of information and together with Guy Prentice of the National Park Service's Southeast Archaelogical Center located an NPS version of a local map from William Drayton's 1821 *Memoirs of the American Revolution*.

The painting of soldiers from the 3rd South Carolina Regiment for 1779, including one Catawba warrior and several "men of color," appears courtesy of the Culture and Heritage Museums of York County, South Carolina. Michael Scoggins of that museum is also the director of the Southern Revolutionary War Institute. Charleston may be preoccupied with Fort Sumter and secession, but interest in the Revolution thrives in the backcountry.

Notes

Preface: Why _1775_

1. Frank H. Horton, "The Building of America," _Illustrated American_ 11, no. 123 (June 25, 1892), p. 287.
2. Gwenda Morgan, _The Debate on the American Revolution_ (Manchester, U.K.: Manchester University Press, 2007), pp. 58–59.
3. Ibid., pp. 62 and 69.
4. John S. Shy, _A People Numerous and Armed_ (Ann Arbor: University of Michigan Press, 1976), p. 317.
5. Ibid., pp. 183–84.
6. Mark Kwasny, _Washington's Partisan War_ (Kent, Ohio: Kent State University Press, 1996), p. xv.
7. Arthur M. Schlesinger, _The Colonial Merchants and the American Revolution_ (New York: Frederick Ungar, 1957).
8. Ray Raphael, _The First American Revolution_ (New York: New Press, 2002); Ivor Noel Hume, _1775: Another Part of the Field_ (New York: Alfred Knopf, 1966); Lewis Pinckney Jones, _The South Carolina Civil War of 1775_ (Lexington, S.C.: Sandlapper Store, 1975).

Chapter 1: The Spirit of 1775

1. Charles Royster, _A Revolutionary People at War_ (Chapel Hill: University of North Carolina Press, 1979), pp. 30–31.
2. Rhys Isaac, "Dramatizing the Ideology of Revolution," _William and Mary Quarterly_, 3rd ser., 33, no. 3 (1976), pp. 381–82.
3. John Ferling, _Almost a Miracle_ (New York: Oxford University Press, 2007), p. 26.
4. Jerrilyn G. Marston, _King and Congress_ (Princeton: Princeton University Press, 1987), p. 53.
5. Michael Kammen, _A Season of Youth_ (Ithaca, N.Y.: Cornell University Press, 1978), p. 256.
6. Bernard Knollenberg, _Growth of the American Revolution: 1765–1775_ (Indianapolis: Liberty Fund, 2003), pp. 202–3.
7. en.wikipedia.org/wiki/intolerable_Acts.
8. John R. Galvin, _Minutemen_ (Washington, D.C.: Brassey's, 1996), pp. 46–48.
9. Allen French, _The First Year of the American Revolution_ (Boston: Houghton Mifflin, 1934), p. xx.
10. Galvin, op. cit., p. xiii.
11. Don Higginbotham, _The War of American Independence_ (New York: Macmillan, 1971), p. 22.

12. Arthur B. Tourtellot, *Lexington and Concord* (New York: W. W. Norton, 1959), p. 23.

13. National Park Service, *Salem: Maritime Salem in the Age of Sail* (Washington, D.C.: Department of the Interior, 1987), p. 46.

14. Higginbotham, op. cit., pp. 11 and 85.

15. William B. Clark, ed., *Naval Documents of the American Revolution* (Washington, D.C.: U.S. Government Printing Office, 1966), vol. 2, p. 324.

16. New Hampshire American Revolution Bicentennial Commission, *New Hampshire: Years of Revolution, 1774–1783* (Concord, N.H.: Profiles Publishing, 1976), p. 10.

17. James S. Leamon, *Revolution Downeast* (Amherst: University of Massachusetts Press, 1993), p. 77, and James D. Phillips, *Salem in the Eighteenth Century* (Salem, Mass.: Essex Institute, 1969), pp. 370–71.

18. Marston, op. cit., p. 51.

19. There were British soldiers on ships—off Norfolk, Virginia, for example—but, save for Boston, none on land until Canada in the North and British East Florida in the South.

20. Terry W. Lipscomb, *The Carolina Lowcountry, April 1775 to June 1776* (Columbia: South Carolina Department of Archives and History, 1994), p. 17.

21. Jeffrey Dorwart, *Fort Mifflin of Philadelphia* (Philadelphia: University of Pennsylvania Press, 1998), pp. xii and 18–25.

22. Edward G. Burrows and Mike Wallace, *Gotham* (New York: Oxford University Press, 1999), p. 225.

23. French, op. cit., p. 148.

24. Ibid., p. 598.

25. John A. Neuenschwander, *The Middle Colonies and the Coming of the American Revolution* (Port Washington, N.Y.: Kennikat Press, 1976), pp. 200–201.

26. The term dates to the 1800–1802 period, when Pennsylvania was labeled the "archstone of democratic politics," but the origins are not precise.

27. George Washington, *Writings from the Original Manuscript Sources,* ed. J. C. Fitzpatrick (Washington, D.C.: U.S. Government Printing Office, 1913–1941), vol. 6, pp. 397–98.

28. Thomas Fleming, *1776: Year of Illusions* (Edison, N.J.: Castle Books, 1996), pp. 431 and 36–37.

29. Joseph Ellis, *American Creation* (New York: Knopf, 2007), p. 20.

30. French, op. cit., p. 714.

31. Ibid.

32. Neuenschwander, op. cit., p. 46.

33. Sydney George Fisher, *The Struggle for American Independence* (Cranbury, N.J.: Scholar's Bookshelf, 2005), vol. 1, p. 230.

34. Lipscomb, op. cit., p. 6.

35. William Moultrie, *Memoirs of the American Revolution* (1802: reprint edn., New York: Arno Press, 1968), vol. 1, pp. 57–58.

36. William E. White, "The Independent Companies of Virginia," *Virginia Magazine of History and Biography* 86, no. 2 (April 1978), p. 155.

37. Royster, op. cit., pp. 25–27.

38. David Ammerman, *In the Common Cause* (New York: W. W. Norton, 1975), p. ix.

39. *A Bid for Liberty* (Philadelphia: William Penn Association, 1937), pp. 14–17.

40. *Naval Documents,* op. cit., vol. 1, p. 7.

41. Helen Augur, *The Secret War of American Independence* (Boston: Little, Brown, 1955), pp. 133–34.

42. Because several Massachusetts enterprises had produced muskets for earlier wars, the province's initial reaction was to favor local gunsmiths, but as the winter of 1774–1775 moved toward a fight, procuring the weapons became paramount.

43. Augur, op. cit., pp. 17–18.

44. Ibid., p. ix.

45. *Naval Documents,* op. cit., vol. 1, pp. 44–45.
46. David H. Fischer, *Paul Revere's Ride* (New York: Oxford University Press, 1994), p. 51.
47. Allen French, *General Gage's Informers* (Cranbury, N.J.: Scholar's Bookshelf, 2005), pp. 10–33.
48. *Naval Documents,* vol. 1, pp. 388–461.
49. Ibid., p. 53.
50. Lipscomb, op. cit., pp. 3–10.
51. Ibid., p. 10.
52. Fischer, op. cit., p. 43.

Chapter 2: Liberty's Vanguard

1. Robert L. Scribner, ed., *Revolutionary Virginia: The Road to Independence* (Charlottesville: University of Virginia Press, 1975), vol. 1, pp. 79–84.
2. Neuenschwander, op. cit., pp. 36–37.
3. Catherine Drinker Bowen, *John Adams and the American Revolution* (Boston: Little, Brown, 1950), pp. 479–80.
4. Neuenschwander, op. cit., p. 9.
5. Alan Tully, *Forming American Politics* (Baltimore: Johns Hopkins University Press, 1994), p. 311.
6. Neuenschwander, op. cit., pp. 66–67.
7. Tully, op. cit., p. 420.
8. Neuenschwander, op. cit., p. 13.
9. Bruce Bliven, *Under the Guns* (New York: Harper & Row, 1972), p. 9.
10. Neuenschwander, op. cit., pp. 207, 160.
11. Wallace Brown, *The Good Americans* (New York: William Morrow & Co., 1969), p. 60.
12. Neuenschwander, op. cit., p. 194.
13. Ibid., pp. 20–21.
14. Ibid., pp. 77, 105, 119, 123.
15. See in particular William H. Nelson, *The American Tory* (Boston: Northeastern University Press, 1992), pp. 21–23.
16. The fullest portrait of the five Virginia conventions can be found in *Revolutionary Virginia: The Road to Independence,* vols. 1–6, compiled for the Virginia Bicentennial Commission and published by the University of Virginia Press in 1975.
17. Walter Edgar, *South Carolina: A History* (Columbia: University of South Carolina Press, 1998), pp. 218–19.
18. Ibid., p. 219.
19. Terry Lipscomb, *South Carolina Becomes a State* (Columbia: South Carolina Department of Archives and History, 1976), pp. 6–14.
20. South Carolina claims are plausible, but there appear to be no records.
21. Harold E. Selesky, *War and Society in Colonial Connecticut* (New Haven: Yale University Press, 1990), p. 227.
22. Richard Buel, Jr., *Dear Liberty* (Middletown, Conn.: Wesleyan University Press, 1980), p. 4.
23. David S. Lovejoy, *Rhode Island Politics and the American Revolution* (Providence: Brown University Press, 1958), pp. 179–83.
24. Ammerman, op. cit., pp. 21–22.
25. As tensions rose in New England during the 1760s, so did British and Tory discussion of abrogating the Massachusetts, Connecticut, and Rhode Island charters. During the winter of 1774–1775, after elements of the Massachusetts Charter of 1691 had been set aside by the Coercive Acts, British government attention refocused on the other two. According to Peter D. G. Thomas in *Tea Party to Independence, the Third Phase of the American Revolution, 1773–1776,* "one possible move was to declare forfeit the charters

of Rhode Island and Connecticut, whose popular institutions of government were deemed a factor in their defiance of Britain" (p. 217). General Gage privately agreed, and Anglicans in Rhode Island had begun urging an end to the charter in the 1760s.

26. Buel, op. cit., p. 30.

27. Oscar Zeichner, *Connecticut's Years of Controversy* (Williamsburg, Va.: University of North Carolina Press, 1949), p. 188.

28. Buel, op. cit., p. 31.

29. Zeichner, op. cit., pp. 191, 196; Buel, op. cit., p. 38.

30. See, for example, Buel, op. cit., pp. 42–80, and Bliven, op. cit., pp. 61–126.

31. Buel, op. cit., pp. 43-44.

32. See Chester M. Destler, *Connecticut: The Provisions State* (Chester, Conn.: Pequot Press, 1973).

33. David M. Roth, *Connecticut's War Governor: Jonathan Trumbull* (Chester, Conn.: Pequot Press, 1974), pp. 10, 14–15, 20, and 72–75.

34. Charles Kingsley's 1855 novel *Westward Ho!*, set in the sixteenth-century North Devon of Drake and Hawkins, Gilbert and Raleigh, painted an English spirit that had already taken the "westward enterprise" across Wales and Ireland to America and was farther questing for the Northwest Passage. The English Americans in the vanguard colonies were only continuing that spirit in their own drive toward the Pacific.

35. Because Connecticut's 1662 charter granted territory westward to the Pacific, it was at odds with a 1664 royal patent extending New York territory east to the Connecticut River. A preliminary compromise was worked out under a 1683 boundary agreement in which Connecticut did well, but a handful of Yankee-settled towns from Rye north to Bedford and Brewster wound up in New York's Westchester County. Disputes continued, as several books document. See, for example, Philip J. Schwarz, *The Jarring Interests: New York's Boundary Makers, 1664 to 1776* (1979) and Clarence Bowen, *The Boundary Disputes of Connecticut* (1882).

36. Three of the five men selected as delegates to the First Continental Congress came from Essex County, and after the Congress adjourned, Essex spearheaded the implementation of the Continental Association in New Jersey. Neuenschwander, op. cit., pp. 39, 58.

37. Marc Egnal, *A Mighty Empire* (Ithaca, N.Y.: Cornell University Press, 1988), p. 282.

38. Glenn Weaver, *Jonathan Trumbull* (Hartford: Connecticut Historical Society, 1956), p. 109.

39. Tercentenary Commission of the State of Connecticut, *Migrations from Connecticut Prior to 1800* (New Haven: Yale University Press, 1934), p. 19.

40. Neuenschwander, op. cit., p. 196.

41. Stewart Holbrook, *Ethan Allen* (Portland, Ore.: Binford & Mort, 1988), p. 133.

42. Richard T. Warfle, *Connecticut's Western Colony: The Susquehannah Affair* (Hartford, Conn.: American Revolution Bicentennial Commission, 1979), pp. 32–40.

43. Thomas Abernethy, *Western Lands and the American Revolution* (New York: Russell & Russell, 1959), p. 2.

44. For Virginia's list of land companies, see ibid., pp. 1–145.

45. Joel Aschenbach, *The Grand Idea: George Washington's Potomac and the Race to the West* (New York: Simon & Schuster, 2004), pp. 123–24, 41–42.

46. Thomas J. Wertenbaker, *Torchbearer of the Revolution* (Princeton: Princeton University Press, 1940), p. 211.

47. Edgar, op. cit., pp. 1-3, 39.

48. Ibid., pp. 36–49, 83–85; George C. Rogers, Jr., *Charleston in the Age of the Pinckneys* (Columbia: University of South Carolina Press, 1980), p. 4.

49. Edgar, op. cit., p. 37.

50. Alice Hanson Jones, *Wealth of a Nation to Be: The American Colonies on the Eve of Revolution* (New York: Columbia University Press, 1980), pp. 10, 170–71, and 377–79), cited by Edgar, op. cit., p. 152.

51. George Frakes, *Laboratory for Liberty* (Lexington: University Press of Kentucky, 1970), p. 10.

52. Ibid., pp. 88–89.

53. William Dabney and Marion Dargan, *William Henry Drayton and the American Revolution* (Albuquerque: University of New Mexico Press, 1962), p. 82.

54. Ibid., p. 130–31.

55. Joanne Calhoun, *The Circular Church: Three Centuries of Charleston History* (Charleston, S.C.: History Press, 2008), pp. 138–71.

56. Dabney and Dargan, op. cit., p. 15.

Chapter 3: Religion, Ethnicity, and Revolutionary Loyalty

1. John Rogasta, *Wellspring of Liberty* (New York: Oxford University Press, 2010), pp. 87–107.

2. Henry S. Commager and Richard Morris, *The Spirit of Seventy-six* (New York: Harper & Row, 1967), p. 267.

3. Brendan Simms, *Three Victories and a Defeat* (New York: Basic Books, 2007), pp. 595–96.

4. Ibid., pp. 341–42, 417–18.

5. George O. Trevelyan, *The American Revolution* (Cranbury, N.J.: Scholar's Bookshelf, 2006), vol. 1, p. 50.

6. Bernard Bailyn and Philip Morgan, eds., *Strangers Within the Realm* (Chapel Hill: University of North Carolina Press, 1991), p. 310.

7. Charles Glatfelter, *Pastors and People* (Breinigsville: Pennsylvania German Society, 1980), p. 310.

8. Pauline Maier, *American Scripture* (New York: Knopf, 1997), pp. 140, 240–41.

9. Paul A. Wallace, *The Muhlenbergs of Pennsylvania* (Philadelphia: University of Pennsylvania Press, 1950), p. 107.

10. For a slightly different set of estimates, see Bailyn and Morgan, op cit., p. 244.

11. Wallace, op. cit., pp. 110–13.

12. Ibid., pp. 116–18.

13. Patricia Bonomi, *Under the Cope of Heaven* (New York: Oxford University Press, 1986), p.187.

14. See, for example, Alan Heimert, *Religion in the American Mind* (Cambridge, Mass.: Harvard University Press, 1966), and Nathan O. Hatch, *The Democratization of American Christianity* (New Haven: Yale University Press, 1989), and for an overview, Mark A. Noll, *The Rise of Evangelicalism* (Downers Grove, Ill.: InterVarsity Press, 2003).

15. William G. McLoughlin, *Revivals, Awakenings, and Reform* (Chicago: University of Chicago Press, 1978), p. xiv.

16. Ruth Bloch, "Religion and Ideological Change in the American Revolution," in Mark A. Noll, ed., *Religion and American Politics* (New York: Oxford University Press, 1990), p. 53.

17. Martin Marty, *Righteous Empire: The Protestant Experience in America* (New York: Dial Press, 1970), pp. 16–17.

18. Ibid., p. 49.

19. Bonomi, op. cit., p. 9.

20. Odd as it may seem initially, there was a huge difference between Anglicans in Virginia and South Carolina and those from Connecticut, New York, and New Jersey. The former had dominated their colonies for a century, were doctrinally easygoing and low-church, strongly opposed the notion of bishops being sent from England, and in 1775 solid majorities favored Patriot politics and the Revolution. The Anglican 10 percent of the churchgoing populations in western Connecticut, New York, and New Jersey, by contrast, represented a later-eighteenth-century growth pattern and an assertive politics. In New York, Anglicanism was established in four counties—New York, Queens, Rich-

mond, and Westchester—and its clergy were closely allied with royal governors. Since the 1760s, the Anglican clergy in the three provinces, most of them royalist and high church in sentiment, had been been working with one another and with the London-based Society for the Propagation of the Gospel (SPG) to persuade the British government to send bishops to promote the Church of England in America. This put them strongly at odds with the Congregationalists in Connecticut and the Presbyterians in New York and New Jersey who led local Revolutionary sentiment. Precise measurements do not exist, but one analysis found that in Pennsylvania, New Jersey, New York, and Connecticut, 52 Anglican clergymen were Loyalists while only three were Patriots. Another fourteen were neutrals. Nancy L. Rhoden, *Revolutionary Anglicanism: The Colonial Church of England Clergy During the American Revolution* (New York: New York University Press, 1999), p. 89. As for their parishioners, among rank-and-file Anglicans in New Jersey, New York, and Connecticut, Loyalists probably outnumbered Patriots by three to one. Pennsylvania was something of a transition zone, where a significant Anglican minority (probably 25 to 35 percent) took the Patriot side.

21. Randall Balmer, *A Perfect Babel of Confusion* (New York: Oxford University Press, 1989), pp. 119–20 and 137–43.

22. Bonomi, op. cit., p. 175; Alan W. Tully, "Ethnicity, Religion, and Politics in Early America," *Pennsylvania Magazine of History and Biography,* vol. CVII, 1983, pp. 503–4.

23. James B. Bell, *A War of Religion: Dissenters, Anglicans and the American Revolution* (London: Palgrave Macmillan, 2008), p. 76.

24. There is no need to debate whether New York and Pennsylvania circa 1775 were already gestating America's first political parties. The question here is more confined: were ethnicity and religion emerging as the leading shapers of politics and Patriot versus Loyalist loyalties in the thirteen colonies? Evidence seems especially strong in New York, New Jersey, and Pennsylvania, which had higher ratios of non-British inhabitants than the other ten colonies, as well as eleven to fifteen religious denominations. This pluralism, far from muting cultural differences, stimulated an active politics aimed at both self-protection and aggrandizement. Benjamin H. Newcomb, *Political Partisanship in the American Middle Colonies, 1700–1776* (Baton Rouge: Louisiana State University Press, 1995), p. 4. Politics took further religious coloration during the quarter century before the Revolution by controversies over Quaker domination in Pennsylvania, and in New York by resentment of the favoritism to Anglicans based on the Anglican church's four-county establishment. Alan Tully, *Forming American Politics: Ideals, Interests and Institutions in Colonial New York and Pennsylvania* (Baltimore: Johns Hopkins, 1994), p. 424. Between 1769 and 1772, imperial issues played a growing role, which intensified religious divisions because both the Pennsylvania Quakers and the New York Anglicans were unable to manage or straddle this agenda, and by 1775 new alignments were taking shape, pushing a new credo to the fore. Presbyterians were the leading denomination in Pennsylvania, New Jersey, and New York, accounting for 20 to 30 percent of the churchgoing population, and they dominated the early Revolution in all three provinces. Charles Inglis, a Loyalist Anglican rector in New York, stated that he did not know a single Presbyterian minister in the synod of New York and Philadelphia who was not an active Whig. Leonard J. Kramer, "Muskets in the Pulpit," *Journal of Presbyterian History 31,* December 1953, p. 231. Anglicans and Quakers were the biggest losers. One study offering an ethnic-religious interpretation of the Revolution in Pennsylvania captured the 1775–1777 upheaval: "Before the separation from England, the Quakers and Anglicans controlled 63% of the seats in the Assembly. Fifteen months after the Declaration of Independence, Presbyterians, [German] Reformed and Lutherans controlled over 90% of the seats in the Assembly . . ." Wayne L. Bockelman and Owen S. Ireland, "The Internal Revolution in Pennsylvania: An Ethnic-Religious Interpretation," *Pennsylvania Magazine of History and Biography 41,* April 1974, p. 149.

25. Richard W. Pointer, *Protestant Pluralism and the New York Experience* (Indianapolis: Indiana University Press, 1988), pp. 54–62.

26. John F. Woolverton, *Colonial Anglicanism* (Detroit: Wayne State University Press, 1984), pp. 15, 18, and 37.

27. Bell, op. cit., pp. 26 and 118.

28. Bonomi, op. cit., p.170.

29. Ibid., pp. 49 and 218.

30. Woolverton, op. cit., p. 232.

31. Bonomi, op. cit., p. 210.

32. In Maryland, North Carolina, and Georgia, Anglican clerics were not as likely to support the Revolution as the Patriot-minded Anglican clergy of Virginia and South Carolina. Vestries did not match those in Virginia, and other local considerations created more Loyalist sentiment. In Maryland, for example, the proprietary Calvert family had a role in clergy selection. In any event, one tabulation is as follows: Maryland, 24 Loyalists and 22 Patriots; North Carolina, eight Loyalists and seven Patriots; and Georgia, three Loyalists and no Patriots. James B. Bell, *A War of Religion: Dissenters, Anglicans, and the American Revolution* (Basingstoke, England: Palgrave Macmillan, 2008), pp. 232, 238, 240.

33. Woolverton, op. cit., p. 123.

34. Bonomi, op. cit., p. 201.

35. Woolverton, op. cit., p. 29.

36. Pointer, op. cit., p. 25.

37. Carl Bridenbaugh, *Mitre and Sceptre* (New York: Oxford University Press, 1962), p. 221.

38. Ibid., pp. 233, 234, and 236.

39. Ibid., pp. 246–47 and 256–57.

40. Bonomi, pp. 206–7.

41. Bridenbaugh, op. cit., p. 20; Bonomi, op. cit., p. 199.

42. Bonomi, op. cit., pp. 187, 172.

43. Ibid., pp. 202–3.

44. Bell, op. cit., p. 167.

45. Ibid., pp. 146–47.

46. Ibid., p. 166.

47. Ibid., pp. 162–164.

48. Bonomi, op. cit., p. 96.

49. Bell, op. cit., p. 42.

50. Bonomi, op. cit., pp. 191–94.

51. Bell, op cit., p. 78.

52. Bloch, op. cit., p. 52.

53. Ibid., p. 49.

54. Simms, op. cit., p. 583.

55. Ibid., p. 584.

Chapter 4: A Revolution for Economic Self-Determination

1. Linda Colley, *Britons* (New Haven: Yale University Press, 1992), pp. 1–9.

2. David S. Lovejoy, *Rhode Island Politics and the American Revolution, 1760–1776* (Providence, R.I.: Brown University Press, 1958), pp. 36–37.

3. Arthur M. Schlesinger, op. cit., pp. 607–13.

4. Woody Holton, *Forced Founders* (Chapel Hill: University of North Carolina Press, 1999), p. 9.

5. Erna Risch, *Supplying Washington's Army* (Washington, D.C.: Center of U.S. Military History, 1981), p.335.

6. Jack P. Greene and J. R. Pole, eds., *Blackwell Encyclopedia of the American Revolution* (Oxford, U.K.: Blackwell Publishers, 1994), p. 59.

7. Jack P. Greene, *The Quest for Power* (Chapel Hill: University of North Carolina Press, 1963), pp. 108–109.

8. Virginia Harrington, *The New York Merchant on the Eve of the Revolution* (New York: Columbia University Press, 1935), p. 106.

9. John McCusker and Russell Menard, *The Economy of British America, 1607–1789* (Chapel Hill: University of North Carolina Press, 1991), p. 239.

10. Eric Robson, *The American Revolution* (London: Batchworth Press, 1955), p. 7.

11. Jason Goodwin, *Greenback* (New York: Henry Holt. 2003), pp. 60–61.

12. Harrington, op. cit., p. 11.

13. T. H. Breen, *The Marketplace of Revolution* (New York: Oxford University Press, 2004), p. 120.

14. Holton, op. cit., p. 55.

15. Jack P. Greene and Richard M. Jellison, "The Currency Act of 1764 in Imperial-Colonial Relations, 1764-1776," *William and Mary Quarterly,* 3rd sers., 18, no. 4, October 1961.

16. Joseph A. Ernst, *Money and Politics in America, 1755–1775* (Chapel Hill: University of North Carolina Press, 1973), pp. 252–55.

17. Marjolene Kars, *Breaking Loose Together* (Chapel Hill: Omohundro Institute/University of North Carolina Press, 2002), p. 67.

18. Merrill Jensen, *The Founding of a Nation, 1763–1776* (New York: Oxford University Press, 1968), pp. 379–80.

19. Ibid., pp. 52–55.

20. Curtis Nettels, *The Emergence of a National Economy, 1775–1815* (New York: Harper Torchbooks, 1962), p. 23.

21. McCusker and Menard, op. cit., pp. 338–41.

22. Greene and Jellison, op. cit.

23. Knollenberg, op. cit., p. 19.

24. Ernst, op. cit., p. 101; Ammerman, op. cit., pp. 66–68.

25. McCusker and Menard, op. cit., pp. 355–56.

26. Greene and Tellison, op. cit., p. 517.

27. Leslie V. Brock, *The Currency of the American Colonies, 1700-1764* (New York: Arno Press, 1975), p. 560.

28. Conrad Edik and Kathryn Viens, eds., *Entrepreneurs* (Boston: Massachusetts Historical Society, 1997), p. 1.

29. Margaret Newell, *From Dependency to Independence: Economic Revolution in Colonial America* (Ithaca, N.Y.: Cornell University Press, 1998), p. 235.

30. Greene and Jellison, op. cit., pp. 486–87.

31. A. Roger Ekirch, *"Poor Carolina": Politics and Society in Colonial North Carolina* (Chapel Hill: University of North Carolina Press, 1981), p. 10.

32. Ernst, op. cit., pp. 30–31.

33. Greene and Jellison, op. cit., p. 518.

34. Ernst, op. cit., p. 370.

35. Michael A. McDonnell, *The Politics of War* (Chapel Hill: Omohundro Insitute/University of North Carolina Press, 2007), p. 33. McDonnell's estimate synthesized the views of Lawrence Gipson, T. H. Breen, and Woody Holton.

36. T. H. Breen, *Tobacco Culture* (Princeton: Princeton University Press, 1985), p. 128.

37. J. F. Shepherd and G. M. Walton, *Shipping, Maritime Trade and the Economic Development of Colonial North America* (Cambridge, England: Cambridge Press, 1972), p. 132.

38. Ronald Hoffman, *A Spirit of Dissension: Economics, Politics, and the Revolution in Maryland* (Baltimore: Johns Hopkins University Press, 1973), p. 20.

39. Zeichner, op. cit., p. 82.

40. Russell Menard, "The South Carolina Low Country," in Ronald Hoffman, John J. McCusker, Russell B. Menard, and Peter J. Albert, eds., *The Economy of Early America* (Charlottesville: University of Virginia Press, 1988), pp. 258–59.

41. Ekirch, op. cit., p. 18.

42. Robson, op. cit., p. 42; John C. Miller, *Origins of the American Revolution* (Boston: Little, Brown, 1943), p. 15.

43. J. H. Plumb, *England in the 18th Century* (Harmondsworth, U.K.: Penguin, 1966), p. 126.

44. Breen, *Marketplace of Revolution,* op. cit., pp. 241–42.

45. Ibid., p. 20.

46. Miller, op. cit., p. 16.

47. Breen, *Marketplace of Revolution,* op. cit., pp. 42–43 and 100.

48. Ibid., p. 255.

49. Ibid., p. 326.

50. David M. Roth and Freeman Meyer, *From Revolution to Constitution: Connecticut 1763 to 1818* (Chester, Conn.: Pequot Press, 1975), pp. 8–15.

51. Zeichner, op. cit., pp. 78–81; Mann, op. cit., pp. 60–67.

52. Holton, op. cit., pp. 64–65.

53. Ibid., pp. 61, 39, 64–65, and 216–17; Isaac Samuel Harrell, *Loyalism in Virginia* (Durham, N.C.: Duke University Press, 1926), pp. 26–27.

54. Hoffman, *Spirit of Dissension,* op. cit., pp. 129, 138, 143, and 149.

55. Greene, *Quest for Power,* op. cit., pp. 420–24.

56. Oliver Dickerson. *The Navigation Acts and the American Revolution* (New York: A.S. Barnes, 1963), p. 112.

57. Holton, op. cit., p. 48.

58. Miller, *Origins,* op. cit., p. 14.

59. Holton, op. cit., pp. 49–58.

60. Hoffman, *Spirit of Dissension,* op. cit., pp. 30–31.

61. Miller, *Origins,* op. cit., pp. 14–16.

62. Nancy F. Koehn, *The Power of Commerce* (Ithaca, N.Y.: Cornell University Press, 1994), pp. 101–2.

63. Brown, *Good Americans,* op. cit., pp. 6–7; Holton, op. cit., p. 52.

64. Thomas Barrow, *Trade and Empire: The British Customs Service in Colonial America, 1660-1775* (Cambridge, Mass.: Harvard University Press, 1967), p. 256.

65. Oliver Dickerson, op. cit., p. 169.

66. Lawrence Gipson, *The Coming of the American Revolution* (New York: Harper Torchbooks, 1962), p. 62.

67. Lovejoy, op. cit., pp. 31–32.

68. Dickerson, op. cit., pp. 179–84.

69. Ibid., pp. 182–83, 214–15.

70. Ibid., p. 210, 224–49.

71. Barrow, *Trade and Empire,* op. cit., pp. 175–80.

72. Ibid., p. 176.

73. Ibid., p. 180.

74. Robert M. Weir, *Colonial South Carolina* (Columbia: University of South Carolina Press, 1997), p. 163.

75. Lovejoy, *Rhode Island,* op. cit., p. 19.

76. Ibid., p. 33.

77. Barrow, op. cit., pp. 247–48.

78. William Nelson, *The American Tory* (Boston: Northeastern University Press, 1992), p. 4; Kars, op. cit., p. 40.

79. Brown, *Good Americans,* op. cit., p. 240.

80. Robert A. East, *Connecticut's Loyalists* (Chester, Conn.: Pequot Press, 1974), p. 20.

81. Raphael, op. cit., pp. 14–20.

82. Jonathan Powell, "Presbyterian Loyalists: A 'Chain of Interest' in Philadelphia," *Journal of Presbyterian History* 57 (1979), pp. 135–58.
83. Holton, op. cit., pp. 3, 29–33.
84. Harrell, op. cit., p. 180.
85. Mann, op cit., pp. 130–31 and 137.
86. Schlesinger, op. cit., pp. 16–49.
87. John W. Tyler, *Smugglers and Patriots* (Boston: Northeastern University Press, 1980), pp. 241–42.
88. Harrington, op. cit., pp. 348–51.
89. Thomas M. Doerflinger, *A Vigorous Spirit of Enterprise: Merchants and Economic Development in Revolutionary Pennsylvania* (Chapel Hill: University of North Carolina Press, 1986).
90. Thomas M. Doerflinger, "Philadelphia Merchants and the Logic of Moderation, 1760–1775," *William and Mary Quarterly,* 3rd ser., 40, no. 2 (April 1983), pp. 214–17.
91. Ibid., p. 217.
92. Tyler, op. cit., pp. 245–46.
93. Ibid., pp. 249–50; Doerflinger, *Vigorous Spirit,* op. cit., pp. 192–93.
94. Tyler, op. cit., pp. 18, 248.
95. Harrell, op. cit., p. 49.
96. Hoffman, op. cit., p. 165.
97. Miller, op. cit., p. 17.
98. Robert O. DeMond, *The Loyalists in North Carolina During the Revolution* (Hamden, Conn.: Archon, 1964), p. 52.
99. Breen, *Tobacco Culture,* op. cit., p. 200.
100. C. Robert Heywood, "Mercantilism and South Carolina Agriculture," *South Carolina Historical Magazine* 60 (1959), p. 20.
101. Weir, op. cit., pp. 211 and 146.
102. Laura H. McEachern and Isabel M. Williams, eds., *Wilmington-New Hanover Safety Committee Meetings 1774–1776* (Wilmington, N.C.: Wilmington-New Hanover County American Revolution Bicentennial Committees, 1974), p. 38.
103. Joseph J. Malone, *Pine Trees and Politics* (Seattle: University of Washington Press, 1964), p. 54.
104. Ibid., pp. 141–43.
105. Edward Byers, *The Nation of Nantucket* (St. Petersburg, Fla.: Hailer Publishing, 1987), pp. 142, 144.
106. Arthur Bining, *Pennsylvania Iron Manufacturing in the 18th Century* (Harrisburg: Pennsylvania Historical and Museum Commission, 1987), p. 136.
107. Ibid., p. 140.
108. Ibid., p. 122.
109. Hoffman, op. cit., p. 34.
110. Bining, op. cit., p. 137.
111. Edward Countryman, "The Uses of Capital in Revolutionary America," *William and Mary Quarterly,* 3rd series, vol. 49, no. 1 (1992), p. 26.

Chapter 5: Urban Radicalism and the Tide of Revolution

1. Adapted for *1775* from Benjamin Carp, *Rebels Rising: Cities and the American Revolution* (New York: Oxford University Press, 2007), p. 225.
2. Jack P. Greene and J. R. Pole, *Colonial British America* (Baltimore: Johns Hopkins University Press, 1984), pp. 27–29.
3. Carl Bridenbaugh, *Cities in Revolt* (New York: Knopf, 1968), pp. 216–17.
4. Because no British census was taken until 1801, these are estimates, by no means agreed upon, taken from volumes ranging from encyclopedias to G.D.H. Cole and Raymond Postgate, *The British Common People, 1746–1946* (London: University

Paperbacks, 1961), p. 26, to Paul Langford, *A Polite and Commercial People, England 1727–1783* (Oxford: Oxford University Press, 1989), pp. 418–20.

5. John Phillips, *Electoral Behavior in Unreformed England* (Princeton: Princeton University Press, 1982), p. 120.

6. Alfred Young, "English Plebeian Culture," in Margaret R. and James C. Jacob, *The Origins of Anglo-American Radicalism* (Atlantic Highlands, N.J.: Humanities Press International, 1991), pp. 188–89.

7. Nash, *Urban Crucible,* op. cit., p. xii.

8. Paul A. Gilje, *Liberty on the Waterfront* (Philadelphia: University of Pennsylvanaia Press, 2004), p. 103.

9. Young, op. cit., p. 193.

10. Russell Bourne, *Cradle of Violence* (Hoboken, N.J.: John Wiley & Sons, 2006), p. 142. He attributes the description to Benjamin Irvin.

11. Ibid., p. 205.

12. Ibid., chap. 5, "The Sailors' Liberty Tree."

13. Jesse Lemisch, *Jack Tar vs. John Bull* (New York: Garland Publishing, 1997), pp. 125–33.

14. Burrows and Wallace, op. cit., p. 211.

15. Jesse Lemisch, "Jack Tar in the Streets," *William and Mary Quarterly,* 3rd ser. (July 1968), p. 400.

16. Gilje, op. cit., pp. 99–100.

17. Bourne, op. cit., pp. 153–63.

18. Gilje, op. cit., p. 102.

19. Bourne, op. cit., p. 79.

20. Carp, op. cit., pp. 28–32.

21. Gary Nash, *The Unknown American Revolution* (New York: Viking Penguin, 2005), p. 24.

22. Burrows and Wallace, op. cit., p. 215.

23. Walter J. Fraser, *Patriots, Pistols and Petticoats* (Columbia: University of South Carolina Press, 1993), pp. 55–57.

24. Bourne, op. cit., pp. 182–98.

25. Peter Linebaugh and Marcus Rediker, *The Many-Headed Hydra* (Boston: Beacon Press, 2000), pp. 115–16 and 230.

26. Ibid, p. 232.

27. Doerflinger, op. cit., p. 174.

28. Nash, *Urban Crucible,* op. cit., p. 150.

29. Fraser, op. cit., p. 2.

30. Weir, *Colonial South Carolina,* op. cit., p. 170–71.

31. Lemisch, *Jack Tar in the Streets,* op. cit., p. 397.

32. For further analysis in this vein, see Linebaugh and Rediker, op. cit., p. 156.

33. Ibid.

34. Ibid., p. 219.

35. Ibid., pp. 220–21, 241.

36. Ibid., p. 151.

37. Bourne, op. cit., pp. 64–71.

38. Burrows and Wallace, op. cit., pp. 182, 193.

39. Dickerson, op. cit., pp. 212–15.

40. Linebaugh and Rediker, op. cit., p. 219.

41. Ronald Schultz, *The Republic of Labor: Philadelphia Artisans and the Politics of Class, 1720–1830* (New York: Oxford University Press, 1993).

42. Burrows and Wallace, op. cit., p. 199.

43. Ibid., p. 216.

44. Countryman, *People in Revolution,* op. cit., p. 164.

45. Nash, *Urban Crucible,* op. cit., pp. 76–79, 110, 162.

46. Koehn, op. cit., p. 27.
47. Charles S. Olton, *Artisans for Independence* (Syracuse, N.Y.: Syracuse University Press, 1975), p. 2.
48. Bridenbaugh, *Cities in Revolt,* op. cit., pp. 268–69.
49. Gary Nash, *Race, Class and Politics* (Chicago: University of Illinois Press, 1986), p. 243; Bridenbaugh, *Cities in Revolt,* op. cit., p. 272; Olton, op. cit., p. 122; and Sharon V. Salinger, "Artisans, Journeymen and the Transformation of Labor in Late 18th Century Philadelphia," *William and Mary Quarterly,* 3rd ser., 40, no. 1 (January 1983), p. 67.
50. Bridenbaugh, *Cities in Revolt,* op. cit, p. 272.
51. Walsh, Rogers, and Fraser, op cit., pp. qx–x, 73–74, and 11–16.
52. Schultz, op. cit., p. 22.
53. Ibid., p. 39.
54. Ibid., p. 45.
55. Richard Alan Ryerson, *The Revolution Is Now Begun: The Radical Committees of Philadelphia, 1765–1766* (Philadelphia: University of Pennsylvania Press, 1978).
56. Ibid., p. 182–90.
57. Steven Rosswurm, *Arms, Country and Class* (New Brunswick, N.J.: Rutgers University Press, 1987), p. 251.
58. Ibid., p. 253.
59. Ryerson, op. cit., p. 112.
60. Ibid., pp. 112–15, 134–35.
61. Rosswurm, op. cit., p. 57.
62. For militia details in Virginia, see McDonnell, *Politics of War,* op. cit., pp. 92–102, 105–130. For Maryland, see Hoffman, *Spirit of Dissension,* op. cit., pp. 170–77.
63. This group includes, among others, Don Higginbotham, Walter Millis, Piers Mackesy, and John Shy, which is to say most of the major military historians who have written about the Revolutionary era.
64. Galvin, op. cit., p. xiii.
65. Higginbotham, op cit., p. 12.
66. Raphael, op cit., chap. 5; Galvin, p. xx.
67. Higginbotham, op. cit., p. 59.
68. Zeichner, op. cit., p. 179; Joan Nafic, *To the Beat of a Drum: A History of Norwich, Connecticut During the American Revolution* (Norwich, Conn.: Old Town Press, 1976), p. 51.
69. Buel, *Dear Liberty,* op cit., p. 166–67.
70. Seleskey, op. cit., pp. 166–67.
71. Ibid., pp. 225–26.
72. Roth, op cit., *Connecticut's War Governor,* pp. 33–34.
73. Ibid.; Zeichner, op. cit., pp. 183–209; Kwasny, op. cit., pp. 4–6.
74. Kwasny, op. cit., pp. 21–22.
75. Darrett B. Rutman, "The Virginia Company and Its Military Regime," in Rutman, ed., *The Old Dominion: Essays for Thomas Perkins Abernethy* (Charlottesville: University of Virginia Press, 1964), pp. 1–20.
76. Shy, *A People Numerous and Armed,* op. cit., p. 33.
77. Ibid., p. 35.
78. McDonnell, op. cit., pp. 78–160.
79. Frakes, op. cit., pp. 170–74.
80. Greene, *Quest for Power,* op. cit., p. 309.
81. James M. Johnson, *Militiamen, Rangers and Redcoats: The Military in Georgia 1754–1776* (Macon, Ga.: Mercer University Press, 1992), p. xiv.
82. J. Paul Selsam, *The Pennsylvania Constitution of 1776* (New York: Octagon Books, 1971), p. 22.
83. Nash, *Urban Crucible,* op. cit., p. 146; Selsam, op. cit., p. 25.

84. Ibid., pp. 169–70.
85. Ibid., p. 178; Selsam, op. cit., p. 41.
86. Selsam, op. cit., pp. 74–76.
87. Nash, *Urban Crucible*, op. cit., pp. 243–44.
88. C. H. Firth, *Cromwell's Army* (London: University Paperbacks, 1962), pp. 15–20.
89. McDonnell, op. cit., p. 92.
90. Higginbotham, op. cit., p. 10.
91. Shy, op. cit., p. 174.
92. Ibid., p. 175–76.
93. Piers Mackesy, "The Redcoat Revived," in William M. Fowler and Wallace Coyle, eds., *The American Revolution: Changing Perspectives* (Boston: Northeastern University Press, 1981), p. 182.
94. Ibid.
95. Kwasny, op. cit., p. xv.
96. Ibid., p. 330.
97. Mackesy, "Redcoat Revived," op. cit., p. 182; Millis, *Arms and Men,* pp. 34–35.
98. Shy, op. cit., p. 187.
99. Royster, op. cit., p. 10.
100. Kwasny, op. cit., pp. xi and 12.

Chapter 6: Challenge from the Backcountry

1. Bernard Bailyn, *Voyagers to the West* (New York: Random House, 1986), pp. 14, 15, and 36.
2. Jack Greene, "Independence, Improvement and Authority," in Ronald Hoffman, Thad W. Tate, and Peter J. Albert, eds., *An Uncivil War: The Southern Backcountry During the American Revolution* (Charlottesville: University of Virginia Press, 1985), pp. 3–4.
3. Grady McWhiney, in *Cracker Culture: Celtic Ways in the Old South* (Tuscaloosa: University of Alabama Press, 1988), traces the term and the culture back to eighteenth-century Celtic herdsmen. In 1766 a colonial official explained to Lord Dartmouth that Crackers were a "lawless set of rascals on the frontiers of Virginia, Maryland, the Carolinas and Georgia, who often change their place of abode." *Cracker Culture,* p. xiv.
4. Louis De Vorsey, Jr., *The Indian Boundary in the Southern Colonies* (Chapel Hill: University of North Carolina Press, 1966), pp. 90–92.
5. Ibid., p. 111.
6. Tom Hatley, *The Dividing Paths: Cherokees and South Carolinians Through the Revolutionary Era* (New York: Oxford University Press, 1995), pp. 204–15.
7. Ibid., p. 180–83.
8. Bailyn, *Voyagers,* op. cit., p. 36.
9. Ibid., pp. 30–32.
10. De Vorsey, op. cit., pp. 9–10
11. Michael Bellisles, *Revolutionary Outlaw* (Charlottesville: University of Virginia Press, 1993), pp. 146–47.
12. De Vorsey, op. cit., p. 81.
13. Robert D. Mitchell, "The Southern Colonial Backcountry," in David C. Crass, Steven D. Smith, Martha A. Zierden, and Richard D. Brooks, eds., *The Southern Colonial Backcountry: Interdisciplinary Perspectives* (Knoxville: University of Tennessee Press, 1998), p. 10.
14. Bailyn, *Voyagers,* op. cit., p. 3.
15. Richard J. Hooker, ed., *The Carolina Backcountry on the Eve of Revolution* (Chapel Hill: University of North Carolina Press, 1953).
16. Stephen Marini, *Radical Sects of Revolutionary New England* (Cambridge, Mass.: Harvard University Press, 1982), pp. 1–53 and 63–81.

17. Holton, op. cit., p. xxx.
18. Hatley, op. cit., p. 137.
19. L. W. Turner, op. cit., p. 11.
20. Bellesisles, op. cit., pp. 91–92.
21. Kars, op. cit., pp. 79–93.
22. Klein, op. cit., pp. 48–49; Hatley, op. cit., pp. 180–83.
23. See, for example, Hatley, op. cit., Klein, op. cit., and Jim Piecuch, *Three Peoples, One King* (Columbia: University of Souh Carolina Press, 2008).
24. Colin Campbell, *The Western Abenakis of Vermont, 1600-1800* (Norman: University of Oklahoma Press, 1990), p. 207.
25. James H. O'Donnell III, *Southern Indians in the American Revolution* (Knoxville: University of Tennessee Press, 1973), p. 18.
26. Piecuch, op. cit., p. 74.
27. Ibid., p. 54.
28. Hatley, op. cit., pp.141–45, 152–54.
29. Ibid., p. 189.
30. Ibid.
31. Ibid., p. 199.
32. Piecuch, op. cit., p. 70.
33. Edward J. Cashin, "Sowing the Wind," in Harvey Jackson and Phinzy Spalding, eds., in *Forty Years of Diversity: Essays on Colonial Georgia* (Athens: University of Georgia Press, 1984), pp. 243, 245.
34. O'Donnell, op. cit., p. 30.
35. Holton, op. cit., p. 14.
36. Lovejoy, *Religious Enthusiasm in the New World,* op. cit., pp. 215–22.
37. In Massachusetts, as in Virginia, Baptist leaders at odds with the province's dominant religious elite found it politic to come to terms. During the early 1770s, the priority of Bay Colony Baptists, led by Isaac Backus, perhaps 5 to 8 percent of all churchgoers, had been to oppose the Congregationalist state church and seek relief from paying local taxes that went to support it. After the fighting began in 1775, rank-and-file Baptists largely took the Patriot side, as did preacher Backus and the regional Warren Association, but they gained some of their demands for freedom of conscience and greater relief from taxation and certification laws. Marini, op. cit., p. 23. Official disestablishment of the Massachusetts Congregational Church took another half century.
38. Like Anglicanism in the southern backcountry, by the 1770s the Congregationalist establishment in southern New England could not provide ministers for many of the new towns in northern hills, to the benefit of Baptists and other radical sects who filled the gap, often with itinerants. In the future Vermont, Baptists and other sects sometimes took root under New York auspices, and Patriot Ethan Allen actually whipped one Baptist preacher holding office as a New York justice. A. M. Henessy, *Vermont Historical Gazetteer,* vol. I, Burlington, Vt., 1868, Arlington section. In New Hampshire, Anglicans were those most disposed to Loyalism, but Baptist neutralism has been well documented. In 1776, Baptists had only eleven parishes and five clergymen in the province. "Of the five Baptist ministers three signed the Association test and two opposed it. . . . Furthermore, in ten of the towns where Baptists predominated considerable numbers refused the [Patriot loyalty] Test." Richard F. Upton, *Revolutionary New Hampshire* (Hanover, N.H.: Dartmouth College Press, 1936), p. 61. According to another study, Baptists in New Hampshire "were lukewarm to the Revolution and to the Congregational leadership thereof because they saw a threat to their weak church in its battle for equality before the law." Charles B. Kinney, *Church and State in New Hampshire* (New York: Columbia University Teachers College, 1955), p. 84.
39. Bellesisles, op. cit., p. 260.

40. Wesley M. Gewehr, *The Great Awakening in Virginia, 1740–1790* (Gloucester, Mass.: Peter Smith, 1965), p. 117.

41. Kars, op. cit., pp. 180–85.

42. John W. Brinsfield, *Religion and Politics in Colonial South Carolina* (Easley, S.C.: Southern Historical Press, 1983), p. 150.

43. Gewehr, op. cit., p. 213.

44. As in Massachusetts, Virginia Baptists faced an immediate choice in 1775: Would they rally? On August 14, 1775, the General Association of Virginia Baptists petitioned the Virginia Convention to allow Baptist ministers to preach to those of their brethren who were enlisting. However, at that same meeting, papers were prepared for circulation at churches stating that while the colony was contending against Britain, Baptists should maintain strong unanimity among themselves and petition for all religious privileges previously denied them. William Parks, "Religion and the Revolution in Virginia," in Richard Rutyna and Peter Stewart, eds., *Virginia in the American Revolution: A Collection of Essays,* Vol. I (Norfolk, Va.: Old Dominion University Press, 1977), p. 50. Regimental and battalion chaplains were provided for by the convention in several 1775 resolutions, but in some cases, Baptist ministers did not serve as chaplains but as company commanders. Preacher William McClanahan became captain of the Culpeper Minute Battalion in the summer of 1776. William J. Terman, *The American Revolution and the Baptist and Presbyterian Clergy of Virginia* (Michigan State University: doctoral dissertation, 1974), pp. 176–177.

45. Candor has become less common in recent decades. However, from the 1930s through the 1970s, Southern Baptist publications and scholars were reasonably forthright in discussing some of the dubious patriotism, leadership, and unacceptable behavior of Separate Baptists in the Carolinas between the 1760s and the period a quarter century later when mergers of Regular and Separate Baptists subdued the latter's behavior and Baptists in general took on more middle-class characteristics. Mercer University's *Baptist* series included a biography of early Baptist stalwart Richard Furman that discussed how Revolutionary-era differences between "emotionally rowdy" Separates and "deliberately restrained" Regulars kept the two at odds. In that same account, Baptist leader and historian Morgan Edwards, who played down Separate deviations, was dismissed as "an Englishman and a Tory whose British sympathies during the War for Independence so discredited his reputation among Baptist leaders that the records of the Philadelphia Association, in which he had once been a central and commanding figure, contain no reference to his plans for a general chartered organization of Baptists." James A. Rogers, *Richard Furman* (Macon, Ga.: Mercer University Press [reprint], 2001), pp. xxxiii, 169–70).

46. This is a difficult subject. Over the last few decades, Methodist historians have been more willing to discuss the disloyalty charges made against Methodists in Maryland between 1776 and 1779. Similarly, a book published in the bicentennial year by the Reformed Church in America included a chapter acknowledging the fact that a large minority of Dutch Reformed Church adherents in New York and New Jersey had been Tories or neutrals: James Van Hoeven, ed., *Piety and Patriotism* (Grand Rapids, Mich.: W. B. Eerdmans, 1976), pp. 17–33.

47. David A. Benedict, *A General History of the Baptist Denomination in America and Other Parts of the World* (Boston: Manning and Loring, 1813), vol. 2, p. 29, quoted in Rogers, *Richard Furman,* op. cit., p. 14.

48. Kars, op. cit., p. 112.

49. Ibid., pp. 128–29.

50. Ibid., pp. 86–93.

51. Leah Townsend, *South Carolina Baptists* (Florence, S.C.: Florence Printing Co., 1935), pp. 122–75.

52. Hooker, ed., op. cit., pp. 112–13; Townsend, op. cit., pp. 123–24.

53. Townsend, op. cit., p. 125.

54. J. F. McGregor and B. Reay, eds., *Radical Religion in the English Revolution* (Oxford: Oxford University Press, 1984), pp. 199–201.

55. Historians agree that very few records of Separate Baptist churches in the South Carolina backcountry survived the war. Neither did many of their buildings or congregations. Most of the latter do not seem to have put themselves back together until the late 1780s or 1790s. Considerable detail on the churches and their chronological gaps can be found in Leah Townsend, *South Carolina Baptists* (Florence, S.C.: 1935), chapters 4–5. In consequence, no profile can be compiled of these churches' antinomian characteristics during the 1760s and 1770s. When the congregations did reconstitute, Townsend noted (p. 180), "regularization was so rapid as associations gathered in the groups that the names Separate and Regular disappeared and only Baptists remained." She added that "some of the old Separate Baptist meeting houses were in or near the scene of many [Revolutionary skirmishes]" and a curator of the South Carolina Baptist Historical Society concluded that "Baptist ranks were split between Patriots and Tories, the result being that some upcountry churches split or vanished. The guerrilla warfare in the upcountry also meant that few church records from the revolutionary war era survived." J. Glen Clayton, "South Carolina Baptist Records," *South Carolina Historical Magazine*, vol. 85, no. 4, 1985, p. 319. One author has catalogued some of the Baptist churches that became battlegrounds or were nearby. Daniel W. Barefoot, *Touring South Carolina's Revolutionary War Sites* (Winston-Salem, N.C.: John F. Blair Publishers, 1999).

56. Divergent Presbyterian groups in Pennsylvania-settled Chester County began holding common services in 1759 and the Reverend William Richardson is credited with unifying them and naming the church in 1770. Roadside marker erected by the Chester County Historical Society, 1964.

57. Rogers, *Richard Furman,* op. cit., p. 28.

58. A. E. Smith, *Colonists in Bondage* (New York: W. W. Norton, 1971), p. 48.

59. Ibid., pp. 118–21.

60. Kenneth Morgan, *Slavery and Servitude in Colonial North America* (New York: New York University Press, 2000), p. 44.

61. A. E. Smith, op. cit., p. 4.

62. Ibid., pp. 5–7.

63. Morgan, op. cit., p. 61.

64. A. Roger Ekirch, *Bound for America* (Oxford: Clarendon Press, 1987), p. 116.

65. Several books and articles have elaborated on these plans and possibilities. Among the more notable are George W. Kyte, "Some Plans for a Loyalist Stronghold in the Middle Colonies," *Pennsylvania Magazine of History and Biography,* vol. 16, no. 3, July 1949, pp. 177–90, and Carl Van Doren, *A Secret History of the Revolution* (New York: Viking, 1941).

66. Don Jordan and Michael Walsh, *White Cargo* (New York: New York University Press, 2007), p. 259.

67. Hatley, op. cit., p. 184.

68. Smith, op. cit., p. 259.

69. Ekirch, *Bound for America,* op. cit., p. 193.

Chapter 7: The Ideologies of Revolution

1. The thesis held by several historians that support for the Revolution was strongest in areas where long-settled populations were of English descent clearly has some validity because the old-settled and heavily English colonies of populous New England and Virginia were in the vanguard of the Revolution. On the other hand, proponents— Canadian Willam Nelson, British military historian Piers Mackesy, and others—tend to overlook the exceptions. In Massachusetts, Patriot support was softer in the old Plymouth colony district; Anglican populations of English descent in southwestern Connecticut, lower New York, and New Jersey were substantially Loyalist; so were the

long-settled and largely English Quaker populations in and around Philadelphia, western New Jersey, and Nantucket. Many poor whites and watermen of English descent in southern Delaware and the Eastern Shore sections of Maryland and Virginia were Loyalists. The idea of "Englishness" per se being critical has to be qualified.

2. In 1860, parts of New England gave surprising support to the presidential candidates who were pro-southern (nominee John Breckinridge) or in favor of compromise and peace (Constitutional Union nominee John Bell). Many Massachusetts cotton manufacturers opposed a war. Boston gave Bell, whose running mate Edward Everett was a prominent "Cotton Whig," a quarter of its vote. In southwestern Connecticut, where Anglican Loyalism had been substantial in 1775, about a third of the vote was cast for Breckinridge and Bell. Local industries made carriages for the South, and Episcopalians leaned Democratic in response to the Congregationalist or evangelical Republicans. For more detail, see Kevin Phillips, *The Cousins' Wars* (New York: Basic Books, 1999), pp. 423–25.

3. Bernard Bailyn, *The Origins of American Politics* (New York: Vintage Books, 1970), pp. ix and x.

4. Carl Bridenbaugh, *The Spirit of '76: The Growth of American Patriotism Before Independence, 1607–1776* (New York: Oxford University Press, 1975), pp. vii, 4–7.

5. Ibid., p. 89.

6. During the mid-to-late 1760s, Stiles and several middle-colony Presbyterian leaders worked to bring about a "Union among all the anti-Episcopal churches," but it never took official form. See Bridenbaugh, *Mitre and Sceptre*, op. cit., pp. 270–76. While Stiles was ministering in Newport, Rhode Island, he advocated a union between the Congregationalists and Calvinist Baptists.

7. Richard L. Merritt, *Symbols of American Community, 1735–1775* (New Haven: Yale University Press, 1966).

8. Richard Koebner, *Empire* (Cambridge, U.K.: Cambridge University Press, 1961).

9. Albert H. Smyth, ed., *Writings of Benjamin Franklin* (New York, 1905–7), vol. 2, pp. 205–8, sec. 22.

10. Richard Koebner, "Two Conceptions of Empire," in Jack Greene, ed., *The Reinterpretation of the American Revolution, 1763–1789* (New York: Harper & Row, 1968), p. 121.

11. Koehn, op. cit., p. 15.

12. From an analysis by Frederick the Great, quoted in H.A.L. Fisher, *A History of Europe* (Boston: Houghton Mifflin, 1939), p. 785.

13. Louis Hacker, "The First American Revolution," *Columbia University Quarterly* 37 (1935), pp. 259–95.

14. Koehn, op. cit., pp. 59 and 105.

15. Ibid., p. 77.

16. Ibid., p. 49.

17. Ibid. For Pitt, p. 131; for Burke, pp. 59, 77, and 105; for Shelburne, pp. 23, 97; for Rockingham, p. 108; and for Grenville, p. 61.

18. Holton, op. cit., p. 57.

19. Barrow, op. cit., p. 248.

20. St. George L. Sioussat, "The Breakdown of Royal Management of Lands in the Southern Provinces," *Agricultural History* vol. 3, no. 2, April 1929, p. 7.

21. Langford, op. cit., pp. 298–99.

22. John Phillip Reid, *Constitutional History of the American Revolution: The Authority of Law* (Madison: University of Wisconsin Press, 1993), p. 167.

23. Charles H. McIlwain, *The American Revolution: A Constitutional Interpretation* (Ithaca, N.Y.: Cornell University Press, 1958) p. 118.

24. Reid, op. cit., pp. 172–73.

25. Ibid., pp. 163–73.

26. John M. Murrin, "Magistrates, Sinners and Precarious Liberties," in Hall, Murrin, and Tate, eds., *Saints and Revolutionaries* (New York: W. W. Norton, 1984), p. 188.

27. John Phillip Reid, *In a Defiant Stance* (University Park: Penn State University Press, 1977), pp. 21–22.

28. Ibid., pp. 27–40 and 55–64.

29. Bonomi, op. cit., p. 187.

30. William Sweet, *The Story of Religion in America* (Grand Rapids, Mich.: Baker Book House, 1973), pp. 177–78.

31. Mark J. Larson, *Calvin's Doctrine of the State* (Eugene, Ore.: Wipf & Stock, 2009), p. 97.

32. N. S. McFetridge, *Calvinism in History* (1882), p. 11.

33. John Lothrop Motley, *History of the United Netherlands* (New York: Harper & Brothers, 1861), vol. 3, p. 121; vol. 4, pp. 547–48.

34. McFetridge, op. cit., p. 113; John Fiske, *The Beginnings of New England* (Boston: Houghton Mifflin, 1899), p. 58.

35. German historian Leopold von Ranke (1796–1896), is widely quoted saying that through his beliefs, "John Calvin was the virtual founder of America." French ecclesiastical historian Jean-Henri d'Aubigné (1794–1872) called Calvin "the founder of the greatest of republics. The Pilgrims who left their country in the reign of James I . . . were his sons, his direct and legitimate sons; and that American nation which we have seen growing so rapidly boasts as its father the humble Reformer on the shores of Lake Leman." D'Aubigné, *History of the Reformation in the Time of Calvin* (New York: Carter & Brothers, 1863), vol. 1, p. 5. To Dutch historian Robert Fruin (1823–1899), "In Switzerland, in France, in the Netherlands, in Scotland and in England, and wherever Protestantism has had to establish itself at the point of a sword, it was Calvinism that gained the day." Abraham Kuyper, Stone Lectures, quoting Robert Fruin, *Tien Yares uit den Tachtigjarigen Orlag 1588-1598,* 6th ed. (Den Haag, 1904), p. 217. Hippolyte Taine, a French historian of atheist belief, called the Calvinists "the true heroes of England. They founded England, in spite of the corruption of the Stuarts, by the exercise of duty, by the practice of justice, by obstinate toil, by vindication of right, by resistance to oppression . . . They founded Scotland; they founded the United States; at this day, they are, by their descendants, founding Australia and colonizing the world." Loraine Boettner, *The Reformed Doctrine of Predestination,* supra. section 6, note 7. Emilio Castelar, a Catholic who in 1873 became president of the Spanish Republic, observed that "it was necessary for the republican movement that there should come a morality more austere than Luther's, the morality of Calvin, and a Church more democratic than the German, the Church of Geneva. The Anglo-Saxon democracy has for its lineage the book of a primitive society—the Bible. It is the product of a severe theology learned by the few Christian fugitives in the gloomy cities of Holland and Switzerland, where the morose shade of Calvin still wanders." *Calvin Memorial Addresses* (New York: General Assembly of the Presbyterian Church in the United States, 1909).

36. Loraine Boettner, *The Reformed Doctrine of Predestination* (1932), Section VI, "Calvinism in History," http//biblecentre.net/theology.

37. Fiske, op. cit., p. 59.

38. Keith Griffin, *Revolution and Religion: The American Revolution and the Reformed Clergy* (New York: Paragon House, 1994), pp. 15 and 84.

39. Bloch, "Religion and Ideological Change," op. cit., p. 46.

40. Bailyn, *Origins of American Politics,* op. cit., p. 11.

41. Bernard Bailyn, *The Ideological Origins of the American Revolution* (Cambridge, Mass.: Harvard University Press, 1992), pp. 118–20.

42. Bernard Bailyn, "The Central Themes of the American Revolution," in Stephen G. Kurtz and James H. Dutson, eds., *Essays on the American Revolution* (Chapel Hill: University of North Carolina Press, 1973), p. 8.

43. Bailyn, *Origins of American Politics,* op. cit., p. x.

44. Ibid., p. 38.

45. Bailyn, "Central Themes," op. cit., pp. 8–9.

46. Ibid., pp. 4, 7, 10.

47. Bailyn, *Ideological Origins,* op. cit., pp. 94, 153.

48. Two well-received examples are Stephen Budiansky, *Her Majesty's Spymaster* (New York: Viking Penguin, 2005), and Alan Haynes, *The Elizabethan Secret Services* (Stroud, Gloucestershire: Sutton, 2000).

49. Derek Hirst, *Authority and Conflict: England, 1603–1658* (Cambridge, Mass.: Harvard University Press, 1986), pp. 184–201.

Chapter 8: Fortress New England?

1. Henry Wadsworth Longfellow, "Paul Revere's Ride, 1775" (1860).

2. French, *First Year,* op. cit., pp. 23–24.

3. Ibid., pp. 17–18.

4. French, *General Gage's Informers* (Cranbury, N.J.: Scholar's Bookshelf, 2005), pp. 10–32.

5. French, *First Year,* op. cit., p. 11.

6. Peter D. G. Thomas, *Tea Party to Independence: The Third Phase of the American Revolution, 1773–1776* (Oxford: Clarendon Press, 1991), pp. 139, 159, 160.

7. Charles R. Ritcheson, *British Politics and the American Revolution* (Norman: University of Oklahoma Press, 1954), p. 195.

8. John Prebble, *Culloden* (New York: Atheneum, 1962), pp. 245–47.

9. *Naval Documents,* op. cit., vol. 1, pp. 65–66, 69–70.

10. Ibid., pp. 165, 167, 179, 181, 188; *Essex Gazette,* April 18, 1775; Taunton, Gerry Tuoti, "Encampment Recreates Life During Revolutionary War," *Taunton Gazette,* August 8, 2009.

11. *Naval Documents,* op. cit., pp. 173, 179, 183, 185–87.

12. French, *First Year,* op. cit., p. 20.

13. *The War of the American Revolution* (Washington, D.C.: Center of Military History, U.S. Army, 1975), p. 89.

14. Gage had received information, dated April 15, that "the [Massachusetts] Congress have determined on raising an Army if the other New England colonies would join them. The Army is to consist of 18,000 men 8,000 of whom are to be raised in this province, 5,000 in Connecticut, 3,000 in New Hampshire and 2,000 in Rhode Island." French, *Gage's Informers,* op. cit., 234.

15. French, *First Year,* op. cit., p. 67.

16. Bowen, op. cit., p. 522.

17. Gage knew little about the besieging army's disorganization but felt his own weakness. Graves declined to act offensively save for the immediate preservation of His Majesty's ships. *Naval Documents,* op. cit., vol. 1, p. 500.

18. Rossie, op. cit., pp. 76–77.

19. French, *First Year,* op. cit., p. 78.

20. Nathaniel Bouton, ed., *Documents and Records Relating to the Province of New Hampshire from 1764 to 1776* (Nashua, N.H.: State Printer, 1878), vol. 7, pp. 442–44.

21. French, *First Year,* op. cit., p. 142.

22. I. W. Stewart, *Life of Jonathan Trumbull, Senior* (Hartford, Conn.: Brown & Gross, 1878), pp. 181, 213.

23. Schlesinger, op. cit., pp. 561–62.

24. L. W. Turner, op. cit., p. 88.

25. Crane, op. cit., p. 129.

26. Albert E. Van Dusen, *Connecticut* (New York: Random House, 1961), pp. 144–45.

27. Robert A. East, *Connecticut's Loyalists* (Chester, Conn.: Pequot Press, 1974), pp. 22–27.

28. David M. Roth, op. cit., p. 34.

29. Schlesinger, op. cit., pp. 445–46.

30. East, op. cit., pp. 24–29.

31. Steiner, op. cit., pp. 50–51.

32. Roth, op. cit., pp. 66–67.

33. Stewart, op. cit., p. 221.

34. East, op. cit., pp. 22–27; Steiner, op. cit., pp. 45–52.

35. See Buel, *Dear Liberty,* op. cit., p. 80, and subsequent chapters. Connecticut's mobilization peaked in September 1776. Buel heads the unfolding chapters as follows: "Exertion," "Attrition," "Signs of Strain and Exhaustion."

36. Bellesisles, op. cit., pp. 186–216.

37. Rossie, op. cit., p. 3.

38. Ibid., p. 5.

39. James Kirby Martin, *Benedict Arnold: Revolutionary Hero* (New York; New York University Press, 1997), p. 75.

40. Rossie, op. cit., pp. 31–33.

41. Ibid., pp. 9–10.

42. Ibid., p. 11.

43. *The War of the American Revolution,* op. cit., pp. 90–91.

44. Rossie, op. cit., pp. 16–25.

45. Howe was sympathetic enough to the colonies to become a peace commissioner in 1776 as well as the British military commander. Burgoyne, too, had briefly hoped for a peace-making role.

46. *War of the American Revolution,* op. cit., p. 91.

47. Rossie, op. cit., p. 62.

48. Chester M. Destler, *Connecticut: The Provisions State* (Chester, Conn.: Pequot Press, 1973), p. 12.

49. Edward Fales Jr., *Arsenal of the Revolution* (Salisbury, Conn.: The Tri-Corners History Council, Revised Issue 1997), p. 17.

50. Adam Ward Rome, *Connecticut's Cannon: The Salisbury Furnace in the American Revolution* (Hartford, Conn.: The American Revolution Bicentennial Commission of Connecticut, 1977), pp. 10–11.

51. James P. Walsh, *Connecticut Industry and the Revolution* (Hartford, Conn.: The American Revolution Bicentennial History of Connecticut, 1978), p. 62.

52. Rome, op. cit., p. 9.

53. Destler, op. cit., p. 56.

Chapter 9: Declaring Economic War

1. Koehn, op. cit., pp. 129, 142–43.

2. Ibid., pp. 143–46.

3. Jensen, op. cit., pp. 325–26.

4. For the details of Edinburgh's Porteous riots, see, for example, John and Julia Keay, *Collins Encyclopedia of Scotland,* pp. 782–83.

5. P.D.G. Thomas, op. cit., p. 52.

6. Ammerman, op. cit., p. 131.

7. Jensen, op. cit., pp. 505–15; Ammerman, op. cit., pp. 83–84, 150–53.

8. Ammerman, op. cit., p. 106.

9. Jensen, op. cit., p. 560.

10. Schlesinger, op. cit., p. 444.

11. Jensen, op. cit., p. 538.

12. Schlesinger, op. cit., pp. 454, 459–60.

13. Burrows and Wallace, op. cit., pp. 223–24.

14. John E. Selby, *Dunmore* (Virginia Independence Bicentennial Commission, 1977), p. 21.

15. Schlesinger, op. cit., p. 463.
16. Ibid., p. 463.
17. P.D.G. Thomas, op. cit., p. 139, 169, 177.
18. Ibid., pp. 208–10, 193.
19. Jeffrey J. Crow, *A Chronicle of North Carolina During the American Revolution* (Raleigh: North Carolina Division of Archives and History, 1975), p. 17.
20. Lord Dartmouth and the American Department were not overburdened with useful reports from the thirteen colonies: "Official reports with any semblance of regularity came only from Massachusetts, New York, New Jersey, Pennsylvania and Virginia." Peter D. G. Thomas, op. cit., p. 131. By 1775, Josiah Martin of North Carolina had also become a regular correspondent.
21. Ammerman, op. cit., p. 103.
22. Ibid., pp. 106–7.
23. Ibid., pp. 107–8.
24. Ibid., p. 107.
25. Jensen, op.cit., pp. 531–32.
26. Schlesinger, op. cit., pp. 451–52.
27. Ammerman, op. cit., pp. 104–8.
28. Robert L. Ganyard, *The Emergence of North Carolina's Revolutionary State Government* (Raleigh: North Carolina Division of Archives and History, 1978), p. 32.
29. McEachern and Williams, op cit., p. xi.
30. Lipscomb, *South Carolina Becomes a State,* op. cit., pp. 10–11.
31. Breen, *Tobacco Culture,* op. cit., pp. 46–57.
32. Holton, op. cit., p. 94.
33. Ibid., p. 95.
34. Ibid., p. 111.
35. Jensen, op. cit., p. 517; and Hoffman, *Spirit of Dissension,* op. cit., pp. 138, 143.
36. Holton, op. cit., pp. 126–27.
37. Robson, *American Revolution,* op. cit., p. 30.
38. Knollenberg, op. cit., pp. 70–72, 95–96, and 118–19.
39. P.D.G. Thomas, op. cit., p. 166.
40. The act in question was the Treason Act of Henry VIII (1543).
41. Richard Platt, *The Ordnance Survey Guide to Smugglers' Britain* (London: Cassell, 1991), p. 11.
42. G. J. Marcus, *A Naval History of England: The Formative Years* (Boston: Little, Brown, 1961), p. 404.
43. Fred Anderson, *Crucible of War* (New York: Knopf, 2000), p. 700.
44. Jensen, op. cit., p. 495.
45. Breen, *Tobacco Culture,* op. cit., pp. 190–93.
46. Schlesinger, op. cit., p. 519.
47. Ryerson, op. cit., p. 115.
48. Ammerman, op. cit., p. 103.
49. Jensen, op. cit., p. 516.
50. Schlesinger, op. cit., pp. 531–33.
51. Ibid., pp. 566–67.

Chapter 10: Five Roads to Canada

1. Rossie, op. cit., pp. 4–7, 31, 36–37.
2. Francis Parkman, *A Half-Century of Conflict* (New York: Collier Books, 1962), p. 22.
3. Kenneth McNaught, *The Pelican History of Canada* (Harmondsworth, U.K.: Penguin Books, 1969), p. 25.
4. Mark Kurlansky, *Cod* (New York: Penguin, 1998), pp. 37–45, 73–74, 83.
5. Ibid., p. 78.

6. Marcus, *Naval History of England,* op. cit., p. 404.
7. Christopher Magra, *The Fisherman's Cause* (New York: Cambridge University Press, 2009), pp. 147–48.
8. C. H. Van Tyne, "French Aid Before the Alliance of 1778," *American Historical Review* 31, no. 1 (October 1925), p. 30; Marion Huibrechts, *Swampin' Guns and Stabbing Irons: The Austrian Netherlands, Liège Arms and the American Revolution, 1770–1783* (Catholic University of Leuven, Belgium: Doctoral Dissertation, 2009), vol. 2, p. 210; Van Tyne, op. cit., pp. 33–34.
9. P. J. Marshall, ed., *The Oxford History of the British Empire: The Eighteenth Century* (New York: Oxford University Press, 1998), p. 373.
10. McNaught, op. cit., pp. 48–50.
11. Thomas H. Raddall, *The Path of Destiny* (New York: Popular Library, 1957), p. 16.
12. Peckham, *The Colonial Wars, 1689–1762* (Chicago: University of Chicago Press, 1962), pp. 30–31, 64, 66–67, 70–71.
13. Ibid., p. 161.
14. Ibid., p. 170.
15. Ibid., pp. 70, 222–23.
16. Ibid., pp. 71–73.
17. Parkman, op. cit., pp. 122–33.
18. Ibid., p. 124, 130.
19. Ibid., p. 132.
20. North, *Race, Class and Politics,* op. cit., p. 196.
21. Bridenbaugh, *Cities in Revolt,* op. cit., pp. 60–61.
22. North, *Urban Crucible,* op. cit., p. 114.
23. Ibid., p. 152.
24. Magra, op. cit., pp. 151–58.
25. *Naval Documents,* op. cit., vol. 1, pp. 233, 284, and 350.
26. John B. Brebner, *The Neutral Yankees of Nova Scotia* (New York: Columbia University Press, 1937), p. 305.
27. *Naval Documents,* op. cit., vol. 1, pp. 233, 284, and 350.
28. Rossie, op. cit., p. 41.
29. Raddall, op. cit., pp. 17–18.
30. Ibid., p. 19.
31. Ibid., pp. 19–21.
32. Ibid., p. 23.
33. Brebner, op. cit., pp. 308–13.
34. McNaught, op. cit., p. 52.
35. Raddall, op. cit., p. 88.
36. Ibid., pp. 81–83.
37. Arthur Lefkowitz, *Benedict Arnold's Army* (New York: Savas Beatie, 2008), p. 23; Thomas Desjardin, *Through a Howling Wilderness* (New York: St. Martin's, 2006), p. 10.
38. Lefkowitz, op. cit., pp. 76–78.
39. Ibid., p. 157.
40. Ibid., p. 151.
41. *Writings of George Washington,* op. cit., p. 67.
42. Paul A. Stevens, *A King's Colonel* (Youngstown, N.Y.: Old Fort Niagara Association, 1987), pp. 17–23, 40–41.
43. Ibid., p. 36.
44. Ibid., pp. 35–37.
45. Ibid., p. 43.
46. Ibid., p. 47.
47. Mary Fryer, *Allan Maclean, Jacobite General* (Toronto: Dundurn Press, 1987), pp. 128–137, p. 141.

Chapter 11: The Global Munitions Struggle, 1774–1776

1. Huibrechts, op. cit., vol. 1, section 3.2, p. 64. Her information is from Public Records Office CO5/231 National Archives, Whitehall, July 5, 1773, circular letter of Dartmouth to all governors in America and the West Indies.
2. Ibid.
3. Ibid., vol. 2, p. 298.
4. Risch, op. cit., p. 339.
5. Ibid., p. 349.
6. Ibid., p. 340,
7. Potts, op. cit., p. 28; Risch, op. cit., p. 340; George Washington to John Hancock in J. C. Fitzpatrick, ed., *Writings of George Washington*, vol. 3, pp. 394–95; Augur, op. cit., p. 36.
8. Risch, op. cit., p. 331.
9. Ibid., p. 342.
10. Potts, op. cit., p. 29.
11. Fitzpatrick, op. cit., vol. 3, p. 384.
12. James B. Hedges, *The Browns of Providence Plantations: Colonial Years* (Providence: Brown University Press, 1968), p. 219.
13. Huibrechts, op. cit., vol. 1, pp. 109–10.
14. Augur, op. cit., p. 35.
15. David Syrett, *The Royal Navy in American Waters, 1775–1783* (Aldershot, U.K.: Scolar Press, 1989), p. 30.
16. Augur, op. cit., p. 35.
17. Ibid., p. 36.
18. Desjardin, op. cit., pp. 145–46.
19. Potts, op. cit., p. 32; David Lee Russell, *Victory on Sullivan's Island* (Haverford, Penn.: Infinity Publishing, 2002), pp. 215–24.
20. *Warren-Adams Letters* (Boston: Massachusetts Historical Society, 1917), vol. 72, p. 116.
21. Harlow G. Unger, *John Hancock* (New York: John Wiley, 2000), pp. 179–84.
22. Samuel Flagg Bemis, *The Diplomacy of the American Revolution* (Bloomington: Indiana University Press, 1957), pp. 3–15, 255. He cites approvingly both E. S. Corwin, *French Policy and the American Alliance of 1778* (Princeton: Princeton University Press, 1916) and Elizabeth Kite, *Beaumarchais and the American War of Independence* (Boston: Badger, 1918).
23. Ibid., p. 18.
24. Augur, op. cit., p. 117, quoting French historian Henri Doniol.
25. Desnoyer to Vergennes, November 1774, Huibrechts, op. cit., p. 249; York, op. cit., p. 26; Neil R. Stout, *The Royal Navy in America* (Annapolis, Md.: Naval Institute Press, 1973), p. 162.
26. Potts, op. cit., p. 26.
27. Ibid., pp. 26–27.
28. Ibid., p. 27.
29. Huibrechts, op. cit., p. 157.
30. Ibid., p. 250.
31. Augur, op. cit., p. 18.
32. Ibid., p. 65.
33. J. Franklin Jameson, "St. Eustatius in the American Revolution," *American Historical Review* 8, no. 4 (July 1903), p. 695.
34. Magra, op. cit., pp. 166–68.
35. Potts, op. cit., p. 25.
36. Hugh Thomas, *The Slave Trade* (New York: Simon & Schuster, 1997), p. 326.
37. Potts, op. cit., p. 25; Augur, op. cit., p. 20.
38. Syrett, *American Waters*, op. cit., p. 30.

39. Belgian scholar Huibrechts's goal in her massive doctoral dissertation was to show how the arms industry in the Prince-Bishopric of Liège, and nearby in what was then the Austrian Netherlands, contributed to the flow of weapons and munitions to the American rebels. But in conducting intensive research in Continental archives generally ignored by English-speaking historians, she also considerably expanded the information available on the flow of weapons and munitions to America from other parts of Europe.

40. Huibrechts, op. cit., pp. 147–48.

41. French, *First Year,* op. cit., pp. 125–26.

42. Selby, *Dunmore,* op. cit., p. 21.

43. Orlando W. Stephenson, "The Supply of Gunpowder in 1776," *American Historical Review* 30, no. 2 (January 1925), p. 272.

44. Samuel Adams to James Warren, *Letters of Delegates to Congress,* vol. 2, letter 303, p. 297.

45. George C. Daughan, *If By Sea* (New York: Basic Books, 2008), p. 60.

46. Stephenson, op. cit., pp. 274–75.

47. Ibid., p. 47.

48. Augur, op. cit., p. 36.

49. French, *First Year,* op. cit., p. 272.

50. Augur, op. cit., p. 59.

51. Risch, op. cit., p. 335.

52. Adams to Warren, *Letters of Delegates,* op. cit.

53. York, op. cit., p. 28.

54. Potts, op. cit., p. 31.

55. Huibrechts, op cit., vol. 2, p. 170 (Dutch powder mills); Huibrechts, vol. 2, p. 181 (cutting off water to St. Eustatius); and Jameson, op. cit., p. 690 (exports from Bengal).

56. York, op. cit., p. 29.

57. Henri Doniol, in his six-volume history of the participation by France in the establishment of the United States, published between 1884 and 1892, drew on French archives but did not publish other documentation of Benjamin Franklin's presumed plotting, which has limited the attention of later historians. In a nutshell, Doniol stated that "Franklin, before returning to America [he left in March 1775], treated with armorers or merchants of England, Holland, France, for supplies and transport of munitions of war to the colonies. These operations were in part concentrated in London and Beaumarchais was aware of them." Henri Doniol, ed., *Histoire de la participation de la France a l'etablissement des Etats Unis d'Amerique,* vol. I, (Paris: 1884–1892), p. 133.

58. Augur, op. cit., p. 65.

59. Potts, op. cit., p. 136.

60. Ibid., p. 33.

Chapter 12: The Supply War at Sea

1. Mackesy, op. cit., p. 65.

2. David Syrett, *Shipping and the American War, 1775–1783* (London: University of London/Athlone Press, 1970), p. 243.

3. Ibid., p. 244.

4. Michael Lewis, *The History of the Royal Navy* (Fairlawn, N.J.: Essential Books, 1959), pp. 158–59.

5. Tagney, op. cit., p. 118.

6. Paul W. Wilderson, *Governor John Wentworth and the American Revolution* (Lebanon: University of New Hampshire Press, 1994), p. 241.

7. James L. Nelson, *George Washington's Secret Navy* (New York: McGraw-Hill, 2008), p. 8.

8. Tagney, op. cit., p. 19.
9. Magra, op. cit., pp. 142–43, 154–55.
10. Nelson, *Secret Navy,* op. cit., pp. 21–22.
11. Ibid., p. 7.
12. Syrett, *Shipping,* op. cit., p. 123.
13. *Naval Documents,* op. cit., vol. III, p. 82.
14. Fowler, op. cit., pp. 16–19.
15. Nelson, op. cit., p. 82.
16. Magra, op. cit., p. 187.
17. Ibid., p. 189.
18. Nelson, op. cit., pp. 132 and 4.
19. James Volo, *Bluewater Patriots* (Lanham, Md.: Rowman & Littlefield, 2006), p. 63.
20. Syrett, *Shipping,* pp. 18, 24–25.
21. Ibid., p. 243.
22. Syrett, *Shipping,* op. cit., pp. 137–38.
23. Buel, *In Irons,* op. cit.
24. Syrett, *American Waters,* op. cit., p. 27.
25. Lipscomb, *Carolina Lowcountry,* op. cit., pp. 8–9.
26. Nelson, *Secret Navy,* op. cit., p. 51.
27. Magra, op. cit., pp. 184–86.
28. *Naval Documents,* op. cit., vol. I, p. 857.
29. Fowler, op. cit., p. 29.
30. Nelson, op. cit., pp. 58–60.
31. *Naval Documents,* op. cit., vol. I, p. 1287.
32. Gardner W. Allen, *A Naval History of the American Revolution* (Cranbury, N.J.: Scholar's Bookshelf, 2005), vol. I, p. 63.
33. Nelson, op. cit., pp. 212–15.
34. Ibid., pp. 105–6.
35. *If By Sea,* op. cit., p. 46.
36. Nelson, op. cit., pp. 126–31.
37. Fowler, op. cit., pp. 54–60.
38. Allen, op. cit., pp. 40–41.
39. Ibid., pp. 43–46.
40. Ibid., p. 42.
41. Ruth Y. Johnston, "American Privateers in French Ports," *Pennsylvania Magazine of History and Biography,* vol. 53, no. 1, October 1929, pp. 352–53.

Chapter 13: The First British Southern Strategy, 1775–1776

1. Hume, op. cit., p. 164.
2. Ibid., p. 399.
3. Kars, op. cit., p. 208.
4. Dabney and Dargan, op. cit., pp. 92–93, Jones, op. cit., pp. 32–33.
5. Coleman, *American Revolution in Georgia,* op. cit., pp. 48–49.
6. Rankin, op. cit., p. 35.
7. Ibid., p. 32.
8. Ibid., pp. 28–29.
9. See especially David K. Wilson, *The Southern Strategy: Britain's Conquest of South Carolina and Georgia, 1775–1780* (Columbia: University of South Carolina Press, 2005), pp. xi–xvi and 1–4.
10. Eric Robson, "The Expedition to the Southern Colonies, 1775–1776," *English Historical Review* (October 1951), p. 538.
11. In 1775, Wilmington, Brunswick, and the Lower Cape Fear were the wealthiest section of North Carolina, the principal seaport district, and the source of vehement

earlier demonstrations against the Stamp Act. That year, Lower Cape Fear residents again took the lead in July by capturing and burning Fort Johnston, the main British installation at the mouth of the Cape Fear River. The district produced a disproportion of the province's early Patriotic leadership, witness one book entitled *Hartnett, Hooper and Howe: Revolutionary Leaders of the Lower Cape Fear* (Wilmington: Lower Cape Fear Historical Society, 1979). The three—Cornelius Hartnett (the Samuel Adams of North Carolina), William Hooper (signer of the Declaration of Independence), and General Robert Howe—probably did represent a more concentrated leadership roster that any other North Carolina town could boast. H. G. Jones, former curator of the North Carolina Collection at the University of North Carolina, complained "that one small area of the country should produce [three such leaders] . . . is remarkable, and that their importance should remain obscure for two centuries is a measure of the influence of New England historians of the nineteenth century" (book jacket, *Hartnett, Hooper and Howe*).

12.   Malcolm Ross, *The Cape Fear* (New York: Holt, Rinehart, 1965), p. 7.

13.   Rankin, op. cit., p. 31.

14.   Ibid., pp. 31–32.

15.   David Lee Russell, *The American Revolution in the Southern Colonies* (Jefferson, N.C.: McFarland & Co., 2000), p. 85.

16.   Robson, op. cit., p. 539.

17.   Ibid., pp. 540–41.

18.   Ibid., pp. 541–42.

19.   Ibid., p. 543.

20.   Ibid.

21.   Ibid., p. 544.

22.   Ibid., p. 545.

23.   Ibid., p. 549.

24.   Ibid., p. 553.

25.   Wilmington does have an obelisk commemorating Cornelius Hartnett and there is a national military park at Moore's Creek. Otherwise, though, there is very little that presents, amplifies, interrelates, or commemorates the events of the ten months between the capture of Fort Johnston in July 1775 and May 31, 1776, when Britain's vaunted Southern expedition gave up on North Carolina and sailed away to even greater ignominy in Charleston Harbor.

26.   Syrett, *Shipping,* op cit., p. 198.

27.   Ibid, pp. 206–207.

28.   See, for example, John Steven Watson, "The Reign of George III, 1760–1815," in *The Oxford History of England,* op. cit.

29.   French, op. cit., p. 318.

Chapter 14: Is Falmouth Burning?

1.   Neuenschwander, op. cit., p. 139.

2.   Hast, op. cit., pp. 56–59; Michael Kranish, *Flight From Monticello* (New York: Oxford University Press, 2010), pp. 68–83.

3.   Burrows and Wallace, op. cit., p. 242.

4.   *Naval Documents,* op. cit., vol. 1, pp. 499–500.

5.   Bridenbaugh, *Cities in Revolt,* op. cit., pp. 17–21 and 98–103.

6.   *Naval Documents,* op. cit., vol 1., p. 125.

7.   Ibid., p. 279.

8.   Ibid., pp. 363.

9.   Elaine F. Crane, *A Dependent People: Newport, Rhode Island in the Revolutionary Era* (New York: Fordham University Press, 1985), p. 121.

10.   Ibid., p. 123.

11. Nelson, op. cit., p. 59.
12. *Naval Documents,* op. cit., vol. 1, p. 1236.
13. Charles O. Paullin, "The Connecticut Navy of the American Revolution," *New England Magazine,* 35, 1907, pp. 715–16.
14. Wilderson, op. cit., pp. 263–64.
15. Burrows and Wallace, op. cit., p. 226; Bliven, op. cit., pp. 35–38.
16. Thomas Wertenbaker, *Father Knickerbocker Rebels* (New York: Scribner's, 1948), p. 63.
17. Bliven, op. cit.
18. Burrows and Wallace, op. cit., p. 227.
19. Lovejoy, *Rhode Island,* op. cit., pp. 186–87.
20. *Naval Documents,* op. cit., vol. 1, p. 549.
21. Tagney, op. cit., pp. 154–60.
22. *Naval Documents,* op. cit., vol. 2, p. 1144.
23. Tagney, op cit., pp. 163–64.
24. Ibid., p. 151–53.
25. Buel, *Dear Liberty,* op. cit., pp. 43–46.
26. Marga, op cit., pp. 212–13.
27. Lipscomb, *Carolina Lowcountry,* op. cit., pp. 16–18.
28. *Naval Documents,* op. cit., vol. l, pp. 293–94.
29. Russell, *The American Revolution in the Southern Colonies,* op. cit, p. 70.
30. French, *First Year,* op. cit., p. 20.
31. *Naval Documents,* op. cit., vol. 1, pp. 1252–53.
32. Ibid., pp. 1281–83.
33. *Naval Documents,* vol. 2, op. cit., p. 7.
34. Ibid., p. 324.
35. Ibid.
36. Ibid., p. 513.
37. Nelson, op. cit., p. 139.
38. *Naval Documents,* op. cit., vol. 2, p. 420–21.
39. Volo, op. cit., p. 38.
40. Thomas Macy, *The Hannah and the Nautilus* (Beverly, Mass.: Beverly Historical Society, 2002), pp. 17–28.
41. *Naval Documents,* vol. 2, p. 471.
42. Leamon, op. cit., pp. 70–71.
43. Tagney, op. cit., p. 226.
44. John E. Selby, *The Revolution in Virginia* (Williamsburg, Va.: Colonial Williamsburg Foundation, 1988), p. 63.
45. Rhode Island, *The American Guide Series* (Boston: Houghton Mifflin, 1937), p. 426.
46. Letter to John Page, *Papers of Thomas Jefferson,* vol. 1, pp. 250–51.
47. Hast, op. cit., p. 59.
48. Kranish, *Flight from Monticello,* p. 82–83.
49. *Naval Documents,* op. cit., vol. 2, pp. 7–8.
50. Volo, op. cit., p. 72.

Chapter 15: Red, White, and Black

1. Kranish, op. cit., p. 93; Holton, op. cit., p. 214.
2. Simon Schama, *Rough Crossings* (New York: HarperCollins, 2006), p. 16.
3. Ibid., p. 8.
4. Smith, *Colonists in Bondage,* op. cit., p. 262.
5. Schama, op. cit., pp. 3–18; Alfred W. Blumrosen and Ruth G. Blumrosen, *Slave Nation* (Naperville, Ill.: Sourcebooks, 2005), pp. 35–38.
6. Schama, op. cit., p. 66.
7. McDonnell, op. cit., p. 23.

8. Colin G. Calloway, *The American Revolution in Indian Country* (Cambridge, U.K.: Cambridge University Press, 1995), pp. 12, 16, 85–100.

9. Ibid., pp. 26, 88–89, 92, 95.

10. Ibid., p. 93. General Gage's proposals for British use of Indians are collected and cited in Allen French, *First Year*, op. cit., p. 408.

11. Calloway, op. cit., pp. 68–76.

12. William T. Hagan, *Longhouse Diplomacy and Frontier Warfare* (Albany, N.Y.: Office of State History, 1976), pp. 11–12.

13. Allan W. Eckert, *The Wilderness War* (Boston: Little, Brown, 1978), pp. 70–71.

14. J. Edwin Hendricks, *Charles Thomson* (Cranbury, N.J.: Fairleigh Dickinson University Press, 1979), p. 16.

15. Distrust of Dunmore's motives in October 1774 grew in the spring of 1775 as his April and May behavior became hugely suspect in Patriot eyes. However, the chronology of Dunmore's changing relations with the Shawnee after the October battle and initial peace talks is not clear. Dunmore took some of the Shawnee warriors given to him as hostages back to Williamsburg that winter, but during the winter they were treated as guests, and by April and May, they seem to have been as much bodyguards for Dunmore as hostages. According to Charles Campbell's *History of the Colony and Ancient Dominion of Virginia* (Philadelphia: 1860), pp. 607–8, Dunmore armed his Shawnee "hostages"on April 20. In February, John Connolly, his western lieutenant, visited the governor in Virginia and was instructed to secure the Indians for the king. Thwaits and Kellogg, supra., p. 19. It is easy to see why Virginian suspicions might have been rising that winter.

16. Hume, op. cit., p. 164.

17. Reuben Thwaits and Louise Kellogg, *The Revolution on the Upper Ohio* (Madison: Wisconsin Historical Society, 1908), p. 18.

18. Ibid., p. 137.

19. Gregory Schaaf, *Wampum Belts and PeaceTrees* (Golden, Colo.: Fulcrum Publishing, 1990), pp. 31–32.

20. Colin G. Calloway, *The Shawnees and the War for America* (New York: Viking Penguin, 2007), pp. 59–65.

21. Coleman, op. cit., pp. 113–14.

22. Kenneth Morgan, *Slavery and Servitude in Colonial North America* (New York: New York University Press, 2001), p. 44.

23. Holton, op. cit., p.178; Jordan and Walsh, *White Cargo,* op. cit., p. 270.

24. McDonnell, op. cit., p. 128.

25. A. E. Smith, *Colonists in Bondage* (New York: W. W. Norton, 1971), pp. 283–84.

26. Jordan and Walsh, op. cit., p. 254.

27. "unrelieved horror," Sharon V. Salinger, *To Serve Well and Faithfully* (Westminster, Md.: Heritage Books, 2007), p. 114; "horses or cows" and "parcel of sheep," Jordan and Walsh, op. cit., p. 253.

28. William Eddis, *Letters from America,* quoted in Jordan and Walsh, op. cit., p. 257.

29. David Waldstreicher, *Runaway America* (New York: Hill & Wang, 2004), p. 22.

30. William Eddis, quoted in Jordan and Walsh, pp. 256–57.

31. Gary B. Nash, "Poverty and Politics in Early American History," in Billy G. Smith, ed., *Down and Out in Early America* (Philadelphia: University of Pennsylvania Press, 2004).

32. Salinger, op. cit., p. 128; Smith, op. cit., pp. 7–8.

33. Roger Ekrich, *Bound for America* (New York: Oxford University Press, 1987), pp. 21 and 27.

34. Waldstreicher, op. cit., p. 140.

35. Ekirch, *Bound for America,* op. cit., p. 119.

36. Bailyn, *Voyagers,* op. cit., pp. 206, 255–56.

37. During the 1750s, Maryland governor Horatio Sharpe had estimated that his province alone had 9,000 indentured servants and convicts, totaling about 6 percent of the population. Bailyn, op. cit., *Voyagers,* p. 255. Virginia probably had at least as many; and Pennsylvania, despite fewer convicts, probably had 6,000 to 8,000 indentured servants.
38. Bailyn, *Voyagers,* pp. 255–56.
39. McDonnell, op. cit., p. 261.
40. Hoffman, op. cit., p. 201.
41. Ibid., pp. 245–58.
42. Hoffman, op. cit., pp. 116 and 135; *White Cargo,* op. cit., pp. 257–58.
43. Smith, op. cit., pp. 262–63.
44. Benjamin Quarles, *The Negro in the American Revolution* (New York: W. W. Norton, 1973), p. 72.
45. Sylvia Frey, *Water from the Rock* (Princeton: Princeton University Press, 1991), p. 60.
46. Quarles, op. cit., p. 60.
47. Ibid., pp. viii–ix.
48. Ibid., p. 78.
49. Sylvia R. Frey, op. cit., pp. 45–80.
50. Ibid., p. 45.
51. Ibid., p. 53.
52. Ibid., pp. 53, 60.
53. July letter, Hume, op. cit., p. 327; officers sent, Hume, op. cit., p. 283.
54. Frey, op. cit., p. 55.
55. Ibid., pp. 54–55 and 66–67.
56. Ibid., pp. 66–67.
57. Ibid., p. 67.
58. Hoffman, op. cit., p. 148.
59. Jeffrey J. Crow, *The Black Experience in Revolutionary North Carolina* (Raleigh: North Carolina Divisions of Archives and History, 1977), p. 56.
60. Ibid., p. 58.
61. Frey, op. cit., p. 62.
62. Crow, op. cit., p. 61.
63. Ibid., pp. 57–58.
64. Frey, op. cit., p. 56.
65. Robert A. Olwell, "Domestick Enemies," *Journal of Southern History* 55, no. 1 (February 1989), pp. 28–33.
66. Sylvia Frey, "Between Slavery and Freedom: Virginia Blacks in the American Revolution," *Journal of Southern History* 49, no. 3 (August 1983), p. 385.
67. Olwell, "Domestic Enemies," op. cit., p. 46.
68. Gordon Burns Smith, *Morningstars of Liberty: The Revolutionary War in Georgia, 1775–1783* (Nashville, Tenn.: Boyd Publishing, 2006), pp. 56-57.
69. McDonnell, op. cit., pp. 227–28.
70. The details can be found in Patrick Charles, *Washington's Decision* (privately printed, 2005), pp. 134–35.
71. Ibid., pp. 61–77.
72. Alan Gallay, *The Indian Slave Trade* (New Haven: Yale University Press, 2002), pp. 8–9.
73. Pekka Hämäläinen, *The Comanche Empire* (New Haven: Yale University Press, 2008), p. 14.
74. Ibid., p. 79, 153–54.
75. Giles Milton, *White Gold: The Extraordinary Tale of Thomas Pellow and North Africa's One Million European Slaves* (London: Hodder & Stoughton, 2004), pp. 99, 222, 270–71.

Chapter 16: Divided National Opinion and Britain's Need to Hire Mercenaries

1. John Brewer, *The Sinews of Power* (New York: Knopf, 1989), p. xvii.
2. The 36,000 figure comes from Stephen Conway, *The British Isles and the War of American Independence* (New York: Oxford University Press, 2000), p. 13.
3. William Urban, *Bayonets for Hire* (London: Greenhill, 2007), p. 253.
4. Paul Langford, *A Polite and Commercial People, England 1727–1783* (Oxford: Oxford University Press, 1989), pp. 228–29.
5. Three books illustrate this new depth and complexity on divisions within Britain during the American Revolution: Paul Langford's *A Polite and Commercial People, England 1727–1783* (1989), Linda Colley's *Britons: Forging the Nation 1707–1837* (1992), and Stephen Conway's *The British Isles and the American War of Independence* (2000). All three looked beyond the old insistence on British unity and documented considerable disunity, Colley to the point of perceiving a civil war in the English-speaking world. All saw Tories and the Church of England regaining political importance in the 1760s. The mobilization of Irish and Scottish Catholics for service in the British Army during the American Revolution was manifest, and Langford reiterated Sir George O. Trevelyan's early-twentieth-century point about how even in England, British military recruitment fared best in old Jacobite strongholds.
6. George O. Trevelyan, *History of the American Revolution,* op. cit., vol. 2, pp. 7–8.
7. Watson, op. cit., p. 203.
8. Brown, op. cit., p. 156.
9. For greater detail, see *The Cousins' Wars,* chap. 6, "Support for the Revolution within the British Isles."
10. John Sainsbury, *Disaffected Patriots: London Supporters of Revolutionary America 1769-1782* (Montreal: McGill-Queen's University Press, 1987).
11. Kathleen Wilson, *The Sense of the People: Politics, Culture and Imperialism in England, 1715-1785* (Cambridge, U.K.: Cambridge University Press, 1995), pp. 287–433.
12. James E. Bradley, *Religion, Revolution and English Radicalism* (Cambridge, England: Cambridge University Press, 1990), p. 320.
13. Colley, *Britons,* op. cit., p. 139.
14. Conway, *British Isles,* p. 140.
15. Bradley, op. cit., pp. 360–409.
16. Paul Langford, "Old Whigs, Old Tories and the American Revolution," *Journal of Imperial and Commonwealth History* (January, 1980), pp. 124–26.
17. James E. Bradley, *Popular Politics and the American Revolution in England* (Macon, Ga.: Mercer University Press, 1986), p. 127.
18. See especially T. M. Devine, *Scotland's Empire and the Shaping of the Americas, 1600-1815* (London: Penguin Books, 2003), chap. 14, "Empire and the Transformation of Scotland."
19. Conway, *British Isles,* op, cit., p. 184.
20. Belief that Catholics in Ireland were supporters of the American Revolution dies hard. Ulster Presbyterians in the north of Ireland were lopsidedly pro-American, but the Catholic clergy, gentry, and merchants in the south were getting policy concessions and beginning to profit from the empire. Professor Owen Dudley Edwards noted that in an Irish-American bicentennial summer school in 1976 "a range of scholars as divergent in other respects as Professor John Murphy, Dr. Conor Cruise O'Brien, Dr. David Doyle and myself acknowledged that our independent investigations had all moved to the same conclusion of Irish Catholic hostility to the American Revolution." Owen Dudley Edwards, "Ireland and the American Revolution," in Owen Dudley Edwards and George Shepperson, eds., *Scotland, Europe and the American Revolution* (New York: St. Martin's, 1978), p. 124.
21. David Smurthwaite, *Battlefields of Britain* (Exeter, U.K.: Webb & Bower, 1984), pp. 174–75.

22. Conway, *British Isles,* op. cit., pp. 154–55.

23. Trevelyan, *History of the American Revolution,* op. cit., vol. 2, page 34.

24. Bruce Lenman, *The Jacobite Clans of the Great Glen* (Aberdeen: Scottish Cultural Press, 1995), p. 205.

25. French, *First Year,* op. cit., p. 315.

26. Conway, *British Isles,* op. cit., p. 157.

27. Bradley, *Religion, Revolution,* op. cit., p. 386.

28. Conway, *British Isles,* op. cit., p. 15.

29. Conway, *British Isles,* op. cit., pp. 128–164; Langford, op. cit., p. 542.

30. Conway, *British Isles,* p. 13.

31. Ibid., p. 15.

32. Trevelyan, *American Revolution,* op. cit., vol. 2, p. 46.

33. Ibid., pp. 51–52.

34. Lenman, op. cit., pp. 184–85.

35. Lenman, op. cit., p. 207; Philip R. N. Katcher, *The Encyclopedia of British, Provincial and German Army Units, 1775–1783* (Harrisburg, Penn.: Stackpole, 1973), pp. 69–73.

36. Richard B. Sher and Jeffrey R. Smitten, eds., *Scotland and America in the Age of Enlightenment* (Edinburgh: Edinburgh University Press, 1990), p. 91.

37. David Dickson, *Old World Colony: Cork and South Munster, 1630–1830* (Cork, Ireland: Cork University Press, 2005), pp. 366–73.

38. Conway, *British Isles,* op. cit., pp. 184–85 and 249.

39. Owen Dudley Edwards, "The Impact of the American Revolution on Ireland," in *The Impact of the American Revolution Abroad* (Washington, D.C.: Library of Congress, 1976), p. 135.

40. Conway, *British Isles,* op. cit., p. 140.

41. Ibid., p. 185.

42. Ibid., p. 190.

43. Rodney Atwood, *The Hessians* (Cambridge, U.K.: Cambridge University Press, 1992), p. 153.

44. Charles W. Ingrao, *The Hessian Military State* (Cambridge, U.K.: Cambridge University Press, 1987), p. 136.

45. Trevelyan, *American Revolution,* op. cit., vol. 2, p. 35.

46. Atwood, op. cit., p. 24.

47. Trevelyan, *American Revolution,* op. cit., vol. 2, p. 41.

48. Ibid., pp. 36–37.

49. Atwood, op. cit., p. 24; Trevelyan, *American Revolution,* op. cit., vol. 2, pp. 35–36.

50. Ingrao, op. cit., pp. 1, 138–40.

51. Edward Jackson Lowell, *The Hessians and Other German Auxiliaries of Great Britain* (New York: Harper & Bros., 1884), pp. 25–26.

52. Peter Taylor, *Indentured to Liberty* (Ithaca, N.Y.: Cornell University Press, 1994), pp. x–xi.

53. Trevelyan, *American Revolution,* op. cit., vol. 2, p. 52.

54. Ingrao, op. cit., pp. 2–3, 137.

55. Atwood, op. cit., p. 178.

56. Hume, op. cit., pp. 409–10.

57. Philip Davidson, *Propaganda and the American Revolution, 1763–1783* (New York: Norton Library, 1973), p. 371.

58. Langford, op. cit., p. 384.

59. Atwood, op. cit., p. 18.

60. Trevelyan, *American Revolution,* op. cit., vol. 2, p. 36.

61. Watson, op. cit., p. 204.

62. *Gazette van Antwerpen,* 1775, quoted in Huibrechts, op. cit., p. 110.

Chapter 17: The Chesapeake—America's Vulnerable Estuary

1. Ira D. Gruber, *The Howe Brothers and the American Revolution* (Chapel Hill: University of North Carolina Press, 1972), p. 136.
2. Ernest M. Eller, ed., *Chesapeake Bay in the American Revolution* (Centerville, Md.: Tidewater Publishing, 1981), p. 16.
3. Eller, op. cit., p. 315.
4. Augur, op. cit., p. 69.
5. Hoffman, op. cit., p. 147.
6. Hoffman, op. cit., 164–65; Eller, op. cit., pp. 285–86.
7. Eller, op. cit., pp. 212–15; Geoffrey M. Footner, *Tidewater Triumph* (Centerville, Md.: Tidewater Publishers, 1998), p. 46.
8. F. C. Spooner, *Risks at Sea: Amsterdam Insurance and Maritime Europe, 1766–1780* (Cambridge, U.K.: Cambridge University Press, 2002), pp. 101–2.
9. Eller, op. cit., p. 316.
10. Ibid., p. 297.
11. Ibid., 106.
12. Gene Williamson, *Guns on the Chesapeake* (Westminster, Md.: Heritage Books, 2007), p. 48.
13. Hoffman, op. cit., p. 143.
14. Eller, op. cit., p. 381.
15. Hoffman, op. cit., pp. 154, 167.
16. Ibid., pp. 170–75.
17. Ibid., pp. 185–92.
18. Hume, op. cit., p. 269.
19. Hast, op. cit., p. 54.
20. Eller, op. cit., p. 11.
21. Adele Hast, *Loyalism in Virginia: The Norfolk Area and the Eastern Shore* (Ann Arbor, Michigan: UMI Research Press, 1982), pp. 66–68.
22. Eller, op. cit., p. 171.
23. Ibid.
24. *Revolutionary Virginia: The Road to Independence,* op. cit., vol. 5, p. 46.
25. Eller, op. cit., pp. 222–23.
26. Eller, op. cit., p. 157; *Guns on the Chesapeake,* op. cit., p. 97.
27. Lincoln Diamant, *Chaining the Hudson* (New York: Citadel Press, 1994), p. 88.
28. Jeffrey Dorwart, *Fort Mifflin of Philadelphia,* op. cit., pp. 20–21.
29. Hast, op. cit., pp. 33–34, 69.
30. Eller, op. cit., p. 78.
31. *Revolutionary Virginia,* op. cit., vol. 4, p. 169.
32. Eller, op. cit., pp. 220–23.
33. Jean Lee, *The Price of Nationhood: The American Revolution in Charles County* (New York: W. W. Norton, 1994), p. 135.
34. Gay Montague Moore, *Seaport in Virginia: George Washington's Alexandria* (Richmond, Va.: Garrett & Massie, 1949), p. 35.
35. Eller, op. cit., p. 173.
36. Ibid., p. 134.
37. *Naval Documents,* op. cit., vol. 3, pp. 1349–50.
38. Eckenrode, op. cit., p. 108.
39. Hume, op. cit., pp. 282–83, 389.
40. Eller, op. cit., p. 69.
41. Charles J. Truitt, *Breadbasket of the Revolution* (Salisbury, Md.: Historical Books, 1976), p. 5.
42. Keith Mason, "Localism, Evangelism, and Loyalism: The Sources of Discontent in the Revolutionary Chesapeake," *Journal of Southern History* 56, no. 1 (February 1990), p. 24.

43. Hoffman, op. cit., p. 226–27.

44. Smith, *Colonists in Bondage,* op. cit., pp. 262–63.

45. McDonnell, op. cit., p. 144.

46. Ibid., p. 145.

47. Selby, *Revolution in Virginia,* op. cit., p. 274.

48. Mason, op cit., pp. 30–31; Truitt, op. cit., pp. 110–13.

49. M. Christopher New, *Maryland Loyalists* (Centerville, Md.: Tidewater Publishing, 1996), p. 46.

50. This is discussed in somewhat more detail on p. 138 and pp. 592–93 of *The Cousins' Wars,* as well as in Carl Van Doren, "Some Plans for a Loyalist Stronghold in the Middle Colonies," *Pennsylvania History Magazine,* 1949.

51. Dee Andrews, *The Methodists and Revolutionary America, 1760-1800* (Princeton: Princeton University Press, 2000), pp. 45–62.

52. Hoffman, op. cit., p. 227; William H. Williams, *The Garden of American Methodism* (Lanham, Md.: Rowman and Littlefield, 1997), p. 40.

53. Russell, *The American Revolution in the Southern Colonies,* op. cit., p. 127.

54. New, op. cit., p. 79.

Chapter 18: The American Revolution as a Civil War

1. Jones, *The South Carolina Civil War,* op. cit., pp. 7, 13, 60.

2. Winston S. Churchill, *The Age of Revolution* (New York: Bantam Books, 1963), p. 172.

3. Leiby, op. cit., p. 94.

4. Brief details on the choice of sides and actual military confrontations in English North America can be found in *The Cousins' Wars,* pp. 57–60. Two recent books of related interest include Timothy B. Riordan, *The Plundering Time: Maryland and the English Civil War, 1645–1646* (Baltimore: Maryland Historical Society, 2004); and Susan Hardman Moore, *Pilgrims: New World Settlers and the Call of Home* (New Haven: Yale University Press, 2007). A considerable group of New Englanders returned to Old England to participate—religiously, politically, or militarily—in the Civil War and the Cromwellian aftermath.

5. Kwasny, op. cit., p. xvi.

6. Bonomi, op. cit., p. 178.

7. Wallace Brown, op. cit., p. 80.

8. See especially A. M. Everitt, *The Community of Kent and the Great Rebellion* (Leicester: Leicester University Press, 1986).

9. This is not intended to be a learned endnote. But just as cultural, ethnic, and religious explanations of the divisions within Britain circa 1775 have become more important, that also seems to be true in explaining the divisions of the 1640s.

10. Anne Osterhout, "Frontier Vengeance: Connecticut Yankees vs. Pennamites in the Wyoming Valley," *Pennsylvania History* (Summer 1995), pp. 337–47.

11. Henry S. Young, *The Treatment of Loyalists in Pennsylvania* (Ph.D thesis, Johns Hopkins University, 1955), pages unnumbered in copy.

12. Phillips, *Cousins' Wars,* p. 162.

13. Bellisles, op. cit., pp. 107–10.

14. These units included the American Legion, American Volunteers, British Legion, Butler's Rangers, DeLancey's Brigade, Emmerich's Chasseurs, Johnson's Royal Greens, King's American Dragoons, King's American Regiment, King's Orange Rangers, Loyal American Regiment, New Jersey Volunteers (multiple battalions), New York Volunteers, Prince of Wales' American Regiment, Provincial Light Dragoons, Queens Rangers, West Jersey Cavalry, and West Jersey Volunteers. Source: Katcher, op. cit., pp. 82–102.

15. Jones, op. cit., pp. 32–34.

16. Ibid., p. 48.

17. Ibid., p. 61.
18. Ibid., pp. 67–74.
19. Ibid., pp. 77–78.
20. Ibid., p. 76.
21. Ibid., p. 78–79.
22. Kars, op. cit., p. 208.
23. Rankin, op. cit., pp. 28–31.
24. Robert M. Dunkerly, *Redcoats on the River* (Wilmington, N.C.: Dram Tree Books, 2008), pp. 74–75.
25. Rankin, op. cit., pp. 37–39.
26. Henry Belcher, *The First American Civil War* (London: 1911, reprint edition Cranbury, N.J.: Scholar's Bookshelf, 2005).
27. For a fuller sampling and discussion of the many names used, see Appendix 1 in *The Cousins' Wars,* pp. 613–14.
28. For a fuller examination and discussion, see Figure 5.1 on page 163 and Figure 9.1 on p. 365 in *The Cousins' Wars.*
29. Greater detail appears in Appendix 2, "The Cousins' Wars as a Conspiracy Chain," in *The Cousins' Wars,* pp. 615–17.

Chapter 19: The Declaration of Independence—a Stitch in Time?

1. Neuenschwander, op. cit., p. 131.
2. David Armitage, *The Declaration of Independence* (Cambridge, Mass.: Harvard University Press, 2007), p. 48.
3. Ibid., p. 33.
4. Julian Boyd, ed., *The Papers of Thomas Jefferson* (Princeton: Princeton University Press, 1950), vol. 1, p. 323.
5. No consensus exists, but many argue that only President of the Congress John Hancock and perhaps Secretary Charles Thomson signed on July 4; the New Yorkers were still without authorization and only signed in August, and some others did not sign until even later.
6. Boyd, op. cit., p. 134.
7. Ibid., pp. 199–202.
8. Ibid., p. 419.
9. Joseph Ellis, *American Sphinx* (New York: Vintage Books, 1998), pp. 59–60.
10. *The Writings of Thomas Jefferson* (ed. 1869), vol. 7, p. 304, quoted in Carl Becker, *The Declaration of Independence* (New York: Vintage Books, 1958), p. 25.
11. Armitage, op. cit., p. 21.
12. Ellis, *Sphinx,* op. cit., p. 45.
13. Stephen E. Lucas, "Justifying America" in Thomas W. Benson, *American Rhetoric: Context and Criticism* (Carbondale, Ill.: Southern Illinois Press, 1989), p. 78.
14. Pauline Maier, *American Scripture,* op. cit., p. xvii.
15. Garry Wills, *Inventing America* (New York: Vintage Books, 1979), p. 323.
16. Maier, op. cit., pp. 168–71.
17. Malcolm Kelsall, *Jefferson and the Iconography of Romanticism* (London: Macmillan, 1999), pp.1–11.
18. Phillip Papas, *That Ever Loyal Island: Staten Island and the American Revolution* (New York: New York University Press, 2007), pp. 63–64.
19. Armitage, op. cit., p. 34.
20. Becker, op. cit., p. 129.
21. Maier, op. cit., pp. 37–38.
22. Ellis, *American Creation,* op. cit., p. 49.
23. Maier, op. cit., p. 66.
24. Ibid., p. 64.

25. Armitage, op. cit., p. 36.
26. "What is being cried for is aid from France," Wills, op. cit., p. 348; the apparent objective was "to enable the rebellious colonies to enter into diplomatic and commercial alliances with other powers," Armitage, *Declaration of Independence,* op. cit., p. 84.
27. Wills, op. cit., p. 326.
28. Lucas, op. cit., p. 78.
29. Armitage, op. cit., p. 34.
30. Wills and Maier make this point, but so do historians focused on Virginia and Maryland. It is not only Woody Holton's thesis in *Forced Founders,* but the basis of his title. For Maryland, Ronald Hoffman in *A Spirit of Dissension* makes a similar argument in his chapter entitled "A Reluctant Independence."
31. In his book *A People Numerous and Armed,* historian John Shy, taking this view, cited Weldon A. Brown, *Empire or Independence: A Study in the Failure of Reconciliation* (Baton Rouge: University of Louisiana Press, 1941), pp. 90–107. Shy also noted a letter dated May 31, 1776, from George Washington to John Augustine Washington in *The Writings of George Washington,* ed. John C. Fitzpatrick (Washington, D.C., 1932), vol. 5, pp. 91–92.
32. Shy, op. cit., p. 19.
33. Lovejoy, *Rhode Island,* op. cit., p. 192.
34. Boston and Huntington—Hazelton, pp. 267, 256; Savannah—Coleman, op. cit., p. 79.

Chapter 20: The Battle of Boston: A Great American Victory

1. French, op. cit., p. 259.
2. Ibid., p. 258.
3. Ibid., p. 531.
4. Ibid., p. 332.
5. Ibid.
6. Ibid., p. 259.
7. Syrett, *American Waters,* op. cit., p. 9.
8. French, op. cit., p. 345; Syrett, op. cit., p. 29.
9. Fowler, op cit., p. 41.
10. French, op. cit., p. 531.
11. Ibid., p. 531.
12. Nelson, op. cit., pp. 317–21.
13. Benjamin H. Irvin, *Samuel Adams* (New York: Oxford University Press, 2002), p. 103; Pauline Maier, *The Old Revolutionaries: Political Lives in the Age of Samuel Adams* (New York: W. W. Norton, 1980), p. 9.
14. John C. Miller, *Sam Adams* (Stanford, Calif.: Stanford University Press, 1936), pp. 343–44.
15. Details on this historiography can be found in Maier, *Old Revolutionaries,* op. cit., pp. 3–50.
16. Irvin, op. cit., pp. 103–4.
17. Miller, *Sam Adams,* op. cit.
18. Miller, op. cit., pp. 134–65.
19. Ibid., pp. 163–65.
20. Irvin, op. cit., p. 91.
21. Galvin, op. cit., p. 44.
22. Miller, op. cit., p. 266.
23. Ibid., pp. 270–71.
24. For Philadelphia, see Richard Ryerson, *The Revolution Is Now Begun,* pp. 36–37; for New York City, see Edwin G. Burrows and Mike Wallace, *Gotham,* pp. 214–15.
25. John Cary, *Joseph Warren* (Urbana: University of Illinois Press, 1961), p. 136.
26. L. Kinvin Wroth, ed., *Province in Rebellion* (Cambridge, Mass.: Harvard University Press, 1975), p. 21.

27. Leamon, op. cit., p. 56; Coleman, op. cit., p. 50.
28. Maier, *Old Revolutionaries,* op. cit., p. 21.
29. Ibid., p. 12.
30. Wroth, *Province in Rebellion,* op. cit., p. 52.
31. Cary, op. cit., pp. 160–61.
32. Bowen, op. cit., p. 480.
33. Ibid., p. 161.
34. Ibid., p. 158.
35. Nelson, *George Washington's Secret Navy,* op. cit., p. 260.
36. Joseph Galloway, *Historical and Political Reflections on the Rise and Progress of the American Rebellion* (London, 1780), pp. 68–69.
37. French, op. cit., p. 259.
38. Ira Gruber, *The Howe Brothers and the American Revolution* (Chapel Hill: University of North Carolina Press, 1972), pp. 54–55.

Chapter 21: Canada: Defeat or Victory?

1. French, op. cit., p. 149.
2. Ibid., p. 386.
3. Buel, *Dear Liberty,* op. cit., p. 42.
4. Arthur F. Lefkowitz, *Benedict Arnold's Army* (New York: Savas Beatie, 2008), p. 134.
5. *Fort Ticonderoga Museum Bulletin,* Spring 1989, p. 73.
6. Ibid., p. 72.
7. French, op. cit., p. 379.
8. John Adams, *Life and Works,* vol. 2, p. 419. The sentence is unfinished in the original.
9. John H. G. Pell, "Philip Schuyler: The General as Aristocrat," in George Athan Billias, ed., *George Washington's Generals and Opponents: Their Exploits and Leadership* (New York: Da Capo Press, 1994), pp. 63-73. Pell is sympathetic to Schuyler. But he presents the Acland episode in detail.
10. Higginbotham, op. cit., pp. 109–10.
11. John H. G. Pell, "Philip Schuyler, Esq: An Unfinished Biography," *Fort Ticonderoga Museum Bulletin* 15, no. 2, (Spring 1989), p. 71.
12. Higginbotham, op. cit., p. 112.
13. *The War of American Independence,* p. 111. To Higginbotham, "the withdrawal was an incredible performance," a severe blow to American morale. Loyal seigneurs in Montreal celebrated by "a grand mass with a Te Deum."
14. Brendan Morrisey, *Quebec 1775: The American Invasion of Canada* (Oxford, U.K.: Osprey, 2004), p. 41.
15. *Fort Ticonderoga Museum Bulletin,* op. cit, p. 69.
16. French, op. cit., p. 383–84.
17. Morrissey, op. cit., p. 41.
18. "Diary of the Reverend Benjamin Trumbull," *Fort Ticonderoga Museum Bulletin* (Spring 1989), op. cit., pp. 108–12.
19. French, op. cit., p. 416; Morrissey, op. cit., p. 42.
20. Jacques Castonguay, *Les défis du Fort Saint-Jean: l'invasion ratée des Américains en 1775* (St. Jean, Quebec: Les Éditions du Richelieu, 1975), p. 119.
21. Thomas Desjardin, *Through a Howling Wilderness* (New York: St. Martin's, 2006), p. 125.
22. Lefkowitz, op. cit., p. 63.
23. Desjardin, op. cit., p. 126.
24. Martin, *Benedict Arnold, Revolutionary Hero,* p. 150.
25. Desjardin, pp. 145–48.
26. Ibid., p. 128.

27. Ibid., p. 122.
28. *Howling Wilderness*—Sault-au-Matelot, pp. 196–97; Montgomery's death, pp. 177, 196–97; *Benedict Arnold's Army*—Morgan's opportunity, pp. 251, 256. *Benedict Arnold: Revolutionary Hero*—Morgan's opportunity, pp. 176–177.
29. Martin, *Benedict Arnold*, op cit., pp. 64–66.
30. Ibid., p. 76.
31. Ibid., p. 92.
32. Ibid.
33. French, op. cit., p. 382.
34. A. T. Mahan, *The Major Operations of the Navies in the War of American Independence* (Boston: Little, Brown, 1913), p. 3.
35. Mackesy, op. cit., pp. 56–57.
36. Syrett, *Royal Navy in American Waters*, pp. 39–40.
37. Rossie, *Politics of Command*, p. 76; in *First Year*, p. 598, Allen French noted his own agreement with Adams's thesis.
38. French, op. cit., p. 427.
39. Raddall, op. cit., pp. 88–89.

Chapter 22: Lord Dunmore's Second War

1. Selby, *Lord Dunmore*, op. cit., pp. 8–9.
2. Hume, op. cit., pp. 28–30.
3. Holton, op. cit., p. 34.
4. Hume, op. cit., pp. 142–47.
5. Ibid., pp. 215–19.
6. Ibid., pp. 221–25.
7. Holton, op. cit., pp. 140–43, 148, 151–52.
8. Ibid., p. 144.
9. Holton, pp. 145, 147, and 148.
10. Hume, op. cit., p. 342–46.
11. Selby, *Dunmore*, op. cit., p. 68.
12. Hume, op. cit., p. 28.
13. Selby, *Dunmore*, op. cit., p. 16.
14. Ibid., p. 28.
15. Selby, *Revolution in Virginia*, op. cit., p. 56.
16. Kranish, op. cit., p. 234.
17. Ibid., p. 74.
18. Selby, *Dunmore*, p. 11, and Hume, op. cit., p. 164, quoting from unpublished mid-twentieth-century Ph.D. theses by Keith Berwick and Percy Caley.
19. *Revolutionary Virginia: The Road to Independence*, vol. 3, p. 223.
20. Williamson, *Guns on the Chesapeake*, op. cit., p. 74.
21. Hume, op. cit., p. 348.
22. Ibid., p. 352.
23. Ibid., p. 355.
24. *Revolutionary Virginia*, vol. 4, op. cit., p. 322.
25. Hume, pp. 358–63.
26. Holton, *Forced Founders*, op. cit., p. 158.
27. Ibid., p. 159.
28. *Revolutionary Virginia*, op. cit., vol. v, pp. 6–7.
29. Ibid., p. 9.
30. Ibid., p. 10.
31. Selby, *Dunmore*, op. cit., p. 70.
32. *Revolutionary Virginia*, op. cit., Vol. v, p. 10.
33. Ibid., op. cit., vol. 5, p. 11.

34. Kranish, op. cit., p. 80.
35. Selby, *Dunmore,* p. 49. Selby points out that a story in *Dunmore's Gazette* on January 15 touched on Virginian responsibility but was not followed up.
36. Sir Henry Clinton, *The American Rebellion* (New Haven: Yale University Press, 1954), pp. 24–25.
37. Selby, *The Revolution in Virginia,* op. cit., pp. 104–5.
38. Selby, *Dunmore,* op. cit., p. 57.
39. Ibid., pp. 59–60.
40. Ibid.
41. *Guns on the Chesapeake,* op. cit., p. 144.
42. Kranish, op. cit., p. 90.
43. Ibid., p. 88.
44. Syrett, *Royal Navy in American Waters,* op. cit., p. 20.

Chapter 23: Whaleboats, Row Galleys, Schooners, and Submarines: The Small-Ship Origins of the U.S. Navy

1. French, *First Year,* op. cit., p. 109.
2. William M. Fowler, Jr., *Rebels Under Sail* (New York: Scribner's, 1976), p. 28.
3. George Daughan, *If By Sea* (New York: Basic Books, 2008), p. 17; Fowler, op. cit., p. 26.
4. Fowler, op. cit., p. 26.
5. Ibid., p. 28, Daughan, op. cit., p. 26.
6. French, *First Year,* op. cit., p. 365.
7. Lipscomb, *Carolina Lowcountry,* op. cit., p. 7.
8. Ibid., p. 8.
9. Ibid., pp. 8–20.
10. French, *First Year,* op. cit., p. 367.
11. Allen, op. cit., p. 43.
12. Besides the *Hannah,* the names of Washington's eight schooners were *Franklin, Harrison, Hancock, Lee, Thomas, Washington,* and *Warren.*
13. Manstan and Frese, *Turtle: David Bushnell's Revolutionary Vessel* (Yardley, Penn.: Westholme, 2010), pp. 44–58.
14. *The War of the American Revolution* (Washington D.C.: Center of Military History, U.S. Army, 1975), pp. 93–96.
15. *Naval Documents of the American Revolution,* op. cit., vol. 2, pp. 302–3.
16. William T. Munson, "Privateering in Vineyard Sound in the Revolution," Woods Hole Museum occasional paper, pp. 3–4.
17. Rossie, op. cit., p. 15.
18. *Naval Documents of the American Revolution,* op. cit., vol. 1, p. 630.
19. Ibid., vol. 2, p. 869.
20. Ibid., vol. 2, p. 935.
21. "Battle of Brewster Island," www.history.com/this-day-in-history/battle-of-brewster-island.
22. James Warren to John Adams, *Naval Documents of the American Revolution,* op. cit., vol. 2, p. 1017.
23. Ibid., vol. 1, p. 1019.
24. Ibid., vol. 1, p. 1022.
25. Ibid., vol. 1, pp. 1059–60.
26. Joseph E. Garland, *The Fish and the Falcon* (Charleston, S.C.: History Press, 2006), p. 138.
27. Fowler, op. cit., pp. 48–49.
28. *Naval Documents of the American Revolution,* op. cit., vol. 2, p. 28.
29. Tim McGrath, *John Barry* (Yardley, Penn.: Westholme, 2010), p. 85.

30.   Daughan, op. cit., pp. 87–89.

31.   Ibid.

32.   Selby, *Dunmore,* op. cit., p. 55.

33.   Volo, op. cit., pp. 181 and 186–88.

34.   Nelson, op. cit., p. 82; Magra, op. cit., p. 183.

35.   Nelson, op. cit., p. 251.

36.   Ibid., p. 284.

37.   Kurlansky, op. cit., p. 83.

38.   Footner, *Tidewater Triumph,* op. cit., p. 47.

39.   Ibid., p. 49.

40.   Manstan and Frese, op. cit., p. 46.

41.   Ibid., p. 55.

42.   Ibid., p. 56.

43.   Ibid., pp. 262–63.

44.   Ibid., p. 269.

45.   William B. Clark, "American Naval Policy, 1775-1776," *American Neptune* 1 (1941), p. 26.

46.   Donald A. Yerxa, "Vice Admiral Samuel Graves and the North American Squadron, 1774–1776," p. 381.

47.   Ibid.

Chapter 24: Europe, the Bourbon Compact, and the American Revolution

1.   Simms, op. cit., p. 504.

2.   Ibid., p. 517.

3.   Ibid., p. 515.

4.   Ibid., p. 592.

5.   Ibid., p. 473.

6.   Cummins, supra, p. 30.

7.   William Langer, *An Encyclopedia of World History* (Boston: Houghton Mifflin, 1968), pp. 471, 536–37.

8.   Lydia Black, *Russians in Alaska* (Fairbanks: University of Alaska Press, 2004), pp. 79–91.

9.   Herbert K. Beals, trans., *For Honor and Country: The Diary of Bruno de Hezeta* (Portland: Oregon Historical Society, 1985), p. 26.

10.   Black, op. cit., p. 91.

11.   Beals, op. cit., p. 26.

12.   Ibid., pp. 39–43.

13.   Ibid., p. 26, quoting Fisher, *Bering's Voyages.*

14.   Black, op. cit., p. 79.

15.   Light Townsend Cummins, *Spanish Observers and the American Revolution* (Baton Rouge: Louisiana State University Press, 1991), pp. 23–24.

16.   See, for example, Stanley J. Stein and Barbara H. Stein, *Apogee and Empire: Spain and New Spain in the Age of Charles III, 1759-1789* (Baltimore: Johns Hopkins University Press, 2003).

17.   Besides *Spain and the Independence of the United States* by Thomas E. Chavez (Albuquerque: University of New Mexico Press, 2002), the standard reference is Juan Francisco Yela Utrilla, *Espana ante la independencia de los Estados Unidos,* 1925 (reprinted Madrid: Collegio Universitario de Ediciones Istmo, 1988). Another more recent Spanish-language volume is Eric Beerman, *Espana la independencia de los Estados Unidos* (Madrid: Editorial MAPFRE, S.A., 1992).

18.   Cummins, op. cit., p. 27.

19.   Ibid., p. 30.

20.   Ibid., pp. 4–5, 25–26, 32–35.

21. Ibid., p. 34.
22. Potts, *French Covert Action in the American Revolution,* op. cit., p. 95.
23. Chavez, op. cit., pp. 31, 49.
24. Cummins, op. cit., p. 4.
25. Ibid., pp. 52–81.
26. Ibid., pp. 113–14.
27. Chavez, op. cit., pp. 188–94.
28. Jonathan Dull, *The French Navy and American Independence* (Princeton: Princeton University Press, 1975), p. 243.
29. Ibid., p. 245.
30. Stein and Stein, op. cit., p. 346.
31. Robert Thonhoff, *The Texas Connection with the American Revolution* (Austin, Tex.: Eakin Press, 2000), pp. 46–49.
32. Simms, op. cit., pp. 516–17, 535.
33. Robson, *American Revolution,* op. cit., p. 29.
34. Simms, op. cit., p. 574.
35. Ibid., pp. 546, 521.
36. Ibid., p. 559.
37. Ibid., p. 572.
38. Ibid., p. 567.
39. Stout, op. cit., p. 162. On August 8 and 31, and September 3 and September 23, according to Stout's review of Admiralty records, Adm. 1/45.
40. Simms, op. cit., pp. 644–45.
41. Ibid., pp. 640, 636.

Chapter 25: The Southern Expedition of 1775 and the Limitations of British Power

1.   Robson, "The Expedition to the Southern Colonies," op. cit., p. 535.
2.   Center of Military History, op. cit., p. 113.
3.   Simms, op. cit., pp. 589–90.
4.   French, *First Year,* op. cit., p. 700.
5.   David Lee Russell, *Victory on Sullivan's Island* (Haverford, Penn.: Infinity Publishing, 2002), p. 117.
6.   Peter Force, ed., *American Archives,* sers. 4 (Washington, D.C., 1853), vol. 4, p. 440, quoted in Wilson, op. cit., p. 4.
7.   Sir John Fortescue, *The War of Independence: The British Army in North America, 1775–1783* (London: 1911; reprint Greenhill Books, 2001), p. 21.
8.   Rankin, *North Carolina Continentals,* op. cit., pp. 34–35, Russell, *American Revolution in the Southern Colonies,* op. cit., p. 79.
9.   Wilson, op. cit., pp. 25–34. The number of Patriots in the battle depends on whether one counts only those on the battlefield (1,050) or includes other forces not far away (1,900).
10. Ibid., pp. 33–35.
11. Dunkerly, op. cit., p. 98.
12. Rankin, op. cit., p. 58.
13. Ibid., p. 54.
14. Patrick O'Kelly, *Nothing but Blood and Slaughter: The Revolutionary War in the Carolinas* (Booklocker. com: 2004), vol.1, p. 103.
15. Russell, *Victory on Sullivan's Island,* op. cit., pp. 146–47.
16. Dunkerly, op. cit., p. 108.
17. Rankin, op. cit., pp. 66–68.
18. Ibid., p. 60.
19. Ibid., p. 62.
20. O'Kelley, op cit., pp. 42–43.

21. Lipscomb, *South Carolina Becomes a State,* op. cit., pp. 17–18; *Lowcountry,* p. 11.
22. Lipscomb, *Lowcountry,* op. cit., pp. 16–17.
23. Ibid., p. 17.
24. Ibid., pp. 20–21.
25. Russell, *Victory on Sullivan's Island,* op. cit., p. 161.
26. Russell, *American Revolution in the Southern Colonies,* op. cit., p. 74.
27. O'Kelley, p. 50.
28. Lipscomb, *Lowcountry,* op. cit., pp. 22–23.
29. Ibid., p. 26.
30. Ibid., p. 27.
31. Ibid.
32. *Naval Documents of the American Revolution,* op. cit., vol. 1, pp. 1,022 and 177.
33. Ibid., p. 1196.
34. Ibid., vol. 2, pp. 120–21; McGrath, op. cit., p. 54.
35. Wilmington-New Hanover Safety Committee Minutes, op. cit., pp. 70–72.
36. *Naval Documents of the American Revolution,* op. cit., vol. 1, p. 638.
37. Lipscomb, *Lowcountry,* op. cit., p. 26.
38. Russell, *Victory on Sullivan's Island,* op. cit., p. 220.
39. Mackesy, op. cit., pp. 43–44, 158–159; Simms, op. cit., pp. 589–90.
40. Mackesy, p. 408.

Chapter 26: 1775: A Good Year for Revolution

1. Syrett, *American Waters,* op. cit., p. 1.
2. Trevelyan, op. cit., vol. 2, p. 58.
3. Mackesy, "The Redcoat Revived," op. cit., pp. 182–83.
4. Nelson, op. cit., p. 260.
5. Buel, *In Irons,* op. cit., pp. 39–40.
6. Ibid., pp. 44–45.

Bibliography

Abernethy, Thomas. *Western Lands and the American Revolution*. New York: Russell and Russell, 1959.

Allen, Gardner W. *A Naval History of the American Revolution*. Cranbury, N.J: The Scholar's Bookshelf, 2005.

Ammerman, David. *In the Common Cause*. New York: W. W. Norton, 1975.

Anderson, Fred. *Crucible of War*. New York: Knopf, 2000.

Andrews, Dee. *The Methodists and Revolutionary America, 1760–1800*. Princeton: Princeton University Press, 2000.

Armitage, David. *The Declaration of Independence*. Cambridge. Mass.: Harvard University Press, 2000.

Aschenbach, Joel. *The Grand Idea: George Washington's Potomac and the Race to the West*. New York: Simon & Schuster, 2004.

Atwood, Rodney. *The Hessians*. Cambridge, England: Cambridge University Press, 1992.

Augur, Helen. *The Secret War of American Independence*. Boston: Little Brown, 1955.

Bailyn, Bernard. *The Ideological Origins of the American Revolution*. Cambridge. Mass.: Harvard University Press, 1992.

———. *Voyagers to the West*. New York: Random House, 1986.

———. *The Origins of American Politics*. New York: Vintage Books, 1970.

——— "The Central Themes of the American Revolution" in *Essays on the American Revolution,* Stephen G. Kurtz and James H. Dutson, eds. Chapel Hill, N.C.: University of North Carolina Press, 1973.

——— and Philip Morgan, eds., *Strangers Within the Realm: Cultural Margins of the First British Empire*. Chapel Hill, N.C.: University of North Carolina Press, 1991.

Balmer, Randall. *A Perfect Babel of Confusion*. New York: Oxford University Press, 1989.

Barefoot, Daniel W. *Touring South Carolina's Revolutionary War Sites*. Winston-Salem, N.C.: John F. Blair, 1999.

Barrow, Thomas. *Trade and Empire: The British Customs Service in Colonial America, 1660–1775*. Cambridge, Mass.: Harvard University Press, 1967.

Beales, Herbert K., tr. *For Honor and Country: The Diary of Bruno de Hezeta*. Portland, Ore.: The Oregon Historical Society, 1985.

Becker, Carl. *The Declaration of Independence*. New York: Vintage Books, 1958.

Belcher, Henry. *The First American Civil War*. London: 1911; reprinted, Cranbury, N.J.: Scholar's Bookshelf, 2005.

Bell, James B. *A War of Religion: Dissenters, Anglicans and the American Revolution*. London: Palgrave Macmillan, 2008.

Bellesisles, Michael. *Revolutionary Outlaw*. Charlottesville, Va.: University Press of Virginia, 1993.

Bemis, Samuel Flagg. *The Diplomacy of the American Revolution*. Bloomington, Ind.: Indiana University Press, 1957.

Benedict, David A. *A General History of the Baptist Denomination in America and Other Parts of the World*. Boston: Manning and Loring, 1813.

Billias, George A., ed. *George Washington's Generals and Opponent*. New York: DaCapo, 1994.

Bining, Arthur. *Pennsylvania Iron Manufacturing in the 18th Century*. Harrisburg, PA: Pennsylvania Historical and Museum Commission, 1987.

Black, Jeremy. *War for America*. Stroud, Gloucestershire, England: Alan Sutton, 1991.

Black, Lydia. *Russians in Alaska*. Fairbanks, Al.: University of Alaska Press, 2004.

Bliven, Bruce. *Under the Guns*. New York: Harper & Row, 1972.

Bloch, Ruth. "Religion and Ideological Change" in *Religion and American Politics,* Mark Noll, ed. New York: Oxford University Press, 1990.

Blumrosen, Alfred W., and Ruth G. Blumrosen. *Slave Nation*. Naperville, Ill.: Sourcebooks, 2005.

Boettner, Loraine. *The Reformed Doctrine of Predestination*. Grand Rapids, Mich.: Eerdmans, 1932.

Bonomi, Patricia U. *Under the Cope of Heaven*. New York: Oxford University Press, 1986.

Bourne, Russell. *Cradle of Violence*. Hoboken, N.J.: John Wiley & Sons, 2006.

Bouton, Nathaniel, ed. *Documents and Records Relating to the Province of New Hampshire from 1764 to 1776,* vol. 7. Nashua, N.H.: State Printer, 1878.

Bowen, Catharine Drinker. *John Adams and the American Revolution*. Boston: Little Brown, 1950.

Boyd, Julian, ed. *The Papers of Thomas Jefferson*, vol. I. Princeton: Princeton University Press, 1950.

Bradley, James. *Popular Politics and the American Revolution in England*. Macon, Ga.: Mercer Press, 1986.

———. *Religion, Revolution and English Radicalism*. Cambridge: Cambridge University Press, 1990.

Brebdner, John B. *The Neutral Yankees of Nova Scotia*. New York: Columbia University Press, 1937.

Breen, T. H. *The Marketplace of Revolution*. New York: Oxford University Press, 2004.

———. *Tobacco Culture*. Princeton: Princeton University Press, 1985.

Brewer, John. *The Sinews of Power*. New York: Knopf, 1989.

Bridenbaugh, Carl. *Mitre and Sceptre*. New York: Oxford University Press, 1962.

———. *Cities in Revolt*. New York, Oxford University Press, 1970.

———. *The Spirit of '76: The Growth of American Patriotism Before Independence 1607–1776*. New York: Oxford University Press, 1975.

Brinsfield, John W. *Religion and Politics in Colonial South Carolina*. Easley, S.C.: Southern Historical Press, 1983.

Brock, Leslie V. *The Currency of the American Colonies, 1700–1764*. New York: Arno Press, 1975.

Brown, Wallace. *The Good Americans*. New York: William Morrow, 1969.

Brown, Weldon A. *Empire or Independence: A Study in the Failure of Reconciliation*. Baton Rouge, La.: University of Louisiana Press, 1941.

Buel, Richard. *Dear Liberty*. Middletown, Conn.: Wesleyan University Press, 1980.

———. *In Irons*. New Haven: Yale University Press, 1998.

Burnett, Edmund C. *Letters of the Members of the Continental Congress,* vols. I–IV. Washington, D.C.: 1921–36.

Burrows, Edwin G., and Mike Wallace. *Gotham*. New York: Oxford University Press, 1999.

Byers, Edward. *The Nation of Nantucket*. St. Petersburg, Fla.: Hailer Publishing, 1987.

Calhoun, Joanne. *The Circular Church*. Charleston, S.C.: The History Press, 2008.

Calloway, Colin G. *The Western Abenakis of Vermont*. Norman, Ok.: University of Oklahoma Press, 1990.

———. *The American Revolution in Indian Country*. New York: Cambridge University Press, 1995.

———. *The Shawnees and the War for America*. New York: Viking Penguin, 2007.

Carp, Benjamin. *Rebels Rising*. New York: Oxford University Press, 2007.

Cary, John. *Joseph Warren*. Urbana, Ill.: University of Illinois Press, 1961.

Castonguay, Jacques. *Le Defis du Fort Saint-Jean: L'Invasion ratee des Americains en 1775.* St. Jean, Quebec, Canada: Les Editions de Richelieu, 1975.

Cashin, Edward. "Sowing the Wind," in *Forty Years of Diversity: Essays on Colonial Georgia.* Harvey Jackson and Phinzy Spalding, eds. Athens, Ga.: University of Georgia Press, 1984.

Charles, Patrick. *Washington's Decision.* Privately printed, 2005.

Chavez, Thomas E. *Spain and the Independence of the United States.* Albuquerque, N.M.: University of New Mexico Press, 2002.

Christi, Ian, and Benjamin Labaree. *Empire or Independence, 1760–1776.* New York: W. W. Norton, 1976.

Churchill, Winston S. *The Age of Revolution.* New York: Bantam Books, 1963.

Clark, J.C.D. *The Language of Liberty, 1660–1832.* Cambridge: Cambridge University Press, 1994.

Clark, William, ed. *Naval Documents of the American Revolution*, vols. I–III. Washington, D.C.: U.S. Government Printing Office 1964–1966.

Clark, William B. "American Naval Policy, 1775–1776," *American Neptune*, vol. I, 1941.

Coleman, Kenneth. *The American Revolution in Georgia.* Athens, Ga.: University of Georgia Press, 1958.

Colley, Linda. *Britons.* New Haven: Yale University Press, 1992.

Commager, Henry S., and Richard Morris. *The Spirit of Seventy Six.* New York: Harper & Row, 1967.

Conway, Stephen. *The War of American Independence.* London: Edward Arnold, 1995.

———. *The British Isles and the War of American Independence.* New York: Oxford University Press, 2000.

Countryman, Edward. "The Uses of Capital in Revolutionary America," *William and Mary Quarterly*, 1992.

Crane, Elaine F. *A Dependent People: Newport, Rhode Island in the Revolutionary Era.* New York: Fordham University Press, 1985.

Crow, Jeffrey J. *The Black Experience in Revolutionary North Carolina.* Raleigh, N.C.: North Carolina Division of Archives and History, 1977.

Cummins, Light Townsend. *Spanish Observers and the American Revolution.* Baton Rouge, La.: Louisiana State University Press, 1991.

Dabney, William, and Marion Dargan. *William Henry Drayton and the American Revolution.* Albuquerque, N. M.: University of New Mexico Press, 1962.

Daughan, George. *If By Sea.* New York: Basic Books, 2008.

Davidson, Philip. *Propaganda and the American Revolution 1763–1783.* New York: Norton Library, 1973.

DeMond, Robert O. *The Loyalists in North Carolina During the Revolution.* Hamden, Conn.: Archon Books, 1964.

Desjardin, Thomas. *Through a Howling Wilderness.* New York: St. Martin's, 2006.

Destler, Chester M. *Connecticut: The Provisions State.* Chester, Conn.: Pequot Press, 1973.

Devine, T.M. *Scotland's Empire and the Shaping of the Americas, 1600–1815.* Washington, D.C.: Smithsonian Books, 2003.

DeVorsey, Jr., Louis. *The Indian Boundary in the Southern Colonies.* Chapel Hill, N.C.: University of North Carolina Press, 1966.

Diamant, Lincoln. *Chaining the Hudson.* New York: Citadel Press, 1994.

"Diary of the Rev. Benjamin Trumbull," *Fort Ticonderoga Museum Bulletin*, vol. XV, Spring 1989.

Dickerson, Oliver. *The Navigation Acts and the American Revolution.* Philadelphia: University of Pennsylvania Press, 1951.

Dickson, David. *Old World Colony: Cork and South Munster, 1630–1830.* Cork, Ireland: Cork University Press, 2005.

Doerflinger, Thomas. "Philadelphia Merchants and the Logic of Moderation, 1760–1775," *William and Mary Quarterly*, vol. 40, no. 2, April 1983.

———. *A Vigorous Spirit of Enterprise*. Chapel Hill, N.C.: Omohundro Institute/University of North Carolina Press, 1986.

Donovan, Robert Kent. "The Popular Party of the Church of Scotland and the American Revolution," in *Scotland and America in the Age of Enlightenment*. Richard B. Sher and Jeffrey E. Smitten, eds. Edinburgh, Scotland: Edinburgh University Press, 1990.

Dorwart, Jeffrey. *Fort Mifflin of Philadelphia*. Philadelphia: University of Pennsylvania Press, 1998.

Dull, Jonathan. *The French Navy and American Independence*. Princeton: Princeton University Press, 1975.

Dunkerly, Robert M. *Redcoats on the River*. Wilmington, N.C.: Dram Tree Books, 2008.

East, Robert. *Connecticut's Loyalists*. Chester, Conn.: Pequot Press, 1974.

Eckenrode, H.J. *The Revolution in Virginia*. Boston: Houghton Mifflin, 1916.

Eckert, Allan W. *The Wilderness War*. Boston: Little Brown, 1978.

Edgar, Walter. *South Carolina: A History*. Columbia, S.C.: University of South Carolina Press, 1998.

Edik, Conrad, and Katheryn Viens, eds. *Entrepreneurs*. Boston: Massachusetts Historical Society, 1997.

Edwards, Owen Dudley. "The Impact of the American Revolution on Ireland," in *The Impact of the American Revolution Abroad*. Washington, D.C.: Library of Congress, 1976.

———. "Ireland and the American Revolution," in Owen Dudley Edwards and George Shepperson, eds. *Scotland, Europe and the American Revolution*. New York: St. Martin's Press, 1978.

———, and George Shepperson, eds. *Scotland, Europe and the American Revolution*. New York: St. Martin's Press, 1978.

Egnal, Marc. *A Mighty Empire*. Ithaca, N.Y.: Cornell University Press, 1988.

Ekirch, Roger. *Poor Carolina: Politics and Society in Colonial North Carolina, 1729–1776*. Chapel Hill, N.C.: University of North Carolina Press, 1981.

———. *Bound for America*. Oxford: Clarendon Press, 1987.

Eller, Ernest M., ed. *Chesapeake Bay in the American Revolution*. Centerville, Md.: Tidewater Publishing, 1981.

Ellis, Joseph. *American Sphinx*. New York: Vintage Books, 1998.

———. *American Creation*. New York: Knopf, 2007.

Evans, Emory G. "Trouble in the Back Country," in *An Uncivil War: The War in the Southern Back Country*. Thad W. Tate and Ronald Hoffman, eds. Charlottesville, Va.: University Press of Virginia, 1985.

Everitt, A.M. *The Community of Kent and the Great Rebellion*. Leicester, England: 1966.

Ferling, John. *Almost a Miracle*. New York: Oxford University Press, 2007.

Firth, C.H. *Cromwell's Army*. London: University Paperbacks, 1962.

Fischer, David Hackett. *Paul Revere's Ride*. New York: Oxford University Press, 1994.

Fisher, H.A.L. *A History of Europe*. Boston: Houghton Mifflin, 1935.

Fisher, Sydney G. *The Quaker Colonies*. New Haven: Yale University Press, 1921.

———. *The Struggle for American Independence,* vol. I. Cranbury, N.J.: Scholar's Bookshelf, 2005.

Fiske, John. *The Beginnings of New England*. Boston: Houghton Mifflin, 1899.

Fitzpatrick, J.C., ed. *George Washington: Writings from the Original Manuscript Sources,* vol. VI. Washington, D.C.: Government Printing Office, 1913–1941; Etext.virginia.edu/Washington/fitzpatrick.

Fleming, Thomas. *New Jersey*. New York: W. W. Norton, 1984.

———. *1776: Year of Illusions*. Edison, N.J.: Castle Books, 1996.

Footner, Geoffrey M. *Tidewater Triumph*. Centerville, Md.: Tidewater Publishers, 1998.

Force, Peter, ed. *American Archives,* series 4, vols. 4–5. Washington, D.C.: 1853.

Fortescue, Sir John. *The War of Independence: The British Army in North America, 1775–1783*. London, 1911, reprint Greenhill Books, 2001.

Fowler, Jr., William. *Rebels Under Sail*. New York: Scribner's, 1976.

Frakes, George. *Laboratory for Liberty.* Lexington, Ky.: University Press of Kentucky, 1970.

Fraser, Walter J. *Patriots, Pistols and Petticoats.* Columbia, S.C.: University of South Carolina Press, 1993.

French, Allen. *The First Year of the American Revolution.* Boston: Houghton Mifflin, 1934.

———. *General Gage's Informers.* Cranbury, N.J.: Scholar's Bookshelf, 2005.

Frey, Sylvia. "Between Slavery and Freedom: Virginia Blacks in the American Revolution," *Journal of Southern History,* vol. 49, no. 3, August 1983.

———. *Water from the Rock.* Princeton: Princeton University Press, 1991.

Fryer, Mary Beacock. *Allan Maclean, Jacobite General.* Toronto, Canada: Dundurn Press, 1987.

Gallay, Allan. *The Indian Slave Trade.* New Haven: Yale University Press, 2002.

Galloway, Joseph. *Historical and Political Reflections on the Rise and Progress of the American Rebellion.* London: 1780.

Galvin, John R. *Minutemen.* Washington, D.C.: Brassey's, 1996.

Garland, Joseph E. *The Fish and the Falcon.* Charleston: History Press, 2006.

Gewehr, Wesley. *The Great Awakening in Virginia, 1740–1790.* Gloucester, Mass.: Peter Smith Publishers, 1965.

Gilje, Paul A. *Liberty on the Waterfront.* Philadelphia: University of Pennsylvania Press, 2004.

Gipson, Lawrence H. *The Coming of the Revolution, 1763–1775.* New York: Harper Torch Books, 1962.

Glatfelter, Charles H. *Pastors and People, Volume II—The History.* Breiningsville, Pa.: Pennsylvania German Society, 1981.

Goodwin, Jason. *Greenback.* New York: Henry Holt, 2003.

Greene, Jack P. *The Quest for Power.* Chapel Hill, N.C.: University of North Carolina Press, 1963.

———. *Peripheries and Center.* New York: W. W. Norton, 1986.

———. *Understanding the American Revolution.* Charlottesville, Va.: University Press of Virginia, 1995.

———. "Independence, Improvement and Authority," in *An Uncivil War: The Southern Backcountry During the American Revolution.* Ronald Hoffman, Thad W. Tate and Peter Albert, eds. Charlottesville, Va.: University Press of Virginia, 1985.

———, and Richard M. Jellison. "The Currency Act of 1764 in Imperial-Colonial Relations, 1764–1776," *William and Mary Quarterly,* third series, vol. 18, no. 4, October, 1961.

———, and J. R. Pole, eds. *The Blackwell Encyclopedia of the American Revolution.* Oxford: Blackwell, 1994.

Griffin, Keith. *Revolution and Religion: The American Revolution and the Reformed Clergy.* New York: Paragon House, 1994.

Gruber, Ira. *The Howe Brothers and the American Revolution.* Williamsburg, Va.: Institute of Early American History and Culture, 1972.

Hacker, Louis. "The First American Revolution," *Columbia University Quarterly,* 1935.

Hagan, William T. *Longhouse Diplomacy and Frontier Warfare.* Albany, N.Y.: Office of State History, 1976.

Harrell, Isaac S. *Loyalism in Virginia.* Durham, N.C.: Duke University Press, 1926.

Harrington, Virginia. *The New York Merchant on the Eve of the Revolution.* Gloucester, Mass.: P. Smith: 1935.

Hast, Adele. *Loyalism in Virginia: The Norfolk Area and the Eastern Shore.* Ann Arbor, Mi.: UMI Research Press, 1982.

Hatch, Nathan O. *The Democratization of American Christianity.* New Haven: Yale University Press, 1989.

Hatley, Tom. *The Dividing Paths: Cherokees and South Carolinians Through the Revolutionary Era.* New York: Oxford University Press, 1995.

Haywood, C. Robert. "Mercantilism and South Carolina Agriculture," *South Carolina Historical Magazine,* vol. 60, 1959.

Hedges, James B. *The Browns of Providence Plantations: Colonial Years.* Providence, R.I.: Brown University Press, 1968.

Heimert, Alan. *Religion in the American Mind.* Cambridge, Mass.: Harvard University Press, 1966.

Hendricks, J. Edwin. *Charles Thomson.* Cranbury, N.J.: Fairleigh Dickinson University Press, 1979.

Higginbotham, Don. *The War of American Independence.* New York: Macmillan, 1971.

Hirst, Derek. *Authority and Conflict: England, 1603–1658.* Cambridge, Mass.: Harvard University Press, 1986.

Hoffman, Ronald, John McCusker, and Albert Menard. *The Economy of Early America: The Revolutionary Period, 1763–1790.* Charlottesville, Va.: University Press of Virginia, 1988.

Hoffman, Ronald. *A Spirit of Dissension.* Baltimore: Johns Hopkins University Press, 1973.

———. "The Disaffected in the Revolutionary South," in *The American Revolution.* Alfred Young, ed. DeKalb, Ill.: Northern Illinois University Press, 1976).

Holbrook, Stewart. *Ethan Allen.* Portland, Ore.: Binford and Mort, 1988.

Holton, Woody. *Forced Founders.* Chapel Hill: Omohundro Institute/University of North Carolina Press, 1999.

Hooker, Richard J., ed. *The Carolina Backcountry on the Eve of Revolution.* Chapel Hill, N.C.: University of North Carolina, 1953.

Horton, Frank H. "The Building of America," *Illustrated American*, vol. II, issue 113, June 25, 1892.

Huibrechts, Marion. *Swampin' Guns and Stabbing Irons: The Austrian Netherlands: Liege Arms and the American Revolution, 1770–1783.* Leuven, Belgium: Catholic University of Belgium, doctoral dissertation, 2009.

Hume, Ivor Noel. *1775: Another Part of the Field.* New York: Knopf, 1966.

Ingrao, Charles W. *The Hessian Military State.* Cambridge, England: Cambridge University Press, 1987.

Ireland, Owen S. *Religion, Ethnicity and Politics.* University Park, Pa.: Pennsylvania State University Press, 1995.

Irvin, Benjamin H. *Samuel Adams.* New York: Oxford University Press, 2002.

Isaac, Rhys. "Dramatizing the Ideology of Revolution," *William and Mary Quarterly*, vol. 33, no. 3, July 1976.

Jameson, J. Franklin. "St. Eustatius in the American Revolution," *American Historical Review*, vol. 8, no. 4, July 1903.

Jensen, Merrill. *The Founding of a Nation.* New York: Oxford University Press, 1968.

Jones, Alice Hanson. *Wealth of a Nation to Be.* New York: Columbia University Press, 1980.

Jones, Lewis Pinckney. *The South Carolina Civil War of 1775.* Lexington, S.C.: Sandlapper Store, 1975.

Johnson, James M. *Militiamen, Ranger and Redcoats: The Military in Georgia, 1754–1776.* Macon, Ga.: Mercer University Press, 1992.

Johnson, Ruth Y. "American Privateers in French Ports," *Pennsylvania Magazine of History and Biography* 53, December 1929.

Jordan, Don, and Michael Walsh. *White Cargo.* New York: New York University Press, 2007.

Kammen, Michael. *A Season of Youth.* Ithaca, N.Y.: Cornell Uuniversity Press, 1978.

Kars, Marjolene. *Breaking Loose Together.* Chapel Hill, N.C.: Omohundro Institute/University of North Carolina Press, 2002.

Katcher, Philip R. *Encyclopedia of British Provincial and German Army Units, 1775–1782.* Harrisburg, Pa.: Stackpole Books, 1973.

Keay, John, and Julia Keay. *Collins Encyclopedia of Scotland.* London: HarperCollins, 1994.

Kelsall, Malcolm. *Jefferson and the Iconography of Romanticism.* London: Macmillan, 1999.

Klein, Rachel. *The Unification of a Slave State.* Chapel Hill, N.C.: University of North Carolina Press, 1990.

Knollenberg, Bernard. *Growth of the American Revolution: 1766–1775.* Indianapolis, Ind.: Liberty Fund, 2003.

Koebner, Richard. *Empire.* Cambridge, England: Cambridge University Press, 1961.

———. "Two Conceptions of Empire" in *The Re-Interpretation of the American Revolution 1763–1789.* Jack P. Greene, ed. New York: Harper & Row, 1968.

Koehn, Nancy F. *The Power of Commerce*. Ithaca, N.Y.: Cornell University Press, 1994.

Kranish, Michael. *Flight from Monticello*. New York: Oxford University Press, 2010.

Kwasny, Mark. *Washington's Partisan War*. Kent, Oh.: Kent State University Press, 1996.

Kurlansky, Mark. *Cod*. New York: Penguin, 1997.

Kyte, George W. "Some Plans for a Loyalist Stronghold in the Middle Colonies," *Pennsylvania Magazine of History and Biography*, October 1952.

Lambert, Robert S. *South Carolina Loyalists in the American Revolution*. Columbia, S.C.: University of South Carolina Press, 1987.

Langford, Paul. *A Polite and Commercial People, England 1727–1783*. Oxford: Oxford University Press, 1989.

———. "Old Whigs, Old Tories and the American Revolution," *Journal of Imperial and Commonwealth History*, January 1980.

Leaman, James S. *Revolution Downeast*. Amherst, Mass.: University of Massachusetts Press, 1993.

Lee, Jean. *The Price of Nationhood: The American Revolution in Charles County*. New York: W. W. Norton, 1994.

Lefkowitz, Arthur. *Benedict Arnold's Army*. New York; Savas Beatie, 2008.

Leiby, Adrian C. *The Revolutionary War in the Hackensack Valley*. New Brunswick, N.J.: Rutgers University Press, 1992.

Lemisch, Jesse. "Jack Tar in the Streets," *William and Mary Quarterly*, July 1968.

———. *Jack Tar vs. John Bull*. New York: Garland Publishing, 1997.

Lenman, Bruce. *The Jacobite Clans of the Great Glen*. Aberdeen: Scottish Cultural Press, 1995.

Lewis, Michael. *The History of the Royal Navy*. New York: Penguin Books, 1962.

Linebaugh, Peter, and Marcus Rediker. *The Many-Headed Hydra*. Boston: Beacon Press, 2000.

Lipscomb, Terry W. *South Carolina Becomes a State*. Columbia, S.C.: South Carolina Department of Archives and History, 1976.

———. *The Carolina Lowcountry April 1775–June 1776*. Columbia, S.C.: South Carolina Department of Archives and History, 1994.

Lovejoy, David S. *Rhode Island Politics and the American Revolution, 1760–1776*. Providence, R.I.: Brown University Press, 1958.

———. *Religious Enthusiasm in the New World*. Cambridge, Mass.: Harvard University Press, 1985.

Lowell, Edward Jackson. *The Hessians and Other German Auxiliaries of Great Britain*. New York: Harper & Bros., 1884.

Lucas, Stephen E. "Justifying America" in *American Rhetoric: Context and Criticism*, Thomas W. Benson. Carbondale, Ill.: Southern Illinois University Press, 1989.

McCusker, John, and Russell Menard. *The Economy of British America, 1607–1789*. Chapel Hill, N.C.: University of North Carolina Press, 1991.

McDonnell, Michael A. *The Politics of War*. Chapel Hill, N.C.: Omohundro Institute/University of North Carolina Press, 2007.

McEachern, Laura H., and Isabel M. Williams, eds. *Wilmington-New Hanover Safety Committee Meetings, 1774–1776*. Wilmington, N.C.: Wilmington-New Hanover County American Revolution Bicentennial Committee, 1974.

McGrath, Tim. *John Barry*. Yardley, Pa.: Westholme, 2010.

McGregor, J.F., and B. Reay, eds. *Radical Religion in the English Revolution*. Oxford: Oxford University Press, 1984.

McIlwain, Charles H. *The American Revolution: A Constitutional Interpretation*. Ithaca, N.Y.: Cornell University Press, 1958.

Mackesy, Piers. "The Redcoat Revived," in *The American Revolution: Changing Perspectives*. William Fowler and Wallace Coyle, eds. Boston; Northeastern University Press, 1981.

———. *The War for America, 1775–1783*. Lincoln, Neb.: Bison Books, 1993.

McLoughlin, William G. *Revivals, Awakenings and Reform*. Chicago: University of Chicago Press, 1978.

McNaught, Kenneth. *The Pelican History of Canada*. Harmondsworth, England: Penguin Books, 1969.

McWhiney, Grady. *Cracker Culture: Celtic Ways in the Old South.* Tuscaloosa, Ala.: University of Alabama Press, 1988.

Macy, Thomas. *The Hannah and the Nautilus.* Beverly, Mass.: Beverly Historical Society, 2002.

Magra, Christopher. *The Fisherman's Cause.* New York: Cambridge University Press, 2009.

Mahan, A.T. *The Major Operations of the Navies in the War of American Independence.* Cambridge, Mass.: Harvard University Press, 1913.

Maier, Pauline. *The Old Revolutionaries.* New York: W. W. Norton, 1980.

———. *American Scripture.* New York: Knopf, 1997.

Malone, Joseph J. *Pine Trees and Politics.* Seattle: University of Washington Press, 1964.

Mann, Bruce. *Republic of Debtors.* Cambridge, Mass.: Harvard University Press, 2002.

Manstan, Roy, and Frederic Frese. *Turtle: David Bushnell's Revolutionary Vessel.* Yardey, Pa.: Westholme, 2010.

Marcus, G.J. *A Naval History of England.* Boston: Little, Brown, 1961.

Marini, Stephen. *Radical Sects of Revolutionary New England.* Cambridge, Mass.: Harvard University Press, 1982.

Marshall, P.J., ed. *The Oxford History of the British Empire: The 18th Century.* New York: Oxford University Press, 1998.

Marston, Jerrilyn G. *King and Congress.* Princeton: Princeton University Press, 1987.

Martin, James Kirby. *Benedict Arnold, Revolutionary Hero.* New York: New York University Press, 1997.

Marty, Martin. *Righteous Empire: The Protestant Experience in America.* New York: Dial Press, 1970.

Mason, Keith. "Localism, Evangelism and Loyalism: The Sources of Discontent in the Revolutionary Chesapeake," *Journal of Southern History,* vol. 56, no. 1, February 1990.

Menard, Russell. "The South Carolina Low Country," in *The Economy of Early Americ.* Ronald Hoffman, John McCusker, Russell Menard and Peter Albert, eds. Charlottesville, Va.: University Press of Virginia, 1988.

Merritt, Richard L. *Symbols of American Community, 1735–1775.* New Haven: Yale University Press, 1966.

Miller, John C. *Sam Adams.* Stanford: Stanford University Press, 1936.

Millis, Walter. *Arms and Men.* New York: Mentor Books, 1958.

Milton, Giles. *White Gold: The Extraordinary Tale of Thomas Pellow and North Africa's One Million European Slaves.* London: Hodder and Stoughton, 2004.

Mitchell, Robert D. "The Southern Colonial Backcountry: A House Divided" in *The Southern Backcountry: Interdisciplinary Perspectives on Frontier Communities.* David Crass, Steven Smith, Martha Zierden, and Richard Brooks, eds. Knoxville, Tenn.: University of Tennessee Press, 1998.

Moore, Gay Montague. *Seaport in Virginia: George Washington's Alexandria.* Richmond, Va.: Garrett and Massie, 1949.

Morgan, Gwenda. *The Debate on the American Revolution.* Manchester, England: Manchester University Press, 2007.

Morgan, Kenneth. *Slavery and Servitude in Colonial North America.* New York: New York University Press, 2000.

Morrisey, Brendan. *Quebec 1775: The American Invasion of Canada.* Oxford, England: Osprey 2004.

Motley, John Lothrop. *The History of the United Netherland,* vols. I–IV. New York: Harper and Brothers, 1860–1867.

Moultrie, William. *Memoirs of the American Revolution.* New York: Arno Press, 1968.

Munson, William T. "Privateering in Vineyard Sound in the Revolution." Woods Hole Museum Occasional Paper, 1999.

Murrin, John M. "Magistrates, Sinners and Precarious Liberties," in *Saints and Revolutionaries.* David Hall, John Murrin and Thad W. Tate, eds. New York: W. W. Norton, 1984.

Nafic, Joan. *To the Beat of a Drum: A History of Norwich, Connecticut During the American Revolution.* Norwich, Conn.: Old Town Press, 1975.

Nash, Gary. *Race, Class and Politics*. Chicago: University of Illinois Press, 1986.
———. *The Urban Crucible*. Cambridge: Harvard University Press, 1986.
———. *The Unknown American Revolution*. New York: Viking Penguin, 2005.
———. "Poverty and Politics in Early American History," in *Down and Out in Early America*. Billy G. Smith, ed. University Park, Pa.: Pennsylvania State University Press, 2004.
National Park Service. *Salem: Maritime Salem in the Age of Sail*. Washington, D.C.: Department of the Interior, 1987.
Nelson, James L. *George Washington's Secret Navy*. New York: McGraw-Hill, 2008.
Nelson, William H. *The American Tory*. Boston: Northeastern University Press, 1992.
Nettels, Curtis P. *The Emergence of a National Economy, 1775–1815*. New York: Harper Torchbooks, 1962.
Neuenschwander, John. *The Middle Colonies and the Coming of the American Revolution*. Port Washington, N.Y.: Kennikat Press, 1976.
New, M. Christopher. *Maryland Loyalists*. Centerville, Md.: Tidewater Publishing, 1996.
Newell, Margaret. *From Dependency to Independence: Economic Revolution in Colonial New England*. Ithaca, N.Y.: Cornell University Press, 1998.
New Hampshire American Revolution Bicentennial Commission. *New Hampshire: Years of Revolution, 1774–1783*. Concord, N.H.: Profile Publishing, 1976.
Noll, Mark A., ed. *Religion and American Politics*. New York: Oxford University Press, 1990.
O'Donnell III, James H. *Southern Indians in the American Revolution*. Knoxville, Tenn.: University of Tennessee Press, 1973.
O'Kelly, Patrick. *Nothing but Blood and Slaughter: The Revolutionary War in the Carolinas*, vol. I. Booklocker.com: 2004.
Olton, Charles S. *Artisans for Independence*. Syracuse, N.Y.: Syracuse University Press, 1975.
Olwell, Robert A. "Domestic Enemies," *Journal of Southern History*, vol. LV, no. 1, February 1989.
Osterhout, Anne. "Frontier Vengeance: Connecticut Yankees Versus Pennamites in the Wyoming Valley," *Pennsylvania History*, Summer 1995.
Papas, Philip. *That Ever Loyal Island: Staten Island and the American Revolution*. New York: New York University Press, 2007.
Parkman, Francis. *A Half-Century of Conflict*. New York: Collier Books, 1962.
Paullin, Charles O. "The Connecticut Navy of the American Revolution," *New England Magazine*, vol. 35, 1906.
Peckham, Howard. *The Colonial Wars, 1689–1762*. Chicago: University of Chicago Press, 1962.
Pell, John H.G. "Philip Schuyler, Esq: An Unfinished Biography," *Fort Ticonderoga Museum Bulletin*, vol. XV, Spring 1989.
———. "Philip Schuyler: The General as Aristocrat," in *George Washington's Generals and Opponents: Their Exploits and Leadership*. George Athan Billias, ed. New York: Da Capo Press, 1994.
Phillips, James D. *Salem in the 18th Century*. Salem, Mass.: Essex Institute, 1969.
Phillips, John. *Electoral Behavior in Unreformed England*. Princeton: Princeton University Press, 1982.
Piecuch, Jim. *Three Peoples, One King*. Columbia, S.C.: University of South Carolina Press, 2008.
Platt, Richard. *Smuggler's Britain*. London: Cassell, 1991.
Pointer, Richard W. *Protestant Pluralism and the New York Experience*. Indianapolis, Ind.: Indiana University Press, 1988.
Potts, James M. *French Covert Action in the American Revolution*. New York: iUniverse Inc. 2005.
Powell, Jonathan. "Presbyterian Loyalists: A 'Chain of Interest' in Philadelphia," *Journal of Presbyterian History*, vol. 57, 1979.
Plumb, J.H. *England in the 18th Century*. Harmondsworth, England: Penguin, 1966.
Prebble, John. *Culloden*. New York: Atheneum, 1962.

Quarles, Benjamin. *The Negro in the American Revolution.* New York: W. W. Norton, 1973.

Raddell, Thomas H. *Path of Destiny.* New York: Popular Library, 1957.

Rankin, Hugh F. *The North Carolina Continentals.* Chapel Hill, N.C.: University of North Carolina Press, 1971.

Raphael, Ray. *The First American Revolution: Before Lexington and Concord.* New York: The New Press, 2002.

Rawlyk, G.A. "The American Revolution and Canada," in *The Blackwell Encyclopedia of the American Revolution.* Jack P. Greene and J. R. Pole, eds. Oxford: Blackwell, 1994.

Reid, John Philip. *In a Defiant Stance.* University Park, Pa.: Pennsylvania State University Press, 1977.

———. *Constitutional History of the American Revolution: The Authority of Law.* Madison, Wisc.: University of Wisconsin Press, 1993.

Rhode Island. *The American Guide Series.* Boston: Houghton Mifflin, 1937.

Rhoden, Nancy L. *Revolutionary Anglicanism.* Basingstoke, England: Macmillan Press, 1999.

Risch, Erna. *Supplying Washington's Army.* Washington, D.C.: Center of Military History, U.S. Army, 1981.

Ritcheson, Charles R. *British Politics and the American Revolution.* Norman, Okla.: University of Oklahoma Press, 1954.

Robson, Eric. "The Expedition to the Southern Colonies, 1775–1776," *The English Historical Review,* October 1951.

———. *The American Revolution.* London: Batchworth, 1955.

Rogers, George. *Charleston in the Age of the Pinckneys.* Columbia, S.C.: University of South Carolina Press, 1980.

Rogers, James A. *Richard Furman.* Macon, Ga.: Mercer University Press, 2001.

Ross, Malcolm. *The Cape Fear.* New York: Holt Rinehart, 1965.

Rossie, Jonathan G. *The Politics of Command in the American Revolution.* Syracuse, N.Y.: Syracuse University Press, 1975.

Rosswurm, Steven. *Arms, Country and Class.* New Brunswick, N.J.: Rutgers University Press, 1987.

Roth, David M. *Connecticut's War Governor: Jonathan Trumbull.* Chester, Conn.: Pequot Press, 1974.

———, and Freeman Meyer. *From Revolution to Constitution: Connecticut 1763 to 1818.* Chester, Conn.: Pequot Press, 1975.

Royster, Charles. *A Revolutionary People at War.* Chapel Hill, N.C.: University of North Carolina Press, 1979.

Russell, David Lee. *The American Revolution in the Southern Colonies.* Jefferson, N.C.: McFarland, 2000.

———. *Victory on Sullivan's Island.* Haverford, Pa.: Infinity Publishing, 2002.

Rutman, Darrett B. "The Virginia Company and Its Military Regime," in *The Old Dominion: Essays for Thomas Perkins Abernethy.* Darrett B. *Rutman,* ed. Charlottesville, Va.: University of Virginia Press, 1964.

Ryerson, Richard Alan. *The Revolution Is Now Begun: The Radical Committees of Philadelphia, 1765–1776.* Philadelphia: University of Pennsylvania Press, 1978.

Sainsbury, John. *Disaffected Patriots.* Montreal, Canada: Queen's University Press, 1987.

Salinger, Sharon V. "Artisans, Journeymen and the Transformation of Labor in Late 18th Century Philadelphia," *William and Mary Quarterly,* third series, vol. 40, no. 1, January 1983.

———. *To Serve Well and Faithfully.* Westminster, Md.: Heritage Books, 2007.

Schaaf, Gregory. *Wampum Belts and Peace Trees.* Golden, Colo.: Fulcrum Publishing, 1990.

Schama, Simon. *Rough Crossings.* New York: HarperCollins, 2006.

Schlesinger, Arthur M. *The Colonial Merchants and the American Revolution.* New York: Frederick Ungar, 1957.

Schultz, Ronald. *The Republic of Labor: Philadelphia Artisans and the Politics of Class, 1720–1830.* New York: Oxford University Press, 1993.

Scribner, Robert L. ed. *Revolutionary Virginia: The Road to Independence,* vols. 1–6. Richmond, Va.: University Press of Virginia, 1975.

Selby, John E. *Dunmore.* Williamsburg: Virginia Independence Bicentennial Commission, 1976.

———. *The Revolution in Virginia, 1775–1783.* Williamsburg: Colonial Williamsburg Foundation, 1988.

Selesky, Harold E. *War and Society in Colonial Connecticut.* New Haven, Conn.: Yale University Press, 1990.

Selsam, J. Paul. *The Pennsylvania Constitution of 1776.* New York: Octagon Books, 1971.

Sher, Richard B., and Jeffrey R. Smitten, eds. *Scotland and America in the Age of Enlightenment.* Edinburgh, Scotland: Edinburgh University Press, 1990.

Shy, John. *Toward Lexington: The Role of the British Army in the Coming of the American Revolution.* Princeton: Princeton University Press, 1965.

———. *A People Numerous and Armed.* Ann Arbor, Mich.: University of Michigan Press, 1990.

Smith, Abbott E. *Colonists in Bondage.* New York: W. W. Norton, 1971.

Smurthwaite, David. *Battlefields of Britain.* Exeter, England: Webb and Bower, 1984.

Smyth, Albert H., ed. *Writings of Benjamin Franklin,* vol. II. New York: Macmillan, 1907.

Spooner, F.C. *Risks at Sea: Amsterdam Insurance and Maritime Europe, 1766–1780.* Cambridge, England: Cambridge University Press, 2002.

Stein, Stanley J., and Barbara Stein. *Apogee of Empire: Spain and New Spain in the Age of Charles III, 1759–1789.* Baltimore: John Hopkins University Press, 2003.

Steiner, Bruce E. *Connecticut Anglicans in the Revolutionary Era.* Hartford, Conn.: American Revolution Bicentennial Commission of Connecticut, 1978.

Stephenson, Orlando W. "The Supply of Gunpowder in 1776," *American Historical Review,* vol. 30, no. 2, January 1925.

Stevens, Paul A. *A King's Colonel.* Youngstown, N.Y.: Old Fort Niagara Association, 1987.

Stout, Neil. *The Royal Navy in America, 1760–1775.* Annapolis, Md.: Naval Institute Press, 1973.

Stuart, I.W. *Life of Jonathan Trumbull, Senior.* Hartford, Conn.: Brown and Gross, 1878.

Sweet, William. *The Story of Religion in America.* Grand Rapids, Mich.: Baker Book House, 1973.

Syrett, David. *Shipping and the American War, 1775–1783.* London: University of London/Athlone Press, 1970.

———. *The Royal Navy in American Waters, 1775–1783.* Aldershot, England: Scolar Press, 1989.

Taylor, Peter. *Indentured to Liberty.* Ithaca, N.Y.: Cornell University Press, 1994.

Tercentenary Commission of the State of Connecticut. *Migrations from Connecticut Prior to 1800.* New Haven: Yale University Press, 1934.

Thomas, Hugh. *The Slave Trade.* New York: Simon & Schuster, 1997.

Thomas, Peter D.G. *Tea Party to Independence: The Third Phase of the American Revolution, 1773–1776.* Oxford: Clarendon Press, 1991.

Thonhoff, Robert. *The Texas Connection with the American Revolution.* Austin, Tex.: Eakin Press, 2000.

Thwaits, Reuben, and Louise Kellogg. *The Revolution on the Upper Ohio.* Madison, Wisc.: Wisconsin Historical Society, 1908.

Tortellot, Arthur B. *Lexington and Concord.* New York: W. W. Norton, 1959.

Townsend, Leah. *South Carolina Baptists.* Florence, S.C.: Florence Printing Company, 1935.

Trevelyan, George O. *The American Revolution,* vols. I–IV. Cranbury, N.J.: Scholar's Bookshelf, 2006.

Truitt, Charles J. *Breadbasket of the Revolution.* Salisbury, Md.: Historical Books, 1976.

Tully, Alan. *Forming American Politics.* Baltimore: Johns Hopkins University Press, 1994.

Turner, Lynn W. *The Ninth State.* Chapel Hill, N.C.: University of North Carolina Press, 1983.

Tyler, John W. *Smugglers and Patriots*. Boston: Northeastern University Press, 1980.

Unger, Harlow G. *John Hancock*. New York: John Wiley & Sons, 2000.

Urban, William. *Bayonets for Hire*. London: Greenhill, 2007.

U.S. Army Center for Military History. *The War of the American Revolution*. Washington, D.C.: Government Printing Office, 1975.

Van Alstyne, Richard W. *Empire and Independence*. New York: John Wiley & Sons, 1965.

———. *The Rising American Empire*. New York: W. W. Norton, 1974.

Van Doren, Carl. *A Secret History of the Revolution*. New York: Viking, 1941.

———. "Some Plans for a Loyalist Stronghold in the Middle Colonies," *Pennsylvania History Magazine,* 1949.

Van Dusen, Albert E. *Connecticut*. New York: Random House, 1961.

Van Hoeven, James. ed. *Piety and Patriotism*. Grand Rapids, Mich.: W. B. Eerdmans, 1976.

Van Tyne, C.H. "French Aid Before the Alliance of 1778," *American Historical Review,* vol. 31, no. 1, October 1925.

Volo, James. *Bluewater Patriots*. Lanham, Md.: Rowman and Littlefield, 2006.

Wallace, Paul A. *The Muhlenbergs of Pennsylvania*. Philadelphia: University of Pennsylvania Press, 1950.

Watson, Steven. *George III*. London: Oxford University Press, 1960.

Warfle, Richard T. *Connecticut's Western Colony*. Hartford, Conn.: Connecticut American Revolution Bicentennial Commission, 1979.

Warren-Adams Letters. Boston: Massachusetts Historical Society Collection, 1917.

Weaver, Glenn. *Jonathan Trumbull*. Hartford, Conn.: Connecticut Historical Society, 1956.

Weir, Robert M. *Colonial South Carolina*. Columbia, S.C.: University of South Carolina Press, 1997.

Wertenbaker, Thomas. *Torchbearer of the Revolution*. Princeton: Princeton University Press, 1940.

———. *Father Knickerbocker Rebels*. New York: Scribner's, 1948.

White, William E. "The Independent Companies of Virginia," *Virginia Magazine of History and Biography,* vol. 86, no. 2, April 1978.

Wilderson, Paul. *Governor John Wentworth and the American Revolution*. Lebanon, N.H.: University of New Hampshire Press, 1994.

Williamson, Gene. *Guns on the Chesapeake*. Westminster, Md.: Heritage Books, 2007.

Wills, Garry. *Inventing America*. New York: Vintage Books, 1979.

Wilson, David K. *The Southern Strategy: Britain's Conquest of South Carolina and Georgia, 1775–1780*. Columbia, S.C.: University of South Carolina Press, 2005.

Wilson, Kathleen. *The Sense of the People: Politics, Culture and Imperialism in England, 1715–1785*. Cambridge, England: Cambridge University Press, 1995.

Wood, Gordon. *The Radicalism of the American Revolution*. New York: Knopf, 1992.

Woolverton, John F. *Colonial Anglicanism*. Detroit: Wayne State University Press, 1984.

Wright, Esmond. *Causes and Consequences of the American Revolution*. Chicago: Quadrangle, 1966.

Wroth, L., Kinvin, ed. *Province in Rebellion*. Cambridge, Mass.: Harvard University Press, 1975.

Yerxa, Donald A. "Vice Admiral Samuel Graves and the North American Squadron, 1774–1776," *Mariner's Mirror* 62, 1976.

York, Niel. "Clandestine Aid and the American Revolutionary War Effort: A Re-Examination," *Military Affairs* 43, 1979.

Young, Alfred F. "English Plebeian Culture and the 18th Century American Radicalism," in *The Origins of Anglo-American Radicalism*. Margaret Jacob and James Jacob, eds. New York: The Institute for Research in History, 1991.

———, ed. *The American Revolution: Explorations in the History of American Radicalism*. DeKalb, Ill.: Northern Illinois University Press, 1976.

Young, Henry S. *The Treatment of Loyalists in Pennsylvania*. Baltimore: Johns Hopkins University, Ph.D. thesis, 1955.

Zeichner, Oscar. *Connecticut's Years of Controversy*. Chapel Hill, N.C.: University of North Carolina Press, 1949.

Index

Page numbers in *italics* refer to maps and figures.